THE FILMS OF FRITZ LANG

GRIFFITH COLLEGE CORK

The Films of Fritz Lang

Allegories of Vision and Modernity

TOM GUNNING

A BFI book published by Palgrave Macmillan

Contents

Preface and Acknowledgments

A preface always hopes to prepare a reader for a book, cajole them into a favourable position from which to approach it, warn them about what not to expect from it, as well as promise something to look forward to. Of course, such precautionary advice can never truly precede the experience of the book, since the reader must have the open book in hand and be engaged in the act of reading already in order to respond to it. But I do want to indicate here, particularly to anyone coming to this book from my previous work on Griffith or essays on early cinema, something about what this book is and what it isn't. It is, first and foremost, a reading of the films and the career of Fritz Lang. Although I strongly believe films should be viewed and listened to first, rather than read through a particular grid, I use the term 'reading' here advisedly. As one of my dominant assumptions in approaching Lang has been the importance of allegory to his work, I believe that as well as being watched and listened to his films do have to be read – that is interpreted, even decoded. This book determinedly picks up the burden of interpretation, a task that certain of the best minds in film studies have advised us to either avoid or defer. I am not insensitive to the motivation for this advice, especially its concern that the sensual and formal properties of cinema have all too often become simple grist for the academic mill of meaning. However, I frankly feel that although interpretation can be a dangerous thing, it forms an essential aspect of our encounter with works of art and that our tack should not be to avoid it (although I would hasten to add there are many other worthwhile things to do with films), but rather to find ways of doing it better. Clearly allegory itself would have to be abandoned entirely as a concept if the act of interpretation were forbidden, or seen as inessential.

I emphasise this from the start because this book departs in many ways from most of my work on early cinema. It is not a work of original research into the production and reception of films. As I hope I indicate in this book, I feel a thoroughly researched historical study of the production and reception of Lang's films still needs to be done, and I hope it will be undertaken (I hope, in fact, to contribute to it). But that is not my principal task. I utilise a great deal of the research that already exists on these aspects of Lang's films, but it does not form the centre of this book. At the centre of the book are the films themselves and the act of viewing them. However, as important as I think the textural level of a film is, I do not believe that this text can ever be approached in isolation, in some pure form. Even without making it the focus of my analysis, the process of production that led to these films and the way they have been received exerts a pressure on the way I have watched them. I strongly agree with Roland Barthes that a thorough formal analysis makes us confront history rather than shielding the text (and the critic) from it. Therefore although this work by no means claims to be a work of historiography, I believe it demonstrates that no area of a film is untouched by history.

Primarily, then, I am trying to come to terms with these films in terms of style and meaning (aspects I find indivisible, and mutually informing), through an act of film criticism. To a large extent, although most film studies is founded in film criticism – that is, the analysis and discussion of individual films – our field has been more concerned with discussing the assumptions and practice of theory and history than of criticism.[1] I try here to use both theory and history, but in order to elucidate individual films and the corpus of a film director. All too often in the last decades of film study film criticism has actually meant using a film text to illustrate or exemplify a particular theory. This may in some sense be inevitable, since theory cries out for practical demonstration, as anatomy depends on dissection. But rather than using theory as a way to open up films to new discoveries, or to test a theory's weak points by pointing out its difficulty in dealing with a film, such approaches tended to scoop out the elements of a film that could be made to correspond to a theory, and then to toss the rest away. More than anything else this process has given interpretation a bad name, since the meaning was already available ready-made in the theory and the film simply served as matter to be processed by it. Few surprises occur in this process. I believe the work of interpretation should involve the progressive discovery and uncovering of a film's structures as well as an unfolding of its surfaces – and all of this must be filled with surprises. This was certainly the process I went through in viewing these films.

In some ways this book may appear old-fashioned, the study of a director's style and corpus. However I do not believe it is. As I try to show in my introduction, I feel film studies jettisoned the concept of the author without thoroughly investigating what it meant in a modern context and in relation to new technology. I believe, in fact, that many of the most promising methods of author-studies (although again I stress that this is by no means the only way to approach films, nor do all films call for it) were not allowed to thoroughly develop; their premature abandonment has stunted the growth of a dynamic film criticism. For instance, the assumption that a moment in a film may develop resonances through the repetition, inversion and transformation it undergoes throughout a director's work has been a guiding principle for me, and I believe provides a tool for interpretation that is more flexible and mercurial than explication by theory. I believe that there is more to explore in this vein and that it should not be curtailed by accusations of romantic individualism that are frankly inapplicable.

If I have tried to avoid approaching Lang's films as exemplary of a central theory, this does not mean I have not used theoretical work in my criticism. On the contrary. My central thesis that Lang's films form a complex and profound meditation on the cinema as a means of representing modern experience guides much (although certainly not all) of my understanding of them. In this the work of the Frankfurt School – but especially of the school's outsiders or fellow travellers, Benjamin and Kracauer – has been a constant guide to my thinking. Lang, after all, was part of the same world. He shared with Benjamin, Adorno and Kracauer (as well as Karl Kraus, Martin Heidegger, Georg Lukacs and Bertolt Brecht – other figures who shaped my understanding of Lang's work) the experience of World War I, the ambiguities of the Weimar period, and the rise of Nazism. Each of them engaged with the collapse of traditional transcendental values, the rise of the modern city, the threat and promise of technology and the nature of modern mass totalitarian movements. Lang was by no means an intellectual and his grasp of these issues often proceeded by the way of the popular genres of serial novels and sensation films. But I believe he faced the same issues in his films as these theorists did in their writings, although Lang's articulation of them contrasts sharply at points with the elucidation the theorists offered. I believe it is not irrelevant that one of

Lang's close friends was Theodor Adorno and that he had an intense relation with Brecht.

It is around the issue of modernity, as articulated particularly by these theorists, that I cluster many of my readings of Lang's films. Here, of course, a continuity with my essays on early cinema can be found. As I hope this book makes clear, I do not consider cinema's interaction with modernity to be a brief encounter lasting only a decade or so, but rather an ongoing and mutually redefining interaction. Whereas the early cinema of attractions primarily expressed the novelty and shock of new technology and the urban environment, I feel that Lang's films (picking up on patterns sketched in the genre that first brought him, as a young scriptwriter, to cinema – the detective film) deal primarily with modernity's systematic nature, its interlocking technologies which I describe as the 'terrain' of modernity: a new landscape of space and time riddled with technological links and devices which seem to extend (and often defy) the human will. The experience of shock and novelty are still operative, but instead of the direct confrontation of the spectator in the sudden burst of the present that characterises the cinema of attractions, the shocks have been absorbed into the system – like the explosion Freder witnesses in the machine room in *Metropolis* which is treated as part of the normal functioning of the city's mode of production.

I wrote this book primarily in 1999, the last year of the twentieth century, well aware that the centennial of Lang's birth (1890) and that of the invention of cinema (1889? 1891? 1895?) had already passed. Ironically, 1999 was also the centennial year of the one film director whose detailed study was never halted or even slowed down by diatribes against the *auteur* theory: Alfred Hitchcock. In many ways the first decades of academic film studies could be seen as the era of the criticism and analysis of Hitchcock and *film noir*, with both areas gaining immensely from the insights and dialectics of feminist film theory (within historical research, the same claim could be made for the importance of the formulation of the Classical Hollywood Cinema and, I hope, Early Cinema). I myself first focused my personal interest in film through the work of Hitchcock (reading Robin Wood's pioneering book on Hitchcock when I was fourteen made me first think about becoming a film critic) and I would never dispute the centrality of his work to our field. But I think that the avalanche of books and articles on Hitchcock over the past decades contrasts strangely with the relative neglect of Lang. In spite of dozens of insightful essays on Lang, no thorough stylistic account of Lang's career exists in English, other than Lotte Eisner's important pioneering, and Frederick Ott's very valuable (but long out of print) survey, both from the 70s and neither providing in-depth analysis. It was this neglect (as much as Rob White's quietly eloquent persuasion that writing a book on Lang need not take several decades of research) that made me decide an English language book which presented a stylistic reading of Lang's career was badly needed, if only as an instigating, rather than a definitive, work.

It is my hope that writing on Lang will become a major preoccupation of film studies in the future, because I believe his work raises different issues from Hitchcock's but equally important ones. In many ways the two directors reflect each other, with, as I claim briefly in a later chapter, Hitchcock beginning his film-making career strongly under Lang's influence and Lang more or less deliberately imitating Hitchcock later on. But I think that their conceptions of psychology and society, while often twining around similar themes of violence, sexual obsession and the ambiguous power of representation, diverge sharply. Lang is less concerned with the psychological complexity of characters, with their interiority (whose existence I think he doubts), than with their interface with social systems, with technology and politics, with the issues I assemble around the term 'modernity'. Hitchcock's films, especially after he came to Hollywood, follow a primarily ascending curve in terms of box-office popularity, critical reception and big budgets, while Lang's curve is almost the opposite. This makes Hitchcock's films more accessible and often more enjoyable, featuring performances by Cary Grant and James Stewart, Ingrid Bergman and Grace Kelly, rather than Dana Andrews and Debra Paget. Lang's films are more charming and often more emotionally engaging. This is due partly to the fact that Hitchcock fashioned the enduring cinematic representation of the drama of individual desire. For Lang individuality and even desire always become subsumed into larger impersonal and often sinister systems – what I have termed in this book the 'Destiny-machine'. By this term I try to indicate that the thematic core isolated by so many of Lang's critics (including himself) – that is, the problem of 'fate' – need not be jettisoned as an old-fashioned metaphysical interpretation. It can be refashioned as a profound insight into modernity. In some ways Lang's more hostile critics of past decades found him conservative, still stuck within the silent era and outmoded methods of Expressionist melodrama. I believe, on the contrary, that in the present era Lang's cold abstraction can appear as the truly modern technique and sensibility that his French admirers always claimed it was.

Hitchcock and Lang meditate equally powerfully on the role of the director in film, not simply as a production role but as an aspect of the film text itself, what Raymond Bellour, writing on both film-makers, refers to as the issue of enunciation. Both film-makers devised ways to make the audience aware of their brooding presence over the world of fiction they engendered through devices within the film. Although in some ways superficial instances of this presence, the manner in which each director appeared in their films provides an allegory of the importance they each placed in reminding the viewer of the director/storyteller behind the film. Hitchcock's appearances are overt and ironic. Lang's appearances (his hand was filmed and intercut as a close-up, he claimed, in each of his films) remained devious, yet heavily symbolic. I believe that an author study is appropriate to Lang's work partly because the issue of enunciation occupies a central role in both his stylistics and his plots (as it does, I think, in a somewhat different way in Hitchcock).

I want to signal here the strong debt I owe to what Thomas Elsaesser has called the 'French moment' of Lang, his reception by enthusiastic and insightful French critics, which began with *Der müde Tod* in the early 20s, but which, for my purposes, blossomed particularly in the 50s and 60s in the journals *Cahiers du Cinéma* and *Positif* (and continues to this day).[2] I would have to confess to a detour through France in my own understanding of Lang and indicate the influence of the always inspiring, if often somewhat obscure, writings of Lang's French commentators. I also have to confess here to the limits of my grasp of German, a language that I love deeply (and which this project allowed me to encounter intensely) but whose true command I could not claim. Consequently I have undoubtedly neglected some German critics of Lang, although I was fortunate enough to benefit from the great insights of Enno Patalas and Frieda Grafe through the French translation of their small but extraordinary book on Lang.

I also want briefly to touch upon the epigraphs which introduce the sections of this work, and on which I probably expended an inordinate amount of time. Although some are ornament, I consider most to be argument (each reader can decide which is which). They signal a range of extra-filmic influences on my understanding of Lang, tracing a relation between German Romantics, especially the anonymous author of the extraordinary nihilist work *The Night Watches of Bonaventura*, American Romantics such as Poe, the Symbolists, especially Baudelaire, as well as German authors contemporary to Lang, including Rilke, Junger, Trakl and Kaiser, as well as Brecht.

If a preface starts with the hope of persuading a reader how to approach a book, it ends in a profound sense of indebtedness. Since my interest in Lang has been lifelong (ever since I went to a screening of *M* at the Bleecker Street Cinema on a visit to New York City at the age of thirteen), I cannot hope to acknowledge all these influences. But I do want to thank the people in New York City with whom I shared my first serious days of film viewing and, at the same time, discovered Lang: John Sonneborn, Mike McKegney, Paul Lawrence, Mark Durand, Rat Magoo, Terry Watkins, Louis Schwartz and Claribel Cone (who made it possible for me to meet Lang). I owe much to my fellow graduate students at NYU who made up an early Lang seminar that was student-run: especially Noel Carroll (who continues to inspire me) and Paul Arthur. Lectures there by Noel Burch strongly shaped my understanding of Lang despite my disagreements with his evaluation of the American films, as did later discussion with Scott Bukatman. In more recent years I returned to Lang in my teaching and must thank students in the various Lang courses I taught at the University of Wisconsin Madison, SUNY Purchase, Northwestern University, the University of Stockholm (including the Stockholm Mabuse group), and the University of Chicago. I must also thank many people who helped out in various ways: Trond Lundemo, Emily Godbey (who helped me with the German, as did Bo-Mi Choi and Anton Kaes, although they are not to blame for any of my errors), Jonathan Crary, Chris Simmons. In addition I want to thank Jan Olsson for making my Stockholm seminar on Lang happen in such wonderful style. More directly involved in the genesis of this book, I owe so much to Rob White who made it happen at every stage and has been the most Socratic of midwives. I want to thank Julia Gibbs and especially Josh Yumibe for helping with illustrations; Thomas Elsaesser, Yuri Tsivian, Vincente Benet, David Levine, Bill Rout, Raymond Bellour for early conversations, and especially the book's early godfathers who read sections of this work (with Jonathan reading it all and providing sage advice and encouragement at every stage) and helped me enormously: Jonathan Rosenbaum, Anton Kaes, Travis Preston and Lewis Klahr. And to Frank Kessler for wonderful comments at the end. And to all of those whom I have inadvertantly forgotten at this stage! I also thank Diane Ofarim with whom many of these ideas were discussed in another context. I want to thank the Solomon Guggenheim Foundation whose generous grant, combined with additional aid from the School of the Humanities at the University of Chicago, allowed me a year released from teaching in which to write the book. I pay tribute with appreciation and love to my wife Deborah for all her support. And finally I want to thank my colleague Miriam Hansen whose work opened up so many of the horizons I explore herein, from her groundbreaking discussions of the treatment of film by the Frankfurt School, especially Benjamin and Kracauer, which has so influenced my understanding, to her unparalleled example of allegorical reading in her treatment of Griffith's *Intolerance* in *Babel and Babylon*.

Introduction
Standing Outside the Films: Emblems

Hilf mir nur meine Rolle zurücklesen, bis zu mir selbst [...]
Sieh, da suche ich mich zu ereilen, aber ich lauf immer vor mir
her und mein Name hinterdrein ...
Help me read my role backwards, till I reach myself [...]
See, there I am trying to catch myself, but I am always running
ahead of me and my name behind ...
The Night Watches of Bonaventura[1]

And so, my life is a running away, and I lose everything and
everything is left to oblivion or to the other man.
Jorge Luis Borges, 'Borges and Myself'[2]

The Inscribed/Imprinting Hand

The screen offers us an image, somehow standing outside or on the cusp of the film which is beginning to unroll. A graphic drawing of a hand reaches towards us showing its palm, on which the simple title of Fritz Lang's most famous film is inscribed,

the single letter *M*. It is as though the hand offers the film to us in this credit sequence, as over this graphic image other letters appear, forming the names of the film's various collaborators. We are in the liminal space that introduces nearly every film, the credits which serve, to use Gerard Genette's term, as a *paratext*, the boundary between the text and the world surrounding it,[3] and which acknowledge that the fictional world we are about to see was *made*, produced by a number of people, whose names now appear before us. This hand stands out in its non-photographic quality as a visual emblem underlying all these names of the makers of this film, a hint of what is to come.

But in its rather contorted depiction, the hand does not really seem to make a generous gesture of offering to the audience. Rather, it displays itself, a hand raised, almost in a gesture of supplication or surrender. It recalls the convulsed and deformed hands of German Expressionist paintings and graphics; its gesture speaks of suffering, as if the letter inscribed on it were a wound, an insignia branded on the palm like an archaic punishment. As emblem of the film's story, it anticipates a moment in which the criminals pursuing Hans Beckert (Peter Lorre), just identified by the blind balloon seller as the child murderer the whole city is pursuing, mark Beckert in order not to lose sight of him in the city night. To do so, one of them inscribes the palm of his own hand with a large white M in chalk (M for murderer, *Mörder*). This chalk mark is then transferred onto Beckert's shoulder as the man pretends to stumble against him. The M proclaims Beckert's identity as the murderer, the man sought throughout the film, lifting him from the crowd of anonymous backs that one might pass in a city street, the crowd into which he had previously disappeared. The mark, then, is the sign of singularity, of guilt, of being picked out from the crowd. But the hand that is inscribed with the M is, therefore, not the murderer's hand, but rather that of the man who marks him. As an emblem for the film, the image of the hand serves as a transfer between the marker and the marked, a common bond between murderer and pursuer, as much as a differentiation. Lang's film works both to establish and to blur categories: between the police and the criminal, the normal and the insane, the guilty and the innocent.

Lang pointed out in interviews that the M inscribed in the palm simply traces over an M already imprinted on the human hand from birth. The three major lines of the palm – those which chiromancy claims stand for life, love and success – intersect to form a figure like an M. Lang, therefore, identifies the M with the traditional sign of fate, the lines imprinted on the palm which occult science allows us to interpret. But whereas everyone's fate is different – and the differing lengths and shapes of these lines were believed to encode and reveal an individual's destiny – the figure of the M is nearly universal. The mark that has such a fatal consequence for Hans Beckert in this film is a mark we all share.

There is another reference contained in this marked and marking hand. Lang has indicated that he made frequent appearances in his own films, a practice we more often associate with a director highly influenced by Lang and whose success Lang, during his later career in Hollywood, would envy and try to emulate, Alfred Hitchcock. But whereas Hitchcock's appearances emphasised his highly recognisable figure, Lang's appearances remain anonymous. He appears not as a face, or a caricature silhouette, but in close-ups of hands, standing in for actors playing characters in his films. Although we cannot identify with certainty which of the close-ups of hands in Lang's films (and there are many of them) actually show his own hand (presuming his anecdote is true), it is not unlikely that it is actually Lang's hand which is marked with chalk in *M*.[4]

This opening image and its associations suggest a large number of the themes that will be central to this book: inscription and identity, the ambiguity of gestures, the body as a sign, the transfer of guilt, the interplay of individuality and universality, of single character and mass – all these are themes that intertwine in Lang's films throughout his career. But, primarily, this book seeks to plot the ambiguous figure of Lang himself and his presence in his films. But what do I mean by the 'figure' of Lang? I do not simply mean the biological, biographical person Fritz Lang who directed these films and with whom I once spent an evening in 1969. This book will not be in any sense a biography. Patrick McGilligan's recent biography of Lang, *The Nature of the Beast*, has opened up new perspectives on Lang's life and I feel sure more Lang biographies will be produced, perhaps questioning and modifying McGilligan's findings.[5] The figure of Lang I seek to trace is constituted by an exchange between this actual historical person and the films he made. Eventually Lang merges with these films and therefore becomes both more and less than the biological, biographic person. Rather than detailing Lang's life and times, I want to capture the way Lang enters his own films, fashioning for himself his identity as a film-maker, forging an image of himself which stands behind, or looms over, his films and the discourses surrounding them. This figure of Lang seems to be, like a credit sequence, part of his films, yet also outside them, connecting them to an enunciating labour, to a source from which they derive. But it is a source whose existence is indicated by the films themselves; a source we find only by reading backwards from them, as though the films, or our careful viewing of them, create the figure of Lang as much as vice versa. In what way did Lang imprint himself in his films, or – to pick up on the reversal suggested by this image of the imprinting hand which first must be marked itself – in what ways do Lang's films imprint him on the audience, on film history?

This is, therefore, a book that tries to tackle the issue of director's style and authorship in a somewhat novel manner. The critique of authorship which was launched in the 60s and 70s in literature and film studies, signalled by key texts from Roland Barthes, Michel Foucault and Peter Wollen, undermined the *auteur* theory, which treated film directors as authors, pronouncing it both methodologically naive and ideologically suspect. Naive because it lacked a true understanding of the Hollywood mode of production and the constraints placed on a director's self-expression; suspect because it staked a meaningful interpretation on a 'theological' account of the author-as-creator. Such a view of the author precluded a more progressive assumption – that meaning is made by readers and viewers in an ongoing interaction with texts whose energy should not be frozen by being referred back to an authoritative source.

If we approach authorship in terms of the director maintaining control over the production of a film, Lang stands out in film history. Lang's assertion of control over his European films is legendary, epitomised in the many stories describing him as a tyrant, driving actors and technicians to extraordinary achievements. His attempt to exert a similar degree of control over his Hollywood films is equally well-known, as evident in its compromises and defeats as in its successes. But even a passing study of Lang also reveals the vital role his collaborators played in his films, including directors of photography, set designers and, perhaps most importantly, his screenwriter and wife, Thea von Harbou. The credits of some prints of *M*, in fact, avoid mentioning Lang as director (although the first writing on the screen declares we are watching 'ein Fritz Lang film'). Instead the credits open with the rubric 'dieser film entstand in gemeinsamer arbeit' – this film comes from a collective project – and then lists Lang's name first in a long column of collaborators. Lang's image of himself as a director in these credits wavers between a claim of ownership ('a Fritz Lang film') and apparent modesty (one of a collective). But just as this book is not a biography, it is also not going to provide a production history of Lang's films, recounting the evolution of each Lang film and the various forces which shaped its final form – as much as that book needs to be written, and as I would love to write it. The focus of my work will remain for the most part on the screen. I will explore the complexity of Lang's imprint on his films through viewing his films, rather than exploring their production.

Lang once characterised himself as a *Handwerker*, a craftsman, rather than an artist. But, once again, with apparent modesty, Lang claims an important stake in his work. In Germany a *Handwerker* takes on the traditional value of direct personal involvement with production, in contrast with the alienated and mechanical labour of an industrial worker. Lang once again asserts the priority of his own imprint on his films through keeping his hand in the process. The hand leaves the imprint of the maker. But the work process of a director of films – which are certainly complex industrial and technological products, created through a detailed division of labour – makes a literal understanding of this imprint impossible. Lang will never leave a simple fingerprint, but an imprint which resembles the mark left on Beckert's back, a sign heavily mediated as it attempts to emerge from anonymity.

The Screening Room: 'Strange but True'

But what clasp is given us by this phantom hand, which is not physically present there in the text to greet the reader or viewer, but only leaves its mark, its imprint? The author does not necessarily efface the reader's part; indeed, the author exists as an invitation to reading. The author, in film as well as literature, is, I would maintain, a creature of the reader's or viewer's desire. Instead of providing the ultimate signification and meaning through presence, the author works by remaining absent. As Foucault's essay 'What is an Author?' makes clear (as well as the writings of literary critics, such as Wayne Booth, who have analysed the multiple registers of narration), the author never simply speaks in their own voice.[6] Between the actual writer and the reader a series of speakers intervene, such as fictional narrators, or what Wayne Booth calls the 'implied author', all of which are contained in the writing and separate the reader from direct contact with the actual writer. As Foucault puts it:

> It is well known that in a novel narrated in the first person, neither the first person pronoun, the present indicative tense, nor, for that matter, its signs of localisation refer directly to the writer, either to the time that he wrote, or to the specific act of writing. Rather they stand for a 'second self' whose similarity to the author is never fixed and undergoes considerable alteration in the course of a single book. It would be as false to seek the author in relation to the actual writer as to the fictional narrator; the 'author-function' arises out of their scission in the division and distance of the two.[7]

Rather than achieving direct communication with a reader, by writing an author splits off their own words so that they take on a life of their own. As Jorge Borges states in his sketch 'Borges and Me', the author is always 'the other man' separate from the living breathing person; the author is the one who writes, or rather who is embodied in the writing. Foucault calls writing 'a voluntary obliteration of the self': 'Where a work had the duty of creating immortality, it now attains the right to kill, to become the murderer of its author.'[8] Barthes, in fact, sees the death of the author as not only the birth of the reader, but as the birth of writing, and of the writer as *scriptor*, one who does not express himself, but rather, like Mallarmé, abdicates, gets out of the way, erases his 'I', in order to let language itself take over.[9] In modern literature, Barthes claims, from Mallarmé through Kafka, Proust and the Surrealists, there is no longer a person behind the text, but rather a play of signification, a 'fabric of quotations', the force of language and writing itself which, as Foucault puts it, 'creates an opening where the writing subject endlessly disappears'.[10]

Film studies, frankly, never lingered over these major theorisations of authorship.[11] It was often assumed any treatment of the author must follow the naive trajectory Barthes denounces: the author as god, as first cause and ultimate meaning of the text to be discovered through the biographical author's 'person, his history, his taste, his passions'. Barthes' proclamation of the death of the author, in the selective manner it has been used in film studies, seemed to reduce the process by which a reader or viewer encounters an author in a text to a hushed and submissive passivity. The possibility of a modern author dedicated not to self-expression but to the play of discourse, particularly relevant in a medium like film where the '*auteur*' rarely speaks directly in 'his own voice', but rather indirectly through sounds and images assembled, performed and in some ways produced by collaborators, remains largely unexplored.

I see the author as precisely poised on the threshold of the work, evident in the film itself, but also standing outside it, absent except in the imprint left behind. I will approach Lang as an author from this perspective, not simply (following Peter Wollen's refining of the *auteur* theory) considering the author as a name for the systematic nature of a group of texts.[12] Not all films invite us to construct their author. In fact, the film medium readily lends itself to authorless discourse. I would claim a director has to struggle to assert authorship, both in the making of the film and in the discourses surrounding it. An authored film shows the signs of this struggle, a struggle by which the author may discover (and reveal to the viewer) something other than her personality or individual 'history, tastes and passions'. The *agon* of authorship in film invites an encounter with the language of cinema, just as the modern author in literature encounters the drives underlying language itself. My exploration of Lang will seek to uncover this encounter with film language, which is also, in a profound sense, the fashioning of its tradition and history. Lang stands as one of the film authors who fundamentally influenced the way film language – editing, composition, lighting, set design, acting – told stories and addressed audiences. Film language's encounter with and reaction to large-scale forms – such as allegory, the adventure story, or the crime narrative and tale of detection – are essential parts of Lang's creation as an author.

We can follow Foucault in claiming that the biographical person in effect dies to produce the author, as Barthes imagines Proust giving up his life in order to produce the novel of his life. I will not be tracing these films back to Fritz Lang's life, but will rather trace the way Lang as an author, as an assembler of images and sounds, makes his hand sensed within the very filaments of the texts. His hand beckons to us to enter his texts and find him, but entices us into a maze rather than setting up a direct encounter. Since there will be no author's hand in this maze to grasp ours and show us the way, we encounter the language of cinema itself and our own work as film viewers. The search for the author takes place in a labyrinth in which at times even the film director himself may have lost his way.

Perhaps there is no better exploration of the paradoxes of film authorship than the screening room sequence in Godard's *Contempt* in which Fritz Lang plays 'Fritz Lang', a German director, now making a film of Homer's *Odyssey* in Cinecitta for producer Jeremy Prokosch (Jack Palance). In this scene, Lang watches rushes from this film which he never actually directed but his fictional character of the same name within the film did. The sequence contains many references to Lang's career, to incidents that Lang himself had reported in interviews. The key instance involves a struggle for control over the film (and the nature of film discourse) with Prokosch. After knocking cans of film across the room, Prokosch bears down on Lang, yelling, 'You cheated me, Fritz', claiming the scene he shot was not in the script. Lang claims it is, but refuses to surrender his own copy of the script to the producer. When a copy of the script is brought to Prokosch he flips through it and gruffly admits the scene is there, 'But it's not what you have on that screen.' Lang responds, 'Naturally, because in the script it is written and on the screen it's pictures, motion pictures it's called.' Prokosch reacts by flinging more film cans, this time in a parody of the classical Greek statue, Myron's *Discus Thrower* (Lang comments: 'Finally you get the feel of Greek culture').

The sequence re-stages an encounter Lang claims he had with Eddie Mannix, the producer of his first Hollywood film, *Fury*.[13] Therefore Lang is playing (or replaying) Fritz Lang based on his own script. But the dialogue also makes an essential claim about film authorship: it is not the script, the written words, that Lang has authored, but their translation into images. Here we encounter Lang's own claim to being an *auteur*, his attempt to control in detail the image as it appears on the screen. The surviving scripts of Lang's Hollywood films make clear how literal this authorship was, with Lang's careful diagrams showing the camera angles and camera movement within the set, the paths of the actors, with sketches conveying the framing and even the gestures of the actors. The words were a libretto for which Lang supplied a full orchestration into images. And as his anecdote makes clear, this control over *mise-en-scène* did not simply add something to the words, but transformed them. Lang's contribution is alchemical, a chain reaction of reinterpretation and visualisation, opening up the film (and the viewer) to non-verbal meanings.

But this sequence of Godard's film also demonstrates the way a modern author (or a cinematic author: Godard as well as Lang) creates a text out of Barthes' 'fabric of quotations'. The film-maker functions less as a *scripto*r than a fashioner of palimpsests, texts written over other texts creating new meanings from the superimposition of old ones. Besides quoting Lang's life (or accounts of his life), the sequence accumulates a thicket of references and quotations, including Palance's parody of Myron's sculpture. Inscribed on the wall is a quote attributed (possibly spuriously) to Louis Lumière: 'the cinema is an invention without a future'. Scenes from a cinematic adaptation of Homer's *Odyssey* are screened, accompanied by Lang quoting in German verses on Odysseus – not from Homer, but from Dante – in which the Italian poet placed his forebear's hero in the Inferno and had him recount the voyage he undertook *after* his return from Troy. The film screened, although supposedly directed by Lang, recalls, with its arcing camera movements around ancient statues, Rossellini's *Voyage to Italy* (a film we see announced on the marquee of a theatre later in the film and the plot of which, as many critics have pointed out, resonates with *Contempt*'s story of the collapse of a marriage). Therefore, we receive Homer's *Odyssey* as passed down through several hands: Dante's sequel and Godard/Lang's cinematic adaptation with a bow to Rossellini. When Prokosch tries to circumvent Lang's direction by hiring Paul Javal, a new scriptwriter (Michel Piccoli), he seals the deal by writing a cheque on the back of his female assistant (Godard would later use the cheques written for the stars and technicians of *Tout va bien* as credits for that film), declaring, 'When I hear the word culture, I bring out my cheque book', a quote transformed from Nazi Reich Marshal Hermann Goering who threatened, 'When I hear the word culture, I take out my pistol.'

But perhaps the most complex quotation in the scene, and the one with the most resonance as an emblem for the film director, comes when Lang quotes in German (he speaks German, French and English in this sequence – the three languages in which he made films – making us aware of the varied texture of language and the need for translation) the last stanza of Friedrich Hölderlin's poem 'The Poet's Vocation':

> Furchtlos bleibt aber, so er es muss, der Mann
> Einsam vor Gott, es schuzet die Einfalt ihn
> Und keiner Waffen brauchts und keiner
> Listen, so lange, bis Gottes Fehl hilft.
> [*translated by Christopher Middleton as:*
> Fearless yet, if he must, man stands, and lonely
> Before God, simplicity protects him, no
> Weapon he needs, nor subterfuge
> Till God's being not there helps him.]

Lang then discusses the variants on the last line, that Hölderlin first wrote 'So lange der Gott *nicht* da ist' which Francesca, Prokosch's assistant, translates for Paul as 'Tant que Dieu ne fait pas defaut' (as long as God does not fail him). Then, Lang states, Hölderlin changed the verse to 'So lange der Gott uns *nahe* ist' (as long as God is near to us). But the final version reverses these and describes man's aid coming from God's being missed, his failure (Gottes Fehl) or as Lang says in French, 'ce n'est plus la présence du Dieu, c'est l'absence de Dieu qui rassure l'homme' (it is no longer the presence of God, it is the absence of God that reassures Man). Lang concludes, 'it is very strange, but true'.[14]

Hölderlin's verse claims the creator's absence as an essential relation to his creation. The sequence in the screening room centered around the representation of gods and heroes. Prokosch intones, 'I like gods. I know exactly how they feel.' Prokosch's identification with the gods revolves around his sense of their power – like his chequebook which can reverse the plot of the *Odyssey* by hiring a new writer. Lang, however, immediately cautions Prokosch, 'Jerry, don't forget, the gods have not created men, man has created the gods.' This is more than a simple statement of Feuerbach-like humanism or atheism. As the author is in some sense the creation of the reader, imagined by the reader as they interact with the text, so likewise, the gods are created by man from the traces, images and signs of their power. The gods shown in these rushes from the *Odyssey* directed by 'Lang' appear only as statues; immobile, inert. The living presence of the gods has departed from this world, leaving only their images behind. Man misses god, and that missed opportunity remains like an unanswered phone call (in German a *Fehlanruf* is the term for a wrong number). Contrary to the approach to the author that Barthes condemns, which claims to uncover the full presence of the author in the text, in this more complex theology (or theory of reading) offered by Hölderlin and Lang (or Godard) absence becomes the author's final ambiguous, but powerful, gift to the reader.

The Interview and the Clock

I claim that I can find Lang within his films, that he has imprinted them with his mark. But things are more complex than that. I am not just reading Lang's films backward in order to reach the real man outside the films. I am claiming that Fritz Lang as author in some sense merged with his films. The author stands on the threshold of his films rather than entirely outside them. The Fritz Lang that existed entirely outside his films (if such a total exclusion were possible) was not Fritz Lang the author about whom I am writing this book. But I am not just saying that the author is immanent in his texts, either. Fritz Lang is a construction, a creation as much as any of his films are, but of a different sort than any single film. Not only is he the point of convergence of all his films, he is also a figure that existed outside them but always in relation to them, directing them from that position. Lang clearly appears as this figure in Godard's film: 'Fritz Lang', a famous German director, author, as Godard's characters indicate, of both *M* and *Rancho Notorious*, yet in some way a fictitious character as well, part of a plot. This is a character with a history becoming a character in a story. But Lang did not have to wait for Godard to create this role for him. He had already played it and, as we saw, provided Godard with the scenario and dialogue for many of its key scenes.

A key anecdote of Lang's role in history appears in *Contempt*, when Paul expresses his doubt to Prokosch that Lang will accept his rewriting of the *Odyssey*: 'In '33 Goebbels asked Lang to take over the German cinema industry, and that same evening Lang crossed the border.' The story of Lang's escape from the Third Reich after a tension-filled meeting with Goebbels, which included the Minister of Propaganda's offer to Lang to assume the leading role in the development of Nazi cinema, forms the eye of the hurricane in recent revisionist accounts of Lang's life. Patrick McGilligan points out that Lang only began to tell the tale of his meeting with Goebbels during World War II.[15] The first version was published in 1943 as publicity material for the release of his Hollywood anti-Nazi film, *Hangmen also Die* and the simultaneous release of an English-language version of his last German film before exile, *The Testament of Dr. Mabuse*, the banning of which by the Nazis supposedly precipitated the meeting with Goebbels. In other words, Lang first told this story as a way of stressing his own involvement with the world portrayed in his films and as a sort of advertisement for them.

Lang later gave increasingly detailed and dramatic recitations of the story many times, in interviews in English, French and German, in versions that have significant variations but all of which seem based on the same central scenario. Nearly anyone who reads them notices a quality to the accounts that is not only dramatic, but cinematic, and not only cinematic, but specifically Langian. In his account of the meeting Lang emphasises a sense of repetition, hard-edged geometry and an experience of alienation that recalls the sets and *mise-en-scène* of *Metropolis*, *M*, or his Hollywood anti-Nazi films. The imagery suggests a labyrinth, like the maze of authorship in which, I suggest, Lang himself may have lost his way:

> You go down long wide corridors with stone flags and so on, and your steps echo, and as you come around the corridor there are two guys there carrying guns. It was not very agreeable. You come to another desk, a third desk and finally to a little room and they say, 'You wait here.' So now you are perspiring a little. The door opens on a long, long office, and at the end of the office there is Dr. Goebbels.[16]

A version Lang told to William Friedkin for an unrealised documentary, quoted by McGilligan, adds these characteristic Langian details to the description of his walk down the corridor:

> [It] had great squares of cement, the walls were black – no pictures, no inscriptions. The windows were very high [so] that you couldn't look out of [them]. I walked and walked on these cement squares. Every step echoed constantly.[17]

The interview with Goebbels varies little in the different versions, except in one detail. In all versions Goebbels explains to him the need to ban *The Testament of Dr. Mabuse* because of the film's ending, but reassures Lang that the Führer knows and loves Lang's films and has proclaimed, 'This is the man who will give us the great Nazi films.' Only in a few versions does Lang raise the issue of his Jewish heritage, with Goebbels responding, 'We will decide who is a Jew.' Lang indicates he outwardly expressed delight to Goebbels while inwardly thinking in panic, 'How do I get out of here?' [18]

This concealed desire is brilliantly expressed in Lang's narrative by another characteristic (and cinematic) detail: a clock: 'Outside the window there was a big clock, and the hands went slowly round.'[19] Lang's concern about the time comes from his decision that he must leave Germany that very evening (saying to himself, 'This evening is the last moment you can be sure of getting out of Germany'), the essential motif of classical cinematic storytelling (developed to perfection in Lang's own films) – the deadline. 'I looked at the clock again. At two-thirty the banks close and how can I get out of here? I didn't get out.'[20]

The rest of the narrative recounts Lang's furtive and secretive crossing of the border that evening, the last he could safely spend in Germany. Unable to get money from the bank he gathers a few expensive objects (a golden cigarette case, a golden chain and, according to a French version, jewellery from a girl friend) and the cash he had around the house and takes a train to Paris, ostensibly for a few days, in fact, never to return to Germany while Hitler was in power. Some versions recount him concealing these valuables on the train (taping them under the bathroom sink, or hiding them in a slit he cuts in the carpet) as he crosses the border.

After Lang's death the cracks began to appear in this story, or at least in its relation to actual events. The sale of Lang's passport to the Stiftung Deutsche Kinemathek in Berlin allowed scholars to determine when Lang actually left Germany for France, and the date was months after the alleged meeting with Goebbels. As McGilligan points out, there is no record of the meeting although Goebbels meticulously recorded his meetings in his diaries.[21] It seems likely, then, that the story is Lang's fabrication, his scenario, or, as Jorge Dana describes it in the narration of his recent documentary on Lang's German films, 'his imaginary film'.

The biographical enigmas this fabrication presents are many. Does it conceal a more ambiguous attitude towards the Nazis and Goebbels than the tale expresses? What about the detail, sometimes included, of the discussion of Lang's Jewish heritage, a part of his identity he rarely mentioned and seemed unwilling to explore? Did Lang, after endless repetitions of the story, grow to believe it himself? I am not going to pursue these biographical issues here. What draws me to this story is its role as an archetypal Lang scenario of suspense, subterfuge and of threat to one's identity, here rendered as an autobiographical tale. Lang in some way made sense out of his own life, and presented it to other people, through this sort of story. Here we see the Langian scenario eclipsing the actual events of his own life.

If Lang is caught in the labyrinth of his own storytelling, the revealing image for me comes in the slowly revolving hands of the clock outside the window. This clock supplies the suspense of the story, the sense of the need for an immediate escape (which the evidence of Lang's passport, with its numerous trips and returns to Germany in the months following the apparent date of his encounter with Goebbels, belies). The turning hands of the clock (McGilligan notes that in the version told to Friedkin, Lang said the clock 'moved *and* moved and *moved*'), its relentless motion stressing Lang's own immobility, stuck in Goebbels' office.[22] But the clock also relates Lang to the world outside this office, a network of clock-determined deadlines – the banks which will close, the train schedules which could take him out of Germany. The clock hands tick towards 'the last moment you can be sure of getting out of Germany'.[23] In the only visual version of this story I have seen, a television interview where Lang tells the tale in German, acting out the various roles, he acts out the motion of the clock, turning his hand and arm one way to indicate the passing of time and his other arm in the opposite direction to indicate Goebbels' ongoing speech.[24] These gestures add a further dimension to Lang's drama: he is caught between two implacable machines, one counting the minutes, the other voicing Nazi ideology and offering the temptation of becoming 'the Film Führer'.

In the next chapter I will discuss the role clocks play in setting up a central device of Lang's films which I call the Destiny-machine. To define briefly a concept I will discuss in detail, the Destiny-machine determines the environment in which Lang's characters struggle, serving in most cases as an obstacle. This corresponds in many ways to the theme of fate or destiny (in *Contempt* Lang introduces his film of *The Odyssey* as the 'fight against the gods') which has become such a cliché of Lang criticism that recent commentators have tended to treat it with scorn. But I think we risk losing the mainspring of Lang's dramaturgy if we simply dismiss the idea of destiny in his films as banal. The point is that for Lang destiny is not a metaphysical concept (and actually not a fight against the gods) but a material one, less a meaning than a structure. Destiny appears in Lang's films, not as a philosophy, but as a machine, whose mechanical nature in most of the films remains very literal. This is not to say that Lang's films are about a Luddite struggle against machines (although *Metropolis* does dramatise such a revolt). The machine in Lang does stand for something beyond itself. But, rather than a metaphor for a view of human nature or metaphysics, the machine is a metonymy, a fragment which stands in for the whole systematic nature of the modern world which Lang sees as a complex determining destiny. In the following chapters I will show how this systematic nature of the modern world is explored in Lang's films, but here in this self-fashioning anecdote we find Lang himself pitted against the Destiny-machine, on the one hand the unstoppable clock marking the boundaries of human social time (when banks close, trains leave and human fates are given their 'last moment' when something is possible) and the equally unstoppable machine of ideological discourse issuing from one of the key inventors of modern propaganda, Joseph Goebbels.

In his story Lang stands fixed between these two forces, immobilised. But as we have learned, Lang himself created this particular scenario, possibly as the only way to make cogent the power the Nazi partyheld at this moment over his identity and future as a film-maker, or perhaps to camouflage his own more ambivalent reactions to Nazi power. In narrating, or rather acting it out, his gestures not only indicate his own actions and reactions, but the motions of the Destiny-machine, as he revolves his arms to capture its mechanical progression. Lang's gesture summons up an image he often recalled, of a lunatic he saw in an asylum when he was preparing *The Testament of Dr. Mabuse*, who thought he was a grandfather clock. In his interview with Peter Bogdanovich, Lang indicates he incorporated this figure into the 'original version' of that film:

> He stood there and made a movement with his arms like a pendulum – and I dissolved to a grandfather clock; one day this man has a feeling that some of his springs have fallen out – so he crawls on the floor and tries to find them.[25]

Whether or not this figure ever actually appeared in a version of *The Testament of Dr. Mabuse*, he does appear in the most interesting of Lang's unproduced scripts, *The Man behind You*. This original story by Lang represents his attempt to make an American version of his Mabuse films and its earliest version was one of Lang's first American projects, one he continued to work on throughout the 30s. Here the man-clock is presented exactly as Lang describes in the Bogdanovich interview, a man who swings his arms like a pendulum and who is presented from the point of view of Dr. Moran (the film's Mabuse-like master criminal) in a dissolve to an image of clockworks which suddenly snap, as the madman crumbles onto the floor in a fit. This patient will only respond to one question: 'What time is it?' and always with the same answer (like the clock outside Goebbels' office): 'Too late.'

I end this introduction of emblems of Lang's authorship with this image of Lang, like his fictional lunatic, acting out the mechanical motions of the clock. In Lang's world (which includes his finished films, his scripts, and his accounts of his life, particularly as they tend toward the fictional) not only are characters threatened by the Destiny-machine, but the very act of authorship as well. Within the *agon* or struggle which authorship initiates, the author becomes subject to systems beyond his or her control, not only the tyrannical system of Nazi power, but also systems like the very order of language which the modern author, described by Barthes and Foucault, surrenders to as he vanishes. But this is not simply a contest of hero and opponent with the stronger force overcoming the weaker. Rather authorship often slips into an identification with the impersonal system. The man becomes the clock and counts off the moments of his own fate. The author becomes captured by his own story. Part of the drama that Lang's films enact is precisely the struggle between the claims to power of an author-like figure and the real power of the impersonal system of the Destiny-machine. In almost all cases the apparent master is revealed to have been a tool all along.

PART I

Reading the Text of Death

Lang's Silent Allegories:

Der müde Tod (1921)

Die Nibelungen (1924)

Metropolis (1927)

The greater the significance, the greater the subjection to death, because death digs most deeply the jagged line of demarcation between physical nature and significance.

Walter Benjamin, *The Origins of German Tragic Drama*[1]

1

The *Märchen: Der müde Tod* –
Death and the maiden

Who Tells the Timely Story of Death?

Watchman, what of the night? Watchman, what of the night?
The watchman said, the morning cometh, and also the night:
if ye will inquire, inquire ye: return, come.

Isaiah 21, 11–12

The subjection that the character Fritz Lang feels to the clock outside Minister Goebbels' window inscribes his place within a system he cannot control. Lang does not describe his dilemma simply in terms of his fear of Goebbels' power and tyranny. His dramatic agony comes from the possibility that he might not be able to make it in time, get to the bank, get his money, make his train – and from the second-by-second frustration of his intentions. Although the theme of destiny as analysed in Lang's films by previous commentators (including Lang) most often opposed individual freedom to a metaphysical determinism ('Man's fight against the gods'), Lang's narratives supply a more dynamic model. The question becomes not which is more powerful, an individual's will or the decree of the gods, but rather who is in control of a system by which events are interrelated and characters' destinies become interlocked, who can make use of its order and power and who will be crushed by it? Will Lang be able to leave the office and carry out his plans by making the connections the

system of train schedules and banking hours allows? Or will Goebbels seem to work in concert with the clock (remember the two interlocking revolving hand gestures Lang made in telling the story) and frustrate Lang's intentions? I would claim Lang never raises the philosophical issue of pure freedom or pure necessity. Rather, his plots trace the attempts by different characters to control or at least work in concert with a system that operates separately from their desires and according to its own mechanical logic. Lang stages again and again the varying relations characters can have with this system which I term the Destiny-machine.

This struggle with a systematic order often becomes staged as a battle to control the narrative structure of the film itself, as if the attempt of these characters to seize control of the Destiny-machine mimicked the power of the director over the film. Lang at points seems to confuse the clear separation between diegetic story and action and extra-diegetic style, as characters seem to assert control over the visual devices of the film itself, especially its editing. In many ways, Lang's 1921 film *Der müde Tod* offers the most elegant convergence between the Destiny-machine and the film's narrative structure. Lang structures his film not only as a story to be followed, but as an emblematic text which must be read and interpreted, cueing viewers to unravel its enigmas and ask questions about its authorship and intentions. He balances his exposition of the Destiny-machine in this film with another device, equally important to his narrative style: moments of revelation, visionary moments in which characters must read reality in a different manner than they did previously. The revelations offered by these visionary moments also provide the film's viewer with a deeper insight into the dynamics of the film in the form of visual emblems which the viewer, as well as the character, must interpret. The interplay between the Destiny-machine and such visionary moments forms one of the basic armatures of Lang's film-making as I will trace it in this book, recurring in various guises and with shifting significances throughout his career.

Although Lang's earlier films, especially *Der Spinnen*, set up many of his basic themes, elements of dramaturgy and *mise-en-scène*, *Der müde Tod* ('The Weary Death', known in France as *Les Trois Lumières*, 'The Three Lights' and in England and the US as *Destiny*) provides the first example of Lang's completely developed system. As only the third film of Lang's long collaboration with Thea von Harbou (whom he married about a year after completing the film), it reminds us how much Lang's cinema was shaped by this collaboration. *Der müde Tod* remains also one of the most perfectly crafted films of the Weimar cinema, perhaps the most beautiful of the *Märchen* films based on folk and fairy tales. The subtitle of the film describes it as 'Ein Deutsches Volkslied in 6 Versen', the six verses corresponding to the film's six reels. In the film's intertitles and 'naive' characterisation Lang and Harbou invoke the style of a popular tale, with its simplicity of psychology, its materialisation of metaphysical figures (the cloaked figure of 'weary' Death himself) and the tale's aspiration to deliver wisdom about the antinomies of life, the intertwining of love and death. But concealed within its self-conscious invocation of an oral tradition of tale-telling *Der müde Tod* offers a complex meditation on cinematic narrative.

The story stands as one of scenarist Harbou's most poetic inventions. A young couple about to wed meet a mysterious figure who joins them at table in a tavern. We learn he arrived in town not long before, bought a plot of land which he proceeded to enclose with a huge wall. Most mysteriously, this wall seems to have no gateway or door, no means of entrance or exit, which baffles and disturbs the burgomasters. The young fiancée leaves the table for a moment and when she returns, finds her lover and the man in the cloak gone. Searching for her lover hopelessly, she is aided by an apothecary seeking mandrakes in the moonlight. At his pharmacy the despairing young woman drinks poison. Immediately she comes to the vast wall of the mysterious figure, in which a door now appears for her. The cloaked figure announces himself to her as Death and asks why she has entered his realm without being summoned. When she explains she is searching for her lover, Death holds out no hope for his return. Taking pity on her, he shows her a vast room filled with candles. Each candle, he explains, is a life, and when it flickers out, the life is lost. Death himself is weary of this role and wishes it could be changed. He therefore offers the maiden a chance to rescue her lover from death.

He shows her three candles (the 'three lights' of the French title) and tells her that if she can save these lives from being extinguished, she may have her lover back. The largest section of the film narrates these three tales, each comprising a reel (or 'verse', as the original intertitles term them) of the film, set in a different historical and cultural milieu: the caliphate of Baghdad; Renaissance Venice; and a fairy-tale vision of China. In each of the tales the same actress who plays the maiden, Lil Dagover, plays a young woman who is threatened with the loss of her lover. In each tale she strives bravely to preserve him, but in each of them he dies and the candle flame is extinguished. Still wishing to see the young woman defeat the decree of fate, Death offers her another bargain: if she can find a life whose time has not yet come, willing to enter the realm of death early, he will give her her lover in exchange, but she must find this soul before midnight. When we return to the framing story in the pharmacy, no time has passed in the human realm. The apothecary manages to knock the poison from the maiden's hand. The clock strikes eleven; she has one hour to find a substitute for her lover. Although she searches among the abject, the old and the infirm, everyone responds with the same refrain: 'Not one day, not one hour, not one breath' will they give up.

The maiden finds that the infirmary is on fire, trapping an infant on an upper floor. She fights her way to the room and Death appears, arms outstretched to receive the babe from her as the fulfilment of their bargain. Instead, the young woman rushes to the window and lowers the baby to its frantic mother below. Apparently perishing in the fire, the maiden is now reunited with her lover in the realm of death.

The simplicity and symmetry of the tale cannot obscure its powerful meditation on the nature of story-telling. As a tale, we watch this film unfold, aware that it is being told, our attention drawn to its structuring devices and to such extra-diegetic processes as casting and scripting. The film's division into six single reel 'verses' (two reels given to the opening, the first ending with the lover's disappearance; the next three divided between the three stories, and the last reel given to the final attempt to find a soul) draws the viewer's attention to the film as a crafted piece of story-telling. Its structure as a series of embedded stories highlights the tale form, as we follow three different stories and the larger framing tale which encompasses them. Likewise, the casting of Lil Dagover as the maiden and Walter Janssen as her lover in a similar role in each tale and the appearance of Bernhard Goetzke (who plays the weary Death in the framing tale as well as the figure who ultimately defeats the lover in each of the embedded tales) draws attention to casting and performance. Lang/Harbou also provide a series of relays between the tales through repetition. The similar narrative structure in each tale of love crushed by tyrants cues the viewer to see them as variants of a single plot, and establishes the film's sense of fatality through repetition of the same story dynamics and identical endings. Each story moves towards its resolution implacably, like destiny. The end of each story is death, as the appearance of Goetzke signals the closure of each tale, Death becoming a figure of fate because it represents the inevitable ending. Story-telling, therefore, provides a perfect image of the struggle against, and surrender to, death, which is destiny. In *Der müde Tod* the story serves as a perfect image for the Destiny-machine, the system whose ending is always the same. And that's why Death is weary.

But who tells the story, who sets the Destiny-machine in motion? The desire to find the figure behind it all motivates the young girl's search for her lover, for the one who has taken him from her and can return him to her. Her search is initiated by an act of reading. The girl enters the realm of Death impelled by the words she reads from *The Song of Solomon* in the Bible lying open in the apothecary's: 'Set me as seal upon thine heart, as a seal upon thine arm; for love is strong as death'. The text proclaims that her desire stands as an equal opponent to the power of death and this contest between them supplies the ongoing motive force for the story. The seesaw opposition between desire's restless quest and the weary carrying-out of duty by Death sets the Destiny-machine in motion. If the girl cannot find her lover, she wants to find the one in charge, the apparent master of the story, he who deter-mines its end and therefore could change it. But Harbou/Lang endow this early master narrator with more self-reflection than the hubristic master criminals of their later films. Death knows he is not his own master, and indeed he is weary of playing out the same scenario from time immemorial. If all humans, all characters in this story, are subject to death, to whom is Death subject?

The film makes this the central enigma of its story-telling, one which it refuses to answer unequivocally, but insists on raising. Within the embedded tales, the figure of Death generally acts as the servant of one of the tyrant characters. In the Arabic tale the gardener El Mot follows the orders of the Caliph and buries Zobeide's lover alive, and in China the Emperor's archer kills the lover of Tiao-tsien. But the Renaissance tale provides an essential reversal; Death appears here as the Moorish servant of the heroine Fiametta, instructed by her to stab a man with a poisoned dagger. Fiametta has plotted that the Moor's victim should be her tyrannical betrothed, Girolamo. But because Girolamo has intercepted and exchanged the note Fiametta sent her lover, her plot is derailed. Instead, her lover arrives at the time appointed for the murder, and receives the fatal wound in Girolamo's place. Death only *appears* to be someone else's servant; in truth, he acts to bring the story to its ironic resolution.

But as Death indicates to the maiden, Death itself has no will, no desire to end human lives. He is not his own master. Is Death then the servant of the story-telling process, subject to the narrative as Destiny-machine? This seems to be the film's logic. When Death indicates he is incapable of returning her lover to the young girl, he explains his impotence by bringing her into the Hall of Flames, and showing her the candles. These inanimate objects would seem to control human destiny and the actions of Death. In each of the tales, the story ends, the lovers die, as the candle burns out. The candle seems to have a causal power, a magical potency that Death, at least as a character, lacks. Further, Lang identifies the power invested in the candle with the devices of the cinema, especially the act of editing. This is evident not only in the last shot of each of the tales which cuts (usually through an overlap-dissolve) to a sputtering candle, but also to the brief sequence in which Lang first demon-strates visually the power of the candle through two key cinematic devices: the overlap-dissolve and parallel editing.

Death leads the maiden over to a candle and surrounds its flame with his delicately cupped hands. Through a trick superimposition, Death seems to lift the flame from the candle, raising it. The flame then dissolves into a naked infant, cradled in Death's hands. Death looks up from the infant and, as his gaze meets the camera, the infant disappears. Death spreads his now empty hands apart. We cut immediately to a woman collapsed weeping over a cradle, then back to Death and the Hall of Flames. The cinematic figuration of this sequence is worth reading closely as one of the emblems Lang offers in this film which demand to be unpacked. Lang's delight in cinematic tricks appears throughout this film (with the Chinese tale performing a homage to the trick cinema of Méliès and Pathé of more than a decade earlier). But beyond the delight in both technology and the amazement it creates, this candle sequence shows that cinematic tricks can convey other realities, an essentially German attitude to the possibility of the fantastic in film, first heralded by Georg Lukacs and Paul Wegener in the early 1910s, and put into practice in Wegener's earlier *Märchen* films.[2] Lang and Harbou continued this tradition, undoubtedly due to its cinematic as well as metaphysical possibilities. Lang employed the overlap-dissolve throughout the 1920s as a means of revealing a deeper reality beneath the surface of things (recall his overlap-dissolve from the lunatic swinging his arms to the clock works which reveal his hallucinatory self-perception). In the first two stories of *Der müde Tod* an overlap-dissolve is used as El Mot or the Moor dissolve into the figure of Death. But in the Hall of Flames the dissolves express the instantaneous power of death – poignantly in this image of the suddenly appearing and vanishing baby, seemingly born and delivered into the hands of Death, simply to evaporate before our eyes.

The parallel cut to the weeping, bereft mother plays no less a role in defining Death's power cinematically. The cut links Death to some other space, somewhere in the world where his power has just struck. The cut follows cause (his taking of the baby) with effect (the mother's grief). The cut across space expresses Death's action at a distance, his power, just as a cut from one end of a phone to the other represents the power of the telephone. If the Hall of Flames represents all the lives of the world (and the narratives that follow stress Death's vast geographical range: from Europe to the Middle East to the Far East), then this room not only represents the time allotted to each human destiny, but a compression of all the space of the globe. Lang concisely expresses this omnipresence with this cut to the weeping mother, somewhere within the vast realm of Death.

Here we enter into the extraordinary narrative complexity of this apparently simple film, which, although it mimes the pre-modern form of a *Märchen*, in fact elegantly produces a peculiarly modern conception of space and time. The Hall of Flames is like a vast switchboard with relays connecting it to all the world's destinies. While this is first expressed by the allegorical use of a symbolic set of the mass of candles, an image Harbou borrowed from the Brothers Grimm's tale 'Grandfather Death', it is more fully explicated through the use of editing. But the most complex aspect of the unique space and time of the Hall of Flames appears with the narrative device of the three lights which represent the three separate tales. Not only do these tales take place in different geographical locations, they also seem to take place in different times. The Arabic tale could be set in the indefinite period of the *Thousand and One Nights*, except for the costume and automatic pistol of Zobeide's European lover which places it in contemporary times (possibly even after the apparently nineteenth-century setting of the framing tale!). The Venetian tale, however, clearly takes place in the Renaissance, and the rather ahistorical Chinese tale seems to refer to a legendary past. The maiden's quest to preserve the destinies embodied in the three lights moves through time as well as space, as if the Hall of Flames stood beyond all earthly demarcations, able to connect with any period anywhere on the globe.

The model for this series of tales from different times and cultures linked in telling the tale of love's betrayal would seem to be D.W. Griffith's *Intolerance* (although Carl Dreyer's 1919 Danish film *Leaves from Satan's Book* may also have served as a model, presenting six episodes of parallel stories in different historical periods, or even before that, the Italian film *Satan*). Griffith, however, gives no diegetic explanation, natural or supernatural, for his cutting between four historical periods (Babylon, Palestine in the time of Christ, sixteenth-century France, and the contemporary US) as he tells the story of 'Love's Struggle through the Ages'. To explain the film's unique blending of these historical periods, Griffith described the editing logic of his film in terms of a viewpoint from which one can see separate historical periods, flowing together, like the view of separate rivers converging when seen from a mountain top. Although Lang/Harbou never intercut the various stories, instead treating each tale as an integral whole, the Hall of Flames operates like Griffith's mountain top, a point outside space and time (recall the allegorical set of the wall without doorways with no access to the surrounding world), but supernaturally connected to all of history and the reaches of the world. Lang/Harbou develop this theme of the realm of Death existing outside time most thoroughly when the maiden is given her last chance to return to the realm of the living and bring back a soul.

In the series of shots which bridge the maiden's entrance into and her return from the realm of Death, Lang shows a masterful control of the temporality of film editing that rivals even *Intolerance*'s radical cutting through history. The editing elegantly figures time's paradoxical role in the realm of the dead, and forever marks the masterful control of time as a hallmark of Lang's narrative style. The most consistent emblem of the Destiny-machine in Lang, the revolving hands of the clock, receives here its first extended treatment in a Lang film. After reading the passage from *The Song of Solomon*, the maiden stares directly into the camera to emphasise her realisation of the words' significance and her decision to confront Death directly. She takes the vial of poison and pours it into a glass. Lang deftly employs the editing technique Griffith introduced to cinema: the power of a cut to suspend an action or gesture. As she pours the poison, Lang cuts to three successive shots. First, a clock (presumably the village clock) fills the screen, its hands marking the hour of eleven. Lang then cuts to a long shot of the village square at night. Then we see a low angle close-up of the night-watchman and his horn as he proclaims (through an intertitle) 'Eleven o'clock and all is well.' Lang returns to the maiden as she brings the glass to her lips. Through the parallel cuts to the clock, watchman and town, Lang places the maiden's act in a specific space and time and emphasises the dramatic importance of her attempted suicide.

Lang then interrupts the action of drinking with another cut, this time an overlap-dissolve to the maiden, matching her previous standing position, but now with no glass in her hand and posed before Death's massive wall in which she discovers the entrance way. Her action has taken her out of space and time into the realm of Death. Lang presents her return to the land of the living (after the tales of the three lights) as a voyage back into time through a strictly parallel sequence. From a shot of the maiden kneeling before Death, surrounded by the candles, we dissolve to the circular form of the clock face. Once again (still?) it marks the eleventh hour. Lang also repeats the shots of the town square and the close-up of the crier and his cry ('Eleven o'clock and all is well'). We see the apothecary looking off-screen in alarm. In the next shot we see the maiden (again? still?) raising the poisoned glass to her lips, but the apothecary rushes into the frame and dashes it from her hands. The maiden's voyage to the realm of the dead, including the stories of the three lights, took no time whatsoever, as Lang indicates literally by the clock fixed on the same minute, and cinematically by the repetition of the previous shots marking the time. Further, the cuts which previously interrupted the act of drinking the poison are here sutured; the action is completed, but differently than we anticipated earlier. Time has, in effect, hiccuped and run backwards slightly, like a scratched record.

The complexity of this control of time shows the modern sophistication of this apparently simple tale, its need to be read carefully. Most of the film takes place within a crease in the fabric of time, between one phase of a fatal action (drinking the poison) and its ultimate interruption (dashed to the ground). The cuts that interrupt the maiden's suicidal action serve, first, to place the action in time, second (the dissolve), to take it out of time, and, finally, to return it to time. We have two realms of time, then: the world of the living, marked by the clock and its implacable movement, and the realm of Death and the three tales, outside of time. But, as we saw, instead of an atemporal release from time's burden, an eternity of dream, poetic inspiration or spiritual delight, the realm outside of time acts as the switchboard in which time's pattern is observed and determined. The candles from Death's realm ultimately synchronise with the clock in the realm of the living; both chart the course of characters and story lines towards death.

If the realm of Death stands outside of time, the stories of Love's quest immerse us into time with a vengeance. Although the three stories take up no time, occur only in the instant between the cup and the lip, within each story time devours and defeats desire. In each of the stories, time is always running out. Not only is the course of each story, like the lives of the lovers, marked by the burning candle. Time also slips through the characters' fingers, like the magic wand in the Chinese story which grows smaller each time it is used and whose disappearance announces the futile nature of the lovers' flight from the archer. In the Venetian story Fiametta's message unwittingly sets the time of her lover's death. Fiametta specifies that Girolamo visit her when the clock strikes ten. When Girolamo treacherously delivers this message to her lover instead, it is her lover who arrives at the appointed time, and who therefore dies. But nowhere is time's role as a narrative deadline clearer than in the last reel of the film, when the maiden returns to the living with a strict schedule.

The clock face now becomes a motif in the narration, hurrying the action along, instead of marking its suspension. Lang cuts to the clock several times, at each point marking the maiden's failure to find the soul she seeks. The refrain each character offers as their refusal to her makes it clear that what they refuse to give up is time: not a day, hour or breath. When the maiden refuses to exchange the baby's new life for her lover's and perishes herself as a consequence, she again leaves the realm of time. We see her walking off, her back to us, arm-in-arm with her lover, Death disappearing from the screen for the last time. But the film does not end with this image of a reunited couple. Instead we see the clock face once more, now having reached the deadline of midnight, the two hands of the clock joined. The last image and intertitle return to the nightwatchman and his refrain, 'Twelve o'clock and all is well'.

The deadline reached in this shot is not that of Death's bargain with the maiden; that deal was abandoned several shots earlier. Instead it marks the end of the film, its final image, the coming to rest of the narrative (like the burned-down candles of the embedded stories), the running-down of the Destiny-machine. But the film leaves us with a machine, the clock itself, rather than a figure who stands behind it. Death, we have learned, does not do his own will, but is subject to a system of limitations whose final image is this clock. The attempt to intervene in this scenario is doomed; it is always already written and simply has to run its course. But this determinist description doesn't quite do justice to the narrative system of Lang's cinema, or of this film in particular. The maiden in *Der müde Tod* demonstrates that her love *is* as strong as death, that Eros and Thanatos stand in equilibrium in Lang's storytelling, weights and counterweights within the Destiny-machine and the ongoing narrative. And in the story's logic her defiance of death begins with an act of reading, her chance encounter with the passage from *The Song of Solomon*.

The Allegory of the Maiden: Reading and Desire

If the maiden's efforts within the film are feckless, she avoids being a passive counter in the game of fate. She also tries to make the system work for her. While the cinematic devices, the cuts and overlap-dissolves, primarily illustrate the unconquerable power of Death, the maiden would seem to claim these devices as well. On the side of Death and the Destiny-machine these devices demonstrate the implacable power of the system; but from the viewpoint of the maiden, these devices invoke the act of reading and interpreting, of visionary moments and recognitions. It is her action after reading the Biblical passage that suspends time; the importance of her act, while failing to regain her lover, should not be minimised. If the author of the narrative in *Der müde Tod* seems ultimately impersonal and absent, the act of reading dynamises the action of the plot. The maiden does not succeed in overcoming Death, but she gradually succeeds in reading his signs. Unlike the caricatured denizens of the village, the maiden possesses a penetrating insight into reality which Lang conveys through cinematic devices of overlap-dissolves and superimposition, even if she herself is initially loath to accept their significance. These sequences give the maiden the visionary role which I claim forms an essential part of the Langian system.

Visionary moments are granted to many of Lang's characters, and they mark and motivate turning points in the plots. For the most part, these are moments when a character sees through the surface of things and gains a vision of the Destiny-machine pulsing beneath, once again recalling Lang's description of the overlap-dissolve in *The Man Behind You*, showing the clockwork ticking beneath the madman's apparently absurd behaviour. These images do not simply visualise a hallucination or a fantasy. In Lang's films, they trigger a moment of realisation and interpretation, a reading of signs, in which the true mechanism controlling reality is perceived by a character. These readings contradict the ordinary view of things and astonish the characters who experience them. Most often the characters become alienated from their previous sense of existence through these visions.

This can be illustrated by one of the most famous images from Lang's *œuvre*, Freder's vision of Moloch, the god of human sacrifices in the machine room of *Metropolis*. An intrusion by Maria and the children of the workers into the upper realms of the futuristic city has made Freder, the son of the Master of Metropolis, realise the sheltered nature of his existence. Drawn by a desire to discover the real nature of the city he lives in, he has penetrated into the depths and watched the toil of the workers as they serve the machines that run the city. One of the machines explodes, killing and injuring several workers, but the work goes on. Aghast, Freder stares at this huge mechanism (referred to in Harbou's novel as the 'paternoster' machine). An overlap-dissolve replaces it with a monstrous set, a demon's face with a fiery furnace for a mouth into which sacrificial victims are herded and passive workers march mechanically. Freder cries out, 'Moloch', the name of the Philistine god denounced in the Old Testament (and the receiver of children as burnt offerings in Pastrone's 1913 super-film *Cabiria*). The vision melts away as Lang dissolves back to the machine and its real life victims.

Visionary moments act as dramatic pivots within the narrative. They reveal to a character a new dimension to reality and most often destroy a previous semblance of harmony or order. The most extended visionary moment in *Der müde Tod* comes as the climax of the maiden's wandering outside the city in the moonlight searching for her lover. When she reaches the massive wall with neither doors nor windows she leans against it as if weary to the point of death, or perhaps in a trance-like state. She looks off and her eyes suddenly widen and her hands stiffen as if in horror. A point of view shot shows a crowd of people of all ages – children and the elderly– and all classes – kings and beggars– coming toward her as phantoms, transparent superimpositions. In contrast to her bodily exclusion by the wall, these phantoms pass through easily. Lang cuts several times between her horrified reaction and her point of view of the phantoms, until we see her lover among the procession of the dead. The maiden stretches her arms to the spectre of her lover but he passes on, merging with the wall as she falls on her knees, hands clasped, begging for his return. As the dead vanish into the wall, she pounds on it and then collapses. It is here the apothecary finds her. The maiden has seen the wall, which so baffled the city fathers, as the border between two worlds: unyielding to the living, welcoming to the dead. The town elders saw the wall only as a material barrier, apparently meaningless and bizarre; she has discovered, through her vision, that the wall must be read as an emblem of the divergence between life and death. The film's most spectacular emblem, this wall (which dwarfs all human figures that pass before it, looming as it does beyond the film frame with no visible limit or edge to it) defines the demarcation between death and life.

But there are two earlier visionary scenes involving the maiden, which, while briefer, signal more fundamental transformations and readings. The first of these comes when Death sits at their table in the tavern. The lovers have just been told by the tavern-keeper's wife that, as a betrothed couple, they must drink from the loving cup. The couple undertake this awkward task, the girl laughing. Lang cuts from their playful clumsiness to a close-up of Death staring fixedly off to the right, towards them. When we return to the couple's innocent fun in the next shot, we realise it takes place under the stern gaze of Death. It may be this awareness of being watched that causes the maiden to look away from her lover. Rather than meeting Death's gaze directly, she glances down at the table in his direction.

There she sees a phantasmagoric scene in two phases. In modern prints this crucial shot is very brief, and its second phase almost subliminal. But the maiden's vision introduces the major transformation of reality in the film, the first encounter with the power of Death. First, she sees an elongated shadow of a skeleton on the table, falling next to a beer glass whose shadow also stretches across the table. The skeleton shadow comes from the figure that tops Death's walking stick, clearly visible in the previous close-up, a skeleton which raises one hand to his brow, as if searching. Suddenly, a rapid overlap-dissolve occurs, and the beer glass transforms into an hourglass casting its shadow. Her point of view transforms the table into a screen on which the emblems of Death are projected, the skeleton as a shadow and the hourglass as dissolved-in figure, as well as shadow. Its imagistic nature lifts these emblems out of the everyday reality of the tavern, becoming a visual puzzle for the maiden to read, a sort of rebus, a premonition of her lover's disappearance. In the midst of the playful celebration of their impending wedding, the figures of time and Death intrude as a vision seen only by the maiden. A scene of everyday life becomes an encounter of opposing emblems: the loving cup against the hourglass, the lovers against the shadow of Death.

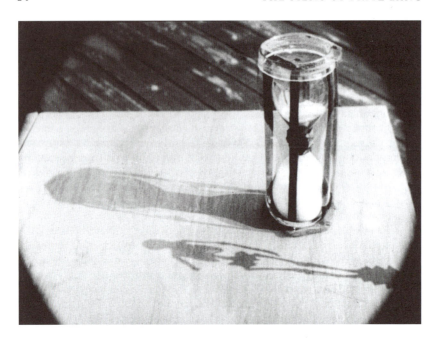

   The visionary moment in Lang represents a rent in the ordinary visual experience
of reality, a moment when other forces shine through and must be read by a character.
But this reading demands a transformation in point of view. The side-long glance with
which the maiden sees the emblems of Death, recalls the use of anamorphosis in Holbein's painting *The Ambassadors* (as the imagery in the procession of the dead recalls
Holbein's engraving series *The Dance of Death*); only a side-long view of this painting

converts the formless figure on the carpet before the ambassadors into a death's head. The visionary moment for Lang wrenches a character out of a previously innocent viewpoint and reveals a world of death writhing beneath the skin of appearances, like Freder's discovery of the deadly exploitation of the workers on which his previous pleasure garden existence has rested. But, in *Der müde Tod*, Lang presents the de-centring effect of this vision with special cogency. The vision itself is prompted by the maiden feeling herself under the gaze of Death, and her own view comes from an askew position which allows the figure to unwind itself, take on emblematic clarity in order to be read. Her reaction, however, is one of horror: she stands up suddenly and shatters the loving cup she shared with her lover, spilling the wine.

While her horror shows she has read the emblem correctly, as we have seen, it will take more than one visionary experience for the maiden to accept the presence of death at the centre of her life. Her immediate reaction to this vision is disavowal, shrugging it off. She passes a hand over her brow as if wiping the vision away, keeps her lover from touching the sharp shards of the cup and leaves the table to attend to her stained dress. Death's attention now turns to the lover as he speaks to him and lifts his glass. In the kitchen, the girl's attention is attracted by some cavorting kittens. She cradles one as the tavern lady drapes another on her shoulder. She opens a door and re-enters the dining room in close-up, wreathed in these living balls of fur, as if this fetishistic immersion in animal life could dispel her vision of death. She looks off-screen towards her lover, smiling. But the point of view shot of the table which follows shows only his empty place. Here Lang offers for the first time what will become, as his career progresses, his ultimate image of the presence of death, a place left empty where people should be. While in no way forming a supernatural image or an explicit emblem for either viewer or character, this image of empty space will haunt Lang's films from this point forward and in all cases be associated with the imminence of death. Its most famous example (and the one which most resembles this shot) appears in *M* when we see the empty place at the table that should be occupied by Elsie Beckmann.

It would seem the maiden cannot read this image; it simply confuses her, precisely because she has chosen to repress her previous vision. In some ways this emptiness presents a more devastating image of death than the vision. There the space is saturated with significance, with the cultural emblems of death. Here we experience death simply as absence, as an emptying-out of a world previously filled with love and laughter. It is this absence that literally impels the maiden's search, inspired most likely by the verses from *The Song of Solomon*: 'I opened to my beloved but my beloved had withdrawn himself and was gone. ... I sought him but could not find him.' If the visionary scene operates to reveal the labour of death beneath the surface of things, this vision also impels an active reading and determined action on the part of Lang's characters, that desperate search for the fulfilment of desire which converts the determinist and potentially static aspect of the Destiny-machine into something other than a simple metaphysical demonstration.

But their role in motivating the maiden's search does not exhaust the emblematic force of these two visionary shots. The mere exit of the lover would be sufficient for that. As a crystallisation of the forces contending within the film, these shots raise the problem of reading images in silent cinema which threaten to freeze action into an allegorical tableau. As Vincente J. Benet Ferrando has pointed out in his fine essay devoted to *Der müde Tod*, this film maintains a tension between a narrative and a poetic axis.[3] Metaphorical images accumulate as the film progresses, generally of inanimate objects, or elements of architecture: not only the emblems already

discussed – the wall, the Hall of Flames, the hourglass, the extinguished candles –
but also the more ambiguous close-ups of the row of coins Death lays down, the
cross with alpha and omega he draws in the dirt, the mandrake in the apothecary's
hand, the raven on the skeleton in the pharmacy, the unicorn sign outside the
tavern, the weeping statue that ends the Chinese tale, and so on. Such seemingly significant images constantly interrupt the unfolding narrative, often with ironic or
frustrating effects (perhaps the most amusing example is the shot of the stone
figure of Aquarius, the water carrier, that appears during the sequence of the infirmary's conflagration, unable to intervene in the narrative action, yet poised as if
ready to do so). The figure of Death, appearing both as character in the narrative
and as symbolic figure, exemplifies for Benet the way these two axes contaminate
and even confuse each other. The excessive role of the poetic axis of figures whose
symbolic significance seems to overwhelm their narrative role poses one of the
enigmas of *Der müde Tod*: how do we as viewers read this film?

While *Der müde Tod* invokes the world of the *Märchen*, the complexity of its
temporality, narration and cinematic emblems reveals its preoccupation with
directing the viewer's attention to the play of filmic language. The film demands that
the viewer, like the characters, do some work, become an unraveler of enigmas,
decoder of emblems and interpreter of allegories. Without exactly mimicking its
historical form, Harbou and Lang offer a cinematic *Trauerspiel* ('Mourning play' or,
roughly, 'non-classical tragedy'), the form of German baroque drama to which
Walter Benjamin devoted his *Habilitationsschrift*. For Benjamin the key to the
Trauerspiel lay in its employment of allegory as a means of expression.[4] His
groundbreaking analysis of this use of allegory launched a rediscovery of the power
of the mode after its scornful dismissal during the Romantic period for its lack of
organic form and its privileging of significance over specific depiction. Few film
historians have paused to reflect on the great resurrection of allegory within silent
cinema, of which mode both *Intolerance* and the early work of Lang stand as
paramount examples. An understanding of the structure of *Der müde Tod* demands
an allegorical reading.

Benjamin relates the baroque obsession with allegory to a fascination with Egyptian hieroglyphics which had not yet been deciphered.[5] As Miriam Hansen has
shown, silent cinema provides a direct parallel to the baroque obsession with hieroglyphics through the recurrent claim made during the 1910s that cinema's pictorial
means of expression resurrected the hieroglyph as a universal language, a claim most
thoroughly, if eccentrically, pursued by American poet Vachel Lindsay.[6] An equally
important parallel could be found in the fact that both the baroque theories of hieroglyphics and Lindsay's speculations were founded on extreme misreadings of the
Egyptian writing as allegories. The ancient guide provided by Horapollo
(mis)interpreted hieroglyphics as allegorical emblems and, in an era before Cham-
pollion's deciphering of the Rosetta stone, was regarded as an authority by baroque
authors.[7] Likewise, Lindsay, in his slightly mad 1916 book *The Art of the Moving Picture*, exfoliated Egyptian hieroglyphics into complete movie plots, superseding their
literal meanings.[8] But Lindsay's eccentric approach to the hieroglyph depended on
his penetrating insight into the language of silent film. In the films of Griffith, the
early films of DeMille, the works of Gance, Dulac, Epstein, the complex rhetorical
experiments of the Soviets, and in most of Weimar cinema we recognise the 'awkward heavy handedness' that Benjamin sees as essential to allegory.[9] These are works
that seek to develop images which will be simultaneously intense and (in opposition
to the Romantic symbol – and to the taste of most modern critics) legible; images

that aspire to writing in pictures, willing to court the artificiality that foregrounds significance over depiction.

If the allegorical mode provides a central context for much of silent cinema and for Lang's work especially, *Der müde Tod* relates most strongly to the melancholy aspects of the mode that Benjamin finds in the baroque *Trauerspiel*. The embedded tales of *Der müde Tod* shares *Trauerspiel's* preoccupation with tyrannical rulers and intriguers and a pessimistic and cyclical view of human history. What these tales of different historical periods share most strongly with Griffith's vast allegory *Intolerance* is the aspect that Miriam Hansen relates to Benjamin's description of history in the *Trauerspiel*: the dramatic presentation of each historical episode as an incident in 'an accumulation of catastrophe'.[10] But in *Der müde Tod* this sense of catastrophe surpasses *Intolerance*. Whereas Griffith exempts his central modern story from the grim ending of death and destruction found in each of the tales of the past, Lang/Harbou make their framing tale into the central allegory of death's power.

In this presentation of the cycles of history as catastrophes, *Der müde Tod* closely approaches Benjamin's model of the *Trauerspiel*: 'Everything about history that, from the very beginning, has been untimely, sorrowful, unsuccessful, is expressed in a face – or rather in a death's head'.[11] The overlap-dissolve in *Der müde Tod*, as in much of Lang, embodies the allegorical vision which, as Benjamin puts it, 'strips objects naked',[12] piercing through appearance to their mournful significance. The dissolve which seems to reveal an image lurking beneath a previous shot, works as an allegorical device *par excellence*, stripping away the surface of the world and revealing the bare bones of significance. Because in *Der müde Tod*, as in the *Trauerspiel*, what lives beneath the surface is the death's head, reality's ultimate significance must be read with the gaze of mournful melancholy.

Thus the narrative resolution of the maiden's search in *Der müde Tod* remains circular, like the recurring pattern of desire's defiance of tyranny and ultimate defeat in each embedded tale. She can only end her search by realising what she had already seen at the beginning: the presence of death at the heart of things. All her searching, her voyage to the other world, her struggles through history, must lead back to this visionary moment at the table, to her acceptance of the mournful melancholy of the allegorical reading. Instead, she flees this realisation with disavowal. But the logic of the story (ies) become(s) more than a lesson in determinism and defeat. The maiden undergoes a process stretching from insight through denial to realisation and acceptance – Benet refers to it as an initiatory drama, or a *Bildungsroman*.[13] The arc of this narrative rehearses in some ways the work of mourning as described by Freud in his great essay 'Mourning and Melancholia' written just a few years before this film.[14] But a close comparison of Freud's description of the 'work of mourning' and the structure of Lang's film shows the way the story in this film remains subject to its emblematic and allegorical axis. Lang's film operates in a space between Freud's *Trauerarbeit* and Benjamin's *Trauerspiel*.

The maiden's denial of her lover's death, her re-enacting of his loss in the embedded scenarios and her final acceptance of his death recalls the gradual process of reality-testing (checking repeatedly to confirm that the lost loved one no longer exists) and final de-cathexis that allows the mourner to accept the fact of death and loss. However, the maiden may accept the fact of her lover's death, but she does not perform the essential re-entry and re-cathexis with the realm of the living that the work of mourning must accomplish (as Death advises her after her failure in preserving the three lights: 'Go to the Living – and live!'). Instead, she seems to descend into that failure of mourning Freud calls melancholia, the same term Benjamin identifies with the allegorical imagination.

Here we enter into a central hermeneutic problem that reveals both the limits and power of allegory. For Freud, mourning collapses into melancholia because of an ambivalence the mourner feels about the lost loved one, a psychological conflict that is not resolved. One might be tempted at this point to use Freud to open up the character of the maiden, to discover the ambivalence that prevents her from successfully completing the mourning process. But I do not believe the maiden can be analysed as a complex psychological character. Neither the *Märchen* nor the allegorical form construct characters in this manner. To attempt to locate and analyse her ambivalence towards her lost lover would distort her essentially non-psychological nature, and misinterpret the mode of this film. There is no hidden depth of characters here; this film's mysteries lie in its emblems and narrative structures.

But if Freud can be used realistically to explain the depth of psychologically conceived characters, this does not exhaust the insights psychoanalysis can offer into a text. Freud's central concepts operate like allegorical dramas, and it is as personifications of conflicting drives that we must see the figures in this film, rather than as neurotic characters. Rather than a static illustration, Lang and Harbou offer a dramatic interaction with Freud's concepts. While the maiden in her defiance of Death in the name of love would seem initially to represent the force of Eros that Freud, following a long Western tradition, opposed to Thanatos, the death drive, her narrative trajectory traces a different story. The repetitive cycle of action undertaken by the maiden brings her closer (with each repetition) to identifying with the death drive itself, which Freud associated with the compulsion to repeat. What seems to convince the maiden of the reality of death in the last 'verse' of the film is not the restoration of her reality testing (the outcome of successful mourning), the failure of her struggle for her lover's survival in each of the stories, but the adamant refusal of all humans to acknowledge their own Being towards Death (underscored by the recurring refrain: 'Not one day, not one hour, not one breath', which literalises the 'verse' structure of this last episode). The pusillanimous nature of their clinging to life causes her to see Death differently – as an outcome which cannot be denied – and also to identify with its power and the release it offers. Increasingly the maiden sees the world from the viewpoint of Death; whereas in the three stories she tried to shelter her lover from the threat of death, in the final verse she acts as Death's agent, trying to obtain a substitute victim. She has moved from the allegorical personification of one drive to its opposite.

It is this identification with death, this movement from defiance to co-operation, that highlights the maiden's descent into melancholia rather than Freud's pathway back towards life through mourning. And if we read this passage into melancholia as a broader allegory rather than as the symptom of an individualised character, it is hard to avoid the conclusion that what is invoked here is a historical trauma, the breakdown of the act of mourning accompanying the massive accumulation of death from World War I, ended just three years before this film, and which Lang himself had survived only after several serious injuries. Like the wall that Death builds in the film, this fact of overwhelming death achieved proportions so great as to prove excessive for previous modes of memorial and mourning.[15] I make this move to historical context not to supply Lang's film with the significance of a grand signifier of historical representation, but because I think it is the social rather than an individual failure of mourning in this film that endows the allegorical form of the maiden's unsuccessful contest with Death with such power.

One must recall that psychoanalysis has a social as well as an individual dimension. The war played a key role in Freud's own writings on mourning, melancholia and the death drive, with the classic essays written during the war (including 'Thoughts for the Times on War and Death' and 'On Transience').[16] The slightly later *Beyond the Pleasure Principle* (published in 1920, the year before the release of *Der müde Tod*), represents a major rethinking of Freud's views, largely inspired by war victims who repeatedly dreamed of their initial trauma, apparently calling into question Freud's notion of the dream as wish fulfilment.[17] Freud ends the short but beautiful essay 'On Transience' with a wish for the success of a national mourning at war's end:

> When [mourning] has renounced everything that has been lost, then it has consumed itself, and our libido is once more free (in so far as we are still young and active) to replace the lost object by fresh ones equally or still more precious. It is to be hoped that the same will be true of the losses caused by this war. When once the mourning is over, it will be found that our high opinion of the riches of civilisation has lost nothing from our discovery of their fragility. We shall build them up again, and perhaps on firmer ground and more lastingly than before.[18]

Freud's own life, his final flight from Vienna to London, reflects the failure of this mourning on a social and historical level. *Der müde Tod* expresses it more directly in its allegory, providing a key not only to Lang's work but to the mood of Weimar Germany.

We sense in the maiden's final action not only a Christian self-sacrifice (glossed in the intertitle as 'He who loses his life shall find it'), but also an erotic surrender to death, in which the maiden mimes and reverses the action which first demonstrated Death's power to her, the appearance of the baby in his arms. Instead of that earlier birth into death, the maiden now delivers the child from the conflagration and into the world of the living. Here we have the action closest to Freud's successful mourning, the saving of a young life. But the maiden remains on the other side, and her act of bringing the baby's life into the world seems to cement her erotic ties to the world of death. It is on the side of death that her lover lies, it is there that she is finally delivered from her compulsion to repeat. The realm of Death becomes a realm of fulfilment, but very much within the terms of Freud's death drive, the ultimate cessation of all movement and desire.

The world of the living remains under the petrifying gaze of melancholia: empty, bereft, filled with people too enervated to live and too cowardly to die. The last reel of the film which separates the maiden from this world envisioned the will of the village's inhabitants to live as the last gasp of feebleness. The final image we have of the world of the living in the film is an image which will haunt Lang's films from this point on – a conflagration – as the infirmary roof collapses in a storm of sparks and flame, causing the crowd below to kneel in awe. Knowing Harbou and Lang's interest in Eastern culture (they had met while scripting *The Indian Tomb* before *Der müde Tod*), the Buddhist image of the world as a burning house from which souls must be rescued may well be the reference here. By the ending of the film, the image of the lover's empty place at the table gains even more salience than the projected shadows of death and time. In true melancholia the image remains empty of significance, except the significance of emptiness itself.

The resolution of *Der müde Tod* takes place on a symbolic level and within an allegorical space. Maiden and lover are reunited in a room that looks like a gothic waiting room between the burning holocaust of the world of the living and the

fields of heaven into which Death will lead them. Here they leave their bodies
behind, as Death seems to peel off transparent phantom selves which rise and are
led by Death through the wall. The flowering field of heaven appears only in one
penultimate shot as the figure of Death, who separated the couple initially, now
unites them as he dissolves away and they walk on, arm in arm, backs to the camera,
out of the film. If Lang offers a vision of bliss and resurrection (that which according to Benjamin redeems the hollowed-out world of allegory), we get only this brief
glimpse of it. To end the film, Lang cuts from heaven to the already mentioned
image of the clock face and the nightwatchman announcing midnight. Time has
run out, the film is over and we are presented with emblems of the Destiny-
machine. We are alone with our own act of reading.

Final Figure: The Look at the Camera

But how does the film resolve its question about narrative and enunciation in relation to its allegorical style? In what way do the figures generated by its melancholic
mode relate to the question of who is telling this story, and how does this act of enunciation relate to the Destiny-machine? Benet relates the question of enunciation and
death in this film to a key cinematic figure in Lang's style, the look at the camera.
Benet points out that there are two points of view within the narrative of *Der müde
Tod*. On the one hand, that of the maiden who focalises most scenes and whose literal
point of view appears in many shots. On the other hand, there is the figure of Death,
the centre of the film's enigmas and emblems to which all paths seem to return. Benet
points out that Death frequently looks directly at the camera, as if asserting a privileged relation to the cinematic apparatus and his dominant role in the narrative.[19]
This introduces one final device that helps us come to terms with this film and which
will also be further developed in Lang's later work: the look at the camera.

The look at the camera is a vexed issue in film studies. Some theorists have
assumed that, as Marc Vernet puts it in his important essay on the subject, a look by
an actor directly into the lens of the camera, 'foregrounds the enunciative instance
of the filmic text and attacks the spectator's voyeurism by putting the space of the
film and the space of the movie theatre briefly in direct contact'.[20] Following this
interpretation, the look at the camera could play a crucial role in a cinematic style
like Lang's which raises the question of the enunciative instance of authorship.
When a character looks at the camera (or in other words, looks out from the screen
towards the viewer) we feel addressed by that look directly and lose the secure invisibility of a voyeur who watches but cannot be seen which is cultivated by most narrative cinema. Avoiding the look at the camera became one of the assumptions
which became codified in the classical Hollywood style. As Vernet puts it, 'the look
at the camera would be the "major interdiction" and the great "repressed of narrative cinema"', precisely because it interferes with the assumption of classical narrative that as film viewers we are discovering a scene unaware of our presence.[21] And
certainly, as a cinema which recurringly raises the problem of enunciation and
authorship, Lang's *œuvre* stands as a *locus classicus* of looks at the camera.

However, the look at the camera does sometimes appear within the shot/ reverse
shot pattern, in which two shots from complementary angles are edited together to
indicate two different aspects of an action, such as a conversation between two
people. One of the cognitive cues for the construction of a shot/reverse shot is the
off screen look of the characters. While not really a taboo, in the classical paradigm
the look at the camera is generally avoided even in a shot/reverse shot. A character

looks off screen, but avoids looking directly into the camera. The shots of Death speaking to the lover at the tavern table and of the lover responding are good examples of this dominant practice. Neither actor looks directly into the camera. Instead, Death looks to the right, while the young man looks to the left. The aiming of these looks to the side of the camera clarifies the spatial relations of the characters within the 180 degree space of the filming: Death looks right toward the young man seated on his right; the young man looks left towards Death. Their sightlines match.

But while the angled look is the rule, there are variations, either through awkwardness or by design. By *Der müde Tod* Lang clearly had mastered the spatial logic of the shot/reverse shot. He understood the role directing a look away from the camera played in clarifying spatial relations, and used it in most shot/reverse shots. But Lang and other directors sometimes create shot/reverse shots with actors looking directly into the lens of the camera. The clearest example of this in *Der müde Tod* occurs in the last 'verse' of the film when the maiden asks the apothecary to give up his life so that she can regain her lover. In close-up the apothecary looks directly into the lens as he voices his adamant refusal. Several points should be made about this sort of look at the camera. We understand that his gaze remains within the world of the fiction; he is looking directly at the maiden and refusing her request. However, this style of shooting is by no means simply a functional equivalent of the more common shot/reverse shot which avoids the direct look at the camera. The effect of the apothecary's look into the camera is startling, supplying a sort of exclamation point to the shot. There are two related reasons for this effect: first, as a less frequent variation from the norm, the direct look strikes the viewer as unusual; second, even if we understand that the character is looking at the maiden, we first experience his gaze as a direct lookout at us from the screen. The startling nature of the variation and of the direct look gives the shot a sort of punch and emphasis. This is even clearer in the scene of the maiden's visionary moment before the wall, when she sees the procession of the dead. Here in medium shot we see her look directly at the camera (especially in the second shot) as she expresses her horror. We understand that her horror comes from her vision of the dead, but Lang expresses the idea that this is no ordinary sight by this dramatic variation. Therefore, the look at the camera does not need to have a Brechtian illusion-destroying effect to play a significant role within a style. Instead, like many key devices in Lang's system, it simply has to play with rupturing the fiction enough to attract our attention.

Other looks into the camera occur that are not part of a shot/reverse shot figure. At several points in *Der müde Tod* characters look at the camera as if seeing something far off. Generally such looks become part of a performance code; they cue us that the character's thoughts are 'elsewhere', that they are deeply moved, or reflective. In some ways such shots function like the soliloquy in classical drama, a moment aside from the other characters, when thoughts or feelings are directly addressed to the audience. The effect of such shots depends heavily on performance that is the type of look the actor directs to the camera. For instance, in the pharmacy the maiden recovering from her terrifying vision and the fainting spell which followed, looks out at the camera in close-up, glassy-eyed and expressionless. We understand that she focuses on nothing, and the direct blank-eyed gaze at the camera makes this a disturbing experience for the viewer, associated with the character's numb despair. A few shots later she discovers the text from *The Song of Solomon*, and her distraction transforms into fully absorbed reading. Having read the passage, she looks up from the page and stares at the camera with a look that is now focused, intent. We feel ourselves transfixed by this gaze, even as we understand it as a sign of her sudden realisation and resolution.

As Benet indicates, Death also has such moments, although their reading in terms of character expression remains limited. Most frequently they remain framed in long shot (as in the look he gives the camera after the baby disappears in his arms in the Hall of Flames, or a similar look given at the end of the tale of the first light, when he dissolves back into the figure of Death over the grave of Zobeide's lover). But Death also delivers looks to the camera that become more powerful through closer framings (which increase the sense of address to the spectator). One occurs when the burgomasters ask Death how to get through the wall that encloses his garden. In medium close-up, after looking left and right (presumably at the town elders), he then looks deliberately into the camera as he delivers the line, 'I alone know the way in'. His look at the camera here emphasises his mystery and other-worldliness. Perhaps most complex is the moment when the actor Goetzke is introduced in the Arabian tale as El Mot the Gardener in close-up and he looks up and stares at the camera. Clearly this is a moment directed to the audience, cueing us to recognise him as the same actor that plays Death, and therefore realise the identity of these two figures.

While most looks at the camera in *Der müde Tod* have roles within the diegesis, the shots particularly of Death and the maiden (who between them have nearly all the looks at the camera) also have an extra-diegetic dimension. They affirm the role of these two figures as narrative agents: Death as the figure of narrative determination, and the maiden as the reader of fate, the character who recognises the pattern of the story she is in. In this sense their looks have an enuciative role, reminding us of the camera as an invisible force of narration to which their looks draw our attention. But does Death have a privileged relation to the camera, as Benet indicates? Certainly, but no more (and possibly less in terms of number of close-ups) than the maiden. And it is precisely the moment the maiden reads the Bible that motivates perhaps the most intense look at the camera. Lang sees the act of reading as being as essential as Death's acts of enunciation.

But if the figure of Death seems to share a privileged position in relation to the camera with the maiden, one could argue that the point of view of Death does more generally claim a primary relation to the camera. Key moments when the maiden looks at the camera involve a vision of death, not only the off screen look at the procession of the dead at the wall, but also the shot in the Venetian story when Fiametta realises she has caused the death of her lover, not of the hated Girolamo. The only pronounced look at the camera by a character other than Death or the maiden that is not part of a shot/reverse shot comes in the Venetian tale as well. After a shot in which Girolamo's henchmen have killed Fiametta's messenger in order to obtain the letter she is sending to her lover, Lang cuts to Girolamo. Girolamo in close-up looks directly at the camera and smiles slightly. The cut links effect to cause, the look at the camera positing Girolamo as the agent of death. In *Der müde Tod* the look at the camera not only expresses connection with the extra-diegetic realm of the film (authorship, narration, the viewer) as an enunciative mark, but also a thematic connection with death, an association Vernet among others have made with the look at the camera in other instances: 'What is seen in the look at the camera is the Invisible, Elsewhere, Death.'[22]

The maiden experiences death in every register in *Der müde Tod*: as a visionary premonition, as an unaccountable and disavowed loss and absence, as a hopeless search for a lost love, as a cloaked figure with a penetrating stare, as a wall that cannot be penetrated, as a phantom lover who cannot be touched, as candles sputtering to their end, as a recurrent narrative she cannot stop or change, as a clock marking the final hour. All these emblems demand to be read, but all reiterate the same meaning. Likewise her search for an enunciative power who could reverse the narrative only results in her always re-living the same scenario. The activity of reading and interpretation brings one not to a fully present author but to an empty site, whose name is death, weary death.

2

The Decay of Myth:
Siegfried's Death, Kriemhild's Revenge

> The parts of the dream which he [the analysand] describes in
> different terms are by that fact revealed to me as the weak spot
> in the dream's disguise: they serve my purpose just as Hagen's
> was served by the embroidered mark on Siegfried's cloak.
> Sigmund Freud, *The Interpretation of Dreams*[1]

While *Der müde Tod* invokes the simple form of the *Märchen* but actually creates a much more complex allegorical form closer to the baroque *Trauerspiel*, both *Die Nibelungen* and *Metropolis* weave allegories out of other symbolic forms: mythological epic and futuristic science fiction. Both films expand from the relatively modest scope of *Der müde Tod* into super-films, epic spectaculars which enlarge the already impressive sets of *Der müde Tod* into complete and complex environments. These super-films seemingly contrast in historical orientation, the two-part *Die Nibelungen* delving into a primordial past, while *Metropolis* speculates on a distant future. However, the purported eras of the two films actually serve the same end – one not unlike the *Märchen* reference in *Der müde Tod*: removing the stories from any direct reference to the contemporary environment (which dominates Lang's crime

thrillers, dealt with in the next section) and allowing them to take place in an entirely constructed and symbolic environment.

Although these two super-films both employ an allegorical cinematic language and make use of the basic elements of the Langian system – the problematic of narration and reading, the visionary moment and the Destiny-machine – they also contrast sharply. While neither film refers to a specific historical period (indeed they both claim to be *outside* history), their opposed vectors of before and after history do represent extremely different orientations. *Die Nibelungen* invokes the power and riches that come from myth and legend, a realm of more-than-human heroes, Valkyries, dragons and dwarves – an ambiguous legacy of magic. *Metropolis*, on the other hand, struggles with the threat and promise of new technology, a promise which it depicts as a sort of black magic. While Lang's treatment of the two eras converges in the vision of mythical heroes and the ambiguous role of magic, they differ sharply in their denouements. *Die Nibelungen* chronicles the disenchantment of the magical world, its betrayal and the apocalyptic consequences of that betrayal. *Metropolis* envisions the triumph of a saviour hero of the future issuing in a millennium whose ambiguity I will explore.

In no other Lang film are the workings of the Destiny-machine more closely allied to traditional images of fatality than they are in *Die Nibelungen*. As Lang's closest encounter with the world of mythology, *The Death of Siegfried* (*Siegfrieds Tod*) presents the mythical as a dark realm of chthonic forces and determinism whose clearest emblem lies in the gap in Siegfried's invulnerability, the spot marked by the falling leaf from the linden tree which kept the magical dragon's blood from touching his skin at that one point, leaving him exposed to danger. But is it anachronistic to speak of a Destiny-machine in this film which portrays a pre-mechanical era? If I intend by this term the way that Lang portrays individual destiny as the product of a complex system of interlocking elements with fatal consequences, the falling of this leaf stands as a perfect example in spite of its apparently natural process. The way Lang portrays this stroke of fate visually, makes this clear.

Siegfried has wandered into the Odenwald (the dark forest where Fafner guards his treasure) after being misdirected by his envious tutor Mime. Encountering the fire-breathing dragon form of Fafner, Siegfried is more than willing to engage him. After slaying the dragon and releasing a flood of his blood, Siegfried discovers the blood's magical properties through a synthesis of the accidental with the mythical. Observing the steaming blood, Siegfried reaches down (out of a boyish curiosity to stick his finger in it?) and touches the flow, then jerks back up and puts his finger in his mouth (the blood's too hot?). Lang maintains careful control of editing on action; different angles of Siegfried's action cut together seamlessly as he tastes the blood.

Lang immediately cuts to a close-up of a bird in a tree (an *ersatz* bird that rivals the robin at the end of David Lynch's *Blue Velvet* for mechanical movement and matches the uncanny artificiality of the now deceased Fafner). Intertitles inform us that the taste of blood enabled Siegfried to understand the language of birds, which now tells him that if the dragon-slayer bathes in the dragon's blood it will render him invulnerable. Siegfried strips naked, and (filmed from a discreet distance) the nude hero kneels before the dragon's flaccid neck and gets under the downpour of blood. Lang cuts to a close-up of the blood's source in the dragon's wound, then to a medium close-up of Siegfried's head and shoulders as he lets the blood pour over his skin.

Lang has detailed the process of gaining invulnerability; now we watch in successive shots its counter action, happening, as it were, behind Siegfried's back. A high
angle shot cuts to the final death throe of the dragon as his tail quivers with one last
recoil. Like a fatal Rube Goldberg machine, this blow sets off a chain reaction:
   1) the tail hits the linden tree;
   2) Lang cuts to the tree's leaves shaken by the blow, as one detaches;
   3) in a separate shot this single leaf floats through the air;
   4) in the same framing as the previous shot of the hero's blood bath, the leaf lands on
      his shoulder, masking off that point from the blood's magic protection.
Although the story of the leaf comes from the medieval epic (and probably derives
from ancient mythic sources) and parallels the myth of Achilles' heel in Greek
mythology, Lang's cinematic narration emphasises its systematic and nearly
mechanical nature, his careful analytical editing linking up the different phases of
the event that will bring about his hero's undoing.

   Die Nibelungen takes place in a world of total design; the massive cement tree
trunks of the Odenwald through which Siegfried rides are as carefully fashioned as the
square turrets of the court city of Worms. Nothing in this film is natural (as evidenced
by the intricate mechanism of Fafner, supposedly operated by seventeen men seated at
complex control panels inside the beast, or the bird that speaks to Siegfried). Nearly
every commentator on *Die Nibelungen* has noted the claustrophobic and artificial
nature of the Odenwald and the jerky puppet-like movement of the Fafner-machine.
Often these have been criticised as primitive flaws in the film's special effects, but their
lack of natural spontaneity reveals, rather, the 'heavy hand' of allegory. There is nothing natural here: nature and myth blend into a second constructed nature through
which a rich vein of artificiality runs. Beneath the film's invocation of a primordial,
mythical world rumbles an appetite for the systematic, schematic and the abstract, the
steady rhythm of the Destiny-machine. The film's main emblem of destiny, Siegfried's
vulnerable spot – seemingly 'naturally' produced – goes through a radical process of
abstraction, appearing finally as a diagrammatic mark on his cloak.

   In the latter part of the film, as Hagen plots to destroy the mythic hero, he
manipulates Kriemhild, now Siegfried's wife, into unwitting complicity. Claiming
concern for Siegfried's vulnerability, Hagen asks Kriemhild to reveal where it lies.
She agrees to mark the spot with a cross stitched in thread on his tunic. In close-up
Lang shows her needlework as she pulls a tangle of threads together until they form
an X. Lang uses his favoured device of an overlap-dissolve here, as the X becomes
superimposed over a shot of Hagen standing before a rack of standing spears. He
selects one, holds it horizontally (creating a cross figure against the vertical rack)
then hurls it into the floor. He has selected the spear with which he will kill the hero.
Lang cuts directly to Siegfried and Kriemhild framed within a rectangular doorway
as she arranges his tunic. As Siegfried moves through the doorway she lingers
behind. Shot from Kriemhild's point of view, a close-up frames the thread-etched
cross on the back of Siegfried's shoulder. In a close reaction shot, we see her concern. This sequence demonstrates the obsessive geometry that determines composition of shots in the Burgundian court. But this constant geometrical abstraction is
not restricted to individual shots. At key moments these motifs interlock and
develop from shot to shot, containing the characters' actions within an expansive
geometrical schema achieved by editing as well as composition.

   The leaf-made spot has become a geometrical figure, a decorative motif, like the
many tapestries, standards, lintels, curtains, shields which make up the highly-dec-
orated, geometrical world of the Burgundians. Lang's cutting embeds the marking

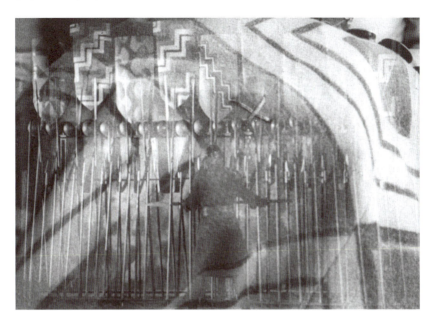

of the spot within a series of processes, (as he had detailed its origin in the leaf fall), but now the actions shown refer to later, anticipated events: Hagen's spear thrust, Kriemhild's mourning. Both the X's position and its role as the mark of fatality recall (or rather anticipate) the M marked on Beckert's back. In both *The Death of Siegfried* and *M* the mark of fatality is inscribed on the characters' clothing, transforming them into unconscious bearers of the plot's progress, inscribed with an alphabet they cannot read, but whose consequences the audience realises. From the mythic hero of a magical world of nature, Siegfried becomes a target: a marked man within the 'civilised' court politics of the Burgundians, a figure in a larger design scripted in terms of his death.

Thus the mythic world of Lang's *Die Nibelungen* falls under the melancholic gaze of allegory. Rather than the transcendent heavenly realm of the gods, the mythical realm which opens *Die Nibelungen* belongs to intermediary beings, heroes and monsters, inhabitants of Middle Earth, not of the realms of Valhalla. The opening image of a rainbow descending from a high mountain recalls not only the landscape painting of Caspar David Friedrich, but Norse cosmology in which the rainbow bridge Bifrost unites the Middle Earth, where man dwells, with Asgard, the home of the gods. Lang and Harbou's film traces a descent from the realm of gods into the human, out of the realm of legend into history. The fatality that rules this film is less the decree of the gods (who are absent) than the downfall of the world of myth.

The conflict between myth and allegory in *Die Nibelungen* is a complex issue. Although allegory frequently and traditionally makes use of the figures of mythology, it nearly always works in a de-mythologising mode, interpreting and 'explaining' the elements of mythology in terms of other systems (later religions, politics, psychology). Allegory represents a stage in the disenchantment and melancholy of the world as opposed to the coherent belief structures of mythology. Can this more melancholic and belated viewpoint be seen in Harbou's and Lang's project in filming *Die Nibelungen*? In discussions of the film both authors indicated their intention to bring the *Nibelungenlied* back to life. Lang declared, 'Above all in the Nibelungen film, I hoped to make the world of myth live again for the twentieth century, to live again and be believable'.[2] But if the task of the film was one of resurrection, Lang was well aware of the difficulties involved in such a task. Indeed, we could claim that one of the master themes of Lang's films throughout his career (from *Der müde Tod* through *The Testament of Dr. Mabuse* to *Fury*, *Woman in the Window* and *The Thousand Eyes of Dr. Mabuse*) has been the difficulties of the return of the dead to the world of the living, the tragedy of revenants who remain in some way caught between two worlds.

For Lang, the most immediate difficulties in creating a modern version of an ancient epic lay in crossing the barriers of time, the exclusivity of class taste and the fundamentals of belief. Lang responded to all these with an almost religious sense of the possibilities of cinema. The *Nibelungenlied* as a literary work, Lang claimed, remained the property of a small elite who have the time to read it. Even having read it, the reader experiences an emotional distance from the behaviour of people in that era, and from the mythical and magical events he can no longer believe. But cinema is the art of all the people; it delivers actions driven by emotions that 'are the same today as they were in all times'.[3] Siegfried and Kriemhild are revealed as people not unlike those of today. As for the unbelievable magical events:

> Today someone who hears of Siegfried's battle with the dragon should not have to take it on faith, but instead he should see it and experience it fully by seeing it. The mystical magic of Brunhild's mountain that stands under the eternal Northern Lights in the middle of the fiery seas should appear visible before him. The magic power of the *Tarnhelm*, with which Siegfried wins the bride for Gunther, should be believable through the viewer's own eyes. In short, it seems to me, that precisely film's specific qualities correspond to the *Märchen*-like aspects of the Nibelungen film, once one succeeds in mastering the technological difficulties – and they were legion.[4]

For Lang, then, film could make a nation's epic myths available to the masses, by focusing on their human emotions and their spectacular visual effects. Film could play an essential role in bringing about a national renewal through bringing a nation's myths to life.

But could such a humanised, democratised and spectacularised version of myth really claim to be a renewal of myth? Sabine Hake quotes conservative critics who felt the film 'destroys those aspects of the myth which still lives on in the German people, since its brilliant visual presentation eliminates the last remnants of imagination and extinguishes almost all memories of the real Nibelungs'.[5] Many reviewers found Harbou's kitsch version of *Die Nibelungen* to be a betrayal of a national treasure. Certainly Lang and Harbou's film must be seen within a context of a wide cultural revival of mythic material in Weimar (and even Wilhelmian) Germany, often trivialised or manufactured for contemporary taste. Even the Nazis were unsure how to view Lang's film –as a part of modern, capitalist mass media cheapening of national myths or as (as Goebbels claimed when he re-issued *The Death of Siegfried* in 1933) a partner in the cultural renewal they were calling for.[6] Many of the film's images – Siegfried's 'stab in the back'; the treacherous Alberich's Semitic features; the Nibelungs' loyalty unto death – were ripe for Nazi appropriation, even if they were not fashioned with this intention.

But the possibility of reviving mythic world views was hotly debated during the Weimar period and not simply from the practical points of view raised by Lang.

Georg Lukacs in his highly influential *The Theory of the Novel* proposed that the 'spontaneous totality of being' that characterises the 'integrated civilizations' that produce epics (such as the Homeric Greeks) was gone forever and could not be resurrected.[7] This analysis strongly influenced the work of Kracauer, Benjamin, Horkheimer and Adorno. Lang may not have been directly aware of this discourse (although Adorno would become a close friend during their shared American exile). But if the impulse towards a renewal of mythology is evident in *Die Nibelungen* and much of the discourse surrounding it, I feel that a close examination of both its narrative logic and imagery supports Lukacs' view, not simply through a failure of the film, but in its portrait of the way the pure products of myth are destroyed as they enter into the realm of history and civilisation. Lang's attempt at the resurrection of myth is stillborn, as Siegfried perishes from the treachery of men. The inevitable nature of this outcome, what Lang and Harbou described as 'the unheard of inexorability from the first sin to the last atonement' hardly chronicles the re-establishment of myth but rather the inevitable slide toward apocalypse.[8] The very diverse realms that intersect so tragically in *Die Nibelungen* contrast sharply with the totality of being Lukacs describes 'where everything is already homogeneous before it has been contained by forms'.[9] Instead, *Die Nibelungen* charts the encounter between 'four completely self-enclosed, almost hostile worlds',[10] inhabited by men and heroes, divine beings and monsters. This sort of divided and fragmented world, I believe, relates more strongly to the the fallen world of allegory than to the vibrant coherent world of myth.

Lang and Harbou described the four realms in which *Die Nibelungen* took place: the forest realm of the young Siegfried filled with mystery and supernatural figures: the dwarf Mime, the dragon Fafner, the elf Alberich; Iceland, the equally mythic kingdom of Brunhild, the Valkyrie; Worms, the civilised cathedral town, site of the Burgundy court of Kriemhild and her brother Gunther; and the steppes where Attila the Hun, leader of the oriental hordes, rules.[11] The first two realms partake of mythical power and magic. Worms provides the central stage of *The Death of Siegfried*, the court society to which Siegfried voyages searching for Kriemhild; Attila's realm, the obverse of this world of civilisation, but still an all-too-human, rather than divine realm, supplies the killing field of the second *Die Nibelungen* film, *Kriemhild's Revenge*. While Lang and Harbou differentiated these four separate realms through their differing meanings, characters and dominant visual designs, the film tells the story of their mutual contamination.

The figures from the realms of myth, Brunhild and Siegfried, enter the human realm where their powers are exploited or scorned, where they become subjects of intrigue and betrayal. In the final shot in *The Death of Siegfried* their dead bodies rest together in the cathedral, the image of Worms' civilised order. Characters whose origins lay in the elemental realms of dark forests and frigid mountains become absorbed into the plots of court intrigue, betrayal of trust, and the hero's martyrdom that typified the *Trauerspiel*. As in *Der müde Tod*, Lang and Harbou use a traditional form, in this case myth and epic, to create an allegory of decay and death. In contrast to the earlier film, however, Thanatos struggles against civilisation and its discontents rather than Eros.

Using contrasting visual styles to mark the four different realms, Lang and his designer Otto Hunte made key distinctions between them in atmosphere and tonality. The forest of Siegfried's first adventures fills the screen with an organic morphology in which trees, rocks and living beings seem to blend into each other. The cave in which Siegfried and Mime operate their forge takes the form of a dragon's head: the cave entrance an eye; exposed rocks, snarling teeth; a tree, a snout horn. While a fresh breeze or a ray of sunlight never penetrate this mythical world (fog is more frequent and, as we have seen, the only instance of fluttering leaves brings fatal consequences), to describe it as inert would be wrong. Rather, the contorted trees and hills appear to sheathe demonic forces, like Alberich hiding in the hollow tree which seems to absorb his form. Lang's favourite trick sequence of the film – the dwarves bearing the treasure of *Die Nibelungen* slowly becoming petrified – supplies the central image for this world: a world of mythic power slowly turning to stone.

Lang and Hunte's inspiration for the visual design throughout the film stems undoubtedly from Wilhelm Worringer's influential book *Form in Gothic* (first published in 1912). For Worringer Gothic design was a hybrid of the two opposed forces of empathy and abstraction:

> This is not a case of the harmonious interpenetration of two opposite tendencies, but of an impure, and to a certain extent uncanny, amalgamation of them, a requisition of our capacity for empathy (which is bound up with organic rhythm) for an abstract world which is alien to it.[12]

In this film the uncanny quality comes from an absolute elimination of the contingent, natural or accidental, in favour of the heavily designed, calculated and predetermined, so that even the fall of a leaf can set in motion the Destiny-machine. Yet this world seems less soulless than, as Sabine Hake has put it, petrified – the rhythms of life frozen in the mode of abstraction. It is a world in which the violence of allegory becomes visible, as significance wrestles with organic form, converting it into anguished yet ossified images, like Alberich himself frozen into a gothic stone carving after his defeat by Siegfried.

But if this gothic will-to-form pervades the film, the four different worlds express different stages in its petrifaction. In the world of the forest, one sees the uncanny, monstrous life forms still lurking at the threshold of animal and mineral kingdoms. Each of Siegfried's battles converts his victims into gothic ornament: Fafner becomes a grotesque gargoyle spewing blood, the dwarves decorate a titanic chalice, Alberich turns into a contorted sculpture. In the court of the Burgundians the barely contained threat and energy of the forest world becomes tamed through symmetry and geometrical abstraction, as the repeated motifs of heraldry mark both space and characters with a new level of civilised order. The mythic energies are still alluded to in bird-like and dragon-like decorative motifs, but the dominant form is that of the arch which seems to undergo a constant play of permutation as Lang cuts from shot to shot within the palace of Worms. The arch marks the entranceway of the main gate by the drawbridge, the entrance to the cathedral and the entrance to the throne room in which Siegfried first pays homage to King Gunther and asks for Kriemhild's hand. Narrower more vertical arches form the windows in the living quarters of the Burgundians.

In *Die Nibelungen* Lang has worked out a visual style in which monumental set design interacts with (and to a large degree determines) the placement and composition of actors as well as the composition of the camera frame. Few films have reached such perfection in total composition. But as commentators from Kracauer on have noted, this overwhelming sense of design never serves purely pictorial ends.[13] The structuring of space traces (and seems to lay out) the relentless progression of the narrative. The brute violence of Fafner and the magical cunning of Alberich, so easily defeated by Siegfried in the film's first episodes gives way to a colder and more disguised violence and cunning, more orderly and therefore more efficient. The geometrical perfection of the Burgundian court exemplifies the workings of the Destiny-machine.

Concern for the total composition of the cinematic image, in which space, articulated through set design, lighting and composition, played as expressive a role as the performance of the actors typifies the Weimar art cinema (including *Der müde Tod*). But in *The Death of Siegfried* the total composition becomes so saturated with resonances from the narrative action that the film seems to demand Siegfried Kracauer's comment, 'these patterns collaborate in deepening the impression of Fate's irresistible power'.[14] Yet Kracauer ignores the dramatic drive toward abstraction that propels the film; his identification of the fatality in the film with 'the grip of primitive passions', or the 'anarchical outburst of ungovernable instincts and passions' misses the point.[15] *The Death of Siegfried* weaves an allegorical reading of the presence of Death through the decline, rather than the resurrection, of the mythical and primitive.

As in *Der müde Tod*, *Die Nibelungen* self-consciously calls attention to its narrative form by dividing each film into seven '*Gesänge*', songs or cantos, each corresponding to two 35millimetre reels. This not only makes a reference to the form of the film's source, in this case the medieval epic *Die Nibelungenlied*, but carves up the film's narrative into significant blocks. Although *Die Nibelungen* does not focus on the formulaic form of the tale as *Der müde Tod* does (with its three stories with similar plot structures and recurring characters), it does foreground the act of narrating, especially in *The Death of Siegfried*. As David Levin points out, the major characters of the film, Siegfried and Kriemhild, first learn of each other through tales told of their beauty or prowess.[16] An oral account of the town of Worms and the beautiful Kriemhild inspires Siegfried to set out on his adventures at the beginning of the film, images we see as visual equivalents of the tale he hears. While the *Erste Gesang* (first canto) ends as the fatal leaf lands on Siegfried's back, the second *Gesang* begins with the image of Volker the Burgundian minstrel performing for the court at Worms the epic of Siegfried the Dragon-slayer. We could assume that the previous *Gesang* was actually sung in its entirety by this minstrel. Siegfried's next adventure, his gaining of the treasure of the Nibelungs from Alberich, is also framed by Volker's performance (the intertitle announcing, after Siegfried picks up the sword Balmung, 'So sang Volker'). The most mythological section of Siegfried's story, then, is presented through the mediation of the oral tradition, and a specific narrative performance. Similarly, the arrival of Siegfried and Gunther in Iceland, the kingdom of Brunhild, is forecast by a wise woman who casts runes. Her reading of the future is actually a reading of simultaneity, as Lang uses parallel editing to reveal the truth of her prognostications. Each stage of Siegfried's journey is read by the woman in the runes: his arrival on the shore, his crossing of the sea of fire, until a sentry rushes in to announce the hero's arrival at their gates. Lang not only visualises the content of these spoken tales, but in this case draws a parallel between the wise woman's reading the runes and the cinematic technique of parallel editing.

The division of the film into *Gesänge* plays another role, allowing narrative structure and the treatment of the film's image to intertwine. In *Der müde Tod* the division into verses mirrored the transitions across different temporalities and each reel/verse ended with an image of narrative closure which became an emblem of Death. *Die Nibelungen*, especially *The Death of Siegfried* operates in a similar manner, but relies on the story-freezing capability of images more than the closure of individual episodes. Each *Gesang* ends at a moment when the workings of the

Destiny-machine crystallise into a clairvoyant visuality. The first *Gesang* of *The Death of Siegfried* ends at the moment the leaf lands on his back. The second ends as Gunther and Siegfried make their pact promising Siegfried Kriemhild's hand if he wins Brunhild for Gunther. The shot presents a symbolic gesture fraught with ambiguity, the hands of the two kings joined in medium close-up with Hagen's baleful stare posed behind.

The closing of the third *Gesang* contrasts two images: first presenting Siegfried meeting Kriemhild after his successful return from Iceland, then Brunhild and Gunther. In a shot that exemplifies the film's obsessive pursuit of symmetry, Siegfried approaches from the left, Kriemhild from the right, each in absolute profile perpendicular to the camera axis, looking like matching halves of some primordial blonde androgyne. They meet in the exact centre of the frame, their embrace further framed by a rectangular doorway in the background and the converging highly decorated beams in the ceiling. The brightly lit space of the set, the decorative motifs, the actors' movement and appearance all speak of harmony and order, union and future happiness. However, the following shot, the very last shot of this *Gesang,* reverses this composition. In the dark set of Brunhild's bedroom, dominated by a huge arch over the bed alcove, the deceiving Gunther and betrayed Brunhild express their despair and lack of trust. Brunhild sits collapsed on the floor while Gunther stands over her. He reaches for the torch which illuminates the room and extinguishes it, as an iris closes over the shot.

The endings of the fifth and sixth *Gesänge* revolve around emblematic close-ups. The penultimate shot of the fifth *Gesang* presents an extreme close-up of Gunther against a nearly abstract white background (a shot compositionally different from all but a few shots in the film – all dealing with the death of Siegfried – in its lack of any anchoring decorative motif), as he gives in to Brunhild's jealousy of Siegfried and announces the hunt at which Siegfried will be the quarry. The final shot shows

Hagen disappearing through a curtained doorway as if going backstage to prepare the spectacle ordered by his king. In the close-up Gunther looks panicked and out of control and towards the end of the shot he looks directly at the camera, a quite infrequent practice in *The Death of Siegfried*. The look expresses Gunther's seizing control of the narrative action at this moment, arranging the plot in which Siegfried will die. However, it is Hagen who closes the *Gesang*, as he will the next one. The shot ending the sixth Gesang seems to respond directly to this shot, a medium close-up of Hagen after he has killed Siegfried, gesturing towards the camera as he declares in the intertitle: 'The Hunt is Over!'

Harbou/Lang used the interruption provided by the breaking into *Gesänge* to create a unique structure for the film. On the one hand, the final image of each *Gesang* presents a crystallisation of the narrative action, a key turning point in the plot, so that one could almost construct a synopsis by stringing them together: the fallen leaf, Gunther's pledge, the doomed marriage of Brunhild and Gunther, Gunther's agreement to betray his friend, Hagen's accomplishment of the deed. But there is more than summary offered in these images. Each of them has a dialectical aspect, highlighting the action of the Destiny-machine, as one element of each composition questions another: Siegfried's apparent invulnerability is undone by the leaf; Gunther and Siegfried's handshake is regarded sceptically by Hagen; the unity of Kriemhild and Siegfried is contrasted by the smouldering resentment of Gunther and Brunhild; Gunther's claim of control is contradicted by Hagen's celebration. As the film progresses, the dialectics of the final images of the *Gesänge* become more complex, moving from elements within the frame to a contrast between the final shots of two separate *Gesänge*.

Each of these images anticipates a future which will undo the apparent moments of control, harmony or invulnerability. These potential reversals are not witnessed by the characters, who remain ignorant of the plots into which they are pulled. It is the structure of the film which renders them visible to the viewer, the enunciating force of the film which asks us to read them as the fate of the characters and the workings of the Destiny-machine. Thus the narrative structure of *Gesänge* plays a similar role to the set design in creating an enclosed world of fatality. But the growing sense of fatality does not come from the mythical forces, the legendary and super-human elements whose power is constantly defeated and attenuated in the film. These final images stress the power of the world of Worms, the deceitful handshakes, the sham marriages, the staged hunt with a human victim. It is the death of the myth that *The Death of Siegfried* chronicles, as finalised in the last image of the seventh *Gesang*, the final shot of the film. In this tableau of the destroyed mythological figures, Siegfried's body lies within the highly ordered and symmetrical space of the cathedral, Brunhild at his feet, dead from her own dagger, and Kriemhild mourning at his head.

The accenting of these final images that comes from the division of the film into *Gesänge* creates a structure of double reading for the audience not unlike the two poles of the narrative and the poetic that Benet finds in *Der müde Tod*. But in this epic film the emblematic nature of these shots refers directly to the progression of the narrative: we read them not simply for a metaphorical reference but as anticipations of what is to come as the story unfolds. Thus the allegorical dimension of *Die Nibelungen* is sutured to its narrative form and particularly to its unfolding (rather than to its cyclical repetition as in *Der müde Tod*). We are asked to read two narratives, on the one hand following the intrigues and passions of the characters, but on the other hand following a fatal scenario which seems to make use of those individual passions rather than springing from them.

Brunhild's jealousy and rage certainly provide a complex motivation for much of the plot; her unspoken love for Siegfried (as if recognising him as a fellow creature from the mythic age they both belong to) and her rage at his naiveté in making himself available to Gunther and Hagen's plotting are beautifully implied in Harbou's script. However, she gains nothing from her role in the destruction of Siegfried, as her suicide at his bier acknowledges. Her passion too has become a lever within Hagen and Gunther's plotting. Hagen stands at the centre of this intrigue (Kracauer calls him 'Fate's pace-maker'),[17] but the enigma of his motivations creates the moral ambivalence that rules *Die Nibelungen*. The contrasting motives of jealousy of Siegfried and loyalty to his sovereign seem inadequate as an explanation for Hagen's actions, and this opaque quality makes him the pre-eminent agent of fate in the film. As David Levin has shown, Hagen scurries about doing the narrative's bidding, making the fatal connections between characters, as visualised in the shot which closes the second *Gesang* of Hagen glowering behind Gunther and Siegfried's clasped hands.[18] Hagen arranges Siegfried's deception of Brunhild for Gunther, tricks Kriemhild into marking Siegfried's tunic, arranges the final hunt. But Hagen doesn't direct and stage manage these scenes in order to advance his own aims. Instead, he seems to be working out a predetermined pattern, the course of the narrative as the course of destiny.

Individual passions, rather than providing the source or explanation or motivation for the unfolding of the plot, are employed by a grand design in order to achieve its nearly diagrammatic symmetry. One could plot the relations between characters of the court of Worms in this manner:

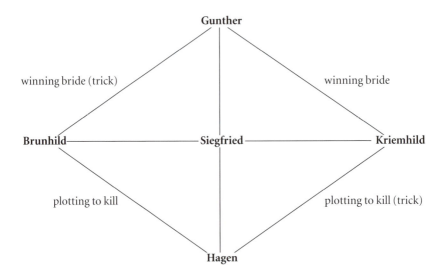

Siegfried stands at the centre of a number of groups made up of three or four characters who, working in concert, accomplish the major narrative actions after Siegfried comes to Worms. The top half of the diagram deals with marriages. Siegfried conspires with Gunther to win him Brunhild; Gunther then gives Kriemhild to Siegfried. The bottom part of the diagram deals with murder. Brunhild conspires with Gunther and Hagen to bring about Siegfried's death; Hagen tricks Kriemhild into an unwitting role in the conspiracy by marking the point of

Siegfried's vulnerability. These parallel actions chart Siegfried's angular relations in the diagram. But he is also caught between the characters on the axes. On the horizontal axis, Brunhild and Kriemhild have opposed relations to him, love and hate, founded in Siegfried's ambiguous role in Brunhild's own wooing. The film works out this play of oppositions by Brunhild's dark clothing and hair as opposed to Kriemhild's glimmering blonde paleness, and stages it in almost diagrammatic fashion in their furious argument on the steps of the cathedral of Worms. Likewise, Siegfried is caught between Gunther and Hagen on the vertical axis, with Gunther moving from the friendship pledged in their handclasp to the betrayal of the hunt staged by Hagen.

As opposed to the short formulaic form of the tale that shapes *Der müde Tod*, Harbou and Lang construct *Die Nibelungen* through the gradual unfolding of the stages of action of the epic. Each stage is brought to a point of clarity that achieves an almost emblematic immobility in the final shot of each *Gesang*. But the ongoing force of the narrative similarly resolves itself into a diagrammatic simplicity, as if the cross inscribed on Siegfried's back could stand as a synopsis of the whole story and of his final destiny. The structuring of the film into *Gesänge*; the arrangement of space through set design, actors' placement, lighting and camera framing; the pattern of events and the logic of characters – all seem to refer back to the same infrastructure, a code by which the abstraction of the Destiny-machine slowly rises to the surface and into complete visibility.

This rise into visibility defines the role of the visionary scene in Lang's films. The visionary scene refers to a shot or series of shots in which we see a character's subjective vision which no longer corresponds simply to the visible world, but shows in symbolic or allegorical form the workings of the impersonal forces behind the narrative. These are scenes that must be read or interpreted by both characters and audience, although their meaning (as in *Der müde Tod*) may be disavowed or remain opaque. There are two pronounced visionary moments in *The Death of Siegfried*, both associated with Kriemhild and both taking the film's drive toward abstraction to its furthest point. As in *Der müde Tod* they are visions of death.

As Benjamin's discussion of the *Trauerspiel* makes clear, it is not simply that death can stand as an allegorical figure (for the vanity of life, for instance), but rather that death represents the actual work of allegory, its stripping away of the surfaces of nature through its melancholy gaze to reveal the death head beneath.[19] In *The Death of Siegfried* death's role does not end with the perishing of Siegfried, but with the dying out of the realm of myth he and Brunhild represent, the abstraction of its magic into the calculations and intrigues of the court of Worms. The movement out of the forest of symbols into the geometrical order of the Burgundians, from the timeless realm of myth into the realm of history and civilisation is a movement into the fallen world of death, a soulless duplicitous world which can only await its apocalypse. Thus what Kriemhild perceives in her visions signifies more than the death of her husband. In contrast to the maiden in *Der müde Tod*, Kriemhild does not simply experience death as the opponent to love, the figure of personal loss. The death head that Kriemhild perceives condemns the world she lives in.

Before I turn to a discussion of Kriemhild's two visions, the frequently discussed 'Dream of the Hawks' and the tree which turns into a skull, I want to point out another more hidden figure of the death's head in the film. This shot is not a visionary scene as I have defined it, since it does not present the viewpoint of any character. Rather it is a puzzle picture offered to the audience, one which I imagine has been seen before, but which I have not found discussed in previous commentaries.

In the fifth *Gesang* Siegfried has brought to Worms the treasure of the Nibelungs. Gunther and Hagen watch Siegfried and his vassals in the courtyard below from the arched windows. They are joined by Brunhild. Those who will in the future conspire to kill Siegfried are brought together, although at this point none of them has articulated a desire for his death. Gunther stands within the arch looking down on Siegfried, Hagen stands on the left side of the arch, while Brunhild approaches and stands beside Gunther on the right. Backlit against the white light from the window, the figures are silhouetted (as Hagen will be when he throws the fatal spear at Siegfried, or Gunther when he proclaims the treacherous hunt both framed against a similar white light). The high arched window takes on the form of a skull as the three dark figures outline eyes and nose orifices on the white ground. Recalling a long tradition of *vanitas* trick pictures (including Holbein's anamorphic *The Ambassadors*) in which the gestalt of a skull can be assembled out of other elements, Lang briefly, almost subliminally, anticipates the outcome the union of these three characters will have on the character they view from above. The proleptic nature of this diagrammatic visual figure (at this point Gunther still professes love for Siegfried) indicates that the plan pre-exists its conscious articulation.

If few viewers have picked out this visual trick on Lang's part, Kriemhild's visionary scenes have sometimes been criticised for their over-legibility. Both make explicit the drive towards abstraction that underlies the film. The first is the 'Dream of the Hawks', an extraordinary sequence which Lang lifts out of the rest of the film by a number of means. The sequence makes a dramatic shift in modes, moving from 'live action' to animation. (Lang is one of the few directors to include animated sequences in his films, something he continues to use even in Hollywood in *The Secret Beyond the Door* in 1947. Hitchcock provides a parallel in both *Sabotage* and *Vertigo*). This sequence is literally a film within a film with a different *auteur*, the experimental German animator Walther Ruttmann. The film recalls both the

techniques and forms of Ruttmann's extraordinary *Opus* series (1921–4) and has a place within Ruttmann's *œuvre*, excerpted from Lang's film (as the sequence was eliminated from the American release of *Siegfried*, apparently because it stopped the flow of narrative and confused audiences). However, Ruttmann clearly took the scenario for his animated film from the formal vocabulary of Lang's film.

The brief sequence begins with an abstract grey arch shape rising from the bottom of the screen, echoed then by the similar rise of a series of black arches. Here Ruttmann animates the formal permutations on the arches which appear throughout the film in the doorways, gateways and windows of the sets. Out of a swirling white comet-like form a white bird appears, and is pursued by black wing-like forms, permutations of the earlier black arches. Taking more precise bird forms, the black figures seem to peck at the white bird, until a series of white pointed shards converge and the dream ends abruptly. These shapes reflect the colour oppositions between Siegfried, always shown in white, and his strongest opponents Brunhild and Hagen, who are always dressed in black. It also picks up the wing motif of Hagen and Brunhild's helmets. As a sequence of animated heraldry, the dream also reflects the absorption of animal imagery into geometrical abstraction in the decorative motifs at Worms.

The dream is presented as Kriemhild's premonition when Siegfried first arrives at Worms. As such, it even precedes the first meeting between Siegfried and Kriemhild, but already lays down the scenario for his ultimate destruction. This prefiguration creates an atmosphere of fatality, but its visual abstractions are equally important. Here only the morphology of form, primal opposition of colour and shape, express Siegfried's downfall. As a heraldic emblem the sequence subjects the narrative of the film to its melancholic gaze and strips it down to elemental oppositions, imagery reduced to its most abstract aspects. Like the maiden's vision of death in the tavern in *Der müde Tod*, Kriemhild's prophetic dream provides no apotropaic power; forewarned is not forearmed.

Later, in interviews given during his Hollywood career, Lang described Kriemhild's second visionary scene as part of a 'symbolic' style he had abandoned.[20] As a visual emblem, it comes closest to the maiden's initial vision of the shadow of Death in *Der müde Tod* and literally enacts Benjamin's evocation of allegory as the petrified primordial landscape of the death's head. We see successive images linked by Lang's favoured symbolic transition, the overlap-dissolve. First we see Siegfried standing next to a blossoming tree, waving farewell to Kriemhild as he heads off to the fatal hunt. Then the figure of Siegfried fades out and the blossoms disappear from the tree, revealing only the bare branches sweeping the ground. These branches whiten and outline two dark circles. In the next dissolve the dark circles become staring empty eye sockets as the white branches weave themselves into the shape of a skull. The shots carry the same significance as the premonitory dream, and gradually merge into the visual mode of animation, as the recognisable photographic basis of the image fades out, and the shot transforms into a graphic image on a black ground, a death's head occupying no space but the space of significance. The figure of the hero fades away, the blossoming nature dies and then gives way to an emblem which paradoxically stares at camera and viewer through sightless eyes.

In the American release version, *Siegfried,* these images occur as another premonition of Kriemhild's as Siegfried departs for the hunt, doubling and reinforcing the message of her earlier dream, and indeed this is the way Lang remembered the images functioning in the later interview: as 'foreboding' Siegfried's death. However, in the original German version these images only appear *after* Siegfried's death, as

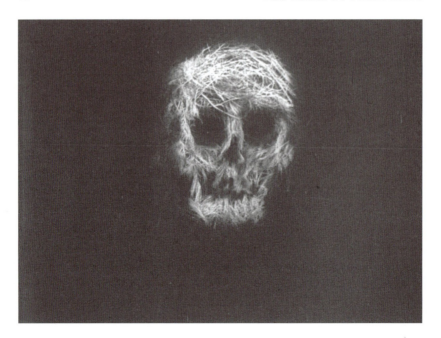

Kriemhild kneels beside his body in their palace quarters. Siegfried's wave farewell did appear as he departed for the hunt (and, in fact, Kriemhild speaks before he leaves of disturbing dreams of his death). But the farewell shot is repeated as a flashback after his death, and then gives way to the visionary images just described. In Lang and Harbou's original text these emblems do not serve to predict the course of the narrative; rather they are its ultimate significance and *telos*. The hero is dead, the world of nature and youth has given way to the figure of death.

I will not deal with the second half of *Die Nibelungen*, *Kriemhild's Revenge*, in as much detail as *The Death of Siegfried*. Although an extraordinary film, it is less complex. Similarly broken into seven *Gesänge*, *Kriemhild's Revenge* nonetheless basically follows one central narrative movement, which is impelled by the ending of *The Death of Siegfried*: the carrying-out of Kriemhild's revenge on Hagen for the murder of her husband. In contrast to the halting rhythm constructed from successive tableaux of *Siegfried*, *Kriemhild* explodes with action and barrels through its plot with a single-minded purpose. No diagrammatic pattern rules the action of this film; instead the magical world of transformation and the courtly world of deception here give way to a pure savagery of retribution. In contrast to the dialectically interrelated three worlds of *The Death of Siegfried* and its central conflict between two worlds of myth (Odenwald and Iceland) and civilisation (Worms), *Kriemhild* has only two worlds: Worms and the wild steppes of Etzel and the Huns, and it abandons Worms in the beginning of the second *Gesang*. It is in *Kriemhild's Revenge* that Kracauer's description carries some weight: primitive passions are released with Kriemhild's hatred. The battle no longer pits the dying world of myth against the deceptive world of civilisation, but the eruption of savage and chaotic violence against the defensive order of civilisation.

But to understand the energy of this battle and its direct linear structure (in contrast to *The Death of Siegfried's* crisscrossing conspiracies and alliances) we must dwell on the end of *The Death of Siegfried* and its final emblems of death. Although all four films dealt with in this section resolve themselves into allegories of death, they are far from identical in meaning and mode. Death is surrendered to in a sort of erotic melancholia in *Der müde Tod*. Although Kriemhild will also surrender to death in the final image of *Kriemhild's Revenge* – and I will dwell on certain similarities in these final scenes – the tone and significance of her surrender is very different. Kriemhild fully identifies with death, not simply as its agent, but as the embodiment of its power of destruction. Although endowed with a social significance, death remained essentially a personal issue in *Der müde Tod* – the loss of a lover. I would claim that Kriemhild's final vision of death in *The Death of Siegfried*, no longer a premonition since his death is accomplished, is a vision of the death of the whole world: not simply the hero and husband, but the flowering branch, and the tree, root and bole, become the death's head. The final abstraction of *The Death of Siegfried* is the logical outcome of the life-denying world of civilisation at Worms, a vision of its own death. The final act of *Die Nibelungen* becomes presaged in this emblem: it must be destroyed. This emblem announces a new allegorical mode, as Lang and Harbou had already moved from the *Märchen* to the Epic. What lies ahead is simply the apocalypse, the revelation of final things.

Lang and Harbou could hardly claim originality in envisioning the downfall of civilisation from the invasion of Eastern hordes. The vitality and chaotic movement of the Huns contrasts diametrically with the sense of space and order in Worms. Primal energies seem to be liberated on the steppes and the stampeding, mounted Huns provide the closest thing to nature and spontaneity in *Die Nibelungen*. But what is liberated here is violence, not renewal, as if the Huns were simply the other side of Worms, its designated avenger. It is Kriemhild's apocalyptic vision which turns the Huns' savagery into a final righting of the balance, a redressing of Worms' crimes. With the death of her husband, Kriemhild sees only a world of death and she employs the savagery of the Huns to wipe away the imposture of civilisation and make literal her vision of a landscape of death. Kriemhild drives the Huns to create the holocaust of the Burgundians.

Although *The Death of Siegfried* constantly foregrounds the issue of narration by the embedded tale sung by the minstrel Volker, or the structural importance of the division into *Gesänge*, the questions of enunciation raised in *Der müde Tod* about who bears responsibility for the tale's unfolding are rarely articulated in the first *Die Nibelungen* film. The force of narration remains impersonal, embodied in the diagrammatic nature of the story, the sets, and the structure of the *Gesänge*. Although a variety of characters lay different sorts of claim to the narrative – such as Volker the minstrel, or Hagen and Brunhild as the arrangers of intrigues – no-one can truly claim it, even in as problematical a manner as the figure of Death in *Der müde Tod*. The look at the camera remains relatively rare in *The Death of Siegfried*, with the significant exception of Gunther's wild-eyed stare in close-up as he agrees to the killing of Siegfried and announces the false hunt. As mentioned earlier, Gunther at this moment seizes control of the narrative action and directs it, staging the scene. However, consistent with his pusillanimous character, he cannot maintain this hold, as his hesitation at the hunt shows, and the sixth *Gesang* actually ends with Hagen departing, apparently to implement Gunther's proclamation. Therefore, narrative control is attributed to no one character in *The Death of Siegfried*, and no-one claims a special relation to the camera. Only with the ambiguous sightless stare of the death's head in Kriemhild's final vision are we possibly introduced to the enunciator of the film – the stare of death, which certainly introduces the enunciating viewpoint of the film to follow, *Kriemhild's Revenge*.

The lack of a dominant claim of narrative authority in *The Death of Siegfried* sharply contrasts with *Kriemhild's Revenge* where Kriemhild single-handedly directs narrative action and recurrently stares directly at the camera (as does her consort and tool of revenge, Etzel). Her stares nearly always express her devotion to revenge, first as the visual accompaniment to the oaths she offers, or gets others to offer, to destroy Hagen, then as implacable instigator, director and witness of the destruction of the Burgundians. She stares resolutely at the camera as she makes her oath at Siegfried's tomb before leaving Worms; as she gets Etzel to swear before their marriage; as she asks Etzel to invite her brothers to his castle; when she offers the Huns gold for Hagen's head; and as she demands Rudiger keep his oath and engage Hagen in combat. Her unflinching stare at the camera during the feast, as preparations are made for the massacre, and during the attacks and then the burning-out of the Burgundians (even as her brothers call to her, 'Sister, see your work!' displaying the body of her younger brother, she does not blink) not only indicates her relentless will to revenge, but identifies her stare with the force of death itself.

Kriemhild's appearance transforms itself entirely between the two films, as she abandons her innocent white to take on the dark colours of Brunhild and Hagen. However, she is not simply garbed in black, as some commentators have said. Instead complex white gothic spirals cover her in a maze-like inscription. But most striking is the transformation of her eyes and her posture. Her eyes are outlined in black and seem excessively widened, creating an unflinching stare which make(s) her (and Etzel) resemble a Sumerian idol. She stands stiffly and rarely turns her head, instead shifting her eyes as her gaze moves from character to character. This is a dead woman walking – and staring – which is why, once her revenge is accomplished, she dies so suddenly, collapsing like an abandoned marionette.

Kriemhild's apocalyptic vision at the end of *The Death of Siegfried* becomes realised as the holocaust at the end of *Kriemhild's Revenge*. The world is filled with death: the heaped-up corpses of the Huns, the orderly, arranged bodies of the Burgundian knights. Kriemhild's response to the ferocity of the Burgundian's defence is an unbending posture and an unflinching gaze. As her look at the camera indicates a privileged relation to the apparatus of visibility, one could describe her posture and viewpoint as like a camera, recording, in horror as much as delight, the carrying-out of her revenge. But the recording that Kriemhild-as-camera engages in is not simply passive. She witnesses, but she also directs: she is the author of the conflagration ('Sister, see your work!'). She will stand unmoved until the final deaths, the killing of Hagen and Gunther are accomplished. It is she who will turn the battle into a holocaust by ordering the burning of the palace. In the midst of the flames *Die Nibleungen*'s most literal narrator figure, Volker the minstrel, accompanies the inferno with a song of death, which, heard outside, even sets the Huns into a rhythmic swaying. As he plays this final song of death, Volker too stares directly at the camera. What he shares with the woman now destroying his world is the viewpoint of narration as the chronicling of death. In her double identification with the camera and with death, Kriemhild embodies the viewpoint of annihilation, the cinema of apocalypse, the final fiery destruction and purging of the world, its delivery into the hands of death; she will expire in the penultimate shot of the film.

As in *Der müde Tod* the end of the film represents the triumph of death, the ceasing of the last resistance to its demands. Narration and closure become imaged as a process of surrendering to death. But whereas *Der müde Tod* briefly presents us with the reunion of lovers and the flowery fields of heaven, *Kriemhild's Revenge* shows the devoted wife releasing the soil soaked with her husband's blood and collapsing in a world emptied out, burnt out, by her revenge. But if the endings of the two films contrast in tone, the scenography of their climaxes mirror each other. Each ends with a conflagration, a holocaust imaged as the fate of mankind. The maiden in *Der müde Tod* goes into the fire to rescue a young life, while Kriemhild stands outside to make certain no-one escapes the flames. The happy ending allowed in the earlier film (to the extent that it is happy) stays within the realm of the personal, the reunion of individual lovers. In *Kriemhild's Revenge* the work of mourning does not simply descend into melancholia, but releases itself as revenge against the world of the living, as rage and holocaust. The horror of the ending of *Die Nibelungen* extends broadly, laying waste to the world. Lang and Harbou move between these two films from an allegorical use of the *Märchen* to a truly apocalyptic vision. As we will see, Lang is not yet through with this image of conflagration, nor it with him.

3

Metropolis:
The Dance of Death

The Allegory of the Machine

> Allegoricists, like alchemists, hold dominion over an infinite
> transformation of meaning, in contrast to the one, true, word
> of God.
>   Susan Buck-Morss, *The Dialectics of Seeing: Walter Benjamin*
>   *and the Arcades Project*[1]

Metropolis remains the albatross around Lang's neck, condemned, or at least partially condemned, by critics and film-makers (including, at points, Lang himself).[2]
Since its first release, every generation seems to have found a new reason to be suspicious of this film, whether for its naive romanticism about solving the problems
of technology; its harbouring of – if not Nazi sympathies – at least a susceptibility
to Nazi ideologies; or its blatant gender stereotyping. While all these attacks hold

some truth, what is hard to explain is why this rancour against *Metropolis* continues to be renewed, continuing to generate new reviews and essays. The enigma to be explained is not the controversy the film inspires, but its continued popularity, its constant citation in pop culture (Madonna's video, *Express Yourself*, a London musical, the film *The Bodyguard*) as well as in highly regarded cultural sources (Rotwang's mechanical hand on *Dr. Strangelove*, the machine room explosion in Philip Glass and Robert Wilson's *Einstein on the Beach*, the references in Pynchon's *Gravity's Rainbow*).

But if *Metropolis* has remained a topic of heated discussion since its release, its reception has hardly been stable. Its current popularity cannot be attributed simply to a disco makeover for its re-release by Giorgio Moroder in 1984. Anyone, like myself, teaching the film over the decades noticed a sudden rise in student enthusi-asm for it – with or without Pat Benatar and Loverboy on the soundtrack. The very element that caused most critics to abjure it, the naive resolution of the heart medi-ating between head and hand, was offered as the final words of wisdom in Madonna's *Express Yourself* video. Although I will not argue this point fully here, I would claim that *Metropolis* was received as a postmodernist work in the 1980s. A new sensibility embraced its blend of kitsch and monumentality, mechanical sexu-ality and over-the-top melodrama, powerful political critique matched by cartoon solutions, all conveyed through its exquisite sets and masterful visual style. In a postmodernist context *Metropolis*'s contradictions could be seen, not as an inherent flaw, but as the sign of a work divided against itself (a fissure attributable, claimed many, to the Harbou/ Lang collaboration – with the good due to Lang and the bad to 'that Nazi bitch'). Its schizoid nature found a home in the 1980s, on a level of appropriation, if not of critical evaluation, and its overt employment of allegory was intuitively, if rarely articulately, embraced by audiences and artists.

We are also faced with the irony that the best-known and most popular of Lang's silent films survives in the most incomplete form of any of his major films. *Metropo-lis* was Lang and Ufa's super-film, the most elaborate and expensive film made in Ger-many to that date and one which was to crown Germany's challenge to Hollywood as an international maker of films. Lang and Harbou had already made the claim with *Die Nibelungen* that by drawing on its past Germany could produce a cinema that would rival and surpass Hollywood. With *Metropolis*, Lang claimed, the technology of motion pictures which the Americans understood pragmatically would be given a 'spirit', a meaning and significance Hollywood films lacked.[3] This was a common claim by German technicians and engineers from the Weimar into the Third Reich, that German technology was superior to other nations because it was based on spir-itual values.[4] However, *Metropolis* so overspent its budget that it drove Ufa into the red (and ultimately into financial dependence on Hollywood corporations), and the mixed reviews *Metropolis* received at its opening led to the cutting of the film for its international release and for its secondary release in Germany.[5] Unfortunately no print of the original release was preserved, and the print most commonly circulated is based, ironically, on cuts made for the American distribution of the film.

The cuts were drastic. The second version reviewed by German censors for gen-eral release was nearly a quarter shorter.[6] The American version made some addi-tional cuts. Whole subplots (such as Georgi the worker's trip to Yoshiwara, the pleasure quarter) were cut, characters eliminated (Desertus the monk, head of the sect of gothics, Joh Fredersen's mother) as well as the back story of Joh and Rot-wang's rivalry over Hel, Freder's mother. Attempts to restore the film have recovered a number of previously missing scenes and stray shots, but still more than twenty per cent of the film originally released has disappeared. Therefore, I will discuss Thea von Harbou's novel in some depth in this chapter, since it reflects much of the original design of the film.

I detour here into the contemporary reception of this film because, of all the films I deal with in this section, *Metropolis* flaunts its allegorical emblems and devices most flagrantly. Just as Benjamin, writing his book on the baroque *Trauerspiel* in Weimar Germany felt that this seemingly archaic form held the key to the contemporary use of allegory in Expressionist art, I think the embrace of the allegorical in the postmodern has facilitated the contemporary revival of Weimar art and cinema.

Both *Der müde Tod* and *Die Nibelungen* rise to moments of emblematic allegorical clarity out of other narrative forms, the *Märchen* and the epic. The narrative structure of each film seems initially to be determined by the fairytale or the legendary epic, but the importance of figural emblems, especially cued through the visionary scenes, reveals a more dominant allegorical intent. In both these films the allegorical revelation is closely tied to the discovery of the Destiny-machine and the figure of death. It is the exposing of the mechanical pattern and force beneath the apparent tale or legend that lifts these films into the allegorical mode. In *Metropolis* allegory, as well as the theme of the mechanical, lies on the surface, with the science fiction genre serving simply as the modern genre most attuned to the allegorical mode. Harbou makes clear in the epigram to her novel version of *Metropolis* that her tale is not intended as a simple prognostication of the future, but as a figural commentary on the present (a fact underscored by the date given for the action, 2026 AD, one century from the time of the film's completion). 'This book is not of today or of the future. It tells of no place. ... It has a moral grown on the pillar of understanding.' The no-time, no-place of *Metropolis* open into the realm of significance and instruction: the mode of allegory.

How does allegory as a mode function to bend representation or narrative towards the task of significance and instruction, and particularly how does silent cinema take on this task? To answer this we need to catch allegory at work. The classical definition of allegory saw it as a development of the *trope*, the turn of phrase that deviates from literal meaning (allegory in Greek means 'inversion' or 'speaking other than one seems to speak'[7]). But as developed in classical rhetoric, allegory does not serve as a simple synonym for a trope, but as its extension. Thus rhetorician Richard Lanham defines allegory as 'extending a metaphor through an entire speech or passage'.[8] Angus Fletcher offers the classical distinction between trope and figure, *trope* being a play on single words, an isolated instance, while *figure* deals with larger groups of words.[9] An allegory, then, could be defined as a text which uses tropes by grouping them into larger figures which regulate the whole text.

If Benjamin's *Origin of German Tragic Drama* supplies the treatment of allegory both most contemporary and most revelatory for Lang's silent films, the most thorough contemporary study of the forms of the mode is Angus Fletcher's *Allegory: The Theory of a Symbolic Mode*. While Benjamin's work reaches a greater depth in contemplating the melancholia of allegory, and I will return to it at the end of this chapter, Fletcher's work replicates a wider range of allegorical structures that allow us to analyse *Metropolis* in detail. A masterful work of critical syntheses and originality, Fletcher's approach to allegory supplies us with several essential tools for making sense out of Lang and Harbou's film. A great deal of the disfavour which *Metropolis* inspires comes simply from an unfamiliarity with the allegorical mode, an unfamiliarity which often masquerades as a judgment about taste and therefore obscures the nature of Harbou and Lang's film. Fletcher's analysis of the form of allegory allows us to decode the enigmas of characterisation, acting and plot resolution in this film, and its strange melange of attraction and repulsion, its blending of sexuality and the mechanical.

It is important to remember that modern critical commentary on allegory began as condemnation, first in the work of Goethe who denounced the allegory in favour of a new understanding, originating in Kant, of the innate power of the symbol.[10] For Goethe the symbol puts us in contact with an idea in an indirect and mysterious way, while allegory remains conventional and rational. Bringing these concepts into an English tradition, Coleridge perhaps said it most clearly when he translated the opposition between allegory and symbol into the conflict between the organic and the mechanical.[11] Whether realist or romantic, nearly all of nineteenth-century aesthetics aligns itself with the organic form as opposed to the mechanical. In contrast, silent cinema – the 'art of the machine' – understood its affinity to allegory, and Lang perhaps more strongly than any other director.

Metropolis is the allegory of the future as the triumph of the machine. And the machine in a variety of manifestations becomes the central allegorical figure of the film. I have already discussed the key visionary scene in *Metropolis*, Freder's vision in which he sees the central machine of the city transform itself into a demon, the cannibalistic, pedophagic god, Moloch. I will return to this scene later. But in many ways even more central to the film's allegorical structure is the figure of the robot. Fletcher in his attempt to explain allegory's determinedly non-psychological, non-realist and non-organic approach to characterisation first describes allegorical characters as demonic, as if each were possessed by a monomaniacal force. However, he finally declares:

> The perfect allegorical agent is not a man possessed by a daemon, but a robot, a Talus, and finally after certain prototypical creations, as in Mary Shelley's *Frankenstein*, this type of agent is fully exploited by a twentieth-century author, Karel Capek whose play *R.U.R.* makes robots out of creatures who look exactly like human beings.[12]

Although *R.U.R.* (the play which introduced the term 'robots' and chronicled their revolt against their human masters and inventors) undoubtedly influenced Harbou and Lang's image of the robot in *Metropolis*, Fletcher could have easily replaced Capek with Lang. The image of the robot dominates *Metropolis*, not only in the false Maria created by inventor Rotwang, but also in the performance styles of the workers (in their dehumanised mechanical actions as soulless slaves – as well as their chaotic 'machine-gone-wild' riot of destruction instigated by the robot Maria). In many ways the robot (and the demonic aspect of the mechanical it represents) takes over *Metropolis*'s imagery and action, diverting energy from its rival parables of order and rationality or spiritual awakening which attempt to contain this demonic energy.

Metropolis stands, therefore, as the Lang film that is most blatantly allegorical. Here he wrestles most directly with the demon of allegory and in a sense overcomes it, never returning to the form as explicitly again (although never abandoning it entirely). But the victory may be pyrrhic. Likewise *Metropolis* stages man's encounter with the machine front and centre, there is no need for anyone to have a visionary revelation of the machine pulsing beneath the surface; it stands as manifest content.

It is the over-explicit nature of this film that makes many viewers, trained to hunt out subterranean meanings and organic symbols, so uncomfortable. But if Lang and Harbou's allegory at points appears too obvious, the process of reading it reveals, as in Freder's vision, demonic energies that pulse beneath the tropes and subvert any final comfortable interpretation.

The Universal Language of Silent Film

> The internationalism of filmic language will become the
> strongest instrument available for the mutual understanding
> of peoples, who otherwise have such difficulty understanding
> each other in all too many languages.
> Fritz Lang, 'The Future of the Feature Film in Germany'[13]

Every allegory, and certainly every modern allegory, foregrounds the act of reading and even offers a lesson in how it should be read. *Metropolis* offers its lesson as instruction not only in the act of reading allegorical figures but in the specifically cinematic creation of tropes or hieroglyphics. Lang demonstrates the work the film-maker undertakes to wrench the image away from simple reference. The tutor text for this mode is revealed appropriately as a story within a story, a visual parable that translates a sermon delivered by the film's moral centre, the female prophetess Maria: the story of the Tower of Babel.

The selection of this particular Biblical text for visual translation and ideological re-interpretation marks *Metropolis*'s culmination of the millennial ambitions of the silent film. Vachel Lindsay's invocation of the hieroglyphic as the foundation of a new film language was made within a broad millennial claim for cinema as a new language for mankind: 'The invention of the photoplay is as great a step as was the invention of picture writing in the stone age.'[14] In a particularly American reinterpretation of the hieroglyphic, which had been traditionally understood as an enigmatic, priestly language sheltered by its obscurity from the understanding of the profane, Lindsay saw the motion picture as a mode of iconic communication whose images where accessible to the great international masses, legible and visible at once: to see a moving picture was to understand it. However, beyond this immediate accessibility, the visual hieroglyphic for Lindsay contained layers of meaning, and pondering its 'spirit meaning' would open its viewers to a new vision of the world.[15] Miriam Hansen, in her brilliant discussion of Griffith's *Intolerance,* has cannily inserted Lindsay's discussion of the hieroglyphic and the potential of film as a new language into the tradition of the universal language, a millennial concept like Lindsay's, which centred on the Biblical image of the Tower of Babel. As Hansen points out, the view of silent film as a universal language, based partly on gesture and physiognomy, found European advocates as well (such as Béla Balázs, to give an example more likely to be influential on Lang and Harbou than the American Lindsay).[16]

Choosing the Tower of Babel as an allegory for this new universal language of silent cinema reveals the tensions at the heart of Lang's allegory, for, as Hansen says, 'the Tower of Babel stands not only for the project of a universal language but also for its opposite, the impossibility of such a project'.[17] In the Bible, it is man's hubris in building the tower whose top reaches to heaven that *causes* the diversity of human languages. Jehovah, witnessing a project ambitious beyond anything

humans have yet attempted, declares: 'Here they are one people with a single language and now they have started to do this; henceforward nothing they have a mind
to do will be beyond their reach' (*Genesis*, chapter 11, verse 6). His confusion of the
single language into multiple tongues subverts the building of the tower by divine
intervention. Therefore the rebuilding of the tower, the creation of a new universal
language will always carry a suggestion of titanic revolt. Harbou and Lang's retelling
of the Tower of Babel parable involves, as do all of the film's numerous Biblical references, not a pietistic reference but an allegorical refashioning of the original
meaning.

Maria tells the tale of the Tower of Babel to the workers of Metropolis deep
within the catacombs in the depths of the city. It functions primarily as a political
parable about class and power divisions, introducing Maria's central trope, one of
the oldest in the history of allegory, the city-state as a human body, with workers
conceived as 'hands' and planners as 'brains'. Harbou moderates the hubris of the
project behind the construction of the tower by inscribing it with a motto which
gives divine and human glory equal billing: 'Great is the World and its Creator. And
Great is Man'. Rather than descending as divine punishment, the confusion in languages derives from a primal division in labour, as those who conceived of the
tower gather labourers – hands – to realise it. The labourers do not understand the
architects' noble motives, but only experience the pain of their own enslavement;
while the architects have no awareness of the workers' suffering. Harbou's novel
glosses this confusion in communication as a breakdown of the primal word 'Babel'
into opposed meanings for each class:

'Babel!' shouted one, meaning: Divinity, Coronation, Eternal Triumph!
'Babel!' shouted the other meaning: Hell, Slavery, Eternal Damnation![18]

Harbou's re-reading of the Tower of Babel has a certain power, locating the origin of
the dispersal of mankind not in divine jealousy, but in the breakdown of the unity
of labour, and hence language. However, the limits of Harbou's political insight are
also naturalised by her allegory: the division of labour is not questioned, nor are the
power relations inherent in it revealed. Instead, it is 'natural' that the 'hands' and the
'brains' have different tasks. The only problem is one of communication.

Many of these allegorical figures were commonplaces of Weimar culture which
was deeply embroiled in a debate on the nature of technology and political power.
Harbou most probably adopted this image, as well as many others in the film, from
Oswald Spengler whose *The Decline of the West* had declared, 'the center of this artificial and complicated realm of the Machine is the organiser and manager. The
mind, not the hand holds it together.'[19] The portrayal of the natural masters of society as architects, planners or engineers occurs both in Weimar science fiction and in
the 'reactionary modernism' of Weimar's right-wing engineers themselves.[20] The
idea that the working classes simply needed to be informed of the planners' ideals to
become contented predicts the role of propaganda as a major agent
of social change and consensus. As Kracauer commented, discussing the final
scene of *Metropolis*, where the heart is proposed as mediator between brain
and hand, '[Goebbels], too, appealed to the heart – in the interest of totalitarian
propaganda.'[21]

Although parsing the reactionary and progressive elements in *Metropolis*
between Lang and Harbou seems to me suspicious (and possibly sexist), the articulated moral of the film seems to lag behind the play of figural language. If generally

Lang can be held responsible for the visualisation of the film text, nonetheless Harbou's mastery of allegorical figures within her novel shows a figural imagination which certainly inspired the film's visual style. At the same time, the visualisation of the Babel sequence in the film, although its basic figures derive from the parable as told in Harbou's novel, serves as a demonstration of the visual tropes at the command of a film-maker as articulate as Lang.

The sequence is embedded within Maria's meeting in the catacombs. It is framed by two shots of Maria looking directly at the camera at the beginning and ending of the sequence, in one of the clearest examples of Lang's use of the look at the camera as a sign of authorship, since these images convey Maria's words. The opening shot frames Maria in medium long shot against the altar covered with tall candles. She begins the shot with her face raised, as if getting inspiration from above. She then lowers her face until her gaze meets the camera. Wide-eyed, actress Brigitte Helm speaks, as she raises her left hand in a broad gesture. In a title she announces she will tell the story of the Tower of Babel. The following shots are to be understood as visualisations of the sermon. Each shot is marked by streaks of halo-like light in their corners, which function like quotation marks, marking the images as being at a different level of reference from the images which surround them.

The composition's first image of the parable reflects the last image of Maria. Again a figure stands on a raised platform speaking to a group below him. Like Maria, he also gestures broadly as he speaks. Intertitles convey the content of his speech: the desire to build a tower which will reach the heavens and to inscribe it with the motto: 'Great is the World and its Creator and Great is Man'. The image of this desire appears magically in the next shot, a huge multi-tiered tower against a starry sky, recalling the painting of the Tower of Babel by Pieter Breughel. However, a dissolve places this image in context, as the tower appears as a model surrounded by several men. The tower, so immediately imaged, is only a plan, and the long-haired, elegantly-gowned men surrounding it merely contemplate it, emblematically taking the pose of Rodin's 'The Thinker', chins resting on closed fists.

The next intertitles indicate the men's impotence, their inability to build the tower they imagine so vividly. The imagistic response to their need for workers comes in a brilliantly executed composite shot. This is probably the shot that cameraman Karl Freund described as a multiple re-printing of a shot of a thousand men to make them look like six thousand – a trick necessary, he claimed, because Ufa could not find enough extras willing to shave their heads![22] That motivation is unlikely, since the effect of this elegant composite shot is far from illusionistic. Instead, we see five columns of bald slaves converging toward the centre. At the centre we have another element in this composite, a circularly framed and closer shot of the slaves, emphasising their lowered bald craniums. The image addresses the viewer through its shape and artificial quality (as the previous images of the parable have also taken place in the more minimal and shallower space of stylised sets). The space of this shot has no real previous life equivalent; its composite nature makes it a purely cinematic image whose reference is metaphoric. The shape itself acts as a trope, based on the synecdoche introduced in Harbou's text, the workers as 'hands'. We see the converging columns as the outspread fingers and the circular insert as a palm. This composition of roiling bodies also functions as a symbolic close-up of a hand, one of Lang's most powerful visual tropes.

The next two shots develop Harbou's contrast between hand and brain, ideal plan and physical labour. We see the speaker from the opening shot kneeling in rapture before a vision of the tower. The flat space of this vision, surrounded by con-

centric circular nimbuses, marks it as immaterial, floating in air. But the following shot visually conveys the material resistance of the tower's building material. The first shot to be set in a real exterior shows slaves pulling a huge block of stone (like the wall in *Der müde Tod,* its monumental size is expressed by looming beyond the edges of the frame of this extreme long shot). Lang stresses the physical strain and effort of the workers by cutting into a medium shot of the slaves grimacing and cursing as they pull at their wooden yoke.

Ideals and physical force collide violently in the following shots, perhaps Lang's most ingenious combination of dramatic set design and cinematic framing to create dynamic action within a visual trope. A huge staircase dominates most of the frame. As in the Worms' cathedral steps in *The Death of Siegfried* (and undoubtedly influenced by the use of stairs in the experimental theatre of Reinhardt and Jessner), the stairs in this set not only create a powerful graphic image, but also stress shifting power relations and hierarchies. At the top of the massive staircase and occupying the very top edge of the frame, stands the visionary speaker from the first shot. Once again he speaks, his arms outstretched as he gestures. If the stairs lift him to the top of the frame and express his position of power, his distance from the camera carries a different message, reducing him to a tiny figure. His puny physical presence contrasts sharply with the massive and very physical figures of three slaves standing in the foreground. Their subordinate position below the speaker stands in tension with their dominant presence. This tension ignites in action, as the slaves raise their hands in defiant reaction to the speaker's gestural rhetoric.

A title follows with the single word: 'Babel', Harbou's primal word with polar signification for the masters and the slaves. The title itself is animated, as if bringing signification to life: the word drips (with blood? sweat?). The workers rush forward and, almost magically they turn into a huge mass of workers, which, filling the frame rushes up the stairs to converge violently on the speaker. The stairs now stage a

revolt against hierarchy, as if Lang were quoting Eisenstein's *Potemkin*, reversing the direction from Eisenstein's down-thrust of the Tsarist repression in this dynamic uprush of rebellion. The visual transformation from a handful of figures to a charging mass is not, however, achieved by an optical trick, but from the careful framing of the shot. The masses emerge from below the frame, presumably at the bottom of the stairs, while those first visible stood on another platform closer to the camera. The visual tropes beautifully expresses the reversal of hierarchy and power, the few rebels becoming a sea of humanity. The next shot expresses the same idea more abstractly. In the background we see the vision of the tower ringed by the shining nimbus. In the foreground a series of hands rise, backlit and forming dark silhouettes, progressively blocking out the tower with angry gestures. The final shot completely reverses the first view of the tower, against the same starry background, but now it lies a shattered ruin. The speaker's motto 'Gross is die Welt und sein Schöpfer. Und Gross ist der Mensch' shimmers in arcs above it, now an ironic epitaph.

Harbou's moral, which sprouts from this parable of ruin, is rendered legible as we return to Maria, now framed in medium close-up, her eyes fixed directly on the camera and spectator. She gestures emphatically with her hands as the intertitle gives her words: 'Between the brain that plans and the hands that build there must be a mediator'. As Lang cuts back to her after the intertitle, her eyes still fixed upon us, Brigitte Helm grasps her left breast and intones (through the intertitle): 'It is the heart that must bring about an understanding between them'. No doubt this is Harbou's message, inscribed as the epigraph to her novel as well. But does the tower sequence teach us anything more than this schoolboy dictum? Certainly on the visual level, it also serves as a lesson in the construction and reading of visual emblems, cueing us to scrutinise the visual form and framing for meanings, contrast, similarities, synecdoches and symbolic arrangements in space. What should we make of the pronounced visual similarity between the speaker/visionary in the parable and the speaker/visionary Maria who delivers it? Within the parable the visionary is blind to the forces around him and is destroyed by them. Does the parable predict the same fate for Maria? Of course, one can also see a contrast here. The visionary scene of the tower has no mediator; the only thing that bridges that deep gulf between the speaker and the masses huddled at the bottom of the stairs is violence. In the cathedral set, also dominated by a massive stairway, Maria will resolve the violence of the masses, but not until the end of the film. But at the very least, this sequence tells us not simply to believe in the moral as stated in words but in the acts portrayed in images. The final image showing the results of the revolt, the ruined tower, serves to overturn the optimistic but naive slogan above it.

Visual emblems in *Metropolis*, then, operate less as inert translations of a verbal moral than as site for the play of opposed energies, or as Fletcher puts it, daemons – active agents who embody a single purpose and identity endlessly repeated and replayed, like a perpetual motion machine.[23] Like the seesaw of master and slaves (one goes up, while the other goes down), this rhythmic energy pulses beneath the allegory. In this way the allegorical image possesses a magical function, the possibility of concentrating the energy of its demon to a specific purpose. As Fletcher makes clear, the demonic portrayal employed by allegory is given to polarisation and dichotomies rather than mediation, to explosive struggles and internecine battles.[24] The Tower of Babel teaches this in the mutually destructive war of master and servants. It would seem the mediator Maria prays for is designed to deliver them from allegory as much as from enslavement or ignorance.

Demons of Energy: Who Rules the City of Metropolis?

In their structure and mechanics, all larger cities of the white
world are identical. Situated at a midpoint of a web of rails,
they shoot off their petrified street-threads over the country
side. Visible and invisible networks of rolling traffic crisscross
and undermine the vehicular ravines and twice daily pump
human beings from the limbs to the heart. A second, third,
fourth network distributes water, heat and power, an electrical
bundle of nerves carries the resonance of the spirit.
                            Walter Rathenau, *On the Critique of the Times*[25]

If allegory employs demonic energies in explosive situations, what holds it
together? For Fletcher containment comes from a specific type of allegorical figure
which subordinates other figures into the central trope. He calls this central figure
the *kosmos*. Fletcher uses this term for its two meanings, one familiar, the other forgotten: first a universe, and second, an adornment which reveals the wearer's rank
within a hierarchy. Fletcher makes the kosmos perform all the tasks he considers
essential to an allegorical image, especially creating a hierarchy in which the various
demons of energy can contend.[26]

   Is there such a complex image in *Metropolis* which corrals its various demons into
a structured whole? It obviously consists of the city of Metropolis itself, whose
highly hierarchical spatial levels not only determine symbolic meanings, but stage
the tensions of dramatic actions and encounters. The city Metropolis takes its spatial
order from the Tower of Babel itself (in fact, in Harbou's novel the main building in
which Joh Fredersen has his offices is called 'The New Tower of Babel'): a vertical
structure which aspires to reach the heavens and proclaim the technical triumph of
humankind. As in the parable, the main narrative of *Metropolis* explicates the structure of the city and narrates its (near) destruction.

   This city is nothing if not hierarchical, with the first third of the film basically
tracing and exploring (and re-exploring) its various layers and levels. The opening
prologue introduces the machines that power the city: the repetitive motions of pis-
tons and drive shafts ordered into a ten hour shift (the Langian clock face here
rationalised into a round number and setting the only pattern for a worker's life),
and the whistle of released steam, energy turned audible, that marks the end of one
work round and the beginning of the next. But the structure of the city is best
described by the elevator ride which the mechanised labourers take from their place
of work to their home in the depths of the city. The elevator sets a vertical trajectory
of the city and the narrative to come, although somewhat disingenuously. At the
end of the ride we have not yet reached the depths of the city.

   The class-based nature of this vertical hierarchy is next established as the purgato-
rial imagery of the depths is contrasted with the paradisial images of the pleasure gardens and playing arenas of the rulers of Metropolis and specifically Freder, son of Joh
Fredersen, the Master of Metropolis. The opening scenes set up an image of order
and hierarchy which, while it may be unjust, appears at least to be unquestioned. It is
disturbed by a displacement from the depth, when the pleasure gardens are invaded
by Maria (with a gaggle of urchins from the lower slums of Metropolis) who
demands that Freder recognise the kids as his 'brothers'. The power of this visitation

to wrest Freder out of the order of Metropolis comes less from the moral appeal for common humanity or the psychological motivation of erotic attraction to Maria (although the film allows space for both) than the central allegorical question of power and agency. What is behind all this? What really lies in the depths? Here lies the constant question in Lang's films. A system is revealed, but the question lingers – who controls it, whom does it serve?

Freder's two voyages into the depths of his city discover layers he had not known of before and raise new questions about who wields power in Metropolis, undermining his unquestioned faith in the vertical order of the city in which power radiates from his father's intellect and control down to his minions, the workers and machines. In the first voyage he discovers the realm of the machines and has the visionary experience which reveals the demonic power of the city, embodied in the Moloch machine screaming to be fed (the steam whistle now revealed as a demonic cry rather than marking the orderly progression of time). After being rebuffed by his father when he returns to the surface, Freder makes his second voyage below and takes on the identity of a worker (embodied in the worker's uniform and cap emblazoned with a number). The allegorical high point of Freder's incarnation as a worker comes in his symbolic crucifixion on the dial wheel which dissolves into an image of the inhuman ten hour clock. But on this second voyage he discovers an even deeper level to the city, one previously unknown even to his father, the catacombs in which he hears Maria deliver the sermon on the Tower of Babel. Each voyage calls into question his father's power. The first reveals the demonic machine god Joh Fredersen may serve as an acolyte rather than use as a tool, while the second introduces a feminine prophecy that forsees the results of hubris and ignorance in ultimate destruction. How does power move through the vertical city of Metropolis, then? From top to bottom? Or radiating from the demonic centre, the voracious maw of the machine issuing its demands? Or ascending from the female voice calling for repentance in the city's lowest depths?

The city operates as a demonic machine using and releasing energy, either in an orderly manner (the steam whistle, the clock) or in an explosive one (the 'accident' Freder witnesses in the machine room which immolates the workers). But in fact, in this demonic system of production, order and explosion are not opposed to each other, but simply different parts of the one cycle ('Such accidents are inevitable', Joh Fredersen says, dismissing his son's alarmed report). This cycle will be writ large in the action of the film, the workers' revolt incited by Joh Fredersen and his tool, the false Maria, the demonic robot, giving way finally to a new order as father and son are reunited. The revolt and restoration then are less a new beginning, perhaps, than the large form of the cycle of order and catastrophe on which the city is founded. We will return to this possibility when we consider the allegorical language of the end of the film.

There are three centres of figuration in *Metropolis*. The first circles around the figures of the machine and images of modernity and rationality: the machine room itself, the robot Maria, and the city of Metropolis. All of these figures involve a combination of potentially explosive energy contained by repetitive and orderly motions; chaos and uniformity form the polar extremes of this centre. These images supply the major science fiction elements of the film, and are clearly associated with a dystopic future. The second centre clusters around images associated with the past and particularly the gothic, as if props and sets left over from *Siegfried* somehow formed the ur-level of the city of Metropolis. The madonna Maria, the sorcerer Rotwang, the locales of the catacombs and the cathedral form this cluster; its polar elements are the

religion of love preached by Maria and the black magic of demonic technology mastered by Rotwang. Mediating between these two centres are the images associated
with Freder as hero. As Roger Dadoun points out,[27] Freder performs archetypal
heroic functions, very much like Siegfried's exploits in the early *Gesänge*, the journey
into the underground, the quest for the pure maiden, the encounter with the monster. However, although Freder is posed as a simpler hero than Siegfried (he is not
defeated by the secular world of civilisation and betrayal), he is also more vulnerable
and even feminine, repeatedly given not only to the visions which were the privilege
of the women characters in Lang's earlier films, but subject to fits of fainting. Freder
propels the narrative action initially, but his visions seem to baffle and defeat him.
These three centres constantly intersect with each other and key moments of *Metropolis* can be understood as emblematic tableaux in which the different centres superimpose themselves. For instance, Freder's first encounter with the Moloch machine
brings the three centres into alignment and produces the first vision: the machine as
medieval demon, the undermining of the order of Metropolis' modernity and order.

Gothic Modernism: Technology as Modern Magic

> It forces the entrepreneur not less than the workman to
> obedience. *Both* become slaves, and not masters of the
> machine, which now for the first time develops its devilish and
> occult powers.
>
>   Oswald Spengler, *The Decline of the West*[28]

Insufficient attention has been paid to the role of the clash between the gothic and
modernity in this film, which often displaces the more manifest conflict between
classes. The revolt in *Metropolis* is staged as a conflict between master and workers,
a struggle resolved so legibly – and yet so unsatisfyingly and naively – in the film's
articulated moral. But in many ways this workers' revolt, the result of the false robot
Maria operating as an *agent provocateur*, takes the form of a sham battle. The true
conflict in *Metropolis*, the one which actually produces and energises the film's
system, comes from the collision between the gothic and the modern.

Lang in later interviews made rather cryptic remarks about the central role
magic played in his original concept of the film. Speaking to Peter Bogdanovich, he
said:

> Mrs. Von Harbou and I put in the script for *Metropolis* a battle between modern
> science and occultism, the science of the medieval ages. The magician was the evil
> behind all the things that happened: in one scene all the bridges were falling down,
> there were flames, and out of a Gothic church came all these ghosts and ghouls and
> beasties. And I said 'No I cannot do this.' Today I would do it, but in those days I did
> not have the courage. Slowly we cut out all the magic and perhaps for that reason I
> had the feeling that *Metropolis* was patched together[29]

Much of this statement remains obscure, especially why Lang didn't dare to include
the creatures coming from the gothic church (perhaps concern about a sacrilegious
uniting of the Church and the demonic?). But he certainly signals the key opposition
between the imagery of the gothic and the modern in the film.

While Lang indicates he eliminated much of the gothic imagery from the film, plenty remains, radiating from, as I said before, two centres: Maria and the medieval Christian imagery associated with her, and Rotwang who drags along with him a whole baggage of medieval magic and demonic images. One can undoubtedly see the influence of Spengler's sweeping theory of history here, pervasive in its influence on Weimar culture, with its description of Western man as 'Faustian' and the impulses toward mastery of nature through the machine as having its roots in the 'gothic'. Yet if Spengler's ideas seem sprinkled throughout Harbou's novel and screenplay, the gothic never entirely loses its opposition to the modern, and its associations with the ancient. The gothic exists in the core of the modern, providing another function of the 'layers' of the city of Metropolis. Metropolis is not simply a new modern city but a palimpsest whose layers (like the layers of ancient Rome that Freud invokes as an image of the way the past persists in the unconscious)[30] contain the traces of previous belief systems. Lang makes it clear that these repressed layers are only slumbering and can be called back into life.

'In the centre of the city stood an old house,' says the intertitle introducing the home of Rotwang the wizard inventor. The image shows a squat windowless medieval building with a sharply peaked roof like a gothic arch huddled among the steel girders and skyscrapers of Metropolis, as if the city had grown up around and over it. As R. L. Rutsky points out, the house (like Maria's catacombs) seems 'to hide a power that has been repressed by Harbou's functional, technologically rationalized world, a power that is figured in the connection of these structures to the spiritual, to the religious or to the magical'.[31] Harbou's novel describes the house as 'older than the town'[32] and relates that it was built by the supernatural power of an evil magician. When modernisers tried to pull down the house, it responded with a malevolent power, killing those who attacked it. It remained as an ancient relic until the inventor Rotwang chose it as his home. Rotwang, whom Lang describes as the source of evil in the film, combines the images of the modern and the gothic in the Spenglerian figure of the Faustian scientist. He is a master of technology, whose own hand is mechanical, the inventor of the race of robots ordered by Joh Fredersen. But the visual portrayal of his surroundings marks Rotwang as a medieval wizard, a trafficker in spirits and demons.

Lang and his designers created every aspect of Rotwang and his surroundings to blend modern associations with medieval ones. The desk in his study is illuminated by a coil of electrical light tubes, but the walls are filled with ancient tomes. His costume recalls a monk's robe, but a robotic hand emerges from its sleeves. His laboratory is honeycombed with electrical wires, and contraptions, but recalls traditional representations of an alchemist's lair. The effect of all this is not contradictory. Rather, new technology, especially those aspects which are part of the future predicted by *Metropolis*, such as robots and automatically opening and shutting doors, are presented by Lang and Harbou as a form of magic. Inscribed on the wall behind Rotwang's ultimate creation, the robot which the novel names Futura, is the inverted pentagram of the sorcerer. Harbou mines here an already well established series of similes even without the contributions of Spengler's theory of the scientist as the Faustian man. American journalists had christened Thomas Edison 'The Wizard of Menlo Park' after the invention of the phonograph, and Villiers de l'Isle Adam literalised this in his portrayal of Edison in *L'Eve Futur*, his symbolist novel of the creation of a female robot that greatly influenced Harbou. The future as a return to the repressed and forbidden energies of the past – this constitutes one of *Metropolis*'s allegories of modernity.

The house of Rotwang forms a node of images of the gothic past in Harbou's system. Her novel speculates the house may be older than the cathedral which faces it across the street. In the surviving prints of the film the cathedral's presence has been reduced, but it still plays a key role. In the novel the cathedral stands as another reminder of past ages, crowned with an image of the Virgin on its highest tower (an image of faith in contrast to Rotwang's house of magic) and ornamented with gothic figures and gargoyles (presumably the ones that Lang refers to as coming to life during the city's catastrophe). Joh Fredersen, the Master of Metropolis, has long desired to pull it down as well, but a strange pressure sect known as the 'gothics' headed by a monk named Desertus demand its preservation. Desertus and his following are not included in the version of the film we now have, but the cathedral still plays a central role in the images that remain.

After Freder's encounter with Maria in the catacombs where she gives her sermon on the Tower of Babel, she agrees to meet him the next day in the cathedral. Maria has been imprisoned by Rotwang, while Freder, wandering through the cathedral searching for her, becomes attracted to the gothic statues that adorn it. He contemplates an arrangement of figures: the Seven Deadly Sins flanking a figure of Death, portrayed as a scythe-bearing skeleton about to play a deadly tune on his leg bone flute. This arrangement returns us to a major source of allegorical emblems for Harbou and Lang, the Dance of Death. The figures representing the sins, as well as the skeleton itself, seem frozen in arrested motion, expressing that 'restless activity' that Worringer saw as characteristic of the gothic style, and evident in Holbein's etchings of the Dance of Death.[33] The moment when these figures seem to come to life in Freder's vision will occupy the central moment in the intertwining of *Metropolis*' allegorical strands and their fusion into a vision of the apocalypse.

The gothic cathedral shelters this image of Death as master of the dance. The imprint of death rests as well on the third realm of the past, this one buried in the depths of the city of Metropolis – and again Rotwang's house serves as a place marker. As the house without windows faces the ancient cathedral, it also rests over the most primordial part of Metropolis, so neglected that even Joh Fredersen, whose mastery of the city becomes increasingly tenuous, remains ignorant of it: the catacombs, described in Harbou's novel as 'the city of graves over which the city of Metropolis stands … the thousand year old Metropolis of the thousand year old dead'.[34] The interconnected topology of gothic spaces is completed by the fact that Rotwang's house contains a secret passageway down to this space.

Instead of meeting Maria in the cathedral of the Virgin, Freder encounters the Dance of Death. His previous inspirational meeting with his beloved prophetess also took place in the realm of the dead, the necropolis that forms the root of Metropolis. This moment of transfiguration for Freder in which he accepts the mediator role Maria prophesies for him, corresponds to the hero's descent into the underworld described by so many twentieth-century theorists of myth and romance, the encounter in the depths with the realm of the dead from which the hero emerges with the promise of salvation. Harbou knowingly employs this archetype, but it is her complication of it that makes it interesting. Every image of the gothic as religious renewal in this film meets its demonic and deathly counterpart. Maria's sermon is followed by her capture by Rotwang inside the tombs, a capture seemingly accomplished by his wielding the beam of an electric flashlight which terrifies Maria by illuminating the skeletal remains around her and then creeps up her body like a crawling male gaze with a slow slimy tactile violation. (Lang himself described it this way: 'This beam of light pierced the hunted creature like the sharp claws of an animal, refused to release her from its grasp, drove her unremittingly forward to the point of utter panic.')[35]

As I stated earlier, for an archetypal hero, Freder is amazingly ineffective. His voyage to the underworld yields revelations, but his return to the surface is beset by missed appointments, temporary imprisonment, fainting fits and sick-bed fever-dreams. His role as saviour becomes shunted aside as the film's demonic energy kicks into high gear. This may reflect Harbou's inability to construct action under any form other than chaos or, in the last reel, 'sensation film' heroic rescues and cliffhangers. But this lack of action by the mediator hero reflects the film's profound ambivalence about its own messianic vision. No-one, other than the demons, wants to take action in this film; action leads only to chaos. The religious figures, the blessed side of the gothic equation, are capable only of visions. Maria herself refuses to take any role other than that of John the Baptist, the forerunner and announcer of the Messiah to come. As the anointed one, Freder becomes lost in the labyrinth of Metropolis's gothic neighbourhoods and his own visionary psychosis.

Only the demonic side is capable of creation and destruction. The ultimate sequence of gothic modernism takes place when Rotwang creates the film's synthesis of the energies of magic and technology, false Maria, the robot. This justly famous sequence employs all the spectacular resources of modern technology to produce the image of scientist as wizard, as currents of electricity arc through the set and liquids bubble in strange containers. Rotwang methodically rushes from one switch to the next, checking readings, turning dials, merging himself with his equipment so that neither man nor apparatus appear as master or tool, but rather are fused into one technological project. The rhythmical pattern of the cutting, the use of superimpositions fuses cinematic devices with the creation process, both spectacularly visual, and hard-edged in their precision (interestingly, Harbou's novel does not describe the robot's creation). This mechanical rhythm, first introduced in the opening images of the film and reprised in the scenes in the machine room, finds its ultimate embodiment in the robotic Maria who will gather it into herself and bring it to the point of explosion and chaos.

But, for all its heavy equipment, the means by which the robot is created remains mysterious: imagistic and metaphoric rather than technological. The end result is the transfer of Maria's physical likeness (and presumably some quality of her organs and flesh) to the metallic Futura. This is a process of mechanical reproduction in at least two senses. First the obvious parody of birth, the attempt at reproduction by the male wizard/scientist without a female partner. But while the foaming liquids, shooting sparks, the pulsing machines and the rods Rotwang handles burlesque some processes of procreation, what we see primarily takes the form of photographic superimposition. Over the metal endoskeleton first a pulsing heart, then systems of circulation are superimposed. Although Rotwang directs the process, Lang continually cuts to the true Maria, encased in a glass tube, her body banded by metal rings, electrodes plugged into her helmet. She seems unconscious, yet dimly aware of the process. The process aims at producing a simulacrum, a copy. Raymond Bellour, in fact, describes the sequence as a whole as a reflection of the cinematic medium, 'the actual process of substituting a simulacrum for a living being directly replicates the camera's power to reproduce automatically the reality it confronts'.[36] Villiers' description of the creation of his female android Hadaly portrays Edison employing his motion picture device, the 'cylinder of movements', to transfer the gestures of the model to her simulacrum. The final stage of Lang's process is marked by a close-up of Futura, the metallic robot whose inhuman eyes stare at the camera. Then, through Lang's recurring metaphoric device, the overlap-dissolve, we see the face of Maria appear, her eyes closed. Her eyes stretch open into a stare at the camera. Lang cuts to the source of the simulacrum, a close-up of the true Maria in her electrode helmet, as her head collapses into a deeper unconsciousness. We cut back to robotic Maria as she stares piercingly at the camera.

The final moments of the process link it to Lang's visual vocabulary and use of allegory in silent cinema. Like a photographic process, Maria's face and figure have been imprinted onto the machine. We have watched the transfer of identity: that process which film theorist André Bazin saw as the truth of photography and which Lang shows here as the technological triumph of the lie and the demonic – the illusory power of false appearance. The final overlap-dissolve recalls the visionary scene earlier in the film, Freder's encounter with the demon face of the machine Moloch, but here the process is reversed. Instead of a gaze which penetrates past the surface to a revelation of the true nature of things, the overlap-dissolve cloaks the metallic armature with the appearance of flesh. Magic acts at antipodes to vision, it camouflages the actual mechanics of existence. Robot Maria's stare at the camera asks again the question that echoes throughout the film, resting on a variety of characters: who holds power in Metropolis, who can control its energies?

Robotic Maria's forthright but cold stare serves as a direct challenge, a parody of the visionary gleam of the real Maria as she preached the coming salvation in the catacombs. The creation scene is bracketed by shots of Freder trapped by the trick doors of Rotwang's cellars, screaming Maria's name helplessly. The saviour has no role in the cloning of his prophetess. Through its proliferation of looks at the camera, its multiplication of saviour and anti-Christ figures, Metropolis overloads the allegorical mission of its film and threatens to reduce it to a hall of mirrors reflecting competing authorities, counterfeit identities and spurious images. In Metropolis Lang and Harbou bring the allegorical language of silent film to an end, bringing it to a climax and staking its high-water mark from which, in the years remaining to it, it can only recede. The mechanically driven figures of allegory in Metropolis confront and parody any attempt to revitalise the symbols of religion and magic and thereby tip the film into a sustained vision of the apocalypse. If Die Nibelungen dramatised the decline of the world of myth and magic into the decadent world of civilisation and double dealing, Metropolis stages the failure of an attempt to revive the energies of the gothic through a fusion of religious salvation and technological magic.

Oedipal Nightmares, Allegorical Riddles

Berlin, your dancing partner is Death![37]

Metropolis continues to produce visionary scenes of a more and more ambiguous nature and Freder becomes increasingly undone by them. Released almost disdainfully by the magical devices of Rotwang's house after the creation of the false Maria, Freder rushes home to his father. There he sees the deceptive scene of (what he takes to be) Maria in his father's arms. Quite simply, he freaks. The next ten minutes or so of the film are so bizarre, so fully loaded in their visual rhetoric, so complex and even contradictory that no analysis could ever exhaust them. Roger Dadoun who offers a psychoanalytic interpretation of this sequence admits this overcharge of material, saying, 'so complex are the displacements and overdeterminations that there is scarcely an image in the film that cannot occupy the most surprising positions at any of the forty-nine levels of Talmudic interpretation'.[38] But if we follow the thread of an allegory-machine gone wild, spewing out a torrent of filmic rhetoric, we can follow its progression to the film's final apocalypse and its perverse destruction and reconstruction of its saviour hero. This series of visionary scenes contrasts sharply with the moments of insight granted to the maiden in *Der müde Tod* or Kriemhild in *The Death of Siegfried*, or even Freder's vision of Moloch. In contrast to the terrifying but piercing brevity of those visions, these are baroque and hysterical sequences, imaged as hallucinations and nightmares. They also play a psychological role for the character of Freder that was avoided in the earlier films.

The first hallucination sequence demonstrates Lang's alliance with the avant-garde of the late 20s, the 'pure film' montage experiments and the animation of Walther Ruttman and others. Lang does not simply rip off this tradition here; he uses it not only expressionistically to portray a mind stretched to its limits (through the use of rapid montage and a loss of spatial co-ordinates), but also as a visualisation of his own will-to-abstraction, his visionary claim that abstractly organised schema and allegories operate beneath the surface of reality.

Lang first presents Freder's view as an obscuring of sight. As he rushes in the door and sees Maria and his father entwined, he stares at the camera in disbelief and backs away. Lang cuts to the first of a series of nearly subliminal shots, white circles of light either enlarging or approaching the camera, like bright flashes obscuring vision. The next few shots develop this dissolving grasp on vision. Freder raises his hand and passes it before him, as if simultaneously trying to wipe out what he sees, and touch it to see if it is real. A point of view shot follows of Joh and Maria holding each other, their faces turned toward Freder. This image wavers and goes out of focus. Freder holds out his hands as if beseeching them.

The following images move from vision obscured to pure hallucination. The image of Joh and Maria becomes surrounded by a border of Joh's office spinning at a dizzying rate. Freder seems to lose his balance, as if the floor rocked beneath him. The spheres of light are supplemented by star-like bursts, scratched directly on the surface of the film. Lang pushes the crisis of vision past abstraction into the very materiality of the film strip, losing its emulsion before our eyes. The scratches explode around Freder as well. Then comes a series of subliminal shots (each under a second): we see a close-up of Maria, her hairstyle and makeup marking her as the sensual robot clone (rather than the pure prophetess) as shapes spin around her. Cut to the spheres of light bursting. Cut to a close-up of Joh, then a fade to black.

The following extremely brief shots are no longer based on elements present in Joh's office, but move into the visionary. We see a close-up of Maria almost identical to the last shot of the creation of the robot, staring at the camera. Lang cuts in a close-up of Rotwang grinning demonically against a black background. Then a close-up of the image of Death the flute player, surrounded by cubist swatches of light. Then a return to the first close-up of Maria, only now prismatically reflected into multiple images, as the outer images spin. The final barrage of images place Freder in an abstract but violent space as the room disappears and scratches, arcs of light and spheres burst around him and he continues to lose his footing. Freder lifts his arms and seems to plunge through this abstract nightmare, plummeting through horizontal bands of light which pass over his body.

Freder's attempt to bring his message of salvation up from the underworld here encounters its strongest check, a descent into madness, an almost classically Freudian nightmare of Oedipal terror. But before we follow through the Freudian kink Harbou has tied in the hero's quest, we need to explore this moment as an archetypal Langian visionary moment. It performs the same role all such scenes take on, the revealing of the system of forces beneath the surface. The quick succession of close-ups at the centre of the sequence not only provides a riddling answer to Freder's own disbelief at seeing his beloved in his father's arms, but also addresses the central question of the film: who truly rules Metropolis? The succession of shots beginning with the false Maria followed by close-ups of Joh, Maria at the moment of creation, then Rotwang, spell out in telegraphic montage the order of her creation: 'This woman was ordered by Joh Fredersen, she is a robot created by Rotwang.' Likewise the prismatic multiplied image of Maria not only conveys Freder's vertigo, but hints at the process of mechanical duplication that stands behind the robot Maria. Freder, however, cannot read or decode the message. The riddle of creation also proposes a succession of 'masters' (and a mistress) of Metropolis: Joh, the robot, Rotwang, Death. Death as the master of Metropolis not only links this central enigma back to previous Langian visions, but prepares the way for the apocalyptic finale of the film.

But Freder does not understand his vision and this leads to his complete regression. Not only does he break down emotionally during this sequence, he loses the ability to stand upright, regressing to an infantile state. The next shot after the fade to black that ends his tumble through space shows him tucked in bed, ministered to by father and nurse. Unlike the maiden's disavowal of her vision of death in *Der müde Tod* which does not develop her as a psychological character, Freder's disavowal draws explicitly on Freudian scenarios that Harbou weaves into her script and novel. Cuts in the current version of the film have obscured the back story, but the primal forces are still very clear. Harbou works as creatively with her Freudian themes as she does with the Biblical material. The development of Freder as an archetypal hero intertwines with both Christological and Freudian patterns to create an extraordinary maze of reference from which no analyst may ever emerge unscathed.[39]

What a hoot this film is! Although it is easy to see the prophetess Maria as a sexist stereotype of feminine purity (and she is that), tracing her roles leads us into a mare's nest of gender contradictions. In relation to the Christ myth she primarily plays the role of John the Baptist, the forerunner of Christ. But her name and her association with virgin purity also align her with the mother of God. But if the hero's romance demands (as it literally will in the film's climax) the love for, and rescue of, a pure maiden, Maria cannot be Freder's mother, without creating a scandal. But if the plot avoids literally acting out this regressive Oedipal fantasy, Harbou constantly throws it back in our face, and most obviously in this (primal) scene. What is this trauma-producing moment, as Roger Dadoun was perhaps the first to point out,[40] but Freder rushing into his parents' bedroom to witness the primal act of darkness? The splitting of Maria into pure virgin and mechanical whore so often noted in this film loses none of its ideological charge in this reading. But it becomes that much more psychologised, if not pushed to the point of psychosis: these polarities are the rival fantasies a boy has about his mother, a sign of his inability to accept adult sexuality. Thus the imagery of regression given Freder, stumbling like a toddler who has forgotten to walk, arms outstretched for support.

The novel makes explicit Freder's longing for a mother, more precisely for Hel, his biological mother who died bringing him into the world. Maria appears as the explicit reflection of this lost mother throughout the book. When Freder first sees Maria in the pleasure gardens Harbou's prose describes what he sees: 'the austere countenance of the virgin. The sweet countenance of the mother'.[41] Freder wanders the streets of Metropolis looking up at the image of the virgin atop the cathedral and calls out: 'Mother, look at me.'[42] Harbou casts her saviour as a lonely mama's boy lost in the big city. This dead mother also broods over the creation of the robot. Hel was the wife of Rotwang, a love he has never abandoned and memorialises in a monument he has created to her in his house. She was taken from him by Joh Fredersen, and the two men hate each other for this reason. At the film's climax Rotwang has gone mad and believes Maria actually to be Hel, his lost wife (and Freder's lost mother) and climbs the cathedral with her in tow. The processes of mechanical reproduction in this film constantly recycle the image of the lost mother/lost wife through a play of substitutes and doubles.

In a nearly Gnostic manner Harbou recasts the Christ aspect of Freder's hero tale as an Oedipal drama, longing for union with his virgin mother, attempting to wrest her from the control of his father. Joh (the invented first name intended to recall the God of the Old Testament) Fredersen corresponds to one Gnostic view of the Old Testament God as learning the lesson of compassion through his son's sacrifice. The film makes Freder's crucifixion explicit in his martyrdom on the dial wheel of the machine room (crying out to his father), and Harbou in the novel lays on Christ references with a trowel. But Freder's mission of salvation must also be an Oedipal revolt against his father, as his hallucination sequence makes clear. The need to reconcile Freder with his father, as well as the masters with the workers, strains Harbou's mythopoeisis to the breaking point. The scenes of resolution and reconciliation remain unsatisfying partly because Harbou does not truly seem capable of thinking through (or accepting) any of the scenarios offered by her material: the resolution of the Oedipal complex, the Christian sacrifice, or the workers' revolution. Instead, imagery of breakdown and chaos dominate. The allegorical vision of Lang and Harbou remains an apocalyptic one, dominated by the figure of castration rather than identification with the father, Death rather than resurrection, capitulation rather than revolution.

To understand the power of this apocalyptic imagery we need to go back to Freder's continued fever-dream hallucination. The scene which follows his plunge through the floorboards opens with Freder tucked cozily in his bed at home. In the sequence to follow Lang systematically plays with the devices of parallel editing and shot/reverse shot in order to create a visionary scene of remarkable spatial ambiguity. Parallel editing, the earliest major editing figure mastered by silent film-makers, intercuts two separate series of images occurring at the same time in different places in order to indicate simultaneity. On the literal level this editing rules the sequence. Lang cuts between Freder on his sick-bed and the soirée Rotwang and Joh Fredersen arrange to introduce the robotic Maria to male high society, supposedly to test the believability of her fleshly incarnation; two separate events happening at the same time at some distance from each other. On the other hand, shot/reverse shot, especially when combined with an eyeline match, presents a single dramatic space by cutting between two opposed angles within it, usually to indicate a back and forth exchange, such as a conversation or an exchange of glances. Most often such shots are angled to the side of the characters talking and/or looking, but, as discussed earlier, Lang occasionally films them with direct 180 degree reversals, having characters look directly into the camera. The added intensity of this manner of shooting usually indicates for Lang some heightened emotion or threat.

In this sequence Lang complicates things by blending these two editing figures, thereby contradicting their spatial codes. He intercuts Freder with the soirée in such a way that it seems he is witnessing (or imagining?) the events. At first only parallel editing seems involved. Robotic Maria appears on stage and does an orgiastic dance as men in evening wear ogle her. (Brigitte Helm swivels her hips in a manner here that leads me to believe either that she truly has ball bearings in her joints, some sort of special effect was used, or, alternatively, that there are more mysteries in creation than I have yet experienced.) Meanwhile Freder rests at home, his brow smoothed by an attentive nurse. The editing contrast stresses his infantile regression. Awakened by a clumsy servant, Freder sits bolt upright in bed, his eyes widened and staring at the camera. The force of his movement up and towards the camera is multiplied by a cut to a closer shot of him leaning forward, staring. Such a forceful stare leads one to expect a point of view shot and Lang cuts directly to a shot that is clearly designed to catch a male gaze, Maria twirling in her scanty costume.

As if reassuring us about the conventional nature of the shot/reverse shot, Lang then cuts to a medium shot of the onlookers at the soirée, staring at the spectacle and chewing their lips in lust. He then introduces a more avant-garde editing figure, the jump cut: the editing together of actions within a single space with a marked temporal ellipsis so that they seem to jump from one position to another. The remainder of Maria's dance is cut in this manner, jumping, for instance, from Maria kneeling and twisting her torso, to Maria standing lifting her legs, to Maria turning her head from side to side. Lang continues to intercut this with the ogling men, but these images, too, become more abstract, giving way to a composite shot of several unblinking eyes in close-up, until one single staring eye fills the screen. This fantasia on the male gaze returns to Freder, likewise staring enraptured in close-up. Lang clearly encourages us to read Freder as also witnessing the dance, whether through clairvoyance, hallucination or pure sexual fantasy. These sexual visions contend with his regression. After Maria kneels down, her legs spread provocatively, Lang

cuts to Freder smiling as the nurse's hand enters the frame from left, strokes his brow and offers a glass of water with her other hand. Freder closes his eyes and drinks sensuously, leaning his head back in her supporting hand. But, after giving into this moment of infantile oral satisfaction, he opens his eyes again and leans forward toward the camera, his eyes fixed on visual pleasure.

At this point Lang signals that we are abandoning the parallel editing between separate, but real, events, however strangely linked by a preternatural gaze, and entering the realm of pure hallucination and vision. Maria rises from the cabaret stage mounted on a huge monstrous statue, holding a chalice in one hand. Lang intercuts Freder staring and the woman on the beast. We cut back to Freder's astonished gaze. A long shot shows the beast and Maria on a platform, the platform itself supported by the statues of the seven deadly sins from the cathedral. Lang cuts again to Freder. We see Maria and her beast as the men rush forward, arms outstretched. Cut back to Freder. The more insistent intercutting of Freder marks this as his vision. But more importantly, the imagery tips not simply toward the subjective but the allegorical and referential. As the finale for her act, robotic Maria does a *tableau vivant* from *The Book of Revelations*, the whore of Babylon with her golden goblet and the beast whereon she sits with seven heads and ten horns.

Here Lang develops the film's most complete apocalyptic vision, as Freder's gaze no longer links us to the events of the soirée but to entirely allegorical scenes. We return to the sculpture of Death and the seven deadly sins in the cathedral. But their immobility gives way as Death jerkily sways his thigh bone flute, like a parade master raising his baton. In a close-up, recalling the brief shot in Freder's earlier hallucination, Death raises the flute to his lipless mouth and plays. Cutting back to long shot, the statues step from their niches stiffly, as if still contending with, not overcoming, their inert stillness. In close-up Death continues his music. This image of gothic statues come to life fulfils Worringer's description of the gothic as a frozen

moment of energetic gesture and Fletcher's image of allegorical agents as images brought to life in a halting mechanical manner. They recall Futura, the metal robot that moves beneath the synthetically reproduced flesh of the false Maria. This grotesque Dance of Death blends the mechanical and the allegorical in one image. Then the sins dissolve away and Death has the dancing floor to himself.

The next images take us deeper into Freder's delirium and propose an allegorical riddle that ties his Oedipal conflicts back to the question of who wields power in Metropolis. Intercut with Freder's visionary trance-like stare, Death comes forward. Lang cuts to one of the *leit motifs* of the film, the steam whistle that marks the cycle of ten hour working shifts in the city of Metropolis. Like the nightwatchman's cry in *Der müde Tod*, it is an aural marking of the passing of time, the mechanical progression of the Destiny-machine, here embodied in the whole city organised as one vast mechanism. When the whistle blows, as Harbou phrases it in her novel, all the machines of the city demand to be fed on living men.[43] In its time-marking, rationalised aspect, the steam whistle appears as the tool of Freder's father, Joh, linking up with a series of images that unite Joh with the clock and its almost sadistic measurement of time. A huge clock face looms over Joh's office at the top of the New Tower of Babylon. During Freder's ordeal at the dial machine, Lang cuts to Joh Fredersen glancing at his watch, shown in close-up, then back to Freder moving the dial hands. In the next few shots the dial becomes a clock face with numerals and minute hands as Freder appears crucified upon the hands of time. He appeals then to his father in a parody of Christ's words on the cross. The answer and his deliverance come with the steam whistle. The steam whistle embodies, then, both aspects of power in Metropolis, the rationalised order represented by Joh's methodical calm, and the demonic hunger, fed on human flesh, of the Moloch machine. Now in Freder's vision both demand and order are tied to Death. Freder claps his hands over his ears at the piercing noise.

In the penultimate image of the delirium, Death is shown in front of the cathe-dral, his scythe in his hands, swinging the blade as he moves forward, swiping at the camera. The image of the Grim Reaper, the gothic image of death, derives partly from the reaping angels described in *Revelations* harvesting the souls of the world. But his accoutrements, the hour glass and the scythe, also derive from a classical ref-erence, the god Kronos, the Greek god of time, and father of Zeus. Kronos in Hesiod's *Theogony* castrates his father Uranos with a sickle given him by his mother. He in turn devours his own children until killed by Zeus. I have no doubt Harbou, with her love of mythology, was aware of these associations with the Grim Reaper, and used them to articulate her blending of Oedipus and Christ in Freder. Freder reacts to this figure with his greatest panic. In the last image of the sequence, Lang shows him flailing his arms in alarm as if trying to ward off the blow from the scythe. Beautifully, Lang images Death's attack as an attack on the film image itself: a huge arcing scratch appears over the image of Freder, marking in a supernatural way the curving stroke of the scythe in this visionary reverse angle. To affirm its cas-trating power, the scratch passes over Freder, as if cancelling him out. Once again he loses consciousness.

On one level the allegorical figure here encourages a psychoanalytic decoding: Freder as terrified by the castrating power of his father, a reading very much in line with the scene previous to this delirium, his horror at the primal scene of Joh and Maria. The Freudian primal scene, as Laplanche and Pontalis put it, 'gives rise to sexual excitation in the child while at the same time providing a basis for castration anxiety'.[44] Freder's fantasy acts out both of these, combined with an image of the mother figure as literally a whore. Freder seems unable to deal with the threat his father poses. But if the allegory is not simply read as a case of character psychosis, but as a serious answer to the riddle of power in Metropolis, we recognise what the flash-images in Freder's earlier hallucination hinted at. Behind the two extreme

faces power assumes in this city of modernity – the rationalised image of the clock
face and the devouring maw of the monster (both images associated with the castrating god of time, Kronos) – stands a figure of primal terror – lack and castration
itself, and a desire for the absolute wiping clear of all representation, the scratching
away of the film's emulsion, the desire not only for death but for the end of everything – apocalypse.

   Are we to read this central sequence of *Metropolis*, then, psychoanalytically, or
allegorically? One of the triumphs of Lang's visual language and Harbou's
mythopoesis in this sequence is to render psychoanalysis as a modern allegorical
language as rich in figures and exemplary narratives as any sacred text. *Metropolis*
converts psychoanalytical imagery into visual tropes as creatively as the medieval
cathedrals did the Holy Scriptures (and their host of other sources). At the same
time, the chaos of this film, its interbreeding of references, its syncretism of sources
– from mythology, from the Bible, from Freud, from sensation films – makes it
impossible to disentangle a psychoanalytical reading from the others (mythic and
allegorical) offered. One can no more read Freder's dream simply as an Oedipal
fantasy and leave it at that, than decode its mythic references and ignore the psychoanalytical references. We are mired deep within the allegorical imagination and
its processes. This blasted allegory gives the film much of its postmodernist feel; the
processes for making significance still function, but there remains no single master-
text for making sense of the damn thing.

Apocalypse without End, Endings without Conviction

This Babylonian confusion of words
Results from their being the language
Of men who are going down.
That we no longer understand them
Results from the fact that it is no longer
Of any use to understand them.
                    Bertolt Brecht, 'The Babylonian Confusion'[45]

The final third of this film chronicles the destruction of the city of Metropolis primarily by forces unleashed by the robotic Maria, and therefore with the collusion of Joh Fredersen, the figure of instrumental rationality, and Rotwang, the figure of demonic technology. As almost all viewers have noticed, Joh Fredersen's action seems to be lacking a motive (in fact the supplier of the English language intertitles felt compelled to manufacture one not present in the English language version, describing Fredersen's desire to eliminate the workers and replace them with robots, aware of the gap in Harbou's character logic). In her novel Harbou responds theologically rather than psychologically to this lack with an allegorical scene in which Freder encounters his father standing before a cross sparking with electricity in the machine room as the whole city is shaking with explosions. He begs his father to save the city, but Joh Fredersen declares it is his will the city must be destroyed so that Freder can build it up again and redeem its inhabitants. Whether or not this scene was ever part of the original film, it still remains inconclusive. Freder does not accept his father's mission but remains incapable of stopping the city's destruction.

The motiveless destruction of Metropolis may reflect Lang's own vision, an attitude found in accounts of Lang's own titanic efforts during the film's production, as well as in the Tower of Babel parable: an unparalleled energy of creation matched by an equally powerful nihilism, a desire to smash creation into shards. Witnesses of Lang's filming have described his delight in personally precipitating the conflagrations that tend to mark the climaxes of his silent films. Designer Eric Kettelhut described Lang shooting the magnesium flares-tipped arrow which initiates the holocaust of Etzel's palace in *Kriemhild's Revenge*. Cameraman Fritz Arno Wagner reported Lang's glee in pushing the red button that caused the explosion of the chemical factory in *The Testament of Dr. Mabuse*. And Harbou reported that Lang himself threw the torch onto robotic Maria's funeral pyre.[46] The director's hand intervenes here personally to immolate the world he has conceived. The authorial fantasy becomes a fantasy of destruction.

The ending of *Metropolis* simply extends the conflagrations which end *Der müde Tod* and *Die Nibelungen* with longer duration and more elaborate sets. Although on one level the film can be seen as a reactionary, cautionary tale about the destructive power of workers' revolt, the film actually displaces its political discussion of power into a nihilistic denunciation of the world, expressing the melancholic world-denying nihilism that Benjamin associates with the allegorical mode. Here lies the film's power. However, the film backs away from its nihilistic vision and attempts to reinstall Freder as an action hero, rescuing the children Maria first proclaimed his brothers, from the flood (but failing to rescue what he believes is his beloved from the flames, as the robotic Maria is burned by the crowd), then, least originally of all, rescuing Maria from Rotwang and flinging the magician from the top of the cathedral (like a recycling of Universal's 1923 *The Hunchback of Notre Dame*, precisely the mechanical sort of American costume film Lang had claimed he was determined *not* to take as a model).[47] These unconvincing heroics are followed by the film's most tepid allegory, one which intentionally or unintentionally seems to self-destruct before our eyes.

Resolution comes quickly to this film, as if the business of tying up loose ends should be accomplished as soon as possible. Within a single reel we see: the rescue of Maria; the destruction of Rotwang (having become the scapegoat of the film, at least for its resolution); the burning away of the illusory flesh of the false Maria; the accession to manhood of Freder (marked mainly by his climbing ability); the transformation of Joh Fredersen (embodied in his hair turning white as he watches his son's peril among the cathedral towers); and the pacification of the workers (presumably by the combined terror and pity of watching the robot's immolation and Freder's hairbreadth rescue). We now get the staging of Harbou's motto: 'The mediator between brain and muscle must be the heart'. The workers form a flying wedge and toddle up the stairs of the cathedral where the motto will be staged. The hierarchical stairs with Freder, Joh and Maria at the top and the orderly geometrical pyramid of workers seems designed to reverse the powerful image of revolt in the Tower of Babel sequence. The workers are led by Grot the foreman who approaches Joh Fredersen, hands in his pockets like a bashful adolescent too shy to ask for the next dance. Joh stands like a prom queen unable to overcome his stiff reluctance. Maria urges Freder to emerge from the corner he has withdrawn into and act like a good host and help the guests mingle, intoning, 'there can be no understanding between the Hand and the Brain unless the Heart acts as mediator'. Freder takes the hands of the reluctant couple and pulls them together into the handshake that now ends all existent versions of the film.

Everyone hates this ending. I will not try to redeem it, but there are things worth pointing out about it. First, it is an extremely literal allegory, a tableau of personification in which the characters line up to form a sentence, spelled out in front of us, reading left to right, HANDS (Grot) BRAIN (Joh) and between them HEART (Freder). Further, its artificiality is stressed: we see it staged before us within the theatrical porch of the cathedral with Maria acting like a kindergarten teacher patiently directing her bored charges. But these aspects of super-legibility and artificiality also reflect the allegorical mode, so it would be inconsistent to fault this sequence for them. More complex issues are raised, however, if we scrutinise the personifications performed for us. Joh Fredersen remains the brain of Metropolis, no change there. Freder apparently has won his right to represent the heart by his compassion for the workers' children. And the hand, the workers – are represented by Grot. Who is Grot? We have seen him earlier as the spy who brings Joh the plans found on the dead workers, and communicating to Fredersen over a television telephone about the workers trying to wreck the machines. He defied the workers as they approached his machine, then led them to capture and burn the robotic Maria. In other words, the workers here are represented by a management spy and informer, who cares only for the machines of Metropolis. And the heart is the boss's son, who at one point donned the workers' overalls for part of one shift that almost killed him and has been wearing his former silk duds ever since. The tableau staged for us shows the boss congratulating his spy and *agent provocateur* with his son cementing the deal. Kracauer, determined to discover the contraband concealed

within this tableau, gave it this interpretation decades ago: 'The whole composition denotes that the industrialist acknowledges the heart for the purpose of manipulating it; that he does not give up his power, but will expand it over a realm not yet annexed – the realm of the collective soul.'[48] Georges Sadoul also noted that the workers approach the cathedral like the subdued automata they appeared to be when they went to work in the beginning of the films and asks, 'Shouldn't we see here an internal critique of an imposed ending?'[49]

Are we supposed to read this sequence this way, can we argue for an authorial intention? Nothing in Harbou's novel indicates cynicism about her motto (but this scene of reconciliation is also absent from it). The Tower of Babel sequence (which I presented as a guide to reading allegorical figures in the film) ends, as I noted, with an inscribed motto (Great is Man) which is belied by the imagery of ruin beneath it. But Lang, for all his discomfort with the ending of this film, never claimed he visually undercut it. Perhaps the discomfort the ending causes most viewers comes partly from the film itself, an underlying nihilism which it cannot articulate explicitly. Or this may simply be a case where the melancholic nihilism of allegory has so outrun any attempt at an optimistic narrative resolution that even if taken at face value this final tableau proves inadequate, not only as political thinking, but as an aesthetic strategy. Or if this tableau of reconciliation is not to be read against the grain, then it perhaps should be read cynically, as the fulfilment of Joh Fredersen's master plan, with the revolt operating within the total system of Metropolis much like the explosion in the machine room, an unavoidable spate of violence easily absorbed into the cycle of inhuman production, a release of demonic energy – like Metropolis's steam whistle, containable within the re-established cycles of work. Anton Kaes has also proposed to me another approach: that *Metropolis* is conceived basically as a series of sensations, a film of disparate attractions rather than narrative integration, and that

Lang simply didn't care that much about pulling it all together in a final satisfying coherence. The final tableaux would then be a cinematic equivalent of the Looney Toon proclamation of closure – 'That's all Folks!'

Burn Witch Burn

> CHIEF ENGINEER: For the first time a gap opens in a system
> that has been flawless all the years. The pendulum swings wild!
> The machine has stalled. … It's the machine that's running
> wild and it's running wild because its works are moving to a
> different rhythm. … The tumult becomes a face grinning its
> hideousness into their horror-frozen minds!
>   Georg Kaiser, *Gas II* [50]

The last truly powerful image in the climax of *Metropolis* comes with the burning of Maria. The burning reverses the process of creation already discussed, with the fleshly sheath melting from the metallic armature. As such it literalises a typical Langian visionary revelation. The crowd draws back in horror as they see the metal robot tied to the stake. If the allegorical centre of *Metropolis* lies in the revelation of a demonic energy at the core of the rational system of modern technology, it appears for the last time in this bizarre immolation. The apocalypse in *Revelations* purges the world with a great holocaust and prepares the way for a new heaven and new earth. Here the flames uncover an interior that cannot be burned, the robot as image of death standing amid the flames. This unconsumed residue, this leftover from disaster, returns us to one of the allegories of *Metropolis* which never seems to be thoroughly digested, the figure of the false Maria.

The gender stereotypes and polarity of the film, as already noted, portray the flesh and blood Maria as virginal and pure: Brigitte Helm's body language remains asexual, motherly when she kisses Freder and entirely lacking in sensuality. The robotic Maria, however, possesses every cliché of carnality, and Helm does an amazing job of keeping these signs of sexuality coming. Not only are hair and makeup transformed, but facial expression and bodily posture telegraph an errant sensuality. Robotic Maria doesn't simply dance semi-naked in nightclubs, entice men in evening dress to fight duels and commit suicide over her, and invert Maria's message of peace and patience into one of violence and revolt – her total body language stands at antipodes to Maria's. Whereas Maria's hands are usually folded in front of her as she stands rather rigidly and moves with stately symmetry, robotic Maria stands with legs apart, runs, holds her hands above her, forming grasping claws, or pulls provocatively at her bodice, and thrusts her head and pelvis out. Her movements remain jerky, her head, particularly, darting from side to side like a lizard's, her body bent forward as she speaks to the workers. But this liveliness and sensuality are attributed to the *machine*, while rigidity and repose are the attributes of the (supposedly) living woman.

Andreas Huyssen first directed critical attention to *Metropolis*'s relation to a long tradition that tied technology to the cultural image of the feminine, embodied in his quote from art collector Eduard Fuchs: '… the machine which coldly, cruelly, relentlessly sacrifices hecatombs of men as if they were nothing is the symbol of the man-strangling Minotaur-like nature of woman'.[51] Huyssens points out that the duality of the virginal Maria and her destructive mechanical twin not only reflects patriarchal fears of woman, but also contrasting views of technology: the machine as obedient passive servant to man, or as an untamable destructive force. Huyssen also relates this diametrically opposed attitude towards technology to *Metropolis*'s dual inheritances: from Expressionism which distrusted technology and from *Neue Sachlichkeit* which embraced the machine's rational order. The climactic witch-burning becomes for Huyssen a purging of both fear of woman's sexuality *and* of the unpredictable energy of technology, making way for a new rational order.

In perhaps the most thorough and complex essay on *Metropolis*, R. L. Rutsky has complicated Huyssen's schema, emphasising the film's desire to avoid choosing between these two alternatives, and attempts to find mediation through figures which seem to combine opposed traits. According to Rutsky both the realm of the purely rational (Joh) or the instinctively sexual (robotic Maria – notice how the workers again drop out of the schema) are portrayed as incomplete and deadly.[52] I think Rutsky's reading of the film's logic holds, but we run into the same problem, the inability of the film to portray this mediated wholeness convincingly, an inability which may be a backhand virtue rather than a vice. Just as the film cannot imagine Freder as a convincing saviour, and cannot truly come up with a new melding of religion and technology to 'heal' the rift within the city of Metropolis, it does not succeed in raising a new cathedral of humanity. Rutsky convincingly relates the film to the architectural fantasies circulating through Weimar culture, from Paul Scheerbart's *Glasarchitektur* and Lionel Feiniger's Cathedral of Socialism to Albert Speer's 'Cathedral of Light' designed for the Nuremberg Party Rallies.[53] But this is not what the ending of the film portrays. As Rutsky admits, the enthused vitalised crowds attending the Nuremberg rallies in *Triumph of the Will* have little in common with the pacified and re-mechanised workers Sadoul noted at the end of *Metropolis*.[54] Perhaps the ultimate image of *Metropolis*'s fortunate failure in achieving the aesthetic and religious renewal of the technological state would be Lang's image of the supernatural creatures fleeing from the collapsing church. Walter Benjamin, speaking of the baroque allegoricists, complained that 'these allegories fill out and deny the void in which they are represented just as ultimately, the intention does not faithfully rest in the contemplation of bones, but, faithlessly leaps forward to the idea of Resurrection'.[55] The resolution of *Metropolis* also makes this faithless leap, but seems to lose its footing, while the aesthetic energy of the film remains true to 'the contemplation of bones'.

But the issue of sexuality's relation to gender, the riddle of the false Maria remains. It is not simply that the false Maria figures the feminine as technological, she also embodies sexuality itself. Clearly part of the horror of the crowd at the final image of Maria at the stake lies in the fact that instead of bones revealed beneath the fire-consumed flesh, one sees the machine, an image neither of life nor death. Beneath the whore of Babylon runs the mechanism of modernity. In this respect Huyssen's technological reference should not be to Vaucason's flautists, but to Henry Adams' revelation at the Gallery of Machines at the 1900 Paris Exposition of the common element shared by the dynamo as the force of modernity and the Virgin as the force behind the gothic cathedrals: energy. Sexual energy and mechanical energy for Adams had the common denominator of force, or attraction.[56] If the motives of Joh Fredersen and Rotwang in the creation of Futura as a sensual version of the virgin Maria remain obscure in terms of narrative logic, the sequence of robotic Maria's performances makes clear that the fascination of their experiment lies in the energy and attraction generated by the exploitation of mechanical sex as a visual spectacle. A charismatic performer who excites upper-class young men to acts of violence against themselves and each other and working class audiences to orgies of destruction against machines, the robotic Maria demonstrates an untapped explosive energy equal to the mysterious Gas which powered Georg Kaiser's Expressionist play so influential on Harbou's script.

Sex as energy and as a means of stimulation, if not control, takes the visual form of a woman as the focus of the male gaze. But once that form is taken away, only the metallic works are revealed. Freder's panic at this vision marks it as another figure of the terrifying lack at the centre of this film, while the horror shared by the crowd as well reveals it as not limited to his unsuccessful Oedipal trajectory. This image reveals the void Benjamin found at the centre of allegory as much as a Lacanian lack, and the strongest moments of the film confront (and equate?) both. Feminist readings of this film have not proposed Harbou's script as a feminist work, and more than her ultimate Nazi affiliation seems to argue against such appropriation. Harbou (or Lang) do not seem capable of a truly feminist critique any more than of a Marxist, Freudian or Christian resolution. Instead, we have a text whose allegorical energies seem unable to coalesce into a single grand narrative, but rather ceaselessly generates reference to nearly all the narratives – political, religious, occult, aesthetic, sexual – that circulated through Weimar culture. The energy in *Metropolis* becomes increasingly centrifugal, images escaping from the grand narratives to which they belong. Rutsky, for instance, points out that *Metropolis* utilises some of the key images Klaus Theweleit isolates from the writings of members of the Freikorps to express their unconscious terror of women, such as the overwhelming flood.[57] But if the flood can be associated with the robotic Maria through her role in destroying the machines, it is also opposed by the angelic Maria, who strives to rescue the children from the rising tides. More important, however, might be the image of the masculine body armour, particularly as embodied in Ernst Junger's steel-clad bodies of warriors and industrial workers.[58] One must observe Harbou's brilliant, and perhaps feminist, inversion of this image. The woman as an object manufactured for the male gaze wears her flesh on the outside, her metallic sheath within.

Harbou's understanding of the gender roles in this film may not be limited to the skin deep contrast between the Madonna and the whore of Babylon. Not only, as Huyssen points out, do the sequences of robotic Maria's performances reveal the working of the male gaze in an unparalleled critical fashion, the image of the robotic Maria stands less as liberated female cyborg, than the deconstruction of the attractions of commercial sexuality.[59] The crowd, after being aroused by robotic Maria's erotic gyrations, punish her and burn her flesh away. Their moment of triumph turns to horror, however, when her body armour is revealed, standing like a final allegorical emblem, invulnerable to their flames. The robot at the stake (invoking Joan of Arc – whose heart, according to legend, would not burn as much as the witch) and the crowd's horror provides an endlessly generative allegorical enigma, in contrast to the inert illustration of final reconciliation offered on the cathedral steps. It is perhaps this understanding of the feminine masquerade as a different form of body armour, skin deep with a metallic core to shield the centre from the male gaze, that attracted Maria's modern counterpart Madonna, who knows a thing or two about the apotropaic power of donning the costume of a slut.

As I mentioned, the ending everyone hates and which is ritually attributed to Harbou, does not appear in her novel. Instead, the novel ends by invoking again the absent women that hover over the story, Hel, Freder's mother, Joh's dead wife and

Rotwang's lost mistress. This finale is arranged by another withdrawn mother, Joh Fredersen's estranged mother (who lives in a farm house with a thatched roof and a walnut tree which Joh has transplanted to a rooftop in the city) and has always opposed her son's work. Joh returns to her, chastened and humbled, and she gives him a letter she has been keeping, written by Hel shortly before her death. The letter closes by quoting the Bible: 'I am with you always, even unto the end of the world.' Harbou's novel opens with the motto about the heart as mediator, but closes with a message from a dead woman, and a protest against separation. In the last lines Joh Fredersen repeats the message of ultimate reunion in a manner which stresses its apocalyptic horizon: 'Until the end of the world ... until the end of the world'.

PART II

The Mastery of Crime

Lang's Urban Thrillers:

Dr. Mabuse, the Gambler (1922)

Spies (1928)

The Testament of Dr. Mabuse (1932)

But there is no stone in the street and no brick in the wall that is not actually a deliberate symbol – a message from some man as much as if it were a telegram or a post-card. The narrowest street possesses, in every crook and twist of its intention, the soul of the man who built it, perhaps long in his grave. Every brick has as human a hieroglyph as if it were a graven brick of Babylon. Every slate on the roof as educational a document as if it were covered with addition and subtraction sums.

G. K. Chesterton, 'A Defense of Detective Stories'

4

Mabuse, Grand Enunciator: Control and Co-ordination

The Sensation-film and the Spaces of Modernity

> Just as the detective discovers the secret that people have
> concealed, the detective novel discloses in the aesthetic
> medium the secret of a society bereft of reality, as well as the
> secret of its insubstantial marionettes.
>
> Siegfried Kracauer, 'The Hotel Lobby'[1]

But what if *Metropolis* had originally ended like Harbou's novel, with Joh reading his dead wife's letter containing a promise of eternal love, 'until the end of the world?' As I noted, apocalyptic energy still hums in this promise, perhaps a wish for the world's end as much as for eventual reunion. But this final letter from Hel also introduces another device in Lang's cinema, one which stretches from his earliest surviving film until his last: the message from a dead person.[2] The opening sequence of surviving prints of the first film of Lang's *Spiders* diptych, *The Golden*

Sea, shows an old man emerging from a cave and picking his way among rocky cliffs to the edge of sea. Lang cuts between the man and a pursuing Indian. The old man writes a message on a piece of cloth, crams it into a bottle and prepares to throw it. Lang cuts from the old man winding up for the pitch to the Indian drawing his bow taut, then releasing an arrow. The old man propels the bottle into the ocean and simultaneously receives an arrow in his back and falls dead. The sequence ends with an iris out on the bottle floating out to sea.

The motif of the message and its relative independence from its sender will reappear in numerous Lang films in Germany and America (think, for instance, of the suicide note that opens *The Big Heat*, or the message contained in the editor's strong box that briefly exonerates Dana Andrews at the end of *Beyond a Reasonable Doubt*) and I will return to it several times in this book. For the moment I want to use it to focus on Lang's extraordinary reliance on the pathways and media of messages in his films, ranging from the signal fires which announce Gunther's homecoming in *The Death of Siegfried* to ringing telephones in nearly every contemporary-era film. Lang's view of the world, particularly the modern world, as a geography crisscrossed and demarcated by the constant circulation of messages, messengers and message delivery systems provides another image of the Destiny-machine, one more topographical than the omnipresent clock face, and ultimately an image of modernity wrenched away from the mythological and legendary forms of his more overtly allegorical films.

Metropolis attempts to provide an allegory of modernity, and part of its unresolved quality comes from the difficulty of representing modernity as something visible, even from a transcendental viewpoint. Although Lang never fully abandons the allegorical mode, his contemporary films evolve in a different genre, the detective/adventure film. Like science fiction, the detective genre provides fertile ground for allegorical devices, as G. K. Chesterton and others demonstrated, but it also supplies allegory with an alibi, as it absorbs transcendent mystery into a more tangible form of the mysterious. As Kracauer says, 'The composition of the detective novel transforms an ungraspable life into the translatable analogue of actual reality'.[3] When Lang entered the film industry, according to his own accounts writing scenarios while convalescing from war wounds sustained during World War I, it was the genre of detective and adventure film which originally attracted him. From the beginning of the 1910s or a bit earlier the emerging narrative cinema had embraced the detective and crime film as a genre that provided ready-made plot formulas familiar to a mass audience and also challenged film-makers to develop visual means for telling economic and fast moving stories with a certain degree of complexity. The French first developed detective series with Nick Carter (at Eclair) Nick Winter (Pathé) and Nat Pinkerton (Eclipse), soon followed by films of master criminals, *Zigomar*, *Fantomas*, *Les Vampires*. The Nordisk company in Denmark, a major source for films in Germany before World War I, supplied early Sherlock Holmes films as well as the exploits of the oriental criminal Dr. Gar el Hamma. Shortly before the war, Germany began the extremely intriguing series of girl detective films, *Miss Nobody*, as well as a number of crime features by directors Franz Hofer and Max Mack. During the war the enormously successful Stuart Webb series was initiated by director Joe May and star Ernst Reichert. According to some sources, one of Lang's first scenarios, *Der Peitsche* was sold to the Stuart Webb Detective Company. More certainly, Lang sold one to the detective rival to Webb that Joe May created after breaking with Reichert, Joe Deebs, for a film May directed as *Die Hochzeit im Exzentrikklub* in 1917.

Critics have often spoken of the debt Lang's films owe to the serial form, an insight of great importance in spite of an error in terminology. This detective tradition does not derive primarily from the film serial, the ongoing narrative form released in weekly instalments, of which the most popular and influential were undoubtedly the films Pathé released starring Pearl White, *The Perils of Pauline* and *The Exploits of Elaine*. Of more direct influence on Lang were the *series* films such as the detective and criminal films mentioned above which consisted of self-contained films all featuring the same character (and sometimes actor). These films were often feature-length and most were not portioned out in weekly segments. However, the narrative form of the series and the serials, as well as other self-contained adventure films were similar. They consisted of a concatenation of exploits by heroes or villains, whose narrative momentum seemed unstoppable. Based on conflicts between sharply opposed characters or groups of characters, and measured out in battles, defeats, successes, deceptions, captures, and escapes, their structure is additive rather than being based on the resolution of a central conflict. Encounters between detectives and criminals multiply as individual films or series continue, with new obstacles appearing on the horizon as soon as old ones are dispensed with.

This popular adventure detective form should be distinguished from the classical detective story as it developed (or atrophied) particularly in England as the rationalist puzzle based on intricate clues, the pastime of academics and politicians. The series-based detective stories were a more popular form based on a succession of exciting sequences (derived largely from their origin as *feuilletons*, serial fiction) rather than a tightly plotted central mystery awaiting a clever resolution. The battle between detective and criminal in a potentially endless series of encounters, mysterious locations borrowed from the gothic novel and death-defying situations taken from adventure novels, made up the loose and baggy form of these works, quite in contrast to the precision of an Agatha Christie mystery or even the economy of a hard-boiled Dashiell Hammett novel. The early detective films owed a great deal to the cinema of attractions, the form of early cinema made-up of spectacular visual moments strung loosely together, and even *Dr. Mabuse, the Gambler* still shows this rather loose form of a series of sensational adventures and episodes held together by a central conflict.

The term generally used for this form in Germany was 'sensation-film' (like the sensation-dramas and novels of the late nineteenth century from which they spring), accenting their structure around a series of sensational scenes rather than character-based drama. 'Sensation' referred to the direct visceral effect the scenes were designed to have on their viewers, with moments of heightened danger, suspense and terror, as well as a spectacular visual presentation. This modern genre conceived of its viewer or reader in a materialist manner: as a bundle of sensations to be played upon, and the successful artist knew how to evoke responses from carefully arranged stimuli. Rather than the traditional viewer coming from novels and theatre who was addressed through character psychology and dramatic conflicts, the viewer of the sensation-drama and film was pummeled and shocked, directly shaken by the events portrayed. This distinctly modern dramaturgy of shock, aimed at physical excitement rather than mental engagement, was the bane of the Film Reform movement in Germany from the early 1910s on. Based on a mechanistic theory of spectator and mass psychology that cloaked an alarm about both the conditions of modernity and the rise of mass culture, the Film Reform movement attacked film generally and the sensational film in particular as deleterious to the audiences' moral, mental and physical health.[4] Like the other daily 'shocks' of

modern life, the cinema seemed to undermine a sense of moral and mental equilibrium and a calm rational sense of the self. As late as 1924 Lang wrote an essay to
defend the sensation-film, claiming its violence and gruesome situations were no
worse than the incidents found in the popular *Märchen* and epics of traditional literature.[5]

In this article Lang defends the sensation-film and sees two vital centres of film-
making in 20s Germany: the art cinema typified by *The Cabinet of Dr. Caligari* and
the sensation-film designed for the masses. Lang is consistent throughout his career
in proclaiming his view that film is a democratic art form and that art films must be
accessible to large audiences. His own film-making, he proclaimed, attempted to
create works of art that could also be successful with general audiences. Linking the
sensation-film with traditional popular forms was one method of creating this
artistic/popular synthesis, directly applied in *Der müde Tod* and *Die Nibelungen*. In
the sensation-film Lang believed he had found a form that could be simultaneously
traditional and modern, popular and artful.

Lang's earliest surviving film *Spiders* displays his inheritance from the sensation-
film. The first film of this two-film series, *The Golden Sea*, employs motifs from the
feuilleton literature which had been accumulating stock characters and situations
for nearly a century. The message found in a bottle, the remnants of an ancient
civilisation, quests for hidden gold mines, secret criminal organisations complete
with hidden headquarters and occult emblems and codes, balloon ascents and
parachute jumps, battles with giant snakes, rescues from human sacrifices, desperate encounters in subterranean caverns, an athletic upper-class hero adventurer
(Kay Hoog) and an exotic female villainess (Lio Sha) – all of these are the rich, if
well-worn, devices of the boyhood reading of Lang's generation: Alexandre Dumas,
Wilkie Collins, Jules Verne, Karl May, H. Rider Haggard. *The Golden Sea* adds little
that is new to this tradition, other than the impressive sets by Hermann Warm and
Erich Kettelhut of the supposedly 'Incan' (stylistically Mayan) temples.

Few critics, however, have seemed to notice the emergence of Lang as a truly innovative sensation-film-maker with the second *Spiders* film, *The Diamond Ship*. In
between he had filmed the quite powerful *Harakiri* which turns its Madame Butter-
fly plot of a Japanese woman seduced and abandoned by a European officer into a
drama of paternal interdiction and shame (the father performs the first hara-kiri, the
daughter the last at the film's end) and religious fatality, exemplified by the figure of
the *bonze* who pursues the heroine throughout the film trying to force her to return
to her role as priestess (like the priest in Murnau's *Tabu*). But it is precisely from the
exoticism of both *The Golden Sea* and *Harakiri* that *The Diamond Ship* departs in
order to create the first of Lang's truly modern thrillers. In his 1924 article discussing
the sensation-film, Lang admitted the debt his film, *Dr. Mabuse, the Gambler* owed to
the sensational tradition, but had also claimed his film's appeal was due to its portrayal of its time (the subtitle for the Mabuse film is 'ein Bild der Zeit' – 'an image of
the times'). Mabuse showed the 'man of today', Lang claimed, 'not simply some man
from 1924, but *the man* of 1924'.[6] This, Lang declared, was the ultimate vocation of
the cinema, to provide a record of contemporary times.

The contemporary sensation-film, the urban thriller, deriving from the tradition
of detective and master criminal stories, novels, plays and films, provided Lang with
his ultimate allegory of modernity. While the cinema may well have an affinity with
the tradition of magic and myth, it has also – from its origins – claimed the privilege
of mirroring its own times. Lang's belief that future generations would be able to
understand this century simply by opening a film tin which contains a condensed

version of that earlier period may be naively put[7], but a close examination of his contemporary films shows his claim of representation went beyond a naive realism. As he stated in this article, the portrayal of contemporary reality would need a 'foundation of stylisation, just as much as the past centuries have'.[8] The image of his times that Lang constructs through the detective and sensation genre quickly becomes as complex as his allegorical representations of the past and the future.

The Diamond Ship profits greatly from the collaboration of Karl Freund, master of German camera stylistics and later cameraman on *Metropolis* (as well as Murnau's *The Last Laugh*). The opening sequence flaunts both Freund's originality and Lang's substitution of the modern for the exotic. The first action of the film takes place in a large American city of skyscrapers, as the Spider gang pull off a jewel heist from a bank vault. Lang and Freund shot this heist as a high angle long shot, the overhead view transforming the bank's cubicles and corridors into a checkerboard maze of gridded space as doorways open and close and the gang (attired in top hats and domino masks) play hide-and-seek with the nightwatchman. Lang intercuts the robbery with a cop on the beat outside, law and order unaware of what takes place behind the building's' facade. Lang/Freund may have taken their visual approach from Maurice Tourneur's masterful gangster film of 1915, *Alias Jimmy Valentine*, which portrays the safecracking of a bank vault in a similar manner, a high angle looking down into a labyrinth of cubicles and hallways as the burglars make their way to the safe and then try to avoid the nightwatchman. Tourneur's sequence works better as drama. His slightly higher angle looks more clearly into the cubicles and makes the burglars' pathways and dodging of the watchman easier to follow and more suspenseful. Lang's shot is not quite high enough and the geometry of the partitions dominates over the human actions. But while this may be awkward dramatically, this shot presents the first instance of a major Langian stylistic device, the topographical view which renders a locale as a geometrical field within which human actions and pathways seem to trace out pre-existent pathways. Production stills at the Cinémathèque Française reveal that Lang apparently shot – but did not use – a similar overhead view of the ransacking of the warehouse office building in *M*, in the search for the child murderer, a sequence which would have therefore directly recalled this one.[9]

The Diamond Ship finds Lang ready to mine the existing visual and narrative vocabulary of the detective-crime-sensation-film, and to use it to explore a contemporary environment. The sequence that immediately follows the diamond heist takes place in a hotel lobby, a recurring locale in the film, and for Siegfried Kracauer one of the essential emblems of the detective genre. For Kracauer, the hotel lobby exemplified the empty, purposeless and anonymous space of the modern world based on the *Ratio*, the calculating intellect and the reified relations between alienated individuals under capitalism:

> Remnants of individuals slip into the Nirvana of relaxation, faces disappear behind newspapers and the artificial continuous light illuminates nothing but mannequins. It is the coming and going of unfamiliar people who have become empty forms because they have lost their password, and who now file by as ungraspable ghosts.[10]

In the hotel lobby in *Spiders* anonymous guests pass without interacting, negotiating a complex flow of crisscrossing trajectories. Two men pass in top hats, but one hesitates to identify them with the masked bandits. Lang cuts to a medium shot of an elegantly dressed woman sitting with her newspaper in the background. Lio Sha simultaneously announces and conceals her presence: the emblem of the Spider gang sits pinned to her gown like a delicate ornament rather than a sinister sign. But the muted reaction of the men in top hats, picked out by Lang's cut to them in medium shot, leaves no doubt that we are now dealing with an action with two levels: the appearance of everyday and purposeless action of the lobby cloaking criminal activity. The men sit casually next to Lio Sha and pick up newspapers. In close-up we see their hands creep beneath the newspaper, touch Lio Sha surreptitiously and hand over the stolen diamonds. The modern world (and Kracauer's study of the detective genre shows that the literary genre had fully absorbed this lesson) provides a variety of concealing surfaces, such as the codes of anonymous behaviour in the hotel lobby that provide the perfect camouflage for devious purposes.

The detective genre relies heavily on disguise and deceptive appearance; early detective films adopted these highly visual devices more than ratiocination or the scrutiny of clues. (As Carlo Ginsburg demonstrates, the two are interrelated: 'Reality is opaque, but there are certain points – clues, symptoms – which allow us to decipher it.')[11] Mysterious appearances could also become spatialised. As a direct descendant of the gothic novel, the detective genre, especially the sensation-film, showed a fascination with subterranean spaces, secret passageways and hidden rooms – spaces concealed within spaces. Although the fascination with such hidden spaces comes from many sources, psychoanalytical and phenomenological as well as historical, Lang (and his predecessors, such as Victorin Jasset, director of *Zigomar* and Louis Feuillade, director of *Fantomas* and *Les Vampires*) explored strange interstices of spaces that were peculiarly modern, even if more unusual than the hotel lobby.

Rosalind Williams has explored the hold such underground spaces have on the modern imagination, supplementing an ancient fascination with caverns and underworld realms with the development of modern technology.[12] The mine supplied the first images of a totally technological environment as Lewis Mumford pointed out.[13] The subterranean spaces such as the Incan gold mine in the climax of *The Golden Sea* and the pirate's cave in the penultimate adventure of *The Diamond Ship* are natural spaces that have been created or appropriated by man. As in *Metropolis*, the modern city was, as Willams puts it, an excavated city, digging into its depths to lay a technological infrastructure.[14] The tradition of the urban thriller endowed this modern environment with mysterious associations deriving partly from the legendary caves of treasure (such as Alberich's cavern in *Die Nibelungen*), but also with peculiarly urban topography and the expansion of human technology into the bowels of the earth.

The Spiders' subterranean headquarters beneath Lio Sha's house bristle with modern technology, constructed of riveted steel plates like a battleship with a mechanical sliding door. In *The Golden Sea* Lio Sha uses a closed circuit television to watch her underlings. Using a switchboard with multiple hook-ups, her Chinese minion arranges a meeting of unscrupulous diamond merchants to evaluate the gang's booty in *The Diamond Ship*. Likewise, the police raid which Kay Hoog arranges against the Spiders is described by an intertitle as a 'modern' raid. Unlike the club-swinging but ineffective cop patrolling outside the despoiled bank, plainclothes detectives loiter outside Lio Sha's house as anonymous passersby, communicating while seeming to share a light for a cigarette, or pick up a piece of litter. Kay Hoog dramatically descends to the house's roof from an aeroplane (a ploy included more for its technological edge than its surreptitious effect, one presumes). Lio Sha

learns of the police invasion of her stronghold through an alarm bell and immediately pushes a concealed button which opens a secret elevator by which the diamond merchants can evade the police. Another turn of a switch, and the same
elevator becomes a compressor in which Hoog and the police are nearly crushed.
Released from this mechanical vice, Hoog pries open yet another secret passageway,
only to glimpse the Spider gang and their accomplices speeding away in a waiting
getaway car. As Lio Sha said, her organisation functions like a machine, and control
over the anonymous space and the subterranean passageways that modern technology opened up demonstrates how smoothly her machine fits into the mechanical
routines and rationalised spaces of modernity.

The exotic continues to play a key role in *The Diamond Ship*, but becomes
absorbed into the subterranean structures of the modern metropolis. Thus Kay
Hoog discovers a key-shaped talisman covered with obscure figures on the body of
a guard killed during the raid (another message from a dead man). Decoding it with
the aid of an antiquary, Hoog discovers it is the pass-key to a secret subterranean
city that exists beneath Chinatown. Entered through secret doorways and passageways, this subterranean space contains the repressed and dangerous elements of an
exotic society: opium dens, caged tigers, criminal meetings, and oriental guards
with weapons whose intricate blades resemble insignia. The idea of a secret city of
vice which existed within the everyday city was a basic trope for the modern metropolitan experience, the 'city of dreadful delight' that Judith R. Walkowitz describes,
the locale of one genre of the sensation-novel, the 'Mysteries of the Great City'
which sprang from Eugene Sue, with its 'literary construction of the metropolis as a
dark, powerful, seductive labyrinth …'.[15] Thus the working-class areas of the
metropolis, often populated by immigrants with foreign speech and habits, became
figured as unexplored territories, filled with danger and excitement. Kay Hoog's
descent into the hidden bowels of Chinatown (like Freder's descent to the depths of
metropolis) literalises a powerful social fantasy of the era.

The Spiders' relation to the ancient and exotic is constantly mediated by modern
technology and contemporary modes as if the primitive and the technological met
in a form of modern magic. A Yogi's visionary trance which reveals the whereabouts
of the Buddha-head diamond the Spider gang seeks is brought on by a gang
member using modern hypnosis (which he later uses to control Ellen Terry, the kidnapped daughter of a London diamond merchant). The Spiders' ship sailing
around the world in search of the legendary magical diamond stays in touch with
its network of spies through a wireless, and abruptly changes course based on new
information received over the airwaves.

Although the search moves from India to the Falkland Islands, it returns to
London for the climax which takes place again in the anonymous space of a hotel.
In the hotel, criminals and agents crisscross without acknowledging each other
beneath the everyday surface of hotel business. At the lobby desk, among the traffic
of other guests and bellboys, the members of the Spider gang register under false
identities (Dr. Telphas disguised as a bearded old man with Ellen in a hypnotic
trance identified as his daughter), as do turbaned agents for the Asian Committee,
also in pursuit of the diamond. Within their room the disguised members of the
gang identify themselves through secret gestures, but cannot evade surveillance.
Lang intercuts Kay Hoog and a Pinkerton detective spying on them through binoculars, while the Indian agents eavesdrop on their conversation from the next room.
One member of the gang is captured in the lobby by hotel detectives whom a
moment before had seemed to be guests idly reading newspapers.

As an unabashed sensation-film, *Spiders* introduces the repertoire of plot situations and images of intrigue and mystery from which Lang will continue to draw throughout his career. But even before his grand experiment to transform the sensation-film into an 'image of its times' in the first Dr. Mabuse film, Lang demonstrates that the tradition of the crime thriller supplies many links to the themes of modernity he will develop further. As G.K. Chesterton had claimed as early as 1901, the detective genre became the form 'in which is expressed some form of the poetry of modern life'.[16] In many ways the detective genre serves as a form in which modernity is both displayed and de-familiarised, modern urban spaces and technology providing a modern form of mystery that Lang (and his predecessors in the genre) freely combined with older motifs of the exotic and magical. With Mabuse, however, Lang brings a new degree of organisation to this amalgam, moving away from the image of the Destiny-machine as mythical and magical.

The Terrain of Modernity:
Space, Time and the Mastery of Communication

> The advent of modernity increasingly tears space away from
> place by fostering relations between 'absent' others,
> locationally distant from any given situation of face to face
> interaction. In conditions of modernity, place becomes
> increasingly phantasmagoric …
> Anthony Giddens, *The Consequences of Modernity* [17]

Both Lang's and Decla-Bioskop's publicity stressed the contemporaneous quality of *Dr. Mabuse, the Gambler*. The film, according to Decla-Bioskop, was not simply a sensation-film or a detective film, but an image of the times (*Zeitbild*). 'The world which the film presents to us is the world in which we all live today.' While German films of history and legend had been successful in export, it was hoped that *Dr. Mabuse, the Gambler* would be the first 'German film in modern dress' to have a worldwide success.[18] As Lang found in allegory his mode for exploring realms of myth/legend/fairytale, the detective-crime-thriller would provide him with a skeleton key to contemporary life. Numerous critics have tagged the detective as the exemplary fictional invention of modernity. The use of causal reasoning, penetration into the modern metropolis, exploitation of disguise and the blurry borders of personal and social identity, scrutiny of the smallest physical items and elements of everyday behaviour for the imprint of revelatory clues; the frequent use of technology for surveillance – all these traits mark the detective as a character who negotiates the modern environment with unique mastery. Simultaneously reflecting a positivist belief in the accessibility of knowledge through close and systematic observation, and new systems of social control through a panoptic system of surveillance, the detective sketches the ideology of modernity until it breaks into a violent confrontation and the repression upon which order is founded becomes explicit.

But perhaps even more unique a product of the modern imagination is the detective's evil twin, the complementary character who appears as a reaction to the detective's force and knowledge, the master criminal – not simply a clever or prodigious criminal with a long array of crimes to his credit, but the criminal as organiser, head of a vast conspiracy. Balzac's Vautrin provided the model and Balzac

understood the secret complicity between master criminal and detective in modelling his fictional character on Vidocq, head of the Parisian Sûreté who used his early
experience as a criminal to construct the modern Parisian police force and to found
one of the first private detective agencies. Two aspects of Vautrin define the master
criminal: on the one hand a vast system of underlings whose intricately organised
interactions mirror those of a vast industry, and a desire for power itself, rather than
simple personal gain or revenge, as the motivating force behind the criminal's activity.

The master criminal's role as executive of a large organisation clearly separates
him from the simple cunning thief, highwayman or avenger. Conan Doyle
described one of the prototypes, Holmes' nemesis Professor Moriarty:

> He is the Napoleon of crime, Watson. He is the organiser of half that is evil and
> nearly all that is undetected in this great city. He is a genius, a philosopher, an
> abstract thinker. He has a brain of the first order. He sits motionless, like a spider in
> the centre of its web, but that web has a thousand radiations, and he knows well
> every quiver of them. He does little himself. He only plans. But his agents are
> numerous and splendidly organised.[19]

Doyle stressed another aspect of the master criminal, already evident in Vautrin, a
relative invisibility: not only is he difficult to capture, but even proving his existence
becomes a problem for his detective nemesis. Thus the common ground between
detective and criminal becomes the ability to watch without being observed. As the
ordinary criminal threatens the state's monopoly on violence, the master criminal
threatens the state's unique employment of the panopticon of surveillance and
information-gathering.

As he quickly became part of the popular literature, the master criminal refined
rather than lost his nearly Nietzschean will-to-power, focused as a desire to disrupt
the complacency of bourgeois society, modelled on political opposition groups and
other conspiracies (such as Sue's use of the Jesuits in *The Wandering Jew*), as well as
worldwide criminal networks. This almost abstract nihilism is best captured in the
opening lines of the epic adventures of master criminal Fantomas launched in 1911
by Marcel Allain and Pierre Souvestre (and filmed two years later by Louis Feuillade):

> 'Fantomas.'
> 'What did you say?'
> 'I said: Fantomas.'
> 'And what does that mean?'
> 'Nothing … Everything!'
> 'But what is it?'
> 'Nobody … and yet, yes, it is somebody!'
> 'And what does the somebody do?'
> 'Spreads Terror!'[20]

The nearly abstract, enigmatically named character, origin of such terror, provided
pulp writers with the ultimate figure of hubris and energy. Lang flirted with the
master criminal in a skilful but still limited (especially when compared to her prototype, Irma Vep in Feuillade's *Les Vampires*) manner in Lio Sha, head of the Spiders
gang. But in Norbert Jacques' Dr. Mabuse, Lang found a character who could fully
develop the issues of authorship and control in relation to the Destiny-machine

through his mastery of a vastly radiating, and distinctly technological, web. Lang himself defined the master criminal as:

> ... the man who prepares his crimes quasi-scientifically before executing them himself or having them carried out by others with a mathematical precision. ... Dr. Mabuse, who declares, 'I am the Law', is the perfect criminal, the puppet master who organises off stage the perfect crime. He is in open conflict with all existing institutions, he is the great gambler who gambles on the stock market with money, with love and with the destiny of people, but who never leaves anything in his crimes to chance.[21]

Decla-Bioskop publicity for the film further defined the type, saying Mabuse 'doesn't just want to amass a fortune, he wants to be master – master of the city in which he lives, master of the land in which he dwells, master over all men'.[22] With Mabuse, Lang creates not only his ultimate figure of urban crime, but his most complex enunciator figure, the author of crimes who aspires to be a demi-urge in control of his own creation, Lang's own *doppelgänger* as director and author who will haunt Lang for nearly the full extent of his career (from 1922 to his last film in 1960).

As Allain and Souvestre announced the phantasmal nature of their villain/hero in their opening dialogue, in the first scene of *Dr. Mabuse, the Gambler* Lang places Mabuse in the centre of the terrain of modernity and its network of events and messages against a background of the rationalised space and time of the contemporary environment (a sequence with no direct parallel in Jacques' novel). In the opening sequence Lang tackles the way one form of technology interacts with another to create the abstract and fully co-ordinated grid of space and time that forms the terrain of modernity. Sociologist Anthony Giddens characterises modernity as phantasmagoric through its various techniques of the abstraction of space and time, 'emptying out' and 'disembedding', divorcing them from the local and particular and creating a universal context for interaction. This abstract system cannot be visualised in a single shot or image, but rather becomes evident in the way different spaces and time interrelate in a film, producing a unique playing-field for the master criminal. In this sequence (and in effect throughout the film as a whole) Lang creates an image of the new 'empty' and standardised space and time of modernity, based on uniform measurement and systematic interrelation, in a manner unmatched in any earlier film I have seen and unmatchable in any other art form. The dominant mechanisms employed are the pocket-watch, the railway and the telephone – interacting with the cinematic device of parallel editing.

Mabuse sits at his desk apparently passive, waiting for his henchman Spoerri to transform him into the elderly, bearded, well-dressed bourgeois whose photograph he has just handed him. As he hands the photo over his shoulder, his other hand holds his pocket-watch which engages his full attention. A close-up follows of the watch, its circular form filling the screen. This form is immediately echoed by a circular iris which opens on a high angle shot of a train moving towards and past the camera. We cut to inside a compartment of this train, showing two men seated across from each other, the one on the right apparently dozing, the one on the left checking a briefcase on the seat next to him which we then see in close-up. After cutting over to the apparently dozing man (who seems to glance at the briefcase as well), Lang returns to the briefcase in close-up, only this time he uses an overlap-dissolve which reveals the business contract inside. It is the theft of this document that will be Mabuse's first move in his plot to de-stabilise the stock market.

After this dissolve, we return to the supposedly sleeping man, actually Mabuse's henchman, as he surreptitiously removes something from his pocket – a weapon perhaps? No, the close-up shows it to be another pocket-watch, showing the time to be 8:18. Once again the close-up of a watch triggers a cut to another location, as we see a man waiting beside a car. He too fishes something from his pocket and the succeeding close-up reveals another pocket-watch, the time now 8:19. In the following shot the man seems galvanised by this sight and begins cranking his car, then gets in. We return to Mabuse at his desk, framed a bit more closely as Spoerri begins to arrange his hair. His eyes remain riveted on the watch as if it enabled him to see the scenes we have just witnessed thanks to parallel editing.[23] Without taking his eyes from the watch, his other hand moves to the left of the frame towards the telephone on the desk. We cut back to the train compartment, Mabuse's henchman is still surreptitiously looking at his watch. Another close-up follows showing the watch: it is 8:20. We cut back to long shot as the henchman rises, stretches and then abruptly throttles the commercial courier. We cut to a long shot of the road as the car approaches the camera, framed by an arching underpass. In the next shot we see the train travelling over an embankment.

Shot from outside the train from a slightly low angle, the henchman appears at the compartment window and tosses out the briefcase. Lang cuts to a slightly high angle of the car's driver as he looks up. The following shot of the back seat of this open car shows the briefcase landing perfectly on the upholstery. The two lines of action, train and car, brought together and the exchange made, we now cut in another element: a man shot from a low angle perched on a telephone pole like a repairman, framed within a circular iris. Watching something from his perch, he waves his cap in a broad signalling gesture, then connects some wires. We return to Mabuse at his desk, watch still in one hand, but the other arm fully stretched out to the telephone. With a sharp, almost mechanical jerk, he pulls the receiver to him and swivels his head away from the watch, looking up expectantly. We cut to the man on the telephone pole as he picks up a receiver and speaks into it. A title gives the coded message of success: 'Va Banque'. Mabuse, receiver to ear, stares towards the camera exultantly, almost demonically. He slowly puts the receiver down. The title gives his reaction: 'Bravo Georges!'. Cutting back to a medium long shot, Mabuse hangs up the receiver and leans back in his chair, relaxed for the first time.

This justly famous opening sequence exemplifies Lang's mastery of the co-ordination of space and time through parallel editing. The various elements of the heist – Mabuse at his desk; the henchmen on the telephone pole watching and conveying the action to Mabuse; the train compartment in which the robbery occurs; and the car which passes beneath the train overpass at the precise moment the briefcase is thrown from the window, are cut together in a manner which not only narrates the events but portrays them as interlocking parts of a grand plan, the mobile mechanism of Mabuse's criminal design. Extending the discoveries of the Griffith school of parallel action, Lang co-ordinates separate points in space in terms of a rigorous and unswerving temporality. These events literally unwind like clockwork, capturing, as Ravi S. Vasudevan has observed, the uniquely modern culture of space and time: 'rather than our being given an awareness of different events taking place, it is one event, divided into specific functions, that unfolds before our eyes'.[24] Mabuse appears as the evil genius of modernity, able to extend his power through space through his careful control of time, like a spider sitting in the centre of a technological web.

But if Mabuse, like Moriarty, sits at the centre of a network which conveys his power to its furthest reaches, what constitutes the strands of that web? Clearly there are several elements that form the web of modernity as Lang conveys it. Mabuse's watch, held in his hand and consulted, provides the reference point by which the separate actions become one event. The watch, which immediately finds its *doppel-gängers* in the hands of the train murderer and the chauffeur (as well as visual echoes in the circular irises and the arching underpass), conveys the synchronised nature of the action, a plan devised by Mabuse with a scenario timed to the second. As Mabuse and his henchmen stare at their watches, Lang shows us the precisely determined events unfolding at their allotted moment. This sort of temporal precision depends on a third emblem of the modern culture of space and time, the railway. The theft of the commercial contract and murder of its courier is timed to take place at a precise moment, a unique position within the system of time-space, shortly before the train reaches the overpass, so that the contract can then be tossed to the automobile passing below. Mabuse's plans depend, then, on a system already obsessed with precise timing and schedules. Giddens has pointed out the terrain of co-ordination a railway timetable implies:

> A timetable, such as the schedule of times at which trains run, might seem at first sight to be merely a temporal chart. But actually it is a time-space ordering device, indicating both when and where trains arrive. As such it permits the complex co-ordination of trains and their passengers and freight across large tracts of time-space.[25]

As in the railway, Mabuse's precise timetable does not simply express an anal concern with punctuality, but forms the linchpin of a scenario based on transfers and exchanges. Mabuse's criminal conspiracy is less an anarchistic threat to order than a parasite dependent on the systematic nature of modernity.

The telephone's ability to cross space instantly and the precision of railway schedules rely on a geography of interlocking technologies (the railway, the pocket-watch, the telephone system) that creates a system in which action can be co-ordinated and regulated without, as Giddens says, direct face-to-face interaction. Power and command, as well as obedience and subordination, are technologically mediated. These technical devices evolved in interrelation to each other, as precise railway schedules demanded precise portable time-pieces (originally called 'railway watches') and systems of electric communication (first the telegraph and then the telephone) grew up along railway routes. Lang's sequence makes us experience this interlocking technological landscape as a lived and dramatic event, conveyed through the new technology of film, especially through one of its specific means of representation, editing. Lang's editing models itself on the telephone's ability to carry instantaneous messages across space, and on a new temporality founded on instants and synchronisation. It images modernity as a carefully gridded playing-field of calculation and power. Mabuse's body as he sits apparently immobile at his desk stretches between these two devices, the watch and the telephone. His nearly mechanical interaction with them – marked immobility giving way to sudden jolting motion – makes him seem a part of the mechanism, the relay between two devices. As Mabuse grasps the receiver his demeanour is transformed, as if electrified by a current carried over the wire. We inescapably feel that Mabuse has been plugged in, connected to a source of power.

Before *Metropolis*, Lang created in Mabuse his most effective allegory of modernity, one whose power came partly from its literal as well as its emblematic nature.

Although the aura of the magician still hovers around Mabuse's disguise as Sandor Weltmann, the hypnotist who knows the secrets of the Indian fakirs, Lang and Harbou did not need to draw on images of medieval magic to explain his extraordinary control and power. Mabuse remains within the conditions of his times because he can exploit time itself in its systematic, abstract and instrumental modern nature.

The Mechanical Production of Counterfeit Identity

> The mathematical character of money imbues the relationship of the elements of life with a precision, a reliability in the determination of parity and disparity, an unambiguousness in agreements and arrangements in the same way as the general use of pocket watches has brought a similar effect in daily life. Like the determination of abstract value by money, the determination of abstract time by clocks provides a system for the most detailed and definitive arrangements and measurements that imparts an otherwise unattainable transparency and calculability to the contents of life …
>
> Georg Simmel, *The Philosophy of Money* [26]

Before Mabuse takes his phone call, *Dr. Mabuse, the Gambler* presents an emblematic shot of its main character. The film opens with a close-up of a series of cards spread out for the camera, held in Mabuse's hand. Mabuse draws several from a pile to the right, adds them to his hand and fans them so they are all visible. This opening close-up, as Noel Burch has pointed out, dynamically starts the film with a view of a detail rather than an establishing shot, the image evoking the title of the film, Mabuse, *the Gambler*.[27] However, these are not playing cards. Instead they appear like *cartes de visites*, hand-sized photographs introduced in the nineteenth century bearing one's portrait to be exchanged with friends and relatives. The format persisted into the twentieth century, especially for theatrical portraits of famous performers and had already been adapted by the cinema in the 1910s to promote stars. Mabuse's hand holds a series of character poses, like a succession of images of a famous actor in his most characteristic roles. The shot blends two realms of reference: gambling and role playing. Lang's title, *Dr. Mabuse, der Spieler*, has at least a double meaning. A *Spieler* is a player, a gambler, but also an actor, and this sequence unites both in its imagery.

It also invokes two sorts of liminal prologues used in early silent cinema, both popular in the decades before *Dr. Mabuse*: the emblematic shot and the actors' prologue. The emblematic shot appeared first in early cinema, with a shot that in some manner summarised or invoked the subject matter of the film without actually portraying an event in the film's story. For instance, *Raid on a Coiner's Den,* produced in 1904 by the British Gaumont Company, opens with a close-up of three hands, one holding a pistol, one handcuffs and a third money. The shot encapsulates the action of the film rather than portraying a diegetic event. The actors' prologue appeared around 1910 and was particularly popular from 1914 to 1916 when film companies were introducing stars as a way to market their films. They consisted generally of a sequence at the opening of the film in which actors would present themselves to the audience, sometimes within a stage set and sometimes bowing towards the camera, with intertitles following giving their names and often the names of the characters.[28] Not infrequently the actors would appear both as performers and then, with an overlap-dissolve, in costume as the characters they played; for example, the introduction of Robert Warwick who plays Jimmy Valentine in Tourneur's film. In the 1913 *Fantomas* Louis Feuillade had already used the actors' prologue not only to introduce performers, but to show the various disguises employed by his master criminal: Dr. Chalek, the pimp Loupart and the mysterious 'man in black'. These prologues stress their non-diegetic nature with intertitles identifying the actors *as actors* and often by taking place in an abstract setting, against a blank background (as in *Fantomas*) or on a stage set.

The image of a hand 'holding all the cards' is, of course, an image of control and power. The images on the cards, the series of character poses, portray Dr. Mabuse's various character disguises; we see (along with a couple I don't recognise from the film) Mabuse as the stockbroker; the elderly businessman; Dr. Mabuse the psychoanalyst; the Dutch gambler; the conjurer Sandor Weltmann; and as the drunken sailor. What Mabuse controls is his own multi-faceted identity, which is to say, the way other people see him; he is a master of appearances, an illusionist, an actor. With a brief overlap-dissolve, Lang cuts to the reverse angle, a medium shot of the man who holds the cards, Mabuse, as he collapses the cards and deftly shuffles them, then places them on the table. The gestures not only return us to his role as professional gambler, but to his skill and control. Feuillade supplied a prologue to *Fantomas* which not only introduced his actor, but revealed his various disguises (something the novel avoided doing). Lang, however, does not address the audience outside the story with this sort of non-diegetic prologue. Instead he embeds this revelation into the opening of the story, so that the identities appear to be revealed *by Mabuse*, to the audience; Lang does not assert his extra-filmic presence. For the moment he lets Mabuse hold all the cards. As we shall see, Mabuse's character as master of appearances and role playing, as controller of other people's destinies, works out an analogy with the film director or author. As mentioned earlier, Mabuse stands as the archetypal Langian figure who attempts to maintain control of the film's narrative action and the processes of the Destiny-machine by becoming the master criminal organiser, the energy at the centre of the technological web. But Lang in *Dr. Mabuse, the Gambler* explores the subject of his subtitle, *An Image of the Times* through his title character. Almost systematically Lang constructs Mabuse's power through the various aspects of modernity. In the opening robbery he establishes Mabuse's relation to technology and the imbrication of space and time it allows. In the sequences that immediately follow, Lang uses Mabuse to explore the 'disembedded' nature of modern identity, of a money economy and of the fascination of gambling.

Placing the shuffled pack of cards before him. Mabuse draws one, the elderly businessman, which he hands to his underling, Spoerri, to use as a model for his transformation. In spite of his imperious air in both speech (title: 'Spoerri, have you taken cocaine again?') and gesture (the card thrust back over his head without a glance at Spoerri who trembles at his master's impatience), Mabuse remains in a sense a *tabula rasa*, awaiting the imprint of his chosen face. But it is precisely in Mabuse's ability to assume different identities that his power lies, his extraordinary control over appearances which allow his nefarious activities to occur under the appearance of everyday, simple or even negligent actions. In the scenes that follow he conveys essential information written on a bank note carelessly dropped into a false beggar's hand, and has a rendezvous with a member of his gang under the cover of a traffic 'accident'. When he visits his counterfeiting den, he arrives as an apparently drunken sailor and receives the key to the door hidden in a ball of yarn a woman throws at him as if in disgust at his lurching intoxicated gait. It is when he seems most inactive that Mabuse becomes most fiendishly effective.

The game of disguises in the detective and crime genre rests on an aspect of the genre every bit as essential as the tracking down of clues and the use of ratiocination, but often deprecated in the critical literature (which sees the genre as an intellectual game rather than the 'poetry of modernity'): the effacement and control of identity. Walter Benjamin, however, focused on this aspect of Poe's 'The Mystery of Marie Roget' (the third and most neglected of Poe's Dupin stories which are generally seen as the foundation of the detective genre) when he proclaimed, 'the original social content of the detective story was the obliteration of the individual's traces in the big city crowd'.[29] Nineteenth-century police departments expended much energy devising ways to keep track of the individual identity of criminals and convicts, evolving systems of surveillance and information archives, employing the new technological resources of photography, the systems of measurement and cataloguing of body parts devised by Bertillon's anthropometry and Galton's fingerprinting, thereby processing identifying marks so that any individual could be seen as a unique combination of standard traits easily catalogued and traceable. But if the forces of order employed all the means of the rationalised sciences of observation to reduce individuality to points on a graph, the criminal (at least in fiction) used the devices of illusion and theatre, grimacing when mug shots were taken, multiplying fictional aliases, and mastering makeup and costume to ward off the penetrating gaze of the police.[30]

But once again, Mabuse's fictional identities do not so much attack the system as exploit its structure for his own ends. It is therefore essential that he both understand and adapt to the modern world. He assumes an identity that is proper for the situation he puts himself into, molding identity to contexts: the stockbroker at the Bourse, the psychoanalyst at the society party, the elderly capitalist in his limousine, even the political radical at the working-class café or the drunken sailor in the slum alleyway. In modernity, individual identity becomes largely determined by its role within a profession, institution or social event, and Mabuse never appears in any of his roles out of place. Instead, as in the opening sequence, his power comes from the ease with which he situates himself within a pre-existent web of interlocking pieces.

This is nowhere clearer than in the film's second set piece, Mabuse's manipulation of the stock market. As with all of Mabuse's disguises, his role as a stockbroker not only reflects the structures of modernity, but immediate Weimar current events as well. The sudden drop in the value of the mark in the late summer of 1921 had led to what historian of the inflation era Gerald D. Feldman has called 'an orgy of stock speculation'. Stock market investment took the form of a frenzy, so that by November of 1921, when *Mabuse* began shooting, the Berlin exchange was so overloaded with business it opened for only one day a week.[31] Mabuse acts as behind-the-scenes author in this sequence, as well as costumed lead player. The theft of the commercial contract on the train (itself so carefully co-ordinating different elements) now fits into the larger scheme of Mabuse's manipulation of the stock market. The intricacy of his plot seems designed to demonstrate Mabuse's symbiosis with the arbitrary nature of the rise and fall of stock prices. It is not that Mabuse has stolen information that will allow him to make a killing on the market. Rather, the theft gives him *control* of information. Like a skilled author or dramatist, Mabuse asserts his authority by managing information, first withholding it, then releasing it at precisely the most effective moment. Mabuse counts on the news of the theft of the commercial contract to cause prices in the stock involved to plummet. Buying them once they have reached rock bottom, he then arranges that it will be revealed that the contract has been found, apparently unopened. In reaction, the stock prices rise again. Mabuse does not need the information contained in the contract; he simply uses its appearance and disappearance as a lever to manipulate the mood on the floor. Mabuse's power may still rely on moments of violence, such as the assault in the train compartment, but it is his mastery of the abstraction of the stock market system that proves his most powerful weapon.

Lang fashions the stock market sequence, as he did the opening heist, through the co-ordinated rhythmic interaction of several elements, functioning like a machine, and regulated by the huge clock which dominates the set of the Bourse. Although contained within a single space, the drama again stretches between two apparatuses, the clock, and, on the left, the board listing stock prices, which is continually serviced by minions who erase one price and inscribe another (Lang will parody this price quote board in *M* with the blackboard at the beggars' headquarters listing the prices of leftover food, which undergo similar fluctuations). In between the two is a tumultuous sea of speculators whose top hats rock back and forth with each new price. After the newspapers report the theft of the contract, Lang shows a bearded speculator (probably coded as Jewish) taking off his glove and conveying a secret signal to his underling.[32] An iris isolates an immobile figure amid this chaos, whom we recognise as one of the faces from Mabuse's cards: Mabuse himself with top hat and trimmed moustache, calmly observing all as he puffs on his cigar. Lang cuts rhythmically from broad long shots to details of the frenzied price changes and the anguished looks on the brokers' faces. Mabuse climbs up on a desk and mechanically raises his arm to announce he is buying.

Lang cuts away to frenzied activity in the offices where an exhausted messenger delivers the news of the discovery of the intact commercial contract. We cut back to the floor where Mabuse towers above the rest, still immobile, no longer buying. In medium shot he glances off screen, and Lang cuts for the first time to a shot centring only on the clock (another unusual clock face, this one showing twenty-four hours) as it marks five minutes to the closing hour. Mabuse remains standing still above the frenzied crowd. The office boys throw out leaflets announcing the discovery of the contract from a balcony just below the clock face. They rain on the crowd below and the prices on the board begin to mount. Mabuse continues standing on his desktop, hands in pockets, barely shaking his head as he refuses to sell to the hands raised beseechingly towards him. Then, after a glance at the changing price board, his arm goes up again and he announces, 'I am selling'. A cut to the clock and the attendants ringing bells announces the closing of the market. A shot of the price board shows the figure 1300, from the price of 178 at which Mabuse had begun to buy. Lang ends the sequence with the figure on the board and then a shot of the now empty exchange room, littered with the detritus of the battle, leaflets, papers, stockbrokers' abandoned hats. Over this empty devastated space Lang superimposes a close-up of Mabuse as the stockbroker. Then the stockbroker's face fades away and it is Mabuse's face without disguise that stares at us from the stock exchange floor.

Although not dealing with the modern co-ordination of space and time displayed in the opening sequence, Lang here visualises the abstraction and mechanical rhythm of a money economy typified by the stock exchange. For Giddens,

money is one of the major means of the 'disembedding' of modernity. Like the technologies of communication and transportation Mabuse employs in the opening robbery, money is, as Giddens puts it, 'a means of time-space distantiation. Money provides for the enactment of transactions between agents widely separated in time and space.'[33] The whole institution of the stock exchange expresses this disembedding of space and time as shares are exchanged, and their relation to complex industries or services becomes reduced to the column of numbers rising and falling on the blackboard. As Giddens puts it, 'Today "money proper" is independent of the means whereby it is represented taking the form of pure information lodged as figures in a computer print out'. Although the technology of Lang's stock exchange remains primitive compared to today's computerised systems of trading, the sequence demonstrates the disembedding abstraction of money as a game manipulated by an unscrupulous player.

Human beings in this sequence are shaken like marbles in a tin pan by the collision of information, the clock and the rise and fall of prices. If Mabuse seems unmoved by this tumult, it is precisely because he identifies with it so thoroughly. His control of the system takes the form of melding with it, becoming part of it. The sudden gestures of his arm, his surreptitious glance at board and clock show his almost mechanical alignment with them. The shots which end the sequence summarise his influence with a firmly written round number on the board, and an image of emptiness, a space now bereft of human presence. Lang will use both numbers and empty spaces in his films from now on as emblems of the triumph of abstract systems, of the Destiny-machine. The superimposition of Mabuse's face as the ultimate shot of the sequence performs several roles. First, it announces his dominance and clearly displays his manipulation of disguise and identity as a major tool. The shot proclaims him the motivating force beyond this scene, the author appearing before the now empty stage. But, like the vision scene of Moloch in

Metropolis, it also puts a face to the system, marking Mabuse as the demon of abstraction, disguise and control – of modernity.

Mabuse's pranks on the stock exchange reveal money as pure exchange value and disembedding abstraction: the series of wildly ranging figures no sooner written on the board than erased and replaced by another. Money as a pure play of figures opens up the modern terrain as that realm of abstraction and information that Georg Simmel described as characteristic of the modern economy and the modern metropolis:

> since money measures all objects with merciless objectivity, and since its standard of value so measured determines their relationship, a web of objective and personal aspects of life emerges which is similar to the natural cosmos with its continual cohesion and strict causality. This web is held together by the all-pervasive money value, just as nature is held together by the energy that gives life to everything.[34]

In the opening sequence Mabuse's plans skated upon the frictionless surface of railway timetables and electronic communication; in the stock market sequence he navigates through the swells and depressions of stock prices, confident in the interwoven web of information and demand, clock-time and money as the ultimate measure and means of exchange of all things.

Mabuse's comfortable fit within the systems of modernity does not undermine the obvious fact that he manipulates these systems with force and violence. But rather than undermining them, he relies upon their smoothly-functioning calculability. Mabuse operates by pushing the 'empty' abstraction of time and money ever further. His multiple manufactured identities reflect the abstraction inherent in his major criminal enterprises: stock market manipulations, the manufacture of counterfeit bills (in subterranean factories manned by the blind) and gambling. All of these processes undermine any notion of the unique and genuine, subverting in particular any connection between money and intrinsic value. Money works in Mabuse's schemes precisely because it has no value other than that with which it is momentarily endowed by panicked (and misled) buyers or sellers, ignorant dupes passing forged notes, or concupiscent gamblers hoping to find in their wager a way to compel fortune to smile on them.

As I indicated earlier, Mabuse in this sequence does not just represent the inherent abstraction embodied in a modern money economy or the stock exchange but embodies more immediate events in the Weimar economy. For filmgoers in the Weimar republic the simultaneously arbitrary and dire nature of money and prices was not a theoretical concept, but a matter of survival in everyday life. Besides chronicling the stock market speculation of late 1921, Mabuse and his manipulative relation to money and prices – both the stock market manipulation and his printing of counterfeit money – made him the image of the galloping inflation of the period. As historian Gerald Feldman says, the Mabuse character 'was a genuine and conscious product of the inflation'.[35] Inflation had been a very real problem in Germany since the end of World War I, one which the fledgling republic avoided facing straight on, and which was complicated (and perhaps obscured) by the controversy over the payment of war reparations to the allies. By 1922 the price index compared to the pre-war period was nearly 350 per cent.[36] Early 1921 had seen a brief stabilisation, but by November of 1921, when *Dr. Mabuse, the Gambler* began shooting, the value of the mark had dropped to one quarter what it had been at the beginning of the year.[37] The film was released (Part I in April and Part II in May, 1922) as the inflationary spiral was increasing once again. But by August, spurred partly by the chaos following Rathenau's assassination, it had moved from galloping inflation (a yearly rate of 50 per cent or more) to hyper-inflation (*monthly* increases of 50 per cent or more).[38] By the end of 1923 this index had reached multiples of the thousand millions.[39] Whether reflecting the already serious inflation of prices at the time it was released, or the truly surreal demonstration of the arbitrary relation between goods and money that the film shortly anticipated, the image of Mabuse's sinister manipulations of stock prices became emblematic for the experience of hyper-inflation. Feldman's history of the inflation period, *The Great Disorder*, actually calls 1922, 'the year of Dr. Mabuse', and Lang himself, in the film's sequel, *The Testament of Dr. Mabuse* in 1932, has his detective Lohmann recall Mabuse as a personality from the inflation era. In retrospect, Mabuse's role as the prophet of a degree of chaos that had not yet transpired reveals the strength of Harbou and Lang's 'image of the time' as an exaggeration of forces already in motion, unaware that the times themselves would soon exaggerate them beyond their imaginations.

Mabuse's symbiosis with the inflation era, derives from more than the stock market sequence and permeates the film. The frenzied pursuit of pleasure in the nightclubs and gambling halls of *Dr. Mabuse, the Gambler* captured the culture and attitudes of those who were either profiting from the inflation (the *Schieber*, those dealing in black market or illegal goods – such as Schramm the owner of the grill *cum* nightclub whose career from peddler to wealthy inflation profiteer Lang chronicles in a four-shot, beautifully elliptical, mini-movie) or those who, seeing the value of their savings or wages evaporate were, as Feldman puts it, 'willing to live for the day and to spend their money as quickly as they got it'.[40] Mabuse's role as a printer of counterfeit currency also offered a commentary on the Weimar Republic's tendency to respond to the economic problems by simply printing more money. Thus when hyper-inflation arrived in August, Adolf Hitler could revile 'this weak republic [which] throws its pieces of worthless paper about wildly', as if he were describing the final scenes of Mabuse in his clandestine printing press wallowing in his now worthless currency.[41]

If the forged bank note, a piece of paper with a spurious claim to legal tender based on a (manufactured) resemblance, circulates throughout this film as the emblematic sign of Mabuse's simultaneous faith in, and manipulation of, the money economy, gambling takes us into the true centre of Lang's exposition of his times. For Dostoevsky, gambling, especially roulette, formed the antithesis of calculation, the capitalistic logic of self-denial, exploitation and investment that he associated with Baron Rothschild.[42] But nonetheless it was money in its abstract accumulation and dissipation (like the figures melting on the stock market blackboard) that impelled even the Russian gambler narrator to see in this random succession of numbers the possibility of challenging fortune itself, '... a sort of defiance of fate, a desire to challenge it, to put out my tongue at it'.[43] Dostoevsky's gambler scorns the calculations made by other gamblers on the likelihood of a number showing up, and when he wins it is due to an 'astonishing regularity' of a number recurring that 'throws inveterate gamblers who calculate with a pencil in their hands out of their reckoning'.[44] Walter Benjamin in his discussion of the image of the gambler in Baudelaire realises the profound connection between the modern world of empty abstraction and the gambler's passion. Winning cannot be calculated because no game depends on a previous one, therefore, no experience accumulates as a basis for future action. Like the factory worker on the assembly line, Benjamin claims, the gambler deals with a time that is emptied out, inaccessible to

experience, sharing with the worker 'the futility, the emptiness the inability to complete something. … Since each operation at the machine is just as screened off from
the preceding operation as a coup in a game of chance is from the one that preceded
it, the drudgery of the labour is, in its own way, a counterpart of the drudgery of the
gambler.'[45] The repetitive rhythm of gambling, always awaiting the 'ivory ball that
falls into the *next* compartment, the *next* card that lies on top'[46] captures the hellish
time of modernity as a succession of autonomous empty instants. The gambler in
effect 'kills time' as he or she plays, an experience (or lack of experience) that Lang
visualises by cutting from his romantic hero/victim Edgar Hull as he begins to
gamble under Mabuse's hypnotic suggestion, to a clock whose hands turn rapidly
from two o'clock to nearly five o'clock. Time passes relentlessly, but unnoticed.

It is the mingling of apparent passion and boredom that makes the gambling hall
such a dramatic setting for Mabuse's plots. Each gambler awaits not only the next
chance to win, but also the *next sensation*. Benjamin describes this psychology of
the passions via a famous lithograph of a gambling hall by Senefelder:

> Each man is dominated by an emotion; one shows unrestrained joy; another distrust
> of his partner; a third dull despair; a fourth evinces belligerence; another is getting
> ready to depart from the world. All these modes of conduct share a concealed
> characteristic: the figures presented show us how the mechanism to which the
> participants in a game of chance entrust themselves seizes them body and soul, so
> that even in their private sphere, and no matter how agitated they may be, they are
> capable only of a reflex action.[47]

As in the stock market, the gamblers whose identity Mabuse assumes – Hugo
Balling, or the Dutch professor – fit in perfectly with the other eccentric characters
at the gaming tables. These gambling halls are themselves disguised: from the dive,
Andalusia (which detective von Wenk penetrates with the password 'pineapple' and
gets the response 'cocaine or cards?') to the elegant Petite Casino which has devised
a cabaret stage which can descend from above and conceal the gaming tables in the
event of a police raid. But Mabuse lacks the gambler's surrender to pure chance and
empty time; he, in fact, plays another game while appearing to gamble (Carozza,
Mabuse's mistress, calls it 'gambling with human beings'). Mabuse's hypnotic control over his gambling victims sets him outside the game, as both observer and
manipulator. Once again the cards he holds in his hands are not the true pieces of
the game, which are the human beings he manipulates at the gambling table, relying on both their passions and their passivity to his hypnotic suggestions.

Benjamin places Baudelaire, as well, in a position outside the game, that of the
spectator who watches the gamblers, quoting from the poem 'Le Jeu':

> I saw myself in a corner of that hushed den
> watching it all, cold mute – and envious!
> envying the stubborn passion of such men,
> the deadly gaieties of those old whores –
> all blithely trafficking, as I looked on,
> in honour or in beauty – whatever they could sell!
> Horrible that I should envy these
> who rush so recklessly into the pit,
> each in his frenzy ravenous to prefer
> pain to death, and hell to nothingness![48]

This role of spectator is taken by one of the most uniquely sketched and performed characters in Lang's *œuvre*, Countess Told (played by Gertrude Welcker). Known as 'Lady Passive' the countess haunts the gambling halls but never gambles herself. Instead she prefers to watch the 'passions released by gambling as reflected by others', seeking neither sympathy nor insight, but simply 'sensations of a very special kind to make life bearable' and counter her 'sluggish blood'. A connoisseur of her subjects, she draws the attention of von Wenk (the state's attorney investigating Mabuse) to the hysterical reaction of a Russian émigré woman, saying 'she is marvellous when she loses'. The blubbery woman's crying fit draws the countess to her feet, her own svelte, detached curiosity contrasting to the obese woman's uncontrolled sobs. But the countess indicates that her craving for 'intense living … the exceptional, the sensational' has never truly been satisfied. She also attends spiritualist seances for a thrill, but her detached amusement breaks up the circle of believers. She begins to doubt the existence of the sort of experience she seeks. Like the audience for popular films, Countess Told is seeking sensations, though with an aristocratic air. Such atomisation of time into hollow instants, empty or filled with a requisite stimulation, characterises the world Mabuse moves in.

Von Wenk and Mabuse each offer Countess Told alternatives to her boredom. They both involve abandoning her position as passive spectator of sensation and taking a more active role. Von Wenk offers the countess a role in his investigation, a move from watching *Spielers* (gamblers) to becoming a *Spieler* (an actress). He attracts her by describing his search for 'The Great Unknown' (explaining, 'I don't know the enemy I'm pursuing, I only know he exists'). However, when he persuades the countess to pretend to be a society woman arrested in a gambling raid placed in the same cell with Cara Carozza, Mabuse's mistress, in order to worm Mabuse's identity out of her, Countess Told becomes disgusted with her role of make-believe. Carozza describes her overwhelming passion for Mabuse. 'Who he is nobody knows! He is there, he exists! He stands over the city – huge like a tower – he is damnation and eternal bliss! He is the greatest man that ever lived! And he loved me!' Thrilled by this passionate panegyric, the countess suspects such devotion may be the 'intense life' she seeks. She refuses to aid von Wenk any further.

Mabuse offers the countess a different position within the game, not the *Spieler* who acts a role, but the player who manipulates the pieces. The countess complains to him about her role as passive spectator, 'that everything that can be seen from a car, from a box in the theatre or from a window is either disgusting or of little interest … it is at least boring'. Mabuse responds with his claim that, 'There is only one thing that is interesting any more. Playing with people and the destinies of people.' He scorns her invocation of the grand passion she learned of from Carozza (just as he has scorned Carozza – and the countess remains unaware that Mabuse was the great love Carozza described!) saying, 'There is no such thing as love – there is only desire – There is no fortune, only the Will-to-Power.' The *Spieler* Mabuse invokes is the game master, the author of the piece, the grand enunciator. To demonstrate the power of his will over the destiny of others he has the countess witness his experiment on her husband, seated at the table across the room playing cards. Focusing his gaze in close-up Mabuse looks off screen. In this last scene of Part I of *Dr. Mabuse, the Gambler*, Lang reverses the order of the first two shots of the film: showing first Mabuse's gaze, then a shot of cards in a player's hands. But the hands aren't Mabuse's, they are the Count Told's, who suddenly manipulates them as he deals. The cut joins the gaze of one character with the hands of another, as the will of Mabuse is carried out by the mesmerised Count Told. The count's unwitting card trick is seen by the other players and he is denounced as a cheat by angry guests, as he sits there bewildered by his own actions. The countess rises to her feet, once again the excited spectator of a gambling drama, but this time she faints into the arms of Mabuse who carries her off.

The Grand Enunciator and the Power of the Gaze

> I felt then as if the frightful gaze of the horrifying eyes were controlling my innermost being and taking complete possession of me.
>
> E. T. A. Hoffman, 'Der Magnetiseur'[49]

Lang interweaves Mabuse's identity as the *Spieler*, the player of the game of human destiny, with the theme of theatrical illusions both practically and imagistically. Besides Mabuse's disguises and role playing which literally make the whole world his stage, the film is filled with theatrical spectacles, usually erotic shows designed for the male viewer. These include: the nude *tableaux vivants* of the birth of Venus (Kettelhut described Lang's careful attention to the visual impact of this young Venus' pubic hair)[50] and Apollo pursuing Daphne as she turns into a laurel tree; la Carozza's high-kicking dance with carnival heads sporting huge phallic noses at the Folies Bergères; the woman in a tuxedo dancing to jazz in Palais Schramm; or the semi-nude dancer who descends from the ceiling in the Petite Casino to conceal the gambling tables. The focused gaze of desire is parodied during the *tableaux vivants* as a middle-aged man wipes his pince-nez to get a better look, before his wife snatches them off his nose. But it is Mabuse at this same nightclub who introduces the true power of the gaze as he picks up his opera glasses to examine, not Carozza on the stage, but Edgar Hull in the audience.

Lang gives Mabuse the first marked point of view shot of this scene, coming into focus and masked to indicate a view through opera glasses. The camera pans slightly and rests on Hull, an iris closing in to frame him in a circular vignette. Hull watches the erotic spectacle on the stage (as Carozza loses her dress), but Mabuse's gaze remains fixed on the young millionaire. While Carozza's spectacle is given tumultuous applause from the audience, including Hull, Lang cuts into a close-up of Mabuse staring directly at the camera. Although Mabuse's look at his underlings earlier in the film has often been withering, this is the first portrayal of the occult powers of his vision, his ability to hypnotise victims at a distance, bend them to his will through a focused stare. Lang uses the device of the look at the camera, partly to indicate the intensity of this look, its terrifying force, but also, I would maintain, as an extra-diegetic claim to power, like the other hubristic or metaphysical enunciator characters in Lang's silent films, Death in *Der müde Tod*, Kriemhild in *Kriemhild's Revenge*, the two Marias, Rotwang and Fredersen in *Metropolis* and Haghi still to come in *Spies*. By his direct gaze, Mabuse stakes a claim over the visual apparatus of the film and its narrative destiny.

Mabuse's gaze operates in two ways. The first method, which creeps up on its victim unaware from the back, he uses here on Hull and, later, at the Tolds' soirée, to force the count to cheat. The gaze operates as a ray of power coming from Mabuse's eye and hitting its victim in the back of his head (both Hull and Told reach back and hold the back of their necks when they feel its influence). The second mode calls on all of Lang's visual flair, and involves the figure of the shot/reverse shot, as Mabuse looks directly into the eyes of his victim and the victim receives his gaze. This first appears when Mabuse, disguised as Hugo Balling, plays cards with Hull in the Incognito club. Lang shows Hull's viewpoint: his own hand of cards in the foreground, Balling staring towards him from the background. Lang then reverses the angle and shows Hull holding his cards from Balling's viewpoint. Cut back to Balling, now framed more closely, still staring. Reverse angle to Hull as he slowly puts down his cards, declares he has lost (although we saw he had the winning cards) and stares blankly into the camera.

The real visual pyrotechnics come when Mabuse, disguised as the Dutch professor, encounters States' attorney von Wenk (also in disguise) at the club, Andalusia. Mabuse's gaze is again associated with an optical device, a pair of antique spectacles which he unfolds and flashes in von Wenk's direction, attracting his attention (Mabuse's grotesque makeup in this sequence and the spectacles lead one to associate the figure with E.T.A. Hoffmann's demonic oculist Coppelius from 'The Sandman'). Lang cuts between von Wenk and close-ups of the glittering spectacles as Mabuse plays with them, the closer framings and a masking around the glasses endowing them with a sense of power. Von Wenk's eyes flutter, as if he were fighting off sleep, and he swallows hard, his eyes becoming fixed on the camera. In reverse angle, Mabuse holds the spectacles and likewise looks at the camera. In response to von Wenk's question, Mabuse answers that these are Chinese spectacles from Tsi-Nan-Fu.

The state's attorney seems to shake off Mabuse's influence, and the game begins. However, in the wide shot of von Wenk arranging his money, black masking closes in around him and Lang cuts to an extreme close-up of Mabuse's eyes also surrounded by darkness and dramatically lit from one side. The mysterious words *Tsi-Nan-Fu* are repeated in an intertitle. Von Wenk takes his cards with a laboured movement, as if going into a trance. A point of view shot shows his cards, but a dissolve makes the same mysterious words appear on them: *Tsi-Nan-Fu*. An extraordinary shot follows. We see Mabuse across the table, apparently from von Wenk's point of view, but the space of the table seems to have changed. Mabuse and his cohorts seem far away a product both of a wide angle lens and most likely an actual greater distance than in previous shots, allowing for the trick camera movement that follows. A combination of a lighting change and dark masking wreathes everything in the frame in obscurity – except Mabuse's head which sharpens in illumination and seems to float uncannily in a black void. This disembodied head, abstracted from all space, seems to move towards the camera, or to enlarge, its eyes fixed on the lens (Lang has tracked in towards Mabuse here, although the elimination of surrounding space makes the motion ambiguous: arc wc arc moving forward, or is the head rushing towards us, or even simply enlarging?). Finally the face with its unswerving, baleful eye fills the entire screen, as its mouth grimaces, demanding (via an intertitle) that von Wenk take the next card. This trick shot expresses all the power Lang places in Mabuse's gaze. It lunges towards the character and towards the audience, its thrust and size bearing down on us with a hypnotic willpower, expressing a command. The camera's movement follows the trajectory of the gaze, giving it an almost ejaculatory power.

Rather than simply returning to a reverse angle of von Wenk fighting off this mystical influence, Lang uses another trick shot. Shot from above (an angle which will have increasing importance in Lang's visual vocabulary, and already used in the bank robbery in *Spiders*) von Wenk reaches to turns his cards over, but beneath them the magical words *Tsi-Nan-Fu* sparkle. He vainly tries to cover them with the

cards. The battle of wills continues in shot/reverse shot, Mabuse continuing to stare at the camera in close-up, widening his eyes demonically as he demands again that von Wenk take a card. Von Wenk, however, refuses and in reverse angle we see Mabuse nearly collapse from this failure. As his head falls forward, the black iris around him opens, expressing his loss of concentration, and cementing the link between Mabuse's powers and the devices of the cinema, so many of which – lighting, framing, masking, editing, camera movement – have been associated with his hypnotic power in this brief sequence.

Lang's alignment of the power of cinema with hypnosis pulls in a broader discourse on the nature of film, one intimately linked with the Film Reform movement in Germany and with concerns about the effects of this new medium. Hypnosis and mesmerism, introduced as topics allied with occult sciences at the end of the eighteenth century, had by the beginning of the twentieth become the basis for a broad social theory based on the underlying idea of 'suggestion', the term introduced by Hippolyte Bernheim to explain the effect attributed to hypnosis. European concern about the gains of democracy and the growth of mass culture often took the form of a new 'psychology of crowds', and theorists such as Gustave LeBon and Gabriel Tarde claimed that the 'crowd' or the masses were especially susceptible to the power of 'suggestion', a sort of hypnosis that could have social and even political effects. The new medium of the cinema was eyed with suspicion as a means of this sort of suggestion, ranging from its influence on impressionable children who would imitate the criminal actions they saw in sensation-films, to a long-lasting (surviving in some ways in contemporary French metapsychologies of the cinema) claim that cinema itself had hypnotic powers. From nearly the first exhibitions of cinema, when a New York journalist in 1896 described audiences at motion pictures as sitting 'spellbound in darkness', hypnosis has been attached to the new medium as a metaphor (and sometimes as an actual explanatory system).[51] French film theorist Raymond Bellour, citing Lang's Mabuse films as a major source, has been one of the main proponents of the homogeneity between hypnosis and cinema.[52] My interest lies less in asserting the validity of this comparison as metapsychology than in observing the work it does in Lang's film and the sources Lang draws upon.

The main comparison the Film Reformers (and, indeed, later theorists) made between cinema and hypnosis focused on the situation of the film viewer. The darkness of the theatre, the immobility of the viewer and, most of all, the visual fascination and concentration of a flickering light-filled image recalled one method of hypnosis (according to L. Loewenfeld's classic German text book from 1901, *Der Hypnotismus*, 'the oldest and commonest' method), visual fixation on 'seductively glittering devices'.[53] Similar descriptions of film viewing were used by the surrealists to compare it to dreaming, and in the 1970s to explain the cinematographic apparatus's place in the 'ideological state apparatus' manufacturing willing subjects for ideologies. The Dutch professor's manipulation of his Chinese spectacles may be intended as a visual fascination of this sort, as is the faceted crystal Sandor Weltmann holds before von Wenk.

For the most part Lang emphasises the power of Mabuse's gaze, rather than the visual fascination of his victims (some of whom, like Hull in the theatre, or Count Told at his soirée, don't even make visual contact with their hypnotist). But Lang draws strong connections between Mabuse's gaze and the role of spectatorship (Hull, for instance, may not see Mabuse at the Folies Bergères, but is visually enthralled by Carozza's performance at that moment). The most powerful demonstration of the relationship between spectatorship and hypnosis comes with one of Mabuse's final avatars, the psychic performer Sandor Weltmann.

Mabuse advises von Wenk to attend Weltmann's performance as a demonstration of the dark powers of the will. The performance takes place in a conventional theatre with Weltmann performing within a proscenium stage. He announces as his

first demonstration an experiment in mass suggestion. Weltmann moves to the
side, closes his eyes and concentrates. Through an overlap-dissolve, a desert landscape appears on the stage's back curtain. From the depths of the landscape an Arabian caravan emerges, crossing over the stage and descending into the audience
(horses, camels and all), parading down the central aisle, to the astonishment of the
spectators. Then, Sandor makes a sudden sweep of his arm, and the caravan vanishes, greeted by enthusiastic applause.

In this sequence Lang presents Mabuse as an embodied visual illusion apparatus.
The spectacle he conjures appears as sort of super-cinema, appearing first on the
curtain and then expanding into three dimensional haptic space. The *mise-en-
abîme* of the audience perceiving and applauding Weltmann's mini-movie and the
audience we constitute as we watch Lang's film becomes an emblem for the issues
Lang raises about enunciation in this film. Sandor controls the gaze, both his own
and that of his victims. Can he claim, in some sense, to control the movie we are
watching? If I understand Bellour's claim correctly, he sees Mabuse as an illustration of the apparatus theory (articulated in the 1970s in similar ways by Christian
Metz and Baudry) of the cinema which sees film as gaining power over its viewers
through enforcing a process of psychological regression to a state of visual hallucination.[54] Lang would have been familiar with a simpler version of this analogy
through the jeremiads of the Film Reformers. But it seems to me that rather than
simply embracing the identification of Mabuse with the cinematic apparatus, Lang
engages it dialectically, both as a film-maker and as a story-teller. Sandor's performance is a high point of Mabuse's power, his identification with the actual powers
of the film he exists within. He presents himself as the creator and master of his
world. But I would claim Lang questions this complete control and that the remainder of the film enacts its dialectical reversal. Lang's drama of vision remains more
dialectical than the pure enthralment of the spectator. Mabuse's mastery of the Destiny-machine has taken many forms, all of them manipulating the 'empty' forms of
modernity: the disembedded co-ordination of space and time; the fluctuations of
the money economy; and the gamblers' surrender to the mechanics of desire. He
now claims the apparatus of cinema itself. But the other side of the Langian system,
the visionary scene, still has a role to play.

The first appearance of a classically Langian visionary scene, in which a character
perceives the actions of the Destiny-machine beneath a concealing surface, comes
in the midst of Weltmann's performance and seems to be immediately closed down.
Having invited von Wenk onto the stage for a demonstration, Weltmann holds a
crystal before him and repeats the magical phrase '*Tsi-Nan-Fu*'. The words first jog
a flashback to the gaming tables of the Andalusia, then Lang cuts to a close-up of
Weltmann facing the camera. In a seamless overlap-dissolve Weltmann's wig and
beard dissolve into the makeup of the Dutch professor, and then, his gaze ever
closer to the camera lens, we see the slightly smirking face of the psychiatrist
Mabuse. In an intertitle von Wenk stutters, attempting to vocalise his sudden discovery: 'It's Doctor – Doctor – Ma –'. Mabuse makes a pass over von Wenk's brow
rendering him somnabulistically compliant.

Mabuse now brandishes the envelope containing the command he is forcing his
enemy to follow. At a perilous moment of visionary insight and discovery, Mabuse
re-establishes control with the script he has written for von Wenk to enact: to drive
his car at high speed over a cliff. This command is also accompanied by a mysterious word: 'Melior', and as von Wenk drives maniacally towards his doom, the word
precedes his automobile and seems to draw him on. Von Wenk's men pursue him

and pull him from his car, as the driverless vehicle plunges over the cliff, the machine fulfilling Mabuse's command. Rescued in a sensation-drama cliffhanger, von Wenk informs his men of the insight he gained, the identity of Dr. Mabuse.

Playing with Time

> *Remember!* Time, that tireless gambler, wins on every turn of
> the wheel: that is the law. The daylight fades … *Remember!*
> Night comes on: the pit is thirsty and the sands run out …
> Baudelaire, 'The Clock'[55]

Fittingly, the last day at Mabuse's hideout includes a close-up of an alarm clock awakening his henchmen. But as they head outdoors they find the street filled with police. Alerted, Mabuse looks out the second-storey window and from a high angle (that allows Lang again to stress the topographical geometry), he sees a semi-circular arc of police. As the alarm clock at the beginning of this last sequence announces that Mabuse's time is up, in symmetry to the opening sequence, a phone call now shows that his space has become utterly circumscribed. As Mabuse orders the barricading of the windows and begins to burn incriminating documents, a middle-aged woman leads von Wenk to a telephone in a shop on Mabuse's block. Lang cuts to a woman switchboard-operator making the connection. Mabuse looks over at the telephone and answers it. In medium close-up we see von Wenk speaking on the phone, then we cut to Mabuse seeming aghast at this technological invasion of his domain. Lang cuts between the two ends of the telephone line as von Wenk demands Mabuse's surrender and Mabuse laughs in scorn, declaring the autonomy on which his power rests: (through an intertitle) 'I feel here like a state within a state with which I have been in a state of war for a long time!' When Mabuse hangs up on his caller, we see von Wenk jiggling the receiver and we return to the switchboard-operator who tries vainly to restore the connection. Von Wenk hangs up angrily. But if Mabuse asserts his independence over the phone by severing the connection, this action nevertheless announces his downfall. The technological web no longer responds to his desires, but carries messages he tries to refuse.

The ensuing battle between Mabuse's gang barricaded in his apartment and the forces of the state most certainly set the model for later American gangster films (Hawks's *Scarface* in particular), but it more fully expresses a German context. Mabuse's claim to be a state within a state not only expresses his megalomania but also the fragmentation of power, especially the control of force and violence in Germany after the war. The images of warfare in the city streets, especially when the police force gives way to the military armed with grenades, certainly recall the battles between Freikorps and revolutionaries in various German cities. These, among the most realistic images in a film often classed as 'Expressionist', strongly support Anton Kaes's claim that for the Weimar cinema, as for Germany generally, the image of the war was a traumatically repeated and never resolved theme.[56]

His henchmen dying, his stronghold invaded by troops, Mabuse escapes through a subterranean passageway, one of his secret networks through the city. As in *Spiders,* this subterranean corridor demonstrates his knowledge of the city's inner workings, what Rosalind Williams calls 'the substructure of modern life'.[57] However, the image of Mabuse, his head bandaged, slogging through a tunnel filled with sewer water, does not express mastery, but a desperate man, his surface empire crumbling, a sewer rat escaping as best he can. His escape route leads to the most hidden part of his domain, the secret counterfeiting operation manned by blind workers. As Mabuse emerges from the trapdoor, Lang cuts to a reaction shot of the blind, disturbed by this unaccustomed noise, rising from their work and casting their sightless eyes towards Mabuse. Mabuse himself seems startled by their presence and drops the trapdoor. A close-up of the reverse side of this door shows its self-locking mechanism as its bolt shoots into place. Mabuse's henchmen had explained earlier that, when locked, there is no way to open this door from above.

The locked door seals Mabuse's fate, entrapping him in this small dungeon, reducing the reach of his empire to a small underground space, the kingdom of the blind. The cutaway to the lock closing provides an emblematic image of the Destiny-machine, no longer at Mabuse's beck and call, following its own implacable rules. Why does Mabuse drop the door? Clearly this is a reverse of *deus ex machina*, the plot machinery now working to entrap and destroy its former master. But Mabuse's reaction to the blind, causing him to forget how his own mechanism works, spawns associations as well. Mabuse's power has been the power of the gaze, both his own occult visual powers to compel others by focusing his stare and the ability to attract the gaze of others, to fascinate them as a performer. Here he confronts the image of lack, of the sightless, whose absence of sight he has previously exploited. Although the meek body language of the blind as they hesitatingly retreat from Mabuse into a corner shows they pose no physical threat to him, they confront him with an image of absolute powerlessness, the inverse of his former glory. They cannot see, and he cannot fascinate them.

Mabuse scurries about the room trying the doors he has himself made impregnable. Like later Lang characters caught in locked rooms, Beckert in *M* and Kent and Lilli in *The Testament of Dr. Mabuse*, he tries his pocket-knife on the locked door. He thinks for a moment of his gang members, Hawasch and Fine, killed in the police raid, who had access to this secret factory and can no longer aid him. Then, fully aware of his impotence, Mabuse perceives the surrounding space in a new way. Whereas previously the whole world seemed to respond to his will, now his last domain becomes populated by spectres of his own imagination. Recalling the death of his underlings seems to summon up visions of those Mabuse himself had killed, who appear as black-habited, white-faced transparent phantoms looming before him in every corner of the room. First Edgar Hull appears, then vanishes; then, in another spot (each figure given via Mabuse's point of view), Pesch, the henchman he had killed after his arrest; then Count Told, holding up a playing card. A phantom of Cara Carozza walks towards Mabuse, hands outstretched. Mabuse huddles in a corner more terrified than his blind workers who creep towards him.

Lang has intercut Mabuse's entrapment with von Wenk's interrogation of gang members Spoerri and George. Spoerri finally breaks and tells von Wenk about the secret counterfeiting plant, while Mabuse's fatal influence continues as George hangs himself in his cell. As George tosses his suspender around the bars of his cell window to form a noose, Lang cuts to Mabuse cowering before his blind employees, an overlap-dissolve transforming them into his black-clothed victims. Hull and Told beckon him toward a table for one last game of cards. Hull hands him the cards and Mabuse shuffles and deals. When he shows his hand, Told points his finger and declares 'Cheat!'

Mabuse rises in anger and the wraiths vanish suddenly like the illusions in Weltmann's mental theatre. We are at the high point of Mabuse's madness as he stares into the empty space that his vision had just filled with the victims of his own crimes. Gathering the counterfeit bills from the table, in a fit of manic joy he tosses them in the air around him surrounding himself with a shower of worthless paper, the riches of his counterfeit kingdom. But then his face contorts in horror and he looks over his shoulder. We see from his point of view a large wheel-like shape with spokes radiating from a centre, presumably part of the printing press for the counterfeit bills. In a direct anticipation of the Moloch vision in *Metropolis*, the wheel takes on the face of a fiend with glowing eyes and then (through overlap-dissolve again) a gnashing maw with claw-like, snapping arms.

Mabuse backs away from this vision dominating the background of the shot, as he falls prostrate in the foreground on the table covered with counterfeit bills. The machines flanking either side of the devouring sun-faced monster also transform into threatening entities. Each possesses glowing eyes, while the figure on the right takes on a human form with huge muscular arms and a scaled back and begins to rock up and down. Mabuse collapses to the floor and we see him burrowing into a heap of false money, hiding his face as he crumbles the paper around him. The police arrive, led by von Wenk opening the door with the key Spoerri had identified. Before they enter the cellar an intertitle proclaims: 'The Man who had been Mabuse'. This abject figure sits on the floor, his mouth slack, folding his false currency and staring at the camera with dull, sightless eyes. He grabs the bills without looking at them, as if blind (one more masquerade to avoid capture? or the ultimate loss of his visual power?). Von Wenk and another officer raise him to his feet as he gathers a heap of counterfeit money to his chest desperately. As they lead him out, the bills fall from his hands one by one. An iris closes over Mabuse being led up the stairs, to end the film.

The last scene of *Dr. Mabuse, the Gambler* functions like an extended visionary scene, revealing to Mabuse the true nature of his power. In contrast to most of the

visionary scenes in the allegorical films, this one is coded as madness. It resembles in many ways the extraordinary scene where Count Told wanders his apartments alone pursued by his doubles (or quadruples) who likewise sit down at a table with him for one last card game. But Mabuse's vision expresses more than his subjective state, and Lang frequently associated visionary scenes with unusual mental states, dreams, and hypnosis, for example. What sets them apart, however, from a pure hallucination like Told's is their revelatory role, unmasking the forces actually operating in the films. Mabuse discovers several things in his madness. First, that he has surrounded himself with the dead, as both foes and allies whom he has killed confront him. Second, he realises his own impotence, his inability now to make anything work for him; his own mechanism entraps him, his money is valueless, his crimes haunt, rather than exalt, him. The vision of the demonic machine poses another literal image of the Destiny-machine, threatening and devouring and subject to no master other than its own repetitive actions, titanic energy and insatiable demand.

This is the apparatus that Mabuse believed he had mastered in all its forms: the people whose destinies he played with; the false money he manipulated; the engines of destruction he devised – even the visual illusions he seemed to summon up for others. All these things now confront him and declare their independence from him. He is their subject now, no longer their enunciator. The power in his eyes is extinguished and his final identity mimes that of his most abject labourers, the blind, with shaking hands, unfocused gaze and repetitive motions. The man who could manipulate and transform his identity ends up without one – the man who *had been* Mabuse. He is now restricted to the *tabula rasa* that underlay all his identities, the blank paper awaiting the counterfeit stamp. His power finished, the film ends precipitously. The iris which closes it no longer expresses Mabuse's focused gaze or power of enunciation. He is led haltingly out of the film.

5

Haghi

The Evil Genius/*Mauvais génie*

> I have not resisted the introduction of masks, for the more
> masks there are one on top of the other, all the more fun it is
> to pull them off one after the other down to the penultimate
> satirical one, the Hippocratic and the last fixed one, which
> no longer laughs or cries – the skull, hairless fore and aft,
> with which the tragicomedian departs in the end.
> *The Night Watches of Bonaventura*[1]

Lang told Lotte Eisner that *Dr. Mabuse, the Gambler* had originally opened with a
brief documentary prologue:

> a brief breathless montage of scenes of the Spartacus uprising, the murder of
> Rathenau, the Kapp putsch and other violent moments of recent history. Lang
> maintains that when it first opened this sequence was intact. [...] Originally, Lang
> recalls, the opening montage was linked to [the first] scene by two titles: the first,

WHO IS BEHIND ALL THIS?
The second title, a single word which rushed towards the spectator, growing and
growing until it filled the entire screen:
                I[2]

Certain details of the description cause me to doubt this claim. The assassination of
Rathenau by members of the Freikorps, for instance, took place two months after
the Berlin premiere of the first part of *Dr. Mabuse, the Gambler*. Of course, Lang
could have forgotten the details (it could have been the murder of Matthias
Erzberger in 1921 by Freikorps members that he intended, for instance), but the
confused political thinking of the prologue as described – attributing workers'
uprisings, attempted military coups and right-wing political murders all to the
same source – would seem an example of the worst sort of political obscurantism.
Even the more likely claim by Erich Pommer that Mabuse was modelled on a
Spartacist[3] (which would fit in with Mabuse denouncing von Wenk as a 'god-
damned blood hound', the term Noske had claimed for himself in suppressing the
Spartacist revolt)[4] has the virtue of clarity, even of a horrific sort, over such non-
political thinking.

But I think it is more likely that Lang was mis-remembering the opening of his
1928 film *Spies*. As Nicole Brenez has pointed out, *Spies* also opens with a 'breathless
montage', not of actualities but of a series of crimes – thefts of secret documents and
murders – the frenzied responses of the police and other agents, and ends with a
police officer looking towards the camera and declaring 'Good God, who is at the
bottom of all of this?'[5] In the original German version this is followed directly by a
shot of Haghi looking towards the camera and declaring 'I am.'[6] In many ways *Spies*
will directly develop the master criminal/grand enunciator introduced in *Dr.
Mabuse, the Gambler*, including casting the actor who had played Mabuse, Rudolph
Klein-Rogge, in the part of Haghi. But *Spies* also poses a dialectical response to the
previous film with a number of scenes simultaneously striking in their similarities
and remarkable in their reversals.

Film style changed a great deal in the five years between *Dr. Mabuse, the Gambler*
and *Spies* and Lang seems in many ways anxious to re-invent his own style in this
film. The film Lang had to make everyone forget was *Metropolis* whose enormous
scope had nearly bankrupted Ufa, and whose grand pretensions had left most
reviewers (and apparently audiences) cold. Bailing out of Ufa, Lang set up his own
production company, Fritz Lang Film GmbH, which would still release through Ufa.
As its first production, *Spies* seems to cast off the baggage of the super-film: no grand
elaborate sets, a story rooted in contemporary events, little overt stylisation or allegorical tableaux, a city that was a recognisable location with both detailed realistic
sets and even location shooting. Panchromatic film stock seems to be used more frequently here, producing a broader scale of grey tones and rendering the faces (and
the makeup) of characters more naturalistic. Further, Lang begins in this film to
favour much closer framing and builds up scenes through fragments rather than the
broader, more architectural, long shots of his earlier films. Lang frames more dar-
ingly here and off screen space becomes a major player in his style. Huyssen described
the tension within *Metropolis* between Expressionist and *Neue Sachlichkeit* themes
and styles.[7] The tension is still visible in *Spies* (with a few scenes drawing overtly on
Expressionist elements, such as Matsumoto's vision of the murdered couriers), but
the new sobriety or objectivity of the later style dominates. *Spies* stages its intrigues
within a hard-edged world dominated by the pursuit of information and the

rhythms of the machines, characterised more by speed, mobility and precision than the massive heaviness of the machines in *Metropolis*.

Haghi's retooling of the Mabuse persona displays this increased simplification and even de-dramatisation. Mabuse's appearance in the first scene as a man nearly immobile in the centre of the technological web, directing his criminal enterprises from his desk like a modern executive, becomes the dominant image of Haghi, who sits through most of the film at his modernist Bauhaus-like desk, fitted with a series of push-buttons, a large transparent clock and fluorescent lights. Communicating through intercom, telephones and pneumatic tubes, he is also confined to a wheelchair, seemingly paralysed, yet able to exert his power over people's destinies nonetheless. Haghi's role as business executive operates as more than a simple metaphor or momentary disguise. Like Joh Fredersen of *Metropolis*, Haghi oversees a large operation, the Haghi Bank. The Haghi Bank functions as another of Lang's disguised and duplicitous spaces: housing both a public bank and – hidden behind secret walls and passageways – a cell of spies. Lang has claimed this aspect of the film was based on the Soviet trade legation ARCOS in London in the 20s which was revealed to be a front for spies.[8] The idea of substituting a commercial bank for a Soviet trade delegation recalls the blurring of political orientation found in Lang's supposed *Mabuse* prologue, but it also ties Haghi's plot of world domination closer to Mabuse's dark mirror of capitalism than to international relations. Haghi's proclaimed desire to control the world recalls Mabuse's claim to be a 'state within a state in a state of war', a tyranny based on personal power rather than international politics.

In place of Mabuse's score of kaleidoscopic disguises, Haghi maintains a limited, though powerful, control over his appearance. His primary disguise mirrors the camouflaged nature of both his enterprise and the building which shelters it. At his desk in his secret office, concealed behind mechanical sliding doors, Haghi dresses entirely in black, his dark hair combed in sharp angles, his goatee taking on a devilish air (which Lang claims was based on Trotsky's and Brenez finds similar to Lenin's),[9] while his sudden movements and gestures and his fiery eyes bespeak rapacity and energy. But when his faithful mute nurse wheels him into his other more old-fashioned public office, his beard, moustache and temples are greying and he wears a suit and tie. The interior secret spaces of the Haghi Bank, where the spies live and work, look stripped-down and functional, dominated by one of the few monumental sets in this film, a multi-level, crisscrossing metallic stairwell which creates a Piranesian space of repetitive, entrapping geometry. It is a space made-up of connecting spaces, stairways, doorways and corridors, swarming with activity, machine-like in its hard-edged structure and regulated movement. Its windowless, confined oppression recalls the workers' spaces of *Metropolis*, adding a new bounded claustrophobic aspect to Lang's spaces which previously (as with the wall in *Der müde Tod*, the palaces of the Burgundians or of Etzel) favoured unbounded extension.

Haghi's other disguised identity folds in on itself. As Agent 719 (who also performs as the variety theatre clown, Nemo), he acts as a double agent within the government's Secret Service. Here Haghi's game with identity becomes most complex. As a stage performer whose act forms the finale of the film, Nemo directly recalls Sandor Weltmann, the hypnotist and master of illusions in *Dr. Mabuse, the Gambler*. However, when I discuss Nemo's performance at the end of this chapter, I will note its dialectical reversals of Weltmann's performance. A reversal in name already announces the reversal in conception: 'Man of the world' the literal translation of the last name, 'Weltmann', announces mastery, while the first name, 'Sandor', a form of Alexander, doubles the reference, evoking the world conqueror. The name emblazons Mabuse's ego and megalomania. But 'Nemo'– Latin for 'no-one' – evokes the flip side of Mabuse's ability to be anyone – the fact that he is *no-one*, merely a *tabula rasa* awaiting the imprint of a false identity.

Haghi's ploy of deceiving the Secret Service through his cunning use of the persona of Nemo invokes the archetypal figure of cunning and deception in the western tradition, Odysseus. In order to escape from the Cyclops Polyphemus, Odysseus exploits the ambiguity of his name which can also sound like 'Udeis' – No-one. Adorno and Horkheimer analyse Odysseus as the archetype of the bourgeois self, estranged from nature, triumphing through deception and cunning. His word play exemplifies the formalism of bourgeois society, in which any individual fits into a slot determined by the laws of language and contract.[10] If Mabuse encounters the emptiness of his counterfeit identity in his madness at the end of the film, it would seem Haghi counts upon and exploits it from the beginning.

There is undoubtedly another reference contained in this name, and Lang's love of adventure literature makes it hard to ignore: Jules Verne's Captain Nemo, the ambiguous hero/villain of *Twenty Thousand Leagues under the Sea*. Nemo carries out a terrorist campaign against the civilised world from the subterranean (or rather sub-aquatic) base of his technological marvel, the submarine *Nautilus*. Captain Nemo's tyranny, his mastery of technology, his mysterious identity and the war he wages against the reigning political powers of the earth, all relate him to Lang's master criminals. In his final appearance, in Verne's *The Mysterious Island*, Nemo is revealed to be the Indian Prince Dakkar, leader of the Sepoy rebellion, whose hatred of British imperialism eventually becomes a hatred of the entire modern world, using his genius for advanced technology to fight modernity with its own tools.

Whatever the associations Lang and/or Harbou counted on in adopting this name, the persona of Nemo provides a perfect pivot for the revision Haghi brings to the Mabuse archetype. *Dr. Mabuse, the Gambler* opens with the emblems of Mabuse's control over identity, the cards of identity held in the gambler's hand. A more ambiguous shot buried towards the end of *Spies* – Haghi sitting before his dressing room mirror putting on his Nemo makeup – expresses his gambit with identity. Mabuse slips disguises on and off as the situation demands. The false identity cards he holds delineate the opposition between his true face, his actual identity as master organiser and authority, and the masks he assumes. When Nemo sits before the mirror in the penultimate scene of the film, we do not immediately recognise the face we see. Unlike Mabuse, Haghi does not possess a stable face behind the mask. The face we have assumed to be his own, the physiognomy he displays in his private office – the devil's peaked hair and dark goatee – turns out to be just one more disguise. His most effective disguise, that of double agent 719, employs no makeup, no moustache or goatee, no dramatic wig. When Lang presents Agent 719 conferring with Jason, the head of the Secret Service, he films him from behind, a device which simultaneously cheats by withholding a good view of him from the audience, but also indicates something mysterious about the man (and even points towards his identity as Haghi, the character most frequently filmed from the back).

Nemo-Haghi-719 sits before the mirror preparing his makeup before his final and fatal performance on stage. The scene recalls a previous scene in which Jason and Donald Tremaine (the film's hero and crack Secret Service agent) meet with Agent 719 in the same dressing room. Introduced by a shot of posters announcing the clown Nemo, the earlier scene presented Haghi examining himself carefully in the mirror as he supplied the finishing touches to his already made-up face, turning and speaking to Jason and Tremaine. Lang relishes the irony of the scene: the man the agents are pursuing sits before them, disguising himself beneath their gaze. He is also arranging Tremaine's death, handing him the tickets he has reserved for him in the train compartment he plans to destroy in an elaborately managed train wreck. Haghi manipulates appearances here perhaps even more elegantly than Mabuse. But again the differences define the re-orientation of this film. In *Mabuse* Lang immediately lets us in on the trick: we see Mabuse donning his disguises from the opening, so that we always know he is behind the manipulation. In this scene, the audience can only appreciate the irony of Agent 719's identity in retrospect. We do not learn he is Haghi until nearly the end of the film. The donning of makeup recalls the revelations in *Dr. Mabuse, the Gambler*, but here the hidden identity remains opaque: we are not given the true face behind the mask. The narration in *Spies* conceals more from the audience; in David Bordwell's terms, it is less communicative.[11]

We learn Haghi's identity as Nemo only in this second scene before the mirror near the end of the film. Whereas the earlier scene with the Secret Service agents began with the posters of Nemo, this sequence cuts from a 'Wanted' poster for Haghi. The portrait is a double one, showing Haghi's face with and without his goatee and moustache. Haghi's bare face, never seen before in the film, has an uncannily naked quality, as if stripped of power, while the facial hair on its *doppelgänger* seems like graffiti drawn on by a mischievous boy. Lang cuts to Haghi, filmed from the back once more, but the mirror reflection shows his face. He reads the newspaper with the 'Wanted' announcement in it, lowers it and examines his reflection with a critical air, scrutinising it, as an artist might a blank canvas. Flanking his reflection on the right, taped to the mirror, are two drawings of Nemo's clown makeup. Haghi crushes the newspaper into a ball, tosses it over his shoulder and begins applying makeup. Elegantly, Lang resolves the final enigma of the film, the common identity of Agent 719, Nemo and Haghi, letting the audience into the secret a scene before Tremaine and Jason discover it. The clown's makeup, a mask we watch Haghi himself create as a final desperate attempt at escape, reveals the vulnerability of Haghi's play with identity more than his control. Rather than the winning hand, disguise now offers Haghi only a way to efface his newly publicised face with the garish makeup of a fool. Appropriately, a publicity photo for the film shows Lang himself applying the Nemo makeup to the face of actor Klein-Rogge.[12]

It is Haghi's role as master criminal, master of technology and organisation, and as grand enunciator which supplies a sense of *déjà vu* to this film, in spite of its many canny inversions of the Mabuse figure. As Mabuse *redivivus*, Haghi claims the same degree of control over other characters that his predecessor did and likewise encounters a similar downfall. The master criminal's role as enunciator becomes more refined in this film. Several traits create the figure of enunciator in Lang's cinema. First, on the diegetic level, such figures assert control over events and people, so that they operate as motive, cause, author, stage manager and director of the main plot of the film. But this control over the events of the film bleeds over into a paradoxical assertion of control over the film and its visual presentation itself. The first and most powerful of these gestures comes from the look directly at the camera. Lang uses this technique in a variety of situations, expressing, at least, the shock and intensity of effect that comes from this generally tabooed look. But in most cases it asserts the character's power. This power can be exerted over other characters, as in the hypnosis sequences in *Dr. Mabuse, the Gambler*. But the shock effect of these same sequences comes from paradoxically placing the viewer in the character's position, as if Mabuse's penetrating gaze and control were directed at the audience as well. As Raymond Bellour claims in his seminal article 'Le regard de Haghi' (The Look of Haghi):

> It seems that Haghi looks at me. He, the 'master spy', spies me out, observes me, nails me in my seat. Me? Who? The spectator. But how can it happen that Haghi becomes my spectator?[13]

The second major cinematic technique of the grand enunciator comes with a seeming control over the editing of the film, as if the cuts from shot to shot responded to the master criminal's will. This is introduced in *Dr. Mabuse, the Gambler*, but taken further in *Spies*. In the opening robbery of *Dr. Mabuse, the Gambler* the parallel editing expresses Mabuse's precise control and planning and seems an extension of his power. Similarly, a cut to Mabuse often displays his role in an affair, tracing cause to effect. When the police official reports to von Wenk that Mabuse's accomplice Pesch has just been assassinated en route to the prison after a mob led by an agitator stopped the prison van, the official declares, 'Heaven only knows who incited those people!' As if in answer to the question, we cut to an irised shot of Mabuse taking off his disguise as the political rabble-rouser. Like the superimposition of Mabuse's face over the stock exchange floor, these cuts tie Mabuse to events as their author and prime mover, the man behind it all.

Spies cuts back to Haghi in an even more systematic manner, creating an editing logic which goes beyond tracing effects to their cause. When Haghi declares he is behind all of the events of the opening, he seems to respond to the police official's question. He assumes an omniscience that only the film's narration can have. The cuts to Haghi from Jellusic's suicide, or from Tremaine's first scene at the Secret Service office, as he examines the photographs he has had taken of the agent surreptitiously, indicate that Haghi sees all, not only through his agents but, as it were, through the editing. His preternatural visual acuity, stressed by his look at the camera in several of these shots, combines with the editing here, as if he saw across the cuts to distant places, spying out his victims.

The intensity of Mabuse's gaze at the camera conveys his supernatural powers of hypnotic suggestion, his ability to bend others to do his bidding through the focused power of his will. Haghi's gaze at the camera plays a more abstract role. Often such shots are isolated; he looks out from the screen rather than at another character, the reverse angle of his gaze not given. Haghi's gaze floats in the abstracted space of the close-up and the interstices of crosscutting between scenes. His look at the camera, rather than conveying the literal power of his gaze (like Mabuse's mesmerism), becomes an emblem of his control, his omniscience, his plotting, his authorship. Haghi arranges more intricate dramas for his victims than did Mabuse, dramas which he seems simultaneously to direct and take delight in witnessing. Haghi's authorship in *Spies*, his control over people's destinies, plays out as theatre even more explicitly than Mabuse's similar games did in the earlier film. Bellour hesitates to describe Haghi as the narrator of the film, and this is certainly proper literally, and semiotically.[14] Instead he describes him as 'Less the hero of the film than its evil demon'.[15] The phrase he uses here – *malin génie* – is undoubtedly intended to recall the *mauvais génie* of the end of the first of Descartes' *Meditations on First Philosophy*, the ultimate paranoid vision of Western metaphysics:

... some malicious demon [*mauvais génie* in Descartes's French version; *genium malignum* in the Latin] of the utmost power and cunning, has employed all his energies to deceive me: I shall think that the sky, the air, the earth, colours, shapes, sounds, and all external things are merely the delusions of dreams, which he has devised to ensnare for my judgement.[16]

Descartes' *mauvais génie*, rather than Nietzsche's superman, provides the key reference for Lang's master criminals. As grand enunciators they are not simply storytellers, nor are they the overcoming of the human, but rather demi-urges, creating a complete *mise-en-scène* of deception.

The Staging of Desire

So I will then, since I cannot read myself back out of my role,
read on in it to the end and to the *exeunt omnes*, behind
which the actual I will then though probably stand. Then I
can tell you whether beyond the role something else exists
and the I lives and loves you. (Ophelia to Hamlet)
The Night Watches of Bonaventura[17]

The sudden cuts to Haghi in the midst of action he has arranged reach a literal climax in the seduction of the Japanese agent Matsumoto by Haghi's agent, the seductress Kitty. Matsumoto had observed Tremaine's first romance with Sonja with a spy's detachment. After her disappearance he approached Tremaine, drinking away his sorrow in a tavern, to tell him he has simply been tricked by a beautiful spy. Lang cuts from their conversation to Haghi preparing Kitty for the next phase in his plot, her seduction of Matsumoto. The irony of this juxtaposition underscores Haghi's control of characters' destinies, even (especially?) when they think they are impervious to such manipulation. Once Kitty is installed in Matsumoto's house, after she draws his pity by appearing to him as a homeless waif, wet and cold in a rainstorm, Haghi's plan goes into high gear. When Haghi fails to get the treaty he seeks from the Japanese couriers he has murdered, he relies on Kitty to steal it from Matsumoto's home. In the English language prints, as Kitty seduces Matsumoto a close-up of Haghi's face staring at the camera as he puffs on a cigarette fades in and fades out, converting the intimate scene into a perverse *ménage à trois*. In the original German version this shot comes as Matsumoto, having discovered the treaty is missing and realising his betrayal of his obligation, commits *seppuku*, Haghi's face appearing at the moment of the self-inflicted death blow. Whether cut in at the moment of sex or death, Haghi asserts his mastery of the drama, his omniscience and omnipotence, and his alignment with the cinematic apparatus, cutting through space and time, seeing all.

Although Haghi does use some of the tools Mabuse employed (such as his blackmail of Lady Leslene over her addiction to opium), his major coups come from his staging of desire in his manipulation of Tremaine and Matsumoto. Mabuse had used Carozza to manipulate Hull, but this was secondary to his control of the young man through hypnosis and the threat of blackmail. While the sequence of Tremaine awaiting Sonja's visit directly recalls Hull's anticipation of Carozza's call, the two romances move in opposite directions. Hull's interest in Carozza never rises above

an infatuation, and Carozza views his devotion with contempt. But we witness the pain Sonja's betrayal causes Tremaine and the process of Sonja falling in love with him. Desire, which according to Mabuse is simply the desire to possess what you want, becomes an emotional drama of passionate love and painful loss in *Spies*.

Crosscutting to Haghi's coaching of Kitty undercuts any possibility of viewing her love affair with Matsumoto as anything other than a sad farce (the melodramatic trappings of Kitty's account of her family – a single cut away to a father holding a whip and an obese mother with holes in her stockings drinking – don't fool us, even as they take in Matsumoto). But Lupu Pick's extraordinary performance gives the betrayal a tragic dimension (anticipating Chris Cross's encounter with another Kitty in *Scarlet Street*), as he acquaints us with the power of a passion suddenly ignited late in life in a man dedicated to discipline and self-control. Whether Haghi's face looms in the centre of Matsumoto's ecstasy or at the moment of his death, Matsumoto undergoes the humiliation of living through the plot he himself had earlier perceived behind Tremaine's romance with Sonja. The close-up of his satisfied face, sleeping the deep sleep of the just-after, is followed by one of Lang's most poignant shots of betrayed love, as Matsumoto's hand reaches out and gropes among the pillows for the absent Kitty.

As Matsumoto leaves Tremaine in the tavern after informing him his lost love was an agent (and he a duped fool), Lang cuts to close-up of Matsumoto's hand, on which the first drop of the storm in which he will discover Kitty, soaked and shivering, falls. The shot seems oddly extraneous, until one relates it to the fall of the linden leaf on to the back of Siegfried. As the leaf's fall marked a spot of vulnerability which would prove the hero's undoing, this drop of rain presages the downpour which will transform Matsumoto's life and undermine his emotional reserve. Brief and apparently casual, unlike the fatefully protracted fall of the leaf in *The Death of Siegfried*, this close-up of a drop of water on a man's hand strangely evokes a poignancy not previously seen in Lang – like a tear shed for this man unable to acknowledge or resist his own desires, or to weep at his own fate. The restraint evident in his every gesture, even his superior knowledge, cannot withstand the attraction of desire laden with pity.

The poignancy of the Matsumoto subplot works to enrich the love between Tremaine and Sonja. Although Tremaine, like von Wenk, challenges Haghi on his own ground – he, too, is a master of disguise and fake identities, keenly observant – he quickly falls into his prescribed role in the spy's staged drama. His meeting with Sonja shows him only too eager to play hero to a damsel-in-distress (again *Spies* provides the prototype for scenes in later Lang films – as it marks the increased role desire plays in his later scenography – this scene anticipating, as Lotte Eisner pointed out, Travers' rescue of Marion Menil in *The Thousand Eyes of Dr. Mabuse*).[18] With his mastery of the situation and of disguise, Tremaine is able to conceal Sonja from the police who are seeking her for shooting a man. Tremaine transforms from his grubby tramp disguise, via a lightning change to an oriental dressing gown as he confronts the police, his face concealed by shaving cream (a costume that evokes both Matsumoto in the robe and Nemo in the whitened face), and then, finally, appears as the well-dressed, clean-shaven leading man to woo Sonja.

Sonja, however, disappears, whether as part of Haghi's plot or due to her own growing discomfort with betraying Tremaine (to whom she is already attracted). Instead of the lovely woman grateful for her rescue, when Tremaine returns to the room in which she was hiding, all he finds is an open door and an empty room. A note from Sonja says they should never meet again. As he dashes out the door after her, Tremaine encounters, not Sonja, but Matsumoto standing in the doorway to his room, who ceremoniously bows. Tremaine somewhat hesitantly returns the bow. The two men stand framed in their respective doorways, bobbing heads at each other like slightly askew mirror images. Instead of the expected love scene, so carefully built up to and anticipated by the audience as much as the characters, Lang stages this formal encounter between *doppelgängers* slated to play similar roles within Haghi's plot.[19]

Sonja begs Haghi to take her off Tremaine's case, but he refuses, forcing her – following his dictation – to write a letter to Tremaine arranging a further meeting. The sequence ends with a close-up of Sonja's hand addressing the letter as Haghi's hand places it before her. Haghi is the author, although the hand that writes is Sonja's. Lang fades out from Tremaine's address to a close-up of the number on the door of his hotel room, then to a close-up of a hand reading the letter which arranges a meeting between them. In yet another close-up, Tremaine's hand turns over the envelope of Sonja's message bringing her address close to the camera. We then dissolve to Sonja's front door, as a Japanese agent approaches (as part of Matsumoto's surveillance). Lang embeds the beginning of this love affair in the crisscross of messages and addresses, espionage and counter-espionage and in the explicit plotting and direction of Haghi. The flow of information and messages central to Lang's films from the first becomes foregrounded even further in *Spies* where the acts of transcription and inscription, of writing and dictating, eavesdropping and broadcasting constitute the major moves of the spies against each other. That desire is kindled in this environment and channelled through these circuits brings Lang's conception of the Destiny-machine to a new level of abstraction. The image of the machine and especially of the clock will never disappear from Lang's rhetoric. But the systems of communication and information (already displayed in the stock exchange sequence of *Dr. Mabuse, the Gambler*) become increasingly dominant in his plotting and intertwined with scenes of erotic desire. The meeting in Sonja's apartment, the first love scene of the film, displays this imbrication of desire and surveillance and sketches a new face for the Destiny-machine.

Tremaine and Sonja play out their love scene with coy charm and a series of displacements. Tremaine kisses her hand and Lang cuts to the samovar on her table letting off steam, then cuts back to the couple who glance over to the samovar and laugh. Sonja then offers Tremaine a series of treats: tea, sugar lumps, liquor, cookies, cigarettes – all of which he refuses. Knowingly, she looks at him and asks, 'Isn't there anything you do want?' In close-up the two faces move toward each other in profile. In the following close-up Tremaine takes Sonja's hands in his, and they caress each other. Lang then cuts to a surprising series of images delicately moving us away from this tender scene: first, Sonja's window, its cactus plants and curtains backlit by daylight. Superimposed over this we see a lamp being illuminated. Sonja's window seamlessly dissolves to a shop window (the first time this important Langian motif has been featured) as shutters come down over it, indicating it has closed for the night. Over the closed shutters, a clock (a much more familiar Lang motif) with a swinging pendulum appears. Both clock and shop window fade out and a pile of evening papers fades in, another sign of time passing. We return to Sonja's windows, now showing the darkened evening. Lang cuts to a close-up of Sonja's and Tremaine's hands still intertwined.

This cutaway sequence acts partly as sardonic jab at censorship. We certainly assume that Tremaine and Sonja made love as evening came on, Tremaine finally asking her for what he really, really wants, with these innocuous images serving as convenient displacements for forbidden sights. Have they actually remained chastely hand-in-hand? Sonja and Tremaine's surprised reaction to the sound of a paper boy on the street hawking the evening edition explains this all-too-innocent courtship: they have lost all sense of time. This is the promise offered by desire in Lang's films, to escape from time, to escape from the ongoing Destiny-machine. But while the cutaway images express the couple's inattention to passing time, they also indicate its ongoing progress, ticking away in spite of them. Lang ends the love scene by focusing again on the systems of surveillance that continue to ensnare the lovers whether they are aware of them or not. A superimposition reveals that a delicate vase in Sonja's apartment conceals a radio transmitter. Their love scene, including their plans for their next meeting at the Cafe Danielle, has been broadcast to the Japanese spies, where it is recorded and transcribed, while a typescript of the information is also carried to Haghi's desk by pneumatic tube. Haghi gives further orders on the telephone before we return to the couple's final embrace.[20] This lovemaking is scripted by one group of spies, transcribed by another, with one of its actors, Tremaine, entirely unaware of this, and seeming only to follow his heart's desire. In Haghi's plot, love can be predictably generated and regulated, processed into information and orders.

The pattern of interruption in Tremaine's romance with Sonja recurs in the ensuing nightclub scene. Sonja dances dreamily, eyes closed, in Tremaine's arms, when a hand enters from off screen to deliver her a note behind Tremaine's back, like a prompter's note to an errant performer. A message from Haghi (who is shown to be watching her in his banker's makeup and transfixes her with his gaze) directs her to dump Tremaine and return to entrapping the foreign officer, Jellusic, another of Haghi's plots. Distracting Tremaine's attention, she darts out. Having lost her for the second time, Tremaine pursues and encounters two affronts to his lover's pride. Tracing her to her meeting with Jellusic, he glimpses her as she dashes from his apartment building. When Tremaine demands to know who the lady was that just left, the creepy military officer (Fritz Rasp in all his unpleasantness) who is plotting to betray his country, misleadingly lets Tremaine think Sonja is his lover. Rushing to Sonja's address, Tremaine rings the bell and gets no response. The door swings open eerily. Tremaine walks into the gaping darkness. The apartment is as empty as a struck set. The plethora of decorative objects that made the apartment such an ideal site for a tryst are gone. Tremaine flicks on his flashlight to look around. The beam passes over empty walls, exposed wires hanging where lighting fixtures had been – the place is stripped. Lang has created one of his most powerful images of emptiness, the void which in later films frequently substitutes for the allegorical presence of the death's head of the earlier films as an image of ultimate lack and loss. The new importance of erotic desire in Lang's narrative shapes such emptiness into an image of erotic loss. Tremaine staggers out stunned.

Building Identity from Fragments

> Photography made it possible for the first time to preserve
> permanent and unmistakable traces of a human being. The
> detective story came into being when this most decisive of all
> conquests of a person's incognito had been accomplished.
> Since then the end of efforts to capture a man in his speech
> and actions has not yet been in sight.
> Walter Benjamin,
> 'The Paris of the Second Empire in Baudelaire'[21]

For Noel Burch, *Spies* represented a masterpiece of elliptical cutting and story-telling. Lang's temporal fragments in this film interlock with his increased use of closer framing, and off screen space. Although Lang had certainly used temporal compression and close-ups to great effect in previous films, there is no doubt that *Spies* employs them both more frequently and systematically. Burch correctly directs attention to the opening of the film, the 'breathless montage' already mentioned.[22] Actions are filmed in close-up and as brief fragments of actions and the viewer is asked to put them together. In the first shots of the film, hands crack a safe, and open its door; cut to a close-up of hands placing documents in an envelope; cut to a low angle shot of a man on a motorcycle. Rings radiating from a radio tower indicate a message being broadcast. These images fuse together to yield a summary image: an article from a newspaper, announcing 'Embassy Looted: Notes of Secret Pact Stolen'. The next two shots seem to pose a dialectical reversal of a sequence from *Dr. Mabuse, the Gambler*. In one beautifully conceived shot, we see a well-dressed older man riding in the back seat of an open car. In the background, another open car approaches and shots are fired as the older man crumples. In the following close-up a hand enters the frame and grabs a leather briefcase from the car's seat. In two shots Lang manages to compress the murder of a courier and the theft of a secret document which took more than twenty shots in the earlier film. Lang has chosen compression over detailed precision, and the effect seems even more modern and accelerated.

Many scenes show this combination of fragmentary close-ups (often without revealing their larger spatial context) with temporal ellipses. The sequence of

Tremaine and Sonja 'holding hands' works this way. The shooting drama in the hotel that brings Sonja to Tremaine begins with a close-up of Sonja's hands firing a revolver. No cut to long shot or reverse angle ever reveals her target or her situation, or even her facial expression. We only see her full figure as she rushes into Tremaine's hotel room and collapses histrionically in his arms. Ellipses work doubly in the sequence of Matsumoto's seduction. The cut from Kitty's embrace of Matsumoto fully dressed to the close-up of his face expressing – first – sensual satisfaction – and then panic, not only avoids the censorable act of passion but also eliminates Kitty's theft of the treaty during Matsumoto's blissful sleep. Ellipses also allow scenes to blend one into another, as when Sonja's and Tremaine's idyllic tryst ends with her rushing to the icons she has on her wall, removing from a prayer book an amulet of the Madonna and Child which she brings towards the camera, holding it in her palm in an extreme close-up. The close-up bridges the next scene as we cut to a long shot of Sonja and Tremaine in the back of a cab, and she gives him the amulet as a love token and protective charm.

This narrative and visual compression plays a strong role in the increased overall abstraction of this film. While *Dr. Mabuse, the Gambler* introduced this new abstracted modern environment, we can see that Lang continued to refine his sense of modernity, creating not only a more streamlined style, but taking *Mabuse*'s questioning of a stable identity one step further. Haghi abandons the more flamboyant and theatrical style of Mabuse's disguises and his nearly supernatural use of hypnosis as a means of control in favour of more elaborate staging and plotting, allowing characters' own pursuit of desire to bring them under his control. But Haghi's less spectacular modes of manipulation are possible because of his even greater visual surveillance.

I spoke earlier of the spies, agents of both Matsumoto and Haghi, processing Tremaine and Sonja's love affair into information. The images of their words being listened to over the concealed microphones, written down, then typed in duplicate, exemplifies not only the acceleration of technological mediation in this film, but also the transformation of human actions and even individual identity into exchangeable signs. Lang always dealt with the replacement of characters by signs, but in the earlier allegorical films, this process retained something magical about it, as if there was some transfer of power between Siegfried and the embroidered cross on his tunic, or Brunhild and her bracelet. While the world of Mabuse is a decadent world in which a community of religious meaning would be impossible, the shards of the supernatural and magic still exist and are gathered up by Mabuse as part of his bag of tricks in his pursuit of power. Some residue of the object's power persists through all of Lang's films, even as the realm of practical magic fades away. Sonja's protective amulet retains something of this quality in *Spies*, both in its rich evocation of her person and in the role it has in protecting Tremaine. Tokens given by lovers remain fetishes in Lang, retaining the original magical meaning of the term and exuding an eroticised pseudo-magic. But, for the most part, the world of *Spies* has suffered a pervasive disenchantment, and, rather than retaining an afterglow of magical power, most signs circulated in this film express dehumanisation and abstraction.

Photography in *Spies* exemplifies this reduction of human identity to a sign that can be disseminated. When Donald Tremaine first arrives at the Secret Service headquarters in his tramp disguise, his photograph has already passed Haghi's desk. Haghi's modernistic desk acts a clearing-house of information brought to him by agents and the varied technological equipment his desk contains (telephone, pneumatic tube, intercom). It is partly by means of gathering photographs, images of people, that Haghi asserts his power over them. Tremaine discovers one of Haghi's agents working in the Secret Service office itself, photographing him surreptitiously with a miniature camera concealed in the lapel button of his suit. But he didn't notice that another agent on the street (disguised – as Tremaine is – as a tramp) had already taken his picture while apparently reaching for a cigarette-butt abandoned on the sidewalk. Lang cuts from Haghi examining this photo of Tremaine through a magnifying glass to a close-up of Tremaine himself in Jason's office. The cut not only asserts Haghi's all-seeing control, but his enunciative capability, triggering the close-up with his lens. The omnipresent surveillance that Haghi achieves mimes, of course, the techniques of the modern police force and police state in gathering, processing and categorising images of potentially dangerous or troublesome citizens.

The technological and state apparatus tracing and recording of individual identity gave birth, as I indicated in the last section, to the detective genre with its scenography of tracing guilt and identity and the counter-actions of criminals to maintain their invisibility. Photography played an important role in this evolving practice, as Walter Benjamin had observed. Photographs are used by both sides in *Spies*, the government Secret Service and Haghi's spy organisation. In Chief Burton Jason's Secret Service office, photographs form part of a large archive, thick books that Jason pulls out to show photographs of agents. He first shows Tremaine the photos of all the agents that have been killed in the pursuit of Haghi. Later Tremaine finds Jellusic's photograph in a similar book of people under surveillance. Haghi blackmails Lady Leslene with a photograph of her taken on her Tuesday and Friday evening visits to an opium den. Even more methodically, Haghi creates individual dossiers based on photographs, fingerprints and other informa-

tion on each of the agents he targets. Sonja is given the first of these as Haghi assigns her to Tremaine. The neatly folded, pocket-sized identity file Sonja contains two photographs of Tremaine (both in his tramp disguise), his fingerprint and his agent number (326). Sonja wrinkles her nose at the grubby-looking guy. The scenario is repeated when Haghi hands a photograph of Matsumoto to Kitty. Here the card holds only one photo, a name and address ('Prof. Akira Matsumoto, 17 Strand'). Kitty, in one of those precisely calibrated Langian performances of successive gestures, examines the photo at arm's length, then draws it slowly closer to her, her eyes moving over it as if memorising Matsumoto's features. Then she raises an eyebrow, parts her lips, and, as she lowers the photo, licks her lips slowly with her tongue. In both cases Haghi's photo-card fixes the identity of his future victim with his face and some essential numbers (agent code or address). Possession of the photograph indicates control, under the calculating, yet bitterly sensual, gaze of the female agents to whom he hands the files. Ironically, after Sonja has been separated from Tremaine by Haghi, we see her sitting on her bed tenderly caressing the images she formerly wrinkled her nose at. Her hand moves over it as if magnetising it with her desire.

The photograph fixes identity and renders the photographed subject vulnerable to Haghi's control. The shot of Haghi examining Tremaine's photograph and fingerprint through a magnifying glass visually expresses not only his scrutinising gaze but his dominance over the image and its subject, like a scientist examining an insect fixed on a pin. His photographic surveillance can even see through an agent's disguise. Thus when Haghi finds his own image published in the paper (with and without goatee) as he sits before his mirror, he realises his own defences are crumbling. The photographs kept by the Secret Service exude a similar fatal quality: first, the volume of dead agents which Jason shows Tremaine, which he says he hopes will never include Tremaine's photograph; later, the album of photographed agents which leads to Jellusic's identification and ultimately his suicide. To be photographed in *Spies* becomes a harbinger of death, with only Tremaine managing to avoid this fate, perhaps by the counter magic of his photograph becoming a fetish of lost love for Sonja, and the recipient of her caresses.

Most of the photographs in the film are accompanied by numbers, whether the agent codes contained in Jason's volumes, or the codes and addresses inscribed on Tremaine's and Matsumoto's dossiers by Haghi. The substitution of numbers for names by the Secret Service represent only the most extreme instance of the film's pegging of people with figures. The film accumulates numbers as key switching points in the plot. There is the absurd number that Jellusic gives for his claim check at the telegraph office (the square root of 37083 + 6); the addresses of Tremaine's hotel room and Sonja's house ('Olympic Hotel, Room 119/120'; '24 Park Street') which follow one another in the exchange of letters; the number of the taxi Sonja takes when she disappears, given to Tremaine by the street urchin. Of course, any film taking place in the modern era is likely to generate as many or more numbers than these. But in *Spies*, numbers stand in for characters, marking both their appearance and their disappearance and the impersonal system of information management and control that surrounds them.

Given the significance of numbers in this espionage plot, it is not surprising that when Sonja sees a number written on a slip of paper in Haghi's office, it sticks in her mind. Haghi convinces Sonja to smuggle a treaty out of the country by promising to spare Tremaine and release her from the espionage organisation. As she exults over this possibility, an odd little camera movement brings the paper into view, framed just below Haghi's clenched fist resting on his desk. Sonja reads the note: LDZ 33 133 no. 8. It seems to cause her to hesitate. She stares at Haghi with narrowed eyes and asks him to restate his promise not to harm Tremaine. After staring right at the camera, Haghi picks up the piece of paper. In close-up, he folds it deliberately, covering the number and nods to Sonja. In the previous scene Haghi sent his henchman to purchase tickets for a train compartment bearing this number and we recognise Haghi's plot against Tremaine. His gesture of folding contradicts his gesture of nodding agreement – if we recognise that these numbers now represent Tremaine's place in Haghi's plot. In the following scene – Haghi's meeting with Tremaine and Jason in the dressing room as Nemo – Haghi hands Tremaine a card with the same fatal number, LDZ 33 133 no. 8, his reservation in the railway sleeping car Haghi has arranged to wreck in the train tunnel.

Sonja and Tremaine are on board different trains, each sent off on different missions, each unaware that in different ways they are being manipulated and betrayed by Haghi. In one of his finest diagrammatic arrangements of plot coincidences (whose brilliant visual power distract one from its narrative contrivance), Lang has their trains arrive at opposite sides of a platform at the same time. Lang composes this alignment of the two characters through an expressive geometry arranged within a realistic set, avoiding the Expressionist distortion or monumental symmetry of the earlier films, but brilliantly creating a symbolic space. The camera frames Sonja from within her train compartment as she unpacks. In the background, perfectly framed through Sonja's window, we see into a compartment in another train across the platform. Tremaine enters this other compartment and also unpacks. For an instant it almost looks like the couple share the same space as they carry out their everyday tasks. But this is, of course, impossible; when Sonja notices Tremaine through her window, she hides from view, terrified of blowing her cover and endangering both of them. We then see her point of view of Tremaine's compartment, now framed within the window of his train, as he lowers the window shade. Briefly the couple were brought together in an image of illusory common space. Almost immediately the separation between them, spatial and emotional, asserts itself, and the vision of her lover, so desired and so feared by Sonja, slips from view, as her train pulls out of the station.

Sonja leans out of her window, straining for a glimpse of her beloved. Instead what she sees gliding by are the numbers on his train car: 33 133. Once again, a person disappears and all that remains are numbers. Sonja stands back from the window. Her fingers trace the numerals in the air: 33 133. This number sequence becomes the mantra that leads into the sensation-scene of the film, the spectacular train wreck in the tunnel. Lang uses the numbers not only as a suspense device to foreshadow Tremaine's fate, but as a rhythmic motif which, blending with the rhythm of the train, serves as one of his most complex and subtle portrayals of the Destiny-machine and its newly emphasised interaction with the erotic rhythms of desire. Sonja cannot get the number sequence and its possible significance out of her head, its unconscious persistence carrying an emotional power. Lang relates the number to a series of rhythmic elements, a ticking clock, and the click-clack of the train wheels on the track, the repetitive arrangement of the numbers, two threes on either side of a one, creating a nearly hypnotic effect.

The number sequence's persistence and strange power becomes identified with the forward drive of the train itself, as Lang superimposes the numbers over the drive-shaft turning the wheels of the engine. Then Sonja's small travel clock is shown with the numbers arcing beneath it, like a swinging pendulum. Sonja

pounds her temples as if trying to either drive the numbers from her mind, or force herself to remember their significance. In one of the most exquisite images in silent cinema to evoke sound, the crystal containers of Sonja's perfumes jiggle together, their soft ringing releases the same suite of numbers: 33 133. Lang cuts again to the numbers superimposed over the train wheels, only now they multiply and follow the track, disappearing along the vanishing point of the rail, and flash on and off. Sonja cradles her head and sways. Operating partly as a sound cue – the rhythm of the wheels sounds like the repetitive pattern of the numbers – the superimposition of the numbers over the train recalls the superimposed magical words in *Dr. Mabuse, the Gambler* – *Tsi Nan Fu* or *Melior* – which expressed Mabuse's hypnotic power over von Wenk. *Spies* again avoids the overt staging of the supernatural, but it strongly evokes the hypnotic rhythm of the train as correlative to the Destiny-machine, Haghi's plot which is driving these two lovers away from each other, and towards Tremaine's doom.

But as the trajectories of the two trains bear the lovers away from each other, Lang's cutting brings them erotically closer, intercutting and associating their actions and gestures. As Sonja first traces the numbers in the air, Lang cuts to Tremaine's servant giving him Sonja's amulet which he discovered on the hotel room floor where Tremaine had thrown it after Sonja's disappearance and apparent betrayal. A close-up frames this love-token in Tremaine's palm, recalling the tenderer emotions at the moment it was first given. As the rhythm of the train dominates the sequence, Lang not only cuts between Sonja and the wheels, but between Sonja and Tremaine as each settles into their sleeping berths, simultaneously adjusting their clocks. Tremaine's berth jiggles with the train's motion, an obsessive rhythm that unites the pair even as it moves them further apart. The rhythm rocks Tremaine into slumber. This sensuous montage recalls Lang's

lyrical and erotic evocation of his own love of railway sleeping cars, as quoted by
Frederick W. Ott:

> I can lie for hours, hands under my head, and stare into the night. The rolling of the
> wheels which has for me an ever new changing rhythm, the soft movement of the
> body, the whistle of the locomotive, the swarms of falling stars of its sparks, the
> consciousness to be carried from one place to another without having anything else
> to do but lie still dreaming the dreams of youth […] all this combines for me to [sic]
> a condition of intoxication which inspires me again and again.[23]

Thus the train rhythm evokes hypnosis, sleep and eroticism blended together, even
as it also marks the progress of Haghi's plot to kill Tremaine. The actions of Haghi's
agent uncoupling the car (no. 33 133) from the train in order to strand it in the
tunnel, directly in the path of the oncoming express, are intercut with Tremaine's
slumber. But as his detached car rolls to a halt, the change in rhythm and the inertia
of its final stop causes Sonja's amulet to slip from the pocket of his jacket stowed in
the luggage rack above his berth. It falls on Tremaine and awakens him. The three
shots that embed his awakening in the motion of large machinery and the laws of
physics – a long shot of the train car stopping; a medium shot of the amulet slipping
from the coat pocket; a medium shot of Tremaine roused by its impact – recall the
Rube Goldberg-like tracing of cause and effect in the fall of the linden leaf in *The
Death of Siegfried*, moving from large causes (a dragon's tail, a railway car) to apparently small effects (a leaf falls, a piece of jewellery drops) which, in fact, have large
consequences (Siegfried's fate, Tremaine's salvation).

This fitting together of fragments reaches a climax as the train wreck Haghi has
arranged takes place. In a dramatic low angle close-up we see a hand throw a switch.
Cut to the train rails realigning. In the next few shots the express barrels into and
through the tunnel. Tremaine sees it coming, as the collision shatters the car, splintering wood and twisting metal.[24] As if awoken by the impact miles away, Sonja sits
up in her berth in terror. Lowering her compartment window she finds herself in a
station with scurrying railway officials, and hears the fatal number once more:
'Thirty Three One Thirty Three'. Told there has been a wreck in the tunnel, Sonja
puts her hand to her head. Lang gives a quickly montaged flashback as she puts
together all the pieces: the number of Tremaine's car passing through the frame; the
close-up of the slip of paper next to Haghi's fist; Haghi folding the paper, then staring out at the camera. The number inscribed on a piece of twisted metal follows, the
emblematic summary of this sequence of events. In close-up Sonja stares at the
camera in horror. Then Lang fades in and out on another abstracted close-up of
Haghi staring directly at the camera and blowing out cigarette smoke, like the
author's signature on the apparently completed drama.

Haghi works through abstraction and fragmentation, the master tools of
modern processes, whether bureaucratic or industrial. He fits these crafted pieces
into a mosaic of his own design, like the railway wreck we have just followed in
detail. Lang's style mirrors Haghi's processes as it narrates them. No previous Lang
film has contained as many close-ups (it seems the whole narrative could be carried by simply piecing together the dozens of close-ups of hands found in the
film). But as we have seen before, Lang only appears to relinquish the position of
authority to his over-reacher characters. The rhythms of desire can pulse through
the machinations of the tyrant. Like Mabuse, Haghi will find his systems of manipulation closing in on him.

Finale: Bringing Down the House

It happened that a fire broke out backstage in a theatre. The
clown came out to inform the public. They thought it was a
jest and applauded. He repeated his warning, they shouted
even louder. So I think the world will come to an end amid
general applause from all the wits, who believe that it is a joke.

Søren Kierkegaard, *Either/Or*[25]

Master criminals, from Fantomas to Haghi succeed more in managing *coups de
théâtre* than in accomplishing their immediate goals. Creatures of adventure fiction
more than rational agents, their plots seem designed for thrills rather than effectiveness. Morrier, Haghi's agent in the train, could simply put a bullet in Tremaine's
head as he sleeps, rather than counting on the deadly effect of a massive train wreck,
just as Mabuse could undoubtedly have got rid of von Wenk in a more simple
manner than by hypnotising him to drive a car over a cliff. We are dealing here with
genre conventions rather than common sense, and the genre demands elaborate
theatrical plotting and effects which portray the master criminal as a manager of
spectacular effects rather than logical action. Such genre conventions provided the
perfect context for Lang to develop the workings of the Destiny-machine and the
master criminal's claim to authority and authorship as grand enunciator.

Lang's scenario of power ultimately removes control from the master criminal as
enunciator. Following the long-established schema of the master criminal's rise and
fall, Lang also details the Destiny-machine slipping from the enunciator's grip. The
denouement of Lang's drama does not simply rest on the criminal's failure to
destroy his enemy, but in his loss of control of his own elaborate system. In *Dr.
Mabuse, the Gambler* it is not simply von Wenk's survival of Mabuse's plots, but
rather his penetration of Mabuse's system of disguise, his invasion of Mabuse's
stronghold (first by telephone and then by an armed incursion), as well as the coin-
cidental closing-down of Mabuse's own escape hatch that dismantles Mabuse's control of the Destiny-machine. Perhaps this is why, as the balance of power shifts in
Spies after Tremaine escapes the train wreck unscathed, Tremaine and Sonja
(reunited and in pursuit of Haghi's henchman Morrier) pass a newsreel cameraman perched on a bridge manically filming the site of the train wreck. Phantom of
cameramen to come (in *Fury*, of course, but also Gerda Marus's next role as film-
maker on the moon in *The Woman in the Moon*), he plays an emblematic role. Since
the cameraman is too preoccupied to help them, the couple simply 'borrow' his
motorcycle and sidecar for the film's climactic chase.

The chase of Morrier by Tremaine and Sonja demonstrates that Haghi's network
at first remains intact. Recalling an image from the opening of *Dr. Mabuse, the
Gambler*, an agent observes the car chase from a telephone pole and communicates
its progress to Haghi. As his car enters the city, Morrier crashes through a revolving
door and drives into the lobby of a grand hotel which is broadcasting over the radio
a dance band from its dining room. His revolver blazing, Morrier rushes into the
dining room and heads for the microphone. Once there, he uses the radio hook-up
to broadcast a message to his boss, telling of Sonja's betrayal and of the danger closing in on him. That any radio broadcast can convey information to Haghi expresses
Haghi's central control of the technological network of communication, rather

than common-sense likelihood. But if it expresses Haghi's control (indicated by the cuts to Haghi and his assistant listening to the broadcast over headphones), its message announces his downfall. Like von Wenk's phone call to Mabuse, Haghi's communication system has been penetrated by bad news. Haghi's reaction is intercut with Morrier's suicide by poison, he slowly takes off his radio headset; then his hand raises as if trying to grasp something but falls, angry and empty.

The raid on Haghi's bank parallels the raid on Mabuse's stronghold, but if the earlier climax inspires the final shoot-out with the gangster in Hawks's *Scarface*, the raid in *Spies* is not a dramatic shoot-out, but a less conventional contest pitted against a specific time deadline. Just as *M* divides its climax between two sequences – the seizing of Beckert by ransacking the warehouse and the theatrically staged 'trial' at the brewery – *Spies* first mounts a raid on Haghi's headquarters and then entraps the man himself during his stage performance. The first action launches an assault on Haghi's system, penetrating the duplicitous, disguised nature of the Haghi Bank, a commercial business on one side, an espionage network on the other; the second raid penetrates Haghi's personal disguise as Nemo and makes an assault on his identity.

Haghi, clinging to his control of appearances, makes a strong counter-attack as the police begin their raid. Franz Tremaine's chauffeur, and Sonja find their way down a side street blocked by a pushcart-seller, peddling coconuts. The peddler throws two of his wares at the car, which promptly explode as gas bombs. When the police invade the bank lobby, clearing out customers and employees, Tremaine receives a note from a bank guard. Informing him of Sonja's and Franz's capture, the message constitutes Haghi's last scenario. He demands the police withdraw within fifteen minutes or his hostages will die. Like the alarm tripped by the nightwatchman in *M*, this threat does not stop the search for Haghi, but rather gives it a dramatic and punctual deadline. Tremaine is now acting against Lang's ultimate image of the Destiny-machine – the clock.

The sequence of rifling through the Haghi Bank in search of both Haghi and Sonja resembles the warehouse search in *M* spatially as well as temporally. Like Schränker's gang, Tremaine's agents attack the walls, vaults and doorways of the bank with blowtorches and pneumatic drills. But the game of 'beat the clock' remains subject to Haghi's control, as Lang's editing makes clear. Haghi orders his guards to execute Sonja in seven minutes, pointing off screen. Lang cuts to one of his monumental clocks showing seven minutes to six, then back to Haghi and the guards who nod at his commanding gestures. Using the temporal deadline as a way to channel shots into the suspenseful simultaneity that marked the heist that opens *Dr. Mabuse, the Gambler*, Lang cuts to Tremaine checking his wristwatch. As gas begins to fill the bank, Lang cuts back to the guards, then to the clock, marking one minute to six. In close-up the guards begin to turn the door handle. Inside, the prisoners struggle with their bonds, Sonja using her teeth to untie Franz. Cut back to the clock, now showing six o'clock. In a strong use of off screen space, Lang shows the guards entering the room as shadows cast upon the wall by the opened door.

The search ends as Tremaine's agents burst through the wall separating the commercial bank from Haghi's headquarters. Sonja and Tremaine reunited, Haghi's hidden headquarters turns lethal as the gas fills the bank. The two sides of this duplicitous locale have collapsed into one; Haghi's camouflaged space has been breached. The orderly stairwell swarms with panicked workers. Stressing the subterranean nature of Haghi's network, Lang shows the sidewalk coverings raised as Haghi's minions emerge from the depths to escape the deadly gas. As in the final

collapse of Mabuse's 'state within a state', the over-reacher's plan of world domination ends in cloacal imagery, refugees pouring out from their underground lairs
accompanied by evil fumes, like rats from a sewer.

Haghi stages both his last act in the bank and his final exit from his headquarters
as a *coup de théâtre*. He announces to Sonja and Franz, 'Soon you will know the
great secret – death – but first you will learn one of my secrets!' From his nearly constant position, seated behind his desk, Haghi tosses away his omnipresent cigarette
and rises, the camera tilting up slightly with him as he stands erect. Lang cuts to
Sonja tied to a chair with Franz tied next to her. The following shot exemplifies
Lang's more flexible use of the frame and off screen space in this film. Haghi passes
through the foreground, in front of Sonja and Franz, his body cropped below the
waist as he moves off screen left. As Sonja and Franz stare off after him, a rectangle
of light appears on the wall at the right of the frame, light coming in from the door
Haghi opens off screen. Haghi's dark shadow now appears within this lighted area,
a shadow play devised as his final theatrical exit. He passes through and the wall
darkens as the off screen door closes.

Haghi's ultimate disguise lay in his pretended handicap. His confinement to a
wheelchair underscored his uses of technology to maintain his power of surveillance and communication, the photographs and reports delivered to his futuristic
desk matched by his orders issued through telephone and intercom. The falsity of
this disability was another secret the narration of *Spies* had withheld from its audience. Its unveiling as a theatrical moment demands an audience within the film, as
Haghi flaunts his mobility and strides past Sonja and Franz like a self-satisfied exhibitionist. Exiting the film frame, he casts his silhouette on the back wall like a private movie projected for his captive audience. This shadow recalls Hagen's looming
shadow that precedes him as he enters the chamber where Kriemhild sits beside the
dead body of Siegfried, as it also anticipates the first image of Hans Beckert in *M*,
the shadow looming before Elsie Beckmann.

But this carefully staged exit, showing Haghi suddenly, almost miraculously,
mobile, while his audience sits bound in wide-eyed restraint, offers the last image of
Haghi's complete control. Revealing his lack of physical handicap seems paradoxically to establish a new vulnerability, as his technological prostheses collapse
around him. Haghi's farewell performance balances his claims to authorship and
mastery with ultimate failure. Haghi's final refuge lies in his theatre and his persona
as Nemo the clown. Scampering and dancing, acting the fool in baggy pants, slap
shoes and fright wig, Haghi has truly become 'no-one'. Nemo appears to us framed
within a proscenium stage, seated at a grand piano. As this burlesque pianist, seated
on a too-short kitchen chair, his hands resting on the keys like the paws of a plain-
tive puppy, Nemo presents a parody of Haghi at his desk imperiously manipulating
its buttons and telephone receivers. Apparently unhappy with the music he makes,
Nemo pulls out a comically small revolver and shoots a couple of the gargantuan
notes which float above his piano.

Haghi/Nemo's final space – his final stage – is open on three sides. Lang cuts to
one side with a long shot of the audience laughing and enjoying his antics, the theatre orchestra and conductor in the foreground. Then Lang shows another side, the
wings, the unseen space where illusions are prepared and stage mechanisms are
concealed from the audience, as Tremaine and Sonja appear. Next we see the hidden
side of a performer, Nemo's back, as Lang frames him against the audience. Holding
a saxophone which he will incongruously play with a violin bow, Nemo acts not
only as performer but as director as he addresses the orchestra conductor and calls

for 'a little sad music'.[26] He dances a bit then pauses, looking off screen. Nemo's point of view of the orchestra pit reveals detectives with drawn guns aimed at the stage. Laughing a bit, Nemo resumes his dance, moving in the opposite direction. Another point of view reveals a detective taking aim at him from the other end of the pit.

Pulling out a revolver apparently to shoot an oversize flea taken from his pants (as he had previous shot a large fly flying over him and the oversized musical notes), Nemo fires furiously into the wings. Sonja and Tremaine dodge out of the path of the bullets. Nemo stares into the now empty wings. Switching to a view of the other side of the stage, Nemo sees a detective aiming at him from the edge of a flat in the wings. His realm of performance now restricted to only a few square feet, without chance of escape, Nemo turns and looks directly at the camera and laughs hysterically. This is Haghi's last look at the camera, and it functions (even within the diegesis) as a look at an audience. This long shot differs from the looming close-ups of Haghi smiling sardonically at the camera so frequent in the film, dominating his abstract space. Yet, if he is caught on his own stage, captured in his true (?) identity, powerless to escape his enemies, Haghi still has one thing he can control: the perception of the audience. His laughter barks defiance as he raises the revolver to his head. Enacting his own destruction as he fires a bullet into his skull, Haghi/Nemo staggers. He raises his hand one last time: performing his last gesture of command, he orders the curtain to come down.

This final action of *mise-en-scène*, of control and direction, shows the paradoxical nature of Haghi's authorship. In contrast to Mabuse who appears to have lost all power in the last shots of the film, Haghi maintains the possibility of not only a final act, but a final dramatic production, a final control over his performance, a final illusion. Nemo crumples on the stage, but the last shot of the film shows the curtain closing, obeying his orders, as members of the audience leap to their feet in tumultuous

applause. There is no more deeply ironic ending in film history. Lang's recurring address to his audience through looks at the camera receives a bitter twist here. The end of Nemo's act is the end of the film. Unlike Hitchcock's *The Thirty-Nine Steps*, patterned on *Spies* in many ways (one being the similarity of their theatrical denouements), we do not get a final scene in the wings allowing us an exit from the realm of illusion. We are abandoned in the position of spectators, just as it is demonstrated that an audience never gets a full view of things and must remain duped.

In my earlier contrast of the theatrical performances in *Dr. Mabuse, the Gambler* and *Spies*, I compared the mastery claimed in the name Sandor Weltmann and the elusive nature of the name Nemo. The two scenes show other similarities and reversals. Both present illusions to a duped audience, but Weltmann demonstrates the power of his hypnotic will to cloud men's minds, while Nemo stages his own suicide as a side-splitting farce. Weltmann ends his act with his written command to von Wenk, his scenario extending his power beyond the theatre. Nemo makes do with his circumscribed space, and indeed creates his illusion based on the fact that the audience cannot see the drama occurring in the wings and orchestra pit. But if Weltmann represents Mabuse at the height of his powers, while Nemo's performance presents Haghi's demise, Nemo's final act also contrasts with Mabuse's final abjection. Nemo sacrifices himself in order to maintain the illusion of his final appearance. If the interior drama of the films dealing with master criminals/grand enunciators lies in a struggle over the control of the cinematic and narrative apparatus, we must see Nemo's last moments as equivocal. The Destiny-machine in terms of his own system of disguise and manipulation has slipped from Haghi's grasp. But his very last look at the camera and command to bring down the curtain, not only ends his own act, but the film itself. The darkness of the closing curtain becomes the final darkness of the screen and screening room. *Spies* ends with its master criminal's clear defeat, but his fate as grand enunciator seems sealed with his death. The act of authorship and the death of the author merge in the blank screen.

6

The Testament of Dr. Mabuse

A Message, Condemned to Death, Has Escaped

No-one can fight his way through here, even with a message
from a dead man.

Franz Kafka[1]

Does Haghi's final act, an act of self destruction followed immediately by an artistic
direction ('Curtain!'), mirror that death which the act of writing, or the act of
authorship – according to Barthes, Foucault and Derrida – demands? Haghi's last
actions not only kill himself but also 'kill' the film, as his command to close the curtain dovetails with Lang's act of killing the lights, fading to black to end the film.
Unlike the end of *Dr. Mabuse, the Gambler* where the Doctor's defeat signalled his
loss of authorship, as he became the audience of his own hallucinations, Haghi
remains in control – at least of the production of illusion. He does not relinquish
his place at centre stage. But to see this act as Haghi's victory distorts the ending,

since his project was world domination. It is not truly Haghi who triumphs on the music hall stage, but the clown Nemo; Haghi is defeated, Nemo is applauded. As with Mabuse, Haghi's hubristic command over the destiny of others, his megalomania, comes to an end. Nemo's act, however, scores a 'big finish'. It is Haghi as Nemo, as 'no-one,' that manages this artistic finale.

Lang teaches us, through his crime films, that the author writes through counterfoil, by the impression left by the writing implement, rather than through direct expression – such as the unmediated voice. There is a wonderful scene in *Spies* which illustrates this mediated idea of writing and the circuitous routes a messages might take as it slips away from its sender. In a telegraph office an unsavoury man lounges on one of the desk cubicles supplied for writing messages. Shielding his actions from view with his body, he places something under the desk's blotter, pockets the pencil and replaces it with one of his own. In a brief (but lovely) tracking shot, Lang's camera follows as his hand moves over to the next desk compartment and tears the pencil from its cord holder, then continues to the next cubicle where he smashes the point of another pencil. He exits satisfied with what looks like an act of random vandalism (I remember wondering how often he had visited my neighbourhood post office in Brooklyn when I first saw this film).

Tremaine enters, tries the first two compartments, then settles on the one with the intact pencil. He writes a message which we see in code, then – dissolved in – translated.[2] He moves to the window to give it to the telegraph operator. As he leaves, the vandal returns, heading directly to the first compartment. In close-up we see the cubicle's blotter – a large white sheet covered with swirls of ink, scribbles, words going in different directions, a palimpsest of layers of inscription, the detritus of the message-making process. The hand lifts the blotter, revealing beneath it a dark rectangle, obviously a sheet of carbon paper. The hand removes this as well, unveiling a white sheet of paper with a perfectly legible message, Tremaine's coded original, which the hand takes away. The next shot shows the agent reading it into the telephone and a cut shows Haghi listening at his desk.

Like so much in *Spies*, this sequence shows the processing of matter into information, like the broadcast and transcription of Sonja and Donald's languid afternoon dalliance. But the sequence also renders visible the mediations that messages and their interceptions go through: the act of writing snakes through the byways of the mechanics of inscription, the employment of codes and surreptitious imprinting, electronic transmission. Here the writer is betrayed by the traces he leaves, while the true author of the action, the plotter Haghi, makes use of these unconscious imprints. In *Spies* the Destiny-machine seems to bifurcate. There are still images of large-scale machines, creatures made of metallic moving parts, but the transmission of words and information – even more of the letters and numbers which form no recognisable words – tends to express the film's most sinister systems. The intercutting leading to the train crash in the tunnel brings these two modes together, cutting between Sonja and the apparently meaningless succession of numbers that everything in her world seems to transmit to her, and the railway system itself – tons of metal switched onto a collision course.

Haghi's agent spies out Tremaine's intention by exploiting the process of writing itself, the trace left behind by the writer. The surreptitiously placed carbon copy converts the act of writing from authorial intent into unconscious betrayal. Like Freud's 'mystic writing-pad' the carbon retains the trace of writing even after the writer believes he has erased the message.[3] But the beginning of this shot, just before the spy uncovers his secret recording of Tremaine's writing, briefly reveals an image which announces the even more complex topography of inscription found in *The Testament of Dr. Mabuse*: the blotter itself, with its crisscrossing lines of writing, its truly meaningless heap of graphemes, its superimposition of traces, notes, graffiti. If Tremaine's untranslated code message appears mysterious before its translation, we sense nonetheless an intention behind it. It is a message even if we can't read it. But this messy blotter defies decoding and exists as pure 'noise', the materiality of writing without a code.

The blotter directly foreshadows an image from *The Testament of Dr. Mabuse*. As Dr. Baum lectures to his students about his prize patient, Dr. Mabuse, he gives (in the form of a case history) a synopsis of *Dr. Mabuse, the Gambler*. The students listen, showing a range of reactions, from boredom to intense, almost hysterical, involvement (a woman with a monocle, looking like a Galton photograph combining the features of Lang and Harbou, calmly puts on lipstick, while a young man grips the edge of his desk as he listens). But when the lights in the lecture theatre are lowered and Baum projects an image of Mabuse himself hunched over in his hospital bed, the students all react identically and simultaneously, straightening their backs and staring forward at this image in fascination, a group reaction as perfectly choreographed as the workers' movements in *Metropolis*. Baum explains that eventually Mabuse's uncommunicative catatonia gave way to a motion of his hand (Baum mimes it for his students) which the doctor interpreted as a desire to write. Mabuse was given pencil and paper which, Baum says, he covered with meaningless scribbles. This is the next image Baum projects, a slide showing two pages of Mabuse's 'meaningless scribbles'.

These meaningless scribbles recall the blotter from *Spies*; Baum's patient observation of Mabuse's writing eventually uncovers a meaning – like the revelation of the carbon imprint of Tremaine's message hidden beneath the blotter. He explains that after two years of Mabuse's apparently aimless scribbling single words emerged, then whole sentences. The second slide Baum projects shows a series of rhythmically curved lines of writing covering a page, resembling calligraphy exercises in their graceful but mostly illegible forms, contrasting sharply with the violent jumble and harsh broken lines in the first two examples. Baum explains that as the writing became readable and comprehensible it recorded Mabuse's obsession with crime. These writings outlined plans of crimes, worked out to the smallest detail, in essence, we could say, scenarios of action.

Baum traces Mabuse's writing, beginning with an apparent involuntary motion of the hand which he interpreted as a desire to write and supplied with tools. This initial 'writing on air' (as Baum does when he demonstrates it for his students) forms a motif in Lang's last three German films before exile. We see it in *Spies* as Sonja tries to remember where she encountered the number sequence 33 133. In *M*, Inspector Lohmann traces out the word 'Ariston', the brand of cigarettes Franz Beckert smokes, trying to recall a detail from the mass of facts collected in the police investigation. In these instances Lang portrays writing as first of all a hand gesture, and as an attempt to recall something dimly remembered. In *Testament*, this process of recall takes on a more complex form, as Mabuse seems to be recalling (summoning up) his former self. But the return to full self-consciousness, the cure – if Baum is actually attempting that – never comes. Mabuse remains nothing more than a writing machine, otherwise not communicating, until he dies. His compulsive gestures express the force of writing itself, as if Mabuse's body were its tool. He himself produces a complete range of writing forms – from a jumble resembling the blotter in *Spies* to the legible criminal plans, like the counterfoil revealing

Tremaine's message. Mabuse evokes the automatic writing of the spiritualist (or surrealist), an act of pure transmission, rather than expression. There is no 'writing cure'; Mabuse does not find himself at the end of his text. Rather, he writes himself out, generating his own death sentence. He is not writing his memoirs, but, as the film title tells us, his testament, the legacy of the dead to the living.

The traces of Tremaine's coded message picked up by the carbon paper concealed by Haghi's agents show the independence that writing can have from the author that held the pen, and we recognise the *modus operandi* of *Spies*, to intercept and re-route messages, to complicate the intended connection between sender and receiver. 'Transmission and interception are the two major and complementary figures of Langian narrative', claims Nicole Brenez.[4] The truth of this statement appears in the opening scenes of every Lang thriller we have examined: the death of the old man as he throws the bottle in the sea in *Spiders*; the theft of the commercial contract in the opening sequence of *Dr. Mabuse, the Gambler*; the theft of the documents and the shooting of the agent about to name the culprit that opens *Spies*. *The Testament of Dr. Mabuse* is no exception, but it supplies a variation to Brenez's dichotomy of transmission or interception that may have even more significance: the message that goes astray, escapes, that wanders or gets lost rather than being re-directed or received.

After a dramatic prologue in which Hofmeister, a former police detective, spies out a new criminal conspiracy and barely escapes with his life, a telephone call from Hofmeister to Lohmann attempts to inform him of the brains behind the plot (attempts therefore to articulate and to answer the question so clearly formed in the other master criminal films, 'who is behind all this?') But Lang refuses to let this happen, delaying the connection in every possible manner. Lohmann is on his way to see the opera, *Die Valkyrie*, when his secretary takes the phone call. Lohmann, fearing he will miss the opera, refuses to take the call, tiptoeing out the door and yelling back, 'Tell them I'm dead!' As the secretary tells him the call is from Hofmeister, Lohmann himself grabs the receiver, tells him to go to hell and hangs up. Lang shows us Hofmeister seated at a desk as he realises the connection has been interrupted. He looks haggard as he puts the receiver down and runs his hands through his hair. He toggles the receiver bar again to re-establish the connection. Lohmann, who hasn't left, speaks to the secretary of his affection for Hofmeister who was thrown off the force for a foolish mistake. The phone rings again and the secretary hesitantly answers. We see Hofmeister bent over his desk as he speaks desperately into the phone saying, 'It's a matter of life and death.' Agitated, the secretary holds out the receiver to Lohmann who reluctantly takes it, complaining he is going to miss the first act again.

Lang intercuts between Hofmeister and Lohmann, as Hofmeister continues jabbering, explaining that he is on the trail of a gang of counterfeiters and is afraid for his life. Lohmann answers that he is on the line and Hofmeister expresses delight. Lohmann begs him to make it brief. Hofmeister, however, pauses, suddenly looking off to the left and pointing his automatic off screen. Then he relaxes and asks Lohmann to wait a moment. He puts the receiver down, wipes his brow and composes himself, then speaks into the phone again. Hofmeister asks Lohmann to take down what he is going to tell him and Lohmann dispatches his secretary to listen in on the extension and transcribe it. Hofmeister say he knows the name of the head of the gang. Lohmann asks who it is. Hofmeister, seated at his desk, is about to tell when the screen goes black. In the darkness we hear Hofmeister scream, 'The lights have gone out!' and beg Lohmann for help. For a few brief instants flashes of light illuminate the room as we hear gunfire. Lohmann calls Hofmeister's name into the phone and tells the secretary to trace the call. Suddenly from over the telephone we hear Hofmeister's voice as he sings a love song in a quavering voice. Horrified, Lohmann says, 'he must have gone mad with fright'.

The sequence's suspense revolves around the difficulty in making the telephone connection. At first Lohmann refuses to answer, then he hangs up. When the call is placed again and finally Lohmann is speaking to Hofmeister, it is Hofmeister's own fear and nervousness which delay the communication. We learn he knows the leader's name, but just as he is about to give it and has Lohmann and the secretary fully receptive at the other end of the line, he is interrupted again, this time, presumably, by the murderous gang. Lang, brilliantly aware of the interaction between the visual and the aural in film, expresses this interruption, which might have been simply conveyed by the line going dead, in two ways. First, visually: instead of cutting out the sound, he cuts out the visual image and has the screen go dark. The darkness provides a grim echo chamber for Hofmeister's piteous cries, and a visual way to convey the impact of gunshots as brief bursts of illumination in the darkened room. Then, aurally: Hofmeister's madness is conveyed not by silence but by noise. The phone line still carries his voice (audible to us over the wire for the first time) but no longer carries meaning. As with Mabuse's scribbles, no meaning is transmitted. The promised name is suspended, as if the phone connection had been put on hold.

The opening sequences of *The Testament of Dr. Mabuse* separate messages from their senders by severing their connection with receivers. Lohmann does not hear Hofmeister's information initially, therefore Hofmeister's message remains suspended. Mabuse remains silent and his reams of automatic writing seem to be addressed to no-one. Lohmann spends much of the rest of the film trying to understand Hofmeister's message, while Dr. Baum casts himself as Mabuse's heir apparent, not only deciphering his plans, but eventually feeling compelled to enact them. As we will see, Baum's relation to Mabuse's writings becomes one of complete subjection, behaving as if he were their servant. The writings themselves have this force, even after Mabuse's death, perhaps even doubly so. Disembodied, homeless messages seem to prowl through the film in search of someone to receive them, decode them (in Lohmann's case), enact and embody them (in Baum's case).

Something similar seems to happen to the film's own rhetoric. Whereas the openings of *Spies* and *Dr. Mabuse, the Gambler* strove to tie the film's power of editing and enunciation to its master criminal protagonists, *Testament* takes a different approach. No master criminal oversees the opening action. But if *The Testament of Dr. Mabuse* does not open with a demonstration of the power of its main character, its cinematic narration does not becomes any less overt. In fact, the contrary is true. Whereas the overt narration in the openings of *Spies* or *Dr. Mabuse, the Gambler* soon became naturalised by being tied to the master criminal character, both camera movement and editing in *Testament* follow the film's pattern of dispersal, as if searching for some figure that could command them, make them settle into a single association. The film opens with a truly dramatic tracking shot, a technique Lang premiered in the film that immediately precedes this one, *M*. The shot fades in on a doorway in an attic or basement storeroom, a deafening pounding noise on the soundtrack. No-one comes through the door. No-one enters the frame. Instead, the camera pivots to the right and begins to nose its way through this bizarre locale, past an incongruous melange of objects: old chairs and bottles, hanging lamps, an elaborately carved picture frame, bicycle wheels. Smaller objects vibrate with the pounding rhythm, as the camera continues searching – but for what? It picks its way among the crates and cupboards, brushing past a coiled rope hanging from the rafter, and then tilts down, abruptly revealing Hofmeister hiding behind one of the crates, terrified.

Although in some ways the shot recalls the stunning tracking shots which explore the Beggars' Union Hall in *M*, its purpose is very different. In, *M*, Lang uses the mobile camera to reveal the picturesque details of an unusual environment, picking out curious details: a man playing cards, beggars arranging half-smoked cigars, the manager changing the price of the leftover sandwiches. The shot is descriptive and scene-setting, provoking and satisfying our curiosity about the underside of Berlin. But the opening shot of *Testament* baffles us initially, moving through a space with little intrinsic interest, expressing an unexplained urgency underscored by the nerve-wracking soundtrack. At the end of the shot, we understand; we have tracked down Hofmeister who is hiding in fear for his life. As a suspenseful device, the camera movement leads us into the heart of the narrative situation. But typifying the sort of overt narration that David Bordwell indicates even classical films often display in their opening, it also foregrounds the camera's enunciating power, leading us by the hand before the dramatic situation has been revealed.[5] Acting like a prowling character smelling out its victim, the camera discovers Hofmeister totally independently of the gang's uncovering of his hiding place a few moments later. But who impels this disembodied force? There is no immediate (or even ultimate) answer.

Unlike most classically constructed films, in *The Testament of Dr. Mabuse* such overt narration is not restricted to this opening sequence. Here the editing between sequences draws attention to itself in a manner just as striking as the cuts to Mabuse, or Haghi, in the earlier films, but again without making a connection to a single overseeing consciousness. Noel Burch calls the playful relations set up in this film between the final shot of one sequence and the initial shot of the following one, 'rhyme'.[6] Although his definition remains rather vague, he clearly refers to the way these shots share some common element, formal or semantic, so that one of the shots seem to reply, reflect, comment on, or even parody the other. Burch finds the roots of this in the earlier Mabuse film, and indeed, it does derive from the free-ranging cutting of the earlier films. But instead of connecting scenes and actions back to Mabuse (or Haghi), in *Testament* these cuts refer us only to the film's own omniscient and playful narration. The narrative force remains disembodied, like the opening camera movement, strongly sensed, but not tied to an enunciator character.

The first three sequences bridge broad gaps in space and time with these formal echoes, creating, as Burch says, an apparent continuity across the spatio-temporal discontinuity of the shift between scenes. The first sequence, Hofmeister's attempted escape from the Mabuse gang, ends with an oil drum exploding, filling the frame with flames. As the shot fades out, the voice of Lohmann from the following scene can be heard exclaiming 'Feuerzauber!' (Fire magic). One assumes the voice comments on the flames we see, but, as the next scene fades in on the police headquarters, we realise Lohmann is discussing the musical motif of Wagner's *Die Valkyrie*. This sequence ends with Hofmeister's mindless singing over the telephone and Lohmann's reaction, 'He must have been frightened out of his wits.' Lang cuts directly to a medium shot of Dr. Baum facing the camera and announcing that, 'such cases are not unusual', that sudden frights or terrors can produce a mental collapse. We assume he is speaking about Hofmeister, but in fact this is the opening of his lecture to his class on Dr. Mabuse. This lecture ends with his description of the criminal plans that Mabuse produces, crimes worked out to the smallest details. Lang cuts from the lecture hall to a long shot of Mabuse's gang assembled, listening to a lieutenant explaining that, if they follow the 'doctor's plan' nothing can go wrong. This scene ends with the lieutenant on the phone saying incredulously, 'Lohmann is there himself?' Lang cuts to Lohmann examining the scene of Hofmeister's interrupted phone call. Sound, as Burch had noted, seals most of these rhymes, frequently with what seems to be a continuation of dialogue from one scene to another (a bit like Haghi's apparent gaze across cuts in *Spies*), sometimes with a visual image seemingly described by the sound in the next scene (Feuer), or word taking on flesh ('Lohmann there?' to Lohmann obviously there).

The semantic adaptability of these rhymes reveals the new approach to enunciation and narration taken in this film. Again and again we have to revise our notion of what is being referred to, pulling the references apart as we realise retroactively they don't fit. Discussing similar patterns in *M*, Michel Marie uses the useful term, 'delayed comprehension'.[7] Baum is not speaking of Hofmeister and Lohmann has not seen the explosion, and we must correct our first impression if we are to follow the film's action. It is as though there were a playful demon arranging sounds and images in this film, sometimes providing ambiguous clues (e.g. cutting from Lohmann saying he must find the brute who drove Hofmeister insane to a close-up of Dr. Mabuse staring at the camera – but is Mabuse responsible?), sometimes misleading red herrings. We are aware of our need to become careful readers, separating misleading cues from helpful ones, while catching the formal play in its elegance. But does this play carry a more sinister significance? The cut to Mabuse exemplifies the enigmas of this film and demarcates its difference from both the earlier Mabuse film or *Spies*. Whereas the question 'who is behind all this?' had an answer in the earlier films, *The Testament of Dr. Mabuse* only supplies a sense of infinite regression, embodied (or disembodied) in Mabuse himself (or is it in his writing?).

A testament conveys the will of a dead man. But a message from a dead man, like Mabuse's apparent scribbling, oscillating between apparently meaningless marks or noises and a translatable meaning, brings Lang's obsession with the origin of a message, the man behind it all, the author and grand enunciator, to a crisis, pushing the abstraction already evident in the figure of Haghi even further. As Nicole Brenez has claimed, in *Testament* 'the figure of Evil disperses. One can no longer assign it a body; it has become an idea which transmits itself.'[8] Mabuse appears in Baum's sanatorium as an only slightly animated corpse, his former physical energy gone. In his semi-catatonic condition he has become simply an apparatus of transmission and inscription, automatically writing his testament. In the opening sequences of both *Dr. Mabuse, the Gambler* and *Spies*, flexible cutting through space and time expresses the control exerted by the films' master criminal and grand enunciator, intercutting Mabuse with the crime or cutting back to Haghi as he asserts his dominance through his looks at the camera. In contrast, Mabuse first appears in *Testament* as an image projected in Baum's lecture, an object of apparent study and scientific curiosity, at antipodes to his spectacular demonstration of his enunciatory powers as Sandor Weltmann, master of illusions and of the minds of his audience. Yet Lang shows the automatic response of the student audience to this projected image. What power does Mabuse still hold and how does it operate? This question haunts the film. As Brenez beautifully indicates, dispersal rather than convergence becomes the figure of Mabuse's power – a power that infiltrates and contaminates nearly everything. As writing escapes the hand of the one who wrote it, Mabuse's will-to-power migrates through this film, even after his death.

'Pay No Attention to that Man behind the Curtain'

All visible objects, man, are but as pasteboard masks. But in
each event – in the living act, the undoubted deed – there
some unknown but still reasoning thing puts forth the
mouldings of its features from behind the unreasoning
mask. If man will strike, strike through the mask!

Herman Melville, *Moby Dick*[9]

In *Dr. Mabuse, the Gambler*, Mabuse exerted his powers over others through two
complementary methods. On the one hand his knowledge and manipulation of
modern modes of technology and information ordering, like the stock market or
the currency exchange, makes him a modern criminal *par excellence*. But his other
power, his control over others through hypnosis, while congruent with the revival
of interest in hypnosis in the Weimar Republic and its association with the modern
technique of psychoanalysis, also has an atavistic and supernatural aspect. In *Spies*,
Lang and Harbou restricted themselves to the rational and instrumental conspiracies provided by the modern means of surveillance and betrayal. But in *The Testament of Dr. Mabuse* Lang returns to the hypnotic and supernatural overtones of its
protagonist's previous history, simultaneously performing a retrospective homage
to the silent Weimar cinema.

As befits a character from a silent film, Mabuse remains mute throughout *Testament*, communicating only through his writing which, as we have seen, takes on a
life of its own, or – rather – demands a life of its own through Baum's enactment of
the scenarios it describes. Weimar cinema frequently invoked the magical and even
demonic power of writing – such as the words *Melior* and *Tsi Nan Fu* which
haunted von Wenk in the first Mabuse film. But the power of Mabuse's gaze, which
seemed to flicker out in his eyes at the end of the previous film, rekindles in this
film. The cut to Mabuse that follows Lohmann's statement that he wants to find the
one responsible for Hofmeister's loss of sanity, shows him in a catatonic state staring in front of him, his eyes heavily shadowed. In the shot that follows, the asylum
attendants discuss a change in their patient. He has suddenly stopped his mechanical scribbling and now just stares and sits 'like a corpse'. 'But his eyes, his eyes,' the
servant continues 'could paralyse you.' We cut back to Mabuse in his cell, as the servant voice continues, this time to a full-face close-up in which Mabuse stares at the
camera, recalling shots in the earlier film in which he seemed to claim the camera
with the force of his gaze, and threatens to exert his hypnotic powers. As Lang cuts
back to the hallway, the servant claims he is sure Mabuse could hypnotise people
still, and insists Dr. Baum should be informed.

The replacement of the act of writing by the hypnotic stare seems to equate the
two acts. It is primarily through his writing that Mabuse exerts the power of his will
in this film. This close-up of his stare is the only shot of this sort in the film. Rather
than announcing, as in previous films, the master criminal's attempt to take over
the enunciating power of the film itself, exerting his power directly on the audience
and identifying himself with the look of the camera, this close-up is Mabuse's
farewell to the film, the harbinger of his death. We learn later that Mabuse died that
very morning. Whether, and how, his power continues beyond his death becomes
one of the enigmas of the film, open to alternate interpretations which Lang keeps

alive by an even more complex reference to German film styles of the early 20s and Expressionism.

Baum's desire to implement Mabuse's plans by relaying them to his gang in Mabuse's name takes form as a dementia. But the film also hints that this kind of madness could be understood as Baum's surrender to Mabuse's hypnotic powers which continue after his death. Is Baum simply Mabuse's medium? In what is arguably his most overtly Expressionist sequence, Lang represents Baum's possession by the spirit of Mabuse in a manner that seems to visualise the doctor's psychosis (like the similarly Expressionist sequence of Hofmeister in his asylum cell). But Expressionism, as the representation of extreme states of being, could just as well convey supernatural possession as a hallucination. Lang seems to make this belated return to what was already an outmoded style precisely because Expressionism in film offers him this ambiguity. The unresolved question of madness or possession turns around the central question of this film: what is the ultimate source of messages; in this case, Baum's diseased imagination or Mabuse's hypnotic will?

This flashback to Expressionism is worth lingering over. Although standard film histories often class Lang as a master of Expressionist film, most often this term has simply become a common rubric for the fantastic style of Weimar cinema. Lang and his set designers were certainly influenced by Expressionist graphics, but in most of the films other visual influences (orientalism, romanticism, constructivism and finally *Neue Sachlichkeit*) seem equally important. Lang's strongest use of visual Expressionism occurs in the earlier Mabuse film as part of the 'image of the time', the contemporary reality of the early 20s in which the film takes place. Expressionism, apparent mainly in the artworks in Count Told's house, appears in the film, as Mabuse says when asked about the art movement, as 'a sport' (or pastime – *eine Spielerei*) one game among many that a *Spieler* might take up. Although it would be too simple to approach Lang as an Expressionist film-maker (he once told me that he and Bertolt Brecht were the only people he knew who admitted they did not know what Expressionism meant), Lang did exert a decisive and direct influence on the Expressionist film through his brief involvement with the one film which is generally acknowledged by even the most rigorous of critics to be Expressionist, *The Cabinet of Dr. Caligari*. In numerous interviews, Lang has claimed that it was his idea to construct a framing story for Janowitz and Mayer's script, providing a motivation for the Expressionist design as the visualisation of a madman's fantasy.[10] This transformation has, of course, been denounced both by Expressionists who found it a degraded interpretation of their style and by critics such as Kracauer who proclaimed the revision reactionary, converting a revolutionary parable about the madness of those in authority into a condemnation of critics of authority as insane (Franz's story, and the original script, ends with Dr. Caligari in a straitjacket in one of the cells of his own sanatorium, while the framing story ultimately places Franz in the jacket and cell).[11]

Could we read Lang's return to Expressionism in his last German film as a reference to this earlier film, and specifically to his own revision and reversal of other authors' work? Not only did Lang's revision transform Mayer and Janowitz's original script, it also called into question the validity of the film's interior narrator, creating an ambiguity of narration that became a motif of art cinema for decades to come (from *Caligari* to *Rashomon*). *Testament* questions the source of utterances in a more complex way than simply finding its narrator insane. But it is striking that Baum's relation to his patient, Mabuse, mirrors, and reverses, the central situation of *The Cabinet of Dr. Caligari*. In *Caligari*, the head of an asylum receives a cataleptic patient whom he realises he can make obey his bidding, even to commit murder and abduction. In *Testament*, Baum receives a cataleptic patient who reveals his resources of intelligence and will by writing his plans and compelling (possibly through hypnosis) the doctor to carry them out. After the criminal plans of the doctors in both films have been exposed, they end up patients in their own asylums. Both the similarities and the reversals are striking, as well as the fact that at the end of his German career Lang in effect restores the original ending to *Caligari*. From Caligari to Mabuse, and back again? That Lang's account of the banning of *Testament* and Goebbels' offer to become the Third Reich's 'Film Führer' became his own greatest self-fabrication makes this proliferation of stories and revisions even more dizzying.

If Baum is, in fact, possessed or hypnotised by Mabuse, Lang initially avoids the same portrayal of hypnosis he used in the earlier Mabuse film: the intercutting of the victim and the hypnotised based on the look – especially having each character face the camera directly, gazing into its lens. Instead, Lang creates a more complex and devious play on visual fascination, at first, obscurely subtle and then, spectacularly flamboyant. While writing in his cell under Baum's close examination, Mabuse's gaze does not deviate from the page, even as Baum hovers over him, reading over his shoulder. Lang cuts, rather inexplicably, to the large barred window of the cell, then back to Baum observing Mabuse's unceasing production, directional light from the window strongly highlighting them. Suddenly (almost subliminally – if a sharp discordant note on the soundtrack did not draw our attention to it) a shadow (from the window?) passes over them. Baum pivots abruptly to the left, less as though he saw the shadow than as if its passage triggered his sudden movement. The camera, just as abruptly, pans to the left, perfectly synchronised with the turn of Baum's head. As he stares at the opposite wall, a transparent superimposition of Mabuse stands briefly before him, then fades away. As the phantom disappears, the camera pans further left following another turn of Baum's head and shows the attendant gathering the pages of Mabuse's inscriptions. It pans back to the right to Baum, and, as Lang cuts to a reverse angle, Baum passes his hand over his face and rubs his eyes. He turns and looks again at Mabuse who has been writing without interruption, then looks in the direction of his previous vision.

The action favours viewing the apparition as a hallucination: Baum's own disbelief, or at least bafflement, argues that he himself doubts this vision. But Lang's elaborate and somewhat oblique staging of this vision sequence gives it a unique tone. The progression from the light source (the window), to the shadow, to the wall before which the figure appears, does not employ Lang's most frequent style of a visionary moment: the overlap-dissolve and the apparent penetration of appearances granted the visionary. Instead, it would seem that Baum himself projects this vision on the wall, like an interior movie. There is no seeing through disguises here. Just as Lang moves even farther away from the allegorical mode with the coming of sound, visionary scenes in Lang's sound films take on a more ambiguous quality, more frequently visualising a character's personal obsession than a stark glimpse into the nature of things.

But Mabuse's phantom could be read as his own projection, the phantom body of his writing which will persist after his death – indeed become more powerful and substantial with his death. Mabuse's death happens off screen, apparently soon after the close-up which shows his hypnotic gaze fixed on the camera/audience. We learn of his death as Inspector Lohmann begins to follow the trail of this enigmatic name. As he tells his assistant to phone Dr. Baum and find out if Mabuse is still his patient, Lang uses a device frequent in this film and strongly related to the rhymes between scenes: cutting to a single shot in some other location which either illustrates or counterpoints the character's dialogue. Here the cut supplies a grim irony. We see a close-up of the bare feet of a corpse being tagged with the name 'Mabuse'. In the next shot, Lohmann's assistant reports Mabuse's death. But as Lohmann expresses amazement at this sudden death, Lang fades in on a typewritten note in the hands of Kent, one of the gang members, reading: 'Tonight at midnight – Dr. Mabuse'. The messages continue, projecting their time schedule into the future.

The inter-scene rhymes continue to focus on the question of Mabuse's power. Lang cuts from a gang member warning Kent that, 'the Doctor is stronger than we are' to the morgue where Baum pulls a sheet from the face of Mabuse's corpse to show Lohmann, who has insisted on seeing the corpse himself. Again the meaning of the rhyme is equivocal. Is it ironic? The powerful doctor is now dead. Or is his death a source of power, a literal disembodying that will magnify rather than reduce his influence? The conversation between Lohmann and Baum turns on Mabuse's genius and Baum's nearly accidental mention of his 'testament', which he immediately tries to modify: 'Not a testament in the usual sense, an account [*Niederschrift*] which would only interest a doctor'. Baum ends the sequence as it began, this time covering up the corpse's face with the white sheet, from which Lang cuts immediately to the white sheet of paper bearing the Doctor's message for the gang to gather, 'Tonight at midnight – Dr. Mabuse'. This next shot shows the gang gathered to receive orders.

Lang cuts from the gang assembled at the appointed hour to a close-up of a page of Mabuse's 'testament'. As in the pages projected in Baum's lecture, the writing seems animated, the lines moving in a variety of orientations and patterns. In the centre of the page is the word GAS surrounded by a circle and surmounted by a crude face whose features grow out of the letters. Like the magical words in Lang's silent films, and like the Expressionist calligraphy of both intertitles and imagery in *The Cabinet of Dr. Caligari* (especially the doctor's diary and the words which haunt him during his hallucination and seem to compel him to his crimes: *Du musst Caligari werden* … 'You must become Caligari'), these words tend toward images and seem to vibrate with an energy and will of their own.[12] As in *Caligari* the words seem to play a role in the transformation of the character. As Baum turns the page we briefly glimpse the paper beneath this one, with a similar swirl of letters and images and the central word *Tot* (Dead). Lang cuts to a high angle long shot of Baum in his office seated at his desk hunched over Mabuse's writings.

There follows an extraordinary sequence: one of Lang's most Expressionistically conceived scenes, and most extended visionary moments. But like the earlier brief appearance of Mabuse's phantom, ambivalence rules this scene: is it a supernatural phenomenon, or a hallucination due to a sick mind? In either case, Baum, in contrast to Lang's previous visionaries – the maiden in *Der müde Tod*, Kriemhild or Freder – becomes the victim of his vision. After a close shot of Baum leafing through the manuscript, Lang cuts to a low angle close-up of several archaic artworks Baum has displayed on the top of his bookcase (presumably part of Lang and Harbou's extensive private collection of primitive art), especially a large South Sea Island mask with exaggerated eyes and mouth. A high angle shot of carefully arranged shelves of skulls (including several deformed ones) follows before we return to Baum at his desk. The cutting presents Baum as the object of an uncanny gaze from lifeless, yet disturbingly expressive, entities. This intercutting continues with another elaborate mask, followed first by mummified skulls with tattooed skin and shells for eyes, and then an Expressionist painting of stylised faces with exaggerated eyes. As Baum searches the dead Mabuse's *Testament*, he is silently watched from every corner of the room by eyes that are not human. Baum seems to have found the page he is searching for. The page fills the screen, with large letters reading 'The Mastery of Crime' again surrounded by patterns of letters merging into drawings. We hear Baum's voice issuing from the previous silence, as he reads these words, and then repeats them in a deeper, awed voice, looking up at the camera with an astonished gaze.

The first part of this sequence associated the gaze with inanimate objects, the dead or images of demons and spirits. Now, as Baum looks at the camera and speaks Mabuse's words out loud, we find Lang finally returning to a portrayal of the hypnotic gaze he created in the first Mabuse film. At the same time, Baum's reading of the manuscript recalls scenes of supernatural invocation in earlier fantastic films of the silent Weimar cinema, such as *Faust* or *The Golem*. As Mabuse's writing fills the screen, Baum's voice reads it, intoning Mabuse's philosophy of crime: the committing of apparently meaningless crimes which bring no profit to anyone in order to spread fear and terror. The camera tracks in on Baum as he closes his eyes as if ruminating on these words, or concentrating his thoughts. A strange whispering voice continues the manifesto of crime. Baum's eyes flash open suddenly and he stares into the camera lens. However, rather than lingering on this enunciatory gaze, Lang cuts almost immediately to a 180 degree reverse angle, showing, presumably, what Baum now sees.

Cued by an eerie chord on the soundtrack, we see Mabuse, the source of the whispering voice, seated before Baum, a semi-transparent image perched on the previously empty chair. But this is not the Mabuse we saw earlier in the asylum; the face of this creature has absorbed the stylised features of the primitive masks. In close-up, Baum still stares in horror and fascination at the camera, but there is no power in his gaze. As in the shots of von Wenk as he goes under Mabuse's hypnotic influence, Baum seems caught in a trance. The following reverse angle facial close-up of the wraith of Mabuse shows his mask-like features more clearly (dropping the transparent superimposition). His nose has become a pointed beak, with an edge as sharp as a knife. His eyes have expanded – almond-shaped and huge, like the eyes of ancient Sumerian idols. With mere pinpoints for pupils, they project an inhuman intensity that somehow suits the impassioned, yet feeble, croaking whisper that issues from his mouth.

A long shot of Baum at his desk (but from the opposite side of the camera axis from the earlier long shot) shows him seated across from the transparent Mabuse. But the phantom then divides itself into two; another transparent Mabuse rises from the seated one and appears behind Baum's chair. As the seated phantom continues to transfix Baum with his stare, the standing one places the manuscript before him to read; the two sources of Mabuse's hypnotic influence in this film are brought together, his testament and his gaze. The standing phantom then places its hands on the desk and moves to sit down in Baum's chair across from its *Doppleganger*. Its motion aligns it with Baum's body and as it merges with his space, a drum beat sounds on the soundtrack, and both phantoms disappear. The implication is that they have merged with Baum, become one with him. The image of the phantom being absorbed by Baum's body reverses the ending of *Der müde Tod*, in which Death caused a transparent phantom to rise from the lovers and then led them to the heavenly realm. In its reversal of this action, the imagery of Mabuse and Baum takes on an infernal and perverse tone. Baum succeeds where the maiden failed – he has brought the dead back to life. But Lang shows the horror the maiden escaped, the loss of self which occurs when the dead person lives again by eclipsing its living host.

In *The Testament of Dr. Mabuse* Dr. Baum begins as Mabuse's analyst and becomes his avatar. Once he deciphers the doctor's scribblings, he no longer simply analyses them but takes them as scenarios to be enacted. He gathers a gang around him to carry out Mabuse's plans. The rhyming transition between Baum's lecture and the scene that follows already indicated this direct route from inscription to implementation. Facing the camera as he lectures, Baum declares that Mabuse's scribbles described criminal plans worked out to the finest details. Lang cuts to a group of unsavoury gangsters as a lieutenant similarly speaking before them seems to complete Baum's lecture, but by putting it into an operative mode, declaring that if they follow the doctor's plan nothing should go wrong. This relay of communication constitutes a major structure of Baum's conspiracy, as well as a major theme of the film. Apparently in order to preserve his double life (as respectable psychologist and would-be master criminal) Baum communicates to this gang only indirectly, using the name Dr. Mabuse in all his written communications. This indirect communication seems to demand a *mise-en-scène*, and in addition to the written message, Baum/Mabuse stages highly ritualised audiences of the gang with the crime boss, known as 'the man behind the curtain'.

Lang first introduced the location of his *mise-en-scène* as a single shot scene cut into a longer scene. Two gang members discuss the odd set-up, as one expresses concern over the unorthodox procedures of their criminal acts, especially their lack of profit. The other gangster cautions him with a brief account of this 'predecessor' who was too curious about the boss. The crook's description continues in voice-over, a technique Lang had pioneered in *M*, as Lang cuts to the 'room with the curtain' for the first time. Although the shot serves partly as a visual translation of the gangster's account, it also exceeds that role. The camera shows a door within an apparently empty room with peeling wallpaper. The camera then pans around the room as the voice goes silent, repeating the sort of searching motion that opened the film, passing the drab walls and a bricked up window until it reaches a shabby floor-to-ceiling curtain. The voice-over resumes saying, 'There!', the camera tilts down the curtain, as the crook's voice explains 'we found what was left of him'. On the floor we see the body of a man, one hand grasping the fabric of the curtain in *rigor mortis*. The curtain, we realise, conceals a deadly secret.

Baum's identity as the new Dr. Mabuse and as the 'man behind the curtain' is not explicitly revealed until near the end of the film, but Lang supplies more than enough indications to the audience long before the characters discover it. Many of these are contained in rhymes between scenes, like the cut from the lecture hall to the gang. The first audience with the 'man behind the curtain' follows a similar rhyme. At the asylum one of the servants starts to open Baum's office door, only to be addressed by his off screen voice announcing 'I do not wish to be disturbed!' We cut to the gang approaching the outer door to the 'room with the curtain'. This door opened, another one is revealed behind it, bearing a complex lock, like a door to a bank vault. This is opened with both a combination and a key, and, as it swings open, we see, in the far reaches of the room, the curtain (rendered diaphanous by backlighting) with the dark silhouette of a seated man visible through it. As the room becomes illuminated the curtain becomes opaque and the silhouette vanishes. In a series of alternating 180 degree reversals (which deviate from frontality only with shots of Kent, the sympathetic member of the gang who refuses to be involved in killings), Lang cuts between a long shot of the curtain and the members of the gang as they are issued instructions by a voice that emerges from the behind the curtain.

The sequence of Baum's possession by the dead Mabuse ends with Lang's clearest indication of the professor's implementation of the doctor's plan via the 'man behind the curtain'. Another of Mabuse's pages fills the screen, showing in large letters the phrase, 'Raid on the Railway, Gas Meters and Chemical Factories', each word worked into an image ('Railway' provided with wheels, 'Gas Meter' with a round dial face, the letters of 'Chemical Factory' becoming smoke stacks). As a hand turns the page, Lang cuts to a long shot of the famous curtain from which the voice issues, instructing his minions on the raid on the chemical factory. A close-up shows another Mabuse manuscript being laid down (the location of this paper is not specifically indicated). This plan announces the 'Action against Banks and Currency', with the words 'Inflation' multiplying across the page, along with proliferating circles that become both zeros and coins. Again we see the underlings receiving orders from the off screen voice intercut with the curtain as a plan to place counterfeit notes in banks is detailed by the man behind the curtain.

The final revelation of what lies behind the curtain comes with the climax of the film's rather saccharine and tiresome romantic subplot of the reform of the gangster, Kent, through his love for the office worker Lilli. After Kent fails to show up for a gang operation the pair are kidnapped (by a false beggar, a figure who appears in all of Lang's German thrillers) and taken to the 'room with the curtain'. In the familiar frontal shot of the curtain, the voice announces the lovers' death sentence for treachery. Kent and Lilli look directly at the camera as they respond. Infuriated by the voice declaring that neither Kent nor his woman will leave the room alive, Kent fires his revolver – following the axial logic of nearly all shots in this room – directly at the camera.

The following shot reflects the perverse playfulness of this whole film, disorienting us when we think we know what is going on, deviating just a bit from our expectations with another example of 'delayed comprehension'. We see the curtain and

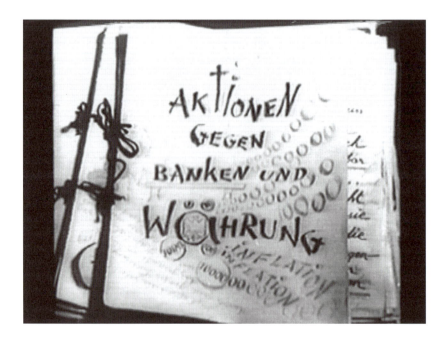

hear the gun shots. The curtain flutters with movement, hands emerge and pull it apart, and we see – Kent and Lilli. After the gunfire we expected a shot of the curtain, a reverse angle shot from Kent and Lilli's point of view, conforming to the alternating editing pattern of all previous scenes in this room. We do see the curtain, but only after the lovers enter do we realise that this is not a reverse angle showing the curtain as Lilli and Kent see it. Instead Lang films the curtain from an entirely new position, from a space it has never entered before – from *behind* the curtain. Rather than a reverse angle, the camera has maintained its previous orientation, but moved back behind the curtain. As Kent and Lilli emerge from the curtain they stop and stare directly at the camera, amazed at what they see off screen. The surprise of re-orienting ourselves about what side of the curtain we are seeing works well to underscore this suspenseful moment, delaying a bit the revelation of 'the man behind the curtain'.

That the man is Baum we are well prepared for. But that is not what the delayed reverse angle delivers. We not only don't see Baum, we see no-one. The sight which stops Kent and Lilli in their tracks is a dark silhouette, a flat cut-out figure of a seated man (now perforated by Kent's bullets) propped up behind a desk which holds both a microphone and a loudspeaker. What we find is not Baum, but Baum's apparatus, the mechanics of voice and listening and a rather pathetic shadow puppet of a human figure. Michel Chion's incisive analysis of this sequence describes the startling effect of Kent and Lilli parting the curtains as if the pair were emerging from the fictional space of the screen, discovering the theatre and the audience.[13] It is hard to escape a sense of self-reflexivity in this sequence. Of course, the reverse shot that follows revealing what the couple actually sees does not – cannot – provide what Chion calls, '*mirage of the absolute reverse shot*', the image of the audience watching the film; but it nonetheless remains self-reflexive; this image of an exposed loudspeaker would be precisely what a viewer would discover if he or she penetrated the screen itself.[14] This exposure of a loudspeaker as the source of the voices of the characters on the screen remains a disorienting experience.

While this technological mediation may preserve Baum's identity from discovery, Baum's use of a private radio broadcast to communicate with his gang recalls the opening of the first Mabuse film and the technological web of communication and surveillance which surrounds the master criminal. But if the original Dr. Mabuse appeared like a prosthetic God due to his technological accoutrements, Baum seems abstracted, rendered somehow bodiless, by them, the awesome 'man behind the curtain' reduced to a cardboard silhouette, a stand-in, a relay between points. Kent's tearing down the curtain, the theatrical prop which has mystified the identity and the power of the 'doctor' who helms the gang, corresponds more closely to the visionary scene in the earlier films than does the scene of Baum's possession. This action exposes the apparatus of the Destiny-machine in this film, the technology of voice and sound that undergirds Baum's machinations. The apparatus itself, aligned here with the apparatus of the new sound film, is exposed, and while the microphone is not Baum, Baum himself by this time is little more than a loudspeaker carrying Mabuse's voice.

However, the revelation does not allow Kent to understand the nature of the trap he finds himself in. The apparatus looks silly, a child's contraption masquerading for a powerful human being. But it does render Baum invulnerable; the bullets pass through the silhouette, but do not touch him. Revealing the mechanism beneath the illusion in this case only perpetuates the mystery. The uninterrupted power of the Destiny-machine immediately makes itself known as the last voice coming over the loudspeaker takes on the role of Lang's ultimate Destiny-machine – the clock. 'You have three hours to live', the voice announces. This off screen voice gives way to another sinister sound from an undetermined locale, a loud ticking that signals the activation of a time bomb.

The Testament of Dr. Mabuse was Lang's second sound film, following *M*. As in the earlier film, sound plays an important role in creating a new environment of terror, especially as a new device for opening up off screen space. Chion's discussion of the film shows how off screen sound, especially the voice of Baum over the loud-speaker, creates a unique uncertainty and terror throughout this film. In the open-ing sequence of the discovery of Hofmeister's hiding place, ear-shattering machine noise not only drowns out all other sounds, but shakes the set with its pounding vibrations. In both that sequence and this one, in spite of (as Chion points out) the extremely different nature of the respective noises, the soundtrack delivers the sound of the Destiny-machine: the terrifying apparatus set in motion by the 'doctor's' gang, channelled through the loudspeaker, ticking off the lovers' last moments as surely as one of Death's candles, and having its origin and impetus in Mabuse's automatic writing.[15]

The very logic of *Testament*, its further development from the earlier master criminal films, relies on the disembodied nature of Mabuse and the Destiny-machine. As Jonathan Crary has described the progression of the Mabuse series as a whole, 'What becomes clear is how the name "Mabuse" does not finally designate a fictional character that Lang returned to several times … Rather Mabuse is the name of a system – a system of spectacular power whose strategies are continually changing.'[16] *Dr. Mabuse, the Gambler* and *Spies* turned on the way the master crim-inal identified himself with the apparatus of the Destiny-machine and then discov-ered his hubristic mistake. In *Testament*, Mabuse is already nothing more than a machine, a series of automatic responses. Baum progressively merges with this mechanical, disembodied will; he is portrayed as its tool rather than its master. Thus Mabuse discards his body and gains another one as he moves into Baum's frame. Neither Baum nor Mabuse need a body to convey their will to underlings; all they need is a voice and an apparatus to carry it.

But does this voice have a source? Kent discovers he cannot confront it. Once it falls silent the voice is replaced by an even more sinister noise – the ticking of the time bomb.[17] As Kent and Lilli first hear it, their eyes dart around the frame, seeking its source. Kent announces that they must find and dismantle the bomb. The sound rhyme that links this statement to the next scene mocks Kent's resolution with the sar-donic wit that marks this film. The ticking of the bomb mixes into the rhythmic tap-ping of a spoon against the shell of a soft boiled egg as Lang cuts to one of the gangsters eating breakfast. Where does the ticking sound come from? Anywhere I choose, responds Lang. Succeeding scenes show Kent and Lilli tearing up the very foundation of this empty room with no exit, splintering the floorboards, prying bricks from the wall, without finding either the bomb or an escape route. Only by turning the room's limited utilities against itself, rupturing a water line to flood the room and buffer the impact of the explosion, do the couple escape the Destiny-machine.

The audiences Baum arranges for his gang to maintain both his anonymity and his power display a theatrical *mise-en-scène*, and a highly theatrical central prop, the cur-tain. But unlike the theatrical demonstration of the power of illusion given by the stage personae of Lang's previous master criminal's – Mabuse's Sandor Weltmann or Haghi's Nemo – here the curtain never rises and the criminal never performs. Haghi's disguise has become literal: there is *no-one* behind the curtain, nobody is there, only a piece of wood and the apparatus channelling a distant voice. As the room fills with water, Lang shows both these props floating abjectly about the flooded room. There is no show behind the curtain, Mabuse is dead. And yet in some sense the show must go on ...

The Same Old Song, but with a Different Meaning
(Since You've Been Gone)

'I know of one Greek labyrinth which is a single straight line. Along that line so many philosophers have lost themselves that a mere detective might well do so, too.'
Jorge Luis Borges, 'Death and the Compass'[18]

Both Baum and Lohmann spend the film dealing with messages sent by others: Baum relaying and enacting the instructions of Mabuse; Lohmann trying to decode the message of crime, read it and trace it back to its source. Both Lohmann and Mabuse are characters brought in from other movies, Mabuse from Lang's first silent super-film, Lohmann from *M*, Lang's first sound film. Lohmann's undeniable corporeality contrasts with Mabuse's mute and ultimately disembodied image. While Mabuse's mode of communication is writing, Lohmann primarily uses the telephone, as would be appropriate for their respective eras of film history. But just as Mabuse gains an eerie voice as he takes over Dr. Baum, Lohmann too must confront the materiality of messages, both Hofmeister's aborted phone call and the hieroglyphics of crime.

After Hofmeister's opening phone call Lohmann next appears in the room from which Hofmeister phoned him. As Lohmann examines the crime scene, trying to reconstruct what happened from the arrangement of objects, his spoken comments are immediately transcribed by a typist (initially off screen – only the clatter of her machine indicating her presence), while the room itself is photographed. Lohmann paces through the room trying to re-enact the past events, the camera panning and following his movements and gestures. Taking on Hofmeister's role, he backs towards the window, which he then examines to see if he could have escaped through it, and decides in the negative. However, examining the window as he closes it, he notices something. Imitating again the role of Hofmeister, backed up against the window by the incoming gang, he moves his hand behind his back in a curious fashion. We soon recognise another 'writing in air' gesture: Lohmann believes Hofmeister has left a message on this pane of glass. Lohmann kneels before it, claiming 'There is writing here.' In close-up we see a number of indecipherable scratches. Lohmann spends the film following Hofmeister's fragmentary messages, this writing on glass and his never-completed phone call.

Lohmann and the police submit the scratches on glass to a series of processes in the hope of making them yield a message. Lohmann demands that the pane be removed and brought to headquarters. There we see it photographed and the photograph scrutinised by experts. One sits over it, tracing the pattern of scratches with his finger, as if its message might be in Braille, or using the recurrent gesture of 'writing in air' as a trigger to understanding or memory. He then begins to make sounds, like a child sounding out a new word: 'Ma bu'. He picks up a pen and traces on the photograph. We cut to a close-up of the photograph on his desk as he completes the tracing. In a shot which brings the themes of writing and transmission of writing through reversal to a climax, we recognise the message spelled out before us backwards: Mabuse. To complete the transference from trace to message the police officer places a blotter over his inked-in pattern. Turning it over, the name magically appears complete and correctly oriented: Mabuse.

The police expert looks at the fruit of his labour and announces, 'It says Mabuse!' Lohmann, walking in at this moment, asks, 'What says Mabuse?' The expert now places the blotter decoded name next to the scratches on the window pane, which reflect him like a mirror. Explaining that Hofmeister must have written with his back to the window, he swivels the windowpane and makes two reversals, upside-down, then left to right. Now, even on the window the scratches seem to announce the name, Mabuse. Properly aligned, the window now reflects Lohmann as he gazes at the writing he intuited was there and now can read. The reversals in the writing reflect the reversals of a mirror, while the reflections of expert and Lohmann remind us of the window's capacity to reflect as well as transmit. It is as though in this brief scene, Lang demonstrates the registers of the sign, from symbolic writing, to iconic reflection, all through the index of the trace. But what does it mean, how do we move from signifier to signified?

Lohmann repeats the name three times as he examines window scratches, blotter paper and, it seems, his own reflection. This accumulation of signs, visual, written, aural, jogs some memory as Lohmann proclaims, 'Yes he was ... the doctor from the Inflation period.' The phrase bridges two scenes, Lohmann's words completed over an image of the multitiered police archive as a Kafka-like assistant shakily climbs a ladder to hand down to Lohmann the dusty file on Dr. Mabuse, which he announces with the title to Lang's film 'Dr. Mabuse, the Gambler'. As I mentioned earlier, when Lohmann enquires about Dr. Mabuse he learns he has just died and all

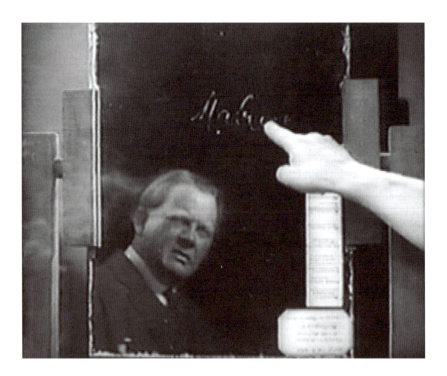

he can interrogate is a corpse. Hofmeister's message leads to the name, the name to the archive and the archive self-referentially back to Lang's film-making. The labyrinth of this detective story is a modernist one, always twisting back to the conditions of its own generation.

What is primary in this film, what lies not just behind the crimes, but behind the name, Mabuse? Hofmeister's message has been read, but has been separated from his voice. Mabuse's testament has been read, but has been separated from his body. For Chion, a voice separated from the body becomes what he calls an *acousmetre*, an unseen, but heard, presence whose mysterious invisibility endows it with a sense of omnipresence and omniscience.[19] Although Baum may embody the voice which controls the gang, it would seem the voice controls him rather than vice versa. Beyond the supernatural or pathological explanations for Baum's possession by Mabuse, Baum has already liberated his own voice from his body via technology. Not only the radio broadcasts as the 'man behind the curtain', but also the recording that Lohmann and Kent discover when they invade Baum's office which has kept servants at bay by announcing 'I do not wish to be disturbed' when the door handle was turned. Significantly, Kent could not recognise Baum as the voice from behind the curtain when he encountered him in person at the police office. However, when he hears Baum's voice 'technologically mediated' (as Lohmann describes it) via this recording device, he immediately recognises it.

One more time Kent bursts through a barrier to get at the voice he hears behind it, he and Lohmann teaming up to break through the door to Dr. Baum's study, only to find no-one there but another device, the gramophone projecting Baum's voice. The empty study still reveals the signs of Baum/Mabuse's authorship, the map spread out on the desk which details the chemical factory he is at this very moment involved in destroying. As Lohmann discovers pages of Mabuse's testament, the handwritten sheets fill the screen, describing the attack. Through an overlap-dissolve, flaming windows appear on the pages of writing and Lang then cuts to a series of images of the chemical factory in flames, the last and one of the most elaborate of his German conflagrations. The visual language short-circuits human agency; it is as though the words themselves provoke the flames and the inferno. Not even Baum's voice is needed, only Mabuse's words.

And what about the other route for Hofmeister's message, the voice 'technologically mediated' by the phone? Lohmann pursues this pathway to the end as well. After disappearing immediately after the aborted phone call, Hofmeister is later brought into an asylum, still jabbering nonsense. Lang portrays his madness as a suspended and repeated moment within the interrupted phone call – Hofmeister still desperate to make his connection and deliver his message. We see him in close-up, his hand to his face holding a non-existent telephone as he mechanically repeats, 'Hello, hello, Commissioner?' The camera pulls back and Lang at his most Expressionist visualises Hofmeister's hallucinatory state, sitting at a glass desk surrounded by crystalline objects: a lamp, bibelots and a glass telephone to the right (although Hofmeister continues to speak into a non-existent receiver). Lohmann enters Hofmeister's asylum cell with the doctor. From Hofmeister's distorted perception, we see superimposed over them a distorted cell with transparent crystalline walls, and the phantom figures of the gang members who terrorised Hofmeister earlier. Switching out of the mode of subjective hallucination, Lang shows Hofmeister seated on a rough prison bench as he recoils with horror and begins his nonsense singing.

The doctor explains to Lohmann that, when Hofmeister thinks he is being watched, he sings and when he thinks he is alone, he tries to call Lohmann. Left alone with Hofmeister, who has begun his pantomime phone call again, Lohmann tries to break through his madness by restoring the phone connection, completing the circuit of information. Taking out his pocket-watch, Lohmann manipulates it so the alarm bell sounds. Using this bell as a Pavlovian substitute for the telephone, Lohmann tries to patch himself into the hermetic world of Hofmeister's madness. He pretends to answer the call: 'Hello Hofmeister, Lohmann here.' But the connection remains elusive. Hofmeister ignores this ersatz telephone call. Lohmann cannot get through on Hofmeister's line, which is stuck in the endless repetition of the traumatic moment before the connection was interrupted.

This sequence provides a fascinating gloss to Lang's treatment of the telephone apparatus.[20] These telephone calls certainly would function – if Hofmeister could make the connection – as all the things we have seen telephone calls represent for Lang: a means of communication; an indication of the social order (Hofmeister calling his superior); and as a forging of a connection across space that allows Hofmeister's surveillance to bear fruit – the exposure of the sinister gang of counterfeiters. But since the connection remains blocked, not only is Hofmeister's message undelivered, but he loses his sanity as well. He remains outside the system in a state of psychosis, condemned to meaningless repetition of his call, his identity and sanity astray in the fissure which has appeared within the system. Indeed, the film ends when Hofmeister finally regains his sanity as Dr. Baum (who has lost his) wanders into Hofmeister's cell and introduces himself as Dr. Mabuse. Hofmeister shrieks the missing name that has now been given him. 'Mabuse!' echoes down the corridors, and Hofmeister emerges from his cell finally to recognise Lohmann and deliver his message, so long delayed: 'The man is called Mabuse, Herr Commissioner, Dr. Mabuse.' While the completed message provides a form of narrative closure, the irony of the film lies in the fact that the name Mabuse has circulated throughout the film continuously, a name which now means absolutely nothing

(Mabuse himself is dead) and yet retains an almost thaumaturgic power. The man who now calls himself Mabuse, Dr. Baum, sits in Hofmeister's cell madly tearing up strips of paper. Power and impotence, brilliance and madness combine in this name, the only message the system seems capable of sending and receiving.

Hofmeister provides a parable about modern identity through the medium of the telephone, as an exemplar of modern systems in Lang. The phone may serve as a simple tool of communication, relating subordinate to superior, sender to receiver, and relaying the message through its apparatus. But, if this system malfunctions, the force of the interruption is more than a momentary check to communication. The sender's whole identity is placed in peril, because his place within the system has been lost. He is thrown into a psychotic position, unable to recognise his surroundings or other people, compelled to repeat the original trauma of the missed connection, or to produce meaningless noise, random songs and hallucinations. Therefore the system does not simply relay messages, it maintains identity and meaning as places within a functioning series of connections.

Two extreme relations to the system are captured in the scenes of Hofmeister's helpless cycles of unsuccessful phone calls, and Mabuse's earlier mastery of space and time as he masterminds a theft through his knowledge and use of railway schedules and telephone link-ups. Mabuse has the illusion that such systems are an extension of his will, and thereby the media of power and corruption. Hofmeister discovers he has no existence when connections fail. Hofmeister is cured when he can finally deliver his message, patching himself back into the world's switchboard. Mabuse goes mad when his systems seem to collapse around him and the state's attorney penetrates his stronghold, his state within a state, by means of a switchboard operator. The system itself seems to invite both madness and corruption: the illusion of power on the one hand; on the other, an identity reduced to being a relay within the system, a relay which can, in fact, lose its connection.

7

M: The City Haunted by Demonic Desire

'Oh Mother I Am Lost!' The Murder of Elsie Beckmann

Out of the deceitful emptiness of a mirror
A face rises slowly and indistinctly
From the horror and darkness: Cain!
The velvet curtain rustles quietly.
The moon shines into emptiness through the window.
I am alone with my murderer.

Georg Trakl, 'Horror'[2]

If *Metropolis* is the albatross around Lang's neck, *M* remains his most universally admired film. The complexity and originality of its structure, the studied ambiguity and ambivalence of its themes, the power of its images and sound guarantee it a place in film history and film criticism no matter how much canons are abjured or the idea of masterpieces viewed with suspicion. Such status and achievement frequently

freezes critical acumen, although in the case of this film at least three brilliant studies, those of Noel Burch, Roger Dadoun and Anton Kaes, have ventured insights
which have deeply influenced my own remarks, and a host of other fine essays and
studies have been produced.[3] No critic can hope to propose a definitive or even a
thorough reading of this film. But I will approach it in terms of Lang's total *œuvre*,
and as a pivotal film, one that turns like a hinge between Lang's silent cinema and
sound cinema, and also (I would maintain even more than the film that follows it
chronologically, *The Testament of Dr. Mabuse*) between his German and his American career. *M* ties up a number of themes from the first part of Lang's career
(although in some respects – such as the homage to the Expressionist tradition discussed in the last chapter – *Testament* provides the true farewell to Germany and
silent cinema), but most importantly it announces new themes and preoccupations.
    The structure of *M* is unique, the high point of Harbou's work as a scriptwriter.
Rather than being built around a central conflict between individuated characters
and/or a heterosexual romance (the classical patterns of narrative cinema and evident in every previous Lang film), *M* takes its form from both process and setting,
an interaction expressed in one of the secondary titles sometimes given the film, *A
City Searches for a Murderer*. The systematic nature of the search, a rational, goal-
oriented process, interacts with the gridded space of the modern city with its networks of communication and intersections already explored in Lang's master
criminal films. But like the highly symbolic spaces of his allegorical films, particularly the court of Worms in *The Death of Siegfried* and the urban and industrial
spaces of *Metropolis*, the city in *M* seems to possess a will of its own; as this secondary title suggests, it could be seen as the protagonist of the film.
    The film's lack of an immediately identifiable protagonist who organises the
point of view of the film marks its greatest difference from previous Lang films
(even *The Testament of Dr. Mabuse* with its mystery surrounding the figure of Dr.
Mabuse and his role in the film, ultimately centres on a conflict between Lohmann
and Baum). As Noel Burch was one of the first to point out, Hans Beckert could
hardly be said to dominate the film's action since he is rarely even seen in the first
half of the film.[4] Although a stronger claim might be made for Lohmann's role in
the action as the detective who guides us through the investigation, he only enters
some twenty minutes into the film, and does not appear in many key scenes (for
instance, he plays no role in the apprehension of Beckert, except in the final minute
of the film). Lohmann's *doppelgänger* in the underworld, crime boss Schranker,
enters the film even later than Lohmann, and although he does organise the decisive
action of the film, the capture of Beckert, he could hardly be said to dominate the
film or its point of view. Instead the film co-ordinates several points of view, presenting a number of semi-autonomous episodes, all centred around the search for a
murderer of children.
    The film does pivot around Hans Beckert, but around his absence rather than his
presence, around the search for this mysterious and initially elusive figure. This may
seem to be merely a ground rule of the mystery genre – the search for and naming
of the culprit – but *M* does not truly introduce any doubt about the identity of the
murderer. Beckert appears early in the film, although in a manner that stresses the
impossibility of grasping him – as a shadow, as a reflection in a mirror. Throughout
the film, as Burch has indicated, Beckert plays hide and seek with us, appearing,
usually indirectly or obliquely, then withdrawing into the darkness, the realm of the
unseen.[5] The film may well pivot around Beckert, but he is the film's blind spot, its
aporia, rather than its point of coherence.

Absence imprints this film from the start and determines the way it uses sound and constructs space. Although *M*'s innovative use of sound forms one of the clichés of film history, this universal acknowledgement cannot render its power banal. Key to everyone's analysis of *M*'s sound design is the way a sound can open up an off screen space, imprinting a space we see on screen with the voice or sound coming from unseen space. As Lang moved away from the broad tableaux of the super-films of the 1920s to the more fragmented space found in *Spies*, the uncertainty caused by the way a frame bounded our visual field became a Langian device. Haghi's exit from his office in that film's climax, revealing his previously undisclosed mobility and casting his shadow on the wall after he passes through the frame, shows Lang's ability to play with the frame as a masking device, concealing and revealing spaces, drawing attention to what lies off screen through shadows and off screen looks. But the soundtrack transforms Lang's frame even more radically. At any moment the frame can haemorrhage toward an unseen area simply by including a sound whose source is not seen. *The Testament of Dr. Mabuse*, as Michel Chion reveals, makes this possibility into an element of the plot – the uncertainty of the source of Dr. Baum's voice.[6] But in place of *Testament*'s exploration of new technologies of voice, *M* explores its spatial dimension, opening seen space into a constant interchange with unseen space.

The first sequence of *M* (called 'The Murder of Elsie Beckmann' by Burch in his useful division of the film into nine parts)[7] stands not only as one of Lang's and Harbou's most sustained achievements in stylistic and narrative mastery, it also serves as a sort of tutor text, introducing the major themes and devices of the film as a whole. Although subject to strong analyses already by Kuntzel, Ropars-Wuilleurmier, and Marie (as well as Burch), it still provides the essential entry point for any reading of the film.[8] As Marie has said, 'it is impossible not to analyse the first sequence, due to its fundamental importance for the later unfolding of the narrative as well as the system of signification it develops'.[9] This is especially true of the use of sound. In the recently restored version of *M*, the credits unroll in silence (other than an apparent gong sounding under the title: *Ein Fritz Lang Film*) until we are plunged into darkness with a black screen.[10] The film will emerge from this darkness with its first sounds preceding the image, a child's voice chanting a nursery rhyme:

Just you wait a little while.

Paradoxically this voice from the darkness has something of the effect of the look at the camera. Located in no represented space, it emerges from the screen in a mode of direct address, speaking in the second person, and tells us to wait for a moment.

The image that soon appears anchors the voice within a space and an action, a small child viewed from above in the courtyard of a Berlin *Mietkaserne*, the tenement blocks with a central courtyard familiar from the drawings of Heinrich Zille. The diminutive child, surrounded by other children, plays a circular pointing game, completing the morbid rhyme:

The man in black will come after you
And with his little chopper
He will make mince meat of you.

She adds, as she points to a child within the circle that surrounds her, 'You're out'. The camera then drifts off to the left, tilting upwards as it moves. As the children's game edges off screen, the child's voice continues, diminishing somewhat in volume, dividing our visual and aural orientation, visually directed left, towards the direction the camera is moving (for what reason?); aurally, right, back towards the children we still hear. Looking upwards we see through a railing the next level of the tenement as a woman moves through the frame. Her attention is drawn by the children's song and she moves to the railing's edge and calls down in irritation, telling them to stop singing 'that awful song!' adding, 'Can't you hear me?' The child's off screen voice falls silent, as the woman heads into the building, muttering. The camera lingers after she leaves and after an instant we hear the girl's voice begin again: 'Just you wait a little while …' as the film's first shot ends.

The very first shot not only sets up the play between on screen and off screen sound, it also establishes the roving and exterior point of view of this film. In one shot we view both the children and the woman, but both of them from pronounced angles: the children from above, the woman from below. The camera does not align itself with any character. Further, it has a will of its own, directing us away from the action and making us imagine events off screen through sound cues. Lang does not cut or move back to the children when they resume their game. Instead the camera remains fixed on a frame empty of people. The high angle recalls other Lang compositions (the 'topographical' views, first introduced in *The Diamond Ship*, which abstract space and action by viewing them from above) and operates here as it does in other films to create a strong sense of the camera as an observing presence outside the consciousness of any character. But never has a single shot so elegantly demonstrated the power of the camera frame as the border between the seen and the unseen.

The second shot (especially in the version which restores its opening) continues this play with off screen space and begins to comment explicitly on the role of sound. The woman who reproached the kids in the previous shot enters from the bottom of the frame in a shot of the tenement stairwell, but before her head bobs into the frame we hear her laboured progress up the stairs, her heavy breathing and the banging of the over-laden laundry basket on each step. This brief beginning of the shot (cut in most available versions of the film) situates us firmly in the social and material realism of this film, a portrayal of environment dedicated to the detailed reproduction of the locales of daily life in all their physical and sensual specificity. The space of the stairway – one of the many in-between, liminal spaces of communication through which people move in this film – awaits the woman's entrance: we see it before we see her, although we hear her approaching. The city is made up of these passageways that connect a series of autonomous little worlds. As in the overhead shot of the jewel heist in *The Diamond Ship*, Lang's viewpoint on the city stresses the determinate geometry of these separate yet connected spaces, as a structure which imposes itself on the lives and movements of the inhabitants.

Lang's 'realism' in this film depends on the geometrical structures in which the rhythms of daily life are caught. The way the woman, both hands burdened with the laundry basket, manoeuvres her elbow to ring the doorbell to Frau Beckmann's apartment, provides a degree of observation of social behaviour few previous Lang films could match. (Similarly, to those able to hear and recognise it, the Berlin accent of this woman provides an aural sign of social specificity.) The sound of the bell once her elbow has angled itself properly, her reluctance to put the basket down even for a moment (presumably because it will be so hard to pick up again – sharp-eyed commentators like Kuntzel have pointed out that the woman is pregnant),[11] the automatic way Frau Beckmann takes the basket from her as she opens the door;

all of these details of sound and gesture root us in a world recognisable in its solid materiality, yet deeply observed as well, never casual. Like much of the *Neue Sachlichkeit* (New Objectivity) movement to which Lang's last German films show an affinity, the effect differs from nineteenth-century realism through its emphasis on non-human patterns, the thing-like nature of reality, its blend of abstraction with the detailed rendering of objects. Lang's use of sound exemplifies this approach. This voice of things renders them much more palpable, but at the same time these sounds are rarely just an attempt to convey the various surrounding sounds of the world. Each sound seems magnified, attracting attention to itself and its source. Thus the woman's heavy tread up the stairs before we see her, the startling sound of the doorbell (the first of many alarming sound signals we hear in this film) carry an almost ominous overtone.

As Lang makes a 180 degree cut in this doorway, transferring us from a focalisation on the pregnant woman to the world of Frau Beckmann (as the first shot transferred us from the children to the woman carrying laundry, setting up a pattern of transfers between characters that will be pursued until the end of the film), Beckmann responds to the woman's complaint about the children's song, saying, 'As long as they're singing at least we know they're OK.' As Robert Bresson has stated, the sound-track invented silence.[12] Lang understood that sound evokes not only the unseen, the off screen, but also outlines it own negative, the unheard, that which has been silenced. Throughout this sequence, Frau Beckmann will interact with a growing silence, to the silence which equals death.

Frau Beckmann puts down the laundry as automatically as she received it, and resumes her rhythmic labor at the scrubbing board, until its repetitive sound is interrupted by another sound signal, the cuckoo of her cuckoo clock. Burch has described the primary formal structure of *M* as an interaction between continuity and discontinuity – that is, between sequences which are based primarily on spatial discontinuity (usually some form of parallel editing) and scenes which unroll within a relatively unified and continuous scenic space.[13] Whereas the classical Hollywood film of the sound era tends to privilege continuity, made up mainly of a succession of scenes acted out within a basically continuous space and time, *M* privileges discontinuity, creating a series of sequences which intercut actions in different locations. It is not until the police raid on the underworld hang-out that *M* presents a scene that is not intercut with another location. Intercutting continues after that scene (as in the famous alternation between the police and the crooks as each side tries to come up with a method for finding the child murderer), but Burch sees a progression toward a greater reliance on continuous scenes, culminating in the lengthy 'trial scene' at the end of the film where Beckert confronts the mob in one long-lasting continuous scene. The pattern of intercutting to other spaces in *M* begins with this first sequence, as we cut between Elsie's mother and Elsie's (interrupted) journey home from school.

But the moment and means by which Lang first introduces a parallel cut to another space demand scrutiny. In the first four shots of the film Lang has taken us on a tour of the living space of the *Mietkaserne*, moving step by step from exterior to interior, from courtyard, to landing, to stairway, through a doorway and into the Beckmann apartment. Now he embeds this domestic space within the city as a whole, using first sound, then editing, and relying on the most persistent of Langian objects – a clock. Lang cuts from a closer shot of Frau Beckmann bent over her scrubbing board to a shot from her point of view of the ornate cuckoo clock on her wall as she hears it mark the hour of noon. But over the shot of Frau Beckmann's touchingly kitschy clock (another one of the striking details that capture the milieu of this tenement family), we also hear, a few seconds later, the booming bell of a larger clock, coming from a church or municipal building somewhere within the city space off screen, outside this apartment. Following the sound, Lang cuts from Frau Beckmann smiling and flicking the soap from her hands to a long shot of the city street in front of the school (the sound of the hour being struck now much louder in this public space and mingling with the beeping car horns of passing traffic) as parents stand waiting for their children to emerge.

I have claimed the city could be seen as the protagonist of this film; while this may put undue strain on the term 'protagonist', there is no question that, at least in these early sequences, Lang does not simply use spatial discontinuity as a formal device, but as the strongest means to create a sense of the space of a city, made up of locations separated from each other, but also interconnected. This atomisation of the city is portrayed by the merging of two Langian techniques: the topographic view and parallel editing. Although the topographical view primarily appears as the overhead god-like perspective that Lang adopts in the film's first shot, it also becomes a less literal means of portraying the city space as a diagrammatic, patterned environment, easily figurable in maps and diagrams, highly rationalised and rendered as both clearly visible and ordered. Parallel editing, although sometimes used for suspense (as in the intercutting between Beckert and the mob in the ransacking of the office building), or as an ideological comparison (as in the cutting between the meetings of criminals and police), provides a primary way of creating this urban topology.

As in the technologically interdependent robberies and raids of the master criminal films, Lang creates a modern environment in which every space interacts with and affects every other one. As in Mabuse's first robbery, Lang uses the clock and modern standard time as a way to interrelate this atomised but interconnected space. Thus, as Frau Beckmann hears the chime of the noon clock, announcing the imminent return of her daughter for lunch, we cut to other parents gathered at the school for the same reason at the same moment. As Georg Simmel pointed out, clock time holds together and regulates the life of the metropolis.[14] But although Frau Beckmann shares time and a concern for her daughter with the other people in the city, there is no true communication between them. The shot of parents in front of the school shows people arranged in independent clumps, not talking to each other, not interacting. The brilliance of Lang's urban topography is that it shows people united in patterns, yet alienated and separate from each other. What they share most deeply as city dwellers is their loneliness and their fear.

The chiming of the city clock continues over the next shot of Frau Beckmann tasting the soup she has prepared for her daughter. From this point until the last five shots of the sequence Lang sets up a very clear pattern of shot by shot alternation, but it does not always involve cutting to another location. Lang cuts constantly from Frau Beckmann to a shot associated with Elsie. In some cases he cuts directly to Elsie – as in the shot which follows immediately: Elsie stepping off the sidewalk near her school, nearly being hit by a car that enters from off screen and then being led across the street by a policeman; or the next pair of shots which cut from Frau Beckmann setting the table to Elsie bouncing her ball and her encounter with Beckert as a looming shadow over the *Litfassäulen*, the circular advertising pillar which bears an announcement of his last murders. But sometimes, as in the following four shots, Lang stays within the space of the apartment, intercutting Frau Beckmann (the anchor of the sequence) with shots that do not show Elsie directly, but rather picture *her absence*. Thus we cut from Frau Beckmann cutting up vegetables for Elsie's soup to her point of view of the clock, now showing 12:20. While the earlier shot of the clock announced Elsie's arrival, this one indicates her delay, her *not* showing up at the appointed time. Sounds coming from the landing (off screen) cause Frau Beckmann to leave the apartment in the next shot and go out there. The following shot of two girls running up the stairs once again shows Elsie's absence: she is not with the girls, as they turn and explain in response to Frau Beckmann's off screen question.

The next pair of shots restores the cutting between distant locations as the cut from Frau Beckmann standing on the landing, first looking up towards the girls, then down into the stairwell, then returning inside. She is filmed from a low angle. The following shot shows Elsie and Beckert purchasing a balloon from the blind toy-seller. It is shot from a high angle, as if matching Frau Beckmann's point of view as she looks down into the stairwell, but the match is not only misleading, it is almost cruel. This scene is precisely what Frau Beckmann *cannot* see (think of her final line which ends the film: 'we should keep better watch on our children'). The high angle surveys the scene, but offers only an obscure view of Beckert from the back. The shot ends as he begins whistling his theme, 'In the Hall of the Mountain King' from the *Peer Gynt* suite; Elsie curtsies and thanks him as he leads her off.

The harsh door bell sounding from off screen opens the shot which returns to Frau Beckmann as she puts the soup tureen on the stove to keep it warm. She crosses to the door, clearly hoping this will be Elsie, only to find a man delivering a new 'thrilling and sensational' instalment of a *feuilleton*. This man has not seen Elsie either and as he continues on his rounds Frau Beckmann walks again onto the landing, ending the shot by looking down into the stairwell. The next shot supplies the point of view shot withheld in the previous pair of shots: a nearly overhead shot of the stairwell, the stages of stairs creating a series of nested quadrilaterals, almost spiral-like in their vertiginous emptiness. This empty shot – empty, that is, of the very thing Frau Beckmann searches for there, Elsie – continues the alternation between mother and images either of her child, her expected arrival, or her prolonged absence. In its stark, almost Expressionistic (yet totally rooted within a realist environment) geometry and abstraction, this shot presents the harshest image yet of Elsie's absence. The mother calls her child's name over this shot for the first time.

The next pair of shots shows Frau Beckmann's return from the landing, shutting the door to her apartment and looking off screen left. The complementary shot provides her point of view of the cuckoo clock (the third shot of the clock in the sequence), which now reads 1:15. The clock no longer marks an anticipated return and break in the routine of housework, or the first stirrings of anxiety. Frau Beckmann reads on its face not just the time but Elsie's prolonged absence and her own growing fear. With a mechanical indifference that seems almost like mockery, the clock strikes the quarter hour.

The cut back to Frau Beckmann shows her twisting her hands on her apron in anxiety. As if drawn by the sound of a peddler calling his wares outside, she walks over towards the kitchen window, the camera panning with her; she opens it and leans out, calling again 'Elsie, Elsie!' The five shots which follow bring this sequence to its end and break the consistent alternation between shots of Frau Beckmann and images associated with Elsie. Frau Beckmann calls Elsie's name five times, twice in this shot of her at the window, her voice becoming progressively more shrill and desperate, never receiving an answer. The cries cluster over the first two shots, while the last three unroll in silence, the silence which is most certainly death.[15]

The first shot seems almost like a stutter in the film's editing. Instead of Frau Beckmann's point of view outside the building, we see the stairwell again, an exact repetition of the earlier shot, but its repetition makes its dizzying geometry even more insistent and inhuman, bereft of the desired child or any other presence. In the following shot Frau Beckmann's voice penetrates into the attic where laundry is drying (as Kuntzel points out laundry is one of the threads weaving through the sequence).[16] This is a deep, cavernous space (it anticipates the cellar that ends the film as well as the office building attic in which Beckert will hide from the mob: liminal, hollow places where people do not ordinarily gather). Deep in the backgrounds we see a child's playsuit hanging. In its poignancy and its growing bitterness the shot recalls a line from an early Brecht poem: '...in the attic/Where they hang the washing up to dry and let it piss'.[17] Although this space is presumably at some distance from the Beckmann apartment, the mother's voice is heard in growing terror. The next shot returns to the Beckmann apartment, but not to Frau Beckmann, who seems herself to disappear from this film, as if expiring in the last gasp of her call. Instead, we see Elsie's place at table, her spoon, soup bowl and rolled-up napkin forming a perfect still life, like the many geometrically precise arrangements of objects that Lang delights in introducing in this film. But this is not simply an aesthetic arrangement. Prepared with motherly care in anticipation of her child's return, it now speaks only of her absence. Like the empty place left at the table at the inn by the disappearing lover in *Der müde Tod*, the image bodes the presence of death in this emptiness. An uninvited and invisible guest has taken its place at Elsie's table. As Kuntzel says, the emptiness previously glimpsed outside the apartment has now entered into the centre of the Beckmann home.[18]

The final two shots of the sequence move not only outside, but presumably far away. The sequence has moved from a city courtyard filled with children to a

suburban area covered with scrub brush. From off screen, out from some shrub-bery, rolls the ball Elsie bounced on her way from school. This shot, looking down at the ground, is paired with a second shot looking up at the sky framed by a utility pole, as the balloon Beckert bought for Elsie (possessing a grotesque humanoid shape, a round head with goggle eyes, a bulbous body and dangling arms and legs) is caught in the power lines. The breeze shifts and the balloon is freed, ascending out of the frame as the shot fades to black. These images present Elsie's murder, an event which, as Lang frequently said, could only be imagined, not pictured.[19] They depict what has happened just off screen, close by, previous to these shots, but very recently. They are, as Lang says, very concrete and material signs of her death,[20] but also of the emptiness that surrounds it, the lack of human agents or victims render-ing it not more palatable, but more deadly and chilling. The inanimate motion in these shots, the ball rolling to a halt, the balloon carried by the wind, emphasises their distance from the human. Lang's tendency, especially since *Spies*, to replace people with objects evinces a new degree of pain in this scene.

Frau Beckmann holds this sequence together, provides its centre. But the sequence extends beyond her, stretching towards her daughter as she awaits her arrival. The mother's consciousness stretches through the city, searching out her daughter, but the city evades her knowledge. The clock-time which regulates the city's space gradually becomes a figure of terror, the Destiny-machine which in this film cannot be claimed by anyone completely, least of all the three characters in this first sequence. The city is first imaged as a space of shared sound, the chiming of the clock which aligns people in carrying out their daily tasks. But ultimately the city becomes a space that sound cannot penetrate. Elsie cannot hear her mother's voice calling her from the window, just as her mother cannot see her from her vantage point. The indeterminate place where Elsie is killed (Marie calls it '*terrain vague*')[21] becomes precisely distance itself, the wasteland, the space of separation that Martin Buber refers to: 'We say "far away". The Zulu has for that a word which means in our sentence form: 'There where someone cries out: "Oh Mother, I am lost." '[22]

But if Frau Beckmann represents the anchor of this sequence (one unfortunately from which Elsie becomes unmoored), the narrative motor, the disturbing element which upsets the equilibrium of daily routine and moves us into the story, from the typical to the unique and sensational, is Hans Beckert, as yet unnamed, except as the *schwarze Mann* (black man, 'man in black') invoked by the children's rhyme. As the anchor to the sequence, Frau Beckmann is visible in nearly half (twelve) of the shots of this twenty-six-shot sequence. In her motherly concern for her child's nourishment and safety, her weary but strong physicality, she is palpably present in the sequence. The *schwarze Mann*, in contrast, is seen directly in only one shot of the sequence (the high angle long shot where he buys Elsie a balloon, which doesn't show his face clearly), but he haunts the whole sequence, permeates it with his absence, his invisible but looming threat.

The introduction of Beckert is justly famous for its dramatic use of off screen space and sound: his shadow looms into the frame, threateningly cast on the police poster describing his crimes and offering a reward for his apprehension, while his surprisingly unthreatening voice compliments Elsie (also off screen) on her lovely ball and asks her name. Besides the cultural association of shadows with evil (and the literalisation of 'schwarze Mann' in this dark silhouette), Lang images Beckert as somehow abstract and insubstantial, in contrast to Frau Beckmann's maternal presence. He does not appear directly in the frame, but only as a shadow and a disembodied voice. Further, this shadow rests upon another indirect representation of Beckert, the poster which describes his deeds. Beckert is a compound of signs of identity and this describes one problem propelling the film story: focusing a range of identifying marks onto Beckert's elusive body, a task achieved only when Heinrich will reverse the situation of this shot (Beckert's dark shadow obscuring the words which accuse him) by imprinting a letter, M, on his dark body.

If Beckert is visible in only one shot, many shots in the sequence evoke him, although not as powerfully as this shadow. Clearly the final shots of the sequence invoke his actions as much as they do Elsie's death (Kuntzel sees the ball rolling to a stop and the fluttering balloon not so much as replacement images of Elsie's death-throes as of Beckert's spasm of pleasure).[23] One of the scandals of *M* lies in the strong relation the children have to their murderer. The first reference to Beckert comes from their mouths as they chant the rhyme the adults do not want to hear. The pleasure the children get from evoking this bogeyman is obvious, and the chant and circle game has a ritual dimension, becoming a chilling invocation of terror. Viewed from above, this circle of children recalls the circular pattern of hands similarly viewed from above in the seance sequence of *Dr. Mabuse, the Gambler*. The children in their innocence call up this figure who destroys them. I am far from blaming the victims here, since I am not dealing with any normal causality which would carry responsibility. Rather children have a bond with the *schwarze Mann*, as they do with all monsters.

Beckert's pleasure in those things that children love forms part of this bond. Like them, he loves sweet things, powdered sugar and tropical fruit, and most especially toys. His admiration of Elsie's ball, his choice of a balloon that would fascinate any child in its grotesque and comic semi-human physiognomy, all of this joined with Lorre's unique voice and physical appearance mark him as belonging in some way to the child's world of immediate gratification; the exact opposite of the voice of the adult world in the opening shot which calls from above in an irritated voice and commands them to stop their songs and game. Any child would think this woman hated children and that Beckert with his immediate engagement with a child's game loves them. The final shots of the sequence do join Beckert and Elsie through their toys, their games; but Beckert unfortunately is not a true child, but an adult whose only means of penetrating a child's world is through their physical destruction. Nonetheless Lang maintains this unique portrayal of Beckert, as alternately a spirit or demon invoked by the children, somehow insubstantial, appearing and disappearing, and as an overgrown child, simultaneously touching and repulsive, powerless and threatening.

M delivers Lang's ultimate vision of urban space, and that encompasses his vision of modern space. I have traced out a transition in the underlying structures of his German films from the semantically rich references of allegory to the more formal and logical networks of modern space based on surveillance and communication found in the urban thrillers. Do these two models have anything in common? They represent totally different ways of organising the world, one, ultimately religious and the other, secular; one, composed of images and figures that refer back to master narratives such as the Bible or mythology; the other, seemingly bereft of narrative and engaged in a purely geometrical subdivision and mastery of information and populations. But Lang reveals their common abstraction and common reliance on a deathly emptiness. The frozen, airless quality that Benjamin finds in allegory becomes a prefiguration of the modern landscape. The death's head that Benjamin finds lurking behind allegory's emblems, Lang reveals as well in the arrangement of the modern city. As Benjamin intuited a relation between baroque allegory and modernist practices, Lang's career demonstrates the progression from one to the other. Ultimately the modern space of *M,* as the opening sequence shows, is read allegorically as well, as the space which measures separation and death.

It is important, therefore, to deal briefly with the film Lang made between *Spies* and *M,* his last silent film, *The Woman in the Moon.* I find this Lang's least successful silent film, a judgement largely based on fairly conventional criteria, those things for which Eisner also criticises it ('lack of sustained suspense').[24] However, prompted largely by comments by Raymond Bellour, I realised I should try to come to terms with it.[25] I discovered that while the film still fails for me as a dramatic work, it represents an ideal point in Lang's work, an experimental extreme, from which I think *M* both profits – and reacts against. Truly this is a film in which Lang seems to bypass character in favour of a drama of technology. The lack of drama or complex psychology in the characters tips its dramaturgy back towards allegory (indeed the drama that is enacted here recalls medieval allegories about Greed, such as Chaucer's *The Pardoner's Tale*).

The central set piece of the film, the launching of the rocket, pays almost no attention to personal drama, focusing instead on the pure spectacle of technology. With the countdown to launch making the Langian obsession with time into the literal substance of the drama, the massive crowds of spectators, the constant intercutting of clocks and dials, the slow rhythms of the rocket's approach into position, the roving beams of spotlights, the Destiny-machine emerges from being a background or subterranean force to take centre stage. More than anything in *Die Nibelungen* or *Metropolis*, this seems to be, in fact, the sequence in Lang's work that most anticipates *Triumph of the Will.* The radio announcer standing before his microphone and dramatically narrating the spectacle to the masses who watch in hyper-enthusiasm – these are the images of mass excitement and devotion that Rutsky noted the lack of in *Metropolis*, if a comparison to Nazi spectacles were made.[26] We see here the masses of *Metropolis* not only pacified but energised, enjoying themselves, having been transformed into spectators of the wonders of technology rather than simply its slaves (but is there a difference?). *M* will provide the flip-side of this vision of united masses as spectators of technology's spectacles, with the image of city inhabitants as isolated, atomised individuals under a regime of terror. The two images present the public and private face of living under fascism as the nightmare of modernity.

In addition, *The Woman in the Moon* is a film about space, in both senses of the word, and therefore Lang's most abstract film. As Jacques Rivette stated, in *The Woman in the Moon* 'the plot primarily served Lang as a pretext for his first attempt at a *totally closed* world',[27] only, instead of enclosure, I would stress the sense of space as total separation, in this film which does paradoxically conflate agoraphobic fear of infinite extension with a claustrophobic fear of entrapment. No other Lang film so thoroughly indulges his love of the diagram, the abstract representation of space. The topographical view from above, the nearly two-dimensional images – not only the actual diagrams and animations in the film, but also the spaceship hurtling across a dark void – the vast expanses of highly illuminated emptiness that form the moon's terrain, all these devices accumulate in this film to create a feeling of agoraphobia, of a Pascalian fear of space itself, of its infinite quantity and extension. If the crowds and radio announcer greet the moon shot as a triumphant moment, the space-travellers themselves experience it in two primary ways; loss of consciousness and terror. Only the old man who goes mad with enthusiasm and, to some extent, the boy, express delight in this voyage.

Lang described his own inspiration for the film as coming from the experience of falling asleep in a train, 'the consciousness to be carried from one place to another without having anything else to do but lie still dreaming'.[28] The key role loss of consciousness plays in the rocket trip to the moon offers experiences such as sleep (and dreams), hypnosis and a consciousness outside of space and time as an analogue of space travel. Even the supposed Langian invention of the countdown recalls certain hypnotic techniques, while the constantly revolving surface of the moon outside the window as they begin to land is almost unwatchable without at least some dizziness (part of my problem with the film has always been that it makes me incredibly drowsy – bored? or something more trance-like?)

Loss of consciousness evokes regression, and the title along with the usual cultural associations of the moon invokes the idea of returning to the mother (notice how the final shot of Helius and Freide alone on the moon as he places his head against her breast recalls the regressive gestures Kracauer analysed in the earlier Weimar 'Street films', which he glossed as 'the desire to return to the maternal womb').[29] But if this regressive fantasy drives the film, Lang seems to express terror rather than comforting submission at this breaching of primal repression. Space travel for Lang entails a space of separation, rather than reunion, and it is this primal terror that drives his characters crazy. The fantasy of returning to the mother evokes the primal trauma of separation. Stated explicitly by most of the characters, it is perhaps most beautifully portrayed when the crew find the boy stowaway and he brings out his comic books to prove he has been studying the moon for a long time. The first images of monsters cause laughter, but the last image of a spaceman parachuting from the moon to earth stops the merriment. Like the fiery brand cast into the lunar cave only to disappear into nothingness, these characters are stranded, terrified of their own separation and isolation. Ultimately this is Lang's most inhuman film, but also a revelatory one; outer space becomes his ultimate nightmare: a world made of emptiness and separation where no-one can hear you scream, 'Oh mother I am lost'.

Formed in Fright: The Topography of Terror

The wasteland grows. Woe to him that hides wastelands within.

Nietzsche

The 'Murder of Elsie Beckmann', the first sequence of *M*, ends with persistent images of emptiness, standing in as images of grief, violence, desire and death, with all three of the suffering and tormented characters – Elsie, her mother and her murderer – exiled from the screen in their paroxysms of sorrow, death and desire – pushed into a space we cannot see, but which echoes through and reverberates within these empty shots. We are left only with places and objects, mementos of the characters we have lost and of the horrors that have taken place. Perverse desire, mother love, childish delight, growing anxiety and terror have snaked their way through the city space Lang has laid out topographically and we are left with this *terrain vague*, this wasteland which grows in the middle of the metropolis.

The following two sequences extend Lang's topographical portrayal of city space, of the interconnections and atomisation of the world of the metropolis, a space gridded and integrated, yet strangely blind to itself, unaware of what happens within it. As Anton Kaes has said, 'Lang's unstated project in *M* – a portrayal of the inherent relation between urban living and danger – is made all the more terrifying by the anonymity and disintegration of the city's social space'.[30] As Kaes shows in his brilliant comparison between Lang and Ernst Junger, for Lang (and here the psychology of Weimar Germany is truly laid bare) city space has become a space of danger and, indeed, of warfare. The city in *M*, as Kaes puts it, is mobilised, that condition of constant fear and readiness which Junger saw as the necessary state of modern man who never moves out of a state of warfare and danger.[31] In *M*, fear simultaneously unites the city in a common emotion, and fragments it, providing, not community, but mutual suspicion.

Like the first sequence, the second sequence of *M*, which Burch nicely titles 'Fear Spreads in the City',[32] begins with sound coming over (or out of) a dark frame, the fade to black which ended Elsie's life and the first sequence. But instead of a child's nursery rhyme we hear the voice of the city, a carefully orchestrated mounting chorus of news vendors, their diverse voices competing with each other and with car horns, announcing an extra edition. The image fades in, showing another high angle shot looking down on a city street as people rush to buy the papers. The second shot, still from a high angle, though somewhat closer to the action, shows a vendor surrounded by people anxious for news, their comments blending with the vendors' hawking. We hear the question 'Who is the murderer?' and Lang cuts to a shot of Beckert, hunched over the windowsill in his apartment, only his back and the top of his head visible.

The sequence shows the sort of sound links and rhymes we traced in Lang's following film *The Testament of Dr. Mabuse*. As in that film (and indeed in all his master criminal films) Lang cuts on the question 'Who is the murderer' (in those films the question is: who is behind all this?) to the perpetrator. But whereas in the master criminal films, the cut expressed the power of the criminal, something else is at issue here. Lorre is writing a letter (a sort of confession, yet an anonymous one) to the press (a word he underlines twice, along with the words *I* and *end*), whistling his *Peer Gynt* leitmotiv. The link holding these shots together is the circulation of information through the city by means of newspapers. Like all modern metropolises Berlin is a city hungry for and inundated by information. But the way this flow of information interrelates essentially alienated individuals is attested to by Beckert's letter, his desire to communicate to the press, to participate in this flow of information, yet remain anonymous.

The following shots continue the links between voices, as sentences are continued and complemented by a series of different speakers. Once again the formal device serves to create the topography of urban information. We cut from Beckert's handwritten text to a printed poster giving the details of the latest murder surrounded by a turbulent crowd, jostling for a better view, the sound of a voice reading the poster overlapping with the end of the shot of Beckert writing. Bystanders ask someone in front to read the poster, which a voice does as the camera pulls back through the layers of people. Some descriptions of the film claim the voice of a radio announcer intervenes here,[33] which would continue the theme of the expansion of information through diverse media, but I confess I don't hear this transition. The reading of the poster mixes into another voice reading the same information which in the next shot is revealed to be a man at a bar reading a newspaper (the overlapping dialogue in these shots, sound preceding the actual cut to another shot, underscores the circulation of information).

The following succession of brief scenes which make up this less than six-minute sequence demonstrates the divisive, rather than community-building effect of the information and the fear it breeds. Lang presents a series of vignettes of typical scenes as the city is gripped by fear. This atomistic narrative approach (each scene has different characters and we never see any of them again) further articulates the fragmentary nature of the citizens of the metropolis, not only mutually suspicious of each other, but each absorbed in their own dramas and reactions to the crisis. Yet every scene is overtly linked by overlapping and rhyming sounds. A group of caricatured bourgeois men (looking like a George Grosz drawing brought to life) seated around a bar table listen as one of them reads a newspaper article which emphasises the deceptive nature of appearances ('candy, a toy, a piece of fruit can be the murderer's weapon'), and asks again the question, 'who is the murderer?' The article adds, 'He is one of us. Your neighbor could be the murderer.'

One of the men nods agreement and accuses a man across the table of being the murderer. The angry pair are separated by the other men, and the accused's cry, 'Slanderer!' is picked up by another voice as Lang cuts to an apartment being searched by a detective and a man, the source of the exclamation, enters from off screen, furious that an anonymous letter has denounced him and prompted the police investigation. The detective's voice explaining that they must follow up every lead because 'any man on the street could be the guilty one' overlaps the cut, with the next shot, showing a 'man in the street' as the phrase 'the guilty one' is heard on the soundtrack. Lang presents another vignette as a young girl asks this old man for the time and bystanders view this innocent conversation with suspicion and confront the man. A crowd gathers, getting progressively more excited and accusing the man of being the murderer. The crowd calls for a police officer. Lang cuts to another high angle topographical view, this time of a double-decker bus with a police officer coming down the stairs apparently in response to the call. But this is another example of the misleading links, the delayed comprehension, discussed earlier in relation to *The Testament of Dr. Mabuse*.[34] This officer is actually arresting a pickpocket caught on the bus. But our mistake is taken up by the crowd waiting to board the bus. When the pickpocket tells the cop he should be out catching the child murderer, the crowd hears only this word and begins pummelling the pickpocket, assuming he is the murderer. Truly the murderer is 'one of us'. In a succession of scenes, Lang shows four different people accused by their fellow city inhabitants. 'One of us' becomes 'the guilty one'. The anonymous crowd cloaks the murderer from detection, but also renders everyone suspicious.

The following sequence (called by Burch 'Police Procedures and their Inefficiency')[35] presents another topographical view of the city and the process of looking for the murderer by intercutting various sequences in diverse locations. In contrast to the process of gossip, accusation and misrecognition in the previous sequence, this sequence follows a rational procedure, the police investigation. Yet this process gets no nearer to the murderer than the actions of blind suspicion and the same fragmented, alienated population is revealed. The sequence opens by picking up and resolving the elements which began the last one. We see Beckert's letter now printed in the newspaper, returning us to the themes of mass media that opened the second sequence. But a hand holding a pince-nez enters the frame and we are pushed into the next sequence, as a government minister berates the chief of police over the phone about the progress of the investigation. This sequence, the most freely roving in *M* in terms of urban space, will be mediated and portrayed through this phone call.

Lang demonstrates again his understanding of the technological nature of the modern terrain. But this sequence contrasts sharply with the phone call which culminates the opening robbery of *Dr. Mabuse, the Gambler*; it does not narrate a moment of intense suspenseful action. Instead, we watch a conversation between a government minister and a subordinate in bureaucratic hierarchy. The sequence is primarily retrospective, as the police chief describes actions they have already taken, providing a systematic description of police procedure. The phone conversation, linking speakers separated in space, naturalises and accelerates the discontinuity evident in the previous sequences, allowing Lang to cut very freely through space (and presumably time) as the exposition of the investigation converts the city into a series of charts and maps, a rational order designed to discover the anonymous murderer, separating him from the masses he dwells among. Lang capitalises on the telephone's extension through space and its role as a network to make his own connections between separate shots taking place in different locations. The phone call brings coherence to this highly discontinuous sequence through another innovative use of sound: the separation of voice from a speaker's bodily presence. We hear the police chief's voice-over as we see the scenes he describes, an innovative technique for the period. The frequent cuts back to the police chief pull these brief bits together, so that he behaves like a sort of switchboard, directing the audience through the shots with his spoken commentary.

The first section of the phone conversation dwells on the processing of evidence, specifically the murderer's letter to the press which prompts the minister's call. We saw this letter as Beckert wrote it; then we saw it reproduced photographically in the newspaper, part of the circulation of news. Now we see it dissected and analysed, scrutinised for clues it might hold beneath its ostensible message. The sequence recalls the processing of information in *Spies* and especially Tremaine's telegraph message. But translation here is not so simple, since the enigma lies not in the meaning of the message but the identity and intentions of its author.

The first cut from the phone call to the images that illustrate it presents a shot of a dossier of fingerprints as the police chief speaks of the difficulty in getting clear prints from Beckert's letter. (Lang's sense of humour is wonderfully – if almost subliminally – evident here: the dossier is for a crook known as 'Four-Fingered Ernst' and the blotter shows four prints with an empty space where the print of the forefinger would be!) As the chief describes the need to compare any print with the prints in their archive, a magnifying glass sweeps over this file and Lang cuts to one of the most famous shots in the film, a police officer writing at a desk as an enormous projection of a fingerprint fills the frame above him, numbered lines pointing out key features. The contrast in scale, the man dwarfed by the huge fingerprint, expresses the power of this processing of identity, the print itself a sort of diagram or blueprint of the individual as caught within the police archives of information and its processing.

Then the handwriting of the letter is scrutinised, the chief's voice-over saying it was sent to a graphologist. Lang cuts to this expert pacing and dictating his report to a female secretary (the process of transcribing is omnipresent) as he claims the shape of the letters reveal a perverse sexuality. The close-up of the writing fills the screen as the graphologist's voice-over continues. But as he ties these letters to the personality of an actor ('*Schauspieler*') Lang cuts to the most direct view of the murderer so far in the film. Beckert is still given to us in a mediated fashion, since we see his face most clearly reflected in a mirror. The shot is chilling, as Beckert appears first to admire himself in the mirror (the apparent narcissism matching the graphologist's claim of an actor's personality), his lowered eyelids and half-opened mouth expressing an almost masturbatory pleasure in his own visage. But then he

uses his fingers to distort his face into a wide-mouthed grimace, his bulging eyes widening as well, converting his previously smugly handsome face into a child's mask, the face of a bogeyman. The graphologist summarises that the writing shows undoubted signs of insanity.

This single shot holds a strange position within this sequence. Everything else portrays facts the police chief knows. This shot exceeds his knowledge. The voice-over which accompanies it is not, in fact, that of the chief, but of the graphologist. His voice leads us into it, but this image, in contrast to the words of Beckert's letter, exceeds his knowledge, showing us things he can only hint at. It would be hard to exhaust or even inventory all the energies released by this shot, our first clear view of the film's shadowy title character. Some of the meanings rest on the surface: Beckert is narcissistic; he is insane; he is split in two, like a *doppelgänger* or a Dr. Jekyll and Mr. Hyde. But his effort to move from a self-image that enraptures him to one which terrifies (him as well?) reaches to the core of his horror. If he is an actor, he is one who performs entirely for himself. In his loneliness, his alienation, the restricted scope and poverty of his anonymous life, he performs spectacular dramas before his mirror. The actor solicits the gaze of others. But M keeps out of sight, hiding throughout the film, afraid to be seen. But alone he displays to himself his own desires. What drama does he perform? Although Beckert is silent in this shot, the only other sound we have heard from him (or will hear from him for many scenes to come) may offer a strong clue. Maria Tatar pointed out that in Ibsen's *Peer Gynt*, Grieg's 'In the Hall of the Mountain King' introduces the sequence where Peer comes to the royal hall of the trolls, who try to transform him into a monster.[36] Although I find her final explication of this wanting, she provides a key insight into Beckert's private drama. Peer comes to ask the king of the trolls for a bride, and must answer correctly the riddle: What is the difference between men and trolls – 'As far as I can see none at all. Big trolls will roast you and little trolls claw you; and we'd be the same – if we dared.'[37] These motifs and Peer's final attempt to escape when the trolls insist on taking out his eyes, all have resonance in Beckert's fantasy life, as we shall see.

What we see in the mirror in horrifying compression is the essence of Beckert's private drama which begins with attraction and ends with repulsion and self-horror. In the private theatre of the mirror Beckert enacts his own transformation into a monster. While he has escaped the gaze of others, he is still imprisoned within his own gaze. This is the most terrifying drama of childhood, the vision of the monster who only appears when one is entirely alone – the bogeyman whom one cannot flee from, because it is one's self. Lorre here is trapped within the reciprocity of his own gaze. He cannot hide from this monster's eyes; the horrifying face that stares out from the mirror is so terrifying because it is a face terrified by itself. The graphologist's analysis of Beckert's handwriting cannot take us into this vision, but Lang/Harbou can, and do.

Lang needs to return us to the prosaic world of the phone conversation after this interior climax, and he cuts back to the minister and then the chief, as the minister demands 'results' and the chief reacts with frustration. The images that follow under his voice-over are more simply illustrative, showing the police stations manned around the clock. The processing of minute details is then shown: a high angle, topographical view of a crime-scene with detectives combing the area, taking photographs, brushing for fingerprints and poking into the bushes. From this rather distant, wide angle view Lang cuts to a close-up of a candy bag handled almost surgically by a detective with forceps. The cut between these two shot sizes is unusual, because it eliminates the focus on the human face and figure which makes the medium shot the most frequent framing of classical film-making. Lang cuts directly from the topographical high angle long shot to a close-up focused on a fragmentary clue. These are the essential spaces for the police investigation and the following shot literally inserts them into a broad rationalised view of the city under the lens of surveillance and investigation.

As the chief's voice-over continues its running commentary, Lang introduces a chart seen from above at an acute angle. In the centre is a three-dimensional mock-up of the locale where the clue was found, placed within a map of the neighbour-hood. A compass uses the crime scene as a centre and describes circles around it, cutting through the city in widening radii. As the chief explains that they interrogated candy shop owners around the site in an ever-enlarging area, Lang cuts to a view of this chart from directly overhead: the crime-scene model becomes the centre of a bull's-eye of concentric circles traced by the seemingly huge compass. These images make literal the topographical view that underlies much of this film and its inherent abstraction. Viewed from above, the city becomes a pattern of lines and forms, intersections and borders, placed within the hard-edged geometry of the compass.

As in the visual abstractions that underlay his earlier allegorical films, these topographical views employ a vision which, like an x-ray, sees through appearances to essential structures. But, as in the technological environments of the master criminal films, in *M* this eye gazes upon a world already suffused with a will towards order and abstraction, the world of the modern city. These images of the city map anchor the logic of this sequence, its ability to coordinate different phases of the investigation as points within a larger plan or system. But the juxtaposition of these shots depicting order to the earlier shot of Beckert making faces in the mirror highlights their disparity. Can this rational order truly encompass the acting-out of horrific scenes of perverse desire? Or does this world of abstract order present the negative of *M*'s fantasy world – a rationalised space where desire is driven underground, made to hide out in the most private and repressed atmosphere, taking on monstrous shapes and distortions?

Even the chief's narration admits the irrelevance of these techniques to the complexities of the case, pronouncing their task hopeless. In a series of three silent shots, a succession of ordinary citizens manning candy stores and snack shops, shake their heads and indicate they saw, or remembered, nothing. The blindness and anonymity of the modern city defeats its rational order of investigation. The final section of the conversation juxtaposes witnesses who did see something, but can't agree on what it was, and images of the police combing the city, walking in closed ranks through the underbrush of parks, checking flophouses and underworld hang-outs. The topographical view of the city persists, but less as an effective tool than an image of the modern world, its archive of facts ('fifteen hundred clues, the documents fill over sixty volumes' explains the police chief), an attempt to make sense of this world, to force it to yield up its secrets.

As I have stated, the topographical dividing-up of urban space may be rendered starkly visible by the search for the child murderer, but it pre-exists it, inherent in the organisation of the modern city. Thus the sense of the extensive atomised and subdivided space of the city appears as much in the middle of the first sequence of a mother waiting for her child to return from school as it does in a police investigation. Lang portrays in *M* a systematic understanding of space and order, precisely the sort of modern space described by Henri Lefebvre, abstracted and subordinated to the needs of power.[38] But Lang also anticipates Foucault, not only in founding this modern space in actions of surveillance and the discursive organisation of the archive, but as thoroughly absorbed into the practices of everyday life. As Anton Kaes has pointed out, Junger's concept of 'Total Mobilization' not only compares the modern society to a state of constant warfare but reveals that these structures are founded on fear, and the terror occasioned by an anonymous serial killer simply throws them into relief. Describing the city-wide search in *M*, Kaes says:

> The mobilization produces a dense surveillance network aimed at making visible what has inexplicably evaded the tightly woven web of controls already in place: criminals and vagrants have identity papers (forgeries are easily detected as the film shows), they are registered and monitored, their fingerprints are recorded; asylums and hospitals keep records of their patients and their medical histories. Telephone lines link the population to the authorities and office buildings have alarm systems directly connected to police headquarters. Plain-clothed detectives control the street, searching in widening circles for every possible clue; neighbors watch each other; parents discipline their children to be wary; and even innocent bystanders are seen as potential suspects. Newspapers and extra editions keep everyone up-to-date at all times.[39]

These techniques of surveillance and order are practised by the whole society, including not only the forces of order, but even the supposed forces of chaos, the underworld.

The famous sequence in which Lang cuts between the meetings of the police and the crime bosses occurring simultaneously on the same subject, the apprehension of the murderer (in Burch's count, the fifth sequence which he entitles – a bit mis-leadingly since there is no common plan – 'The underworld and the police pull together' – *se concertent* in the original French)[40] not only displays a wonderfully witty cutting on gestures which ties the two groups together, but reveals their shared use of surveillance and control through hierarchialised power. Lang's master criminals have always ruled by their precise organisation and order; they are agents of fear, but not chaos. Although Mabuse's testament will speak of spreading chaos, it is part of a carefully calibrated plan (as Baum describes it, 'logical and indis-putable') to attain the mastery of crime, crime as a total system. In a somewhat less theatrical manner, Schränker and his gang organise to restore 'normal' order to the city interrupted by Beckert's murders and the effects they produce. As Roger Dadoun has claimed, in *M* the mob reveals itself as the 'refraction, the imitation, the *counter-relief*' of the legal structures and official codes of power.[41]

Lang undertakes much of this comparison in the form of a parody (most obvi-ously in the stock market blackboard of leftover food in the headquarters of the Beggars' Union where prices fluctuate in a parody of the stock market scene in *Dr. Mabuse, the Gambler*) inspired undoubtedly by Brecht's *The Three Penny Opera*. The opening of the fifth sequence takes on this parodic form as we see the gang members watching the police raid through binoculars (the surveillance of the underworld surveyed by the underworld) and showing a great concern about the exact time. Displaying Lang's fundamental synecdoches of the technological envi-ronment, the pickpocket calls the telephone operator for the exact time, then takes out a half dozen watches and sets them, discarding one which doesn't tick.

Schränker, the crime boss (whose black gloves Lang claimed telegraphed to the audience that he never leaves behind a fingerprint – a perfect example of the under-world as the counter-relief of police procedures)[42] runs the meeting like a chairman of the board, referring to procedures and assuring proper representation at the meeting of each branch of the professions, as well as corporate concerns about funding and public image (in contrast to charismatic master criminals like Haghi and Mabuse who rule their underlings by mystification and fear as much as organisation), denouncing the murderer as an 'outsider' not belonging to their organisation who is disrupting the normal flow of business. Lang begins the intercutting between Schränker's meeting and that of the police with a perfect match on action as Schränker's sweeping hand gesture and spoken sentence is completed in the following shot by the police chief, as both figures open the meeting to discussion. Initially the intercutting is shot by shot, so that police sometimes seem to answer crooks and vice-versa, as if they actually were planning a common strategy. The cops emphasise the problems already detailed in the police chief's previous phone conversation: the lack of public awareness, the unremarkable everyday appearance of the murderer. Smoke fills the respective meeting rooms as frustration builds. A police advisor locates the problem in the fact that the murderer and victim are linked by chance, part of the anonymity of the metropolis, and the murderer leaves no trace behind. The crooks pick up on this sense of contingency, saying that if the police catch the murderer, it will be by accident.

After a period of silent pacing and smoking in both meetings, courses of action are suggested. Both, in somewhat different ways, rely on the rational organisation of the modern city: the police on the archive of documents, the trace left behind by citizens even when they are determined to leave no clue; the crooks on direct visual surveillance of the city determined by a subdivision of urban space. Lohmann's off screen voice in the police meeting suggests that a person as disturbed as the murderer must have had contact with the law before and must have left a record. A systematic investigation of persons released from asylums and prisons must be undertaken. The crooks for their part decide they must apprehend the murderer by permanently watching every square foot of the city. Lang supplies one of his strongest topographical images, an overhead shot of a map of Berlin as Schränker's black-sheathed hand moves over it, pointing. The problem raised about his plan, however, is the same one solved by Bentham's panopticon: how to watch without being seen. Schränker's solution is brilliant, drawing on the blindness and lack of awareness of the modern city so often raised by this film. Who are the invisible people of the metropolis, omnipresent but never regarded? Its abject members, the beggars!

In this world of omnipresent order, even the abject are organised. Schränker can use the beggars not only because they are invisible, but because they are already an orderly systematic group that he can enroll. The process of assigning each beggar his 'square foot' of the city is shown in a convergence of the two emblems of this modern instrumental system: the map and the archive of identity. Lang's roving camera shows the queue of beggars appearing before a desk; a high angle shot shows another city map, demarcated by lines and figures, as each beggar is assigned a territory. The assignment is then recorded in a log book, giving the territory, the beggar's 'union number', and then his name. As in *Spies*, numbers can replace names, as they record one's identity as a place within an organisation, an archive.

Both investigations, police and underworld, leave a paper trace of their process and use the rationalised divisions of space and information as the scenario and guide for their processes. Lohmann receives in his office the list of patients released from mental hospitals, with a file of reports from every institution and another file giving the former patients' present addresses. However, Lang still indicates the porous nature of this web of information. He cuts from a shot of the list of addresses to an apartment building entrance approached by a detective. Lang shows the name on the doorbell (Elizabeth Winkler) then a close-up of the detective's handbook with a series of names crossed out, as he points to the next one on his list, 'Hans Beckert c/o Elizabeth Winkler Gelder St. 15, 2nd Floor'. The police have found Beckert's apartment and in the following scene will even invade his private theatre, the site of his writing and performances before the mirror. But they will not recognise it. And, even more ironically, at the beginning of the shot of the building entrance, we see Beckert go out just before the detective arrives. Many viewers of the film miss this appearance of Beckert, so anonymous is his appearance.

The seizing of Beckert in the office building by the underworld shows the ease of adaptation of the underworld to the systematic nature of modern order. The crooks even become nightwatchmen, making their rounds through the building so as not to set off the automatic alarm. Their adoption of this routine is signalled by another Langian shot of a chart showing the watchman's rounds and the locations of the time clock which must be punched periodically. This chart in the hands of the crooks is matched by the chart of the building in the hands of the cops when the alarm is triggered (the alarm sounds at headquarters and yields, in successive images: a number code, then a file card – with the building layout and location on the back). The crook's search is carefully timed, starting from Schränker's decision that it will begin precisely at eleven o'clock. He counts off the hours they have to wait, and the sequence opens with the chiming of a city clock (reviving not only the theme of time, but a motif from Elsie's murder). Once the alarm is set off, instead of fleeing in panic, Schränker insists they have five more minutes to finish the job. This temporal order mirrors the systematic spatial search of the building (as if Schränker's subdivision of the city for the beggars has shrunk to this one location), as he assigns people to each floor and area. His commands when the alarm is sounded: 'Five more minutes and six more compartments!' Beckert seized, the building is cleared as systematically as it was searched. Lang ends the sequence with a series of silent images showing no movement: the tied-up watchmen, forced doors, smashed partition, as an eerie quiet and stillness prevail.

Lang's new style of abstraction in *M*, epitomised by the high angle topographical shots, also shapes a technique closely related to these shots, and which will appear in nearly every film he makes after this: a high angle view of a complex, geometrically ordered arrangement of objects. In a sense the still life of Elsie's empty place at the table premieres this new device in Lang's *œuvre*. However, most of the arrangements are more complex and less domestic than this one. The first strong examples appear in the aftermath of the police raid on the underworld hang-out. After Lohmann and his cops have examined the papers of the denizens, booked a few and engaged in witty repartee, Lang shows a detective opening a case left behind by a customer, apparently considered to be incriminating evidence. The case unfolds to reveal an *etui* as carefully arranged as a surgeon's, holding every sort of burglary tool. The following shot pans across an extraordinary display of objects, the detritus of the raid, as hands enter placing new finds into precisely sorted categories: first, tools: a power drill, hammers, saws; then, weapons: automatics, revolvers, brass knuckles and knives; next, objects of value, presumably stolen: cigarette cases, spectacle frames, silverware, watches and jewellery, purses and wallets, furs. What is striking in this shot is not simply the accumulation of goods, but their artistic arrangement into symmetrical rows and stacks – hardly the sort of placement likely to result from a police raid. Lang's own obsession emerges here, as if the arrangements of actors typical of the allegorical films – *Siegfried* and *Metropolis* especially – had become miniaturised and frozen. Lang now lavishes on objects the careful *mise-en-scène* his monumental crowd scenes received previously.

Our introduction into the Beggars' Hall shows one of these arrangements in the process of formation, as a beggar lays on a table a series of cigar and cigarette butts, precisely sorted according to the length and type of tobacco, symmetrically displayed. Other beggars, engaged in preparing the supply of leftover food, are arranging half-eaten sandwiches with the same decorative impulse. These arrangements reveal several things about Lang's topographic style. First, the primacy of geometry which rules all his German films can avoid a large-scale stylisation by moving into smaller-scale arrangements, while the sense of an abstract order viewed from an overhead point of view remains constant. Second, if Lang moves away from Expressionist influences to influences from the New Objectivity this move is facilitated by his fascination with objects as much as a turn towards greater realism. The objects which bore emblematic and often enigmatic meanings in the allegorical films here become increasingly opaque, material. As Lang stated in a later interview, 'In my films objects are signs, but very concrete signs.'[43] These still-life arrangements speak of a style that increasingly replaces people with objects, such as the reification underlying the horror of Elsie Beckmann's murder – transformed into a random play of objects, a ball and a balloon. Finally, these arrangements recall simultaneously the many diagrams and maps (often they interact with them, as in the still-life arrangement with map discovered on Dr. Baum's desk at the end of *The Testament of Dr. Mabuse*) but also the key art of the modern consumer society, the arrangement of displayed goods in shop windows. Such windows also become a motif in Lang's films from *M* on, and the use made of them in this film stands at the centre of this modern topography where people and objects are interchangeable and desire is captured through a careful arrangement of things.

Der Schwarze Mann

> … it forced me, by what means I do not know, to lift my eyes
> and imposed on me an image, no, a reality, a strange,
> unbelievable and monstrous reality, with which, against my
> will I became permeated: for now the mirror was the
> stronger and I was the mirror.
> Rainer Maria Rilke, *The Notebooks of Malte Laurids Brigge*[44]

Who is the murderer? This is the question that organises *M* temporally and spatially as a search for one man an attempt to give a criminal a name and a face; to make a criminal act yield up a personal identity: 'the guilty one'. Yet, as has been pointed out, *M* is not a murder mystery. We, the viewers, gradually learn the name and face of the guilty one, long before the other characters do. Rather than identifying the murderer from a range of suspects, this film traces the process of constructing an identity for the obviously guilty one, giving him both a name and a body. Although it may appear that the crime world's investigation is more successful than that of the police, both actually achieve different parts of the objective. Almost simultaneously the police give Beckert a name and address while the mob mark and seize his body. This process of constructing an identity for the murderer not only reveals the panoply of institutions and processes the modern state and metropolis possess for keeping track of their citizens, but also the fundamental loss of identity on which this modern institution is founded, the overwhelming anonymity and loss of a unique, individualised place within a community that necessitates the machinery of categorisation and surveillance. As in *Spies*, Lang reveals that the fixing and tracing of identity rests upon a previous effacement of the person and the community.

Lang's master criminals play on the labile quality of modern identity through a theatrical use of disguise. But Haghi showed that the best disguise is none at all, the ordinary face of an average man that hides behind the mask of Nemo, 'no-one'. However Beckert performs his transformation from nebbish to monster only for himself and his audience of single little girls. He is in many ways conceived as the antithesis of the master criminal. Mabuse speaks of becoming a giant, a titan; one poster for the premiere of *Dr. Mabuse, the Gambler* (possibly patterned on a similar image for both the novel and film of *Fantomas*) shows him as a colossus striding over the city.[45] However Beckert needs no disguise to remain invisible because he is so insignificant and powerless. He cannot command underlings, mesmerise young men and police investigators, make women do his bidding through his charismatic indifference, command technology, or panic the stock market through his control of information. And yet he monopolises the media and terrifies an entire metropolis, upsetting its routines even more than Mabuse's campaign of organised terror. This is the final irony of Lang's German crime films: his least powerful, most anonymous character has the greatest effect.

If the sign of Mabuse or Haghi's power was their apparent omnipresence, their ability to exert their will across a vast terrain through either their criminal organisation, supernatural powers, or their mastery of technology, Beckert's unique ability to evade the forces searching for him comes from his ability to hide. Burch points out that an over-arching 'movement' persists throughout *M*: 'the gradual "unveiling" of the central character' through a series of appearances.[46] Equally importantly, his appearances most often are followed by disappearances, Beckert moving out of visibility. The murderer disappears even more powerfully than he appears, as his absence at the end of the first sequence shows us.

Beckert's initial appearances, as Burch notes, are shadowy, still 'veiled' and strongly visually mediated: he is seen as a shadow, from the back, in a mirror, almost unnoticed as he walks out of frame at the opening of a scene, shot through highly reflective window panes. But his disappearances, his ways of exiting from the scene, become more spectacular and even magical in the second half of the film. After Beckert's first extended sequence in the film (previous scenes had been limited to single shots), the sequence before shop windows which I will discuss later, he withdraws to an outdoor cafe and literally seems to hide from the camera which glimpses him through a hedge. This extremely curious scene consists of a single long-lasting shot (more than a minute and a half) beginning in long shot as Beckert enters the arboured area of the cafe, sits at a table, begins to whistle 'In the Hall of the Mountain King' and orders a cognac. The camera dollies in but stays outside the arbour, showing a rather obscured view of Beckert through the foliage. This unusual framing emphasises both the surreptitious nature of the camera – once again outside the scene viewing it from a distance – its spy-like nature, and Beckert's furtive nature, his hide-and-seek game with the camera. Beckert downs a second cognac, holds his head between his fists, tries to smoke, starts to whistle his theme from *Peer Gynt* again, seems to make his monster face again. Then, when the lights inside the cafe come on and illuminate him, he rises suddenly, pays the bill and leaves, the camera pulling back just before he emerges – as if afraid to be caught in its compromising position.

Beckert's most impressive disappearing act comes just before his capture. It is preceded by his most elusive appearance (heard, rather than seen), but the one which will seal his fate. Over a shot of the blind beggar who sold Beckert Elsie's balloon we hear the off screen whistling of the music from *Peer Gynt* and see a quickly passing shadow. As he recalls the tune, the blind beggar matches his sharp ears with a young man's, Heinrich's, keen eyesight to glimpse Beckert in the off screen distance. In pursuit, Heinrich seems to have lost him, but then glimpses him through the window of a below street level fruit market buying candy for a little girl. This high angle image recalls the shot of Beckert buying the balloon, one of several *déjà vu*-like images scattered through the second half of this film which recall the first sequence.

This sighting leads directly to Beckert being marked with the chalked-on M, and being trailed as he walks with a new potential victim through the streets of Berlin. After Heinrich reports to the underworld headquarters, Beckert is pursued by a myriad of beggars operating in relays. It is as though once marked with the letter M, Beckert has lost a magical invisibility (whereas before it was only the blind who could recognise him). Beckert seems to realise this as he glimpses the mark on his back in a mirror and immediately turns and stares – briefly, but directly – into the camera. This look at the camera (a rarely used device in this film until the final scene) does not claim enunciatory power over the lens and audience, but rather expresses the embarrassment of visibility, being caught in the gaze of the camera. Beckert now sees his pursuers swarming everywhere, and their shrill, whistled signals seem to come from every direction of off screen space, entrapping him. Lang expresses this with a topographical overhead shot as Beckert is literally cornered, standing in the street with a pursuer on every corner of the intersection. Beckert rushes into the large entranceway of an office building, keenly observed by his pursuers in long shot. But, magically, a fire truck, its alarm bells ringing, sweeps through this frame and seems to wipe Beckert off the screen. After it passes he is simply no longer there.

Beckert seems once more absorbed by the anonymous city within which he thrives. An extensive pan and tilt of the empty courtyard and massive architecture, seems to scan helplessly an impassable barrier that shields him. Likewise, as a bell announces the office's closing time (another temporal signal here, as in *Metropolis*, triggering a mass exit) and the crowd of workers leave the building, the beggars do an extraordinary job of looking each person in the face (they are beggars; they can approach people like this) to make sure Beckert is not among them. The cacophony of voices that fills this space underscores Beckert's complete disappearance, swallowed by the metropolis. Beckert has, in fact, withdrawn into the farthest reaches of the building, its storage attic, where we can just distinguish him, huddled among the abandoned furniture, old ledger books, empty bottles. The watchman, finding the door open, makes a quick patrol and, turning the light out and locking the door, leaves Beckert in his hiding place. In the darkness we barely see his silhouette and can just distinguish his laboured, almost asthmatic, breathing.

Beckert will hide/disappear twice more before he is produced for his trial before the underworld in the cellar of the abandoned brewery. First, when he attempts to pick the lock of the attic and suddenly sees the handle to the door turning, then hears the key in the lock. Beckert tiptoes away back into his attic refuge, returning quickly to turn off the light, leaving the corridor dark and empty until the gang opens the door. He huddles among the jumble of odds and ends, listening to the off

67

screen voices of his pursuers closing in, his eyes bulging. Then from off screen a
flashlight beam illuminates him as he stands up, involuntarily fascinated and terrified, staring into the light. The *schwarze Mann* has emerged from darkness. We next
see him in his last (involuntary) disappearing act, as a bundle, carefully wrapped,
twisting and struggling, the largest burden carried off by the departing crooks.

The gang tries to find Beckert, to drag him into the light, for only one purpose, in
order to eliminate him. As Schränker says (in words the Nazi overtones of which are
clear), 'he has no right to live. He must disappear.' Beckert is dragged out of his
anonymity in order to be expunged. As Dadoun argues, Beckert is the ultimate
reject of this society where even the beggars play an organised role. He is the waste
product, the truly abject.[47] Thus he is associated with spaces like the attic storage
room where he finds his last temporary resting place among the other rejected
objects, or the abandoned brewery with its smashed windows and collapsing roof,
appearing like an image from bombed out postwar Berlin. In the organised world
of the city the underworld and the police interact like a hand and a glove, but the
perverse desire of Beckert truly finds no place, other than a place to hide. He
emerges from the darkness of anonymity into the glare of apprehension and identification only as a stage on the road to oblivion.

While the underworld gets Beckert within their sights and marks his body with the
sign of Cain, the police tie him to a name and address, an official place within the city,
as Dadoun again points out, through the systematic investigation of his rejects, an
Ariston cigarette, red pencil shavings, the contents of his waste basket.[48] Lang intercuts the blind beggar's recognition of the Grieg tune with Lohmann recognising the
brand of Beckert's cigarette butt ('A-ri-ston', as he writes in the air) in the detective's
inventory of Beckert's waste basket. Lohmann is able to relate this bit of trash to the
police's archive of facts. Lang cuts from the arcing camera movement which discloses
the M imprinted on Beckert's shoulder to Lohmann poring over the inventory of one

of the crime scenes where Ariston butts were found. The next shot returns to Beckert's apartment with a close-up of the window sill on which he wrote his letter to the press (unexamined in the previous search, since the detective concentrated on the perfectly smooth table). A magnifying glass enters the frame and sweeps across the sill's coarse-grained surface. An extreme close-up through the lens reveals the fatal imprint, the trace of the word 'press'.

Thus Beckert is caught between two literal impressions and inscriptions: the M imprinted on his back which renders him visible, and the mark he himself left as he wrote the confession to the newspaper. Like Tremaine's message caught by carbon paper, this shot reveals the unconscious betrayal writing can leave behind without the writer even realising it. The window is opened and the detective wipes it with his fingertip and finds the red pencil shavings – evidence they were looking for. In close-up he brings them, stuck on the tip of his finger, towards the camera lens. Beckert's self-betraying writing seems poised between the preceding and subsequent Lang films, between Tremaine's telegraph message whose impression is read by the spies, and Hofmeister's message etched in another window (also discovered by Lohmann who refers to it as 'window writing') in *The Testament of Dr. Mabuse*. Lang cuts from Lohmann's excitement at the discovery to the underworld receiving word of the beggars spotting Beckert. From fragments and memories, from cigarette butts and the snatches of a tune, Beckert's identity has been constructed at last. The police have him as well as the underworld. The detectives only miss him because they wait in his apartment and Beckert never returns home again.

But this accumulation of bits of facts, of the refuse of both normal and criminal society, this name and address taken from the police file and this body marked as a target for elimination – how does all of this relate to Beckert's sense of his own identity? Lang provides us with glimpses of him alone, outside the gaze of others, within the scenography of his private fantasies, as in the shot played before his mirror at home. Perhaps the most powerful sequence of the film occurs when Beckert confronts the image of his desire and his monstrosity on the city street.

In his later confession before the underworld Beckert speaks of his need to wander the streets. Marie has even described him as a *flâneur*.[49] In the sequence which occurs during the first police search of Beckert's apartment, he strolls along a Berlin commercial street munching on a piece of fruit. Up to this moment every view we have had of Beckert in the film has been either mediated (the shadow, the reflection) or from behind. This sequence begins the same way, but will also present not only the first extended scene with Beckert, but our first clear view of him. We see him in long shot on the sidewalk as he casually comes into frame, idly attracted by an elaborate window display, tossing his fruit carelessly into the gutter and taking another from his bag. The next shot gives a startling reverse angle and introduces a new motif in the portrayal of Beckert, shooting him through a window which is itself reflecting another scene and projecting it over Beckert – a sort of natural superimposition. This image is famous and yet still powerful. A medium shot shows Beckert (our best view of him so far – nearly half-way through the film!) as he continues to munch his apple, his attention directed at the window display. The image reflected on the glass in front of him shows us what he sees: an elaborately arranged display of cutlery.

Lang and cameraman Fritz Arno Wagner flaunt their mastery of frames and geometrical patterns in this shot. Beckert's head is haloed by the reflection of a large diamond-shaped pattern of knives pointed inward; his belly is rimmed by a rainbow arc of spoons. It is one of Lang's masterpieces of arrangement and composition, but the effect of superimposition gives it a ghostly quality. These patterns seem to radiate out of Beckert, like the metaphysical force lines emanating from characters in an Expressionist painting. But if the Expressionist influence is here, it has also been transformed. Beckert's expression at this moment is casual, as if unaware of the forces that shimmer around him, or aware of them only as shiny attractive objects, drawing the eye of the passerby. He bends down, as if to look more closely at something in the window. We get his point of view shot of the lower part of the display, another carefully arranged series of diverse objects, cases of knives and small scissors, the lozenge of knives no longer visible in this lower framing.

Lang cuts back to Beckert, seen as in the first shot through the glass, framed within the knife pattern, chewing in apparent contentment as he surveys the wares spread before him. Suddenly he reacts: his eyebrows raise, his face freezes, his eyes stare. Lang supplies the point of view shot, this time showing the area of the window previously out of frame. The lozenge of knives is now seen directly, their glimmering forms sharply surrounding a mirror. The mirror reflects a young girl, perfectly framed by the knives as she, too, gazes into the window display from somewhere off screen. Lang returns to Beckert reacting to this vision: he rubs his mouth with his hand slowly, his fingers pulling down the left corner, so that it approximates the monster face he made in the mirror of his apartment, his eyes beginning to bulge as he stares off screen. A brief shot flashes back to the girl in the mirror, then we see Beckert again, as his eyes close and he rocks on his feet as if losing his balance. He straightens up and stares in front of him, his eyes bulging. The point of view shot shows the little girl just slipping out of the mirror which is left empty, reflecting the street and vacant sidewalk, while her dim reflection moves across the window glass. Beckert, viewed from the back, stands in front of the window, the empty mirror to his right as he looks to the left, the direction in which the girl departed. His face is doubled by its reflection in the window. His fingers twitching, his mouth widening, he begins to whistle his theme as he lurches off to the left.

Beckert's madness, the moment of it seizing him, is portrayed both by Lorre's performance and Lang's succession of imagery. The window display introduced here, and soon to be elaborated further, becomes a motif associated with Beckert's obsession. An essential part of the modern urban scene, 'show windows' were intended to use visual curiosity and fascination, 'to arouse in the observer the cupidity and longing to possess the goods' as one merchandising expert, L. Frank Baum, put it.[50] Beckert's highly perverse and repressed desire is stimulated by the devices of the urban consumer culture. These highly illuminated mini-spectacles were designed to release desire through visual stimuli, channelled towards making a purchase. Beckert responds to the first part of their purpose, the visual stimulation and the arousing of desire, but the object of his desire comes from taboo territory. The reflective quality of the window, and especially the mirror, recall Beckert's performance before his own mirror. His private drama has taken over the public space of the street, with a vision of forbidden desire seemingly conjured before his eyes. The vision is fixed for the moment, but then slides away, as if beckoning Beckert to follow.

Lang has devised this mirrored and highly visual environment so that this young girl can appear to Beckert, not as a creature of flesh and blood, but as an image, an image about to disappear. Beckert's relation to his obsession is an imaginary one, based in a virtual reality in which the superimposition of geometrical patterns enforces a sense of entrapment, of predetermined framings. The knives and the mirror seem to impel Beckert towards his next victim. Further, the scenography of bright shiny objects, reflected light, and Beckert's trance-like reaction suggest a

scene of hypnosis, Beckert being taken over by a will not his own. (In his later confession at the 'trial' he claims he has to obey the evil thing inside him.) As Kracauer
put it, 'Evil urges overwhelm him in exactly the same manner in which multiple
objects close in on his screen image'.[51] But this surrender to an alien will takes the
form of a drama, a performance. Given Beckert's fascination by his own image in
the mirror, his absorption in a world of fantasy, this vision of a young girl has also
entered his private world in which he can play a dashing lover and a terrifying monster (and probably never play one without the other). The complex of imagery indicates that Beckert in the throes of his madness enacts his own private movie, the
closest he gets to the enunciatory ambition of the master criminals.

The following shot extends this imagery. The little girl has wandered to another
shop window, this time a book store. But if this seems anodyne compared to the
display of knives which threatened to impale her image in the previous shot, the
visual devices of the window are much more aggressive. A large arrow bounces ver-
tically up and down, pointing to a picture in an open book, while in the background
a circle decorated with a spiral spins, pulling attention towards its eternally withdrawing centre. Such mechanical signs were considered the apex of modern
window dressing, a way to draw strollers irresistibly to your display.[52] Besides continuing the linking of visual attraction and desire, the spiral particularly evokes
hypnosis. As the girl moves from one window display to the next the camera follows
her, Beckert's whistled theme coming from off screen. This is probably the first
example of the 'stalking' camera movement that became a cliché of serial killer films
in the 70s, as the camera's cautious following of the child parallels Beckert's trailing
of her. The camera seems to obey Beckert's will, extending his timid claim at enunciatory command, but it is interrupted almost immediately as this middle-class girl
runs into the arms of her mother, in contrast to the fate of Elsie Beckmann.[53]
Immediately the camera movement and the whistling stops. The camera then
reverses itself as mother and daughter walk to the left. They pass by Beckert, no
longer master of the camera, huddling, in the doorway, his back turned to them and
to us, hiding once more. Emerging, he gazes off screen at them almost wistfully, the
spiral in the window behind him seeming to emerge from his body. He half
scratches, half caresses his hand as he looks off, then turns and gazes directly at the
camera, our first, though brief view of him full face. His previously described withdrawal behind the hedge of the beer garden follows.

The next appearance of Beckert also involves shop windows. After Heinrich, following the blind beggar's suspicion, glimpses Beckert and a new little girl through
the window of the fruit market, he watches as they exit and enact a little drama. The
girl curtsies and offers Beckert a candy, he pulls out a knife in close-up, causing
Heinrich some panic. The following close-up diffuses the drama, but only by offering a substitution: Beckert carefully slices the peel of the orange he offers the girl.
His role as the consumer of little girls as sweet things and cute toys cues us to the
implicit violence in this image. This is the moment when Heinrich chalks the M on
his own hand and, pretending to be just another chance urban encounter, imprints
it on Beckert's shoulder. The beautiful irony of the little girl's solicitous manner as
she returns the potential murder weapon, the knife Beckert dropped when Heinrich
stumbled against him (Marie calls her 'the ideal little Red Riding Hood offering
herself in sacrifice to the Big Bad Wolf'),[54] affirms the bond children seem to have
with this childlike man.

Beckert is now a marked man and his stroll with the little girl is followed closely
by the beggars. But unaware of this, the odd couple proceed arm-in-arm at a

flâneur's pace, pausing in front of a toy store window. This is Lang's most phantas-magorical setting. He shoots Beckert (and the little girl) from inside the store, some of the display of toys visible in the foreground, others reflected on the window pane and seemingly superimposed over the couple as they gawk, mouths open in wide-eyed admiration. A group of dolls and teddy bears sits in the foreground on the display case facing outward, like a miniature audience for the joy of the enraptured pair. Over their heads another mechanical attention-grabber operates, a jumping-jack whose legs enframe them as they gaze into this child's paradise. If Beckert remains partly still a child, attracted to children because he is a reject from the adult world, this would seem to be a moment in which he innocently shares a childlike fascination with his miniature love-object. His face does not show the trance-like fluttering of the eyelids, nor does he show any loss of balance or take on his monster face. He seems simply to enjoy the display, and he apparently asks the girl which toy she likes best and he beams as she points to one. She seems like the bride that Peer Gynt entered the Hall of the Mountain King to ask for, the one for whom he is willing to become a monster.

But Beckert is not a child and he is not innocent. His love of children leads, we know, inevitably to a rage against them, becoming the bogeyman who terrifies and destroys. He already bears the mark of the murderer, the letter M on his back, although he has not realised it yet. But as Kuntzel has revealed, it is present almost subliminally within this scene of toyland. The jumping-jack legs, when stretched wide apart, form an M above Beckert's head, and, further, one can see another dim white M, a reflection on the window, as the legs part.[55] The subliminal becomes explicit in the following shot, from outside the store, as the little girl tells Beckert he's 'all dirty'. The discovery takes place next to the toy display they just looked into, in the shop's doorway.

Here a mirror allows Beckert to search for this dirt the girl has spotted. Another shop window is visible on the left, doubled in the mirror. This one displays rows of both full and half masks of what appear to be children's faces. Starkly white and phantom-like, they witness Beckert's discovery of the mark. At first he sees nothing and asks the child where the dirt is. She points to his shoulder. In medium shot Beckert sees the mark in the mirror; straining to see his own back, he reads it with bafflement. A close-up follows of the M. Still the gracious child-bride of the monster, the little girl tries to wipe it off, as Beckert seems unsure what to think. But as he turns to look over his shoulder in the mirror, he glimpses something which truly terrifies him; he turns quickly and shoots a glance directly at the camera.

On this image my analysis buckles with the previous discussion of Beckert's sudden visibility, his discovery of the pursuers, his final disappearance and eventual discovery. The look at the camera, again, is too brief to assert control over the film Beckert's expression of panic forms the opposite of Haghi or Mabuse's amused confidence. But in being caught in the eyes of others, Beckert's fantasy world also collapses, his private movie, his childlike idyll at the shop window, ends. But his idylls always end in horror. The masks and the children's faces that watch him from the windows as he discovers this dirty mark anticipate his description at the final trial of the horrific turns his private movie always takes: 'And I am pursued by ghosts. Ghosts of mothers. And of those children … They never leave me. They are there, there, always, always. Always … except … except when I do it ….' Beckert is trapped in a private drama, a film with continuous screenings which he cannot control or bring to an end. The child always gives way to the bogeyman, the child-bride and her loving mother become vengeful ghosts. He can only live with this horror by becoming a horror himself and eradicating his child audiences. But now he has been recognised by others, who will end his private drama with a theatrical performance of their own.

The People vs Hans Beckert

Fantastic! Against humanitarian soppiness. For the death
penalty. Well made. Lang will be our director one day.
      Joseph Goebbels' *Diary*, 21 May 1931, after seeing *M*.[56]

With a stump of chalk from his tunic pocket he drew a small
cross on the palm of his hand
   …
As a token of his approval and solidarity would pat anyone
who cursed on the shoulderblade, wherupon the marked
man, white cross on his back, would be caught by the SA
   …
I ran away terrified at home I looked at my back in the
mirror to see if it didn't bear a white cross.
      Bertolt Brecht 'The Chalk Cross', *Poems 1913–1956*

Beckert's brief glimpse of his beggar-pursuer as he turns from the mirror, then flees in panic abandoning his child-bride/victim, could cut directly to his first point of view shot when he is pushed into the cellar of the abandoned brewery.

Falling down the stairs, he turns and screams defiance at his tormentors standing above him, then looks around and becomes silent. The point of view shot shows this grim, subterranean space filled to the gills – the shot pans slowly to include them all – with silent, immobile people seated and staring at him. Beckert has been caught in the gaze of others with a vengeance, the furtive glance of the spy multiplied into a glare of judgement. Burch has pointed out that the film's dominant style of discontinuity in space lessens towards the end of the film. Here in the cellar, the final scene of the film (outside of the two-shot epilogue) stays within a single space and continuous time for nearly fifteen minutes, without a single cutaway to another space.[57]

This return to the uninterrupted scene (with its unity of dramatic space) rather than the sequence (with its intercutting of different spaces) marks the highly theatrical nature of the film's climax. Although this trial is run by outlaws, it not only maintains many of the basic court procedures (another parody of the codes of ordered society appearing in the underworld), such as a variety of testimonies and a presiding 'president', Schränker, it also maintains the theatricality of the courtroom. The cellar overflows with audience, and the scene consists of a series of speeches or performances before them. The basic drama enacted here is the simultaneous establishment and stripping away of the identity of Hans Beckert, murderer.

After Beckert's game of hide-and-seek, and his final discovery, he is, in effect, completely uncovered. Most of our views of him have been mediated by windows, mirrors, views from the back. Now he is displayed frontally with nowhere to hide, stripped of his screens and props, made to confront not only his judges, but his victims and himself. He begins by moving towards the camera after it has moved towards him, his hands outstretched, an ingratiating, if nervous, smile on his face, insisting there has been a mistake. But if Beckert delivers himself to this close-up view, his frame is soon invaded from off screen left, as a hand grabs his shoulder and his expression freezes in terror. The beggar's voice comes from off screen denying there is any mistake. The camera pulls back from the close-up which Beckert dominated, to a wider framing and reveals the beggar holding a balloon identical to the one purchased for Elsie. As he asks Beckert if he recognises it and mentions Elsie Beckmann, Beckert gives a start. Lang cuts 180 degrees to a high angle shot showing the assembled trial members and audience in the background, Beckert in midground gazing up, and in the foreground, in slightly soft focus, the wavering form of the balloon. As it sways in the frame, the balloon alternately obscures, then reveals Beckert's figure standing below.

This is an unbearable moment for Beckert. He backs away from the balloon, stuttering over Elsie's name, 'El ... El ... Elsie ... El', and then shouts denial, 'No, no, no'. But his withdrawal only brings him closer to his judges, as he nearly backs into the table at which Schränker and the other underworld leaders sit. The camera too pursues him as he moves back, seeming to fly in its overhead position past the balloon to keep Beckert in frame. Beckert confronts images from his private drama of monstrosity, the return of the dead. The balloon took on Elsie's identity at her death and seemed to ascend into the heavens. Now it has reappeared in the underworld, an infernal, vengeful presence. It is the visual equivalent of the ghosts of his victims which Beckert will soon confess haunt him continually. But now he is not only haunted by these vengeful ghosts, but confronted by the reality of the mob assembled to judge him. Beckert is caught between them. His backward retreat is interrupted by a shout and a sudden reverse angle cut, and Beckert spins around as Schränker shouts a question about another victim.

The 180 degree reverse angle cutting typical of many Langian scenes of confrontation (such as the meetings with the 'man behind the curtain' in *The Testament of Dr. Mabuse*) dominates this final scene of *M*. Lorre looks directly into the
camera as he responds to Schränker, again claiming he doesn't know these girls,
the camera clearly serving as an accuser and witness. Schränker continues to facilitate the dragging of Beckert's private movie into this public space. He displays to
Beckert a series of photographs of his victims, ending with Elsie Beckmann. After
the first photograph, Beckert again moves backward. But the succeeding photographs are in close-up from his point of view. Unable to distance himself, Beckert first puts his hand in his mouth as if stifling a scream, although the gesture also
expresses the orality so often noted in Beckert's character, his infantile regression.
At its most primal here, he seems to wish to swallow himself in order to disappear,
or to eat the photograph and make it disappear, as he has already consumed the
girl herself like a bit of sweetness. After Elsie's photograph (complete with her ball
– another *déjà vu* image) Beckert turns and runs. But as Schränker has already told
him, there is no way out of here. As in Haghi/Nemo's last performance, space is
enclosed on all sides, except the one open to the audience. There is no off screen
space into which Beckert can move unseen. His disappearing act no longer works:
he is exposed to the glare of visibility and witnesses who remember his acts. His
frenzied attempt to get out the doorway is repressed with brutal physical violence,
as the voices of the crowd cheer his attackers on, suggesting places to hit him ('his
shins!'). Again Peer Gynt's visit to the Hall of the Mountain King is recalled, as Peer
searched vainly for a way out and the trolls called out to bar his way and bite and
kill him.

Schränker restores order and insists on instructing both crowd and prisoner on
the way the order of law will be followed ('we are all experts on the law here: from
six weeks in Tegel to fifteen years in Brandenburg'). A long pan over the grotesque
faces of the convicts sitting in judgement underscores the parodic tone, the almost
carnivalesque inversion of a criminal court. But Lang does not allow us to participate in this carnival with levity. Beckert's anguished and hysterical cries echo
through the cellar, until again a hand enters from off screen and pokes him on the
shoulder. Here another element of parody introduces himself: Beckert's defence
lawyer, picking up his hat in order to tip it in a Chaplinesque gesture of abject dignity. Beckert's demands to be handed over to the police are greeted with ever-
increasing laughter from the audience off screen, the child's nightmare of mockery
at the moment he is being most serious, pleading for his life. Beckert does not have
Nemo's fine-edged sense of irony. He cannot stand being taken for a clown at the
moment of his death. Schränker repeats his demand that Beckert must disappear, a
term taken up by an off screen voice – 'Yes, disappear!' Beckert's most powerful trick
is now being demanded of him, at the same time as any possibility of achieving it
has been taken away from him.

Beckert's monologue that follows is simultaneously one of the finest performances in sound cinema and an extraordinary example of writing for the new
'talkie' by Thea von Harbou. As an act of public self-explication and confession, its
theatrical nature carries enormous power. In essence, Beckert claims he is not
responsible for his acts, that he is compelled to perform them, that he is deeply
split in two ('I can't help myself. I haven't any control over this evil thing inside me.
… It's me pursuing myself'). Lang cuts to a medium close-up as Beckert begins by
addressing the camera most directly, staring into it with a sudden authority, not at
all like his cringing denials earlier in the scene. One thinks of a secondary title the

film was sometimes given: *Dein Mörder sieht Dich an*, 'Your Murder Looks at You'.[58] But his eyes shift to the sides as if scrutinising the site of off screen space, the zone of invisibility, as he describes this force that pursues and drives him. As he recounts his plight in vivid terms – he wants to escape and cannot – we realise that his description of his life subject to his compulsion precisely mimics the imagery of the film ('pursued down endless streets') and ends inevitably in the situation he is now in: wishing to flee from the all-powerful, scrutinising eyes, wanting to escape, but unable to. Because he cannot escape from himself, his own self-scrutinising, self-terrorising mirror drama. His private torment has now found its public equivalent.

His impassioned description cannot help but arouse sympathy, and Lang shows several of the audience nodding in understanding or empathy. His monologue brings us deeper into the horror of the drama he is caught in. As he describes his pursuit by the ghosts of his child-victims and their mothers, Lang shows two mothers listening in horror, showing not so much revulsion or anger, as pure terror, clinging to each other and twisting their handkerchiefs, as if Beckert succeeds in getting them to picture his haunted life. These visions are with him 'always, always, always' – except ... except when he does it.

A new motive is given here for Beckert's murders. He commits them in order to stop the infernal repeating drama, the imaginary snuff film on an endless projection loop, to give himself relief, to make himself unconscious. Lorre's pantomime is at its most extreme here, almost painful to watch. His hands have become claw-like and make strangling motions, gestures replacing words ('When I ...'), his face becomes truly demonic, a sort of spasm passing over it. The face and hands collapse and hang limp and flaccid. His now somnolent face claims, 'and then I can't remember anything'. The murder is the blind spot of his torment, the release from the constant images and torture – oblivion. He has reached what Dadoun describes as 'the abyss of total unconsciousness in which he plunges and disappears when he kills a little girl'.[59] Dadoun further glosses with great insight: 'One could say that he disappears, that he dies phantasmically with or within the real death of his victim. It is therefore he that is killed – but it is also he that kills'.[60] As Dadoun says, Beckert dies only in fantasy. In reality he comes back to life, back to consciousness, back to being tortured by his ghosts. It is a scenario Lang will replay in his Hollywood films with Edward G. Robinson, first as comedy (*The Woman in the Window*) and then as tragedy (*Scarlet Street*). One awakes from an imagined/attempted death/suicide only to find the private movie is still unreeling.

Beckert awakes to be immediately confronted by his crime, as an inhabitant of the modern city in which the news is plastered everywhere. Beckert recalls the scene from the opening of the film's second sequence, the crowds gathered to read of the latest crime. And Beckert tells us he is among them: 'I read and I read ...' But like everyone else in the city he cannot locate the murderer, he cannot recognise himself in what he reads. He acts out his compulsion once more, the drama begins again (triggered by the act of reading?). His utter aloneness with this drama ('Who knows what it's like to be me?') and the self torment of both his interior split between demanding monster and terrified slave ('Don't want to ... Must ... Don't want to ... Must ... Don't want to!') and identification with his victim ('a voice screams! I can't bear to hear it!' as he covers his ears and screams at the same time, attempting to close out the sound of his own suffering). He holds his head and cries 'I cannot ... I cannot ...' One shudders to think of the scene from his own childhood, what encounter with what past monster he is accessing, what experience of torture he has been doomed to repeat as he appears to us now, not as an adult, not even as a monster, but as an abject, suffering, abused child.

There is a sort of anticlimax to the film after this point. Not a failure of dramatic construction, which actually gains increasing suspense as Beckert's fate is debated. But the curiosity, the mystery surrounding Beckert from the beginning of the film, his shadowy oblique existence, has now been exhausted. In Burch's term, he has truly been unveiled before the camera and the audience (of the trial and of the film). He has no more secrets, except the impenetrable ones of human torment and the cycle of cruel madness which both causes it and which responds to it. In effect there is no exit from Beckert's drama. Instead of resolution, Beckert now becomes an object of discourse. Schränker begins by responding to Beckert's performance by taking up a role within it, becoming the monster who wishes to punish Beckert, but who also promises some deliverance in supplying a final end, instead of an endless cycle. He repeats his demand that Beckert be eliminated, disappear.

The argument offered by the defence attorney occupies a curious place in this array of discourse. There is no question that this figure introduced with comic pretensions and self-irony gains considerable dignity and shows true courage as he defends a liberal position: that Beckert is sick and needs to be taken to an asylum, rather than delivered to the rough justice of the mob. Schränker's shrill demand that Beckert 'be snuffed out like a candle' not only recalls Nazi rhetoric of 'living beings unworthy of life', it dwells very much within the paranoid fantasy of Beckert's own madness; the punitive parent. The mocking laughter of the mob as the attorney pleads for humanity directly echoes the response to Beckert when he first appears. The defence lawyer, however, maintains the reflective and deflating Berlin humour so evident in much of the film, as in his opening statement which refers to Schränker as 'our honorable president ... wanted by the police for three murders'. But it is to the lawyer's arguments that the crowd responds with the clearest anticipations (although in 1931 we should perhaps simply say echoes) of Nazi rhetoric. When he refers to Beckert as 'this man', an off screen voice shouts out, 'that is not a man!'

In later years Lang allowed it to be assumed that the film's point of view was that of the defence lawyer, and that *M* was an argument against capital punishment and for the humane treatment of mental patients.[61] In the atmosphere of the film's release this viewpoint was not the most common. Many viewers and reviewers, including liberal or leftist journalists as well as Herr Goebbels, found the film sympathetic to the death penalty and mob justice. In a contemporary review Kracauer attacked these easy interpretations of the film,[62] stressing the ambiguity of Lang's presentation. Lang seems determined not to make a statement here, but to raise a variety of points of view. And indeed it would seem in the aftermath of Beckert's confession no statement is given absolute authority. The defence attorney has rationality, irony and a liberal tradition behind him. Schränker, however, responds to his speech not only with hysteria but also with fear of an endless cycle ('another man-hunt, ... the compulsion all over again and so on and so on to doomsday!').

The emotional response comes from a woman who stands and invokes the dead children and their mothers. She ends with a cry that is taken up by the crowd, 'Ask the Mothers!' This final discourse returns us to the primal pain and separation that opened the film, Elsie and her mother. But this image of motherhood is no longer that of the patient, caring, nourishing mother, but of angry, vengeful mothers, the Eumenides: 'ask the mothers, do you think they will have mercy on him?' It is this question which whips the crowd to the highest point of hysteria, not only shouting,

'Kill him. Crush him' but ready to rush into action, to tear him apart. Having separated Elsie and the other children from their loving mothers, Beckert now encounters the monstrous mother, the mother-murderer. The faces of the crowd as they
call for his murder have become distorted and monstrous, like Beckert's own faces
in the mirror, or when he acts out the moment of murder and oblivion before the
court. According to Dadoun's reading of the mirror imagery in the film, this
accords with Beckert's driving fantasy, the union of murderer and victim becoming
the symbiosis of mother and child, 'M identifies with the child-about-to-be killed,
he identifies with the mother-who-must-murder'.[63] The courtroom scene again
delivers itself up to the primal fantasy of Beckert's own murderous cycle, acted out
now in public before his eyes.

This scene of primal destruction, this *sparagmos* of the guilty one, is interrupted
in mid-action by a *coup de cinéma*, another dramatic use of off screen space. The
mob rushing towards the off screen Beckert suddenly stops in its tracks. With a look
off to the left, they all make the same gesture simultaneously, as carefully timed as
the masses in *Metropolis*, raising their hands (except Schränker who pointedly
delays his gesture a second), as silence fills the cellar. In the following shot, Beckert
looks bewildered until another hand touches him on the shoulder from off screen
(the third in the sequence), and an off screen voice declares, 'in the name of the
Law'. The apparent restoration of order remains elliptical, dramatic in its effects,
incommunicative in its meaning. Lang's final shots emphasise both immediate
restoration of order, but also a strong discontinuity. He cuts immediately to a court
bench in which the judges sit down to pass sentence, but all we hear is a rhyming
complement to the previous voice: 'In the name of the people'. The final verdict is
given to the mothers. But the three grieving women who end the film are not the
vengeful Eumenides seen in the cellars. The one who looks at the camera and speaks
directly to us to end the film is, in fact, Elsie's mother, the caring and nourishing –
and now mourning – Frau Beckmann. She says that 'this' (presumably the verdict
against Beckert and his punishment) will not bring the children back. And as the
image fades into the final darkness of the film she says, 'We, too, should keep a
closer watch on our children.'

The return of Mrs. Beckmann, takes the film back to its opening, something
images and words throughout the final scene in the cellar seem constantly trying to
accomplish. It is, of course, the structure of a murder mystery to try throughout its
length to get back to the primal act, to clear it up and make sense of it. But *M* denies
us that satisfaction. We do indeed learn who committed these murders and we even
learn a great deal about what drives him to them. But the structure of the final scenes
works against resolution: the courtroom debate is not decided in favour of any one
discourse; the rousing to a primitive violence that demands fulfilment in brutal
action is stopped in mid-stride, curtailed; the legal process is stopped in mid-sentence. We are only left with the act of grief and mourning and an address to the audience. One feels Frau Beckmann, in the key address to the camera in this film, makes
a request to us we are not sure we can fulfil: to watch, to watch more carefully …

Like *The Testament of Dr. Mabuse*, and indeed like all of Lang's German films, *M*
exists under the shadow of the Third Reich and the holocaust, one of the last stations
on Kracauer's trajectory from *Caligari* to Hitler. The echoes and anticipations of Nazi
policies appear everywhere for contemporary viewers of this film: Schränker's
leather jacket and cane summon up the image of an SS officer, the rhetoric of final
solutions and eliminations of the outsider, the euthanasia of mental patients, Beckert's inscribed M as the star of David – all recall the Shoah. I believe it is as dangerous

to make these associations automatically as it is to ignore them. Simply to assume an identity between Beckert and the Nazi victims is not only extremely problematic, but was also done as a propaganda device by the Nazis themselves. The Nazis banned *M* in 1933, but appropriated a section of Lorre's final monologue in the 1940 racist documentary *The Eternal Jew* to show simultaneously the dominance of the Weimar cinema by Jews (such as 'the Jew actor', Lorre) and as a portrayal of psychotic Jewish behaviour. Goebbels' claim that the film was proto-Nazi ('Lang will be our director') is no more inherently convincing than later claims that the film is anti-Nazi. Kracauer himself recognised the ambiguity of the film, wavering between different attitudes. It is precisely the manner in which the film is pre-Nazi that makes it so complex. The anxieties about modernity and urban life are inventoried. More than ever before Lang grounds these anxieties in the primal fears of ordinary people, a working-class mother rather than a bored countess, a pathetic, childish psychopath rather than a master criminal hypnotist. It is important not to lose the concrete specificity Lang has brought to this film by creating a series of metaphorical substitutions. But as the concrete world portrayed in *M* generated Nazism, it is on this concrete level that the film can speak to us about its heritage.

Within the narrative that Lang fashioned to describe his own relation to the Nazis, whose climax (we have already seen) revolves around *The Testament of Dr. Mabuse*, *M* also plays a crucial role. Lang claims that the film's working title, *Murderers Among Us*, caused him a number of problems. Anonymous threatening letters were sent and at first the Staaken studio was refused to him as the venue for principal photography. Lang describes the key encounter, once again, in the style of a scene from one of his films. In a heated discussion with the owner of the studio, Lang had grabbed the man by the lapel. Feeling something on the underside, he flipped the lapel over and exposed a Nazi party badge.[64] I make no claim for

the veracity of this anecdote. It seems a bit too dramatic (why would one have to conceal a Nazi badge at the time, anyway?) to ring true. But its scenography employs not only Langian devices but the new concrete 'objectivity' of *M,* the focus on objects. Lang's discovery functions like a visionary scene. He uncovers what lies behind the opposition to his film: the fears the Nazi party had that his title 'Murderers Among Us' referred directly to them, their fear that he, like a Heartfield collage, would expose their monstrous face. But no overlap-dissolve is needed here, no stylised, allegorical imagery: just the object itself, the Nazi badge come out of hiding. As in Lang's allegorical films, the revelation caused a conversion. It was on that day, Lang told Kracauer, that he came of age politically.[65]

Perhaps the most striking thing about *M's* political vision is its mixture of obscurity and terror, an atmosphere which would persist in *The Testament of Dr. Mabuse,* an obsession with fragments, an inability to get a full picture. Although powerful as formal devices, Lang's approaches to the unexpected zones of off screen space in *M* also contrast with the carefully arranged and transcendent visions of the allegorical films, or the grand schemes of the master criminal films. Lang has spoken of his desire in this film to bid farewell to the epic film.[66] But this issue involves more than scale. Lang's vision becomes more barred, more mediated. Instead of visionary clarifications, however dire their message may have been, we see characters whose vision does not so much penetrate the skin of reality as catch their own desires, fantasies and even their own faces, reflected back to them in distorted and monstrous ways. An obscurity and a sort of blindness enter Lang's cinema from this point on. Lang provides a bitter parody of allegory in Elsie's grotesque balloon that ascends to heaven after her death. At this high point in his career as a film-maker Lang questions the possibility of vision and representation, and shows us a world caught in multiplying the images of its own terror.

PART IV

Fritz Lang's America –
The Social Trilogy

Fury (1936)

You Only Live Once (1937)

You and Me (1938)

… I

Who live in Los Angeles and not in London
Find, on thinking about Hell, that it must be
Still more like Los Angeles.

[….]

The houses in Hell, too, are not all ugly.
But the fear of being thrown on the street
Wears down the inhabitants of the villas no less than
The inhabitants of the shanty towns.

Bertolt Brecht, 'On Thinking about Hell'[1]

8

You Ought to Be in Pictures:
Liliom and *Fury*

The Flight of the Refugee

Eat the meat that's there. Don't stint yourself.
Go into any house when it rains and sit on any chair that's in it.
But don't sit long. And don't forget your hat.
I tell you:
Cover your tracks.

Bertolt Brecht,
first poem from *The Handbook for City Dwellers*[2]

We now know the fictional nature of Lang's tale of a sudden flight from Germany, with its secretive departure, nervous border crossing, one final farewell to the land where he had made his career, his fortune and his fame.[3] In fact, Lang left Berlin for Paris after a period of reflection and preparation, and with a motion picture production with his old producer Erich Pommer (who had relocated to Paris) firmly

arranged. Rather than fleeing for his life and trying to beat the clock, Lang left Berlin as, one fellow refugee put it, an 'émigré deluxe'.[4] None of this denies the enormous and undoubtedly traumatic transformation this uprooting brought to Lang's life. Leaving Germany not only meant abandoning a position of enormous power for a strong degree of uncertainty, but also severing relations with his wife and strongest collaborator, Thea von Harbou. The Lang–Harbou divorce was finalised a few months before his final departure from Berlin. The reasons behind it were undoubtedly multiple and personal, but political differences played a role, as Harbou's Nazi allegiances were asserting themselves.[5] Whether or not Lang had truly experienced a 'political awakening' during the shooting of *M*, or in Goebbels' office, his Jewish heritage made an embrace of Nazi ideology impossible. Although some observers claim an initially ambiguous attitude towards the Nazis on Lang's part, by 1934 he was clearly an anti-Nazi.[6] When I spoke to Lang while still an undergraduate I asked him a rather undergraduate question about the role of love in his films. He responded, 'Love! Tell me, if a man is a Communist and his wife is a Nazi, what happens to love?'

Between Lang's German and his Hollywood career, then, there falls a rather brief interlude in Paris, the initial stopping-point for so many Weimar refugees. But unlike compatriots like Wilder, Siodmak, Benjamin or Kracauer, who stayed in France until driven out, Lang soon made arrangements to leave for the US, departing in 1934 with a contract with MGM. The value of Lang's subsequent Hollywood career, in which he spent the bulk of his life as a director (twenty-two years as opposed to fifteen years in prewar Germany; twenty-two films in Hollywood as opposed to some fourteen films in prewar Germany) has been hotly debated. The most definitive and serious dismissal (coming as it does from perhaps the most profoundly observant critic of Lang's German films), that of Noel Burch, describes Lang's post-*The Testament of Dr. Mabuse* career as 'a silence lasting some thirty films' (apparently he doesn't even want to count them!). Even on later reflection Burch claims Lang's American films were 'marginal and second rate'.[7]

I feel that Lang's strongest work was made in Germany before 1934. However, I also feel there is no question that the same film-maker, with the same essential stylistics and preoccupations not only continued to work out the design of his authorship in his Hollywood films, but also developed further some of the most profound insights of the last German sound films. Although Lang did produce some conformist films during his Hollywood career (*The Return of Frank James*, *Western Union*, *An American Guerrilla in the Philippines*), usually at moments of crisis in his career when more experimental films had failed, none of his films are totally bereft of interest. Further, while the best films of the Hollywood period may never surpass the achievements of the best German films, by no means are they markedly inferior.

Primarily we are dealing with a transformation in Lang's method of working, one brought on by external circumstances – especially the increased division of labour in the Hollywood studio and the different responsibilities and degree of control given to the director. There is no question that Lang was hampered by these circumstances – as well as by the loss of Harbou as collaborator. But it is also true that Lang devised methods of working within them. Burch's claim that Lang 'identified himself with that anonymous being … the all purpose Hollywood director' is consistently and directly challenged by the method of work Lang brought to his direction, as well as the many extraordinary films that resulted.[8] Indeed, the issue of authorship becomes that much more intense in Lang's Hollywood *œuvre*, precisely because it cannot assert itself as directly.

Kristin Thompson, in her important essay 'Early Alternatives to the Hollywood Mode of Production', demonstrates that European film directors of the 1920s had much more control over the film process than their Hollywood counterparts. In Hollywood the continuity script for a film was often prepared, not only without the director's input, but as a means of controlling what the director did: he was expected to realise the approved 'blueprint' supplied by the script.[9] Further, his work was overseen by a supervisor or producer whose role was to see the script was followed and that the already agreed-upon budgets and shooting schedules were adhered to. Finally, the editing of the film need not involve the director at all, but was the responsibility of specialised editors working from the continuity script. In Europe, however, the case was quite different:

> Directors were still responsible for many decisions at the scripting stage. The script itself seems to have constrained the director less during the shooting phase. Directors also still had almost complete responsibility at the editing phase.[10]

In fact, Ufa after *Metropolis* (and partly due to the financial failure brought on by *Metropolis*, as well as mutual contracts with Hollywood studios) became more like a Hollywood system, but this is precisely why Lang moved to his own production companies and then to independent producers for his last German films, in order to maintain personal control.[11]

Lang gave up this degree of control when he arrived in Hollywood, but all accounts of his methods of working indicate a constant attempt to assert as much control as he could. Lang's conflicts with nearly everyone in the Hollywood system, from producers to stars to cameramen, involved struggles for power and control. Lang ran up against the producer's authority as much as he encountered friction from union rules which prevented the eighteen-hour shooting schedules he had frequently enforced in Europe.[12] Bereft of his scriptwriter wife, Lang not only lost a collaborator of genius, but also a close involvement at every stage of the scriptwriting. For most of Lang's Hollywood films the greatest loss of control came at the script stage, frequently arriving on set with a script in which his contribution was minimal. Editing posed another problem, but Lang seems to have cajoled most of his editors into letting him participate closely at this stage, almost never abandoning a film after shooting (although never managing the complete control he had in Germany).

Where Lang could assert almost monomaniacal control was at the shooting stage and what one could call the *découpage*, the planning-out of each shot and sequence on paper. Very early in his career Lang began to diagram each shot and scene. Such paper diagrams showed the blueprint of the constructed set, with the angle of view of the camera for each take (and any movement it might make) precisely pencilled in, as well as lines marking out the pathway of the actors as they moved through the scene.[13] These bird's eye views recall Lang's topographical shots and his own drive toward the abstract and diagrammatic. These floor plans were supplemented by sketches of the actual framing, and detailed notes including the actors' gestures.[14] Numerous Lang actors have described his tyranny in determining precisely the movement of their head or hands, the necessity for them to hit exactly the marks Lang had drawn on the floor.[15] Within the realm of authority that the Hollywood division of labour allowed to the director – the actual managing and executing of the shooting itself, converting the script into images – Lang declared himself an absolute despot.

If the claim that Lang abdicated his authority as director on coming to Holly-wood cannot be affirmed, nonetheless the circumscription of his power cannot be denied. In Hollywood, Lang faced a different situation in terms of power and authorship. And his responses to it would be varied, from strong experimental chal-lenging of dominant modes, to quiet conformity, to complexly dialectical subver-sion. Lang's presence in his films, the issue of enunciation so important to the narrative structure as well as the production process of Lang's cinema, becomes more hidden, more subterranean. Like one of his overreaching master criminals, Lang discovers that Hollywood itself could function like a Destiny-machine and that his control of it was always subject to its control over him.

But this transformation possesses its own fascination. Using the terms intro-duced by critic Manny Farber, we could say that Lang increasingly produced 'ter-mite' art, small films whose style hid out in the details of *mise-en-scène* rather than in massive sets or spectacular special effects, less pretentious than the big-budget super-films of his silent career (which would be examples of what Farber called 'White Elephant' art, or as Lang himself called them, *Schinken*, 'hams').[16] Lang in Hollywood made films that do not immediately call attention to themselves and whose signs of authorship are often hidden. As an enunciatory force, Lang begins to bore from within. For the most part, beneath an apparent conformity to Hollywood modes and genres and ideology, Lang fashions extremely personal and often exper-imental works. In this task the continuity with his German work, especially the sound films, becomes obvious. In Hollywood, Lang's work switches its mode, deter-mined undoubtedly by exterior circumstances (are there any other kind?), but his response rewards complex decoding.

Walter Benjamin, writing from exile in Paris, commented on Brecht's first poem in *The Handbook for City Dwellers*, the first stanza of which says:

Part from your friends at the station
Enter the city in the morning with your coat buttoned up
Look for a room, and when your friend knocks:
Do not, oh do not, open the door
But
Cover your tracks.

Benjamin commented: 'Arnold Zweig has pointed out that this sequence of poems has acquired a new meaning in recent years; it represents the city as the refugee experiences it in a foreign country.'[17] Brecht wrote the poems in 1928, Benjamin made his comments in the late 30s. Although Lang in both his homes of exile, Paris and Hollywood, lived in relative ease, the insecurity of the refugee shapes aspects of his new mode of film-making. In a profound sense Lang learned to 'cover his tracks' as a film-maker. When Brecht joined Lang in exile in California a few years later he was disgusted by Lang's adaptation to and enthusi-asm for the United States and Hollywood.[18] But while Lang admitted a strong influence from Brecht and gave him his unmitigated admiration ('the greatest talent of this century in Germany'),[19] Brecht had less sympathy for and, I would say, understanding of, Lang's work. Lang's work in Hollywood particularly accords with the penultimate verse of Brecht's poem, obeying a dialectic that had been in his film-making from the beginning and which responds not only to the refugee's plight, but to the situation of the film-maker working in this technolog-ical mass medium:

Whatever you say, don't say it twice
If you find your ideas in someone else, disown them.
The man who hasn't signed anything, who has left no picture
Who was not there, who said nothing:
How can they catch him?
Cover your tracks.[20]

The lifestyle of the professional spy, the assumption of the persona of Nemo, 'no-one' – these become key to the new stylistics of Lang's Hollywood films. But rather than rendering these films negligible and indistinguishable from the basic Hollywood product, they represent a hermeneutic challenge. Covered tracks must be uncovered.

Lang's first film on leaving Germany, *Liliom*, poses a true puzzle. On the one hand, no film could be more different from the films Lang had just completed; even Lang's Hollywood films would bear more immediate relation to *M* and *The Testament of Dr. Mabuse* than this romantic fantasy. In contrast to *M*, *Liliom* is resolutely continuous in its narrative style, unrolling in a series of unified scenes (with only one 'special effect' of cross cutting – between Liliom and Julie as she 'feels' him stab himself). There is absolutely no use of rhymes between scenes, and rather limited use of off screen sound. Characters frequently look directly at the camera, but such shots are always edited with a reverse angle, so the gaze remains circumscribed by the dramatic space of the scene. There is no thematic of enunciation here. Even the high angle view (other than in its ultimate literal envisioning as a view from heaven) is used sparingly. Further, the tone seems quite at antipodes to a Langian vision: a bitter sweet fantasy focused on a love affair, it has a limited amount of violence, danger or suspense.

One might treat the film as an anomaly for Lang, his passport out of Berlin, rather than a personal project, and indeed, this, rather than the Hollywood films, appears to be the first film in which Lang was not deeply involved in either the selection of the material, the pre-production of casting and planning, or scripting; Pommer assigned Lang the film and made the basic production decisions before his arrival.[21] However, Lang employed his detailed blueprint diagrams for control of the shooting process and he exercised his characteristic tyranny over the selection of props and the control of performances.[22] He also apparently took control of the film's editing, although few Lang films make such limited use of editing strategies.[23] Several shots, in fact, are striking for their length, such as the impressive long take with careful reframings as Madame Muscat tries to woo back Liliom as he washes up and shaves, lasting two minutes.

Lang himself, at least in later years when the film was re-released, spoke highly of it as one of his favourite films.[24] Its comic opera atmosphere, obvious delight in the world of the carnival, and outright, if quite ironic, fantasy, might seem less foreign to Lang's *œuvre* if his project for a similar Viennese fantasy, *The Legend of the Last Viennese Fiacre*, a film first announced (as Bernard Eisenschitz has shown) as his next production after *The Woman in the Moon*, or his delightful script for another Viennese film, *Scandal in Vienna*, which dealt with the turn of the century European tour of Buffalo Bill's Wild West show, had actually been filmed.[25] All these projects share an atmosphere of bittersweet nostalgia and a love of the realm of make-believe.

Liliom intrigues me not as a charming anomaly, nor as an unappreciated masterpiece (if anything it tends now to be overrated), but as a pivotal film between Lang's German and Hollywood *œuvre*. As a romantic comedy, the film focuses on the heterosexual couple much more than most of his German films, and resembles the formula of heterosexual romance that dominates Hollywood feature films and to which Lang would adapt with some difficulty. Of course, nearly all Lang's German films included a central heterosexual romance, but both Lang's direction and often Harbou's scripting subordinated any portrayal of emotional attachment to larger issues of power and revenge (*Die Nibelungen*), spiritual and political renewal (*Metropolis*), or ploys of manipulation (*Dr. Mabuse, the Gambler*). This is not to say that sexual desire does not play a key role in Lang's German films, in fact, it supplies a major motivation for action, challenged only by the desire for power. But a single romantic couple does not motivate the entire story line in most of the films.

M and *Der müde Tod* reveal in different ways the rather unconventional role that desire or love plays in Lang's German cinema. In both films desire propels the action of the film, but although it is a pure, selfless love in *Der müde Tod* and per-verse destructive desire in *M*, both are condemned from the beginning of the film to non-fulfilment. Whereas in most Hollywood films, love and desire move towards the establishment of a couple, with the couple providing a stabilising closure for the film, more often in Lang's films desire can neither be brought to a satisfying ending nor achieve a satisfying equilibrium. Sexual desire can either provide a cynical (as in Carozza and Hull in *Dr. Mabuse, the Gambler*), or a conventional and predictable (as Kent and Lilli in *The Testament of Dr. Mabuse*) subplot. *Spies* stands out by inte-grating its romantic subplots into its major plot of intrigue and power, endowing both Matsumoto's tragedy and Sonja and Tremaine's love affair with a sense of painful betrayal and restless desire. For Lang, desire works best, narratively, when it remains unfulfilled, and the couple, once securely established, doesn't seem to interest him.

Liliom, to my mind, misses being the masterpiece some critics have claimed it is, because the love between Julie and Liliom never feels particularly compelling. Liliom seems motivated more by a certain narcissistic energy, evident in his joy as a carnival performer and his delight in his expected child, which he assumes will be a boy, a miniature Liliom. This attraction accents Lang's view of desire as free-float-ing, bound up with role playing and fantasy rather than heterosexual coupling. Like the false Maria's robotic sex appeal, there is something essentially mechanical about this energy in *Liliom*, embodied in the circular motion of Liliom's merry-go-round (which is emblematically emblazoned with a figure of Eve offering an apple to Adam as the snake coils about them). Liliom can resist Madame Muscat's seduction rather easily, but the lure of the carnival proves almost irresistible. When Madame Muscat attempts to reclaim Liliom, he treats her with undisguised contempt until she begins singing to him the merry-go-round tune. Lang cuts to Julie listening anxiously within their home as she nervously accompanies the off screen tune by turning her coffee grinder, the circular motion involuntarily recalling the carousel. Later, after Liliom's death, Julie will listen to the merry-go-round theme on a phonograph, another circular and repetitive machine.

Desire pulses through Lang's films as primal energy, at points more mechanical than human. In *M*, it compels Hans Beckert to murder. In a fantasy comedy like *Liliom*, it reflects the life-force of Liliom himself, the dizzying excitement of the merry-go-round. It is only during their first meeting on the merry-go-round that Liliom and Julie truly project sensuality and desire. In the later love scenes, Liliom seems politely bored. Sexuality reflects life's energy, not character psychology. Thus, when Liliom is dying, Madame Muscat asks that the carnival pause for a moment.

In one of the film's two great sequences, Lang details the various machineries of delight coming to a halt: first, the merry-go-round's mechanical orchestra, then the spinning merry-go-round itself slowing to stillness (shown as a shadow cast on a wall); the spinning wheels of chance are stopped; the needle is taken off a turning phonograph; a mechanical drummer and an automaton turning the crank of a barrel organ both run down and cease. All these circular motions end, and a silence reigns briefly, in which Lang shows his established image of the Destiny-machine, a clock pendulum still ticking beneath the stilled energies of desire. In this romantic comedy, Lang portrays desire as a life-energy turning about itself, a strangely mechanical vitality that ceases with the coming of death, rather than the foundation of the sentimental and romantic union of a couple.

The film's other crowning moment comes with Liliom's trip to heaven, as beautifully caricatured a piece of cinema as Ophuls or Lubitsch could contrive. Lang returns here to an outright allegorical mode. Lang's images of heaven are, as René Daumal described them when the film was first completed, 'audaciously naive and conventional'.[26] Heaven is made of crudely daubed carnival pasteboard and the only three-dimensional angel Liliom passes during his ascent recalls the mechanical drummer from the fairground. Thus Lang's return to allegory, a form which, as I have said, he never entirely abandons, but which becomes progressively more oblique and problematic for him, here practically chortles with irony. The bureaucratic vision of heaven includes a repetition of Lang's delightful bit of business of an official having trouble stamping a report (earlier seen at the police headquarters during Liliom's life on earth), and a heavenly typist with whom Liliom flirts and who responds by adjusting her makeup. In *Der müde Tod,* Lang provided only the briefest glimpse of the heavenly realm at the end of the film, allowing us only a fragment of transcendence. Here he provides a vision of heaven with no transcendence at all: another Langian office, like the beggars' headquarters, complete with waiting rooms, massive code books carefully consulted, goat-footed messenger boys from Hell and heavenly illuminated signs declaring, 'No Spitting'. Liliom responds to each new familiar bit of bureaucracy, with a resigned and slightly mocking, 'of course!'

But Lang's allegorical energies are not entirely spent in satire. In this forecourt of heaven Liliom must justify his life and be judged. When Liliom defends himself against the charge of being a bad husband, he is confronted with a screen on which the heavenly bureaucrats order the projection of the film of 'Liliom Zadowski, 17 of July, 8:40 AM' from the apparently carefully archived heavenly cinémathèque. Liliom confronts a scene from his life, as we re-see an earlier scene from the film, in which Liliom slapped his wife, angered by there not being enough coffee for breakfast. Liliom, the viewer, is fascinated by this image, especially by Julie and touches her arm, immediately reproached with the cry, 'Touching forbidden!'

Not only is this device of heavenly surveillance one of Lang's most complex Destiny-machines, it functions as a rich and even contradictory node where numerous Langian devices and obsessions intersect (whether or not Lang or the scriptwriter is its source, it does not appear in Molnar's play in which the heavenly officer simply consults the record books for an account of Liliom's earthly behaviour). Ever since *Spies*, Lang had chronicled the means by which individual identity is processed and archived. Nowhere is this process more fine-grained than in this scene in which heaven employs a technological recording device able to capture and replay any moment of one's life. Liliom not only sees this embarrassing moment replayed, but the image itself processed and analysed, as the scene is played one more time, this time with a 'voice-over' soundtrack, an interior monologue of Liliom's thoughts ('thoughts can be recorded as well' says the heavenly archivist) as he grew angry and struck Julie. This image is not only replayed, but actually stilled, the frame frozen, and stepped frame by frame as Liliom makes the fatal slap.

Clearly, this is one of Lang's most self-reflexive moments, an interrogation within his film of the film image itself. But we must go beyond this; too many critics assume a self-reflexive moment is a virtue in itself, a master modernist trope. But Lang is using cinema here in a particular way and it is the work that this self-reflexive device does that must be interrogated. Cinema becomes a device of surveillance, of investigation and demonstration, getting at Liliom's guilt or innocence. It presents, as Godard would claim years later, truth twenty-four times a second. Cinema is, as the heavenly attendant says, an instrument of justice. Further, the scene is observed not only by the heavenly judge but by Liliom himself, who must confront his own image. This stands as one of Lang's great visionary moments, the celestial screen and the manipulation of the image and sound, acting like the overlap-dissolves in Lang's earlier allegories, to reveal the actual nature of things. Here the revelation delivers Liliom's true motives (he regrets the slap even as he does it), but even after the screening, Liliom is unwilling to admit his love for Julie.

Perceptive critics such as Garrett Stewart have noted the relation between this sequence of being forced to witness a self-incriminating film and the climax of Lang's next film *Fury*, in which members of the lynch mob are forced to watch newsreel footage of the criminal acts they had previously denied.[27] Although the tone, the crimes and the actors' demeanour are radically different in the two films, the device is the same. But I would like to draw another comparison which makes a triangular figure between three Lang films shot within five years but in three different countries: *Fury*, *Liliom* and *M*. The parallel sequence from *M*, of course, is Beckert's 'trial' in which he is confronted with objects (Elsie's balloon) and images (the photographs of his victims held by Schranker) which cause him to more or less re-experience his previous crimes (Lorre's mimed monologue of the moment of murder). We can see that all three films stage a scene of judgement and proof of guilt, forcing the malefactor to relive and re-witness his crime, within a theatrical or spectacular *mise-en-scène*, complete with spectators and performance.

In *M*, Lang introduced the situation of a private theatre of perverse sexual fantasy rendered public. The cinematic evidence projected in the two later films deal less with fantasy than with rash actions prompted by emotional reactions (though, of course, Liliom's domestic squabble hardly equals the decision and efforts to burn a man alive taken by the lynch mob in *Fury*, which veer closer to the horror of Beckert's murders). But in all cases the apparatus of judgement penetrates into a disavowed action, an unguarded moment all the characters make an effort to forget. The public theatre restores memory through re-enactment or replaying. This complex theme of replaying one's guilt becomes a central preoccupation of Lang's cinema. Such persistence of themes – not simply a repetition of a similar situation, but a variety of ways of working over, or working out, the same material – constitutes the dialectical continuity of Lang's career. The figure this book traces through various films is not simply a repeated theme, or even iconography. Instead, I am following the way Lang worked through extremely varied script material and came up not only with closely related solutions, but with devices which underwent further development and elucidation from film to film.

This complex of Destiny-machine, visual surveillance, processing of identity, staging of guilt, and visionary moment in *Liliom*'s heavenly cinema returns Lang's allegorical style to its original complexity and strength. From this point on, *Liliom* re-establishes links with the allegory of *Der müde Tod*, both films spinning tales of lovers separated by death. Liliom's revelation of a conscience through the scrutiny of his thoughts during the act of slapping Julie (like Beckert, even as he does the violence, his thoughts shout, 'No, ah, no!') leads to sixteen years in purgatory and the chance to return to the land of the living and see his daughter. As with the maiden in *Der müde Tod,* the visionary revelation is not enough; the protagonist must undergo further trials in order truly to understand the meaning of the vision. In the single day on earth granted to Liliom, Lang doubles the theme of repetition by having his daughter played by Madeleine Ozeray, who also plays her mother Julie (unlike Molnar's play, this theme of repetition is stressed by giving both mother and daughter the same name). While Liliom speaks to his daughter about her father, the adult Julie sits in their caravan and listens to the phonograph playing the song of the merry-go-round as she relives her memories of Liliom. Seeing his face peering in at her window, she re-experiences the supernatural communion of pain she underwent as Liliom stabbed himself, and grabs her breast. When his face disappears, she assumes it was only a hallucination. Meanwhile, Liliom finds the image of his young wife again in his daughter. But his meeting with his daughter replays the same problems he had with her mother. Offended by his criticism of her dead father, young Julie refuses Liliom's gift of a star, a souvenir he apparently pilfered on his way down to earth (and which Lang makes sparkle by scratching the film itself, as he had during Freder's hallucinations in *Metropolis*). Liliom goes after her and tells her he wants to give her something beautiful, but the young Julie orders him out of her yard. Offended by her unyielding manner and her imperiously pointing finger, Liliom slaps her hand.

With this primal repetition Liliom realises he must end his one day on earth, his mission a failure. As Daumal said in his review of the film:

> The film attains its purpose which is to pose the terrible question of the fatality of human actions, to illustrate the idea (which is not Buddhist only!) that in man as in nature the same causes produce the same effects. In other words, if a criminal could miraculously be put in the situation preceding his crime, would he repeat his crime?[28]

The last shot of the sequence is given to young Julie's point of view as she looks for the man who just slapped her, only to see an empty yard with an open gate, another one of Lang's empty frames, the evidence of Liliom's departure from this earth.

Lang has intercut Liliom's interaction with young Julie with another overtly and intentionally naive allegorical image, a huge heavenly balance surmounted by a Masonic eye, symbol of the all-seeing God. As Liliom fails in his earthly visit, the devil piles weights on his side of the balance. But one act restores the balance in Liliom's favour. After young Julie refuses the star, Liliom tosses it into the gutter. Here it is picked up by the film's first allegorical figure, the knife-grinder, who earlier almost succeeded in preventing Liliom's failed robbery attempt which led to his suicide. In heaven Liliom learned that this figure (wheeling his grindstone another one of the film's circular machines and accompanied by the sound of unearthly chimes) is actually his guardian angel. Now the angel throws this discarded gutter star into the balance where it outweighs a multitude of sins. In many ways, this figure recalls the weary Death from *Der müde Tod* as much in his solemn gaunt dignity as in his metaphysical personification (in spite of Eisner's claim to the contrary,[29] this figure is the film's invention; it does not appear in Molnar's play). This figure of a guardian angel as rag-picker retrieving a pilfered star from the sewer is enacted by Antonin Artaud who frequently played small parts in European films (e.g. Marat in Gance's *Napoleon*, Dreyer's *Passion of Jean d'Arc*, the French version of Pabst's *The Three Penny Opera*). Although Lang was probably unaware of Artaud's work as theorist, poet and theatre director, the presence of the man who dreamed most deeply the return of theatre to a state of metaphysics (as well as realising the impossibility of achieving the mythic state he imagined) endows this allegory, however accidentally, with unexpected power.

Of course, Liliom's slapping of Julie's hand causes the balance to sink in the devil's favour and he is about to be condemned to eternal damnation when the heavens hear the voice of the mother, Julie speaking to her daughter (Lang's careful editing allowing Madeleine Ozeray to speak to, and comfort, the younger version of herself) and shedding tears for Liliom. Each falling tear raises Liliom's side of the balance, and a final image of a rainbow or arc of light seems to indicate, intentionally rather crudely, his salvation. This somewhat pat allegory is saved by its knowing *naiveté*. But the true power of this, Lang's last extended allegory, has already been expended in the vision of the celestial cinema and Artaud's gesture of divine abjection.

Meet John Doe: Lang Arrives in America

> Know that our great showmen
> Are those who show what we want to have shown.
> Dominate by serving us!
>   Bertolt Brecht, 'Deliver the Goods'[30]

While Lang's brief sojourn in Paris was immediately justified and accompanied by the production of *Liliom*, it was a full year after Lang's arrival in the US in June of 1934 that his first American film, *Fury*, began production, with script conferences beginning in the late summer of 1935 and shooting beginning in 1936. Travelling first class on the *Île de France*, Lang docked in New York City accompanied by producer David O. Selznick who had negotiated Lang's contract on behalf of MGM, and the newly arrived director was greeted with a great deal of publicity.[31] However, while Lang continued to appear as an 'émigré deluxe', during the following year several projects were proposed by Lang, or proposed to Lang, but none of them ever went into production. Hollywood's policy of acquiring many more properties than they ever produce and even putting under contract more writers and directors than they ever use (in fact, Leontine Sagan, the director of *Mädchen in Uniform*, was also brought back to the US by Selznick on the same boat as Lang, also under contract to MGM, but never made a film in Hollywood, and of course Sergei Eisenstein had been under contract to Paramount in 1930 without any of his proposed projects ever being filmed)[32] was another difference from the film-making methods Lang was accustomed to and one which produced not only frustration but inevitably anxiety and paranoia in the refugee director.

Lang worked on a number of projects searching for one that MGM would approve. The most interesting is undoubtedly *The Man Behind You*, the Hollywood project of Lang's that most immediately recalls his German work.[33] The script centred around a theme Lang and Harbou had considered as a subject when they were first working on *M*, anonymous threatening letters.[34] Messages of unknown but malevolent source recall the many wayward messages we traced in Lang's master criminal films (they also appear briefly in *M* in the second sequence in which the police search the apartment of a man denounced by such a letter). Lang's underlying theme of authorship would be treated richly in this screenplay which basically transplanted a Dr. Mabuse-type master criminal to the US, in the shadowy figure of 'The Professor' who controls the various crime syndicates of a large city and who, Mephistopheles-like, seduces the film's protagonist, the attorney Moran, into a life of crime and madness.

Many motifs from the German films appear in this screenplay – a nightclub with a boxing ring as in *Spies*; the projection of the handwriting of a mental patient as in *The Testament of Dr. Mabuse*; Moran at the ending haunted by the ghosts of his victims as in *Dr. Mabuse, the Gambler*; a lawyer who defends his client by claiming an unknown force within him impelled him to the crime and he therefore was not responsible, as in *M*. The film is filled with Langian references to clocks and time (this is the source of the visionary scene of the human clock mentioned earlier) and scenes most often begin and end with the types of rhymes found in *The Testament of Dr. Mabuse*. Indeed the signature scene of Lang's master criminal films occurs here, as Moran wonders aloud who can be responsible for the strange and obscene notes he finds in his office and Lang cuts directly to the Professor testifying at the police office. Without Lang's *mise-en-scène*, of course, it remains impossible to tell if *The Man Behind You* would have been another masterpiece, or simply a pastiche of earlier films.

Fury does not immediately present such obvious echoes of the German films, although critics soon found a number of shared themes, especially between the attempted lynching that takes place as the central scene of *Fury* and the trial which ends *M*. Clearly, certain shots of the members of the mob from *Fury* could be cut into the crowd listening to Beckert's cries in the abandoned brewery without seeming out of place. But *Fury* defines its place in Lang's *œuvre* through more than surface similarities in theme or style. *Fury* does not present a pastiche of previous films, but rather introduces new narrative forms and develops certain older themes in new directions. Some of these new forms, such as the requisite Hollywood focus on the romantic couple, seem like alien elements embedded (rather than fully assimilated) into Lang's first Hollywood film. Others, like the film evidence presented in the trial sequence, brilliantly bring to a culmination ideas that had been sketched in previous films.

Critics have tended to group together the first three films Lang directed in Hollywood (*Fury*, *You Only Live Once* and *You and Me*) usually stressing their common themes of social criticism (lynching in *Fury*; the 'three-time loser' law and treatment of ex-cons in *You Only Live Once*; and parole laws in *You and Me*).[35] Social commentary certainly became an important element of Lang's early American work and one could argue that politics play a greater role in Lang's American films than in his German career, perhaps supporting Lang's claim of a political awakening after shooting *M*, and undoubtedly the fruit of his new identity as a refugee and his revulsion at the Nazi takeover. However, one can overstate the degree of true political analysis in any of these films; Hollywood explicitly avoids directly the taking of political sides, although during the 1930s Hollywood did see the creation of a series of social problem films (*I Am a Fugitive from a Chain Gang*, *They Won't Forget*, *Heroes for Sale*, *Hell's Highways*, *Gabriel over the White House*) into which Lang's films could fit.

I think Lang's first three American films do form a rough trilogy, even if only ret-rospectively viewed, but they share more than themes of social criticism. One apparently superficial link between them actually played a key role in their produc-tion: their common leading lady, Sylvia Sidney. In the last two films of this group it was Sylvia Sidney who proposed Lang as the director, and her role in creating the trilogy was therefore substantial. Far from being a pre-planned trilogy, these three films were very much separate productions, each produced by a different studio: *Fury* as the completion of Lang's MGM contract, which was not renewed; *You Only Live Once* as a film by independent producer Walter Wanger released through United Artists; and *You and Me* at Paramount with Lang himself, now with some-thing of an established track record in Hollywood, taking the role of producer. In every case, the project preceded Lang's involvement (although Lang transformed greatly the material he was given), and in the case of *You and Me*, a previous direc-tor had even been assigned to the film before Lang was chosen.

But Sidney's performances in all three films, although frequently not to the taste of contemporary audiences, also mark a new role for the leading lady and the romantic couple in Lang's career. The pressure for this comes, of course, from the formulaic romance narrative of Hollywood cinema, and one could chart Lang's progressive ability to make the couple work as the centre of this form of narrative. Lang's allegorical films all have strong female characters and performances. How-ever, with the exception of Gerda Marus in *Spies*, the master criminal films do not have central female characters (Carozza and Countess Told are strong in the first Mabuse film, but remain rather marginal to the plot, while the saccharine perfor-mance and characterisation of Wera Liessem as Lilli in *The Testament of Dr. Mabuse* remain that film's weak point). But all of Sidney's performances creatively express the subjectivity and desire of her characters. Even in *Fury*, in which Lang seems to struggle the most with the role of the romantic couple, Sidney's character maintains the film's moral point of view.

There is a certain poignancy, given Lang's refugee status and still recent divorce, in the fact that two of the trilogy – *Fury* and *You and Me* – begin with lovers about to part, wandering about the city until their train/bus leaves. *You Only Live Once* reverses this by opening with lovers preparing for a reunion – Eddie Taylor's release from prison – which sets up that film's deeply ironic treatment of the romantic couple. But the opening images of *Fury* reveal the problematic treatment Lang brought to the typical Hollywood double plot (in which one line of action, usually driven by the male character, interacts with a base line love story which culminates in the formation of the couple as a stable closure for the film). *Fury* begins with an image of this resolution, cued by a slightly syncopated version of the Wedding March on the soundtrack. An open tome with an ornate page proclaims 'The Fall Bride' as the film begins. The camera tracks left to an artificial dove, then pulls back and reveals a mannequin in a wedding dress. We realise we are looking into a window dis-play and the camera seems to hunt for living characters, tracking to the left. We find the silhouettes of Joe Wilson and Katherine Grant viewed from the back as they stare into the adjoining window display of a bedroom, Joe popping peanuts into his mouth as if he were watching a movie. A reverse angle shows the couple looking through the glass, their faces expressing a sort of embarrassed desire.

The camera movement draws the natural conclusion: from the wedding to the bedroom – the very image of sexual desire under social and legal sanctions. As if to underscore the Hays Code version of Hollywood's representation of sexual fulfil-ment, the bedroom display consists of perfectly symmetrical twin beds, with bathrobe and nightgown laid out. As studies of Hollywood's various forms of self-censorship (and other forms of censorship, including Freud's analysis of the dream-work) have shown, the constraints applied to taboo material are creative in their effect; rather than simply cancelling out desire, they force it to take new forms which express both the constraints and the force of desire seeking an outlet, no matter what.[36] This is particularly obvious in the Hollywood Production Code and other regulations where the game consists of exciting a degree of desire in the audience and simply curtailing its representation in such a manner that it remains vague and free-floating, or is channelled into socially acceptable forms (heterosexual romance leading to marriage and the family). The tension between an ill-defined, free-floating desire and its containment works its way through every Hollywood film in varying degrees, allowing certain films to create, either intentionally or accidentally, complex and sometimes contradictory figures of desire. Hollywood has always known that it was selling the promise of desire and, also, its deferment. Fulfilment, ecstasy, happens off screen, most often after the final shot of the film, outside the confines of representation. But everything in the film, everything represented, points towards it.

Thus Joe and Katherine gaze into the store window – like the movie viewers positioned in front of this film which is now beginning – seeing an image of a fulfilled future which is, for the moment, just a dream, a wish, a desire. And if the movie screen provides one staging area of such dreams, the shop window (as we already saw in *M* and will see in nearly all of Lang's key Hollywood films) poses another dream screen, channelled not towards narrative and ideological resolution but towards consumer cupidity and satisfaction. The desire that Joe and Katherine feel for each other as they walk arm in arm through the city streets facing a long separation, appears before them in its socially sanctioned forms: marriage and instalment buying. In the first line of dialogue, Joe says to Katherine, 'What do you say, kid, are we moving in?'

indicating that they see in front of them their prepared place in the world, already laid out for them. But they are actually on the other side of the glass. Like movie spectators they can look, but cannot enter or touch. The barrier is transparent, but nonetheless maintains their distance from immediate gratification.[37]

Lang in his American career understood he was making films for an audience that expected to have their desires aroused, and to have them portrayed as accessible. Yet at the same time this audience of consumers understood the nature of the shop window. One cannot simply enter. One must stay patiently outside and look. The three films of Lang's first American trilogy play a series of variations on this theme of deferred desire, so basic to the American movie romance. *You and Me* with its department store setting and opening musical number 'You Can Not Get Something for Nothing!' deals with this most explicitly. Even in this rather experimental film Lang will never quite mount a critique of the consumerist logic of displaced and deferred desire. But he will explore its tensions in all three films in different manners. As they walk away from the display, Joe begins to find fault with the ideal bedroom offered him, indicating one could slip and fall on the throw-rugs. Most pointedly (given their mythical status in post-1933 Hollywood) he declares the 'twin beds are out'. Katherine adds provocatively (in the sort of mild *double-entendre* Hollywood generated without trying), 'out like a light'.

But this reverie of future bliss soon switches to the despair of imminent separation. As they walk through the increasingly deserted night-time streets, they pass under a railway trestle. Joe pulls Katherine to him and kisses her passionately. But in the middle of this kiss Lang cuts to the locomotive passing overhead, its wheels turning powerfully. A long established film simile (see Mac and Trina's first kiss in 1923s *Greed*), the cut partly expresses the power of their desire. But more complexly, it also images their separation in the centre of their embrace: Katherine is about to leave on a train, they are walking to the station. Briefly, therefore, in the spinning wheels of the locomotive, Lang offers his first image of the Destiny-machine in this film.

The following farewell scene at the station is filled with images of separation and vain attempts at holding together. In a random accident that receives a large close-up, Joe tears his coat pocket and Katherine (to his embarrassment) immediately sets about sewing it up. The makeshift nature of Katherine's attempt to repair the breach is emphasised by the fact that she must mend his light trenchcoat with blue thread. The dialogue stresses the symbolic nature of this tear and repair when Joe, feeling infantilised by Katherine's motherly act, tries to move away and she pulls him back saying, 'I'm hard to get rid of'. Joe sits back down and adds, 'Like my right arm'. One need not over-analyse these images of separation other than to note the way they, like so many everyday scenes in Hollywood films, seamlessly invoke powerful associations like separation from a mother and loss of bodily integrity (castration, if you wish) to render the emotion of lovers parting.

But if the emotional depth of the scene is quickly accessed, this separation also soon becomes defined in economic terms, the reality principle intervening on the pleasure principle. Joe half moans as he tells Katherine he will be coming to get her just as soon as 'he gets that bank account up to the third floor'. When he weakens and asks Katherine to stay, she reiterates the economic facts: her better job in another state and their need to save for their marriage. Joe comes around and says he understands. Desire is deferred for economic reasons, and the pain this causes is palpable for the viewer (particularly in a period of the Depression when a large proportion of the population was on the move, looking for work, frequently separating families). On the train platform in the rain the lovers exchange mementos (Joe mis-pronounces it as 'mementum' which Katherine, in her motherly mode again, cor-rects patiently); he gives her a bottle of perfume he just bought (along with more peanuts), while Katherine presents Joe with her mother's wedding ring inscribed 'Henry [her father] to Katherine [the name she shares with her mother]' to which she has added 'to Joe'. The close-up of the turning ring unites two generations in a common name and a common coupling, the symbol of marriage that broods over this opening, but which economics render impossible – or rather delay. Joe cannot fit the ring on his ring finger, but places it instead (in a Langian close-up of a hand) on his little finger, an action followed immediately by the call, 'all aboard'. As Katherine boards the train, Joe watches her through the window and the last ges-ture of the sequence completes the opening use of window glass as a barrier. The two of them touch hands on the window; the glass now separates them not only from their vision of the future, but from each other.

The objects and gestures in these opening scenes play double roles. Although concrete objects, they possess a metaphorical valence that shows again that Lang never abandons the hieroglyphic-like allegories of his silent films. Each crystallises aspects of the characters' relation to each other and the world, and their legibility contributes to what some viewers find heavy-handed in Lang's style (one thinks of Brecht's sarcasm about Lang's use of 'effects from the rose theatre anno 1880').[38] Lack of sympathy with this mode on a viewer's or critic's part should not be mis-taken for lack of skill on a director's part, of course. Lang continues to develop the use of resonant objects which he began in his allegorical silent films and, in a more realistic vein, in *M*. But the Hollywood method of assembling a series of character traits in introductory scenes also appears here in a somewhat more blatant manner than in Lang's earlier films. This use of objects to make character traits visible reaches its most over-legible and smarmy moment when Joe, leaving the station, finds a small abandoned dog which he adopts, saying, 'You look like I feel – lonely

and small'. Lang reportedly hated the role this dog plays through the first half of the film (and whose death, he claimed, initially provided the motivation for Joe's revenge!). One can see here the overlap *and* the difference between Lang's and Hollywood's methods of characterisation. For Lang these traits mark and individualise his characters, as they do in Hollywood films as well. But an added dimension of sympathy and identification must be laid on for the protagonist in a Hollywood film, traits the audience shares with the hero and which show both his average guy accessibility (e.g. liking peanuts) and decent humanity (liking small dogs). Lang's Hollywood films frequently rub against this assumption of identification and sympathy with a protagonist, creating strategies of distance that undermine the dominant Hollywood narrative approach.

But beyond the character associations generated by these objects and actions, each of them will have eventual and unforeseen consequences. Lang's careful jigsaw puzzle-like plotting in which every element fits and significant information is methodically seeded early in the film also dismays some critics (I remember Noel Burch saying scornfully in a classroom lecture that if an object appeared in the first scene of a Hollywood Lang film, it was bound eventually to provide a significant plot twist). In this apparently innocent scene in which no animosity toward Joe is present, each of the carefully placed elements – the torn pocket, the blue thread, the peanuts, the ring with its inscription, even Joe's verbal slip 'mementum' – are all preparing his dreadful fate which will unreel months in the future. Each of these details will at some point fix Joe's identity (both falsely – the peanuts, the ring – and truly – the verbal slip, the mended coat), and almost always with dire consequences. The Destiny-machine here is not immediately recognisable, even though the visual presentation of the overhead train, the tearing pocket, and the ring on the wrong finger, should send signals to veteran Lang viewers. But Lang has to some extent covered his tracks, allowing the momentum of the plot to build beneath a series of apparent accidents. Katherine's sewing of the coat does not take on the dramatic density of Kriemhild's marking of Siegfried's tunic, but, as Enno Patalas has pointed out, its effect will eventually be similar.[39]

The hokey, folksy device of Joe's love for peanuts (traditional carnival and movie food, along with popcorn) first turns against him as he is questioned as a suspect in a kidnapping whose one clue (other than a description – a man, 32, of average height and weight – which, as Joe says, 'would fit a million men') is that the kidnapper likes peanuts. The issue of the slippery nature of identity (so basic to all of Lang's work and now to his Hollywood films) seems to pick up where *M* leaves off: from the criminal as the apparently average guy, to, by a logical reversal, the average guy as apparent criminal. Lang has said that the major thing he learned while revising the script for *Fury* was the need for the hero of an American film to be a 'John Doe', an average guy.[40] While Lang clearly bridled at many changes demanded by the Hollywood system, he identified this conception of the hero with democracy and populism and happily embraced it as he did his new homeland. The attempt to make Joe Wilson an average guy, someone the audience could identify with, is evident throughout the first half of this film. Lang's avoidance of pronounced high angle shots (compared at least to the last German films) also seems to indicate a desire to view the world from the perspective of the typical American. But Lang nonetheless maintains his omniscient narration, the strong sense that the film may share the perspective of a character but can never be limited to it. Nor did this idea of an average Joe remove Lang's protagonist from the perils of modern life. The very levelling-out of identity, the depersonalisation that Lang deals with from *Spies* on, constructs society as a series of equivalent slots into which anyone may fit. Joe fits the description and one character trait of a kidnapper. Looking at the wanted poster which also names a 'young woman accomplice', Joe realises Katherine could fit into another slot, and so holds back her name and the possibility that she might clear him.

Emblematically, Joe looks at the camera holding a dish of peanuts, supposedly offering them to the sheriff who is interrogating him, as he learns they were a ploy to get him to betray himself. His blank stare at the camera marks this as a moment of subjection to the camera and the mechanics of the plot, rather than a claim of enunciation and control. As if offering them to the audience (those regular guys like him, possibly also munching on peanuts as they watch the film), Joe is directly caught in the camera's gaze, fixed in his criminal averageness. The second bit of evidence tying Joe to the kidnapping comes as the serial number of one of the bills in Joe's wallet matches a bill in the ransom already paid. Like characters in other Lang thrillers, Wilson has had his identity processed through the systems of modern life, anonymous descriptions, serial numbers of currency, but here, in contrast to *M*, the identification is faulty; it fingers the wrong man.

Lang explicitly contrasted his American John Doe character with the master criminals of his German films: 'So over there [in Germany] the hero in a motion picture should be a superman. Whereas in a democracy he had to be Joe [sic] Doe.'[41] But as Vincente Sanchez-Biosca points out, in the best essay yet written on *Fury*, Joe Wilson eventually takes on the enunciatory characteristics of Lang's master criminals.[42] It is precisely this transformation, as Sanchez-Biosca phrases it, from John Doe to demiurge that defines the curious structure of *Fury*, dividing it in half, a division marked by the apparent dramatic death and subsequent resurrection of its protagonist, who undergoes an almost complete re-creation as a character.[43]

But this transformation of Joe Wilson from average guy to demi-urge enunciator involves a startling reversal of the lesson in democracy and its new narrative demands Lang claims he learned during his first years of exile. Lang reveals a darker view of the average American than indicated in his interviews. Arrested for a crime he did not commit, Joe Wilson is removed from the narrative foreground of the film for a spell, as Lang makes a change in viewpoint that recalls his European experiments. If Joe Wilson initially represented the typical citizen of a democracy, unexceptional and harmless, and later becomes a fascistic character manipulating other people for his own ends, this transmutation is accomplished by a detour away from Joe into an examination of the daily life and citizens of a typical American small town, Strand.

A Whole Town of John Does: The Lynching of Joe Wilson

> With this picture as it is, it must have another ending. That
> such a criminal is insane, that's not punishment. He must be
> destroyed by the people.
>> Lang's account of Joseph Goebbels' explanation for the
>> banning of *The Testament of Dr. Mabuse*[44]

After Joe's arrest, which puts his identity into question, the townspeople of Strand take centre stage in a sequence which recalls the second movement of *M*. Paraphrasing Burch's section title from *M*, we could call this 'A Rumour Spreads Through the Town'. Using the visual and sound rhymes, albeit less marked, that appear in the *M* sequence, Lang traces the multiplying distortions of the news of Joe's arrest. But this is small town America, not metropolitan Berlin, and the means of communication are different. The claim that Joe Wilson is the kidnapper is spread orally, not by print, and is never counterbalanced by a statement of the facts, not until too late, that is. The original source of information is the semi-moronic deputy 'Bugs' Meyers (played with appropriate repulsiveness by Walter Brennan, who would later sentimentalise such roles). Lang's satire of Americana is even more acerbic than his George Grosz-inspired caricatures in the parallel sequence in *M*. The rumour circulates through archetypal American small town gathering places via homosocial, same gender groups: men talking politics at the barber shop, women gossiping over the back fence and in the kitchen or grocery market, men growing more violent at the hardware store and eventually the bar. As opposed to the relatively anonymous forms of mass media in the Berlin of *M*, information in Strand travels orally and personally, and becomes elaborated and exaggerated in each retelling.

Lang's fascination with the average American and embrace of a form of populism which is evident in all films of the social trilogy shows a definite double edge. Whereas he portrays Berliners as capable of either blindly indifferent or rashly over-suspicious reactions, Lang seemed to share some fellowship with these caricatures. But the typical Americans, such as the citizen of Strand, or the woman who turns Eddie and Jo Taylor out of her inn on their honeymoon when she discovers he is an ex-con in *You Only Live Once*, exercise a vein of self-righteous cruelty that Lang skewers mercilessly. He intercuts the gossiping women with chickens clucking (a montage simile that André Bazin would single out as archaic and which Lang himself seemed to feel in retrospect was old fashioned),[45] and the long pan introducing the discussions in the tavern pointedly moves past an advertisement for 'Calves Brains'. Lang not only sketches grotesque types (the potentially homicidal barber who confesses to an impulse to slice through his customers' Adam's apples; the heavy-set woman who claims she is not allowed to say any more about the arrest, waiting to be begged to invent more; the pudgy, middle-aged man who punctuates his comments on the kidnappers by cracking a whip); he also shows the class tensions at the tavern (as lumpenproletariat Kirby Dawson elbows past and intentionally drops egg shells on the self-proclaimed 'leading citizens' at the bar). The common emotion of mob action dissolves such divisions in an orgy of pumped-up morality.

Lang portrays the mob in *Fury* with more horror and condemnation than the group gathered at the end of *M*, in spite of certain similarities as the crowd turns on Lorre. The crowd at the 'trial' in *M* wants explanations as much as it wants the release promised by violence. Many commentators have claimed that Lang's increased bitterness and suspicion of mob action (which remained somewhat ambivalent in *M*) is due to the subsequent Nazi seizing of power and his own exile. This may be true, but *Fury* by no means becomes a displaced allegory about Germany; its violence and social structure is 100 per cent American and carefully observed. Although Lang occasionally cuts back to Joe in his cell and to Katherine (waiting impatiently in the diner arranged for their rendezvous a few miles away), for more than twenty minutes, two full reels, neither of these characters organises the point of view of the film. As in *M* the point of view is free-floating, cutting between a variety of characters as they form themselves into a mob.

The sequence leading to the assault on the jail basically divides itself into two movements, each set into motion by a montage sequence of accelerating passions, and separated by a caesura in which a meeting with the sheriff and calls to the governor hold out the possibility of order being restored. However, each time this break basically allows the second part to become more violent. The first sequence, that of the rumours spreading, has a sense of urgency, picked up both by the elliptical editing from vignette to vignette and by a rhythmic music score. The second movement begins with a second scene in the bar in which Bugs Meyers gives information. His revelation that the cops only found five dollars of the ransom money on Wilson should deflate the rumours of the discovery of thousands of dollars, but Kirby Dawson and a man who identifies himself as a strikebreaker, manage to use it to stir up anger against the sheriff. Lang pans the mob of angry men, all shouting, a few directly at the camera, and with no-one looking another character in the eyes. The shot culminates in a young man who jumps on a table and proclaims 'Hey, come on! Let's have some fun!'

This atmosphere of jollity and high spirits, of carnival (a constantly noted aspect of lynchings in America, especially the thousands of racially motivated ones) makes this second movement so chilling, as violence blends with a feeling of holiday. American lynchings tended to become not only communal rituals of sadism and hatred, but forms of mass entertainment and spectator sport. Lang recalled a riot he had seen and emphasised that it began 'with a casual, "Oh let's have some fun!"' [46] As the crowd issues from the bar, Lang shows a black shoeshine man leaping onto his stand in terror, a reminder of the fact that most lynching victims in the US were blacks, lynched merely for the colour of their skin, a fact unfortunately pushed (like this character) to the margins of Lang's film. Women gaily join men arm in arm in the march, one man grinning broadly with a girl on each arm, as if following a circus parade. But the erotic overtones and grinning faces signal emotional release rather than levity, and Lang stresses the growing anonymous power of the mob with a brilliant shot. The camera tracks along the street at above human height, moving toward the jail's front steps and stops as it confronts the sheriff and his deputies. This is no one person's point of view; rather, the smooth forward thrust of the camera out in front and somewhat above the mob expresses its force, its grabbing of the enunciatory function, its taking control of the story. Joe is only a spectator now, anxiously watching from his jail cell window as his fate is being decided.

The confrontation with Sheriff Hummel recalls elements of the trial sequence from *M*, but with a difference. Hummel speaks for law and order and against the mob, and is greeted by jeers and mocking laughter as was the defence attorney in *M*. However, he also appears as a figure of the law itself and one expects from him something of the almost thaumaturgic power the name of the law exerts at the end of *M*'s trial scene, its ability to stop the mob in its tracks and silence it. Lang here deconstructs the power of the law in a manner he didn't undertake in *M* and which typifies the increased awareness of politics in his American films. The sheriff backs up his claim to represent the law with a threat of force, the National Guard, which he has asked the governor to send. Lang immediately undercuts this, however, by cutting to the Guard in battle gear and fully armed seated in trucks, receiving orders not to set out. A rhyming cut to the governor's office literally completes the officer's question, 'but...'/'...why?' asks the governor of his political boss. The boss explains that in an election year it is bad politics to move troops in on people. Lang makes it clear it is not just the passion of the mob that allows the lynching to happen, but the pusillanimity of politicians.

The cut back to the sheriff still confronting the mob unaware that the force of law no longer backs him up carries a bitter irony. Lang successively strips his words of meaning and his figure of symbolic authority, this overturning of the law accenting the parodic carnivalesque quality of the scene. Sheriff Hummel tells the mob to 'think of your family', and, as if on cue, a woman rushes from the crowd carrying a child and addresses one of his deputies, saying, 'if you stick in with this kidnapper, Milt Grimes you better not come home tonight!' Hummel's declaration, 'You elected me to do my duty and I'm going to do it!' is greeted by an adolescent boy's mockery: 'There's Popeye the Sheriff Man, toot, toot!' to the delight of onlookers. His warning, 'Don't make me use force' is followed by an overripe tomato splattering his face. All of this mockery is delivered in a tone of merriment that accents its volatile nature. The people are enjoying themselves!

Cutting to Katherine as she learns of Joe's plight and tries to get to Strand, Lang interrupts the build-up to the assault on the jail, as gas bombs initially turn the mob back. Lang cuts to a newsreel cameraman filming from a nearby balcony, a stuttering staccato giggle preceding his exclamation, 'Boyoboy, what a shot this is! We'll sweep the country with this stuff!' as the dwindling core of deputies and the sheriff face the mob's attempt on the door with an improvised battering ram and day turns to night. Tear gas and water hoses don't phase the mob once the door is breached, but within the jail they encounter the locked gates to the cells and the keys are out of reach. The images of the mob hanging on the bars recall images of the rioting workers from *Metropolis*. Wilson out of reach of their fury, they decide to burn the jail down. A cut to Katherine again interrupts the action as she arrives in Strand, having apparently run all the way. This cut away, however, represents a significant ellipsis. Things have changed by the time Katherine arrives on the scene.

An eerie silence greets her. The cries and laughter that were heard over the previous shot of the first flames in the jailhouse have ceased. Further, as she turns a corner and runs into the mob, the restless, exuberant turmoil is over. The people stand stock still, their gazes fixed off screen, as if spellbound by some silent spectacle. They hardly notice Katherine as she jostles past them, no sound coming from their lips, their eyes unblinking as they stare off. What has transformed them? The reverse angle long shot showing them gathered in front of the jail in flames, explains some of it. But their zombie-like expressions will be explained only later during the trial, as the district attorney shows newsreels of the action that took place between the shots of the first flames and Katherine's arrival. Katherine pushes forward and a cry goes up, as people point out Joe at the window. We see him framed by bars, looking monstrous amid the smoke and flames. A choker close-up of Katherine aghast, staring wide-eyed into the camera, claims this image as her own. But her anguished expression makes it clear this is an image she is subjected to, one imprinting itself indelibly on her memory, not one she claims as author.

A powerful series of nightmarish images follows, as close as Lang ever got to a horror film. Katherine's classically illuminated face, carefully centred in the frame, is followed by equally extreme close-ups, but now filmed from high or low angles and lit from below, of grotesque faces of the mob. Lang cuts back to Katherine, her face contorted in grief. We see Joe at the window, moving spastically, like a monkey trying to rattle his cage. Then an elderly woman in the crowd sinks to her knees, grasps her hands and begins to utter a prayer. Her solemn reaction is heard over the next image, a woman delightedly pointing out the burning man to her infant child and hoisting the baby to get a better look. A crowd member (previously referred to as 'Goofy', clearly mentally deficient) taking a satisfied bite from a hot dog (another

form of movie/carnival food) as he watches intently. Lang cuts back to a slightly wider framing of Katherine's incredulous, painful stare, the trembling light of the flames playing over everyone from off screen. The mob begins to stone Joe as he clings to the bars and Katherine, in a slightly low angle shot, collapses. A shot follows of the now empty window engulfed by flames.

The aftermath of the lynching finds the town seeking the sort of oblivion it might appear was granted to Katherine when she fainted. A kitchen meeting of housewives of Strand following the burning of the jail invokes the need to forget 'what happened', 'to forgive and forget'. In the face of an investigation by the district attorney, one woman says, 'the responsible business men have decided it's a community and not an individual thing'. In contrast to the previous scene of gossip where everyone had something to say, she assures another woman, 'No one is talking.' Anonymity will be their protection. As the political boss tells the district attorney, 'you can't bring a town full of John Does to trial'. The DA responds that he will be indicting, not anonymous John Does, but twenty-two specifically named 'citizens of Strand, who I can prove are' (here Lang cuts to a pan of the defendants in the trial for lynching, as the DA's voice finishes his sentence which has become his opening argument in court) 'guilty of murder in the first degree'.

In some ways again recalling *M*, the trial that follows serves less to establish guilt than to fix identity. The twenty-two citizens of Strand deny their guilt by denying they are capable of such acts. The series of witnesses the district attorney calls either refuse to identify the defendants as perpetrators, or offer concocted alibis for their whereabouts during the assault on the jail. This refusal by the community to talk, to confess or name names is countered by the DA (and Lang) with a true *coup de théâtre*, or more properly a *coup de cinéma*, the same one Lang had introduced in his previous film, the adaptation of *Liliom*. The judge, jury and defendants are confronted with images from the newsreel taken of the riot and burning of the jail

which clearly show the defendants involved in violent acts. The first images shown
are of the overtly anti-social Dawson; Dawson seems astonished as we cut from
him to the scenes of his actions projected on the screen. But the irony of these acts
of self-spectating sharpens with the next two defendants, Sally Humphreys and
Frederick Garrett, respectable bourgeois, confronted with images of their lawless
selves.

Lang's spectacular use of incriminating evidence not only presents these three
defendants witnessing their own guilt as a movie, but as in *Liliom*, the incriminating
moments are actually presented as freeze frames (the DA describes them as 'stop
action'), a technique sparingly used in the 30s. The stopping of the action fixes the
images of the defendants at their most incriminating. These are the moments that
they hoped would be forgotten. Their projection as emblematic – almost allegorical
– images of their guilt functions as the vengeful return of the repressed. The images
of Humphreys and Garrett are especially powerful: close framings showing them
not only performing their acts of violence, but having the time of their life doing it.
The faces of these 'leading citizens' are contorted and demonic (much more than
Dawson's), but not so much with hatred or anger, as with delight and an almost
orgasmic sense of power. Sally twirls a firebrand above her head, while Garrett, axe
in hand, exults in the spray of the fire hose he has just severed. As Jean Douchet says
in his detailed analysis of this sequence, within these newsreel images we see a
'Dionysian explosion'.[47]

Particularly in contrast with their meek and frightened faces as they watch themselves, one feels these citizens cavorting on the screen never felt better in their poor
repressed lives. Their horrified looks as they watch these images seem to express not
only their fear of discovery, but disbelief before these images of themselves filled
with such power and destruction, a bursting forth of an energy they had always held
in check and now refuse to recognise, and have difficulty even remembering. These
are, in fact, actions which were not shown before in the film, the tossing of fire
bombs at the jail and the preventing of the fire department from putting out the

flames: the orgy of violence and anarchy that followed the seizing of the jail and preceded Katherine's arrival. The still, almost spent, quality of the mob when Katherine did arrive is now explained as post-orgasmic (Dawson was even happily smoking a post-riot cigarette). Garrett's wife stands up after the projection of his image and screams her denial, 'No no it's not true!' then faints, as Katherine had. These are the ultimate visionary images of Lang's cinema, the revelation of the self or of a loved one so horrific, and yet so undeniable, that it can only be expunged by a loss of consciousness.

The courtroom cinema in *Fury* is perhaps the most powerful of Lang's theatres of self-revelation already featured in *M* and *Liliom*. While the guilt displayed in *Liliom* remains rather anodyne by comparison, the idea of the heavenly cinema seems to have inspired Lang for the visual climax to this film. The projection of this newsreel of guilt functions as one of Lang's most powerful visionary scenes, although here the intersection of plot and technology eliminated the need for any supernatural agency. The documentary images portray the monster that lurks beneath normal behaviour, as Sally Humphreys' and Frederick Garrett's faces contort into their moment of murderous ecstasy every bit as much as Hans Beckert making faces in the mirror or re-enacting his sex crimes before the underworld tribunal. As in *M*, private theatres of desire have been re-staged, repeated, in public before a judging audience.

As noted earlier, in contrast to the Berlin of *M*, information in Strand moves mainly by oral communication. During the trial, however, mass communication takes over. We see the radio broadcasts from the courtroom going around the nation, listened to by a variety of people of different classes and in different social situations: from a rural country store to a white-collar office to the boudoir of a well-kept mistress. The progress of the trial is chronicled in newspaper headlines. The sensational moment of the woman collapsing after the projection of the film is immediately followed by reporters rushing to the press room for international phone calls and then headlines which proclaim: 'Identity of Twenty Two Proven' and 'Twenty Two Face Death'. The trial reveals mass media overtaking (and condemning?) the oral culture of Americana, with the newsreel film providing the most advanced technology of surveillance. The identity and guilt of twenty-two citizens of Strand has been fixed by the processes of modernity.

But while the courtroom movie presents the citizens of Strand with their demon *doppelgängers*, images of the self they can repress but can no longer deny (the apparatus having penetrated appearances as resolutely as Freder's vision of Moloch), the trial's investigation of identity has not been completed. It is now Joe's identity that must be established, or rather (as with Beckert in *M*), established in order to be expunged – his death must be proven. Given the lack of his body ('where is the corpse of Joe Wilson?' asks the defence attorney), the powerful newsreel images prove no guilt, if murder cannot be proved with a *corpus delicti*. An essential part of the narrative is still missing.

Because, of course, Joe Wilson is not dead and the apparently apodictic evidence of the newsreel film cannot prove his murder. The cinematic apparatus may work as a vision machine revealing the paradox of demonic identity to Strand's spellbound citizens, but Lang maintains his deep scepticism about the nature of identity, the photographic image and the mass media of modernity. As in *Spies* the indexical and even revelatory nature of photographic surveillance can be manipulated. Far from portraying them as the final arbiters of the truth, Lang repeatedly lampoons the mass media: the cameraman's delight as the jail burns or the radio announcer trying to slip in an ad for 'Nomake MeFat, the magic dessert' before the newsreel is shown. To fundamental questions of identity and life and death the photograph or the mass media cannot supply a complete answer. After the questions raised by the defence attorney the newspaper headlines query: 'Is This Man Alive?' with a photograph of Joe below, the one he sent Katherine during their separation.[48] This question is not as easy to answer as it might at first seem.

'You Can Have the Strand in Your Own Town': Joe Wilson's Private Theatre

> Last time you were in New York you went to 47th St. and Broadway and joined the big crowd of good-looking, well-dressed people that passed through the gay entrance of the Strand ... You wished you could have such a theatre at home – one with pictures like those and a crowd like that. You have a Strand in your town if you have Paramount Pictures! You have the good plays and the good audience.
>
> Paramount advertisement[49]

Movies and especially movie audiences are a recurring theme throughout *Fury*; the courtroom cinema is simply the climax of this motif. In fact, the name chosen for the town in which the lynching takes place, Strand (the incident it is based on took place in San Jose),[50] would have immediately been associated with the movies by audiences in the 30s. The Strand theatre in New York City had been the first great picture palace in the United States, the standard against which all other theatres were judged, and dozens of theatres around the country were named after it.[51] Watching movies and their effects on the audience provide pivotal scenes in *Fury* even before the courtroom climax. Publicity stills indicate that Lang actually shot a sequence, included in the shooting script, but cut from the release print, of Joe and Katherine going to the movies on their last night together on the town. Joe gets into an argument (the still seems to indicate it is with Ward Bond, who doesn't appear in the film as it now exists)[52] over the politics contained in a newsreel, declaring, 'It was the people who made this country what it is today!' articulating the populist sentiment that underlies much of the film. Although the still doesn't show him, the scene in the script also introduced the film's critical attitude toward this naive populism with an African-American character who responded to Joe by saying, 'Brotah, you ought t'get around more!'[53]

But Joe's most bitter comments on 'the people' come with another viewing of a newsreel, not shown directly, but described by Joe in his first monologue to his brothers after he returns, apparently, from the dead. When Joe suddenly appears in his brothers' Chicago apartment, first as an off screen voice, then as a looming backlit and rather monstrous figure, the brothers presumably wonder where he has been (as do we). As if in response Joe says almost paradoxically, 'You know where I've been all day? In a movie'. Joe's brothers exchange glances as if wondering if Joe has gone mad. But his further comments explain: 'Watching a newsreel. Of myself getting burned alive. I watched it ten times or twenty maybe, over and over again, I don't know how much. The place was packed. They like it. They get a big kick out of seeing a man burned to death – a big kick!' This description precedes Joe's explanation of his escape, after the explosion blew his cell door off. Following classical story construction his description of the movie viewing performs several roles: setting up the newsreel that will condemn the citizens of Strand, and showing Joe's near madness from his trauma. But the theme of the endlessly repeating motion picture of his own death and the sensation it causes also introduces a key aspect of the second half of *Fury*, Joe becoming an enunciator of his own drama, constructing and directing a plot against his murderers which will culminate in forcing them to watch the newsreel as he did – as a sign of one's own approaching death. Presumably it is during these repeated viewings that Joe realised the role the films could play in convicting the lynchers, although in Lang's typically withholding narration this is not revealed until much later.

Enno Patalas has compared *Fury* to *Die Nibelungen* – divided into two films, one dealing with the murder of the hero, the second with the avenging of that death.[54] *Fury* does divide into two parts basically at the point that Katherine collapses, with the climax of the successful assault on the jail. This conflagration with its assembled audience also recalls a movie, as well as recalling the scenes of flames and explosions in final or penultimate scenes of so many of Lang's German films (*Der müde Tod*, *Kriemhild's Revenge*, *Metropolis*, *The Testament of Dr. Mabuse*). But rather than following the apocalyptic logic of those allegorical films, *Fury* deals with a monstrous resurrection. As some commentators have pointed out, the second half of *Fury* blunts the film's anti-lynching message.[55] *Fury* is not a message picture, but a fully dialectical fable on the nature of American populism. As Vincente Sanchez-Biosca claims, the holocaust of the jail immolates Joe Wilson as John Doe. From his ashes a transformed character arises who will actually take on many characteristics of Lang's master criminals. When Joe appears in his brothers' apartment, they rush forward to embrace him and then withdraw. This is not their brother, but a revenant from the dead. Joe's nature as an animated corpse aids his new role as a monstrous enunciator.

Sanchez-Biosca described the resurrected Joe in terms that could describe Mabuse or Haghi: 'he will organize a scenario, find a decor, gather the actors and furnish them with evidence, he will build, in a word a *mise-en-scène* complete and tyrannical.'[56] As with Mabuse in *Testament*, Joe will actually gain power through his death, becoming a hidden force behind things:

> Wilson decides to create a mise-en-scène with other actors, other voices which he will manipulate like a ventriloquist. He becomes a phantom who thanks to his incorporeal nature will make himself into a God and move forward along a particularly powerful path of enunciation.[57]

But if Lang here returns to his earlier figure the master criminal (and to his constant theme of the control over the enunciation of the plot), the American version creates new complications.

Lang returns to his traditional means of raising the issues of enunciatory power visually, the look at the camera, and an editing scheme which points to the enunciator figure as the ultimate cause.[58] As Joe tells the story of the newsreel and his escape from the jail, Lang frames him in close-up, addressing the camera frontally. But as he begins to lay out his plot for revenge on the lynchers, Joe's eyeline meets the camera lens directly, as if speaking not only to his brothers but to the audience. Unlike the blank helpless stares at the camera by Joe or Katherine earlier in the film which indicated their complete subjection to a situation beyond their control, now

Joe's expression, determined delivery and glaring, harshly focused eyes – the way he occasionally jabs a finger right at the camera – declare mastery of the situation and the cinematic apparatus. As Sanchez-Biosca puts it: 'Joe takes the stage before the spectator, addressing her and communicating his new strategy of enunciation.'[59]

The courtroom, then, becomes Joe's theatre (he tells his brother he must come to the city where the trial takes place in order to 'be on the scene'), limited only by the fact that he cannot under any circumstances be seen there. Like the other master criminals he makes himself present through technology, especially, as Sanchez-Biosca also points out, through the radio.[60] The first cut to Joe listening to the trial (like other citizens across the nation) seems only to show a passive process. But the second cut to him after a radio announcer comments on the alibis the twenty-two accused have assembled, shows Joe rubbing his hands and muttering, like an omniscient narrator, 'Wait, just wait'. When the district attorney announces his new evidence (the newsreel) Lang cuts to Joe hunched over his radio, nodding and smiling, as if he has arranged what is to come. As Jean Douchet has argued, the projected newsreel serves not only to reveal the lynchers' hidden identity and guilt, but to allow Joe's *mise-en-scène* of revenge to take over the courtroom.[61] The terrifying visions projected on the screen are, in effect, Joe's own nightmare vision as he watched his killers approach. This is the film Joe watched over and over and which he now inflicts on the citizens of Strand, the reverse angle of the spectacle they watched with such absorption as Katherine arrived.

But all of Lang's master criminals ultimately fail and their undoing comes primarily from hubris, from an over-confidence in the power of their scenario and their technological network, their mastery of the Destiny-machine. Is Wilson really, as Douchet claims, the author of this film within a film?[62] That would be too simple, for how can Joe film his own murder? Rather than a demonstration of his power, the film captures Joe's moment of helplessness, the trauma he must return to, repeat, in order to overcome. Joe is as much the victim of this film as its enunciator. And this provides a new complexity and paradox to Lang's drama of master enunciators. The cinema as figure of repetition ('continuous showings at the Strand'), the image and impression left by events, play a multiple role, not only in the newsreel shown in court, but as an image of Joe's own traumatic memory, stuck in the moment of his near-death experience, unable to move past it, unable to come fully back to life.

This metaphor of movies as an image of traumatic experience, endless repeating, becomes focused through the re-introduction of Katherine into the film. Katherine beheld the fiery spectacle of her lover burning amid the flames of the jail with wide-eyed receptivity, unable to avert her gaze, until the moment that the intensity of the image blanks out all consciousness and she faints, marking the dividing point of the film. I compared this scene to the conflagration that ends *Kriemhild's Revenge*, and although their roles in relation to the fire are reversed, Katherine also recalls Kriemhild's wide-eyed stare at the flames which I compared to a camera impassively recording the outcome of her revenge. Katherine makes no claim of authorship for this blaze (as Kriemhild must for hers), but her uncomprehending horror is also like a camera, taking it all in. This comparison gains power when we examine the scene in which Wilson's brothers locate Katherine.

Katherine is seated in her landlady's apartment, staring ahead blankly, nearly catatonic. Such a posture presents a well established image of mental illness (think of Jane in the asylum in *The Cabinet of Dr. Caligari*), but in our context it means more. Katherine is fixed in the position of witnessing the jail fire, frozen in an attitude of horrified spectatorship, in thrall to the traumatic images imprinted on her by the tragedy. Lang makes this literal, when Charlie lights a cigarette. Katherine, who has not moved or responded since the brothers entered the room, turns at the snap of the match striking. She shakes her head in denial and repeats, 'no, no' (like Mrs. Garrett in the courtroom seeing the newsreel of her husband). Lang shows her subjective vision by a superimposition over Charlie holding the match (whose flames have been exaggerated). The last image Katherine saw, the one that blotted out her consciousness, and apparently her reason, appears over Charlie's face: Joe at the jail window surrounded by flames, which crackle loudly on the soundtrack. Katherine screams and stands up, then is reassured by Tom and Charlie.

The psychology here is more tailored to visual storytelling than to actual therapeutic practice, but the intentions and metaphors are clear. Katherine sits staring, unaware of her surroundings because she is constantly witnessing this last scene which has been imprinted on her consciousness, effacing all other reality. The flaming match causes her private movie to bleed into reality and provokes a panic which pulls her back into the real world. But only precariously: once she has recognized Tom and Charlie her eyes drift to the camera lens again and she resumes her fixed stare, saying: 'I saw him behind those flames in that burning jail – his face …' As she collapses in tears and is told (unconvincingly) by her landlady, 'There, there it's all over now', Charlie beams and whispers, 'the witness!' The brothers now have the witness who can place Joe in the jail at the time of the fire. Katherine becomes evidence, much like the newsreel film. She, too, will be forced to re-live her private movie in public.

When Katherine appears on the stand her delivery is shaky, partly because she is being forced to relive her trauma and partly because she has begun to put together the signs that indicate Joe is still alive. The defence attorney in cross examining her raises the issue of this private movie: 'Is it not possible that you did not see Joseph Wilson, but only the image of him your imagination had created in your head?' When Katherine claims she did see him, he responds, 'You can see that picture now, too, can't you?' Katherine admits, 'I'll always see it.' For Lang, such private movies, endlessly repeated, do not indicate a subjective hallucination, a flight from reality. In fact, as visionary moments they rather represent a moment when reality has assumed an essential form, most often so unbearably clear it is painful to watch. Both Joe and Katherine are subject to these endlessly repeating visions and Lang understands that movies, capable of continuous replaying, creating their own repetitive temporality, like a broken record, are the strongest correlative to this visionary experience. Joe's revenge consists in forcing the citizens of Strand to watch this movie as he and Katherine have seen it, with all its pain and terror.

But a new element has entered into Lang's film making, the possibility of a delivery from this endless round of repetition. If we return to the logic of *Der müde Tod*, we could say that the possibility of mourning, of ending the round of repetition of a primal trauma and coming back to life has entered Lang's cinema – at least as a possibility, enforced perhaps by the Hollywood formula of a romantic union as a happy ending. With the romantic formula a new dimension has been given to the master enunciator, a new vulnerability. As Sanchez-Biosca says, all human sentiment places him in peril, and Joe's past love for Katherine conflicts with his disembodied position as the absent author.[63] Listening to her testimony on his radio, he first places his hands over his ears and then switches it off as she says, 'We had been away from each other so long – more than a year.' A close-up follows in which Joe looks directly once more into the camera lens, while an overlap-dissolve superimposes his face over a tracking shot of the twenty-two accused. The shot in one sense affirms his power and authority over his plot and victims, like the superimposition of Mabuse over the stock exchange. But Joe's thoughtful expression also calls his authority into question. After listening to the voice of his lover speak of their separation he sees, not a vision of her face, but of his would-be murderers and potential victims. Is this man alive?

Joe's radio, however, only receives, it does not broadcast; there is a limit to the control it gives him over the scene at the courthouse. After the defence attorney moves for dismissal given the absence of the *corpus delicti*, Joe smashes his radio in fury. His next intervention into the trial must penetrate into the heart of the author's paradox as Lang has posed it. Here again, Lang is not simply continuing a theme from the earlier films, but intensifying it. The issue of authorship becomes more critical in his Hollywood films, as the figure of the master criminal often literally becomes that of the failed artist, whether writer (*House by the River*) or painter (*Scarlet Street*) for whom crime and artistic creation become inextricably intertwined. Wilson sees his master narrative falling apart in spite of the sensation caused by the newsreel which indisputably established the identity and guilt of the accused. But guilt for what action? Joe faces the essential paradox of the modern author: he must prove that he is dead.

To do this, Lang returns to the theme of *The Man Behind You*, the screenplay he first proposed for his American debut: anonymous letters, messages whose authorship has been concealed. Not only does Joe refuse to sign the letter he sends to the judge, he avoids using his own handwriting, pasting letters from a newspaper together to spell words. Wilson even creates a fictive (if vague) identity for himself when he signs the letter 'a citizen of Strand'. The district attorney used precisely this phrase in his opening statement: 'John Doe is not going to trial, but twenty-two citizens of Strand'. Wilson's use of this identity gives another meaning to the superimposition of his face over the shot of the defendants shown in the previous scene. He is not simply dominating them, crafting and deciding their fate. He is in a sense merging with them. As his brothers complain to him later, Joe is becoming a lyncher himself, with twenty-two victims.

Wilson's letter to the judge (which as Sanchez-Biosca states, causes the judge to step down from the bench to place it in evidence, leaving the judge's position for the moment empty)[64] conceals his identity. Joe acts as any criminal would act, trying to cover his tracks. But at the same time, the letter also tries to present incontrovertible evidence of Joe's identity – that is, of his death. The letter avoids any personal reference: no name, no signature, no handwriting. But it encloses the item Joe hopes will serve as the *corpus delicti*, the ring Katherine had given him. The inscription within the ring is read by the district attorney. It has been altered since Joe and Katherine's farewell scene at the station: only the letter K of Katherine's name remains, the rest has been melted by the jailhouse fire, but 'to Joe' is clearly legible. Katherine takes the stand, identifies the ring and supplies the missing part of the inscription, her own name. The completed reading seems to seal the case, as much by the pathos of Katherine's story as by the supplying of a corpus. One of the women accused screams, confesses and begs forgiveness. Joe's plot has reached closure with this dramatic effect of another woman's collapse (in the next scene Joe says to his brothers, 'that must have been some sensation when that woman collapsed' – like a director exulting after opening night).

But, as in all of Lang's tales of authorship, the master enunciator's mastery is never complete. Once again inscription proves fatal, and writing unconsciously betrays itself. Katherine sees the anonymous letter Joe sent and recognises his characteristic mistake: instead of the word 'memento' he has pasted together 'mementum'. Author-ship slips through the error. The sequences surrounding Katherine's testimonies in court have buckled back to the farewell scene at the station. All the identity-defining elements have resurfaced here to be read by Katherine. Coming to the courtroom, in the elevator with Joe's brother, Tom, Katherine noticed the torn pocket of his trench-coat mended by her blue thread. Tom had obviously put on the wrong coat, grabbing Joe's instead. Asked for a cigarette he reaches in his pocket, but to his surprise and Katherine's alarm, pulls out peanuts. Peanuts, the torn pocket, the ring, 'mementum'. Joe has revealed himself in spite of all his efforts to hide and this revelation will destroy his now perfectly completed plot. Is this man alive?

Of course, part of the answer is no. Joe *was* killed in the jail burning and his exis-tence since that point has been imaged as a monster, one of the walking dead. He, above all, has insisted on his own death as the essential element of his revenge plot. On his return to his brothers he does not proclaim his survival but his death ('You can't hurt a dead man and I'm dead! Everyone knows that, the whole country knows it!'). His behaviour, especially his continued separation from Katherine, indicates his decision to remain dead rather than come back to life. The giving up of his ring as the finishing touch for his plot involved not only an objectified version of his renunciation of Katherine, but a mutilation of his own body. When first arrested, he had been unable to take the ring off his finger, bitterly declaring 'maybe you could it cut off, why not!' But to complete his masterpiece of revenge Wilson had accomplished just that: 'Almost cost me my finger getting it off, but it was worth it – it would have been worth the whole hand, two hands!' Joe's willingness to commit self-mutilation comes from his perception of himself as a corpse. Whereas before Katherine had been part of his own body, 'like my right arm', now he can slice off body parts without regret.

Earlier Lang had cut from the courtroom to Joe listening to his radio on the question, 'Where is the corpse of Joe Wilson?' A typical Langian rhyming cut, its complexity unfolds as we trace the themes made cogent by the film. On the one hand it is a question and answer cut, part of Lang's playful omniscient narration, stating: Wilson is not dead, here he is. On another level it is a close parallel to the essential cut of the master criminal films, the cut to the enunciator when someone asks, 'who is behind all this?' But this comparison reveals again the transformation this figure undergoes in this film. The crime at issue is Joe's murder, and in fact Lang does cut to the *corpus delicti*. Joe is dead; he is a corpse until he himself is willing to come back to life. All of this is made explicit in the scene where Katherine follows her trail of signs and finds Joe in his hiding place. She tells him that his pose of being dead cannot be temporary if he allows the accused to be sentenced and exe-cuted. His separation from her will be eternal, because he is dead: 'I couldn't marry a dead man.' Wilson reacts angrily and sails out into the night to celebrate the suc-cess of his plot.

Joe's celebration takes place in a world dominated by death, separation and alien-ation – the world in many ways of Hans Beckert. With minimal dialogue this penul-timate scene of *Fury* shows Lang at his most imagistic and, indeed, allegorical, although (as in *M*) the allegory for the most part remains rooted in concrete objects and events. Joe sits in a German restaurant with polka music coming from off screen, but surrounded by empty tables. The next shot reveals everyone else is danc-ing to the music. Wilson gets the check, saying he doesn't like crowded places. As he walks the street, Lang reprises images from the film's opening. Joe pauses in front of a bedroom display labelled 'For the Newlyweds'. When Katherine's voice from the opening is heard in voice-over, Wilson's reaction indicates this is more than a simple memory. Joe looks terrified; subject to an auditory hallucination, he looks around for its source. Attracted by the loud jazz music issuing from a nearby bar, he rushes over.

Wilson seem to behave now like Poe's 'Man of the Crowd'. Although he left Katherine and his brother in his apartment declaring he wanted to be alone, he is now terrified by his solitude and seeks out pockets of human warmth. But now the isolation he had chosen seems to be inflicted upon him everywhere he turns. He enters the bar and finds it deserted, the chairs already piled on the tables. The lively-sounding music is simply coming over the radio, an ironic echo of Wilson's previous monitoring of the trial from a technologically safe distance. The black barman switches the radio off and takes Joe's order. Off screen chimes mark the entrance of Lang's signature image, the clock, as we cut to it and hear the barman's comment: 'Midnight, and another day'. The workings of the Destiny-machine are now unmistakable. Joe's world is being progressively emptied out; the work of death is apace.

As Joe's resurrection has failed, leaving him in the limbo of the undead, stuck in his endlessly looped movie which he wishes to inflict on the whole world, so the barman's ritual to bring in the new day goes astray. Tearing off a sheet from the cal-endar on the wall ('Today is Friday Nov. 20') he accidentally pulls off the next day as well, exposing the large numeral 22 (the number of the accused) to Joe's horrified gaze. The barman's explanation carries a sardonic pun (his black humour uninten-tional, of course, except to the omniscient narrator and Destiny-machine): 'Two pages must have got hanged together'. Trembling, Wilson pays the tab and beats it. Outside more symbolic environments lay in wait for him, as he passes another shop window, this time an elaborate array of blossoms at a florist. Turning to look at the flowers partly to avoid the gaze of a beat cop, Joe is framed from inside the shop, the flowers surrounding him. The tableau becomes funereal, Wilson surrounded by flowers, a deliberate inversion of the opening of the film.

As in M, the device of the shop window allows Lang to segue into a visionary moment, although here Lang increases the subjective nature of the imagery. Reflected on the glass in front of Wilson are the images of a number of the defen-dants, cued by another voice-over of Katherine's earlier plea for him not to con-tinue his revenge. Apparently this final sequence in the original preview version of the film then proceeded into a full-blown hallucination, recalling the ending of the first Mabuse 'with ghosts shooting up from behind the trees and chasing Tracy', but these Expressionist elements were cut after they caused a preview audience to howl with laughter.[65] Once again, without the film it is hard to judge the success of this sequence as Lang first realised it. But there is no question that the film as it stands now, with only slight suggestions of Joe hallucinating (the voice-over, the reflec-tions), falls more in line with Lang's later development. Instead of superimposed phantoms, Lang confronts Joe with perhaps his most enduring image of the world of death – emptiness. Joe turns from the window display and we see his point of view of an empty city street at night. As he turns to walk down the deserted street, he experiences another aural hallucination – a succession of multiple footsteps fol-lowing him. Apparently in response to the American audience's hilarity at visual ghosts, Lang (or possibly producer Joseph Mankiewicz) transferred their presence onto the soundtrack. Doing so, the scene reaches a new stage of abstraction. Joe looks behind him and we see, as his point of view, perhaps the most empty of all Lang's empty shots, one filled with an invisible energy and intangible malevolence:

a high angle tracking shot of the totally empty dark street striated by off screen street lamps. This rolling shot of nothingness, almost like an abstract field painting, takes on a disembodied threat through the camera movement as the vacant street unrolls before us. No wonder Joe ends up running home.

He dashes up his stairs in a frenzy, slamming the door to his apartment behind him and shouting Katherine's name. As he turns off the light, the threatening theme on the soundtrack ceases and Tracy's mannerisms indicate the hallucination is over. But then we see his point of view as he surveys his apartment – utterly empty, bereft of human presence. In an almost childish voice he pleads over this empty image: 'Katherine, don't leave me alone …' As *Fury* moves towards its ending, the theme of separation that began it re-surfaces, but no longer as a temporary parting, but an eternal, almost metaphysical condition, the divide between the realm of the dead and the living. In a sense *Fury* deals with the theme most explicitly posed in *Der müde Tod* but implicit in several other Lang films (most recently in *Liliom*) of a lover who tries to bring a beloved back from the dead. *Fury* comes the closest to accomplishing this fairy tale task because its character finally does make a decision to return to life.

It is hard to know what to make of the telegraphic and nearly perfunctory nature of the final scene of *Fury*. The verdict is delivered for the twenty-two citizens of Strand. Some are found not guilty, but the bulk are condemned. Hearing his condemnation, Dawson turns around and tries to run out of the courtroom, rushing right towards the lens of the camera. But then he stops short, as abruptly as the mob did at the end of *M*, looking straight into the lens. What does he see? The reverse angle shows Joe Wilson, now looking more like his former self, the well-groomed average guy striding into the courtroom. As Sanchez-Biosca says, this exchange of glances with both characters in turn looking at the camera, ends Wilson's reign as grand enunciator.[66] He delivers himself now over to the rule of law. Lang has indicated his admiration of Tracy's last speech and its delivery and his dislike for the kiss between Joe and Katherine which immediately follows it and ends the film. Both seem to me rushed and uninspired. Tracy's delivery makes Joe's speech sound like a civic lesson and flattens its one crucially significant statement, that he has now realised he can live because he can admit that something of him was burned to death in the jail fire, including his faith in the people and America. Coming to life again entails accepting that part of you is dead. Katherine's kiss seems likewise abstract and unfelt. But it may be simply that Lang has not yet figured out how to resolve the Hollywood romance in the presence of the law. His sense of the pain of separation and the hollowness of emptiness has never been keener. A quick speech and even quicker smooch seem an inadequate resolution to what is certainly one of Lang's most deeply felt films. The work of mourning which would allow these characters to return to life is hinted at, but not imaged. Lang refuses to create a false aura of salvation, but one doesn't know if that is because he cannot yet portray a way back into life out of death, or he doesn't really believe it possible. Perhaps the only fitting way to end this film would be with an image which would make all of us, as spectators, faint away, unable to see any more.

9

You Only Live Once

The Paradoxes of Vision

… wenn man es betrachtet, als ob Einem die
Augenlieder weggeschnitten waren.
… like seeing with the eyelids cut away.

Heinrich von Kleist[1]

For Lang, vision involves more than the simple act of visual perception. Sight has an abstracting force, at once aggressive (that is, probing) and grasping. Sight can pare away the visual world and leave only the essentials. As Frieda Grafe has put it, in perhaps the most incisive description of Lang's visual style, 'Lang is not interested in a reproduction of a reality one has already seen. He wants to reveal, with his instrument, the real power of forms.'[2] Lang renders this aspect of sight not only in

his many diagrams and maps, but in his topographical shots, which view space
from a point which facilitates its abstraction into an essential design. Lang's sense of
composition, illustrated most clearly by his sketches for shots, shows this lust for
the graphic armature of the visual, as opposed to the delight in the textured variety
of a visual field found in directors like Griffith or Renoir. Lang's portrayal of space
takes on a haptic aspect, related to touch, more than the purely visual; it seeks the
outlines of things, the arrangement of objects in space, rather than a dense shimmering panoply of optical delights and textures.[3]

This aggressive sense of sight as probing and grasping often becomes literalised in
an image, such as Rotwang in *Metropolis* violating Maria with the beam of his flashlight, in Lang's words, 'like the sharp claws of an animal, refus[ing] to release her from
its grasp',[4] or the mirror reflecting his next potential victim to Hans Beckert surrounded by knives. This mastering and threatening gaze shares a visual aggression
with the 'male gaze' of classical cinema described by feminist critic Laura Mulvey and
related to Lang's films in detail by Stephen Jenkins in his insightful essay, 'Lang: Fear
and Desire,' the most thorough and observant essay on Lang's career written in English.[5] But I would claim Jenkins, by focusing his discussion on the image of woman in
Lang's films, does not go far enough. A more basic and pervasive visual aggression
underlies the look of desire in Lang, most obviously in his German films, but also
throughout his career (as I hope to demonstrate), what Mabuse would undoubtedly
call 'the will-to-power' and that Jean Roy calls Mabuse's coupling of the look with
power over others,[6] a fundamental desire to dominate the world, the ambition for
systematic mastery which lies behind the project of modernity.

Heidegger calls this modern realm of vision as mastery 'The Age of the World
Picture', in which the world is confronted and organised into a system by man's
technological project.[7] As Heidegger says, in this modern age 'representing is a
making-stand-over-against, an objectifying that goes forward and masters'.[8] In
Lang's cinema a primal desire to dominate the world through vision sometimes (as
in Rotwang's capturing of Maria in order to create her technological double) aligns
with the patriarchal dominance of women, sometimes (as in Maria's dance before
the sons of Metropolis) cynically makes use of male lust, and sometimes operates in
outright opposition to the world of sexual desire (as in Joe's devising of his plot
while denying his desire for Katherine). The male gaze, narrowly defined, certainly
operates in Lang, but it does not exhaust his inventory of vision. Rather, Lang's
cinema allows us to place the male gaze within the context of a broader modern
conception of vision.

But I would not claim that this vision of mastery (which includes not only the
composition of individual shots, but also the editing patterns we have found under-
pinning the master criminal's networks and conspiracies) exhausts Lang's understanding of vision, either. What I have termed the visionary moment, an act of
seeing which tears through the visual fabric of reality, shares a schema of abstraction and grasping fundamentals with the project of mastery, but contrasts sharply
in its overturning of an apparent coherence of the world by revealing another scene
of ultimate significance.[9] The visionary moment does not exalt the seer, but rather
causes trauma, often accompanied by a hysterical reaction of horror, or loss of consciousness. In the vision of mastery the viewer claims power over the object of his
vision. In the visionary scene, the revelation turns the tables: it violently claims the
seer, and reveals to her a scene of emptiness, demonic threat or death.

The archetypal drama of vision in Lang's cinema features an overreacher character (such as the master criminal) who claims visual control. I have described this

scenario as the overreacher trying to merge with the abstract power of the Destiny-machine, that dominating force of modernity which no one person can ever entirely control. The visionary moment frequently overturns this hubristic claim, revealing the Destiny-machine as greater than its supposed enunciator (as when Mabuse encounters his victims and the world of death he has created at the finale of *Dr. Mabuse, the Gambler*). However, visionary moments also occur to characters who make no claim to mastery (the maiden in *Der müde Tod* or Katherine in *Fury*) or only weak ones (Liliom, Freder). The visionary moment reveals the workings of the Destiny-machine, but not necessarily in its technologically tangible form. Rather, it reveals the deathly world view that underlies such claims to mastery or systematic control. The visionary character who is not involved in a project of mastery (such as the maiden, or Katherine) sees through the world of apparent coherence into the dark, inhuman core of the Destiny-machine.

A third scenario of vision plays a key role in Lang's films: an ambiguous visual perception which involves either a character's blindness or incomplete view of the world.[10] Literally blind characters in Lang's films often are acute observers, due to the sharpening of their other senses, such as the blind beggar in *M* who identifies the murderer of Elsie Beckmann by his aural memory, or the blind flower-seller in *Blue Gardenia* who identifies the voice of the mystery woman. Lang also presents fake blind men who take advantage of their feigned impairment in order to observe more closely, such as the agent who trails Jellusic in *Spies*; the beggar in *M* who lifts his dark glasses in order to keep an eye on the children near him; the blind spy in the train compartment of *Ministry of Fear* who turns on the film's protagonist; and, of course, the 'blind' seer Cornelius in his last film *The Thousand Eyes of Dr. Mabuse*. Another very personal (but unrealised) project Lang worked on in the 30s (slated to be the film he would shoot for Paramount after *You and Me*), *Men without a Country*, dealt with spies seeking a powerful secret weapon which turns out to be a ray which will cause mass blindness.[11]

But in a broader, less literal sense, the problem of blindness or mistaken vision plays a key role in many Lang films, and most obviously in *You Only Live Once*. As philosopher George Wilson has said in his extremely perceptive essay on the film, this is 'a film that seems obsessed with the various facets of perception and blindness'.[12] Joan Graham (Sylvia Sidney again), a bright, hard-working assistant to the public defender, loves Eddie Taylor, a small-time criminal who has been arrested three times previously and under the (then current, and recently reinstated in many US states) 'three-time loser' law will be put away for life if he is arrested again. In the opening scenes of the film Joan awaits Eddie's release on parole and their subsequent marriage. Her defence attorney boss, Stephen Whitney, who helps arrange Eddie's parole and who secretly loves Joan (at least she doesn't notice it, although everyone else does) repeatedly wonders what she sees in Taylor. The issue of seeing, or not seeing, what another character sees, structures *You Only Live Once* from its opening.

In the idyllic country inn honeymoon site that Joan spent three years searching for (while Eddie was in prison), the newlyweds describe love in terms of vision. As they sit alongside a lily pond complete with croaking frogs, Eddie explains that frogs mate for life, 'if one dies, the other dies'. Joan responds, 'Like Romeo and Juliet'. Lang cuts to a reflection of the lovers in the pond, upside down as in a *camera obscura*. This figure of reversed vision becomes more complex as one of the frogs leaps into the water and the image of the couple melts into obscurity in the rippling water. As the image becomes distorted, Joan speculates that the frogs 'see something in each other that no-one else can see'. As she speaks, the pond water gradually becomes still and mirror-like again, perfectly reflecting their upside down image.

This intersection between dialogue and visual imagery presents a rich enigma rather than an immediately legible allegory. Do Eddie and Joan see the world upside down? Is their vision of themselves so fragile it can be rendered unrecognisable by a slight disturbance? Or is their image of each other of such underlying clarity that it will re-emerge from any surface disturbance? Love may be blind, but Lang redefines this blindness as a way of seeing differently than other people. Of all of Lang's films, *You Only Live Once* deals most directly with the power of romantic love. Jean-Luc Godard described Joan and Eddie, one of the models for the doomed couple in his epic of *l'amour fou*, *Pierrot le Fou*, as 'the last romantic couple in the world'.[13] In no other film has Lang so focused the themes of his style on a couple and done so with such emotional power and lack of compromise. But from the very beginning the idea of devotion and passion is aligned to questions of vision. This different way of seeing the world and each other, and its clash with other modes of vision, will lead Joan and Eddie unswervingly to both triumph and tragedy.

However much Lang devotes himself to this romantic couple, he does not restrict himself to their point of view. As George Wilson states, 'the problematic character of any single perspective on the action is one of the film's principal preoccupations'.[14] Lang tenderly portrays the lovers' moments of intimacy, but the film's narration also bears an ironic edge. Eddie and Joan's way of seeing is not the only vision of the world, as the frog jumping in the old pond hinted. As Eddie takes Joan into his arms and carries her up the stairs from the courtyard to their honeymoon suite, Lang cuts back to the frogs in the pond. If the couple can see an image of their love (not to mention Romeo and Juliet!) in these slimy amphibians, it is more than Lang asks us to do. Their creepy presence in the middle of this archetypal romantic gesture is disquieting (underscored by a change in the musical soundtrack to a slightly foreboding theme) – a bit like the cut to the locomotive in the middle of the kiss in the opening of *Fury*. Further, the frogs seem to be watching the couple, waiting …

If it is difficult to see Joan and Eddie in this pair of frogs, a more likely substitution immediately suggests itself two shots later: the caricatured middle-aged couple who run this honeymoon nest (Margaret Hamilton, the Wicked Witch of the West herself, and her husband, a lanky Yankee who strikes matches on the seat of his pants). The husband had viewed Eddie with suspicion, declaring to his wife, 'I've seen that feller's face before and I don't like it.' The husband combs through his *True Detective* magazines (with articles such as 'Yeggs Wanted by the Police. Have you seen them?') searching for Eddie's picture, while the lovers are consummating their marriage. This suspicious gaze, the opposite of the look of love that Eddie and Joan exchange, bears down upon the lovers. Lang cuts directly from Eddie carrying Joan upstairs to an open magazine page bearing Eddie's picture, a magnifying glass resting on it. Lang doesn't need to show the inn-keeper's moment of discovery or hear his yelp of recognition. The fatal identification accomplished, the inn-keeper acts as the minion of a process of surveillance which average citizens delight in aiding. The inn-keeper and his wife timidly approach the Taylors' room, then unceremoniously announce, 'Convicts and their wives ain't welcome in this tavern.' Joan and Eddie are kicked out of their honeymoon nest on their wedding night at four a.m.

Father Dolan, the prison chaplain, articulates the theme of blindness and partial or distorted sight explicitly. Dolan, in effect, mediates between the prisoners and the mechanisms of the law, giving prison discipline a human face. Thus he cautions Eddie when he is returned to jail for a crime he did not commit and refuses to see

Joan: 'Eddie, open your eyes, stop walking in the dark.' He preaches a similar gospel
to the warden and his family on the eve of Eddie's execution: 'You see, we all look at
life through the same eyes, but we don't see the same thing.' The character of Dolan
plays badly with contemporary audiences and there is a natural attempt (as in
Wilson's essay) to see him as an ironic figure.[15] Although it is clear that Lang intends
him as a positive character, his complete lack of effectiveness and his role in complicating Eddie's fate make him less an ironic character than one whose good qualities and intentions cannot counterbalance the system in which he plays a role, like
Brecht's *Good Person of Szechwan*. That he cannot see this larger picture – his own
complicity with the prison system, the realm of the Destiny-machine – constitutes
Father Dolan's blindness.

The lynchers in *Fury* or Beckert in *M* were caught because they were unaware
they were being watched, while Lang's master criminals employed elaborate disguises to pass unnoticed under the watchful eye of the law. Eddie Taylor may be a
criminal, but he's certainly no master. His long term experience in prison has
inured him to surveillance. He lives under the scrutiny of suspicious gazes, except
when he basks in Joan's loving looks. These different regimes of vision not only cast
him in different roles, but fragment him. During his stay on death row, Taylor twice
has to present an impassive blank face to attentive guards while carrying out a difficult and even painful action behind his own back. After being told there is a gun
hidden in the hospital isolation ward, Eddie tears his tin cup and uses its jagged
edge to slash his wrist. Lang cuts between close-ups of the tearing of the cup, the
occasionally suspicious guard outside Taylor's cell, and Taylor's face striving to
remain inexpressive despite effort and pain. When Taylor passes out from loss of
blood, he is sent to the hospital, then, after making a scene, condemned to the isolation ward. There, the same fragmentation takes place. As Taylor's face remains
absolutely blank, Lang shows us the close-ups of his hand searching out the seam in
the mattress, opening it and taking out the gun. Lang intercuts this action with the
guard's face at the window to the cell door, his stare now unswervingly focused on
Taylor, but picking up no clue of the action hidden from his view. Taylor's body is
bifurcated into realms of the visible and unseen, as Eddie's face must prepare itself
to meet the gaze of the prison system implacably.

You Only Live Once stages confrontations between different visions of the world,
the lovers who can see something in each other no-one else can and the suspicious
population whose sight is guided by sensational publications and limited to recognising mug shots. But Lang's drama does not consist simply in valorising the lovers'
insight and condemning the population's suspicion. In Lang's world no-one has a
complete view of things and several sequences stage this visual uncertainty explicitly. Perhaps the most spectacular is Taylor's jailbreak just before his scheduled execution. Following his retrieval of the gun from the isolation ward, Taylor takes the
prison doctor a hostage and makes his way into the prison yard at night. In this
nightscape of fog and darkness (which will become an archetypal *film noir* image)
pierced by the beacons searching for Taylor (whom the guards can hear but not see)
Lang pictures an uncertain world. Charged with equal parts violence and uncertainty, it recalls the line from Matthew Arnold that would supply the title for a later
Lang film, 'Where ignorant armies clash by night'.

The siren announcing Taylor's escape from the isolation ward nearly interrupts
Father Dolan's homily about vision to an unsympathetic warden and his wife. Shrill
noises and probing lights invade the warden's bourgeois interior, then Lang cuts to
the prison walls where night and fog have nearly dissolved Lang's haptic space:

guard turrets and bridges barely visible through fog, pierced by shifting lights. The clear space of vision breaks up into swirling mist, pools of darkness and sudden bursts of illumination, shielding the figures who walk through it, turning men into silhouettes and silhouettes into uncertain shadows. The warden tries to overcome his lack of visual mastery with a magnification of his voice over the loudspeaker, telling the guards to shoot to kill Taylor, but to spare his doctor hostage 'if possible'. Exchanges between Taylor and the guards and the warden echo through this obscurity, as Taylor demands that the prison gate be opened or he will 'croak' the doctor.

As the doctor begs the warden for his life, Lang cuts away to a strangely empty shot, barred prison windows viewed from inside, looking out on to the fog-filled night as searchlight beams move back and forth. Presumably this is a transition shot, allowing Lang to introduce a new space and a new wrinkle to the plot, and its relative brevity doesn't allow us to linger over it. But given the plot element it is about to introduce – a telegram arriving with a last minute pardon for Taylor – the shot is worth considering. The arrival of this pardon marks an enormous coincidence, the sort of last-minute rescue that Brecht parodied at the end of *The Three Penny Opera*. This cut away from Taylor's standoff at the prison gates introduces a providential moment, its imagery – beams of light moving in the darkness – hinting at divine intervention. However, even if one took this image as a straightforward allegory, the moment of divine intervention in Eddie Taylor's life won't do him much good.

The lack of visual contact highlights a mutual lack of trust which defines the relationship between Taylor and the law. The warden calls out to Taylor that he has been pardoned, which Eddie takes as a rather bone-headed ploy to get him to give up his gun, and refuses to believe. The warden reiterates, 'You're a free man, Taylor!' Unconvinced, Taylor begins a countdown to twenty, at which point he will blow away the doctor. As Taylor's numbers sound out of the fog and the doctor begs for his life, the warden gives the order to open the gate. Why not? The pardon now makes Taylor a free man, as he said.

But Father Dolan intervenes, stopping the gate from opening. His concern has some logic: Taylor shouldn't leave prison with a gun in his hand, still crazed and not believing in his pardon. He asks the warden's permission to talk to Taylor: 'He'll believe me, he's always believed me.' The warden agrees, as Taylor's countdown echoes through the yard. The sequence that follows provides another thicket of diverse visual and verbal cues, perhaps impossible to reconcile fully. Father Dolan emerges from the fog, which, glowing with light, clings to him like a haloed nimbus. He asks Taylor to put down the gun, to believe in him, to read the message and to realise he is a free man. On an immediate level, Lang seems to construct a fairly pat parable of faith: Dolan, a figure of salvation, offering an ignorant and frightened man a true message and demanding a profession of belief, 'Eddie, won't you believe me?' Eddie responds, 'I don't believe anybody!' Spreading his arms in long shot, subsumed in light (in contrast to Eddie's shadowy figure in foreground), Dolan replies, 'Then I can't open the gate.'

Lang's professed Catholicism (which he has invoked specifically in discussing this film) makes it incumbent on us to consider this reading. Eddie responds to Father Dolan's approach by shooting him, after which Dolan reassures the warden that he has not been hurt and asks him to open the gate for Taylor. One can read this as a succinct Christian allegory. Sinful man in his ignorance and blindness does not recognise his saviour, and actually causes his death. It takes his saviour's willing death, his sacrifice, actually to open the gate to salvation. But a number of other cues in the sequence rub against this reading or render it ironic. Father Dolan first remanded the order to open the gate, keeping Eddie imprisoned. The fog that surrounds him obscures his vision as much as it endows him with a supernatural aura. If Taylor shouldn't have gone out of the gate five minutes' earlier with his gun, why should he be allowed to leave, gun still in possession, now? Most importantly, instead of salvation, when Taylor goes out of the gate he finds that he is now guilty of the crime of murder for which he was about to be executed. Before shooting Father Dolan, Taylor was innocent. The law had finally recognised its mistake and cleared him. Blocking his exit from prison, Dolan involved Taylor in an actual murder and a new guilt, overturning his momentary pardon. As Taylor will say to Joan: 'He made me a murderer.' The gate from which he issues looms above him with a non-celestial motto – not, 'Abandon hope all ye who enter', or 'Work makes free' – but 'Clearance: Ten Feet'. Taylor, briefly a free man, or so he was told, emerges into a hail of bullets, while the wounded Father Dolan looks briefly into the camera lens, collapses and dies.

This central sequence of You Only Live Once not only evokes visual uncertainty, but a host of epistemic conflicts and paradoxes. If one sees a religious reading here, and I think such a reading just as likely as the ironic view of Dolan that Wilson offers, it evokes the paradoxical nature of grace, and seems more like a parable by Kafka or a Jansenist than a reassuring profession of orthodox faith. But if deciding the proper interpretation of this sequence seems an elusive task, its role in Lang's logic of images seems easier to describe. It typifies the shifting nature of Lang's allegories in this film, the subversion of one meaning by another, the juxtaposition of transcendent and ironic meanings. Belief is difficult in an uncertain world in which no-one has a clear view, and freedom especially takes on a contingent meaning.

The uncertainty that dominates this escape sequence does not confine itself to the characters and their partial viewpoints and blind spots. We, the viewers, are left in the dark for a long section of this film. The telegram that arrives during this scene fills in an extraordinary blind spot for the audience, answering the question of who pulled off the film's other big set piece, the robbery of the armoured truck at the Fifth National Bank, for which Taylor had been convicted. Perhaps the most unique aspect of You Only Live Once comes from the presentation of this key sequence, in which Lang refuses to reveal to the audience the identity of the man who lobs the gas bombs and scoops up the loot. This deliberate withholding of information not only supplies the clearest example of an incomplete view (now extended to the audience), but also of the theme of trust in the face of incomplete knowledge.

Like the fog-filled jailbreak, the earlier robbery takes place through an obscuring visual filter, a downpouring of rain. The camera moves in on the back window of a car as the rain beads off it, showing a window shade lowered slightly and two eyes appearing within the slit. The image causes us to shudder; the merging of human eyes with the metallic shell of the machine creating a monster whose shifting eyes express malevolence, the perfect image of Lang's probing, aggressive vision, scanning a space in order to master it. In close-up the eyes shift to the left. In the next shot an armoured truck arrives; armed guards move bystanders back and begin unloading heavy money bags. The shade on the back window closes. In close framing inside the car we see hands open a suitcase and take out a gas-mask, placing a hat in its place; as the camera moves back, we see the man putting the mask on, without getting a glimpse of his face. However, clearly visible inside the hat, are the initials ET. A high angle long shot shows the armoured car continue unloading when suddenly white smoke explodes in the corner of the screen, filling the fol-

lowing shots with a thick and obscuring fog. The next shot shows the gas-masked man throwing gas bombs which continue to explode and fill the air as people scream and collapse, gasping for breath.

The masked man enters the now silent and empty frame (kicking a dying guard away from the back door), gets in the truck and drives off. As the rain continues falling, the truck enters the site of a closed-off road (with a sign warning: 'Detour Danger'), goes around the warning sign and heads off screen. The camera refuses to budge, but we hear a squeal of tires, a crash and then a large splash of water. Lang has obstinately refused to let us see the robber's face (although the initials identify the hat as Eddie Taylor's). Likewise he refuses to let us see what happened to the truck (although the off screen sound indicates an accident).

The most frequent means of withholding information from an audience in classical film-making is to use the limited point of view of a character to filter what the audience learns. Hitchcock's *Rear Window* demonstrates this perfectly, since nearly all the information we gather about whether Lars Thorwald killed his wife comes to us through L. B. Jeffries' point of view. There are a few moments in the film that are not given through Jeffries' viewpoint (e.g. Thorwald leaving early in the morning with a woman while Jeffries sleeps). But the mystery plot, the incomplete and fragmentary clues that gradually establish Thorwald as a murderer, are gathered from the information available to Jeff. It remains a mystery because, in fact, Jeff cannot know everything and must fill in gaps with suppositions. But Lang takes the opposite approach. In a sequence such as the jailbreak, in which characters have different degrees of knowledge (e.g. Taylor's ignorance that the pardon is *bona fide*), Lang lets us know more than they do. Lang's style of parallel editing creates an omniscient point of view, above his characters who have only a partial view (which creates ironical juxtapositions, such as the inn-keeper and his wife preparing to throw Eddie and Joan out while the couple delight in their honeymoon hideaway). Lang does occasionally give us the limited view of a character, at least briefly (e.g. the warden hearing Father Dolan's voice saying he wasn't hit without showing immediately that this is a lie – although in the following shots we learn the truth). Most frequently Lang gives the audience information characters do not have, thereby creating effects of suspense and irony.

But if Lang frequently tells the audience information he withholds from characters, he occasionally also withholds information from the audience, without using the device of a character's limited view. This bank robbery is undoubtedly the most extended and daring of such sequences. Just as omniscience creates a strong sense of an enunciating narrator (as in Lang's ironic or suspenseful sequences), such holding back of information from the audience makes us doubly aware of the narrator's ability to reveal information or withhold it.[16] Lang's framing doesn't show the robber's face until he has his mask on, and it conceals exactly what happens to the truck. In previous films, Lang's mysteries employed similar withholdings (e.g. Beckert's disappearance outside the warehouse, the mystery of Mabuse's messages continuing after his death), but no scene ever flaunted its ability to withhold, to allow us only a partial view of a scene, so flamboyantly. Ultimately Lang makes us, as audience members, aware of the limits of our own vision.

But this sequence goes further than that. It not only won't show us the robber's face until it is covered, it show us something else instead, a near close-up of an object: the hat the robber had been wearing which bears Eddie Taylor's initials. Here, Lang is not simply withholding information through his framing, he seems to be manufacturing evidence, 'framing' Taylor, as it were. At this point the film seems to violate what David Bordwell calls the mystery film's 'fair play' rules with a blatant red herring.[17] One feels the force of enunciation in the way the framing focuses our attention on the hat and the way it is placed so that the initials are clearly legible. But *You Only Live Once* is not really a mystery. This sequence rams the film's themes of partial vision and trust down the audience's throats. We don't simply observe the

limited views of characters or their decisions whether to trust each other. We, the audience, must fill in these limited views and decide whom *we* trust. We encounter the same problems that Eddie Taylor must deal with in the fog. Should he (should we) trust a character he knows to be basically sympathetic (Eddie for us in this scene, Father Dolan for Eddie during the jailbreak)? Should he (and we) believe something that seems highly unlikely, even if we want to believe it (Eddie, that he has been pardoned, we, that, in spite of the hat, Eddie had nothing to do with this robbery)?

Rather than apologising for his manipulation of the audience, Lang relishes it. He absolutely misleads us here. George Wilson's inventive gymnastics to try to keep open the possibility that Taylor *was* involved in the robbery seem to me ingenious, but unconvincing and they basically contradict Lang's stylistic approach.[18] Notice how our tendency to identify Taylor with the robber, while seemingly cinched by the hat, began earlier, triggered by Lang's technique of rhymes between the ending and beginning of sequences, here assimilated to the Hollywood 'dialogue hook'.[19] In the scene previous to the robbery, Taylor, who had been fired from his trucking job for being late, had gone to his boss, hat in hand, to beg for his job. During Eddie's plea, the trucking boss talks to his wife on the phone arranging a dinner party with the neighbours. Eddie pleads that he can't get another job, except from his old gang who offer him 'bank jobs that are foolproof'. Taylor reacts to the boss's callous attitude by socking him in the jaw, clamping his hat back on his head and storming out, with the exit line, 'And I wanted to go straight!' Lang cuts directly from this bit of dialogue to the sign for the Fifth National Bank. The implication is that Taylor has gone right out and robbed a bank, using one of those foolproof schemes.

Likewise, after the loud splash that ends the shot of the truck ignoring the detour sign, our next view of Eddie shows him on foot, totally soaked. The first transition certainly invites (if it doesn't demand) the narrative logic of Taylor's involvement, the second, while less strong, seems to relate the off screen wreck to both Eddie's form of transportation (or lack thereof) and his soaked condition, (although the rain could account for that). But can we trust this sort of narrative logic in Lang? Lang frequently cuts on a rhyme between a sound and an apparent cause which turns out to be merely an association, not a cause at all, often even a joke – such as the cut from the ticking time bomb to the gangster tapping his soft boiled egg in *The Testament of Dr. Mabuse*. Lang teases us with his transitions. Sometimes they supply narrative information or connections (such as the cuts to Mabuse after one of his crimes), but they frequently deliver red herrings, or simple puns. In his playfulness, Lang displays his control over not only images, but their meanings, including misleading or absurd associations. By these jokes Lang lets us know that, if he is not an outright unreliable narrator, he can certainly be a misleading one. When Lang presents a limited frame, one should not assume he focuses our attention on the most important object (in this case, the hat), since the most important point might be that the view is incomplete, even potentially misleading.

The moment when Lang supplies the withheld information about the bank robbery comes nearly twenty minutes later, during Eddie's fog-shrouded escape attempt. As we have seen, although for a moment it seems like a clichéd last-minute rescue, the news of his pardon and its aftermath ultimately transforms Taylor's previously falsely imputed guilt into real guilt. In his omniscient manner, Lang cuts from the telegraph ribbon in the prison office moving across the screen to images of a bulldozer, then chains leading into a Stygian black pool, dredging up (shades of

Psycho) the armoured car from the dark liquid, one of Lang's cloacal visions. A cut closes in on the windshield and a monstrous dead body (until we realise the monstrous face is simply the gas mask). Lang fades back to the telegraph message which now gives the identification of the bank robber as 'Monk Mendall, former cellmate of Taylor's'. This revenant from the dead emerges ultimately to do Eddie no good (we recall Monk warning Eddie as he left prison not to 'high hat' him – another Lang pun?).

Why the delay? What does Lang accomplish by leaving us in the dark about Taylor's guilt or innocence all this time? It is here I think that George Wilson's analysis of the film, perceptive as it is, misses the point, or at least misses the role played by Lang as enunciator. We have been encouraged to see Taylor as guilty, to withhold our complete sympathy from him as he underwent the agony of his trial and imprisonment, his estrangement from Joan, his agony at the approaching execution. (Wilson actually wants to cling to the possibility of Eddie's guilt even after this revelation.)[20] Likewise, we have been encouraged to see Joan's devotion to him as misplaced, as naive (as Wilson also claims we should).[21] Wilson believes we should maintain a scepticism about both these characters throughout the film. This is not an insensitive reading of the film, and it certainly picks up on the relative distance Lang maintains from his characters, his avoidance of a complete Hollywood identification with them.

But I believe Lang counters the partial views all his characters are condemned to in this film with a sort of faith, less Father Dolan's complicit faith which works within the prison system than the rather naive and excessive faith that Joan displays in her devotion to Eddie, a faith which is in a way blind, but which gropes its way through a world in which no-one can ever see everything. If this may sound rather like conventional Hollywood ideology, the film's action proves it is not. Joan's faith does not allow her to integrate into the world any more than Eddie's suspicion does. The unique quality of *You Only Live Once* comes with its progressive nihilism, a nihilism founded in the demonstration that faith and desire have no place in the world as presently constituted.

Identities Assembled and Expunged in a Carceral Society

> Don't be shocked when I say I was in prison. You're still in
> prison. That's what American means, prison.
>
> Malcolm X[22]

You Only Live Once circles around the identity of Eddie Taylor. The film begins with the central question of what Joan sees in him. In a Langian pun as soon as public defender Whitney responds to the question brusquely with, 'How should I know?' Lang cuts to the comic-relief Italian fruit peddler declaring – about some one else (a cop, no less) – 'and he is a cheap crook!' But while this question ultimately bears on Joan's trust and desire for Eddie, it also opens the central enigma of who Eddie is – cheap crook or victim of circumstances in need of a break – the answer to which cannot be separated from how other people view him. Thus Lang's interrogation of viewpoints in *You Only Live Once* intersects with his long-standing interrogation of the construction and deconstruction of identity within modern systems.

No Lang film conducts a more bitter interrogation of modern systems of control: the harsh, suspicious gaze of surveillance, represented most obviously by the guards who watch Eddie in prison. But this gaze extends beyond prison walls. Society at large adopts this carceral attitude of suspicion, like the inn-keepers who throw Joan and Eddie out on their honeymoon. If *M* portrayed, as Anton Kaes demonstrates, the city mobilised in Ernst Junger's sense, Lang's attitude towards this city of total surveillance remained ambivalent, clearly fascinated by the control exerted by both cops and crooks in an attempt to find the child murderer. But in *You Only Live Once* Lang anticipates Foucault in his view of American society as mimicking and reproducing the structure of a prison in its suspicious surveillance and inhuman maintenance of disciplinary protocols.

While circumstances falsely identify both Joe Wilson and Eddie Taylor as guilty of crimes they did not commit, their reaction to these injustices produces diametrically different scenarios. Lang explicitly pinpoints this reversal in a scene where Taylor emerges from court after his conviction to be jeered at by a crowd gathered on the courtroom steps, a group not that different from the mob in *Fury*. Newsreel cameras are there as well, as the crowd throws objects at Taylor as he is led into a paddywagon. Furious, Taylor turns and yells, 'Go ahead, take a good look, you monkeys, have a good time!' In close-up he adds, 'Get a big kick out of it! It's fun to see an innocent man die, isn't it?' The words closely echo Joe Wilson's description of the audience at the newsreel in *Fury*: 'They like it. They get a big kick out of seeing a man burned to death – a big kick!' But whereas Joe took over an enunciatory position, creating, as Sanchez-Biosca says, his own scenario, Eddie Taylor seems fixed in the position of visual scrutiny. The newsreel camera frames him; it can't help fulfil his hatred at the mob's injustice with an undeniable image as the newsreel did in *Fury*. His harangue, in fact, continues uninterruptedly on the soundtrack into the next shot of a guard patrolling the outside of Taylor's cell. While Joe's locked cell ironically protected him from the mob's fury, in *You Only Live Once* the crowd's anger segues seamlessly into the guard's armed surveillance.

Just before Taylor exits the courtroom, Lang presents his guilty verdict in a widely commented on single-shot sequence which displays Lang's continued visual inventiveness in his Hollywood films and one of his most bitter images of the labile nature of identity and truth.[23] The sequence begins as a trenchant example of Lang's ironically unreliable narration, a misleading rhyme with the last shot of the previous sequence. Cops invading Joan and Eddie's new house ordered him to put his hands up. Joan grabs his arm and declares, 'Don't shoot, he's giving himself up.' Earlier Eddie had told her that if he gives himself up it means the chair, but Joan countered that since he is innocent he needn't run away. The cut to the next scene therefore seems to follow Joan's logic: from Eddie's surrender we cut to a close-up of a newspaper front-page, its headline proclaiming: TAYLOR FREED IN MASSACRE! with a photograph of Eddie beaming in relief.

But as the camera edges to the left it reveals its limited perspective and calls into question Joan's clarity of vision. We see another front-page tacked to the wall next to the previous one. It proclaims: TAYLOR JURY DEADLOCKED and shows an image of Taylor with a neutral expression. Then the camera pulls back, revealing a newspaper compositing room in long shot, with three different front-pages on the wall, the third headline announcing: TAYLOR GUILTY with the largest photograph of the three; Taylor glowering hostilely. The phone rings with the jury's verdict; the editor listens silently, then points to the TAYLOR GUILTY front-page, announcing the outcome. The camera moves in on this front-page until it fills the frame, reversing the

message of the opening of the shot. The shot does more than offer a lesson in rel-
ativity and Lang's playful style, making us aware of our ability to leap to (the
wrong) conclusions. Before our eyes the shot literally processes Eddie Taylor's
identity, holding in readiness not simply three different fates, but three mutually
opposed images of Taylor: the relieved innocent, the scowling murderer and the
nondescript average guy. We are not asked to choose between these; instead Lang
demonstrates to us the modern process of construction or deconstruction of a
man's identity. Taylor does not choose either his fate or his appearance. That is
done by people who don't even know him, getting his fate over the telephone, then
releasing it over the wires.

Viewed from this perspective, Eddie's hat, conveniently monogrammed, acts not
so much as a red herring, but as another of Lang's detachable objects that can stand
in for characters. But like Siegfried's embroidered X or Beckert's M, the fatal letters
ET do not define an identity as much as mark it as ready for destruction. As we
have seen in Lang again and again the signs and markers of identity are assembled
in order to be expunged, as the last stage of fixing an identity within the archive
system before cancelling it out. Taylor's identity is composed in the newspaper
office as an appropriate image which will naturalise, and therefore justify to the
readers, Taylor's fate. The impersonality of the telephone call and of the editor's
voiceless gesture shows the working of the Destiny-machine, not so much determining the verdict (as a classical view of Destiny might have it) but rather
embodying the impersonal processes that assemble his identity out of a range of
possibilities.

In contrast to the newspapers in *Fury*, which (like the newsreel) seemed to offer
the truth in opposition to the rumour mill of Strand, the newspaper (and the newsreel) in *You Only Live Once* play a role within an impersonal system that processes
information regardless of people's fate. Taylor had already been fingered as the
murderer in the first newspaper report of the bank robbery. Instead of his face, the

paper bore a large photo of Taylor's hat, an arrow pointing to the tell-tale initials. Above this photo the headline asked a variation of the archetypal Langian question, 'Whose hat is this?' (and in smaller letters: 'answer the question and you find the murderer'). The premise certainly is questionable, but the visual presentation shows the media appropriating another detachable sign of identity, which it asserts will solve a crime. Modern institutions, whether the media or the prison, manufacture and disseminate an individual's identity, able to define and fix guilt and punishment, performing as Destiny-machines.

The first shot focusing on Eddie's hat reveals his precarious hold on his identity in a world of economic uncertainty.[24] Lang cuts from Taylor learning he has been fired to a close-up of this hat, its initials again clearly displayed, resting on a table next to his bed in his boarding house, a torn-out section of the want ads lying next to it. The camera moves past some glasses, then framed photographs of Joan to Monk Mendall lying and smoking on Eddie's bed. The shot certainly sets up how easy it would be for Monk or someone else to appropriate the hat. It also indicates how vulnerable Eddie's identity is to dispersal. Here, in this impersonal boarding house room, he has strewn his stuff about in an attempt to claim the space, make it a temporary home. Later we learn he also has an automatic under his pillow.

Although Eddie's drama first involves getting out of prison with Joan's help, then breaking out of prison without her help, the particularly deadly nature of the Destiny-machine in this film derives from the resemblance of the outside world to prison. As we have seen, the people who run a honeymoon hotel are willing to act as amateur detectives and jail guards. The scene with the boss of the trucking outfit recalls Eddie's earlier scene with the warden, both men regarding their conversations with Taylor as interruptions of other pleasures (the warden munching on a box of candies, the boss talking to his wife on the phone). The reason for Taylor's firing, his deviating from his schedule in order to meet his wife and look at their new home, becomes a grim demonstration of the primacy of schedules over human lives once he returns to prison. Taylor's attempt at suicide threatens to disrupt the schedule of his execution. In the warden's office we see a concerned executioner asking if it will be necessary to postpone the execution. The warden asks the time, as he reaches for another candy, then calls the doctor, who reassures him Taylor should be strong enough, and that they 'will watch him until the time comes'. The warden declares the 'execution will go on as scheduled, 11 p.m.' Just before Taylor's attempted break-out with the prison doctor as hostage, the warden's wife punctuates her metaphysical discussion with Father Dolan by looking at her watch and saying to her husband, 'Daddy, Dr. Hill is late again!' He mumbles through his martini with unconscious irony, 'He'll be along in a minute.'

It is clear that maintaining schedules causes more concern to prison functionaries than the ending of Taylor's life. But Lang's satire grows grim as the resources of the prison hospital are mobilised to save Eddie's life, so that he can then be executed. The preparations for a life-saving transfusion are presented in a brief but strangely sinister montage of medical apparatuses being sanitised, an image of the absurdist Destiny-machine which maintains Taylor's life, precisely so the state can claim a monopoly on the right to end it. Earlier, as Taylor's last meal was prepared, the cook had said to Muggsy (the comic-relief 'screwy' prisoner who will take the meal to Eddie), 'Fine world. First they kill a chicken. Taylor eats the chicken. Then they kill Taylor.' Muggsy gives a double-take, then delivers the beautiful, blackly comic, punch line: 'If I wasn't crazy, I'd worry about that.' It is not simply the inhumanity of the carceral society that Lang captures, but its systematic, paradoxical illogic. The ability to nourish Taylor, to save his life becomes part of his scheduled execution. Even his act of suicide is taken away from him so that the state can demonstrate its control over, and definition of, his life and death, his identity. The state is willing to save a life or to execute, to pardon or to condemn within a brief turnabout, providing it maintains its schedule, and its monopoly on meaning and definition.

The execution schedule, Eddie's death timed for 11 p.m., allows Lang's primary image of the Destiny-machine, the clock, to take over as a metonym for the whole deadly system. Lang begins the scene after Taylor's transfusion with a huge close-up of a clock marking 7:30, its soft ticking dominating an otherwise silent sound-track. Lang reveals Joan sitting on a piano bench, her eyes riveted on the clock. Her sister Bonnie (playing solitaire and covering up the ace of spades, the death card) tells her that there's still time for a last-minute pardon, but Joan shakes her head and voices the ultimate message of the clock as part of the Destiny-machine: 'no, too late now'. Lang returns to the clock at two minutes to eleven, cutting directly from Eddie's escape to an even larger close-up of the clock face. We cut to a close-up of Joan's intently staring face, tears dropping from her eyes. The room is filled with silence, except for the ticking of the clock. Joan rises, placing her hand on the piano keyboard behind her which resounds with an eerie chord. She goes into the kitchenette and with one hand turns on the tap in the sink while the other, in a peculiarly Langian mechanical gesture, opens the door of a cupboard simultaneously. In close-up she empties a powder into a glass of water, preparing the poison she plans to take in order to die at the same moment as her lover. The references earlier to frogs and Romeo and Juliet define this suicide as a romantic act, an act of self-definition, the self-destruction that the state won't allow, even as it makes it inevitable.

We cut from a close-up of the powder pouring into the glass to a typical Langian visual rhyme between sequences: a waitress in a diner fills a cup from the tap of a large coffee urn. Eddie enters the diner and makes his way to a phone booth. This cut away delays the outcome of Joan's suicide in the traditional suspenseful manner of parallel editing, interrupting an action as it unfolds. Lang cuts back to Joan as she lifts her glass. We cut to a new angle of the kitchen, a long shot from behind Joan, showing her face reflected in the glass of a cabinet as she brings the poison to her lips. The shots in this tiny kitchen have echoed with ponderous silence, with only the monotonous noise of the water pouring from the tap. From off screen, suddenly, we hear the ringing of a phone and Bonnie's voice as she answers, 'Hello? Eddie?' Joan repeats the name in an incredulous whisper, then releases the glass which shatters with a crash. She rushes to the phone, sobbing and laughing. We see Eddie in close-up in the diner phone booth saying, 'I'm out.' He gives her the number of a box car, X793621, in which he will be hiding and pleads, 'Come to me.'

Something has happened here that seems to jam the Destiny-machine, if not absolutely, at least temporarily. All the emblems of the system were assembled: the clock, the telephone, even the number Eddie must give as a marker of where he will be. But a fundamental re-routing has occurred which makes this not only a unique film for classical Hollywood, but within Lang's *œuvre* as well. While the Destiny-machine has only been temporarily thwarted, not dismantled, what remains of the film and of Eddie and Joan's life will unwind under the sign of desire as much as the network of the Destiny-machine. The Last Romantic Couple seize a chance to follow a route determined by their desire, as much as an ill-fated attempt to evade the law.

The Re-educating of Joan Graham Taylor

It was my first, my only dream
               Novalis, *Hymns to the Night*[25]

Like the blessed shades by Lethe, my soul now lives with yours
in heavenly freedom and Fate has no more power over our
love.
               Hölderlin, *Hyperion*[26]

I have said that the greatest loss to Lang's film-making caused by his leaving Germany was that of Thea von Harbou, not only her unique contribution but the deep involvement in the scriptwriting process that she offered Lang which he would never recapture. Nonetheless, in Hollywood Lang benefited from many talented collaborations beginning with Joseph Mankiewicz on *Fury* and including Norman Krasna, Dudley Nichols, Nunnally Johnson, Albert Maltz, Ring Lardner Jr., Daniel Taradash, Alfred Hayes, Sidney Boehm, and even Bertolt Brecht! Lang's scriptwriters on *You Only Live Once*, Gene Towne and Graham Baker, gave Lang one of his finest scripts and certainly deserve credit for many aspects of the film I have discussed. Baker and Towne may also be partly responsible for the fact that, other than *Spies*, this is the first Lang film in which a romantic couple not only dominates the action, but expresses romantic desire in a not only convincing but ultimately compelling manner. The extraordinary romanticism of Towne and Baker's script for Frank Borzage's *History is Made at Night*, produced by Walter Wanger immediately following *You Only Live Once*, certainly owes a great deal to it being realised by Borzage, perhaps the greatest director of romantic love stories in American (or international?) cinema. But it is also striking that both *You Only Live Once* and *History is Made at Night* come from the same screenwriters.[27]

You Only Live Once stands as one of Lang's finest films because it was fully able to integrate the passionate love story required by Hollywood formula into a truly Langian scenario without any sense of either compromise or artificial combination (such as we find in the final kiss in *Fury*). Towne and Baker deserve credit for making this couple complexly and believably passionate, as do Sidney's and Fonda's performances. But Lang's contribution was also definitive. As Matthew Bernstein points out in his masterful chronicle of Walter Wanger's career as a producer, *You Only Live Once* recalls another Wanger production, also from a Towne and Baker script, released shortly before *You Only Live Once*, while Wanger was at Paramount. *Mary Burns, Fugitive* also starred Sylvia Sidney as a woman who becomes a criminal through her love affair with a crook.[28]

Although a fully enjoyable film benefitting from strong direction by William K. Howard, nice performances by Sidney and Melvin Douglas and Towne and Baker's witty and intelligent script, *Mary Burns, Fugitive* remains a conformist work. Sidney is attracted to the gangster, but unaware of his crimes. Having to go to jail as his accomplice, she is as much his victim as society's. The film creates a positive couple in Sidney and Douglas (a temporarily blinded explorer that Burns gets a job reading to), expunging the previous bad pairing with the gangster. In the climax Sidney spurns her former gangster lover and actually helps Douglas kill him. Although showing a social sympathy to victims of circumstances like Mary, the film maintains a strong dichotomy between good people and criminals, and Mary moves resolutely from the wrong side of the law to the right one. Her romantic love for Douglas cinches her reintegration into society.

You Only Live Once moves in the exactly opposite direction. Joan Graham begins as a law-abiding (she works in a lawyer's office in the Hall Of Justice), middle-class girl who believes in the dominant ideology of society. Criminals can be reformed by knowing that people trust them. Careful budgeting can make a good life. Eddie should give himself up if he is innocent, since an innocent man has nothing to fear from the law. Each of these illusions becomes systematically and irrevocably shattered in the course of the film. Likewise, as Bernstein perceptively states:

> In *Mary Burns, Fugitive* the faith of one character, the explorer, is enough to save the heroine; in Lang's film, Joan's faith in Eddie and even that of the district attorney [actually Public Defender] (Barton MacLaine) and Father Dolan (William Gargan), is powerless to halt Eddie's prosecution and death.[29]

To any unprejudiced observer, *You Only Live Once* exemplifies the ways Lang could benefit from working new collaborators or even new formulas in his Hollywood films, but also maintain his independence and transform the material he was given, creating works that were far from anonymous or second-rate.

If Lang's German films are not filled with strongly felt romantic couples, strong women characters appear throughout Lang's career and many films are structured in whole or part through a focus on a female character. *Fury* would undoubtedly be less powerful if Lang had not decided to build up Katherine's part and her perspective on the action.[30] Although one thread of *You Only Live Once* is certainly the story of Eddie as a three-time loser, probably the most important arc in terms of character transformation is Joan's. To realise the complexity of Joan's character (and opportunity for character development supplied by the Hollywood emphasis on the 'woman's angle' – the importance of women characters for an audience that studio heads believed was dominated by women viewers), one need only contrast her with the one-dimensional Lilli in *The Testament of Dr. Mabuse*, whose desire to give hope to and reform Kent is similar to Joan's compassion for Eddie, but who remains inert, unaffected by the events of the film (other than getting a very bad cold after her extended swim in Mabuse's secret office).

Like Katherine and Joe in the opening of *Fury*, Joan believes the world holds a place for her and her lover. While the opening of *You Only Live Once* inverts *Fury's* opening separation of the couple by presenting a reunion, the world soon reveals itself to Joan as a place hostile to lovers. Nonetheless, Joan preaches patience to Eddie (as Katherine did to Joe); she has already waited three long years to be reunited with her lover. Our introduction to her as the model competent secretary as she signs for a package (possibly part of her honeymoon trousseau) while dealing with an irate citizen, shows her able to balance work and personal life with grace and efficiency. She packs for the honeymoon with the same excitement that Katherine showed as she prepared for her ill-fated meeting with Joe. Told by her sister that she's 'wacky' to care for an ex-con, she responds almost giddily: 'I love being wacky!', as if she were just another daffy heiress in a 30s screwball comedy (remember Gable's response to the question whether he loves Colbert in *It Happened One Night*: 'Yes! But don't hold that against me. I'm a little screwy!').

But if Joan can view love as wacky, it does not yet represent a threat to her stable position within society. Her love for Taylor represents a concentrated effort to bring him into line with the law. Joan not only pays attention to the official details, she surrounds herself with the institutional documents which inscribe her love within the letter of the law. Their short-lived honeymoon idyll is introduced by a close-up of their names inscribed in the inn's register: 'Mr. & Mrs. Edward Taylor' and then by a shot of their marriage licence, apparently propped up in their room and surrounded by flowers to celebrate and consecrate their fully legal union. Later, after being ordered off the premises, Joan maintains her composure as she assures the inn-keepers they are leaving; her attitude indicates a reservoir of patience, based on faith in her love and in eventually finding a place for it in the world.

The next scene with Joan after the couple's expulsion from their weekend getaway paradise, shows her examining a bungalow with Eddie. The place is dark and empty, but she takes heart as Eddie shows her a receipt for a partial down-payment (another sign of legality) and on the bus home, she inscribes figures into a notebook, creating a monthly budget. The expenses she lists end with 'Gas', as Lang inserts one of his puns and Eddie pulls his truck into a gas station. As is most often the case, Lang's playfulness has a bitter edge: it is here that Eddie learns he is fired (he has screwed up his schedule by looking at the house), and the Taylor family's pursuit of domesticity once more stalls.

If *Mary Burns, Fugitive*, like so many Hollywood films, tells the story of an alienated character's redemption by learning to lead a good life and finding the right man, *You Only Live Once* repeatedly invokes Joan's patient and hard-working belief in the American values of family love and domesticity, only to torpedo it. Eddie and Joan's examination of the house leads naturally to a discussion of children as Eddie pushes the swing outside the house. Eddie's phone conversation with Joan from his boarding house contrasts the lonely male grubbiness of his room with the image of domesticity Joan presents as she prepares their new house, having already moved in. No longer dark and empty, the house seems like another ideal nest for their love – humble, but cosy. Eddie and Joan discuss a housewarming party, a leaking sink ('we'll go into that later,' Eddie says – probably another Lang joke), and he says he can't wait to see the place. Joan's delight is real and she seems assured that their happiness is beginning. Eddie, on the other end of the line, knows that, having just lost his job, these simple domestic acts of moving and papering the walls are reckless. Even if we assume Eddie did carry out the bank robbery, the concatenation of events would make it clear that he was fighting to attain a middle-class respectability, a modest American dream, and the robbery offered a drastic solution to the economic impediments that separate couples.

Eddie approaches the house in the rain, right after the bank robbery and after the shot of the swing swaying again eerily in the storm, as if pushed by phantom children who will never play here. Lang shows Eddie's point of view from the cold and rainy exterior into the brightly lit interior that Joan is making into a home for them. In contrast to Hitchcock, Lang only occasionally uses marked point of view shots, and when he does, they supply a crystallisation of key moments in the plot. The separation between outside and inside, between an inhospitable fugitive existence and an image of warmth and love, is marked by the view through a pane of glass. The bars on the window anticipate the omnipresent motif of the jail sequences to come. Like Joe and Katherine in the opening of *Fury*, Eddie is on the outside looking in, onto a vision of American domesticity, but his exclusion expresses less a promise than a dire fact. The reverse angle as he raps on the glass to get Joan's attention shows him already behind bars, surrounded by darkness, looking over his shoulder. Eddie enters his dream house through the window, turns and pulls out his revolver when the shutter bangs against the window frame. Pulling the shade down immediately, he transforms the intimate setting into a location in a gangster film.

But Joan doesn't see it, yet. As Eddie explains the situation to her and asks for the keys to her car to make a getaway, she tells him, 'You're looking at it all wrong.' She never doubts his innocence, but also never doubts the fairness of the law which will exonerate him. As Eddie agrees to play it her way, the crash of broken glass announces the invasion of domestic space by a state trooper armed with a submachine gun, aimed in through the window. Later, Joan is devastated by the outcome of the trial, but separation from Eddie hurts more than her loss of ideals. Lang continues the motif of separation by glass in the painfully alienated conversation between the couple in the prison as they speak through the small glass ports surrounded by bolted metal. Eddie makes one more assault on Joan's sense of law and order, asking her to smuggle a gun in to him. She reacts with confusion and refusal as Eddie stomps off.

This sequence of separation by glass leads directly into another Langian shop window sequence, as Joan idly glances into the display of a pawn shop. Taking her point of view, the camera drifts over this arrangement of heterogeneous junk: figurines, clocks, musical instruments. Lang cuts to the reverse angle looking at Joan through the window as a passing newsboy hawks the headline: TAYLOR TO DIE TOMORROW. Katherine looks back into the window, her eyes widening. The camera moves in on a revolver. As in other Lang films, the window display provides a scenography of desire, as Joan crosses the line for the first time, from law-abiding citizen. But she is unsure of herself and of her actions, and her plan to smuggle the gun to her lover comes to naught. It is foiled by the prison's metal-detector and also by Father Dolan's intervention, taking the gun from Katherine. In Dolan's office (complete with a towering arch in the decor, smarmy organ music on the soundtrack and a shadow of a cross cast on a chair that consecrates the prison bar motif of this sequence), Katherine surrenders the gun, accepts the inevitability of Eddie's death and clearly decides on her own suicide. Her final bowing to the institutions of society marks these acts as funeral rites. With typical sardonic juxtaposition, Lang follows this scene with the discussion of the killing of the chicken, during which Gimpy hums to himself an off-key version of the film's love theme.

A large number of Lang's films could be described as dealing with an incomplete resurrection, a return of the dead, or a return from death by someone who has trouble actually making it back to the realm of the living. But in *You Only Live Once* both Joan and Eddie re-establish their life and their love after having reached the point of death. It occurs, as so often in Lang's films, literally at the eleventh hour, as Joan stares at the clock moving toward her appointed rendezvous with her lover and with death. But as in *Der müde Tod*, the poison does not reach the maiden's lips, as the telephone call announces a new connection with life.

When Joan leaves to meet Eddie this time, she makes no playful quips about being 'wacky' and no hesitation about violating the law. Joan finds Eddie in the railway yard hiding in an empty car among abandoned crates. She gathers him up in his wounded condition (shot as he was 'escaping' jail) showing both a motherly care and a wifely physical intimacy. The railway yard presents one of those liminal areas of modernity that Lang captures so well, maintaining a hard-edged geometry even through the dark and the fog, as the lovers pick their way through it. Joan, now assured and conscious, moves to the other side, as she pulls up in front of a drugstore display window. There is no hesitation as she looks through the glass. She hurls a brick through to get the medicine she needs to treat Eddie's wounds. Lang cuts to Taylor nearly passed out in the car as he hears the sound of breaking glass. Previously glass shattered as the police stuck their submachine gun into Eddie and Joan's living room. Now it indicates they have broken out, both of them, from both the ideal of American domesticity and the rule of corrupt law. Nowhere else in Lang do characters so directly defy the Destiny-machine, taking what they need, refusing the commodity culture's lessons of patience and feckless fantasy. Joan and Eddie are on the run.

But they haven't escaped. The Destiny-machine hungers for them. Guilt haunts them both, the ghostly image of Father Dolan pursuing Eddie, and Joan tortured by the fact that she ever let Eddie be taken from her. The law interrogates their friends. Average Americans continue to view their flight as a shameless indulgence in lawless luxury. After they rob a gas station for fuel, the attendants empty the till and report it to the police as one more crime of 'Eddie Taylor and his mob'. The visual motif of bars so dominant in the prison scenes continues in the window which frames the gas station attendants, or the barred shadows that surround Joan's sister, Bonnie and her former boss, Steven, as they ponder the fugitives' fate. The entrapping frame of the prison has engulfed the whole society. But Eddie and Joan are in flight, moving, fleeing that entrapment. 'Maybe they will get you,' Joan declares to Eddie, 'but if they do they'll get me too. But they'll have to find us first.' This couple now must move through the landscape leaving as little trace as possible, covering their tracks. Old men chuckle over the fact that the couple must be millionaires with all their loot, 'hiding in a swell place having a good time'.

Lang cuts directly from the old guys' fantasy to a shot of the couple's car fighting its way through a torrential storm. Their lack of comfort and their danger confronts us in every brief scene we see of their life on the road. But something else surfaces in these scenes as well. Eddie, apparently fully recovered, takes good care of Joan. We know from Bonnie's comments that Joan is an expectant mother. The couple's intimacy and care for each other grows under these adverse conditions. In one scene,

apparently after they have just escaped from a shoot-out with the cops, Lang shows their back seat filled with groceries riddled with bullets. This almost surrealist juxtaposition of imagery of nourishment and violence, loaves of bread and cans of milk pierced by gaping bullet holes, provides the most simultaneously touching and tough image of their precarious life, as Eddie encourages Joan to drink some ('you need it' – presumably for the baby) and she sucks milk through the bullet hole.

All the spaces in which Eddie and Joan dwell share this combination of the abject and marginal with the intimate; most obviously their car with its shot-out window, heaped with blankets for warmth and food for survival. The forest shack where they rest while Joan gives birth is designed as a pastoral idyll, as if they were returning to a state of nature (as Godard would point out, becoming *Paul and Virginia*). In place of the combination of physical passion and bridled anger that characterised their scenes in the earlier parts of the film, Eddie and Joan take on a calm grace and confidence with each other, a tone of mutual trust. The rest of the world has dropped away from them; they live like the only remaining people in the world. When Joan arrives at a pre-arranged meeting with Bonnie and Stephen to give up her baby, she seems confused when they ask the baby's name. 'Why, we just call him "Baby"', she answers. She has fully accepted the fact that her relation with her child will never interact with society at large. There is only one Baby, as there is only one Eddie or Joan. This child for a brief time exists outside the entrapping grid of identity that Lang portrays throughout the film, which begins with the act of naming.

Joan does not even seriously listen to Bonnie and Steven's attempt to persuade her to leave Eddie and let them smuggle her to Cuba. She leaves the two of them, her previously embittered sister and Steven who has loved Joan silently from the beginning, in the motel cabin with her baby, a ready-made family. One of the side products of Eddie and Joan's passion, Lang suggests, has been bringing this unlikely couple together. Eddie later says he watched them through the window, recalling his point of view shot of Joan in their home after the bank robbery: 'You and the baby looked so warm and safe, inside a house. We were inside a house once – for a few minutes.' It is not simply the retroactive force of Fonda's performance as Tom Joad in Ford's *The Grapes of Wrath* a few years later that makes this story of a homeless couple resonant with Depression era images of Oakies and other displaced and migratory people. Lang and his collaborators clearly intended the association, counting on a recognition and sympathy for Joan and Eddie's exile from the American dream. 'Lots of people in love get to live inside a house,' Eddie continues. As the couple try to make it across the border to Canada, Lang invokes not only America's migrant population of the 30s, but the plight of the refugee, with the irony that this couple is trying to escape from the land of liberty.

Joan's final moment at the motel after leaving her baby, stages one of Lang's unguarded moments, a trivial action that has dire consequences. She pauses to buy cigarettes from a vending machine in front of the motel office. Lang wished to add another one of his sardonic puns here, and make her buy Lucky Strikes at this ill-fated moment, but in this era before product placement, this was forbidden. The machine being situated in front of the office window and the inn-keeper apparently given to sleeping right next to his safe, what occurs is more than a linden tree leaf coincidence. The inn-keeper wakes up and catches a glimpse of Joan framed by the window. Putting on his glasses he gives her a second look, then compares what he sees with the reward poster of Joan and Eddie plastered on the office wall. The situation recalls the first eviction of Joan and Eddie, being turned out of the Valley Inn on their wedding night. But now it is Joan's picture that an inn-keeper can recall, she too has fallen under the surveillance of suspicious, average American citizens. Further, as the next close-up announces, she has acquired a cash exchange value: a reward of $10,000. The inn-keeper makes a phone call.

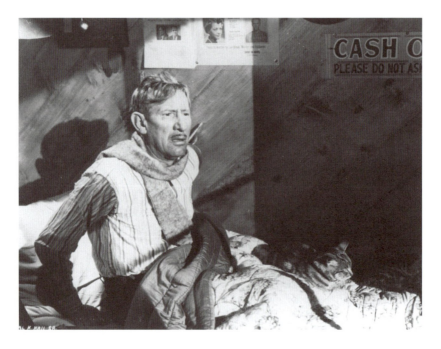

The sequence that follows of Joan and Eddie together in a getaway car trying to make it to the border before daylight, reflects their intimate knowledge, love and trust of each other. 'I never knew two people could be so close', Joan tells Eddie. But their closeness come partly from a surrounding hostile world, and their looks of calm trust for each other alternate with rapid anxious scans of the surrounding territory, as when Joan sees a light between some trees, but Eddie assures her it's only the morning star. When Eddie bitterly recalls their exclusion from their one-time home, she responds with one of Towne and Baker's most expressive bits of dialogue, one I find superior to Ma Joad's rhetorical closing monologue in *The Grapes of Wrath*: 'Maybe anywhere's our home. In the car, out there on that cold star, anywhere's our home.'

But if intimacy rules this sequence, Lang sets the stage for a fatal outcome. The couple share a cigarette, Joan unwrapping the package, recalling the consequences of the purchase. Lang cuts to a view of the road as the car barrels down it, motor humming on the soundtrack, as if even this car/haven can still intermesh with the Destiny-machine grinding now to a final encounter. Further, Eddie hums to himself the film's love theme, just as he did before he learned he was fired, and as Muggsy did as he picked up Taylor's last meal in prison. The depth of desire these two have attained cannot stop the working of the law in its most brutal form. State troopers burst out onto the road firing submachine guns into the Taylors' car.

There is something strangely dream-like about the last minutes of *You Only Live Once*, from the awkward overlap-dissolve as the car apparently turns around at the ambush to Eddie and Joan's mutual denials that they have been hit as they tumble out of their wrecked car. Joan collapses and Eddie carries her in a gesture which, Bernstein points out, Lang added to the script as an echo of his carrying her in his arms to their honeymoon suite.[31] Like the locale for the baby's birth, the forest here is Hollywood studio simulacrum, its idyllic nature undercut by the state troopers

who pursue them. The most powerful image of fatality in all of Lang may be the
point of view shot through the viewfinder of the trooper's rifle, of Eddie Taylor's
back as he carries Joan. The culmination of all the frames within frames which have
entrapped Eddie or Joan throughout the film, it literally embodies the look that
kills, the aggressive eye of the law, whose surveillance is now defined as the hunter's
bead on his prey. As the cross-hairs close in on the couple, Lang's diagrammatic
view takes on its most aggressive mode. That we share the point of view of the state's
hired killer at this most excruciating moment underscores how different Lang's use
of the point of view shot is to Hitchcock's. Far from identifying with the killer, we
wish to disavow our association with this murderous gaze even as Lang forces us
into visual complicity with it.

The following shots of Eddie and Joan take place within this gaze of death. Joan
caresses Eddie, then seems to collapse. But as he calls her name, she revives and tells
him, 'I'd do it again, all over again, glad …' then dies in his arms. Eddie then receives
a bullet in the back and, staggering, manages to give Joan a film-closing kiss. The
violence of this ending demands our attention. Its brutality is uniquely American,
inspired, as the film was, by the real-life deaths of Bonnie and Clyde. This violent
ending was also demanded by the Production Code which would not have permitted the criminals to reach their refuge across the border. But Lang and his collaborators understood how to make this moralistic demand stick in the craw of
American audiences, generating deeper questions about American justice than a
simple evasion of punishment would have. Its nastiness can be underscored by contrasting it to the ending of Jean Renoir's film made in France the same year, *La
Grande Illusion*, where German soldiers refuse to fire on the escaping French prisoners as they make it across the border. Renoir's proclamation of Popular Front
internationalism contrasts sharply with Lang's portrayal of the forces of law and
order of his adopted country, the bastion of freedom. Finally, Lang delivers the closing kiss he squirmed at and handled so awkwardly in *Fury*. Instead of a plot-resolv-
ing, 'all's right with the world', clinch of a romantic couple, this kiss is given by a
dying man to the corpse of his wife.

Of course, for contemporary audiences at least, much of this bitterness is undercut by the final seconds of the film. As Fonda looks up in close-up after being shot, the
soundtrack swells with a soprano choir, the worst moment in Alfred Newman's frequently problematic soundtrack. But if Lang can be relieved of responsibility for the
musical accompaniment (although the score was an area that Lang tried to assert
control over, as Miklos Rosza's account of working with Lang on *The Secret Beyond
the Door* shows)[32] the voice-over that follows is certainly an essential, if problematic
part of the film. Father Dolan's voice calls out, 'Eddie, Eddie. You're free, Eddie! The
gates are open!' Taylor's eyes align with the camera lens for his last moment in the
film, as if the camera were the source of the calling voice. We see (his point of view?)
a long shot of the forest set, light filtering in beams through the trees. The film ends.

What are we to make of this? I always squirm as student audiences on the verge of
being really moved by both the bitterness and tenderness of this ending suddenly
find an easy way out by guffawing at this last-minute, manufactured reassurance.
But if the success of this voice-over remains in doubt, its function and purpose need
probing rather than simple dismissal. George Wilson, trying to redeem the ending,
does what most of us would do, interprets it as ironic, a continuation of the film's
often sardonic bitterness. For him, 'Eddie's dying vision may be only the ultimate
misperception that culminates the vast chain of misperceptions which has led him
to his death'. Thus this 'vision' would be 'the last pitiful illusion of a dying man'.[33]

This is a bold reading which gains authority from its relation to *You Only Live Once*'s theme of blindness which Wilson was the first to isolate, and Brecht would have been proud of it. I would by no means declare it an inadequate reading of the film. But there is no question Lang disavows it.

Asked by Bogdanovich if the statement 'gates are open' was 'meant as an ironic note or as the truth', Lang was unequivocal: 'As the truth … it was not ironic'.[34] Lang invokes his own Catholic upbringing and the hold it had on him to justify it. While relying on intentions is a critical fallacy, I believe it is also important to take the author's statement seriously, especially if it makes us uncomfortable. What would it mean to see 'the gates are open' as the 'truth'? First of all, we need to investigate Wilson's description of this scene as a 'vision' even if he finds it to be an illusion. Does this sequence relate to Lang's visionary scenes? Wilson apparently sees the shot of the forest as a vision of heaven, emphasises that it acts as Eddie's point of view and that 'the light in the forest miraculously brightens'.[35] I am not sure that we are seeing Eddie's point of view, although the editing from his close-up off screen look makes that a possible assumption. But the forest does *not* brighten. The only lighting change, before the fadeout plunges the shot into total obscurity, is actually an increase in shadow. The visual presentation is amazingly ambiguous. As we know Lang was capable of giving truly explicit subjective visions, but does he offer one here?

Sound hallucinations, as a voice-over, echoing previous dialogue occur in the penultimate scene of *Fury*, as Joe hears Katherine's voice. But as in that visionary sequence, and in Lang's silent films, we realise that Lang does not always make a strong opposition between an individual's hallucination and a vision. A vision for Lang (Mabuse's images of his victims, Kriemhild's dream of the birds, Freder's perception of Moloch, Joe's view of a world emptied out of human companionship) can be an illusion which tells the truth about a situation. In contrast there can be hallucinations which simply augur madness (e.g. Baum's encounter with the phantom Mabuse). Can we follow Lang and see Eddie as receiving a vision of the truth at the end of *You Only Live Once*? What would that truth be? The most obvious allegorical reading would be that Eddie and Joan are redeemed. The Production Code may demand their death, but heaven will receive them. The gates that open now are the gates of heaven. Therefore this vision would be of the sort of rebirth Father Dolan said death could be, allowing us to remember our glorious birthright. Again this is a possible reading, less fashionable than Wilson's, but also not inadequate.

But if we probe it, what sort of recompense does it offer? The gate Dolan originally referred to was the gate of the prison. Operating metaphorically here it must mean either the gate of heaven, or the gate of death, or one as the entry to the other (which is Dolan's logic). There is no denying the scene is Eddie and Joan's entrance into death. What strikes me is the deliberate inadequacy of the image of the landscape as an image of heaven. Consider the ending of *Der müde Tod* (the film to which Lang explicitly compared *You Only Live Once*) and its brief glimpse of heaven or *Liliom*, in which heaven is a parody of earth. Even if Lang indicates some belief in transcendence in his plots, his visual style cannot go there.

Two contexts for this ambiguous finale occur to me: one deals with the visual image and its predecessors in high art and the other with the aural phrase, 'You're free', and American gangster films coming after *You Only Live Once*. I will take the latter up first. Dolan's voice-over doesn't promise Eddie heaven, but *freedom*. Within the gangster film cycle during the 30s and 40s, a transformation took place. The strongest requirement of the genre – that the gangster die in the last scene – moves from the astonished reaction of the overreacher gangster discovering his own mortality ('Mother of God, is this the end of Rico?' in *Little Caesar*), or a sardonic joke (the line about gangsters having the best funerals, after Tracy is gunned down in *Quick Millions*), to a more sentimental reaction if the gangster has been rendered more sympathetic (e.g. Cagney's death in *The Roaring Twenties*, followed by the pitying comment, 'He used to be a big shot'). *You Only Live Once* plays a role in this transformation toward more sympathetic gangsters, one continued in Raoul Walsh's *High Sierra* when Ida Lupino greets Bogart's death with the statement, 'Free, free!' In the trajectory of the gangster series, death itself became a deliverance, not necessarily into transcendence, but simply away from the trouble of the world. Wim Wenders may have been thinking of both *High Sierra* and *You Only Live Once* when one of the characters in *Kings of the Road* encounters a roadside crucifix with the figure of Jesus sprung from its cross and says, parodying the voice of an American gangster, 'Double-crossed for the very last time, but now I'm finally free.' In this genre of revolt and retribution, the American cinema developed a fatalistic and materialist deliverance for its tragic hero which the end scene of *You Only Live Once* introduces and exemplifies – except for that damned choir.

But if the words spoken are open to multiple interpretations, what about the final visual image, the forest landscape? The vagueness of this image again strikes me. Is it an image of heaven? What, other than the beam of light (which could recall the searchlights in the prison break), cues us to this interpretation? Is it perhaps, more precisely, the promised land, that is, Canada across the border which seemed to offer a new life to refugees, Joan and Eddie? If so, a more ironic reading seems called for, since Joan and Eddie are denied entrance, rather than passing through the gate. What is undeniable is that the film ends with an idealised landscape, bereft of living human presence. In this regard it might exemplify the inherent virtue of nature before the advent of man and civilisation, a message coherent with Father Dolan's claim that man is born noble but becomes corrupted by society. Perhaps most reflective of Lang's style, however, would be the tradition of landscapes begun in the Renaissance inscribed with the ambiguous Latin passage: *Et in Arcadia ego*. As art historian Erwin Panofsky has shown, the 'I' who was also in Arcadia, the pastoral land of simplicity and happiness in nature, was Death.[36] If, as Lang claims, *You Only Live Once* recalls *Der müde Tod*, this shot might not so much correspond to the brief glimpse of paradise in that film, as to the recurrent presence of Death, the image appearing after the lovers find death instead of deliverance in each story. As that film first cued us, and as Lang has reinforced in nearly every film, one of the primary signifiers of Death in his cinema is emptiness, an empty room, or an empty landscape. Is this lushly illuminated forest more redemptive than the empty suburban lot of *M*?

Does it matter? George Wilson asks us to keep in mind the wonderful title of this film.[37] Does it caution us, as he feels, against expecting fulfilment in some other life? If we return the phrase to the American vernacular expression it refers to (the sort of tag line the recent immigrant Lang found fascinating), the phrase generally comes as a plea to live life to the fullest, to be adventurous. The intensity of desire and fulfilment shines out of the last scene of *You Only Live Once*, as both characters, we feel, 'would have done it all over again – glad'. More than any other Langian couple, Eddie and Joan reach a primal innocence, following their passion beyond the realm of the law. Yet the law is not evaded. *Et in Arcadia ego*.

10

You and Me

A 'Cinematic Hash':
Experimental Cross-breeding among the Hollywood Genres

> Enter, the bear.
> > stage direction Lang claimed to have found in *Othello*[1]

'Every time she says, "I love you", she breaks the law.' This was one of the publicity tag lines by which Paramount (Lang's third studio in three pictures) advertised *You and Me*, teasing the audience with the plot line of Helen (Sylvia Sidney, one more time) who has illegally married Joe Dennis (George Raft), concealing the fact she is on parole (and thus forbidden by law to marry). The poster for the film added this lurid copy:

> The law said she was free … free to worry, free to starve, free to work if she could find a job … **but not free to marry the man she loves!** All the heartache of 50,000 unfortunate girls in the United States packed into the anguished heart-cry of this girl on parole.[2]

The conflict between love and society's restrictions which made *You Only Live Once* such a powerful and bitter film also supplies the basic plot line of most Hollywood genre films – good, bad or indifferent. A primordial tension between law and desire structures both Hollywood film genres and capitalist consumer society, allowing these films to serve as either the ideology or the critique of American culture. (The dilemma of mass culture, as Adorno demonstrates, is that ideology and critique begin to resemble each other.)[3] Hollywood comedies tend to deflate these tensions as simply part of the life lovers learn to live with each other, while melodramas tend to let them inflate to the point they do serious damage. Both genres reveal fault lines within American society and both propose reconciliations – with varying degrees of conformity.

With *You and Me*, Lang jumped into the ambiguities of American film genres feet first and produced a film which he himself pronounced the worst film he ever made, 'it was – deservedly – my first real flop'.[4] Lang seems bent on taking genre conventions to their limits by combining extremely diverse material and contrasting genres – a gangster film *cum* musical *cum* romantic comedy *cum* Brechtian *Lehrstück*. Although *You and Me* was reviled by critics ('the weirdest cinematic hash I ever saw' wrote Russell Malone in the *New Yorker*)[5] and ignored by audiences, I would claim it to be Lang's most experimental Hollywood film and one of his most fascinating, a film in need of rediscovery and re-evaluation. That this film met with general incomprehension and even hostility is not surprising. Lang attempted to forge a new synthesis here between the popular and experimental, stretching Hollywood formulas as far, or farther, than they could reach. Even reviewers who slammed the movie, like Frank S. Nugent in the *New York Times*, admitted, and commended, Lang's ambition 'to break with the Hollywood formula', but felt, 'no director can serve two styles at once'.[6] It was exactly the discontinuous and, to my mind, dialectical, nature of this film which made it so difficult to accept.

A new contract with Paramount allowed Lang to produce his own films and establish a greater degree of freedom than he had previously enjoyed, and he grabbed hold of the opportunity.[7] Lang decided to create a synthesis between his European and (nascent) Hollywood styles, playing Hollywood genres and conventions against each other and exploring modes of stylisation that *M* and *Liliom* had opened up. I have little doubt that Lang's repeatedly stated dislike for the film came from the harsh critical reception it received (even Frank S. Nugent called it 'remarkably bad').[8] Favourable critical notices had supplied the primary clout Lang had in Hollywood, since *You Only Live Once* had not been profitable. The re-negotiating and ultimate cancelling of a three-film deal with Paramount resulted partly from this film's failure.[9] Lang would be unemployed for a while after *You and Me* and had plenty of time to ponder the dire fate of the jobless refugee.

What brought Lang to this pass? A desire to create a Weimar-style cinema from authentic American sources, to surpass Hollywood formulas by using Hollywood genre conventions in an experimental manner. Unlike other 'artsy' films made in the 30s, Lang avoided high art references in *You and Me* and relished its popular art devices. His inspiration undoubtedly came from Brecht and Weill's *The Three Penny Opera*, whose innovative music, staging and politics could still provide hit cabaret tunes. Although Brecht (having fled the Third Reich and now living in exile in Svendborg, Denmark) had no input into this film, *You and Me* represents the high point of Brecht's influence on Lang, a more 'Brechtian' film, I would claim, than the anti-Nazi film, *Hangmen Also Die* that they directly collaborated on during Brecht's Hollywood exile. Lang told Bogdanovich that although there was no direct collaboration, 'Brecht was most responsible for *You and Me*'.[10] This influence is primarily formal, since the explicit politics of *You and Me* remain either muted or muddled. As a *Lehrstück*, *You and Me* states a more explicit political message than any other Lang film, and this stated message, 'Crime does not pay', stays mainly within the vaguely reformist conventional politics of most Hollywood message films. Lang would later mock the film's message, saying (as I remember hearing it in our brief encounter), 'Ja, because crime *does* pay!'[11] However, the message is not quite as simple as it sounds, and the non-explicit commentary of Lang's *mise-en-scène* continues his trenchant critique of American society. The analysis of consumer society and its devious game of stimulating desire and yet insisting on consumers paying the price gives this film its social bite and satire.

Brecht's influence had already been apparent in *M*, mainly in terms of direct borrowings rather than political attitude. The Beggars' Union reflects Peachum's beggars' organisation in *The Three Penny Opera* (without developing Brecht's satire on bourgeois charity), and Lorre, of course, came directly from Brecht productions of *Man is Man* and *Happy End*. But, more pervasively, *M* uses a montage style Brecht and Lang shared to create an extremely non-Aristotelian drama of life and death in the big city. There are strong similarities between Lang and Brecht's modernism: their mutual fascination with techniques of abstraction and their relative ironic distance from their characters. The blindness pervasive in *You Only Live Once* compares with what Roland Barthes describes as 'the blindness of Mother Courage', a narrative form in which neither characters nor viewers are granted total knowledge, although the form makes us aware of the characters' limited viewpoint, at the same time that it implicates us in it; neither character nor viewer are absolved from the tragedies that come from the lack of vision.[12] In many ways Brecht and Lang's views of modernity were profoundly similar. However, the differences between them were equally great (especially Lang's love of melodrama and serial film plot devices, what Brecht disdained as his love of 'surprises')[13] and would make their actual collaboration on *Hangmen Also Die* neither a great Brecht opus, nor a great Lang film.

What did Lang take from Brecht for *You and Me*, then? First, he tried to repeat his success with Lorre and take on another former Brecht collaborator, the composer Kurt Weill who had supplied music for *The Three Penny Opera*, *Happy End*, *The Rise and Fall of the City of Mahagonny*, among other collaborations. Weill had come to the United States after the rise of the Nazis and had even worked for a while on a film score for Lang's previous producer Walter Wanger.[14] His collaboration with Lang was not a happy one, at least on a personal level, although Weill expressed enthusiasm for the project, and apparently much of the music he composed for the film was not used, or was re-written by Boris Morros.[15] But, from the *Sprechstimme* of the opening number 'You Can Not Get Something for Nothing' through to many passages of the score, the modernist influence of Weill's rhythms and tonalities is evident.

The most important influence from Brecht appears in the film's non-continuity, its relative independence of elements. Brecht indicated in his theoretical writings that the elements of a play should be 'knotted together in such a way that the knots are easily noticed … set off one against another', rather than integrated into a seamless whole.[16] Brecht wrote about the opera he created with Weill, '*Mahagonny* pays conscious tribute to the senselessness of the operatic form', its combination of music, drama and spectacle.[17] Likewise, one could say that in *You and Me* Lang pays tribute to the 'senseless' techniques of radical juxtaposition found in popular entertainment. Discussing the form of *You and Me* in the interview with Bogdanovich,

Lang cites the tradition of Shakespearean theatre with its alternation of comic and tragic scenes, applauding popular Elizabethan performances which might introduce a trained bear act.[18] For Brecht such radical juxtapositions worked to liberate the theatre from the illusionism implicit in the Aristotelian theatre of the unity of space, time and action; the relative independence of elements and lack of illusionism created an alienation-effect which could shake a viewer out of aesthetic hypnosis into a state of heightened critical awareness.

Lang's understanding of – or sympathy with – Brecht's new mode of spectatorship was probably limited, and his adaptation of Brecht's techniques to filmmaking was eclectic. Lang saw Brecht's work as a model for a film in which modernist and popular techniques could mesh – very much the Brecht of *The Three Penny Opera*, where entertainment and didactic social purposes come together. Lang hoped to refashion popular cinema as Brecht had popular theatre, creating in *You and Me* a style that could straddle his own formal innovations and Hollywood genre conventions. The conventions of popular form, if not actually being sharpened into alienation-effects, would rub against each other, creating a friction within the usual Hollywood formulas. Lang used Brechtian techniques to create a style for himself within Hollywood, a cinematic practice that could be politically critical and formally experimental, while remaining both populist and popular, drawing on conventional genre elements, but rearranging their meanings. As such *You and Me* should not be seen as a failed synthesis of Brecht with Lang, but rather as a more ambitious undertaking, attempting to blend modernism and populism, a film closely related (as reviewers of the time noted) to other New Deal era experiments in theatre (The Living Newspaper or Orson Welles's Mercury Theatre), public art (the murals of Diego Riviera and others) and documentary cinema (*The Plow that Broke the Plains*, or, more directly, Willard van Dyke's *Valley Town* which included songs by Weill's protégé, Marc Blitzstein).

The plot of *You and Me* develops the themes of Lang's previous Hollywood films of social criticism. But genre conventions can exert an arbitrary magic in transforming tone, and Lang worked this illogical power to the hilt; *You and Me* works over the same disturbing social material found in the previous films in a bizarrely light and ironic manner. Lang has described the film as a fairy-tale,[19] and in many ways it most recalls the tone of *Liliom* in its irony and stylisation. But *You and Me* does not take place in the liminal zones of an earthly fairground or a heavenly bureaucracy, but in a detailed social world of power, threat and legal restrictions. The bitter social analysis evident in both earlier films does not weaken in *You and Me*. Rather, the contrasting light tone, given Lang's ability to play contradictory energies against each other, sharpens the satire. If one recalls the bitter anger of *You Only Live Once*, the very fact that Lang chose the plight of ex-cons as material for a comedy shows the dialectical relation between material and affect that Lang attempts in this film.

It would be a serious mistake to see *You and Me* as a more optimistic film than *Fury* and *You Only Live Once* simply because the conventions of comedy and the musical dominate over those of the gangster film or melodrama. Lang absolutely continues his analysis of American consumer culture and its carceral nature, pushing its implications even further in this film than in the previous ones. The fact that no-one dies or is injured and that lovers are reconciled certainly reduces the affects of bitterness and anger; but the irony of the analysis is no less cutting and Lang's conclusions seem equally bleak. In *You and Me* Lang pursues his comparison of American society to a prison further even than in *You Only Live Once*, but instead of actually setting key scenes in jail and providing nasty caricatures of average citizens, he uses gags and song numbers as tools of analysis and critique.

Like Brecht, Lang uses the musical number for its irrational discontinuity. While *You and Me* operates like a cross-roads where diverse and even opposing genres intersect, the formal discontinuity of the musical genre plays the key structuring role in Lang's experiment. In the Hollywood musical, breaking a film into musical numbers interrupts not only the flow of the diegesis but causes abrupt switches in mode of signification (i.e. from speech to singing, from walking to dancing). As such it poses the greatest challenge to the Hollywood continuity system (other perhaps than outright parody), and marshals techniques to reclaim this sort of dispersal into an affective unity. Musicals manage this, as Rick Altman shows in his magisterial treatment of the genre, by subordinating formal discontinuity to the thematically unifying Hollywood romance – because, after all, love conquers all.[20]

Radical switches from speech to song, movement to dance, sound to music become signifiers of emotional expression, lyricism, delight, passion and longing. As Altman establishes, in no other genre does the Hollywood romance so fully reveal its utopian dimensions.[21] The world is transformed, cut to the figure of desire, driven by a rhythm of arousal and fulfilment. The characters, prevented for one reason or other from speaking their love, can now sing it out loud. Spontaneously, lovers' movements mirror and respond to each other as if regulated by a common heartbeat; the world itself responds to this lovers' moment, supplying a perfect platform for its performance, as passersby join in the dance, provide music, or simply become the perfect audience. The musical number can, of course, express a range of emotions, from melancholy separation, to temporary fury, but for the most part they orbit around the possibility of union and satisfaction.

The genre manages such magical transformations through the device Altman calls the 'audio dissolve', a process of the gradual enchantment of the diegetic world by the possibility of music, as the film moves into the musical number.[22] A series of contingent details suddenly converges to create the audio dissolve, so that dance, song and music seem to erupt naturally out of the fabric of everyday life: such as the sounds of awakening Paris in the opening of *Love Me Tonight* which take on a rhythmic regularity that becomes the beat of the film's first song 'Isn't it Romantic?', or the slapping of the shoeshine rag in *The Bandwagon* that introduces the rhythm of 'With a Shine on my Shoes'. Without the naturalism of diegetic performances (e.g. when numbers are introduced as actual performances, on stage or elsewhere), the audio dissolve celebrates the number's difference from everyday life by making the world change in order to accommodate it, as if infected by rhythm or melody, given over to pure expressivity.

Lang's canny appropriation of the conventions of the musical genre partakes of its promises, but also subverts them. There are three musical numbers in the film (Lang's treatment originally called for more).[23] Two of them make limited use of melody, relying instead on a sort of *sprechstimme*, a highly rhythmic speech using tonality and pitch but rarely breaking into melody, buttressed by other rhythmic sound effects. This avoidance of melody already announces Lang's unique approach to the musical. These numbers (the opening 'You Can Not Get Something for Nothing' and 'Stick to the Mob') stay far away from traditional emotional love songs, providing instead songs of a Brechtian social commentary. The most melodic number in the film, 'The Right Guy for Me', with music by Weill, also uses abrupt changes in rhythm and tone, but, relatively speaking, it becomes the most conventional number, a 'torch' song expressing romantic longing.

'The Right Guy for Me' appears as a diegetic performance number, a song sung in a night club that Joe and Helen visit. The film begins on Joe Dennis's last day before leaving his job at Morris's department store to move to California. As in the opening of *Fury*, Helen and Joe spend this last evening together before she sees him off. The couple walk around town before his bus leaves, and stop in at a nightclub (as Joe and Katherine had gone to the movies). However, instead of an engaged couple splitting up for economic reasons, Joe and Helen have not yet declared their love for each other. After dancing, Joe and Helen discuss their pending separation and Joe's concern he will never meet a girl who will accept the fact that he is an ex-con. As Helen tries to reassure him, a torch singer emerges on the dance floor and begins the film's first number.

The torch song promises a throaty rendition of female desire, usually about the guy that got away, often of devotion to a man who's no good. Helen becomes immediately absorbed by the song, whose first lines recall the problematic of *You Only Live Once*, a woman's devotion to a man whom no-one else thinks is any good:

> They call him good for nothing
> He isn't much to see
> But I've a funny feeling
> He's the right guy for me.

These lines serve as melodic chorus to a ballad that moves in and out of *sprech-stimme*, recounting lovers who meet in a 'waterfront dive, full of wretches and vagabonds' and their subsequent parting.

Undoubtedly the casting of non-singers Sidney and Raft made a conventional love duet sung by the two unlikely. But this song expresses Helen's unspoken desire for Joe, as Lang makes clear by accompanying it with a sort of private movie, or fantasy, of Helen's. The lines of the song are illustrated by otherwise silent scenes, the waterfront dive and the entrance of the longed-for sailor, played by Raft with his sea-bag on one shoulder and a parrot perched on the other. The overt romanticism of these few shots is strongly tongue-in-cheek and bears obvious references to Paramount's most recognisable exotic visual stylist, Josef von Sternberg, with a net-draped sailors' bar right out of *Docks of New York*, and a blonde dressed in feathers like Marlene Dietrich in *Morocco*. Lang intercuts these scenes with a rapt Helen who refuses to let Joe interrupt either the song or her fantasy; her significant glances at Joe show her identification of him with the fatal 'right guy' bound to 'sail away'.

This song plays a curious role. While it performs the conventional role of a musical number of expressing longing, it is not a song of communication. We learn the depth of Helen's emotions for Joe, but *he* does not (he basically sits through the song impatiently waiting to ask Helen if she thinks a girl could ever forget he is an ex-con). The song actually blocks expression and communication between them. Our access to Helen's emotion takes place at one remove, mediated by the singer and her illustrated song and Lang allows an ironic awareness of the clichéd nature of Helen's fantasy to slip in. At this point Helen is more willing to remain within her fantasy of a tragic separation, rather than dare to speak her love for Joe. She evades his question, or at least her own involvement in it, by saying he will meet someone some day, and hurries him off to the bus station.

You Only Live Once revolved around the trope of blindness; *You and Me* centres on silences, things not said or heard, secrets that are kept. Traditionally, blindness belongs to tragedy and the ironies of mishearing and deafness tend to be allied with comedy. Although silences and secrets provide the misunderstandings that drive the plot of *You and Me*, they are more easily (that is to say, less violently) resolved than the misperceptions in the earlier film. While nothing Joe and Katherine could say at the train station in *Fury* could change the economic factors that cause their separation, all Helen needs to do is to tell Joe she loves him, or prompt him to tell her the same thing. At the bus station this sudden confession of love takes place at the last moment. Helen calls out to Joe (as he boards his bus) that, if he had been about to ask her to marry him, she would. Joe tosses his grip out the window and dashes off the bus.

Joe explains he couldn't ask Helen to marry him earlier because of his criminal record, and couldn't stay near her, loving her in silent agony. Helen, however, remains silent about the reason for her previous silence. As Joe unpacks in Helen's apartment after a midnight marriage, he flourishes his completed and defunct parole card, turning it over to display in bold letters its fourth rule: **Do Not Marry.** Anxiously, Helen conceals from Joe her own parole card, still in effect, and we realise the rule is still binding for her. But she doesn't tell Joe and, in fact, backs up her deceit with a plea to him not to mention their marriage at work, since the department store they both work at frowns on employee marriages, this last statement an additional lie to support the first one.

According to Altman, the musical genre takes the romantic couple formula of Hollywood cinema to its extreme. For Altman the musical genre is structured by the dichotomy of gender and works towards the reconciliation and establishment of couples, a narrative pattern exemplified in the song Fred Astaire sings in *Silk Stockings* 'Fated to be Mated'.[24] The very title of *You and Me*, besides expressing Lang's continued populism ('*You and Me*' are the audience, average guys and girls), inscribes this gender duality and inevitable union. As a romantic comedy, *You and Me* follows the traditional pattern: first the formation, then the separation due to misunderstanding, and then the final reconciliation, of the couple. (In the previous films of the social trilogy, separations were caused by violent social forces rather than romantic misunderstandings). But Lang uses the musical numbers against the grain of his romance plot. Besides his oblique love song in 'The Right Guy for Me', Lang uses the musical number less as an expression of the harmony between the couple than as an impersonal narrative voice, or as the expression of social groups.

Lang's original plans for the film included more numbers, tying it closer to the musical genre. Two numbers, only one of which ('Stick to the Mob') made it to the final film, imaginatively develop the 'audio dissolve', the moment when the film passes into the number and music, previously restricted to underscoring, now seems to rule the scene. This rhythmic transformation seems to be the aspect of the genre that most fascinated Lang, much more than the actual music or song itself. Lang's plans for the first marked audio dissolve in the film came with a number (apparently shot, but cut from the final release) called 'The Song of Lies', which followed directly on Helen not revealing that she, too, is on parole and forbidden to marry.

This song would have undercut the euphoria of the decision to express her desire and marry Joe, with the reminder that she has kept something back (unaware of Helen's past, Joe has told her that his prison experience made him suspicious, especially of female 'jailbirds' and that he could never stand being lied to). Contrary to the practice in most American musicals, the singer here would not be one of the characters, but an off screen voice (like the singer of the film's first number 'You Can Not Get Something for Nothing', which I will discuss later). Inspired possibly by the street singer in Brecht's *The Three Penny Opera* (and by Pabst's film version which, in the final scene, has the street singer appear only as an off screen, non-diegetic voice), Lang uses song here as commentary rather than emotional expression. Indeed, the message of the song criticises Helen's emotional impulse, therefore creating the critical distance of a Brechtian alienation-device. But Lang also wanted the song to grow out of the diegetic world of the film, and the musical's audio dissolve allowed this, even while detouring around character subjectivity. In the proposed number, Joe and Helen were given a ride (after their past-midnight marriage) in a milk wagon, and the song would 'grow out of the rhythm of the shaky wheels and be accompanied by a chorus of empty milk cans'.[25] Music arises from the world, fulfilling the promise of transformation that the musical genre holds; but instead of utopian wish-fulfilment, the song would become an impersonal voice of conscience.

This desire to use the musical genre as a means of creating a rhythmically organised soundtrack harks back to the all too brief period of experimentation in the early sound film exemplified by the films of René Clair, which used the musical as a means of creating a sound cinema not limited to the recording of dialogue (indeed *Variety* compared *You and Me* to Clair).[26] Lang's early German sound films had provided models of the imaginative use of sound, including the many sequences which play with the rhythm of sound. The most extended and successful of these is probably the sequence in *The Testament of Dr. Mabuse* in which Dr. Kramm is murdered by Baum's assassination bureau, Section 2-B. The sequence begins with the sputtering of the motor of Kramm's car. He is unaware that he is being followed by the assassin (whose humming motor noise shows that Baum demands his gang keep their carburettors clean!). Stopped at a traffic light, as the assassin gets Kramm in the sights of his pistol, he has his chauffeur begin a rhythmic honking of the car horn. This is taken up by other impatient motorists, each of whom honks with a different rhythm and tonality. Unaware of the dire consequences, Kramm joins in this fatal rhythm, smiling mischievously, and tooting his horn in a high pitched staccato which, combined with the over-all cacophony, covers the noise of the pistol shot that kills him. The traffic signal changes with a clang, motor noises take over from the beeping, but Kramm's car remains, silent and motionless. A traffic cop marches over to the car and raps sharply on the window, then gapes noiselessly at the murdered man within.

For Altman the musical genre images a utopia in which not only are desires fulfilled and couples united, but work and everyday reality give way to play and entertainment.[27] Lang's film seems designed to critique this utopia. But the ideal of a film which organises all its sounds and rhythms, both speech and sound effects, images another sort of utopia, a purely artistic one, a film unified through its form. I can't avoid relating Lang's pursuit of a rhythmic sound film to a fascinating encounter that took place around the same time between another Weimar exile and the Hollywood system: composer Arnold Schoenberg and Irving Thalberg, studio executive at MGM. Thalberg had heard a broadcast of Schoenberg's 'Transfigured Night' and wondered if Schoenberg might compose the score for his impending big-budget film, *The Good Earth*. A meeting was arranged by Salka Viertel, screenwriter and friend of Garbo, wife of Bertholt Viertel, Weimar director of film and theatre (and model for Christopher Isherwood's director in *Prater Violet*) whose household served as the social centre for German émigré culture in Southern California, including such figures as Lang, Feuchtwanger, Adorno, Brecht and Thomas Mann. Thalberg told Schoenberg that he had heard the composer's 'lovely music' and that it had seemed somewhat oriental to him and that since he was preparing a Chinese picture he had thought Schoenberg might compose the score. Schoenberg responded that he did not write 'lovely music', that music and sound in the movies generally was awful and that he would be willing to take the job if he were given complete control not only of the score, but all the sounds in the film – including the way the actors spoke. He had Mrs. Viertel attempt a few sections from *Pierrot Lunaire* to acquaint Thalberg with *Sprechstimme*, and made it clear that in the film music, voice and sound effects must all interrelate, if he were to be involved.[28]

Although it certainly would have been something to see (and hear) – and possibly more bearable than the Academy Award-winning white elephant Thalberg *did* produce – it is probably just as well Paul Muni as Wang Lung attempts no *Sprechstimme* in *The Good Earth*. This anecdote demonstrates the incommensurability of uncompromising refugee modernism and the kitsch production of Hollywood's culture industry. But I would claim that *You and Me* represents an extraordinary synthesis of Hollywood genre film-making and the experimental ambitions of German refugee culture. Both 'You Can Not Get Something for Nothing' and 'Stick to the Mob' are performed in a sort of speaking rhythm that avoids the melodic in favour of the rhetorical. And 'Stick to the Mob' brilliantly marshalls and modulates sound effects to become an organic part of the number's rhythm and tone, operating in a space midway between Schoenberg's *gesamkunstwerk* and the traditional audio dissolve.

'Stick to the Mob' was singled out by American reviewers for special derision. The reviewer for the *New York Herald Tribune* gargled, 'The scene in which he assembles a group of ex-convicts who have decided to go back to their crooked ways and has them chant responses as they remember their stir-crazy days is as phony as anything you will find on the current screen.'[29] It is certainly Lang's most deliberate experiment with the audio dissolve and with non-traditional forms of the musical number. Although Joe arrives at the end of the number, the number is begun by a group of relatively minor characters, including some we only see in this scene. Lang's development of the carceral theme from *You Only Live Once* takes a comic turn here that simultaneously makes it more amusing and more disturbing. *You Only Live Once* severely critiqued the American ideal of domesticity by denying Joan and Eddie Taylor the house they strove for and throwing them on the tender mercies of a life on the road. But the film maintained a dichotomy between the domestic bliss they longed for and the prison environment that separated them. In 'Stick to the Mob,' Lang undermines that dichotomy by invoking the domesticity of the prison as a group of ex-cons wax nostalgic about their 'cosy' former cells.

The sequence takes place in an underworld tavern on Christmas Eve, that ideological nodal point of so many Hollywood films, the ultimate signifier of family, childhood and the fulfilment of wishes through consumer bliss, and which Lang will treat sardonically in the finale of *Scarlet Street* as well as here. We hear a honky-tonk version of 'Silent Night' in the background as the ex-cons sit around a table in silence. A few rhythmic sounds break this reflective silence and set up the audio dissolve to come: Mickey, the gang leader, leans back in his creaking chair, Patsy, the safecracker, cracks some walnuts. A cutaway to an image that recurs in Lang (e.g. *The Testament of Dr. Mabuse*, in Mabuse's cell when Baum has his first hallucination), a barred window showing nothing but the light it lets in, a sort of glowing, imageless screen, provides the visual cue for the start of their prison reminiscences. As Patsy invokes the chicken dinner they got in prison every Christmas, Cuffy begins to drum his fingers on the table. Patsy wonders why, now that you can eat chicken whenever you want, 'you don't get such a kick out of it'. An ideal solidarity surfaces as they long for a time when they were separated from their scolding wives, as Patsy remarks with a sigh (and an oddly intense longing), 'It was a nice bunch of boys up there!' Mickey, who hopes to get the old gang back together, uses this as a cue for an emphatic sound (pounding on the table with his fist) and statement: 'We got to stick together.'

Like 'The Right Guy for Me', 'Stick to the Mob' tells a story, designed to prove Mickey's moral: we got to stick together – a prison memory of the unsuccessful escape attempt of 'Number One, the Big Guy'. No melody intervenes in this sequence, but sounds and dialogue become progressively more rhythmic, a technique Lang referred to as 'pre-scoring', creating a musical number out of sound effects and speech rather than actual music, and which therefore preceded the traditional scoring of the film after it was edited. As the story of Number One begins to be narrated by the various ex-cons in turn, their dialogue becomes blank verse maintaining a metric scansion. Lang has increasingly focused audience attention on rhythmic effects, first, a few scattered sounds, then, the cadence of dialogue. Now he uses a device to make rhythm dominant, the prisoner's code, or Arab telegraph: a Morse code-like staccato tapping that allowed messages to move from cell to cell. In Lang's original treatment this motif ran throughout the film, providing a way for the ex-cons working in Morris's department store to recognise each other and Helen and Joe's final reconciliation was announced by his tapping out the message 'Do you love me?' on the door to her hospital room.[30]

Mickey introduces the Arab telegraph as he recalls attempts to communicate with Number One as he entered prison. 'Remember how it started?' Mickey taps on the table first with the stem of his pipe, then with his knuckles, a tattoo of four little raps. The same pattern is picked up by Cuffy rapping with his fingertips and Patsy with the edge of the playing cards he holds in his hand, each translating the first primal message: 'Can you hear me?' Another ex-con picks up the conversation, rapping out, 'Is the coast clear?' with a spoon, to which another responds, 'The coast is clear,' rapping with the bowl of his pipe. Then Cuffy delicately raps out the question, 'Who are you?' on the rim of his coffee cup. Lang has orchestrated this sequence, not only by the different rhythms of the messages but by the different tonality of the objects used to make them, using, as he explained in his original story outline, everyday things as musical instruments.[31] The repetitive nature of the sound has also allowed the scene to segue into greater stylisation, both visual and aural. An echoing chorus of voices now repeats the lines, as shadows bisect the cons' faces in a lighting style that does not so much recall German Expressionism as presage *film noir*. Suddenly on the soundtrack a definitely non-diegetic noise occurs; in stark contrast to the tapping, a huge metallic vibrating clangs out, followed by a montage of harshly lit, sharply angled, grotesque close-ups of the ex-cons (like those in the trial of *M* or the torching of the jail in *Fury*). The gangsters translate the answer to Cuffy's question: 'Number One!'

Altman describes a visual technique in the musical that parallels the audio dissolve, which he calls (regrettably, to my ear) the 'video dissolve'.[32] The technique involves, first of all, an overlap-dissolve by which one shot or sequence fades into another, briefly becoming superimposed. A general transition device of the cinema (which Lang gave a personal meaning in his many vision scenes), the video dissolve in the musical doesn't simply effect a transition in space or time, but rather marks a movement between ontological realms. The video dissolve ushers us into an idealised memory or dream, a utopian contrast to the everyday world that the musical abhors. Lang uses this device in both 'The Right Guy for Me' and 'Stick to the Mob', partly to stress their discontinuity with the rest of the film. Both numbers visualise fantasies: Helen's romantic longings for Joe and her masochistic absorption in his departure; and the ex-cons' nostalgia for the prison. However, Lang's sequences critique the dream-like quality of these fantasies, rather than endorse and celebrate them as the musical generally does.

The first, very brief, dissolve comes as Jim (a very young Robert Cummings making his screen debut) taps out the question 'How long you in for?' on a tin ashtray. Lang pans to a huge steam pipe (apparently the basement tavern doubles as the boiler room for the *Titanic*) which provides an eerie sync image for the heavy echoing five clangs which follow. Briefly an image of the prison corridor is dissolved in over the pipe, indicating that we are merging with this memory bit by bit. With tonal variations the various gangsters repeat: 'Five years ain't so long'. But Number One responds with an impassioned monologue, heard over a series of obscure images of jail cells, corridors and the silhouette of the big guy himself, proclaiming he *has* to get out. But his plea is met by a chant from the ex-cons that grows in intensity, 'Stick with the mob, do you hear us? Stick to the mob and the mob will stick with you!' A dissolve to the barred window returns us to the tavern.

Joe, who has been avoiding the mob (especially Mickey who left him in the lurch in their last heist), arrives at the tavern in the midst of this chant, dragged there by Gimpy, his childlike ex-con friend (Warren Hymer reprising his comic relief role of Muggsy from *You Only Live Once* with only a slight name change). The chant now focuses the number on the plot's turning point: will Joe return to the mob? He has kept away from them so far; his marriage to Helen and his job in the benevolent Morris store provide his main impetus to continue to do so. However, he has grown increasingly annoyed by Helen's evasions, suspecting she is hiding something. His return here to an all-male environment places both the romance plot and Joe's 'going straight' in jeopardy. His allegiance to the mob is signalled by the device of falling immediately into their rhythm. As he approaches the door to the tavern he taps on it in Arab telegraph the questions, 'Do you hear me?' and 'Is the coast clear?' then taps out a round of drinks for all to the bartender.

In a stylised mode that left contemporary viewers and reviewers scratching their heads about what genre they were in, Joe enters and immediately picks up the gang's rhythmic patter. In fact, Lang went so far as to have George Raft speak in rhyming couplets:

> Although I've gone straight and gotten a job
> Still I seem to belong to the mob.

The gang responds to this in a shot where they all look, and some point directly, at the camera, chanting:

> Think of the Big House once again
> Pal, you were our buddy then!

which dissolves back to the prison corridor. As opposed to the relatively abstract images of the prison in the previous video dissolve, this time Lang merges into a full-fledged flashback, showing Joe in his prison bunk. In a rhythmically-edited sequence which often preserves the cadenced delivery of dialogue from earlier, we learn that Number One is making a break for it. The prisoners say he doesn't have a chance and we hear a percussive accompaniment, of knocks and bangs, followed by a siren.

Lang shows Number One's now empty cell, the bars torn from the window. The prisoners looking out their windows report on his off screen progress, sighting his getaway car. The prisoners clang their tin cups against the bars and chant, 'Stick to the mob!', but the percussion is resolved with the *rat tat tat* of a machine gun, then followed by silence. As Joe whispers, 'they got him', we see the empty cell again, the Langian signifier of death. We dissolve back to the tavern as Mickey delivers the final moral to this parable: 'It don't work going it alone', positioning this as an argument for Joe to rejoin the mob.

The formal *tour de force* of this sequence is undeniable, and represents an innovation not only in Lang' s work but in the genre of the musical. But both video dissolve sequences leave questions in terms of Lang's own stylistics. Are these to be understood as visionary scenes? They certainly use Lang's well-established device, the overlap-dissolve, to provide an opening onto another imagined scene. But they seem to me too simply subjective to have the traumatic and revelatory effect visionary scenes demand, a revelation of a previously hidden reality, rather than simply a memory or desire. Number One's empty cell stands in a long tradition of Lang's images of death, but is too easily recuperated into Mickey's plea for the gang to stick together to actually stand as Joe's vision of death. Lang seems increasingly drawn to subjective images which picture a desire or a memory. But one should not draw the line too firmly. As in *M,* these private fantasies can turn into traumatic revelations, as the character recognises the emptiness or death underlying his or her fantasy or memory. But neither Helen nor the ex-prisoners go that far in these sequences. In some ways 'Stick to the Mob' most closely recalls Maria's Tower of Babel sermon, a similar tale of the disaster of plans carried out without co-operation.

As I mentioned, it was this sequence that most infuriated American reviewers. The *New York Sun* felt the film's 'chanting choruses, stylized direction' destroyed the film's atmosphere, while the *New York World Telegram* disliked its 'musical, farcical and slightly nightmarish interludes'.[33] Lang's radical combination of styles simply confused American reviewers ('a combination of sentiment, melodrama and artiness' complained the *New York Journal American*)[34] and apparently lost audiences, who were cued by advertisements to expect melodrama and got ironic comedy instead. Lang created in *You and Me* a modernist montage of popular genres and devices. No-one knew what to make of it and Lang himself retreated from this sort of experiment, his fingers burned.

You Can Not Get Something for Nothing

> Every day, to earn my daily bread
> I go to the market where lies are bought
> Hopefully
> I take up my place among the sellers
> Bertolt Brecht, 'Hollywood'[35]

The opening musical number in *You and Me* immediately proclaims the film's message and formal innovations. As Lang had planned for the 'Song of Lies', 'You Can Not Get Something for Nothing' is sung entirely by an off screen voice, a supra-diegetic narrator/commentator who never appears on the screen. By divorcing this song from any character, Lang immediately short-circuits the association of song

with individual expression; instead the number functions as the voice of social relations. As in the opening of *M*, the credits give way to a dark screen, over which we
hear the disembodied voice proclaim the first line: 'You can not get something for
nothing!' Lang then fades in on a large sign (presumably over an entrance way) for
the Morris Department Store, the O in Morris, rather exaggerated, like a zero, a
second signifier for nothingness, after the dark blank screen. One wonders … the
magic of the cinema seemed just now to have conjured something from nothing? Is
it, or is it not, possible?

There follows a high angle long shot of the interior of Morris's store, stuffed with
displayed goods and shoppers. The song continues:

> Only a chump would try it.
> Whatever you see that you really want
> You can have – provided you buy it.

These opening images operate as fairly traditional establishing shots, ushering us
into a locale. But the third shot, illustrating the necessity of buying what you want,
presents a close-up of a cash register, rather than a character – the image of the Destiny-machine for this film. Things, and the exchange of things, the cash nexus,
rather than people, rule in this ballad of reification. Rather than introducing us to a
diegetic world of characters and actions, the song number suspends us in a sort of
vestibule to the film, a realm of display, nearly bereft of people, made up primarily
of carefully arranged objects. This musical prologue may well be Lang's visual masterpiece in the arrangement of things, a stylistic fascination that has been present in
his work since *M*. Nowhere has his abstract geometry of arrangement been so perfectly achieved and made so central to a sequence. Further, its range is encyclopedic:
including, as a later line from the song intones: 'candy sticks and/building bricks
/silver chests/ and movie sets/aeroplanes/ and streamlined trains' – as if Lang had

taken inventory of the whole world and placed it all on display – and for sale. How-ever, this is not an exercise in abstract formalism (although the formal pleasures of the sequence are far from minor or irrelevant).

The first three shots after the cash register glide elegantly over glittering silver tableware, fur coats, then sparkling jewellery, lit and shot like advertising layouts, designed to inspire desire. But, after this visual seduction, Lang cuts again to the cash register with a rapid montage of shots of the machine from different angles, as fingers ring up prices, then an extreme close-up of the button marked 'Cash', and the cash drawer popping open in response. The singer reaches a crescendo: 'Remember, they can not belong to you, until you pay for them.' No Hollywood fea-ture film has ever opened so didactically – and yet so engagingly. Lang's formalism intersects perfectly with his theme to illustrate the concept of exchange value. These geometrical arrangements *are* displays, abstract shop windows which we gaze at through the camera, look at the screen, to see. These objects are to be understood as *commodities* offered for sale, their common abstraction resting upon their shared position within a system of universal cash exchange. Their almost ritualistic presen-tation, on the altars of commerce, endow them with the power of attraction that defines the commodity fetish. No human labour is anywhere to be seen. These goods lounge before us like indolent gods.

The song shifts, then, from the eye-popping attractions of shimmering luxury goods to the necessities of life: 'The food we live on/you have to buy', sings the voice as Lang pans over intricate arrangements of vegetables and cuts of meat. The cash nexus applies universally, for fantasy as well as survival, and the song rushes to debunk idealist myths that the best things in life are free:

> You speak of things that money can not buy?
> For instance? Can you name a few? Just try!
> Beauty – to attract the man you love – You have to buy!
> Gems of thought – to cultivate the mind – you have to buy!
> Even vim and vigour and good health you have to buy!
> Sunny skies and mother nature's wealth you have to buy!

Lang's images under these lines re-introduce people, but in abstract settings and shot in a hard-edged, nearly dehumanising manner that recalls *Neue Sachlichkeit* (as does the sequence as a whole). The woman in the beauty shop is hooked up to a multiplicity of electrical wires for her permanent wave, making her appear like a new robotic Maria, or an electronic marionette. The faces of the men in the book stores are wreathed in heavy shadows, the landscapes of nature's bounty are picture postcard images, expressing the rendering of natural beauty as commodity through its depiction. The athletes diving or repetitively hitting a punch bag all seem mechanical, like perfect automatons.

In the song's finale, as the singer belts out, 'Let's see the colour of your dough!', Lang presents cash itself in carefully arranged geometrical patterns, as if the thing itself no longer matters, simply the pattern underlying it, the checker board rather than the counters, the logic of exchange and order. The song ends with its status quo conclusion, a conformist statement which haunts this film as a whole: 'You can not change a plan, arranged by man, since time began.' Is this conformist precept, like the claim 'Crime does not pay', the intended message of this film? On the level of inten-tion it would be hard to prove that Lang had a different message in mind. But even if Lang does express a dangerous resignation here (although his irony prompts us not to take it for granted), his demystifying of the cash nexus and exchange value in a Hollywood comedy remains quite remarkable. What, after all, *is* the relation between something and nothing? Are we condemned to this constant, dehumanised cycle of exchanging one thing for another? The role of wanting, of desire, of lack, in fact, fuels the whole system, as Lang shows. The law itself is inert, at least as a subject for a motion picture, unless desire intervenes and threatens to break it a dozen times a day.

Movie sets are included as one of the possible purchases in this litany, and Lang makes the movies' role clear in a welter of financial deals: cinema as shop window of the world. Paramount took for granted a movie's place within the network of commodities and arranged for *You and Me* (as it did with every film it released) a series of product tie-ins (the earlier, somewhat more subtle, form of product placement, which, as the exclusion of Lucky Strikes from *You Only Live Once* shows, was still taboo). The businesses that paid for potential publicity tie-ins between their products and the film included: Greyhound Bus Lines (Joe's curtailed bus trip); American Servel Stoves (Helen bakes a cake to celebrate her pregnancy, or intends to); Nunn Bush Shoes (Gimpy, the comic relief character, sells shoes at the department store); Taylor Made Blouses (Helen must wear one, I guess); Daisy Churn Kitchen accessories (they do have a kitchen); and as your personal souvenir of the film, a set of *You and Me* cocktail glasses (given that the film was a flop, these must be quite a collectors' item). Lang, the Paramount executives, everyone making films in Hollywood, knew they operated within a tightly woven web of interlocking consumer goods. But in this case, the song makes sure the film's viewers know it as well, not unlike the signed cheque for cast and crew that serves as credits for Godard's *Tout va bien*.

Lang's analysis of the structure of consumer culture segues immediately into the plot line of this film as the song re-introduces the interior of Morris's department store, ending its last line over a high angle, medium close-up of a woman's hand first caressing the fabric of a satin blouse, then grasping and slipping it into her coat. This direct logic of desire and acquisition short-circuits the detour through cash exchange, the essential delay of fulfilment that haunts Joe and Katherine in the opening of *Fury* as they window-shop for future happiness. Lang's pans, skimming over luxury goods, invoked their tactility, inviting/inciting viewers to get their hands on them. But, as a merely visual pleasure, a movie, the image also denies tactile pleasure: looking is free, but touching, grabbing – that takes dough (although, at the movies, even looking is paid for).

This act of appropriation is immediately placed within a grid of looks, as Helen, working as a shop-girl in Morris's, immediately confronts the woman. The dialogue points to the real issue of the film, a society which incites desires that cannot easily be fulfilled. When Helen asks the woman why she did it, she replies, 'Satin. I never had a satin blouse.' She pleads with Helen (who stares directly into the camera in the reverse angle shot), 'You don't know what it is to want something terribly, to want it so much that you …' The woman's explanation is interrupted by the arrival of a floorwalker who asks if there is a problem. Helen in close-up has stared at the camera, expressing the force of her gaze as part of the surveillance of private property. But cueing us to the arrival of the floorwalker, she glances off screen. This is an essential motif in the film: the glance off screen to see if anyone is watching. Helen initially represents the look of surveillance, but she herself is also under a watchful eye, not only from this man above her in the job hierarchy, but, as we learn later, the law itself in the form of her parole.

Helen invents an excuse that satisfies the floorwalker and does not turn the woman in. Clearly the intra-gender plea gets the shoplifter off. As we soon learn,

Helen *does* know what it is like to want something terribly. Her violation of parole by marrying Joe in order to keep him from walking out of her life shows that she also knows what it is 'to want it so much that you ...' would defy the law. But Helen does not possess the conscious rebellion of Joan Taylor in *You Only Live Once*; even after time spent in prison, she retains a hope for a normal life. In that respect, *You and Me* follows a more conformist plot line, the reform of Joe and Helen, ex-cons. But this again is a matter of tone, not an elimination of social criticism. Lang described *You and Me* as a fairy tale because in a sense it is a tale for children, a cautionary tale with a simple moral, but also a tale in which adults behave like children. The regressive aspects of this film provide some of its sharpest satire.

As I stated earlier, the plot of *You and Me* turns on things not said, keeping silent and keeping secrets, communications that pass under code ('Can you hear me?' the refrain of the prisoner's song asks). If Joan kept faith with Eddie no matter how strong the evidence against him seemed to be and only failed him because of her limited knowledge of the world, Helen keeps secrets, like this first one shared between a would-be woman criminal and a female ex-con. The essential device of the woman's genre (the genre which *You and Me*'s advertising promised – 'the heart break story of love on parole') turns on what a woman doesn't say, on her secrets and the complicated reasons why she keeps them. But this aural mode of secrets and silences depends to a large degree on the carceral society Lang had already explored in his previous Hollywood films, especially *You Only Live Once*.

Helen's side-long glance at the floorwalker summons up the panopticon world of constant surveillance that characterises the department store and, moving into society at large, becomes a motif of the film. In the scene in the toy department that follows Helen's encounter with the shoplifter, Cuffy, the ex-con, is trying to sell an obnoxious little girl on the delights of the Goosey-Gander Rocker, but gets a cold response. Glancing over to verify that the child's mother is immersed in gossip and not paying attention, he reverts to his tough guy manner and threatens to wrap the Goosey-Gander Rocket 'around your fat little neck, get me?' When Mr. Morris explains to his wife his policy of hiring ex-cons in his department store in order to give them a second chance, she suddenly gasps with concern and repeats the side-long glance (even though they are alone in his private office) before she asks him, in hushed tones, if perhaps he, too, is an ex-con (which he isn't). Finally, when Joe asks Helen to marry him at the bus station and she asks him, 'Aren't you even going to kiss me?' Joe gives the same cautious glances to the right and the left before he does. Basically every scene in the opening involves the fear of being discovered, an awareness of keeping secrets under a pervasive observation.

Morris's hiring policy in his department store represents a liberal and reformist alternative to the nasty world of suspicious inn-keepers and heartless bosses in *You Only Live Once*. But Morris, while less obviously smarmy and complicit than Father Dolan, does not create a utopia where suspicion and surveillance drop away. Instead, Lang emphasises the way the department store (as the emblem of society's rule of having to pay for what you get) resembles a prison environment. Lang cannily set his story within one of the great emblems of modernity, the high-volume, low-priced store of mass consumption, exemplified by the *Bon Marché* in Paris, Selfridges in London, Wanamakers in Philadelphia and Marshal Field in Chicago.[36] These institutions of the new consumer society not only pioneered a new visual culture based on display as a means of arousing consumer desire, but also a panoptic system of careful surveillance of its customers. The freedom of entrance and exit these stores encouraged, as well as their intoxicating atmosphere of seductive attractions, made shoplifting a new problem (especially, it was claimed, among female customers who were less able to control their impulses). Not wishing to curtail the incitements to acquisitive desire, the stores installed systems of unobtrusive surveillance: mirrors on the ceiling, hidden vantage points for observers, patrolling plain-clothes detectives, all designed to keep their customers under observation.

No store detective character appears in *You and Me*. But the side-long glances indicate that observing eyes are everywhere, whether or not embodied in an actual character. Observers one moment might become observed the next, as with Helen in the opening scene. The department store operates on two levels, a face turned towards the public and a subterranean space where secret violence and desire circulate. Lang introduces this comically with Cuffy's hard-sell of the Goosey-Gander rocker. But if the mode remains comic, actual pain surfaces when Mickey the gang boss makes a visit to Gimpy in the shoe department. Pretending to be trying on a pair of bucks, Mickey grinds Gimpy's hand with his heel in order to extract information about Joe. Gimpy has to smile at passing customers while concealing his pain. His obsequious attitude to Mickey is naturalised by the subservient behaviour expected in his job. Lightly, but trenchantly, Lang introduces us to the Morris department store through a series of exchanges which have violence as their subtext.

The scene introducing Joe involves an even more complicated layering of double meanings and concealed desires. It begins with a Langian joke about framing, a humorous version of the shot of the headlines of Eddie Taylor's verdict in *You Only Live Once*. In the preceding scene, Mickey told Gimpy to tell Joe he wanted to talk to him. In close-up Joe, played by George Raft (identified since *Scarface* with gangster roles) says, 'This is a good racket and I ought to know; there isn't a racket I haven't tried.' The camera pulls back and reveals Joe in the sports department selling a tennis racket to a seductive blonde, who clearly desires Joe more than the racket he holds. The joke acknowledges Raft's star persona, but continues the intertwining of the sales process with metaphors from the gangster genre (decades ago in a graduate seminar Noel Carroll pointed out to me that an earlier scene in the Morris store, in which Patsy manipulates a can opener he is selling as if it were a dial on a combination safe, could be read as a Proudhonian metaphor: 'selling is stealing').

Selling as subliminal seduction dominates the rest of the scene, as the blonde hints at transactions she would rather make. Their discussion about learning new grips, and the classical Hollywood *double entendres* as they move down the escalator together ('Do you play?' 'Tennis, you mean?' 'Yes, you look like you'd be pretty good' 'How are you?' 'Well, I've never had any complaints!' 'Who have you played with? 'Oh a lot of good players ... I'd like to play with you sometime') does more than simply add an erotic undertone to the business of buying and selling. The subtext reveals an aspect of exchange that the film's opening song does not make explicit, but the film does: that what you want isn't necessarily what you buy. Consumer society evokes a promise of fulfilled desire which no commodity can fulfil. Capitalism is fuelled by the devious paths and displacements of desire. Or, as the blonde tells Joe when she agrees to take the racket, 'I'm sold' – a fascinating but revealing inversion. The metaphor of erotic exchange as a cash proposition is not limited to this rather ditsy blonde. Even Helen will say to Joe on their way to get married, 'You're not getting such a bargain, Joe.' Joe's metaphorical response to her is even more disturbing, 'This is going to be a life sentence, kid.' As the film progresses we realise Lang really takes the opening song seriously, but not as a simplistic civics lesson. Its pattern of exchange maps the routes to romance and happiness in modern society, filled with promises, but only sure to deliver ... the bill.

But there is more to the escalator scene. As Joe flirts for the sake of the sale, protected by a double-speak which he only pursues so far (i.e. to the cashier's desk), Helen comes up on the other side of the escalator. This frictionless people-mover, designed to keep traffic moving through the store and increase sales, moves people past each other without physical jostling or contact.[37] Subverting its anonymous transport, Joe and Helen give each other another brief side-long glance, then each puts a hand on the central escalator belt. As Joe keeps up his end of the pseudo-flirtation patter, a close-up shows the secret lovers grasp hands until the contrary movement of the machine pulls them apart. Like Eddie Taylor under guard surveillance, the couple have divided their bodies into separate realms of public behaviour and private actions. That even a liberal and understanding environment like the Morris store demands such conceal-ment shows how pervasive the fragmentation of the modern body has become. This ephemeral touch is the first scene between the couple in the film.

I confess without embarrassment that I, apparently in contrast to most critics, find the scenes of Joe and Helen's initial happiness charming and touching. The very modesty of their circumstances expresses a precarious promise of happiness: the folding Murphy bed that Joe finally discovers behind an ornamental fireplace on their wedding night (as Joe said in *Fury*, no Hays Code twin beds for Lang cou-ples!) and the honeymoon trip 'around the world' – that is, at the succession of for-eign restaurants, their happiness protected by their doting Jewish landlady, Mrs. Levine (Vera Gordon at her most stereotypical, and, I think, charming – the com-plete inversion of the Margaret Hamilton character in *You Only Live Once*). This urban pastoral thrives in their private life, but is constantly under the threat of Joe encountering Mickey and the gang, or Helen encountering her parole officer and revealing her illegal marriage. The law or the mob, as in *M*, represent a common threat. Conflating the eye of the law with the rules of the workplace, Helen explains the need to conceal her marriage to Mrs. Levine, deliberately misdescribing her parole officer as a spotter from the store.

The women's melodrama aspect of the film begins to dominate as Joe and Helen's marriage collapses owing to the tension it takes to maintain Helen's secret. A visit from her parole officer makes her transform their two room apartment back into a single room occupancy with the help of a sliding door. But not only must she conceal her marriage from the her parole officer (who has had a report that she has been seen on the subway with Joe Dennis, an ex-con), as soon as the officer leaves she has to conceal who he was from Joe. Inconsistency and Helen's nervousness ('Did you hear us?' she asks Joe anxiously) make Joe suspicious, but he is stunned when his former gang buddies finally tell him that Helen is an ex-con. He confirms their claim by catching Helen in an unguarded moment. Engaged in the repetitive action of beating the batter for a Christmas cake, Helen answers his questions mechanically: 'How long have you lived here?' 'Six months, I guess.' 'How long were you in for before that?' 'Three years.' Joe walks out on Christmas Eve, willing to rejoin Mickey and the gang in their big heist.

Lang conceived the climax, or anti-climax, of *You and Me*, the attempted robbery of the Morris department store by Mickey's reunited gang and its aftermath, as another number. The opening of the robbery relies heavily on Lang's idea of 'pre-scoring', sound-effects organised rhythmically to act as a score and then blend with the non-diegetic music once it is introduced (one senses Weill's original music strongly here, as well as its often unfortunate re-orchestration). Likewise, Charles Lang's superb cinematography in this film reaches a high point in this sequence as the rhythmic control of light and shadow interacts with careful set design and choreography of movement to create a beautifully worked-out sequence that offers a variation on the raid on the warehouse in *M*.

The sequence begins with the off screen chiming of a municipal clock, as Mickey sits in his getaway car, and a beat cop checks in reporting, 'everything quiet'. Even passersby in the alley behind the Morris store move at a synchronised, slow, rhythmic pace. Joe emerges from the shadows and gives a melodic whistle signal. Gimpy opens the back gates and the alley echoes with their whistled signals as the trucks for the loot are ushered in, burglars enter the building and the musical score accelerates. The dark and eerie emptiness of the art-deco Morris store at night becomes uncanny, as the silhouettes of the gang and the beams from their flashlights move through it. Suddenly the lights are switched on and the gang freezes, confronted by both Mr. Morris and Helen in the toy department. Armed guards emerge from the rocking horses and disarm the bandits as Joe denounces Helen as a squealer.

The sudden illumination of the toy department marks a switch in genre lighting style, from the shadowy urban crime melodrama of back alleys and stairways to a highly lit fantasy set in a stylised environment that veers between the childlike and the grotesque. We veer from *Scarface* to *Alice in Wonderland*. The gangsters are rendered harmless, Damon Runyonesque caricatures, as Gimpy, being searched for his gun, giggles and complains it tickles. As Morris says, 'if you aren't a pretty sight!' a pan surveys this weird collection of mugs, very much at home in a toy department. Further, after the first confrontation, Morris speaks to them as if they were children, and states his position: he is not sending them back to jail – because why should tax payers foot the bill for their keep? 'You're going to work for your living!' Before he leaves, he says sternly, 'I want to see every one of you back on the job tomorrow morning at 8 o'clock – and that doesn't mean three minutes after!' He turns and adds, 'and when you leave, please turn out the lights!'

As they mill about after Morris's exit, grousing, 'I still don't like the idea of being here at eight o'clock in the morning!' Helen demands they take seats and shut up.

More than the pre-scoring of the attempted heist, it is Helen's performance as she lectures the gang that makes this sequence into a sort of (non-musical) number, a direct-address chalk-talk with Helen as professor and the gang as initially reluctant audience. Although her eyes shift as she addresses her diegetic audience, this is the only sustained sequence in the film in which a character addresses the camera frontally and frequently looks right into the lens. Helen is the enunciator here, delivering meaning to her listeners. The gangsters scatter themselves among the toys, exaggerated highlighting and shadows contrasting with the anodyne sur-roundings. These strange creatures are progressively infantilised as they settle into their environment, toying with the things they pick up as they listen to Helen's lec-ture, resembling a monstrous, yet somehow engaging, kindergarten of trolls. Helen evokes school right away, 'the school we all went to' – that is, prison. Lang's series of equations is now complete: prison = department store, work = consuming, prison= school – all part of the disciplinary carceral society. Helen states right away the mes-sage of her talk, the lesson she says she learned in prison: 'Crime does not pay' which is greeted with guffaws from her unruly pupils. Lang, too, used to laugh as he quoted the film's moral, but Helen is not as naive as she sounds

She admits this is the oldest chestnut in the book, but she gives it a new twist, one for which the cash exchange logic of this film should have prepared us: 'it doesn't add up in dollars and cents!' Helen's de-romanticisation of crime takes the form of an arithmetic demonstration of the limited profit margin available to the working-stiff crook. Using a child's blackboard, Helen diagrams an argument against stealing based on the laws of exchange announced since the start of the film – no-one gets something for nothing, not even crooks. This blackboard lecture presents another Langian abstraction, representing power relations with formulas and diagrams.

Helen gets the mob's attention as she adds and subtracts: the return they expect on the fenced stolen goods, minus the necessary expenses (getaway car, trucks to haul the loot, bribes, mouthpiece). Furthermore, Mickey takes a third off the top – so, she

points out, they haven't gotten rid of a boss, they've just traded Morris for Mickey. According to Helen's lightning calculations, each of the crooks would net $113.34 from knocking over the store. 'Only the biggest sap in the world thinks crime pays any dividends', Helen concludes. When Patsy objects that the big shots make a good living, Helen smirks. 'The big shots aren't little crooks like you – they're politicians.' Helen's mathematics and economic logic are flawless: in an era of organised crime, the small provider can hardly make a living.

Lang cuts from Helen's caustic comment to show Mickey, who had been warned he was getting too big, being taken for a ride by the Big Shot's boys. Even Mickey, for all his fascistic mannerisms, is small fry. Our one image of the Big Shot (speaking on the phone to Mickey's mouthpiece), shows just the back of his head, the roll of fat over his collar a direct quote from Eisenstein's agit-prop images of the 20s. Those who do profit from crime are nearly invisible, connected through Mabuse's technological network of the telephone. We cut back to the gang patting Helen on the back, convinced and converted, except for Joe who denounces her as a lying jailbird. The gang finds him gauche and departs, pacified and obedient, even remembering to switch off the lights as they leave.

Lang still has to resolve his woman's melodrama – or romantic comedy – of lovers' misunderstandings. In one brief scene of Helen explaining to the weeping Mrs. Levine that she must leave Joe forever, even though she is pregnant, we are firmly in the weepy mode. Joe, abandoned by both Helen and the mob, in the once again dark and shadowy department store, acts out an almost Expressionist drama of transformation. He picks his way through the dark store, flashlight beam moving among the contorted mannequins until he finds the display case for 'Hour of Ecstasy', the perfume Helen had earlier looked at longingly in the display window. Trying to explain the desire such a commodity inspires, Helen had explained that good perfume 'does something for a girl's soul, kind of'. In need of redemption and reconciliation, Joe now slides back the glass and takes out a bottle.

But as he departs, his flashlight beam hits the cash register, introduced in the prologue and now reaffirmed at the film's end as the (somewhat benevolent) Destiny-machine of the film, the emblem of the maxim 'You can not get something for nothing', briefly reprised in the score at this moment. Even personal redemption costs something. Joe turns back, seeks out the discarded price tag and, like the good salesman he is, writes up the sales slip, not neglecting to add the 30 cents sales tax. As the score reaches a climax, Lang montages a series of close-ups of the cash register, buttons pushed, addition made, cash drawer thrust out, bell rung, a mechanical purr of satisfaction almost audible as Joe drops in his money to the penny. Ecstasy is a commodity to be desired, yet gratification must be delayed, until one can pay for it. Like the moviegoer, Joe has paid for his hour of ecstasy. But satisfying the machine is not yet winning back the girl, and Joe returns to an empty apartment. Seeking her through her parole officer Joe goes even deeper into the thicket of the law. Their marriage, he is told, is void, since a paroled convict cannot enter into a contract. 'You're free from the marriage she "cheated" you into', the officer tells him, but Joe responds, 'I don't want to be free, I want my wife.' Joe also learns for the first time that Helen is pregnant.

The resolution of the film belongs entirely to the comic genre, reconciling irreconcilable differences through the creation of a new, nonsensical society. Joe brings the gang together one more time in order to find the errant Helen. The mob is reconstituted as a family ('she sort of belongs to us, too' Gimpy says), crowded together in smoke-filled rooms like the mob in *M,* as they scour the city looking for

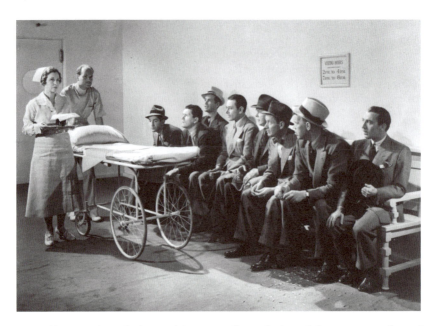

her. Following Altman's thesis of the musical's resolution of the separate realms of genders in a final romance,[38] the all-masculine mob proves their devotion to Helen and reunites the couple. All of them end up pacing the floor in the waiting room of a maternity hospital as Helen delivers, and they all rise simultaneously as the nurse asks for Mr. Dennis.

Likewise, the whole gang stands in waiting as Joe and Helen emerge from their second, now legal, marriage. Gimpy appears for the film's penultimate shot bearing the now legally married couple's infant son. Mob and couple merge in a silly, but also utopian, promise of a new society, one founded on trust and communication, overcoming the alienation of the carceral society that surrounds all of us. Lang knows that this promise can never be anything more than a dream, or fairy tale, and makes us aware of the disproportion between such a promise of happiness and the limited possibility of its realisation. More than the wedding, then, Lang focuses on the infant, that infinitely renewed promise of the newborn that seems already to reveal its betrayal with each passing moment. Gimpy declares, as if it were an absolute principle, 'Well, he's got a right to know what's going on, ain't he?' The last shot is a close-up of this baby presumably demanding his access to knowledge, bawling his head off as Lang zooms in.

This is not a cute baby shot, but almost a disturbing one: infant rage and hunger rather than infant joy. Weill had apparently wanted to have the baby's cries drown out the wedding ceremony itself. Like the baby with no name in *You Only Live Once*, this screaming baby announces a new life and new chances and Lang seems to hit the perfect note of ironic non-resolution. This baby doesn't know yet that he must pay for what he wants. He only knows that he wants something, and will scream bloody murder to get it. But can you get something for nothing? As Lang said to Bogdanovich, even as he made fun of *You and Me*'s didactic message, 'Life has a very peculiar way of making you pay for whatever you get'. As Lang learned after the failure of this, his first American film as producer.

PART V

Framing Desire

The Woman in the Window (1944)
Scarlet Street (1945)
The Secret beyond the Door (1948)
House by the River (1950)

Faust: Was seh ich? Welch ein himmerlisch Bild
Zeigt sich in diesem Zauberspiegel […]
Wenn ich es wege nah zu gehen
Kann ich sie nur als wie in Nebel sehn!
Das schönste Bild von einem Weibe!
Ist's möglich, ist das Weib so schön?

Faust: What do I see with form divine
Upon this magic mirror shine […]
Unless I stand right here in this one place
And do not venture to go near,
I see her only misted and unclear –
A woman of the utmost grace!
Can any woman be so fair?

Goethe, *Faust*, Part I[1]

11

The Woman in the Window:
Cycles of Desire

Prelude to Nightmare: Shop Window Sweetheart

> Least of all, could it have been that my fancy, shaken from its
> half slumber, had mistaken the head for that of a living person.
> E. A. Poe, 'The Oval Portrait'[2]

Lang's social trilogy ran through a series of variations on the shop window and window-shopping. His American career begins with an image which slowly reveals itself as a window display and then discovers Joe and Katherine gazing into the scene, an image of deferred desire. In contrast, Joan Taylor, convinced at last that her love for Eddie means more to her than the law does, smashes the window of a drugstore to get the medicine he needs. Finally, Joe Dennis opens a display case to express his love for the wife he had just reviled publicly, but also makes sure he pays for it. In *The Woman in the Window*, Professor Wanley pauses in front of a

somewhat different shop window after having just deposited his wife and children at Grand Central Station for a vacation in Maine while he teaches summer courses at Gotham College. The three shop windows in Lang's social trilogy contained different sorts of goods and moved from the necessities to the delights of life: a bedroom (shelter), medicine (healing), to the sensual and erotic (the perfume, Hour of Ecstasy). But all of them spoke directly to the needs and desires of John Doe, the average Joe, you and me, the characters as well as intended audience of Lang's populist period. Although his financial circumstances are relatively modest, Professor Wanley cannot be called a John Doe. Likewise the shop window, a posh midtown gallery, hardly recalls the department stores or pharmacies of the social trilogy. What Wanley sees in the window is not really an object that he needs (although, as Baudrillard asks, who decides what we really need?). Rather, it is something he (like Helen in *You and Me*) wants, something desired, which, like the promise of the perfume, has to do with 'the soul, kind of'.[3]

With this film Lang initiated another trilogy: *The Woman in the Window*, *Scarlet Street* and *The Secret Beyond the Door*. As with the social trilogy, Lang did not conceive of this group as an integrated whole beforehand (although the connections between the films in terms of production come closer together – two are for Diana, the production company Lang formed in 1945), and, like the earlier trilogy, these films fall naturally together by starring the same leading lady, Joan Bennett. But besides sharing the same leading lady, these three films are also all melodramas that turn on issues of passion, rather than politics (although Lang's focus on sexual passion most certainly entails a strong social analysis in all these films). In these three films, a work of art tries to either to capture or engender the energy of desire (a fourth film, the neglected and rarely seen *House by the River*, continues this theme and will also be dealt with in this section). Partly exhibiting a common tendency in Hollywood films during the 40s, this series of films not only spawns psychologically more detailed characters with a stronger sense of interior conflict, but also more directly Freudian plots, with psychoanalysis playing an increasingly important role. However, as the shop window theme (which appears in three of these four films) announces, desire itself never entirely escapes definition and appropriation by the commodity culture. While works of art form the central theme in this series, the price paid for art – the dialectic of promise and displacement that fuels a commodity culture, as *You and Me* demonstrated – skyrockets, as human lives are sacrificed.

The scene at the shop window immediately reveals some difference between the two trilogies. No couple, engaged or newly-wed, window-shop at this gallery; rather, a middle-aged man who has just regained a temporary bachelorhood loiters before it. He does not seek a vision of the future, as the couple do in *Fury*, but longs for something else, something he already senses as being in the past. What is looked at is not an object, not even a bottle of perfume, but an image, an image of a woman. The shot therefore doubles the act of looking inherent in the earlier films. The only value one could derive from this portrait lies in the pleasure of viewing it. In the earlier films (at least *Fury* and *You and Me*), visual presentation was a seduction, while glass prevented touching. Here, with a portrait of a seductive woman, dressed in a low-cut gown or negligée, the issue of touch is already deferred, if not culturally sublimated (although evoked, perhaps, even more strongly through its suppression). Framing desire expresses an essential ambivalence. As framed, the image is in a sense appropriated, circumscribed and made available. But the frame also separates the image from the viewer, creating a different ontology, removing it from the immediate grasp.

As such, it embodies the fundamental drama of desire in both Freudian theory and consumer culture: enticement and repression, promise and deferment.

Lang cuts from a long shot of Wanley approaching the gallery, doubled by his reflection on the window, to a medium shot directly centred on the portrait, seen through the window. Likewise framed in medium shot, Wanley looks at it dreamily. The glass window (which reflects passing traffic and pedestrians) echoes another frame, the frame of the picture, stressing that this image, in contrast to the goods in the earlier films, is at two removes from reality. In this trilogy, Lang returns to the issues of ontology and doubling that appeared especially in his German films (including his only partially preserved first collaboration with Harbou, *The Wandering Image*) in which images seem to come to life (e.g. the robots and gothic figures in *Metropolis*). But, even more directly, this new trilogy focuses upon a key theme of *Metropolis*, the woman as image caught within the male gaze. It is in this trilogy that the male gaze and the image of woman, that Stephen Jenkins finds central to all of Lang, truly dominates the films.[4]

As I said earlier, I believe that the instances of the male gaze in earlier Lang films (and there are many, but *Metropolis* supplies the strongest examples) do not by themselves constitute the core of his style. This lustful predatory gaze towards women interlocks with a more pervasive mastering gaze, which we might term the gaze of modernity, surveying space in terms of power and domination. But the gaze of sexual desire, seizing the woman as an image tailored precisely to the desire of the man, becomes a key theme of this new trilogy, closely linked to the gaze as domination and power. Curiously, Jenkins neglects the film which first centres on this theme, *The Woman in the Window*, confining his attention to *Scarlet Street* (admittedly, an even better example). But while one could argue that *Scarlet Street* is Lang's Hollywood masterpiece (and certainly the keystone in this trilogy), that film must be approached as the dark twin of *The Woman in the Window*.

In Lang's films the male gaze does not function as an unquestioned mode of seeing, the basic established position of spectatorship that Laura Mulvey claims it occupies in Hollywood cinema.[5] In many ways the male voyeurs in what I will call the 'framed desire' trilogy encounter the same failure of their dreams of mastery as the master criminals/grand enunciators of the German films. Possessed of an imagined power over the tools of technology (communication and vision), the master criminals believe they control the fate of those around them and even the course of the narrative. However, that control proves illusory and their claims hubristic. The Destiny-machine destroys them, as well. I would claim that in the framed desire trilogy the male characters believe they can assert a control over the image of these women – or these women through their image – only to find that desire and domination are processes belonging exclusively to the Destiny-machine; they become subject to these drives, rather than masters of them. Thus the project of desire discovers itself to be within a frame, in a potentially infinite *mise-en-abîme*.

In contrast to the master criminals who begin their films with sweeping displays of power, the protagonists of the imaginary woman cycle often reveal their relative impotence from the start (in fact, in some ways they become more powerful as the film progresses, although defeated in the end). The casting of Edward G. Robinson, a middle-aged man lacking conventional physical beauty, as two of these protagonists stresses the pathos of these characters. In many ways these figures recall Hans Beckert of *M* rather than Mabuse or Haghi. Beckert's scenes before the shop windows of desire, catching a perverse image of his child-bride, anticipate Wanley's wistful look at the portrait more than the consumer-based window-shopping of the social trilogy. But if these protagonists share Lorre's pathetic qualities and lack of obvious power, what do they share with the enunciator characters?

The Mabuse figures approached crime as a work of total mastery and artistry, as a formal as well as practical triumph. As Nietzschean supermen, crime became for them the ultimate artwork (the complaints by gang members about the impractical nature of the 'Doctor's' plans in *The Testament of Dr. Mabuse*, point up the disinterested aestheticism of these crimes). The films of the imaginary woman cycle move towards an understanding of the artist as criminal (and thus *House by the River* serves as its culmination, *hors serie*). The desire for the woman as image, the mastering male gaze, becomes identified with death as surely as the master criminals' plans of world domination and terror do. But if the protagonists of these American films never aspire to conquer the world, they do attempt to control the object of their desire through becoming artists (painter, architect and, in *House by the River*, novelist), and their artistic callings summon up violence and crimes.

Thus the male gaze is never taken for granted in these Lang films, as it would seem to be in most Hollywood films. Instead, it is scrutinised, criticised, mocked, and – undeniably – participated in. The nakedness of its attraction, exemplified in the reverse angle of Wanley's entranced gaze at the portrait, as if giving in to hypnosis or visual fascination, can even make the male viewer uncomfortable. This position of longing in front of the window was last occupied by Helen in *You and Me* and there is something feminising about Wanley's reaction. In contrast to the unspoken (and generally unseen) position of mastery from which Hollywood films are conceived and received as described in Mulvey's analysis, a traditional male viewer might be embarrassed to align his vision with this middle-aged gawker. Thus Lang follows the shot/reverse shot between Wanley and the portrait in the window by a cut to District Attorney Lalor and Dr. Barkstone, the two men Wanley is about to meet for dinner as they watch him from off screen. Barkstone points and they both laugh as the camera pans to frame Wanley goggle-eyed before the display window.

The male gaze is framed by another view (those off screen watchers omnipresent in Lang's Hollywood films), is immediately recognised, and is laughed at. The conversation between these three middle-aged men describes the woman in the window as 'our dream girl' and turns to the question of representation, image and model. 'Who is she?' asks Wanley, meaning the model, of course, and when he says 'extraordinary portrait', Lalor responds 'extraordinary woman, too, I bet'. Which is the object of obsession, the woman in the window, framed and imaginary, or the woman behind the portrait, absent and imagined? The former is already enframed in a male gaze, but the latter may elude it.

If Lang had acknowledged the Nietzschean superman as the inspiration for his master criminals, the protagonists of the framed desire cycle recall the other end of the spectrum, Nietzsche's Last Man (*letzten Menschen*), an exhausted figure of decadence, dwarfed by habit and repression.[6] Professor Wanley, soon to be named chair of the Psychology department at his college, flanked by his friends representing Medicine and Law, enters into his all-male club for dinner, the victim of routine. Lang bridges a slight ellipsis from this entrance to their after-dinner conversation with an overlap-dissolve which superimposes an ornamental clock dial directly on Wanley's back. The image says it all: Wanley is like a well-regulated machine. Lang's image of the Destiny-machine first appears in this film as the regulator of routines, which spreads a net over every aspect of Wanley's life, a net which both confines and, in a sense, protects him.

During my youthful meeting with Lang, I heard him describe a film he always wanted to make about a man who walked to work every day and always followed the same route. One day, because of roadwork or some such obstacle, he has to deviate from his accustomed path and, as Lang put it, his life changes completely. Although Lang did not detail his plot, it was clear the change was not for the good. We see here a variation on the Destiny-machine as found in either the German films or the Hollywood social trilogy, a variation that seems to support claims that Lang is a determinist. Fateful consequences dwell in the smallest actions and decisions, or, even more, in non-decisions, moments of absent-mindedness or inadvertent breaks in routine. Large consequences sprouting from minor incidents have always kicked the Destiny-machine into high gear, from Siegfried's linden leaf to Beckert's pencil shavings. But rather than a metaphysical fate, I have associated this network of circumstances with the structures of modern urban life, where every trace can be followed up by the archives of a surveillance society.

Brunhild's bracelet, the key to Mabuse's counterfeiting lair, the number Haghi writes on the slip of paper, Beckert's whistling, Joe's love of peanuts, Eddie's hat: these are the clues which (sometimes wrongfully) connect characters to dire scenarios in Lang's films. In the Hollywood films, and especially the enframed desire cycle, dangers loom when the net of habit is broken, when the character is caught off-guard. *Once Off-Guard* is the title of the novel by J. H. Wallis on which *The Woman in the Window* was based.[7] Its message of eternal vigilance reflects a modern paranoia which views every moment as pregnant with lurking dangers. This neurosis appeared not only throughout Lang's later films, but apparently also in his anal-compulsive lifestyle – such as keeping a diary which accounted for every minute of his day.[8] Lang's explanation of this behaviour to a friend as triggered by the accusation that he had murdered his first wife (whose apparent suicide is wreathed in obscurity) is less interesting to me as a biographical explanation of this theme than as another example of the way Lang thought about his life as though patterned on one of his screenplays, with himself constantly under suspicion.[9]

As opposed to the rebels against fate that Lang claims his films chronicled, characters like Wanley or Chris Cross in *Scarlet Street* are creatures of habit and have become their own jailers, complicit with the Destiny-machine. In contrast to Mabuse, they do not identify with the machine in order to bend it to their will-to-power. They abandon their own will to become, as the overlap-dissolve of the clock on Wanley's back visualises, clockwork men. Within these men the Destiny-machine works smoothly, having been internalised. But in both *The Woman in the Window* and *Scarlet Street*, Lang picks up these characters as they experience a last flicker of resistance, a bursting forth of repressed erotic energy that comes, as their internal Destiny-machine clocks should have told them, too late. In the after-dinner conversation the discourses of Law (DA Lalor) and, to some extent, of Medicine (Dr. Barkstone) preach the gospel of routine and repression. As the representative of Psychology, Wanley at first seems to be the most adamant advocate of habit, declaring that on his first night of bachelorhood 'the program' consists of, 'one cigar, another drink and early to bed' ready for his nine o'clock class in the morning. Lalor especially approves of such moderation, saying it's a good thing.

But here Psychology demurs. 'I didn't say it's a good thing', Wanley adds forcefully, 'I only know I hate it; I hate this stolidity, this stodginess I'm beginning to feel.' The clockwork is experiencing friction. He admits he has lost count of the number of drinks he has had, and describes himself as in a 'somewhat rebellious state of mind'. But Wanley also reassures his friends that such rebellion is unlikely to lead anywhere. He is an armchair adventurer, he explains. While he won't set off to a burlesque show, if one of the dancers were to perform in close proximity to his chair at the club, he would be only too happy to watch. He insists that even if the 'alluring young woman in the window next door' were to arise before him and beckon, he would probably run away. His friends departing, Wanley returns to his club's library, selecting a book for an archetypal professor's evening of quiet reading. His reflection appears on the glassed bookcase, however, recalling the window holding the portrait, and hinting that its erotic influence still lingers. He selects from the shelves an edition of *The Song of Solomon*, the archetypal love lyrics of the Western tradition, allowed into the *Old Testament* only by being read as an allegory of divine love, but for centuries known to lovers as the original hot stuff and to school boys as the only description of sexual longing that can be read anywhere with complete impunity.

Within Lang's opus, *The Song of Solomon* already has a meaning from its appearance as the key transitional text in *Der müde Tod*, the text which assures the maiden that 'love is as strong as death' and enables her to enter death's realm to demand her lover back. For Lang, as this film bears out, *The Song of Solomon* evokes not only Eros but Thanatos and, more importantly, a defiance of death in the name of the erotic. The delicately melancholy theme introduced at this moment in Arthur Lange's sensitive musical score sets a mood that is no longer simple mockery. Wanley will confront his own death-by-habit, rebel against it in the name of Eros, but whether the two primal forces of love and death can be separated remains the question of the film. Once the net of habit is pierced, the living death of stagnant routine gives way, not simply to erotic promise, but to violence. Wanley settles into the armchair from which he was willing to watch a spectacle of eroticism. His behaviour balances the temptation to broach limitations with a desire to maintain them. He has one more drink (already over his limit), but he signs for it, maintaining propriety and identity (we later learn this pencil is even inscribed with his initials). He asks the attendant to remind him when it is ten thirty (still intending to get to bed early), but admits he sometimes loses track of time. Wanley teeters on the brink between being always on guard and self-forgetfulness.

Once again Lang uses an overlap-dissolve from Wanley to the same ornate clock (this time his face merging with the clock dial) apparently to bridge an ellipsis in time like the earlier one, as the attendant tells him it is ten thirty. At the end of the film, of course, we learn that this overlap-dissolve deceives us even more than the misleading ellipses in *You Only Live Once*. Lang withholds information from the audience and allows us to follow the path of habit in interpreting this transition as a short break in time. In fact, the dissolve actually cues (or rather *under-cues*, indicates, without giving us a clear sign) a transition into the realm of the unconscious and dream. The dissolve bridges ontological realms and (retrospectively) bears some resemblance to both the vision scenes of the German films and the fantasies and memories of *You and Me*. Once again, Lang presents a subjective experience (hallucination, dream or memory) as a private movie, one which, like Beckert's fantasies, includes images of desire and terror.

Wanley's private movie recalls the films from the Weimar era that Kracauer calls Street Films, and especially the archetypal film of the series, Karl Grune's *The Street* of 1923, which Kracauer describes as illustrating the 'development from rebellion to submission'. *The Street* portrays 'a middle-class, middle-aged philistine who longs for the sensations and splendours of the nocturnal city'. The nocturnal city seems demonically animate, including, as Kracauer points out, tempting shop windows which give rise to fantasies and the looming eyes of an optician's shop sign. Lured by a prostitute, the protagonist becomes involved in a murder and is arrested. Freed when it becomes clear he did not commit the murder, he returns to the security of his wife and apartment and 'now willingly submits to the domestic regime'.[10]

Wanley likewise emerges from his club into an urban nocturnal landscape, stumbling a bit due to the extra brandies. Although initially heading to the left, he is drawn back to the gallery window. On the deserted night-time street he confronts the portrait again. Lang then repeats the shot/reverse shot of portrait and observer, with a change. Earlier, we looked at the portrait through the window, reflections of the street mediating our view, while we viewed Wanley's enraptured expression without glass. The portrait now appears initially without the glass (or at least with no reflection), while Wanley is viewed through the pane, framed between reflections of a ceramic vase and a somewhat anamorphically stretched portrait. Wanley smiles with pleasure, then stares with apparent confusion. The reverse angle of the portrait suddenly presents a double image, another, similar looking woman looming at the portrait's shoulder. The reverse angle shows Wanley doing a double take. The return to the portrait now pans from its doubled image past the window to an (actual) woman standing nearby and smiling.

The ontological doubling has become a tripling: painted portrait, reflection, real (at least within the diegesis) woman. Although staging an archetypal presentation of the male gaze and voyeurism, Lang reveals the gaze as confused, uncertain, perhaps hallucinatory (which, in a sense, it is). The similarity to the first shop window sequence in *M* is striking, although Wanley's slightly befuddled amazement has a different tone from Beckert's entranced hysteria. It also reverses the drama of Beckert's failed encounter; instead of the little girl slipping out of the frame to evade his perverse desire, here the camera moves from representation to reality. The ensuing conversation between Wanley and the woman outside the window is framed with the portrait between them. Wanley speaks in admiration of the portrait's accuracy: 'It's you'. The woman explains that she comes not simply to look at her own portrait, but in order to watch men looking at it (her). Possessed of her own gaze, in this way the portrait's model becomes an image that looks back at the looker.

Once again Wanley's indulgence in the culturally male prerogative of the look becomes caught in another, somewhat amused observation, this time by a woman. Wanley becomes concerned about how he looked to her: 'Did I react properly, ah, *normally?*' The clarification he offers seems to qualify morality with a desire for sexually normal masculinity, stressing again the threat of losing virility that underlies the imaginary woman cycle. The woman confirms his masculinity by distinguishing between two reactions she has noted in men: one, a 'solemn stare – for the painting', the other 'a long, low whistle'. Wanley's reaction is described as 'a long, low, solemn whistle' – apparently a sufficiently normal/proper compromise formation. As Wanley becomes awkward, she takes control and sets the limits on their mutual pick-up: 'I'm not married, I have no designs on you and one drink is all I'm after.'

The woman's appearance, a hat which frames her face in dark feathers, a dark sheath-like dress which constantly glitters with reflected light, projects an almost allegorical image of the temptress. In the bar she and Wanley sit beneath wall decorations of Eve offering Adam the apple, as she invites the professor back to her apartment, to see more artworks, images of her. Wanley demurs that it's late, showing his wristwatch ('Is that late? Eleven?' Her clock runs on a different schedule than Wanley's). His spoken reluctance is answered by a cut to the couple getting out of a cab in front of the woman's apartment. One is tempted to read such ellipses and exaggerations as hints towards the dream nature of the unfolding drama of seduction, especially the sudden attack Wanley suffers from the woman's straw-hatted paramour when he discovers them together. Punishment so swiftly follows temptation that the condensation of a dream seems a reasonable explanation. However, a sharply moral and strongly misogynist allegory on the need to remain ever vigilant against the danger of sexual temptation might seem a more likely motivation for such brutal violence. Wallis's novel, the film's source, which repeatedly refers to the woman as a 'harlot', a 'damned whore', and imagines her covered with blood; and whose protagonist reflects on the fact that his first illicit sexual act ends immediately in murder, certainly offers this sort of reading.[11]

Apparently on taking on the project Lang insisted that the ending be changed, or rather that the ontology and moral status of the ending be transformed.[12] In *Once Off-Guard* Wanley, after killing the violent paramour in self-defence with the help of Alice, the woman who picks him up, tries to conceal his connection with the crime. But, as in the film, his attempt unravels, especially when a blackmailer who suspects the truth enters the picture. In great remorse Wanley commits suicide. Lang insisted that this deadly accumulation of coincidence – from temptation to murder to suicide – be revealed in the end as Wanley's dream, prompted by one too many drinks and presumably the baleful influence of reading *The Song of Solomon*. Does this transformation serve a purpose other than as a trick to get Lang (and his protagonist) out of a truly depressing ending?

Lang admitted this was 'such a corny old trick that it seemed almost new' and from original reviewers down to contemporary student audiences, most viewers moan at the revelation that it was all a dream.[13] But if we compare the film to the grim ending Lang gives to *Scarlet Street* one year later, I think the explanation that Lang simply preferred happy endings is incomplete. Further, discussing the ending,

Lang stressed this was not the first time he had added a framing story to a film and thereby transformed its claim on reality. Lang compared the final revelation of *The Woman in the Window* to the transformation he proposed to Erich Pommer for *The Cabinet of Dr. Caligari*. What Lang stressed was not defusing the fatality of either film, but rather the way each film returns us to the unconscious drama of the character as expressed in his dream or hallucination.[14] In Lang's version, Wanley's punishment does not come from a puritanical conception of retribution (as in Wallis's novel), but from a punishing super-ego that transforms Wanley's erotic wish into a disturbing nightmare. (The film introduces Wanley, as he lectures to his class at Gotham College on 'Some Psychological Aspects of Homicide', standing in front of a blackboard which diagrams Freud's two topographies of the psyche.) In contrast to the puritanical Wallis, Lang felt 'there is no real guilt' in the Wanley character.[15] Instead of a morality tale of the most patriarchal sort, Lang devises a nightmare in which the stir of sexual desire opens up a world of fatality and the gradual destruction of the self. That this vision is self-inflicted, that it dwells within Wanley's psyche, hardly makes it easier to sleep at night.

The image of desire, then, is clearly understood as a masculine projection, and Lang explores the relation such projections have, not only to dreams, but to a whole realm of fantasy and image-making. This does not yield an examination of moral guilt, but a construction of paranoia, the closed world of a precisely interlocking narrative of coincidence, the enframed realm of the perfectly composed picture. Lang's heroes must figure out where they stand in relation to these frames, inside or outside. Locating the frame becomes a complicated question, because (as Lang shows as Wanley gazes through the window at the portrait) both picture and observer can be placed within a frame, and a story may be framed as well. As in *Der müde Tod*, which, as Georges Sturm points out, *The Woman in the Window* echoes in so many ways,[16] the question remains: am I actor or author in this story, and even if I am its author, does that give me authority over its outcome – or does it write itself ... and me with it?

The Paranoid World Made of Glass

> Commit a crime, and the earth is made of glass. There is no
> such thing as concealment. Commit a crime, and it seems as if
> a coat of snow fell on the ground, such as reveals in the woods
> the track of every partridge and fox and squirrel and mole.
> You cannot recall the spoken word, you cannot wipe out the
> foot-track, you cannot draw up the ladder, so as to leave no
> inlet or clew. Always some damning circumstance transpires.
> The laws and substances of nature, water, snow, wind,
> gravitation, become penalties to the thief.
> > Ralph Waldo Emerson, 'Compensation'[17]

Between Joe Dennis paying for his 'Hour of Ecstasy' in *You and Me* and Professor Wanley staying up past his bedtime to sneak in his after-hours art appreciation class, some six years of Lang's career had passed. During the first two years, Lang directed no films, partly due to the failure of *You and Me*. The next year and a half Lang spent at the Twentieth Century-Fox studio trying to prove he could be a contract director.

He directed two westerns, *The Return of Frank James* (1940) and *Western Union* (1941) which made more money than his social films, and he apparently enjoyed the work.[18] The films are quite watchable and quite impersonal and seem designed to prove Burch's claim that Lang became the 'all-purpose Hollywood director'.[19] Was Lang destined to take the route that some other Weimar survivors in Hollywood, such as E. A. Dupont or Joe May, had taken: producing some interesting early work and then disappearing into formula film-making (or even ultimately becoming a Hollywood restaurateur as did May, Lang's first producer)?[20]

A series of films that I will not deal with in detail in this book saved Lang's career as an innovative director: espionage thrillers in which Nazis play the role of villains. While these films could constitute another ersatz trilogy (*Man Hunt* (1941), *Hangmen Also Die* (1943) and *Ministry of Fear* (1944) – the postwar *Cloak and Dagger* (1946) tagging along and spoiling the symmetry), and would reward close analysis, for my purposes they are less accomplished works than either the social trilogy or the framed desire trilogy that precede and follow them. Although ostensibly anti-fascist works, their politics are blunted by propaganda demands (most obviously in *Hangmen Also Die*) and their portrayal of the Nazis limited by stereotypes (the lines 'We have ways of making you talk' and 'Mistakes?! We never make mistakes!' are actually spoken in *Hangmen Also Die*), with only the characters of Major Quive-Smith in *Man Hunt* and, especially, Gruber in *Hangmen Also Die* (brilliantly played by Alexander Granach, the unforgettable Knock from Murnau's *Nosferatu*) rising above the level of music-hall bogeymen.

Most importantly, these films returned Lang to a modern urban environment beset by terror and technological paranoia. As one of the founders of the urban thriller, Lang managed to extend and nuance his sense of an environment of danger in the genre of the espionage thriller. *Man Hunt* becomes powerful as the Nazis trail Captain Thorndike back into London where he hopes to disappear among the crowd.[21] Travelling under Thorndike's passport, the Nazi agent and his cohorts transform the supposedly familiar environment of London docks into a nightmare landscape of deceptive appearances, wrong turns, and dangerous doorways. The fight in the subway reprises Lang's sensation film *topoi* of the underground labyrinth below the city, recalled from *Spiders* (and brought back in some of his last films: *While the City Sleeps*, as well as *The Tiger from Eschnapur* and *The Indian Tomb*). The continuation of the metaphor of the hunt and Thorndike's inability to disappear totally, even as he tries to regress to the state of a burrowing animal, show Lang still developing the issues of modern identity that he introduced in the German urban thrillers.

The opening sequence of *Ministry of Fear*, especially the scenes at the charity fair, are among Lang's most uncanny sequences, reviving the sinister associations that a fairground can have, that Kracauer discovered in Weimar cinema.[22] But Lang creates a strange atmosphere here precisely by stressing the improvised everydayness of this event in which odd behaviour seems triggered by inadvertent actions, such as the fortune teller's mysterious message and the angry confrontation over the cake that protagonist Stephen Neale wins. The most disturbing of Lang's fake blind men appears as a passenger in Neale's train compartment. Offered a piece of the cake, the blind man disturbingly crumbles it in his hands, as if blindness were an affliction of the mouth that rendered ordinary eating impossible. Such an action typifies this new mood of paranoia in Lang: something odd, but not immediately threatening, takes place that holds a hidden and dire significance, like the box of books Neale delivers later in the film which suddenly exploded.

Of all these films, *Hangmen Also Die* comes closest to being a major Lang film. One approaches it with great expectations (Lang's first film as producer since *You and Me*; a collaboration with Bertolt Brecht; the gathering of other Weimar collaborators: Hanns Eisler for the score and the actors Granach and Reinhold Schünzel) which the film's uneven realisation cannot fulfil.[23] The political scenes with the hostages are, to my mind, unimaginative and unoriginal, especially the intoning of the resistance poem, and most of the leads, with the exception of Granach, give wooden, uninspired performances. But the portrayal of a city under the threat of terror provides Lang with a powerful opportunity to take his urban thriller to an extreme of paranoia that recalls *M*. Prague in *Hangmen*, like Berlin in *M*, possesses a dual power system, both the official Nazi authorities and the shadowy institutions of the Czech underground. As Jean-Louis Comolli and François Géré stated, 'opposite the barbarous and ultra-automated Nazi machine another machine is erected, no less ruthless and no less mechanical.'[24]

Thus the Nazi's control of technology, especially radio and listening devices, is countered by the underground's ability to stage manage counter-narratives. When the Nazis bug Mascha Novotny's apartment, hoping that Dr. Svoboda will confess his role in the Heydrich assassination, they hear a manufactured love scene, with dialogue written out by Svoboda (aware of the eavesdropping) for Mascha to deliver. Later Svoboda and Mascha stage a bedroom scene when Gruber visits his apartment in order to conceal an underground leader bleeding to death behind a curtain (a sequence which drove Brecht crazy).[25] Gruber, whose character is conceived as a more perverse Lohmann, eventually sees through this scene because one of its details, a lipstick kiss imprinted on Svoboda's face, is 'too perfect'. Finally, the underground kill two birds with one stone. By manipulating the Nazis' search for the assassin to their own ends, they get rid of a traitor, a beer merchant named Czaka, framing him as Heydrich's assassin. This beautifully contrived conspiracy, by which the underground use the Nazis as their executioner, exemplifies the new paranoid style the anti-Nazi film allowed Lang to develop, as Czaka ends up the victim of two competing narratives, and the stage managing of reality becomes an ironic, but deadly, weapon.

The underground create a system of terror as much as the Nazis in this film.[26] Mascha's terror during her visit to Gestapo headquarters is matched by her earlier terror when she is surrounded by a threatening and mocking crowd of patriotic Czechs when she asks a cab to take her to the Gestapo. But Czaka experiences a complete *mise-en-scène* of betrayal as 'eye-witnesses' (coached by the underground to follow a carefully arranged scenario) implicate him in the assassination. His protestations of innocence are met by Nazi incredulity: 'Are you trying to say the whole city of Prague is conspiring against you?' Purloined objects, such as his golden cigarette lighter with his initials, are placed in compromising locations. Eventually, his own house is made into an incriminating *mise-en-scène*, complete with murder weapon and Gruber's dead body. Buried within the propaganda story of Nazi terror, Czaka's betrayal stands as perhaps the extreme point of Lang's scenography of paranoia: appearances arranged in an elaborate manner to make an innocent man seem guilty of murder. This exceeds the coincidences and misidentifications of *Fury* or *You Only Live Once*, detailing an intentional scheme of entrapment. Lang shows in the last moments of the film that even the Nazis realise Czaka's innocence, but endorse the lie to save face.

Hangmen Also Die develops the paranoid device of the unguarded moment when characters unconsciously betray their identity. Dr. Svoboda reveals his profession as a doctor by his too expert bandaging of Mascha's brother's finger. But more sinisterly, Czaka reveals his role as the traitor to the underground when he laughs out loud at a joke told in German (when earlier his claim that he did not understand German had cleared him of a previous accusation of betrayal). The underground again stage manage a seemingly innocent situation that becomes a deadly confrontation: the telling of the joke by a complicit waiter during a friendly dinner as Czaka reads the menu and cannot suppress his explosive laughter. Caught by an unexpected punch line, Czaka laughs himself to death. The anti-Nazi films, then, allowed Lang to return to his strengths within genre film-making and refine his creation of an everyday terrain of paranoia in which ordinary events reveal themselves in an instant as sinister and deadly.

The Woman in the Window applies these techniques expertly. The sudden violence of Claude Mazard's bursting unexpectedly into his mistress's apartment; slapping her and throttling Wanley; Alice placing the scissors into Wanley's hand as he struggles beneath Mazard; his almost spastic stabbing of the man on top of him – all of this happens so quickly (less than a minute of screen time) that it seems like a magic trick which transforms a wish-fulfilment fantasy into a nightmare. But Lang introduces it with a cut and a coincidence that establish the entrance as part of a careful design. The shot of Mazard entering the door to Alice's apartment building cuts to Wanley laughing as he tries to open a champagne bottle, then cuts his finger as he breaks the wire. The accident introduces the first spilling of blood and motivates Alice to get the scissors (to open the bottle) which will become the murder weapon. There is no visible master enunciator stage managing this coincidence, no Mabuse or Czech underground, only the film-maker Lang, or perhaps Wanley's super-ego as he dreams in the club. But the formal symmetries introduce the paranoia of a world which seems complicit, determined to trap a man.

Paranoia is a term frequently applied to Lang's style, and I have avoided it for the most part, because I feel that it denotes something that gradually develops in Lang's style, truly emerging in his late career. As a term, paranoia straddles psychology and politics with many contested definitions and etiologies. As a form of delusion, its defining characteristic lies in its systematic nature and its relation to a persecution complex. Suspicion of a powerful and coherent system rules the paranoid style of politics which, as Richard Hofstadter said, 'is far more coherent than real life since it leaves no room for mistakes, failures or ambiguities'.[27] If, as I have claimed throughout this book, modernity takes the form of complex interlocking systems of technology, and control or manipulation of such systems forms the great theme of Lang's master criminal films, then not only is paranoia one of Lang's grand themes, but it may be the inevitable byproduct of modernity. As Andrew Sarris said of Lang: 'If this vision be called paranoid, Lang's films might be said to recall the century of Hitler and Hiroshima with the post-Freudian punch-line: "I'm not paranoid. I am being persecuted." '[28] The theme of persecution is essential to paranoia and one can chart a steady change in the status of Lang's protagonists from masters of such systems, to their victims.

Thus although the megalomania of Mabuse, Haghi and Baum clearly relates to paranoia, the emphasis on the criminal's will-to-power creates a different tone to the later films. No question that we are dealing with a paranoid's world in these earlier films, but not from the point of view of the persecuted victim. The lack of a clear-cut protagonist in M begins to tip the tone towards paranoia, a direct result as well of the increased role of surveillance in Lang's plots. The carceral society intentionally produces paranoia as one of the methods of social control employed by the panopticon of surveillance (am I being watched?). Thus Lang's Hollywood social trilogy moves ever closer to paranoia, as the theme of being wrongly accused and condemned dominates both *Fury* and *You Only Live Once*. However, the claims of social criticism made by these films, which denounce the unjust conviction of Taylor or the lynching of Wilson as miscarriages of justice, somewhat undercut the totalising view of paranoia. The injustices in these films are to some degree mistakes, rather than results of a deliberate system. Further, both Wilson and Taylor manage to rebel against the fates dealt out to them, Wilson by attempting to become a mini-Mabuse, Taylor through his outlaw devotion to Joan. Thus, except for the fact that we do not sympathise with Czaka, *Hangmen Also Die* anticipates the full-blown emergence of paranoia in Lang's cinema: Czaka is intentionally framed in a world in which justice no longer needs to assemble proof, but can simply manufacture it.

Paranoia in Lang, as I am defining it, is impersonal. It seems to arise out of the alienated environment of the urban landscape. It does not primarily express the will-to-power of a tyrant, but the formal symmetries of an overly coherent world, almost a work of art. As such, the structures and methods of the Destiny-machine, the basis for paranoia, have not changed much; rather, the point of view from which they are observed has switched. The films of paranoia focus on the victim of the Destiny-machine rather than its self-appointed masters. Paranoia entails a revelation of the Destiny-machine as a crushing force which is set in motion, less by the hubris of a character than by an accidental gesture, a slight infraction of a taboo, a sudden vulnerability, an erotic desire. As opposed to a titanic revolt crushed by the very powers they invoked, the films of paranoia end in pathos, with a sense of loss.

The paranoid victim is not entirely passive; however, the action he undertakes ends up tightening the scenario of entrapment that surrounds him. An accidental participant in the murder, Wanley now takes charge of the cover-up. The first stage of his *mise-en-scène* is the eradication of evidence, washing the murder weapon and, most importantly, disposing of the body. But even as Wanley moves about the woman's apartment with new-found methodical assurance, the decor of mirrored walls that catches and multiplies his image and other details (such as his hat left on the bed – a forbidden action in traditional superstition: a way of inviting trouble, and undoubtedly another Lang joke) hint that his efforts are feckless. We have the recurrent Langian question: who is really in charge of this *mise-en-scène*? But there is no tyrant that reveals his hand on the puppet strings; simply an impersonal order of things which, like Emerson's earth made of glass, reveals and reflects the protagonist's guilt.

Wanley tries to act without leaving a trace, but even as he leaves Alice's apartment to get his car in order to remove the body, we see her examine the vest he left behind as pledge of his return. She finds the pencil with his initials RW left inadvertently in his pocket. Like Czaka's golden lighter emblazoned with EC, or the hat with Eddie Taylor's initials, the pen becomes one of those signs of identity in Lang which gain their significance by going astray, the first sign of Wanley's inability either to suppress or retain his identity. Even his car trip back to Alice's apartment leaves traces: the garage man who demonstrates his knowledge of when tenants come and go, the traffic cop who stops him because he has forgotten to turn on his headlights.

The *corpus delicti* must also be stripped, as the unwilling murderers go through the few things the dead man has on his person. Only a watch with the initials CM indicates his identity (and provides a parallel between Wanley's initialled pencil and the corpse he is disposing of). Wanley directs Alice: all personal effects must be dropped into the East River, the rug must be cleaned thoroughly of blood stains, the scissors boiled, the whole apartment gone over and cleaned to eliminate any sign that either Mazard or Wanley were ever there. Wanley's departure with the body should mark the last contact he and Alice will have with each other, an encounter out of the ordinary partaking of both desire and death and now, hopefully, to be forgotten. He doesn't tell her his name, although he knows hers, Alice Reed, from the apartment buzzer. As Alice watches him from the glass door to her apartment building, we see her image once more doubled by a reflection on the glass, and then see her point of view of Wanley's car taking off, somewhat blurred by the view through the rain-washed pane. Will the incident vanish like a dream, or are they each trapped in their respective frames?

His late night trip into the wilds of Westchester county to discard the embarrassing body outside the city limits, finds Wanley inadvertently leaving more traces of himself, even as he strives to get rid of the evidence of his crime. The highway on this rainy night is manned by sharp-eyed officials: the toll booth attendant who drops Wanley's dime, the motorcycle cop who watches as he just avoids running the traffic signal. As he discards his burden in the woods off the Bronx River Parkway, Wanley's hand and coat catch on a barbed wire fence (the second time he cuts himself in connection with Mazard). Returning to his car, the sound of an oncoming automobile makes him pull out quickly, without discarding Mazard's straw hat. Wanley drives off before the other car sees him, apparently evading detection, but a pan to the right shows us the tire tracks he has left behind in the mud. Police later find footprints as well, from which they can determine his approximate weight and height. Threads of fabric left on the barbed wire fence indicate the type of suit he wore and drops of blood from the scratch give them his blood type. In attempting to rid the apartment of evidence, Wanley has created another crime scene elsewhere and implanted his presence all around it. Wanley burns Mazard's straw hat in his domestic hearth. The next night after he learns the police have threads from his suit, he burns his own jacket in the same fireplace. Who is he trying to efface: Mazard – or himself? Can he erase the existence of one without erasing the existence of the other?

The Woman in the Window becomes Lang's most obsessive demonstration, thus far, of the instability of modern identity. Wanley's stumbling into a world of sexuality and violence reveals primal urges of aggression and sexual desire lurking beneath the surface of a civilised facade, kept in place by routine and habit. But Lang's questioning of identity does not come simply from this demonstration of the 'Divisional Constitution of Mental Life' (as the diagram on the blackboard behind Wanley's opening lecture proclaims), including Freud's division between ego, super-ego, and id. As in the urban thrillers of *Spies* and *M,* as in the films of social protest, and the anti-Nazi films, Lang builds stories out of the process of tracing a man's identity out of an archive of facts, and of an individual's struggle to wiggle through this network of specifications, whether it truthfully detects his guilt (as here) or falsely accuses him (as in *Fury, You Only Live Once,* and *Hangmen Also Die*). Lang's characters can never truly efface their identities, they cannot 'cover their tracks', but, ironically, the indelible nature of their identity does not guarantee either the integrity of their personality or their survival. On the contrary; the identifying traits of Lang's characters are tracked (or constructed, as in the case of Czaka in *Hangmen Also Die*) in order to pronounce their guilt and to destroy them.

While Wanley's drama consists of trying to evade identification and capture by the police, Lang gives it another twist, one which refers back to Wanley's role as the unconscious author of his own drama, the dreamer of his nightmare. Originally, Wanley wished to have a very specific relation to his erotic fantasy, that of a passive author, one who watches his own creation take place before him, like a dreamer. Recall his refusal to go to a burlesque theater, but willingness to watch from his armchair if the woman would come there and perform for him. His voyeurism in front of the portrait shows the same scopophilic passivity, watching the image come to life before him. Once the murder is committed and Wanley seems compelled to take action, a clever device allows him to continue as an armchair spectator of his own case. His friend District Attorney Lalor becomes a major figure in the Mazard investigation and in the nightly dinners at their club, Wanley is treated to the latest news of the case.

Lalor takes nearly sadistic delight in unfolding the investigation to Dr. Barkstone and Wanley, demonstrating 'how the law nails a man'. As Wanley listens, Lalor lays out the evidence which points to the perpetrator, not noticing that the height, weight, economic circumstances and general description match that of his friend. Repeatedly Wanley completes a bit of evidence in classic examples of self-incrimination ('But a trace like that on a barbed wire fence …' 'Did I say a barbed wire fence?' 'Didn't you?' 'No'), which appear as additional unguarded moments of self-betrayal, or even (following the moralistic psychology of Wallis's novel) an unconscious desire to confess. But other factors surface, as well. When Lalor explains that the murderer must have scratched himself, Wanley shows him the scratch on his hand, the very evidence Lalor is searching for, and asks him if it suggests anything to him. While either bravado, or a desire to be caught, or both, may be functioning here, Lalor's analysis, although missing the evidence, hits upon another aspect of Wanley's relation to the crime. 'Yes,' he replies, 'it suggests very strongly that you are eaten up with envy.' Wanley, he claims, is trying to elbow his way into the case and into the spotlight.

In other words, Lalor claims Wanley wants to control the case by hinting he is the murderer. He is torn between a desire to eradicate any trace of his involvement and, I would claim, a certain desire for recognition as the murderer, as the author of the plot rather than its unwitting victim. He aspires to the position of power desired by most of Lang's protagonists, that of authority and authorship, mastery and enunciation. The beautiful irony of the paranoid films is that the victim can only claim that position through self-condemnation. When Lalor takes Wanley to the site where the body was found Wanley inadvertently leads the police in the right direction. Lalor calls out, 'Richard, are you going to be the guide?' This desire to direct the drama, to claim the murder as well as the investigation, motivates Wanley's self-betrayals as much as unconscious guilt or simple absent-mindedness. Slumbering beneath his conscious action, a typical Langian desire to be recognised as the man behind it all stirs inside Wanley, however impotently. There is an impulse to become an artist in this sidewalk connoisseur of portraits (albeit a repressed one) which can only surface as self-betrayal.

Eternal Return

Yet if Hope has flown away
In a night, or in a day,
In a vision, or in none,
Is it therefore the less *gone*?
All that we see or seem
Is but a dream within a dream.

                                      E. A. Poe

The difference between the world of paranoia that I find in the framed desire cycle and earlier Lang films is one of tone and degree. Paranoia certainly characterises all of Lang's films, but I would claim that in this series the source of a malevolent will becomes increasingly pervasive and impersonal, as if it sprang from the environment itself. A sudden arousal of desire in a character triggers this transformation of the environment, so that an erotic impulse entails enslavement to circumstances. This combination of eroticism and paranoia made Lang's films so influential on the series of Hollywood films now known as *film noir*. *Film noir* poses a fascinating thicket for film critics and the temptation, once one enters it, is never to come out; therefore, my comments on Lang's relation to the series must be brief.

Unlike the western or the musical, *film noir* is a term, as James Naremore puts it in the best study of the form, *More than Night*, that was constructed *after the fact* by critics and historians at some distance from the films.[29] It was not, therefore, like established genres, a series of ready-made conventions that both film-makers and audiences could count on being familiar from long exposure. *Film noir*, as presently understood, is less a formula or consistent structure, than what I would call, using a term of Walter Benjamin's, a constellation:[30] a loose group of motifs, stylistic devices and plot lines between which a critic can draw endless imaginary lines connecting them into a shifting series of figures. Therein lies the fascination of defining *film noir* which, as Naremore says, everyone does a bit differently.[31] Nonetheless, in the later 1940s viewers and film-makers sensed something different being introduced into the crime film, which I would claim was a strong injection of the erotic, as if the films of Josef von Sternberg had been crossbred with *Public Enemy* or *Little Caesar*. Thus we get murder mysteries that concentrate less on clever and funny detectives than on a woman who exerts a fatal attraction.

The Woman in the Window and *Scarlet Street* even more so derive a sense of fatality not simply from the opposition to the law which gave the gangster his reputed tragic heroism, but from an erotic entanglement. The key *film noir* from 1944, Billy Wilder's adaptation of James M. Cain's *Double Indemnity*, introduced the figure of a cold-blooded woman who uses sexuality to convince a man to aid her in a crime, setting the model that a series of other *noir* heroines (or villains) followed to a greater or lesser degree in the mid- and late 40s: Claire Trevor in *Murder, My Sweet*, Ann Savage in *Detour*, Ava Gardner in *The Killers*, Rita Hayworth in *The Lady from Shanghai*, Jane Greer in *Out of the Past*, Yvonne De Carlo in *Criss Cross*. All these films, and many other key films in the *noir* series, use this entwining of eroticism and crime to create a new form of thriller founded on a flawed hero with a strong sense of sexual guilt deriving from his surrender to the allure of the fatal woman. This guilt sparks his paranoia, placing him within a world where threats emerge from unexpected quarters, and life becomes doubled: apparently routine on the outside, but devious and criminal (and sexually exciting) undercover. The sequence in *Double Indemnity* where Walter Neff and Phyllis Dietrichson plot a murder under the guise of shopping at a big supermarket clearly parallels the sequence where Wanley and Alice exchange poison in the office corridor in *The Woman in the Window*.[32]

The Woman in the Window and *Scarlet Street* fit within the series of *film noir*, helping to define the fatality of the form. However, when placed within the series of Lang films, certain elements stand out which, while they do not contradict the patterns of *film noir*, do lead to a uniquely Langian narrative. First, the age of the characters played by Robinson in both films contrasts sharply with the young heroes of most *film noirs*. In fact, fatal women frequently use their young romantic dupes to help them get rid of older husbands (most obviously in *Double Indemnity* and *The Postman Always Rings Twice*, where Oedipal overtones dominate). In *Double Indemnity*, in fact, Robinson plays the younger hero's nemesis, the insurance investigator who uncovers the murder plot. Lang's films with Robinson introduce a middle-aged eroticism which has an element of pathos, or even absurdity. The women who exert the fatal attraction may be temptresses, but Alice remains relatively well-intentioned in *The Woman in the Window*, and Katherine, while particularly insincere and predatory in *Scarlet Street*, nonetheless is forced into her role by her slimy pimp. Lang de-emphasises individual responsibility and even psychology, in favour of a fatal environment which seems not only to reflect characters' anxieties, but to trigger a series of fateful coincidences which follow from an unguarded erotic surrender, like a collapsing line of dominoes.

Thus Richard Wanley feels caught in a life of premature stagnation, burdened by a cycle of routine and petty details. He dreams of revolt and erotic possibilities and encounters violence. In trying to undo the effects of his unguarded moment, he discovers a paranoid universe where the same intermeshing petty details now conspire against him with deadly effect. The imprint of his tires or shoes, the case of poison ivy he picks up when he discards the body, slips of the tongue when speaking to his friends – all could lead to his death in the electric chair. In a seemingly benign coincidence (which academics understand the irony of), an announcement in *The Times*, accompanied by a photograph, of his promotion to chairman of his department reveals his identity to Alice Reed, the accomplice he had parted from without revealing his name. With contact between the two characters re-established, the film's narrative begins to repeat itself, recycling its previous elements of being discovered by an intruder and then having to commit a murder.

The final act of this drama opens as a new character comes on the scene, the blackmailer, Heidt, Mazard's former bodyguard. Played by Dan Duryea with oily malevolence, Heidt appears as a resurrection of Claude Mazard. Like Mazard, he invades Alice's apartment to discover evidence of guilt, and like his boss he sports a wide-brimmed straw hat. But instead of slapping Alice around (he does do this, later), he systematically searches the apartment, looking for the traces of the murder Alice was supposed to have cleaned away. In fact, the evidence that first excites his suspicions comes precisely from her tidiness: 'Not a finger mark anywhere, not even where you think they'd be naturally'. In his systematic and rather sadistically threatening scrutiny, he also recalls Lalor, the third character in the film who wears a wide-brimmed straw hat. Heidt acts as a condensation of the two, displaying Mazard's potential violence and lascivious manner (the way he paws through the clothing in Alice's drawers), combined with Lalor's careful assembly of evidence. He does find a few things (the terrain of paranoia can never be thoroughly cleared, it always yields more), most importantly, Wanley's pencil with his initials, hidden in a glove in Alice's drawer – its very concealment indicating its significance. Like Hans Beckert in *M*, Alice and Wanley are now squeezed from two sides, both legal and criminal investigators, as Heidt demands a pay-off.

Alice meets with Wanley to discuss what they should do. Lang tracks along with the couple as Alice explains Heidt's demands, filming them through an iron rail fence that all too clearly evokes jail bars. However, the fence ends abruptly and opens into a gateway as Wanley enumerates the ways to deal with a blackmailer: pay until you're penniless; go to the police and expose your secret; or kill him. Mazard's *Doppelgänger* has come back from the grave, threatens punishment, and must be killed all over again. But important differences separate the two murders. The first was almost a reflex action, unpremeditated: Alice handing Wanley the scissors as he was being choked. This time, Wanley plans everything calmly, obtaining a medicine his doctor friend prescribed for him, a stimulant which, taken in an overdose, causes a massive heart attack. He meets Alice in another public place (he avoids her apartment now), the corridor of an office building, under the cover of casual strangers. (Lang choreographs this scene beautifully – with passersby interrupting their clandestine conversation, including a man who passes through the corridor wearing a straw hat identical to the one worn by Mazard/Lalor/Heidt.) He gives her the money he has raised as well as the stimulant and careful instructions.

Wanley remains off stage during the murder he has planned. Alice plays it as a seduction, beautifully dressed, with romantic music playing as she first tries to charm Heidt into taking less than the full amount of the money. He is suspicious from the start, asking her, 'who told her to say that?' sensing a well-rehearsed cha- rade. Although it is unclear exactly how much Alice is following Wanley's directions (is she really tempted to go off with Heidt? – Lang cuts at this point to Wanley pacing the floor in his apartment, awaiting the outcome of his plot), her behaviour only serves to mask the real intention: poisoning Heidt with a doctored drink. It is her focus on the drink that punctures the performance, as Heidt realises the set-up and refuses the drink he is so persistently offered. He demands the rest of the five thousand he has asked for. Uncovering Alice's hiding place, Heidt also finds the expensive watch with the initials CM (which she had not gotten rid of, as Wanley told her to). Her performance collapses with these revelations, as Heidt scoffs, 'You amateurs!' and demands more money. Alice calls Wanley, who, seated in his arm- chair, hears of the plot's failure.

As I have noted previously, the male characters in *The Woman in the Window* mirror each other: Lalor, Mazard and Heidt, all wearing the same straw hat and all posed in a punishing role towards Wanley. But there is also an identification between Wanley and his victim, marked by Langian identity tokens and their dis- covery/destruction (the burning of Mazard's hat and Wanley's suit; the discovery by Heidt of Wanley's monogrammed pencil and Mazard's initialled watch). It was Wanley's hope that they could clear away all traces that either he or Mazard had vis- ited Alice's apartment that night. Heidt mirrored Mazard not only through the threat he posed to the couple, but by becoming their next victim. When this murder fails, Wanley decides he must commit suicide, taking the same stimulant he had arranged for Heidt's murder. Although the action is fully motivated by the plot (Wanley's inability to pay more blackmail, the failure of the murder attempt), the symmetry is striking: unable to kill Heidt, he kills himself with the same weapon. The mirrored characters align and superimpose: killing Mazard was, in a sense, killing himself, and now that aggression which he had directed outside himself folds back onto him. A dream logic of condensation and displacement seems to shape the drama.

As Wanley sits in his armchair and tells Alice he is 'too tired' to think out their next move, we hear a clock ticking loudly (presumably the large pendulum clock we have seen in his apartment before). As in so many Lang films, the Destiny-machine announces itself through a relay of clocks across the film: the clocks in the club that are superimposed over Wanley, and that announce the time he wished to be awak- ened; Wanley's wristwatch and his concern over the time as he drinks with Alice, progressively violating his evening routine; the illuminated clock outside Alice's apartment building which marked the stages of this night of seduction and murder each time someone entered or exited the apartment; the modernist clock in Alice's apartment which indicated the time she has spent waiting for Heidt to arrive on the evening they planned to murder him. Like these regularly appearing clocks, the progress of the Destiny-machine in this film has been both systematic and pervasive. No criminal organisation, corrupt legal system, German spy ring or underground conspiracy plots the characters' demise. Mabuse's mastery of interlocking technology has become part of the everyday, like the interaction of clock and phone call as Wanley decides to commit suicide. But their lack of drama derives from their efficiency. The paranoid world Wanley stumbled into is, ironically, also a world based on routine, and is routinely destroying him.

Wanley rises wearily from his armchair, pausing to gaze on the photographs of wife and children positioned by the telephone. From a low camera height, Lang frames him walking through two nested doorways to get to the bathroom, perhaps the most beautiful instance of the doubly framed, entrapping compositions frequent in this film, especially in the entrance to Alice's apartment building. The loudly ticking clock and the powders Wanley dissolves in a glass of water recall Joan's suicide attempt in *You Only Live Once*. As in the earlier film, Lang cuts at this dramatic moment to a scene which changes the situation.

Alice Reed hears gunfire in front of her building. Rushing outside, she discovers the police have shot and killed Heidt, who fired on them when they pulled him over for questioning. Going through his pockets, they find the money he took from Alice and the watch with Mazard's initials. Mazard's former bodyguard, who had been a suspect in Lalor's investigation from the start, now seems condemned by the very evidence with which he intended to blackmail Alice. In perfect irony the alignment of events now seems to break the other way. The killing of Heidt has been accomplished, without Alice or Wanley's involvement, and simultaneously they have been cleared of the murder. Does a *deus ex machina* lurk in the wings? Notice again the dream logic of mirrored characters: Wanley begins to kill himself in the manner he attempted, but failed, to kill Heidt. Lang cuts, and, as if by black magic, *Heidt* is killed.

But Lang's paranoid plotting here twists into a new design. Both the parallel with *You Only Live Once* and the *deus ex machina* become derailed (or at least delayed). As in the earlier film, the suicide is nearly prevented by a phone call, as Alice rushes home to call Wanley. In close-up, we see the unanswered phone sitting on the table in Wanley's parlour, nestled among the family photographs, ringing repeatedly as the clock ticks on. On the other end of the line Alice asks the operator to try the number again. We see another close-up of the ringing telephone as the camera pulls back and pivots, showing Wanley slumped down in his armchair, the empty glass in his hand, the clock visible behind him. He rouses himself and looks over at the telephone. He moves the hand grasping the glass a bit, as if making a vain effort to reach for the phone. But his arm goes limp. The camera closes in on him as his eyes glaze over. He moves his head slightly as the camera frames him closely. His eyes move slowly and he seems for a moment to stare directly into the camera lens, then his eyes lose focus and his head slumps, as the telephone continues to ring insistently and the clock ticks on.

This stands as one of the bitterest moments in Lang's cinema, bereft of even the romanticism of the end of *You Only Live Once*. We are in the midst of one of the undelivered messages that haunt Lang's cinema, and the unanswered telephone here spells death as surely as it spelled madness for Hofmeister in *The Testament of Dr. Mabuse*. The irony is sharpened by its contrast with *You Only Live Once* where the telephone brought the voice of a lover and marked a rebirth for Joan, devoted

solely now to Eddie. Here Wanley's one-night stand cannot get through to give him the information that would save his life. Evidence and coincidence combined to clear the guilty couple, but ... too late, says the clock. The ease with which a happy ending *could* have been reached must be kept in mind when one considers the rather different *deus ex machina* that now announces itself.

No cut, no dissolve intervenes from the close-up of Wanley's apparent death. Within the same close framing, a hand enters and shakes the shoulder of the slumped-over figure. On the sound track the repetitive ringing of the telephone had gradually faded out. Now we hear the melodic chiming of a clock, as an off screen voice says, 'It's ten-thirty, Professor Wanley'. The camera pulls back and we see Wanley awakening, seated in his armchair in his club, the attendant standing next to him. As the camera frames him in medium long shot, he looks around – as we do – astonished by the change in decor. Let us linger over the trick for a moment (which, when I met him, Lang refused to explain to me, saying, 'I prefer mystery'.) This single continuous shot begins with the close-up of the telephone table in Wanley's apartment. The camera pulls back and moves to the right, showing Wanley in the chair wearing a dressing gown, the clock on the wall behind him. Then the camera moves in on a 'choker' close-up of Wanley's face. It is, of course, during this close framing that everything is done, the wall of Wanley's apartment removed, the wall of the club moved in, the telephone table taken away and another table substituted, and, most seamlessly, Wanley's robe whisked off (a corner can be seen disappearing at his left shoulder as he slumps over) and the suit beneath it revealed. Thus, when the camera pulls out again, a whole new environment has been assembled.

Lang hoped the elegance of this 'trick' would cover the hackneyed feeling of the 'It's all a dream' revelation. Lang's deep love of trick cinema surfaces here, as he resolves a narrative tangle on a formal rather than a diegetic level (avoiding the happy ending available to him if Wanley had just answered the phone in time) by switching its ontological level. Lang entered this dream with a dissolve which we take for an ellipsis. He backs out of it without any transition, with a trick of continuity. Lang, as a narrator, again misleads and tricks the audience, demonstrates his control and asserts authority. But can any degree of analysis ever overcome the gut feeling one has of being cheated by this resolution? Lang does trick his audience, knowingly and repeatedly, but never without purpose. No-one can deny that an exterior force exerted pressure here, the demand of the Hollywood Production Code (which Lang always fought against) that Alice and Wanley be punished in some form. Lang, secure in his own belief that Wanley committed no serious crime, does everything to avoid punishing him. Thus, he detours away from the cautionary tale, the moralistic and puritanical ending of Wallis's novel.

But does the dream revelation undo the bitter image of Wanley's death, the triumph of an ironic and paranoid world where everything conspires against one, even last-moment salvations? The logic which condemns Wanley to death is not founded in morality, but in Wanley's area of expertise, psychology: it is Wanley's super-ego that demands his death. Although there is clearly a sense of relief and release as the camera pulls back and reveals Wanley alive, returned to an earlier moment before his fateful breach of routine, the primary tone for this awakening (underscored again by Arthur Lange's wistful musical theme) is melancholy – like the sigh that Alkmene gives at the end of Kleist's *Amphitryon* when she realises that both her nightmare and her dream are over and she has returned to a familiar, but limited, reality.[33]

Lang was determined that the last moments of the film should shift into comedy. This is mainly accomplished by a coda (again recalling the ending of *The Cabinet of Dr. Caligari* as well as Freud's concept of the 'dream day' – the elements of everyday life previous to a dream which the dream will take up and transform) in which both

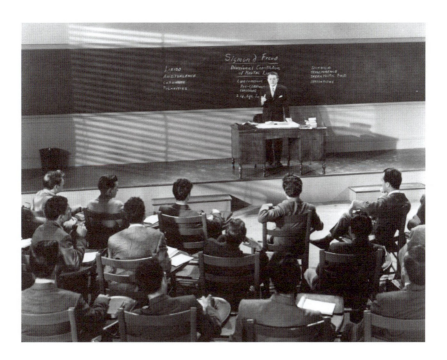

Mazard and Heidt, or at least the actors playing them, reappear. Wanley reassures himself of his identity as soon as he rises from his chair by finding his pencil with his initials still in his pocket. As he retrieves his hat from the hat check man, the actor turns out to be Arthur Loft, the actor who played Mazard. Lang's humour here is pointed. The threatening figure is reduced to a polite and hatless menial who returns Wanley's hat to him (however, as Wanley leaves, Lang shows Loft standing next to a straw hat resting on the shelf behind him!).[34] Outside the club, Dan Duryea is similarly demoted from Heidt, the sinister blackmailer, to Ted, the amiable doorman.

Lang's last laugh is his most bitter. Wanley repeats the deviation from routine that began his dream and walks over for one last look at the woman in the window. The shot/ reverse shot pattern is repeated, only Wanley at first expresses amusement instead of longing. However, when a woman's face once more becomes reflected over the shoulder of the portrait, he expresses terror. Within the euphemisms of the Production Code, the woman is coded as a cheap prostitute, not at all the mysterious temptress clothed in dark feathers that Wanley's dream summoned up. She asks Wanley for a light, but he displays complete panic, almost hysteria, and runs away. No more rebellious eroticism or sense of adventure for him. He has become again the docile creature of routine, a castrated middle-aged man. Wanley dashes off-screen, the prostitute departs wearily, and the portrait remains to dominate the frame. Is there some promise – or threat – still within it? For whom? Who said this was a happy ending?

12

Scarlet Street: Life Is a Nightmare

Mirror Images

This play is ennobled by the distance which everywhere
separates image and mirror-image, the signifier and the
signified. Thus the mourning play presents us not with the
image of a higher existence but only with one of two mirror-
images, and its continuation is not less schematic than itself.
The dead become ghosts.

Walter Benjamin, '*Trauerspiel* and Tragedy'[1]

I have described *Scarlet Street* as the dark reflection of *The Woman in the Window*.
The relation between the two films is as clear as a mirror image, but also as devious;
the apparent absolute duplication of the mirror image (which inspires so many tales
of ontological confusion between image and reality) can hide the duplicity of the
relation between reflection and life, the essential reversal of orientation the mirror
performs. The two films share the same cast of actors – Edward G. Robinson, Joan

Bennett, and Dan Duryea – and nearly the same roster of characters – Robinson as an old man experiencing a sudden rush of erotic longing, Bennett as a seductive *femme fatale* and Duryea as a shady character who hopes to profit from the weaknesses of others. This recurrence of casting and characters over the two films recalls the repeated casting of Dagover, Janssen and Goetzke as lovers and Death in the various episodes of *Der müde Tod*, encouraging us to see them as variations on a theme.

No variation exists without significant differences and *Scarlet Street*'s reflection of *The Woman in the Window* recasts the lights and shadows considerably. Wanley's modest, but undeniable, professional status exceeds the limited achievements of the cashier of twenty-five years, Christopher Cross, as the contrast between Wanley's opening classroom lecture and Chris's opening stammering speech of appreciation to his boss indicates. Likewise, the sophisticated rich man's mistress, Alice Reed, who self-confidently picks up Wanley is a far cry from 'poor, dopey, little Kitty', Katherine March, whom we first see being knocked around by her pimp. Duryea's performances as Heidt the blackmailer and Johnny Prince the pimp carry the most similarities, but his relationship to the characters played by Bennett differ considerably in the two films.

Given the rough similarities in plot situations and imagery, each film explores different tonalities and narrative resolutions in this mirror play. Both films, for instance, end with Robinson walking past an art gallery at night and seeing a portrait of a woman which once embodied his erotic hopes or fantasies, and which now calls forth anxiety, or sorrow. But the extremely different tone of these two denouements constitutes the greatest reversal between the two films. Karl Marx, contemplating Louis Bonaparte's seizing of power and desire to resuscitate the glory of Napoleon I, observed that if history repeats itself, in the process the original tragedy becomes a farce.[2] In retooling *The Woman in the Window*, Lang performed the reverse transformation. Wanley's panicked reaction to the re-emergence of the woman from the window rounds out that film with a farcical guffaw, while Cross's unblinking stare at Katherine March's so-called *Self-Portrait* at the end of *Scarlet Street* is the closest Lang (and perhaps Hollywood) ever got to a tragic vision (or more properly, to anticipate a theme I will develop later, to the form discussed by Benjamin known in German as *Trauerspiel*, 'mourning play').

But there is another mirror image involved in this film, another film reflected and transformed. Beyond its intricate relation to *The Woman in the Window*, *Scarlet Street* is the first Lang film that is a direct remake of a previous film, Jean Renoir's 1931 *La Chienne*. In interviews, Lang stressed that neither he nor scriptwriter Dudley Nichols looked at the Renoir film again, although both admired it from seeing it a decade before.[3] If this is true it was not from lack of trying, since McGilligan reveals that, in fact, they tried hard to locate a print of *La Chienne* for screening, although they may not have been successful in obtaining one.[4] In any case, although the film follows the same plot line (presumably taken from the source of both films, a novel by Georges La Fouchardière), Lang is certainly justified in saying 'not a single scene was copied'.[5] Interestingly, in 1941, Renoir, who, like Lang was exiled in Hollywood at this time, also attempting to adapt his unique film style to Hollywood methods, and Dudley Nichols, who had scripted Renoir's first Hollywood films, *Swamp Water* and *This Land is Mine*, had actually discussed the possibility of remaking *La Chienne* in Hollywood with Nichols scripting and Renoir directing.[6]

Illuminating comparisons of the Lang and Renoir films have been offered by Edward Benson, Thomas Brandlmeier and E. Ann Kaplan, from rather different points of view, so I will not attempt a detailed analysis of the relation between the films.[7] However, a comparison of the final scene of each film (the encounter before a shop window which also holds *Scarlet Street* and *The Woman in the Window* in a double reflection) quickly highlights key elements of Lang's style in contrast to Renoir's. Both films end with the protagonist – Maurice Legrand in Renoir's film, Christopher Cross in Lang's – as a derelict, wandering the city streets. Both stage the final irony of the film: the derelict protagonist passes an art gallery just as a rich collector comes out, having bought a canvas which the derelict actually painted years earlier. Given the same basic location and action, even the same ironic situation of penniless painter whose work is carried off as an expensive commodity, the two realisations create antithetical fictional and stylistic worlds.

Renoir's scene is filmed on location on a real Parisian boulevard in bright sunshine with the sound of passing automobiles filtering from off screen. Legrand and a *clochard* buddy stand looking into a window of a gallery somewhat absently, more as a way to pass time than because anything attracts their attention. Renoir's camera moves away from them, leaving them off screen, until it pauses at the doorway of the gallery as a chauffeur emerges, carrying a painting. The large canvas is the self-portrait Legrand painted years before and which the now deceased Lulu and her pimp Dede sold. The camera pans to the left with the chauffeur as he carries the painting to a car parked curbside and places it in the back seat, the face peering over the back of this convertible. During the pan we briefly glimpse Legrand and his buddy in the background, but there is nothing to indicate they have seen the portrait.

Renoir cuts to a long shot of the pair before the window, as they suddenly begin to run towards the car. Did Legrand finally recognise his work? The end of the shot indicates otherwise. His buddy simply scrambles for a cigarette butt some other passerby discarded on the sidewalk, while Legrand rushes to the car in order to get a tip for closing the door, as we saw him do earlier in the scene. With a somewhat awkward cut (by continuity standards) the next shots show, first, the car pulling away, the portrait still peering over the back like a reluctant passenger, then a medium shot of Legrand, looking in the opposite direction as he examines his tip, and exclaims with delight: 'Victor! Twenty francs!' As the two tramps cross the street, he exclaims, 'Life is beautiful!' The camera pulls back and frames this scene within the rectangle of a puppet stage as the curtain comes down and the film ends.

I will return to the corresponding sequence in Lang's version later in this chapter. For now, I simply want to stress the contrasts with Renoir. Whereas Renoir's sequence basks in the bits of contingent reality that location shooting can provide, Lang's takes place not simply on a sound stage were everything has been arranged and fabricated, but within that closed world of Lang's films which Jacques Rivette was one of the first critics to describe, where everything has been determined.[8] No warmth of a spring day penetrates here, no sunshine, not simply because Lang's scene takes place at night (although that already creates a basic contrast between the two scenes), but because there exists no sense of an atmosphere, nature or reality outside of that of the character's obsession. Renoir's location shooting and open composition typify the director who would be the model for film-making for André Bazin, the advocate of a film style steeped in the openness and contingency of the real. However, Renoir's style can hardly be described as documentary. The camera movement from the *clochards* to the chauffeur carrying out the painting underscores an essential irony with an authorial flourish. But the irony is captured in order to be de-dramatised. Legrand does not see his masterpiece being carried to the car, because it is irrelevant to his life now. It withdraws while he delights over the tip he has received. Renoir's final pullback, framing the scene within the puppet stage that opened the film, primarily serves to contrast this open ending with the tidy drama one might see on the stage. As the puppet announcer said in the prologue to the film, these characters are neither heroes nor villains, just ordinary folks.

It would not be unusual for Lang to deliver to his audience an ironic incident without revealing it to his characters, as Renoir does here. But Lang tends to use such disparities in knowledge as ways of complicating his narratives or creating suspense, rather than resolving them. At the end of *Scarlet Street*, Lang makes sure his character is not only aware of the irony, but also receives its full effect. A tracking shot frames Cross as he wanders along a busy city street on a night shortly before Christmas. As he passes a display window he pauses and a chord on the soundtrack draws our attention to his off screen look. The next shot shows Cross's point of view as he sees (through a plate glass door) the portrait he painted of Kitty which became titled (in an irony I will explore more fully later) *Self-Portrait*, being carried by a chauffeur and an assistant from a gallery. With a trembling and uncanny electronic chord on the soundtrack, the camera executes a breathtaking track-in that keeps the moving painting in the centre of the screen and enlarges Kitty's portrait until her face and staring eyes are framed in close-up and seem to confront the camera.

Lang cuts to a close-up of Chris staring off, his eyes following the painting with a look containing equal parts longing, horror and confusion. In the reverse angle the portrait of Kitty seems to shrink as the two men carry it away from the camera towards a waiting car. Lang now cuts to a new angle of the doorway to the gallery where Dellarowe, the gallery owner, stands with a middle-aged woman wearing a mink coat. He gestures off and says, 'Well, there goes her masterpiece'. Lang cuts to a medium shot of Cross as he begins to walk on. Lang returns to Dellarowe and the woman as the gallery owner says, 'I really hate to part with it.' The woman retorts, 'For ten thousand dollars, I don't think you mind.' As she says this, Dellarowe laughs and Chris crosses in front of them; they move out of frame right as Chris moves off screen, left.

The sequences are executed with almost polar aesthetic assumptions. Not only does Renoir open the sequences to the centripetal energies of a larger environment, he places the sequence's central irony within a *mise-en-scène* which refuses to be dominated by it, any more than Legrand is. Life goes on, in and around the tragedy of Legrand's life; even he is unaware of its deepest ironies. But with the closed-down and even paranoid world of *Scarlet Street*, the film seems designed to contain, enframe and stage this central encounter, forcing its significance on Chris. One might say of Lang, paraphrasing Mallarmé, that the world exists in order to be placed within a frame. The framing in Lang acts as a guide to focus our attention, as it usually does in classical Hollywood film (one of the reasons Lang's interaction with Hollywood was generally more fruitful than Renoir's), and what lies off screen is not a circumambient world indicated by sound and random passersby, but the object of the gaze, and a fateful encounter with an image. Lang not only frames a world, but creates a space of significance which contains and poses emblems and riddles, allegories and demonstrations. It would be foolish to condemn Lang's staging for its nearly allegorical clarity or 'heavy-handedness', any more than to criticise Renoir's direction for its apparently random awkwardness. These are incommensurable and fundamental directorial stances, and the complexity of the allegories of desire in Lang's 'framed desire' cycle spring from this closed-down, artificial world, as much as his silent films' mastery of allegories of fatal landscapes and hidden enunciators emerged from his monumental sets and elliptical montage.

The essential contrast between Renoir's and Lang's handling lies not simply in the contrast of an open versus a closed visual style, or in the different narrative stances (with the irony outside the character's knowledge in Renoir but founded in Chris's point of view shot in Lang). It dwells, I would maintain, in different registers of vision. Legrand's painting is a fact of a visual world: we see it, while Legrand ignores it. But Christopher Cross does more than 'see' the portrait of Kitty. The framing, the camera movement, even the film score, transforms this shot from a simple point of view shot to a truly Langian visionary moment, as the portrait looms before Cross, dominates his visual field and seems to stare right at him. As Stephen Jenkins so rightly claimed (without, however, considering how it complicates the logic of the Mulveyian male gaze through which he reads this film), 'the image looks at Chris who looks back at it'.[9] In a sense this is the ultimate mirror image in this film, an image, like one's face in the mirror, that confronts and looks back at the viewer without losing its status as an image.

That this mirror does not seem to reflect Chris does not forbid this analogy. Although the image is a portrait of Kitty, it was Chris who entitled it *Self-Portrait*. The reversals in gender this self-reflection involves take us into the core of this nightmarish film where the visionary scene reveals not simply a likeness, but an allegory of the instability of identity, and, ultimately, the presence of death in Kitty's staring, yet sightless eyes. Whereas Renoir responds to a visual world which is continuous, varied and all-encompassing, larger than the human drama which takes place within it, and (in the naturalist tradition) rather indifferent to the human desires it thwarts or engenders, Lang creates metaphors, riddles and emblems, even within the Hollywood continuity system, which demand to be read and decoded. For Lang, space is bisected and criss-crossed with both desire and significance.

Jenkins' powerful reading of this film takes us into the nightmare of castration and gender identity within a patriarchal system; but he fails, I think, to realise that *Scarlet Street* excavates the assumptions of this system rather than simply naturalising it within a system of editing and composition based on the male gaze. This is a film which undermines (or encourages us, as viewers and critics, to undermine, through the reflections it provokes in us) the patriarchal system Jenkins argues it exemplifies. The complexity of its use of vision and images (which Jenkins so well captures) should indicate to a viewer that vision and seeing become a *problem* in this film, not simply the domain of male privilege.

In Lang's first treatment of the film, he included another signature window-shopping sequence which not only would have tied it closer to *The Woman in the Window* (and the films of the social trilogy), but also set up a marked antithesis to this final scene. After leaving the office party that opens the film, walking home rather tipsy, Chris pauses in front of a store window where window-trimmers are undressing mannequins as they change the display. Noticing Cross's stare at this sexless nudity, the decorators pull a curtain over the window.[10] Although apparently never shot, the sequence sets up a significant variation on Lang's previous window display scenes. All of Lang's window-shoppers, from Beckert on, make window displays into theatres for projected desires. Like Joe and Katherine in *Fury*, Chris's projection is sexual, but instead of a preview of an intended marriage, this scene displays artificial bodies, lifeless in their nudity, at best a masturbatory fantasy. But in contrast to Professor Wanley's fantasy voyeurism of *The Woman in the Window*, even this pleasure is denied Chris, as the window-trimmers pull the curtain. Of all of Lang's characters, Chris is the most repressed (*vide* his defensive claim to his wife, 'I never even saw a woman without any clothes!' and her response 'Well, I should hope not!'). In Langian dialectics, however, as normal vision is denied to Chris, his visionary powers as a painter are increased. The ordinary voyeurism and its mastering male gaze is denied to Christopher Cross, yet some more primal, both perverted and profound, vision surfaces. At the end of the film he confronts his own vision in the eyes of the portrait of the woman he has killed. No quickly drawn curtain can remove it from his sight, not even the descending curtain of the puppet stage which closes *La Chienne*.

I have described the mirror inversion of the endings of *The Woman in the Window* and *Scarlet Street* as a flip from farce to tragedy, but the relation between the two films as whole works is not that simple. The final dream twist of *The Woman in the Window* reprieves Wanley from a tragic end (in effect removing the vision of ultimate horror and suicide from his sight) and allows the audience to leave the film, as Lang said, with a 'healthy laugh'.[11] However, the mood of most of the film after the murder of Mazard is certainly sombre, and the strong empathy we feel with Wanley encourages more identification with this character than is usual with Lang. It is only at its final moments, therefore, that *The Woman in the Window* could be described as a comedy. In contrast, although the final fate of Christopher Cross is undeniably bleak and its presentation tragic, Lang does not create a warm, empathetic character here. Chris Cross remains weak and pathetic throughout the film; easily duped and manipulated, he stands at antipodes to the typical purposeful and active male Hollywood hero, and resembles more the klutz or hen-pecked husband of American comedies.[12] Even the sympathetic empathy we readily give to Wanley is denied him. Chris at his best has our pity, and a tone of mockery never entirely disappears from Lang's treatment of him. However, the characters who mock him the most – Kitty, Johnny and his wife Adele – are so entirely lacking in sympathetic traits that we resist taking their view of him. Indeed, of all of Lang's Hollywood films, this is the one that maintains the greatest and most complex distance from his characters. If one invokes Aristotle's understanding of comedy as the portrayal of characters that are inferior to us, *Scarlet Street* certainly maintains through most of its course a comic, or at least an ironic and satiric, tone.

Thus, in a sense *Scarlet Street*, in spite of its cheerless plot, adopts an almost comic and satiric viewpoint towards its action, particularly in the first two thirds of the film. While Wanley's middle-aged flirtation with romance caused a chuckle (exemplified by his friends' amused observation of his longing look at the portrait in the window), Chris's involvement with Kitty draws a savage mockery that recalls Sternberg's *The Blue Angel*, Wedekind's 'Lulu' plays and the denouement of Matsumoto's affair (with another Kitty) in Lang's own *Spies*. Renoir's Guignol puppet stage prologue conveys a similar sense of mockery, but this tone does not permeate Renoir's much more humanist film. Lang (and Nichols), however, seem to imitate the tone of Renoir's fairground prologue (especially the barrel-organ music that accompanies it) in the opening shots of their version.

The first images of *Scarlet Street* are filmed from an unusually low camera position, a sort of gutter-eye view of the street, emphasising a fire hydrant, and a passing dog. As Tom Conley has pointed out, there is a definite scatological theme running through the film, part of its mocking attitude, which Lang overtly acknowledged (and one hardly needs Conley's *gematria* to pick it up).[13] In a curious manner, this opening shot gives us no centre to cling to: its low-key *noir* lighting, extremely low camera height and the passersby on the sidewalk in the foreground that obscure the view, all work against its role as an establishing shot situating us in the location of the drama to come. The sound of a hurdy-gurdy dominates, as a car pulls up in front of a restaurant in the background.

The film's second shot gives us a more typically Langian high angle, focused on the car as a chauffeur speaks to a shimmeringly blonde woman framed in the car window, and then runs up the restaurant stairs. The framing now clearly shows the hurdy-gurdy man and his monkey who hops off the organ and climbs over to the woman, who leans out of the window to look at him. Inside the restaurant, the chauffeur speaks to a waiter outside the private dining room where J. J. Holgarth is entertaining his (male) employees. The waiter enters the dining room and whispers something in the boss's ear (obviously, that the lady is waiting downstairs). This relayed message of erotic promise opens the film, linking together its spaces. We don't see the woman again until after J. J. makes his speech honouring Christopher Cross for his twenty-five years of devoted service and then leaves rather hurriedly. As soon as he leaves, the employees rush to the window and peer out at the woman in the car window below; Lang repeats the high angle, with the monkey performing for the lady, as J. J. approaches the car. As one of the employees exclaims, 'Get a load of that dame!' Lang cuts to the only close-up we get of this nameless woman who initiates the action of the film, shimmeringly highlighted, wreathed in furs and jewellery, as she looks out of the car window, still laughing at the monkey's antics.

This image, with its glamour photography, exemplifies the voyeuristic Hollywood male gaze, embedded within the collective point of view of the clerks of J. J. Holgarth and Company, like naughty schoolboys mockingly spying out their boss's indiscretion ('The boss is stepping out!'). Mockery suffuses the scene, not only the clerks mocking their boss but Lang's view of the clerks and their schoolboy gawking. The woman appears not simply as the object of their gaze, but as a spectator herself of the monkey's tricks. The monkey that amuses the woman parallels J. J., the apparent master, as the scene recalls the prologue to Wedekind's first 'Lulu' play, *Erdgeist* in which the various circus animals cavort around Lulu. The tone of the opening of *Scarlet Street* recalls a particular German genre of sex comedy-tragedy which intertwines a savage critique of repressive patriarchal sexuality around a fascination with a vengeful, destructive, female force (Wedekind's Lulu and Sternberg's Lola-Lola) whose portrayal never completely avoids misogyny.

Lang's film draws on this tradition, especially on its intertwining of mockery and horror, but also transforms it. He changes the name of Renoir's heroine, (originally also named Lulu), to Kitty and aligns her with his earlier deceitful spy-seductress whose feminine wiles were rehearsed and directed by a male enunciator. If Kitty, in her manipulation of Chris, reflects this glamorous woman leaning out of a window to laugh at a little monkey, she also develops the problematic of woman and representation introduced in *The Woman in the Window*, a woman whose image is the product of a male gaze, but who does not remain quietly within the frame that gaze creates.

The Fourteen-Carat, Seventeen-Jewel Cashier

> Cashier: The wheel of time turns, crushing any arms stuck in
> the spokes to stop it.
>   Georg Kaiser, *From Morning to Midnight*[14]

Christopher Cross is a riven character, split between his dominant identity as a cashier in the firm of J. J. Holgarth and his marginal identity as a painter, an activity he fits into the remnants of time and space left to him, his leisure on Sunday and his studio, relegated to the bathroom of the apartment he shares with his shrewish wife, Adele. Lang and Nichols fashion Christopher Cross as the extreme case of an oppressed figure, a Kafkaesque clerk, whose one source of joy, his painting, highlights the oppressed nature of his existence. He is Professor Wanley stripped of his dignity, lacking Wanley's degree of self-reflection and protest, and taking Wanley's habit-driven life to near parody. As Wanley entered his club, Lang superimposed a clock on his back, indicating his internalisation of the Destiny-machine. In the opening of Scarlet Street, Lang is more explicit. The banquet in the private dining room we are ushered into is partly in honour of Cross; and J. J. Holgarth rises to make a speech and presentation before he leaves: 'Speaking of time, I have here a fourteen-carat, seventeen-jewel time-piece. And that's only right because the man I am giving it to is a fourteen-carat, seventeen-jewel cashier.'

Chris is a time-piece himself, a carefully crafted precision mechanism, whose limited interiority is both regulated and functional. The watch is passed down the banquet table to Chris and our first view of him (other than as a dark silhouette from the back) comes as he takes the watch, beaming with delight. Urged to make a speech he stammers over the first person singular, a motif that establishes not only his modesty, but his fundamental ontological insecurity: 'Well, I – uh – I – I hardly know what to say ...'.

Nichols and Lang cannily introduce Chris at a moment of recognition and even celebration, rather than in his abject mode (such as clearing up the dirty dishes at home in his frilly apron). The limited terms of his security, identity and self-worth are stated and circumscribed immediately. Even more than Wanley, Cross embodies the man of habits whom any change in routine threatens to disorient. He only reluctantly accepts J. J.'s offer of a cigar, stammering again ('Well, I – I – I, don't usually, J. J. ....') and immediately reacts superstitiously (and surreptitiously) to it being the third one lit by J. J.'s match (a close-up revealing his hidden, crossed fingers, one of many visual plays on his name). Further, he is embarrassed by the erotic. As J. J. leaves and the clerks rush to the window for a glimpse of his mistress, he takes a furtive look, but then withdraws with Charley, another older clerk, as the younger men begin to comment on their boss's sexuality.

Chris does not voice Wanley's mood of rebellion on his first night of semi-bachelorhood; repression is much more ingrained in his character. But the fissures are there, like his stuttering use of the first person, and circumstances proceed to widen them. Like Wanley, he is a bit drunk and stumbles as he descends the restaurant stairs into the street. Furthermore, he scents spring in the rain-drenched air. Offering the shelter of his umbrella to his colleague on his walk to the bus, Chris makes his first deviation and doesn't go straight to the subway homeward-bound for Brooklyn. Lang's camera observes them from high angle shots which capture the glint of light in the rain-streaked city pavement through Milton Krasner's skilful *noir* camera work. The pause as he waits with his friend for the next bus allows Chris uncharacteristically to reflect upon several non-mechanical aspects of his life.

Standing beneath a large illuminated sign for jewellery, this 'seventeen-jewel cashier'[15] confesses that he is lonely. He wonders if the woman they saw from the window really is J. J.'s mistress. Stammering again on the first person pronoun, he says 'I – I – I wonder what it's like ... well to be – to be loved by a young girl like that. You know nobody ever looked at me like that, not even when I was young'. Like Wanley, Chris expresses his distance from the erotic in terms of his age, but indicates that, unlike Wanley, he never had a youth which provided such experiences. His uncertainty with both the first person pronoun and the verb 'to be' hint that

Chris is not truly a mechanical man, but rather someone who has never grown up, who has been cruelly routed from childhood directly into middle age, and whose 'twenty-five years of faithful service' inscribed in his new time-piece represent truly empty time. His main description of being loved – being 'looked at like that' – is both touching in its immaturity and revealing of his lack of mastery of the male gaze.

The invocation of youth leads Chris directly to his means of emotional survival and erotic sublimation: 'When I was young I wanted to be an artist. You know I dreamt I was going to be a great painter someday.' He laughs. 'So, I'm a cashier.' This act of self-definition stages Chris's split. He is a cashier: his inscribed watch says so. But he also paints. 'Every Sunday', he tells Charley, who responds, 'That's one way to kill time. You know Sunday is one day of the week I don't like. I never know what to do with myself.' Charley's life is even more empty than Chris's, a man with a point-less job who suffers uncertainty about what to do with the few hours he has off from it. While Chris automatically identifies with him, he is both more repressed (his discomfort with Charley smoking when he visits, because his wife Adele might object) and yet also possesses something else, an energy which he banishes to a past youth or to the realm of dreams and which he practises only on Sundays and only in the bathroom.

Greenwich Village, the home of bohemians and artists, disorients Chris Cross on his route home. His friend's bus pulls off, leaving Cross and his umbrella alone in the rain standing by another fire hydrant; Lang dissolves to Cross, umbrella still open, wandering through dark and wet cobblestoned streets. A beat cop points out to him that the rain stopped half an hour ago, and we realise he has been wander-ing, lost, for some time. 'These streets are all mixed up in Greenwich village', he complains. Lang and Nichols clearly intend the allegorical and mythic echoes of this protagonist who becomes lost in the middle of his life in an obscure and maze-like part of town. With the roar of the El in his ears, he sees in the distance an almost theatrically conceived scene of a man beating a woman (Enno Patalas describes it as a *tableau vivant*).[16] Like a middle-aged Siegfried (or is he Don Quixote?), Chris sails out to slay a dragon, umbrella at full tilt.

The shot of Cross with his arms up, shielding his face from the blows he expects to receive, makes it clear that knocking Johnny on his ass had more to do with Johnny being drunk than with Chris's prowess. But the continuing roar of the El, like the train passing overhead in the early scenes of *Fury*, cues us that that Chris has plunged into the coils of the Destiny-machine. His acting the hero does not so much introduce a new sense of agency in his life, as an entrance onto a new stage in which his role will be carefully managed and its farce-like nature evident to every-one but himself. As with Wanley in *The Woman in the Window*, Chris attempts to overcome the machine-like nature of his internalised watchworks, only to find he is part of a larger and more deadly machine, fuelled now by his passion rather than his habits. Chris lowers his arms, smiling as he sees Kitty's astonished look at him. Does he take it for that look of recognition, admiration, and – just possibly – desire, he has never received?

In the following scene of Kitty and Chris at a bar, her knowing manipulation of him is obvious. But, in fact, they mutually deceive each other, each assuming another identity as they play a game of guessing each other's profession. Chris's guess that Kitty is an actress is greeted with heavy sarcasm (which he remains unaware of). Although her claim to be an actress is a lie, it provides the basis for her character and performance in relation to Chris, playing first the lonely girl in need of protection (and money) and, later, for Janeway, the naive, but visionary painter. Kitty's guess that Chris is an artist, sets the stage for the rest of the drama, as she divines by accident (or design?) his repressed identity. What perks Kitty's interest, of course, is her inference that he is a *rich* artist, when he doesn't express outrage that a painting by Cézanne could cost $50,000. Without ever lying to her (although he does return to stuttering over the first person pronoun when asked how much his paintings sell for, responding, ' Well I … I … I don't sell my paintings'), Chris creates a zone of uncertainty in which he can imagine himself a painter, while Kitty believes he must be a rich old coot.

At home with his wife Adele, Chris lives an even more desperate, repressed and emasculated life than he does at work. Here at last the Hays Code twin beds enter the boudoir of a Lang couple, and even that proximity seems excessive. All of Lang's discomforts with the Hollywood couple are allowed full range in this nightmare marriage. Stephen Jenkins correctly sees the true representative of repression in this household as being, not the shrewish Adele, but the portrait of her former husband, Homer Higgins, a heroic New York city cop who drowned trying to save a suicide.[17] His larger-than-life image hangs on the wall, looming over Chris with an authoritarian gaze. He embodies, as Jenkins claims, a patriarchal, masculine authority, whose gaze seems directed primarily at Chris, a castrating gaze which contrasts his highly stereotypical male image with Chris's inadequate one (especially when Chris dons a frilly apron to do household chores). The highly realist image has a *trompe l'oeil* effect, since it sports a real medal on its canvas chest, the posthumous award for his heroic demise.

But the portrait of Homer as super-male cannot be taken entirely seriously. Not only does it contrast with the true Homer (who unexpectedly appears later, still alive, and a derelict) who used his apparently heroic death as a getaway from a graft investigation, but Chris himself shows it little respect. Asked by his friend Charley if he painted it, Chris responds with an alarmed denial, and pronounces it 'mud'. As an enlarged and retouched photograph (with a real medal) the conventional and sanitised 'realism' of the painting contrasts sharply with Chris's own modernist and visionary painting. Although it glowers over him and Chris meekly tolerates it, this portrait of Homer Higgins represents only the confining conditions of Chris's life, not the law of his existence. Like the 'Happy Household' radio drama that plays over the dismal home-life of Christopher and Adele, this is a pasteboard ideal, easily seen through, mocked by both Cross and Lang.

But, of course, the irony of Chris's life is that even as he can scorn the muddy vision that produced the trumped-up image of the 'Dear Departed', he cannot truly revolt against it, any more than (initially) he can embezzle money from the huge safe he has charge of, emblazoned with that other patriarch's name: his boss, J. J. Holgarth. When he first takes money from this safe to give to Kitty for her 'studio apartment' where she can live and he can paint, he feels compelled to put it back. As a rebel, Chris remains incomplete and ineffectual. His attempt to get a loan is blocked by the requirement that he would need a 'co-signer' to guarantee the loan. Chris's interaction with Adele alternates flashes of rebellion with regressive returns to submission – angrily telling her he is 'stuck' in their marriage, but immediately letting her smell his breath when she wonders if it is drink that has made him so defiant, or cringing like a whipped puppy when she threatens to give his painting away to the junk-man. With Adele out of the house momentarily, he can look Homer's portrait in the eye, march into her bedroom and fish out some of her bonds which he will cash to bankroll Kitty's new lifestyle. Interrupted by Adele's

unexpected return home, Chris replaces the box of bonds as quickly as an adolescent boy concealing a porn magazine from his suddenly appearing mother.

The sequence of Chris's second attempt to embezzle funds from his boss portrays his subjection to the order of work and authority on several levels, as though
the forces of repression become more salient as Chris's attempt at revolt gains
momentum. It begins with a Langian topographical high angle shot of the office of
J. J. Holgarth and Company, peering into Chris's cashier cubicle (in which he is
visually imprisoned as surely as Eddie Taylor awaiting execution in his cell). The
visual trope is immediately translated into verbal puns, first, when Chris tells the
African-American janitor 'You can let me out in a minute.' As Chris hurriedly takes
money from the safe, Lang cuts to J. J. emerging from his office at the top of the
stairs, viewed from a low angle within Chris's cage. As Chris places bills in an envelope, we hear J. J.'s voice from off screen, saying, 'Just caught you in time'. Chris
looks up, terrified, and we see J. J. standing at his cashier's window, a slightly low
angle of the camera emphasising his towering status, as his statement carries at
least a triple meaning. Chris assumes he has been caught (again a guilty child fearing he can hide nothing from the omniscient parents). In fact, J. J. simply wants
him to cash a cheque, and is glad he caught him before he left (he emphasises the
cheque is 'personal' and most likely it is for his mistress – his action parallels
Chris's, but he can do it legally). On a third level, since the beginning of the film
Chris has been 'caught in time', tangled in the Destiny-machine embodied in his
seventeen-jewel time-piece.

Chris's internalised self-regulating and self-repressing mechanism, however,
does go progressively out of gear in this film. But for Lang, a machine out of whack
is still a machine, perhaps even a more dire one, like the mental patient who
thought he was a clock in his script, *The Man Behind You*, whose clockwork continually breaks down.[18] Within Lang's world, the ultimate Destiny-machine is the
machine out of control. Thus, as Chris moves toward defying his parental authority
figures, J. J. and Adele, he does not experience a liberation from them (except for his
brief delight after he tricks Homer Higgins into returning to Adele), but rather a
sense of guilt and oppression. As possibilities of self-realisation appear to Chris, his
love for Kitty, or the critical recognition of his painting, each is thwarted in some
manner, shunted onto someone else. Johnny receives Kitty's true affection, while
Kitty gets the accolades for Chris's painting. Chris Cross serves only as a transfer
point, a place of intersection, as what he desires, someone else receives.

But at the same time, figures of authority, patriarchal figures like J. J. or parental
figures like Adele, do lose some of their power as Chris's involvement with Kitty
progresses. On the second attempt, in spite of the untimely interruption, Chris does
manage to steal from his boss. And the final unmasking of patriarchal authority
comes with the return of Homer Higgins from his watery grave. The consequences
of the return of the dead dominate Lang's work on both sides of the Atlantic, and as
with all his fundamental themes, he plays a gamut of variations upon this possibility of resurrection and/or haunting. While *Liliom* portrayed the dead's return in a
gentle comedy of regret, Higgins' resurrection gets a burlesque treatment. His
appearance summons up overtones of Oedipal punishment by at first seeming to
refer to Chris's previous theft from his boss. Chris sits in his cashier cubicle and the
same black janitor tells him a 'detective' wants to see him outside. Chris exits the
building anxiously, only to find a derelict with an eye patch, who wonders if Chris
recognises him, and raises his eye patch to aid the process. As Chris realises Homer
stands before him, living and breathing, the debunking of the idealised portrait

reaches completion. Its model appears, not as a monument to an idealised death, but as an abject living body.

This return to life destroys one image of patriarchal authority and gives Chris an opportunity for escape. Homer being alive means Chris is not really married, is no longer 'stuck' but free, free to marry Kitty who had previously claimed she would marry him were he 'free'. However, Homer demands money to conceal this fact and not threaten Chris's marriage. Chris's initial reaction to Homer's demands appears unbelievably submissive, as Chris promises to give Homer access to Adele's bonds when she is out of the house. That even Chris would pay to keep his domineering wife beggars the imagination. But this nadir of his passivity actually becomes the one strong action that Chris takes to claim his liberty. In a sequence dominated by Krasner's most low-key photography and Lang's sinister high angle shots, Chris signals with a flashlight for Homer to enter the apartment. Chris has the last laugh when this apparently ominous scene turns into a carefully planned farce, as off screen screams reveal Adele, very much at home, discovering Homer as he creeps into her bedroom. The errant 'ideal' husband caught, Cross exits merrily, his bags already packed.

But this one act of self-assertion (and Chris's only properly managed *mise-en-scène*) becomes immediately overturned in the following scene, as Chris's brief fling at director/enunciator is cancelled out by a traumatic act of spectatorship. Chris heads directly to Kitty's studio apartment to announce his new-found freedom. Lang fades in on the studio foyer as Chris enters. We hear the song that has become Kitty's theme, 'Melancholy Baby' (first introduced playing on the jukebox in the bar where Kitty and Chris exchange names, and reprised several times since, both in the score as well as Kitty's record of a crooner version), which is playing on her record player as Chris enters the apartment. Kitty's record is scratched so that the needle becomes stuck and endlessly repeats the phrase, 'in love – in love – in love'. As the crooner stutters, Lang cuts to a close-up from Chris's point of view – Johnny's straw hat on the hall table.

Lang cuts to a close-up of Chris's sickly reaction, then back to his point of view, looking into the living room through a glass partition, as he sees Johnny stroll in. Over the reaction shot of Chris we hear the phonograph needle being lifted and the refrain cease, but the off screen voice of Kitty immediately calls out seductively, 'Johnnnneee'. In a long shot tableau, still carefully framed through the glass partition, Kitty enters and embraces Johnny who calls her by his pet name for her, 'Lazy Legs'. Over Chris's astonished and wide-eyed face we hear Kitty intone the film's unforgettable invocation of desire, 'Jeepers, I love you'. Lang conveys the intensity (but also the passivity) of Chris's reaction through the nearly explosive bang as he drops his suitcase to the floor. The sound interrupts the lovers' smooch, as they look off screen, startled. But, by the time Johnny rushes to the hallway and then to the stairway, Chris has vanished. Johnny is furious, worrying that he may have lost his 'sucker', and he, rather than Chris, slaps Kitty in the face.

Filming Chris's vision of the cheating lovers through the glass partition, Lang stresses its theatrical quality, presenting it as a scene framed and at some distance from the viewer, lit from off screen (the light from the bedroom doorway serving as key light) while the performers embrace in a theatrical, rather than casual, manner. The scene replays and cancels out Chris's first vision of Kitty: an even more distant tableau, framed within the structure of the El, and lit by the street lamps, in which Johnny beats her, rather than embraces her (of course, with this sadomasochistic couple, one act is simply foreplay for the other). As Tom Conley astutely pointed out, both scenes reflect elements of the Freudian 'primal scene' in which a child traumatically witnesses

intercourse between his parents, often mistaking it for an act of violence.[19] Does this rather precise Freudian reference (possibly deriving from Nichols, who was as well-versed in Freudian theory as Lang) help us understand the film?

Although I believe Freudian readings can often pull us away from the specific meanings operating within a film text, I think this one explains the intertwining of eroticism and repression in Chris which leads, inevitably, towards violence. The Freudian scenario explains the deeper mechanism of Chris's character, why in contrast to Wanley he goes berserk: his capacity for violence and delusion. Nichols and Lang have constructed Chris as a Freudian man, with a complex psychology. The invocation of the primal scene relates partly to Chris's infantilism – he is the 'melancholy baby' of the song, who wants most of all to 'cuddle up'. But most importantly, it explains Chris's repression in terms of his fear of castration. For Freud the primal scene, sex misunderstood as an act of violence, can traumatically frighten the male child who believes that the Father is castrating the Mother. Chris's avoidance of naked women and his apparent flight in panic after watching the pair's embrace spikes this scene of betrayal with a primal sexual fear. (Notice, for instance, how differently Renoir handles the corresponding scene in *La Chienne*, avoiding emphasis on Legrand's point of view – observing some of the confrontation from an exterior window, a viewpoint no character occupies – and indicating Legrand's shame and building anger, but surely no panic). For Freud, fear of the castrating Father is an essential force in pulling the male child (the melancholy baby) away from the Mother and into identification with the Father. But Chris will only accomplish this identification in a psychotic, violent manner.

The ultimate tragedy of Chris Cross, as I will explore later, consists in his loss of identity, a fate which looms over a number of Lang's characters, including his kinder, gentler *doppelgänger* Professor Wanley. But Lang never explored it more fully than with this man who loses his identity to two different characters and in effect, murders them both: his identity as an artist is given over to his victim, Kitty; while Johnny Prince appropriates his role, first as a lover, and then, as a murderer. Chris Cross is cancelled out by these two contradictory identifications. His failed and deadly identification with Johnny seems to derive directly from the primal scene vision. In spite of an almost identical performance style and costume (e.g. the phallic straw hat so blatantly displayed in several scenes) Johnny's character plays a more complex role in *Scarlet Street* than does Heidt in *The Woman in the Window*. As nasty, slimy, sadistic, cowardly, lazy, ignorant and venial a character as one could find in a Hollywood film, Johnny takes on a disturbing charm through Duryea's creepy performance. His overt sexuality is as caricatured an image of pure phallic maleness as Homer Higgins' portrait is of patriarchal authority. For Lang and Nichols, both are phony at the core, but that does not limit their effects on other characters.

Chris feels an almost instinctual dislike for Johnny which seems to derive less from his dim recognition of him as the man whom he first saw assault Kitty, than a reaction to Johnny's narcissistic masculinity. Johnny haunts Chris, and not simply as an imagined rival, but as a phallic presence threatening to a character whose fear of castration has kept him in an infantile state. When Chris paints his primal encounter with Kitty under the El, the spotlight street lamp and the proscenium arch-like frame of the El are there, but Johnny seems to have disappeared, as Kitty stands alone. But to the right, coiled in the El's pylon, is an enormous snake, clearly Johnny's appearance to Chris as a huge phallic menace. But Lang does not only express Johnny's identification with the snake through Chris's dream-like painting. Lang introduces Johnny and Kitty examining Chris's El painting with an overlap-dissolve that makes the same visual equation. The previous scene ended with Johnny hiding himself at the side of the stoop of Kitty's apartment building in order to avoid being seen by Chris as he left. This medium shot of Johnny dissolves into a close-up detail of the snake in Chris's painting, the coils seeming to grow out of Johnny's body.

Johnny embodies Chris's intertwined fear and attraction to sexual violence. The sex act terrifies him, partly because he misunderstands it as an assault. Therefore only two sexual positions seem open to him: the melancholy baby attached to maternal figures (both Adele and Kitty) who actually have contempt for him, or an identification with Johnny as phallic male violence. (These two poles of sexuality – or of asexuality – also recall the alternation of Hans Beckert's sexual expression between baby-like orality and knifings.) Lang portrays Chris's attraction to a psychopathic phallic violence long before he actually murders Kitty. In an almost surrealist allegory of Chris's sexual dilemma, Lang frames him in the kitchen dressed in his frilly apron, while through the doorway the portrait of Homer Higgins beams down on this perverse scene. Jenkins' analysis recognises the signs of castration in this composition, Chris's apron and subjection to supposedly 'female' domestic tasks under Homer's patriarchal gaze.[20] But what of the huge knife in Chris's hand with which he slices a hunk of liver into strips? The phallic nature of the knife, the moist, pliant meat of the liver, already hint at sexual violence. Lang makes this explicit with Adele's entrance.

Adele shrilly interrogates Chris about his relationship with Katherine March (Kitty). Chris reacts with some fright, as he pretends not to recognise the name. But most importantly, the hand holding the knife raises and points at Adele, a gesture emphasised by a track-in on Chris. (In fact, the following shot, a cut out to the two shot of Chris and Adele, mismatches the position of the knife, as Noel Carroll pointed out to me decades ago, with the knife now resting on the table. This may be an unintentional error in continuity – but a rather uncommon one. It may also be another, admittedly also unusual, way to draw attention to the knife.) As Chris moves towards Adele, his knife still in hand, ostensibly to help her take off her coat, she herself voices what seems still to be an unconscious intention on Chris's part, 'You want to cut my throat?' Chris looks at the knife in his hand as if he just noticed it. As in Sylvia Sidney's accidental reaching for the knife in the dinner sequence of Hitchcock's *Sabotage*, Chris's hand has responded before his conscious awareness. But he still does not put the knife down.

Adele, who has seen Chris's paintings in Dellarowe's art gallery under Kitty's name, accuses Chris of stealing the ideas of a 'real artist' and copying Katherine March's work. 'You're a thief!' she exclaims. 'Holgarth better watch out, or the next thing you'll be stealing his money!' she cries, as she slams the door to her bedroom. Chris, standing in the kitchen doorway stunned by this series of accusations and revelations, finally drops the knife he held. It buries itself upright in the wooden floor. Chris's loss of the knife could be seen as a figure of castration, but the dominant imagery of the sequence points towards his attempt to overcome castration through identification with phallic violence, an identification that is, of course, precarious and ultimately psychopathic. Chris is stunned, not only by hearing his wife confront him with the name of his mistress, but also amazed that she actually accuses him of the wrong crime. He is stunned by the idea that somehow Kitty has appropriated his identity as a painter *and* by the fact that his paintings are on display in a famous art gallery. And he is stunned that Adele, who cannot imagine his extra-marital affair, has seemed to divine his theft from J. J., his first act of Oedipal defiance. Everything in this sequence works in terms of contrast: guilt and abjection balanced by assertion of power, the frilly apron countered by the long knife.

The dropped knife continues this ambivalent see-saw between cringing panic at the threat of exposure and punishment and violent rebellion. Dropping the knife is only half the action. The powerful thrust with which it buries itself into the apartment floor and remains upright (accompanied by an actual clash of cymbals in the score!), stresses Chris's potential violence, not simply his surrender. Jenkins nicely isolates this image of the dropped knife between Chris spread legs (and relates it to other similar images in Lang films), but under-reads it.[21] Lang supplies an essential gloss, however, with another nearly allegorical – and certainly metaphorical – overlap-dissolve. From this close-up of the knife embedded in the floor, Lang dissolves to a shot of Johnny standing in Kitty's studio examining Chris's painting. The position of his body matches precisely the position of the knife as one dissolves into the other. Once again, Johnny, like the knife, embodies phallic violence. But, as this dissolve indicates, he is also in some sense Chris's phallus, the image of what he lacks, as well as what he will claim in a psychopathic way. Chris begins to come unravelled when he realises that Johnny has been doing to Kitty what he wants to do, but has been too repressed to actually carry out. (The non-sexual relation of Kitty and Chris represents an amazing intersection of the mutual repression of the Hays Code and Chris's neurosis!) After getting drunk in a bar, Chris returns, hoping both to forgive and redeem Kitty, whom he believes must be in need of rescue from Johnny (as in the opening), and to ask her to marry him (as he is now free).

But Chris's confrontation with Kitty torpedoes his rescue scenario. As she hears him enter, Kitty calls him 'Johnny', a final and fatal mis-identification. Chris believes she is weeping into her pillow, but she turns and confronts him with raucous laughter, the culmination of her duplicitous 'acting' towards him, revealing at last her real attitude. This scornful and castrating laughter returns Chris to his state of panic, and he backs away from his beloved in horror, bumping against the ice bucket Johnny arranged for their earlier tryst and causing the ice pick to fall. Mechanically, he stoops to pick it up. The picking up of this sharp object parallels and completes his earlier dropping of the knife. In the face of the threat of castration, Chris asserts his masculinity in the only way he can imagine it, as violence. As Kitty continues to mock Chris and even describes the way Johnny would 'break every bone in his body – he's a man!', Chris lunges at her and Kitty pulls the down comforter over her as she screams. We hear the puffy sound of the pick piercing the cover and, presumably, Kitty herself. Lang cuts from this violence to Johnny arriving outside, drunkenly driving his car into a fire hydrant, which causes Marchetti, the restaurant owner, to cry out, 'Look out, Johnny, you killa somebody!' Through the cut, Chris's violence continues its association with Johnny. While Johnny violently enters the apartment building, smashing the glass door, Chris hides at the foot of the stairs, just as Johnny did beside the stoop earlier. That Johnny becomes accused of the murder of Kitty not only provides a beautifully realised twist to the plot, but also the outcome of the film's Oedipal logic. Chris identifies with Johnny in order to kill Kitty. But he must disavow this act of self-assertion, allowing its reality as self-destruction to surface.

Even at the moment of revolt, Chris remains within the vengeful logic of his own repression. As much as Lang mocks the patriarchal system, he also demonstrates its power and violence – its deadly results for all three main characters. The farce of mis-recognition and duplicity, of false idealisations and infantilisations, has fatal consequences. Even in his act of fury and passion Lang stresses the mechanical nature of Chris's actions, his repetitive stabbing of Kitty – he remains the fourteen-carat, seventeen-jewel cashier to the end. This multiple stabbing (among other things in this truly subversive film) upset local censor boards in New York, Atlanta and Milwaukee, and cuts were made reducing the stab to a single thrust, from an original seven (although all prints I have seen have four).[22] The seemingly arbitrary reaction of the censors was mocked by Lang who quipped, 'Is it immoral to stab a woman four times – moral to stab her only once?'[23] But, of course, the censors consciously or unconsciously intuited the sexual association of the repeated thrusts, as well as the added participation this repetitive rhythm invites.

Thus Lang used mechanical and repetitive motifs to express not only Chris's psychology but the nature of his desire as part of the Destiny-machine. The most powerful emblem of this repetitive death drive which underlies the passion in the film (Kitty's and Johnny's as much as Chris's) comes with the motif of the scratched recording of 'Melancholy Baby', Kitty's theme, which not only expresses her laziness (she won't get off the couch to pick up the needle when the record is first heard) but also the obsessive, masochistic nature of her desire for Johnny. Its maddening reiteration of 'in love – in love – in love …' captures the film's view that everyone is, as Chris says to Adele, 'stuck', endlessly repeating the same desires and, just as endlessly, lacking fulfilment. This bleak view extends beyond individual psychology, staking out the broader claim of Lang's increasing pessimism in which desire no longer offers an alternative to the Destiny-machine, but is imbricated with its effective operation.

The Artist's Signature and the Mourning Play of the Melancholy Baby

> We understand that the signature or form is no spirit, but the
> receptacle, container, or cabinet of the spirit wherein it lies; for
> the signature stands in the essence and is as a lute that liest
> still, and is indeed a dumb thing that is neither heard nor
> understood; but if it be played upon then its form is
> understood …
>
> Jacob Boehme, *The Signature of All Things*[24]

In the spring of 1945, as the war against Hitler was building towards a final victory, Fritz Lang announced the creation of a new production company, Diana Productions, which would give him simultaneously the degree of directorial control and the high-budget technical and collaborative support he had desired since he came to Hollywood. This meant that with Diana's first production, *Scarlet Street*, Lang was not only producing his own films again (as he had with *You and Me* and *Hangmen Also Die*) but was the head of a production company dedicated to enabling his own directorial style and signature. There were other partners in the formation of Diana, but all of them acknowledged the primacy of Lang's directorial vision. First came Joan Bennett, the star around whom the company was based, but a star who strongly felt that her work in two previous Lang films (*Man Hunt* and *The Woman in the Window*) was her best and that she 'performed better under his direction than at any other time in my career'.[25] Diana was partly Bennett's initiative as a way to control and promote her star image and as a way to give Lang, whom she greatly admired, a chance to work outside the restraints of the studio system. Bennett was the production company's second largest stockholder after Lang, who held 51 per cent.[26]

While Lang was the linchpin of this new corporation, Walter Wanger, who was Bennett's husband and whose previous independent company had produced *You Only Live Once*, would be the executive producer of Diana films and the executive vice president of the company. Although Lang and Wanger had had conflicts over *You Only Live Once*, the latter, as Matthew Bernstein points out in his study of the producer, saw the real opportunity the new corporation offered. Wanger had been serving as a unit producer at Universal and found he had little chance to work with major directors (before coming to Universal, Wanger had produced films by Borzage, Lang, Ford and Hitchcock). As his attorney suggested to Wanger, '12 per cent of a Lang picture may well be worth more than 50 per cent of a Joe Doakes picture'.[27] Wanger worked out a deal with Universal in which Diana would operate as a semi-independent production company releasing through the studio. Diana would raise the first money for the production through a bank loan. Universal charged for studio space and facilities and supplied the 'second money', the remainder of the budget, and would handle distribution and advertising. A clause in the contract also gave Universal a final cut on the films, although Wanger reassured Lang this clause was rarely invoked.[28] The credits for *Scarlet Street* lay out these interlocking relations. After the Universal logo a title card announces 'Walter Wanger Presents' which dissolves into the next card, 'A Fritz Lang Production'. The names of stars, Edward G. Robinson and Joan Bennett appear next, then (placed within a New York city street sign) the title *Scarlet Street* (with small letters announcing copyright by Universal Pictures, Company, Inc.) and finally 'A Diana Production'.

Although the authority of the star and of the executive producer gave them some say in the way Diana films were made and the relation with Universal gave the studio some authority as well, Diana was founded explicitly on a faith in Lang's direction, and a desire to enable and promote his authorship of films. Lang and Wanger's contracts with Diana both indicated: 'the judgement of Mr. Lang with respect to matters of a purely artistic nature shall control, while [Wanger's] judgement as to all financial aspects of the production ... shall be controlling'.[29] Although, in fact, this tidy division between art and mammon became difficult to maintain in a Hollywood context, the ceding of artistic authority to Lang was something he had long desired. As Bernstein says, 'Diana Productions may not have been Ufa, but it was about as close as an American company in the studio system could come to recreating the encouraging working environment Lang had enjoyed in Europe'.[30] For *Scarlet Street*, Lang was allowed to work for three months with Dudley Nichols on the script, to control casting and to hire Milton Krasner, who had shot *The Woman in the Window*, as cinematographer.

As all these contractual and business arrangements should make clear, the idea of a director as author was not foreign to Hollywood and Lang at this point was the farthest thing from what Burch described as 'the all purpose Hollywood director'.[31] But it is equally clear that, as an author, Lang was a commodity, or more properly, an investment, one whose author-function was defined and circumscribed within the Hollywood practices of production, distribution and publicity. While it is clear that Lang generally did his best work in Hollywood when he was provided with the greatest degree of authority, one cannot abstract his authorship from the system that defined it. At every point in Lang's career the issue of authorship is a complex and dialectical issue on every level, from the process of production to the style of his films. But in a more sympathetic situation like the production of *Scarlet Street*, Lang could grapple with the most profound issues of authorship within his own style with less interference.

Scarlet Street stands as possibly Lang's Hollywood masterpiece, partly because it offers his most complex view of the process of art-making and the identity of the artist/author (an issue that Renoir's film, and especially his filming of the ending, basically ignores). Earlier I described the ending of Lang's film as tragic, by which I hoped to indicate that this final visionary encounter of Chris with his *Self-Portrait* works in a very different way from Renoir's almost comic irony. This might sound self-contradictory, since I have indicated that in classical terms *Scarlet Street*, too, could be considered a comedy, dealing as it does with pathetic rather than heroic characters. If the mockery in *Scarlet Street* seems increasingly hollow as characters die or go mad, aren't we dealing with the pathos of a case study of mentally ill characters, and therefore a tragedy only of the condescending Arthur Miller/Willie Loman sort? If *Scarlet Street* traces a character's movement from neurosis to psychosis, can this really be a tragedy? But *Scarlet Street* does not remain at the level of a psychological case, invoking instead both the demonic and the visionary to become, if not a classical tragedy, a powerful allegory of Eros and Thanatos in the work of the artist and a *Trauerspiel* for an artist's self-martyrdom.

Throughout this book I have used Freudian concepts primarily when they parallel Lang's own allegories, that is when both Freud and Lang emerge as allegorists, rather than as a key to the interpretation of the psychology of either characters or Lang himself. However, with the 'framed desire' trilogy, Lang progressively makes more use of Freudian concepts as ways of constructing his characters (in an era when Hollywood generally was embracing Freudian concepts, albeit in a selective manner). But I would maintain that ultimately it is Lang the allegorist who organises Freudian ideas, rather than vice versa, so that *Scarlet Street* becomes something other than simply a case study. In fact, in this group of films, Freud and the unconscious provide Lang with a clear pathway back to allegory, with the dream-work of *The Woman in the Window* serving as a humorous emblem for the more dire allegories of *Scarlet Street* and *The Secret Beyond the Door*. But while these allegories make use of Freudian concepts, they also produce a surplus of meaning that cannot be dissolved psychoanalytically.

As I stated at the opening of this chapter, classical tragedy does not determine the melodramatic form of *Scarlet Street*. But Benjamin's discussion of the German baroque form of the *Trauerspiel* (which, for Benjamin, includes the Renaissance tragedies of Shakespeare and Calderon) does, I think, provide great insights into *Scarlet Street*'s allegorical drama of artistic creation, including the fact that this later form of tragedy, in contrast to classical models, made room for comedy, especially the cruel joke.[32] The character of the old fool (Polonius or Lear in Shakespeare) shows that even a figure of self-delusion and object of cruel mirth can become tragic in this form without contradiction. The difference between *Scarlet Street* and *Der müde Tod* in their relation to the *Trauerspiel* lies in the greater psychological complexity and interiority of Chris Cross in comparison to the maiden. But Lang does not let this increased psychologism move him towards a greater realism or naturalism (as the contrast with Renoir shows). Rather Chris becomes a character who is turned inside out, his drive to produce images, his role as an artist constantly involved in exteriorising, projecting his fantasies first into images, then, in his madness, through sound.

Chris Cross is a double character, split in two, and his pathetic role as menial cashier and prostitute's dupe runs athwart his visionary talent as a painter. Chris is more than simply a character on the verge of psychosis who never completes his movement through the Oedipus complex. Chris's loss of identity is double, not only does he lose his sexual role to Johnny (both as lover, and in psychotic form, as murderer), he also loses his identity as an artist to Kitty. Tragedy enters with this second loss; while Chris never truly had a sexual prowess to lose, his achievement as a painter constituted his one defence against his reification as a seventeen-jewel cashier and a hen-pecked husband. The quality of Chris's painting in *Scarlet Street* opens this mocking sex comedy onto unexpected depths and ennobles (in a complex way) the pathos of his character.

At the encounter which ends the film, Cross is not simply a smelly vagabond wandering the street on whom life has played a cruel trick, whose punch line –'ten thousand dollars!' – we hear along with him (although he *is* that, too). He is also an artist confronting his work and the full horror it embodies in a flash of recognition; the intensity of pain and longing contained in that encounter rival the bitter irony of its commodification. Chris's encounter with a phantom image of his past achievement recalls the anecdote of the poet Hölderlin, after decades of madness (a time spent as a gardener's assistant), one day encountering a visitor with a copy of Homer. This gardener's assistant, who had once been one of the most profound mediators between Greek and German culture (and hence his significance in Godard's *Contempt*, mediating between Lang and Homer), leafed through the volume of Homer while a complex series of expressions passed over his face. He then put the volume down and returned to his gardening.[33] To understand the tragic dimension of Chris Cross's encounter with this demonic image from his past life as an artist, an image that recalls both passion, rejection and murder, one might think of Hölderlin's own definition of the tragic in his commentary on his translation of *Oedipus Rex*:

> The representation of the tragic is mainly based on this: that what is monstrous and terrible in the coupling of god and man, in the total fusion of the power of Nature with the inmost depths of the man so that they are one at the moment of wrath, should be made intelligible by showing how this total fusion into one is purged by their total separation.[34]

It might seem farcical to see pathetic Christopher Cross as ever hosting a coupling of god and man. But the visionary evidence of his painting, especially this last one, augurs a creativity that is beyond his conscious control. And this final confrontation, as image and artist confront each other and then go separate ways, shows the tragic moment of the wrenching of vision away from this pathetic husk of a human being, this human, all-too-human, *letzte Mann*.

As I said earlier, Chris's painting initially is shoved into the margins of his life, the Sunday he has off from work, the hallway where he stores his paintings and the bathroom that serves as his studio. Lang makes it clear that this is a process of sublimation by balancing the creative act *inter feces et pictor*: Chris sits on the toilet as he paints, a touch Lang introduced with particular delight,[35] another instance of his cloacal vision, but here tied to the creative process. Chris sits there with an excited look on his face, painting a flower that Kitty gave him as a memento the night before, now balanced in a glass on the bathroom sink. As he looks at the flower, he makes brushstrokes in the air, before applying them to the canvas, a gesture undoubtedly illustrating his later comment to Kitty, 'No-one ever taught me to draw, so I just put a line around what I feel when I look at things.' It also recalls the actions of writing words in the air in the German films (*Spies, M, The Testament of Dr. Mabuse*) when characters are trying to dredge up an unconscious memory.

Lang expresses the transformative quality of Chris's painting through a pan that represents the point of view of his friend Charley when he visits. Examining Chris's painting of Kitty's flower, Charley asks, 'Where did you find a flower like that?'

(Kitty asks the same question when she sees the canvas later.) Chris gestures to the daisy in the bathroom glass. Charley queries again, ' You mean you see *this*' – close-up of Chris's painting, a stylised almost mandala-like flower on a dark background – 'when you look at *that*?' – the camera pans over to the wilting daisy on the bath-room sink. Chris responds with a popular explanation of modern art as a watered-down Expressionism: 'Well, yes, that is, I sort of feel it. You see, when I look at that flower I see someone ...' However, Chris's explanation is curtailed by a scream from Adele as she enters the bathroom clad only in a slip. In this hot house of repressed sexuality, the scream seems calculated to guarantee Charley's look at her in her semi-clothed state, rather than any horror at being seen. She slams the door, Chris apologises and retreats with his painting and easel. Adele enters and crosses over to the sink, where she pours the flower from the glass into the toilet. Artistic produc-tion and vision have gone full cycle.

This bathroom exposition of art merits further plumbing. As a signifier of elit-ism, modern art fares almost as badly in Hollywood film as grand opera (think of the stares the cubist painting gets from the detective in Hitchcock's *Suspicion*).[36] As the title of Diane Waldman's survey of the reaction against modernist art in the 40s (the era of *Scarlet Street*) – 'The Childish, the Insane and the Ugly' – indicates, clas-sical Hollywood cinema most often presented modern art as a sign of insanity, evil intentions, or the butt of a joke.[37] Although Chris, too, is portrayed as childish, called ugly by Kitty and ending up insane, Lang and Nichols view his painting sym-pathetically. A fascinating incident in Lang's unproduced spy thriller 'Men without a Country' reveals something, I think, about Lang's view of modern art. One of the spies buys a painting Lang describes as 'surrealist, ultra-modern'. However, the FBI examine it carefully and discover it is actually a detailed map of Diamond Head, a secret American military base that no-one is allowed access to; not even planes can fly overhead.[38] For Lang, modern art contained an enigma, a puzzle whose signifi-cance could be worked out. Like emblems or visual allegories Chris's paintings seem to contain hidden messages, inner meanings he himself could never speak out loud.

Lang based Chris's canvases on the primitivism of *Douanier* Rousseau.[39] The paintings shown in the film, executed by Lang's friend John Decker,[40] are certainly not masterpieces, and seem to waver uncertainly between Rousseau and Walt Disney or Grandma Moses, but they are certainly much more interesting than the paintings usually produced for Hollywood screen painters (think of Cary Grant's 'masterpiece' in Leo McCarey's *An Affair to Remember*!). With the contrast between the 'mud' of Homer Higgins' enlarged photograph and Chris's capturing of feel-ings, the film seems to endorse a fairly conventional explanation of modern art as representing not what one sees, but what one 'feels'. However clichéd this may be as an insight into modernist practice, it sets up an important relation between Chris and the visual world in which we realise that Chris sees differently and perhaps more deeply than other people. But most importantly the paintings are seen as pic-ture puzzles, means of expression which take a detour though the displaced mean-ings generated by repression, and the icons of unconscious desire.

What does he see? Chris's semi-Expressionist explanation indicates a preference for emotions over the simple resemblances of realism. But he also reacts against the hypocritical ideology embodied in the Higgins portrait. If Chris pursues an escape from a simple mundane reality (the wilted daisy on the bathroom sink) to a domain of unspecified feeling, Lang and Nichols seem to short-circuit such idealisation. The scatological theme of painting while seated on the toilet (with original inspira-tion also being flushed away) intertwines with the displaced sexuality rampant in this scene, not only Adele's exhibitionist shriek, but Chris's own unrecognised sexual longing in painting the flower given him by the young woman he has just met. Chris's explanation of what he sees in the flower gets interrupted by Adele's sudden entrance, but he has already described the flower as a person. The traditional symbolic relation between flowers and (particularly female) genitalia certainly functions as at least unconscious material in Chris's painting, with its exaggerated seed-filled centre and unfurled symmetrical petals (and nearby butterflies, another traditional sexual emblem). Painting in his bathroom, like an adolescent finding the one place he can masturbate safely, Chris accesses a primal sexual energy – a sexual energy that has been rendered as a compelling, visual image. In the midst of this scenography of hypocrisy and shame about the body and its functions, Chris has produced a displaced image of sexuality as open, inviting, exotic – even hallucinatory and overwhelming.

Not all of Chris's painting are as clearly readable or as single-minded as this one (although we do see another celebratory flower painting). But the 'feeling' that Chris claims to express in his painting is primarily erotic, as he indicates when he calls his paintings 'love affairs'. His painting of zoo animals expresses a childlike delight and identification with instinctive life, like his spontaneous bird-call when he lunches with Kitty, whistling to the robins building their nest and exclaiming that he feels like a kid again. Chris nearly brims over with an untapped libido, but it is a libido that has not yet reached adult identifications. Chris's visionary talent comes from his childlike openness to a polymorphic erotic delight in vision, matched by a fear of, and therefore repression of, fully adult genital sexuality. The painting of Kitty beneath the El menaced by a monster snake, as I discussed earlier, simultaneously expresses his fear of sexuality and his desire to identify with its darker, more aggressive elements.

Other paintings express an urban melancholy and loneliness – Chris's daily modern life which has crushed his identity as much as his sexual repression (or which is the social form of his sexual repression), reducing him to the seventeen-jewel cashier, rather than the visionary painter of erotic fantasy. Following Benjamin's discussion of melancholy in the *Trauerspiel*, Chris seems ruled by the sign of Saturn/Kronos, the Greek God of time and castration – the forces of repression weighing on Chris Cross, enforcing an attitude of lonely and basically impotent contemplation of the possibilities of the world, reflecting the emptiness of the world he lives in, both socially and erotically.[41]

In its linear, clearly defined haptic forms (Chris's line drawn around his feelings) these paintings also reflect an aspect of Lang's own visual style. Several of them repeat images or forms from the film: Kitty's *Self-Portrait*, Kitty waiting beneath the El, Chris wandering the city streets with his umbrella, Kitty's flower. Yet all of them seem to fix the familiar outlines of things while endowing them with enigmatic significance, the energies of both fear and desire that rule Chris's erotic fantasy-life. Like the overlap-dissolves of Lang's silent films, they present visionary allegories, the visual mode of melancholy, which not only reveal demonic forces beneath the surface of things, but which demand a careful reading and unravelling. If Chris's paintings seem dream-like, it is because they contain fundamental displacements and condensations that transform Chris's unspeakable desires into visual riddles.

In describing the artist 'Katherine March', the critic Janeway refers to her as '*Mona Lisa* without the smile, something hidden'. Although Janeway intuits here the secret of March's identity ('sometimes it seems as if she were two people'), his invocation of the archetypal image of mysterious femininity outruns Kitty and Johnny's con-job deception. This painting in particular goes to the core of Chris's enigmatic sexual identity and like many of Lang's visionary allegories plays a prophetic role within the film. Although Janeway seems to be speaking of Kitty, the woman he believes is the painter, Lang's cut to a close-up of the *Self-Portrait* as Janeway speaks these words, draws our attention to the identity of the painting itself, this image in which two diametrically different people have been merged. This unsmiling Mona Lisa has perhaps caught her baby's melancholy. For, as much as Chris's paintings contain both desire and its repression at their most powerful, as in this *Self-Portrait*, they also reflect the melancholy of the true allegorist, who knows his desire finds no true fulfilment.

The tragedy of *Scarlet Street* does not derive simply from Chris's talent as a painter which ennobles him, or his visionary insight, which is always only partial since he remains blind to both his own deception and even to his sexuality – his images being displacements of his desires. It is the curtailing of the process of self-realisation his painting almost brings him, this sudden interruption of his process of unfurling, that makes him a tragic figure. In spite of Chris, behind his back as it were, his paintings enter into the commodity market and gain a status he never had: he, in effect, realises the dream of his youth, overturning his identity as a cashier. As commodities, his paintings gain an exchange value and Lang satirises this intersection of expression and commerce by extending the exchange in an unexpected direction. Johnny Prince, as the embodiment, not only of phallic sadistic sexuality, but also of egoistic capitalist entrepreneurship, first tries to exchange Chris's paintings for money, then exchanges the identity of the painter, substituting Katherine March, for Christopher Cross. As Prince hands her the brush to make her sign Chris's canvas he demands, 'Right here, just like you'd sign a letter'. This exchange of identities, although of great psychological significance to Chris, has it origins in the commodity market, the Destiny-machine of modernity.

Initially, Lang grants Chris the painter a utopian innocence through this ruse intended to rob him of the cash value of his work. He is allowed to witness the recognition of his paintings without himself becoming part of the commodified world. When he discovers Kitty's appropriation of his identity, he responds with delight, happy with the recognition, indifferent about the money. (Lang told Bogdanovich, 'In my opinion, Robinson's fate in that picture is the fate of an artist who cares more for his paintings than for gaining money.')[42] However, the recognition does effect a change in Chris, a growth of his ego through his new-found (if displaced) authorship. The two scenes in which he 'paints' Kitty show this contrast. Chris's desire to paint Kitty was a motivation for renting her studio, and an obvious displacement of sleeping with her. Kitty delays sitting for her portrait with a calculating coyness. She, too, is a master of displacement (or at least deferment), and when Chris whines that he wants to paint her with particular insistence, she replies, 'Well, I was going to do this myself, but …' She hands him a bottle of nail polish and wiggles the toes of her outstretched leg, saying in a sultry manner, 'Paint me, Chris.' In quiet delight he kneels to the task, as Kitty comments, 'They'll be masterpieces.' The tableau is one of the most mocking and humiliating in the film, and was recreated by Stanley Kubrick in his film of *Lolita* as Humbert Humbert similarly attends to Lolita's tootsies.

But Chris's second painting of Kitty has an entirely different scenography. It occurs as a direct result of his discovery of the success of his paintings (under Kitty's name). Kitty fulfils Chris's childhood wish, voiced (and cancelled out) early in the film, telling him, 'You're a great painter Chris, Mr. Dellarowe said so, and so did Mr.

Janeway – that is, they say I am.' For Chris, the granting of a childhood wish at one remove, still carries magic. Two similes occur to him in rapid succession: 'It's just like a dream', and 'It's just like we were married, only I take your name.' In the toe-painting scene, Kitty's granting of the privilege to paint her toes came right after a discussion of the impossibility of their marrying. But now the manipulation of name and identity becomes a form of marriage for Chris, a merging with his beloved that he welcomes, unaware of its later fatal consequences. Chris's demeanor changes immediately. 'Well', he declares as he almost struts around the apartment, 'that gives me a little authority around here!' He turns and looks at Kitty and says (in a voice with 'authority' as opposed to his previous whining), 'I want to paint your picture Kitty.' He takes off his jacket and sets to work, arranging Kitty, lights and easel. 'Know what we're going to call this?' he says, '*Self-Portrait*'.

   This contradictory act of self-representation creates one of Lang's most complex images, fully expressive of his dialectical concepts of identity and authorship. As Joe in *Fury* tried to cap his *mise-en-scène* of revenge against the citizens of Strand by proving his own death, Chris fully accedes to the authority of being an artist by accepting someone else's signature on his work. In this 'marriage' which gives him his authority, he has taken on his mistress's name, reversed traditional gender roles. His crowning work, his 'masterpiece' will embody this contradiction: Self-Portrait of the Artist as a Young Woman. The possibilities for Chris fork at this point. His identification with Kitty, with a woman rather than a man, his inability to claim his own work, his surrender of his name, could be seen as signs of his own lack of development, his inability to become an adult male who passes on his name, to complete the Oedipal trajectory, and another step towards the madness that will overwhelm him. I wouldn't deny this reading, but I would not claim its inevitability, either. Chris's identification with the image of a woman could also be seen as an essential step in his development as an artist, keeping him alive to his polymorphic childlike perversity, but gaining authority rather than regressing through it. This identification could be seen as a revolt against the hypocritical ideal male identity embodied in the portrait of Homer Higgins, whose 'muddy' vision Chris already rejects, an anti-Oedipal Deleuzian schizophrenia, which could transform Chris from the seventeen-jewel cashier into a pure 'desiring machine'.[43]

Chris's lack of interest in signing his own name to his works and his feminine alter-ego, both recall the fundamental avant-gardist gestures of Marcel Duchamp: signing several works with the name of his feminine alter-ego (whom he had himself photographed as, in drag) Rose Selavy (glossed as *Eros, c'est la vie*). It could also recall the behaviour of more contemporary avant-garde figures, like Andy Warhol who deliberately created uncertainty about his actual contribution to some of his art works, and even occasionally hired other people to masquerade as himself at official functions. Clearly it is a big leap from Chris Cross to the *Brides Stripped Bare by Her Bachelors, Even*. But I am claiming that Chris at this point is not an entirely doomed character, but rather one who is evolving as an artist and as a sexual person.

The shot of Chris beginning to paint his/her/their *Self-Portrait* fades out, and then the programme for the first exhibition of paintings by Katherine March fades in, the series of paintings culminating with a pull back from the now completed *Self-Portrait*, an image of Kitty staring straight out from the canvas. After Janeway's comment about Kitty's secret, the art opening sequence ends with a shot of his review in the paper, which reproduces the *Self-Portrait*. This dissolves to a shot of Chris, seated within his cashier's cubicle, literally under his name and identity so clearly inscribed on the window: Cashier Christopher Cross, smiling as he reads the review of his work under another name. The shot leads into his confrontation with the resurrected Homer Higgins, and I think it is clear that Chris's new-found cleverness in trapping his would-be blackmailer with his former wife and thereby

escaping from his marriage, comes from his recently discovered authority and recognition and perhaps even his new-fashioned, cross-gendered identity.

However, Chris's new identity – his creation of a painting persona which expresses the split in authorial identity and also insulates him from the exchange of art as a commodity – this utopian, polymorphic self – cannot withstand the traumatic primal scene of betrayal he witnesses, which causes his terror of castration to re-emerge. Chris falls back into the coils of the Destiny-machine, into the cycle of desire, jealousy, and violence, instead of the play with appearance and identity that avant-garde art since Nietzsche has promised. Instead of being liberated, once again Chris is stuck – 'in love – in love – in love.' As Chris sits in a bar, traumatised after seeing Kitty with Johnny, the soundtrack delivers one of Lang's hallucinatory voice-overs, the aural equivalent of the visionary overlap-dissolves. We hear Kitty's voice, in an insistent whisper, reprise her declaration of desire: 'Jeepers, I love you Johnny!' It repeats once again as Chris listens to a street corner Salvation Army preacher proclaim the need for forgiveness. The previous scene was so traumatic to Chris partly because the role of lover he wished to play was already taken by the violent, super-male figure of Johnny. Chris remained outside the scene, reduced to watching silently and then panicked flight. He returns to Kitty, trying to take on a traditional male role – protector, rescuer – and to ask her to marry him one more time. Her scorn, as we saw, tips him into madness and an identification with Johnny the punishing phallus.

After his flight from the scene of his crime, we see Chris once more seated in his cashier cubicle, reading about his (again, unattributed) work in the newspaper. But the differing effects of his identification with Kitty the artist and Johnny the punishing male are obvious. Reading the art review, Chris smiled with delight. Now he sits, unshaved, hair tousled, face sagging and flabby, as he reads in horror of the murder, which becomes, in several senses, his suicide ('Famous Painter Slain' says the headline). As in the earlier scene when he read the review of Kitty's show, his reading is again interrupted by the arrival of the law. But this time it is not the debunked Detective Higgins, but the real thing: cops in uniform who go first to J.J.'s office. The patriarch emerges in the film for one last time to fire Chris, but keeps him out of jail, completing the circuit from the opening scene, the final fate of the seventeen-jewel cashier. Chris had thought the police had come to arrest him for Kitty's murder, but instead they expose him for embezzling from his boss. His first Oedipal revolt is punished. 'It was a woman, wasn't it?', asks J. J., chomping on one of his big cigars. Chris nods, speechless, unable to articulate all the ways he might answer that question.

No Perspective: The Cancelling Out of Chris Cross

> The man who hasn't signed anything, who has left no picture
> Who is not there, who said nothing:
> How can they catch him?
> Cover your tracks.
>
>   Bertolt Brecht, 'Cover your Tracks'[44]

Johnny Prince forced Katherine March to take on Chris Cross's identity by signing his works. Chris, whose one desire was to escape his old life, tricked Homer Higgins into revealing his identity to his former wife, by arranging a scene dependent on light and darkness, and made a quick getaway before the lights came on. But then Chris was undone by witnessing a scene he did not arrange and was not supposed to see – his own betrayal by his lover. He murders his lover, an unplanned, mad action. Once again slipping out and leaving no trace behind, he again finds his work attributed to another, this time – bringing this merry-go-round of assumed identities and betrayals full circle – to Johnny Prince.

In a beautifully compressed montage, staged within stylised and abstract settings, Lang encapsulates the trial of Johnny Prince, cutting testimony together elliptically, so that questions raised by one witness are answered immediately by another and a noose of circumstantial evidence is tightened around Prince's neck. Three strands are developed, all hinging on establishing each character's true identity. The first group of witnesses testifies that Katherine March was definitely an artist. The next group testifies that Johnny was a mean son-of-a-bitch. Then both Adele and Chris testify that, contrary to Johnny's claims, Cross could not paint. The sequence ends with Johnny, usually so manipulative and self-assured, looking directly into the camera as sweat beads his face, swearing that Cross is lying. Johnny's look at the camera, a rare instance of this key Langian technique in this film, indicates his subjection to the implacable unrolling of the plot. Johnny the manipulator, recalling Lang's master criminals in his over-confidence – but inferior to them in intelligence and ambition – is being ground finely by the Destiny-machine. In his last appearance in the film, Johnny is glimpsed through one doorway walking down a long corridor into another open doorway – the room that holds the electric chair. As he protests shrilly, this door closes with a slam, an archetypal Langian image of fatality, doubly framed.

A major lacuna occurs in the film at this point, a repressed scene which was definitely shot, but eliminated, apparently after previews. (Lang claims he cut the scene because it appeared unintentionally comic.[45] Bernstein shows that cuts were first suggested by Universal and thinks Wanger may have carried them out over Lang's objection.)[46] On the eve of Johnny's execution Chris takes the train to Sing Sing to witness the final demise of his nemesis. Not permitted to actually attend the execution, in the suppressed scene Chris climbs a power line outside the prison (recalling the lookouts perched on power lines that appear in both *Dr. Mabuse, the Gambler* and *Spies*) in order to have a view of the prison at the moment of execution, to see what Lang describes as 'the glare of light' coming from the death house,[47] and to be near the source of the power that will fry Johnny. Stills from the suppressed scene (especially the one reproduced in Bogdanovich's interview book)[48] indicate this would have been one of Lang's darkest moments, of a nightmarish intensity. Chris Cross transforms from meek cashier, or even visionary painter, to a demonic being, a truly monstrous coupling of man and god at the moment of wrath, the equal, for this brief moment, of the grand enunciators of the German films.

As Jean Douchet points out, in his insightful treatment of this suppressed sequence, this scene harks back to the film's opening and fulfils the promise of the gold watch Chris is given in the opening scene.[49] Chris mounts this power line knowing that Johnny's execution is scheduled for eleven o'clock (the hour of death again and again in Lang films). He clings to the watch that J.J. gave him, lighting a match to be able to see the exact moment and listening for the hum of the electricity through the lines. He peers through the gathering fog trying to see the site of the electrocution, looking, the script indicates, towards the camera. As the watch shows the moment is come, Chris cries out – in the words of the script, 'as if he were invoking the God of Electricity' –- 'Now. Now. NOW!' There may be no scene in all of Lang, certainly none in his American films, which portrays the interweaving of a grand enunciator and the Destiny-machine so succinctly, so emblematically and, it would seem, so powerfully.

Chris throughout the film has lacked authority, whether in his job, his marriage or even in his painting. His affair with Kitty brought this situation to a crisis by arousing an erotic power which began to liberate him as a painter as well as sexually. But the terms of his apparent liberation were, in fact, deceitful and destructive: Kitty would assume his fame as a painter, Johnny would take the sexual favours of his mistress. But Chris's destruction has a tragic dimension because it results directly from his moments of self-assertion. He murders Kitty in a rage, but his exit from his marriage and his framing of Johnny (a painterly act, whose visual metaphor is stressed as Johnny is last glimpsed through the nested frames of the doors to the electric chair), manipulate situations brilliantly, creating masterpieces of devious *mise-en-scène*. Thus mounted on this power pylon, Cross sees himself as murdering Johnny at last, defying Kitty's mockery ('You kill Johnny? I'd like to see you try!'). United with, indeed, *commanding* the God of Electricity, Chris Cross destroys his rival.

All tragedy derives from hubris, and Lang's grand enunciators believe they hold Fate in their hands, that the Destiny-machine operates as their tool. As in *Dr. Mabuse, the Gambler* the master criminal asserts an apparent control over time and powerful technology. In this scene Lang condenses Mabuse's reign of terror into one essential image and one brief moment, Cross, the repressed and guileless cashier, now united with the power of a demonic god, synchronising its deadly force with his own clock, apparently wields the power of death, the divine thunderbolt. For one moment he knows what it is like to be a god – he thinks. But, of course, the power is actually beyond his control; the electricity comes from elsewhere, not from him. Johnny's time is up, but not because Chris declares it. Chris, too is caught in this cycle of time, and it will soon be too late for him, as well.

The script for this scene makes the point that as he climbs up the power line Chris resembles a man on a cross. Throughout the film, Lang and Nichols pun on Chris's name, generating a range of associations. The Christ association set up by his name and highlighted by the imagery of this scene seems rather contradictory and possibly blasphemous, perhaps another reason for Lang suppressing the scene (remember his concern over his demonic imagery related to the cathedral in *Metropolis*). This Chris(t) offers no forgiveness, only vengeance. But in a sense Chris is crucifying himself in this process. In seeming to merge with the gods, he invokes his own madness and destruction. Like a true *Trauerspiel*, from this point on the film dwells in detail on the misery of Chris, his self-martyrdom.

For most of the film, the name Chris Cross has evoked the idea of exchange, particularly all the exchanges from which Chris is excluded, the exchange of paintings without his name being involved, his inability to exchange his wife for Kitty, in spite of his deception of Homer Higgins. But after the murder of Kitty, Cross takes an active role in eliminating himself from the exchanges, making sure Johnny takes the blame. In order to do this Chris has to testify to the truth of his wife's claim (delivered straight into the camera lens) that Chris could not paint. 'I really can't paint', Cross testifies. 'My copies were so bad I had to destroy them.' That Chris's paintings are now claimed to be inferior copies of Katherine March's originals twists the film's mirror play with original and image into a maze. Chris is serious about destroying his paintings, however. If he ever painted again, it would be evidence of perjury, if not of his guilt in the murder. Chris has finally expunged his identity as a painter, even from the last refuge of Sunday mornings on the toilet. The image of the crisscross is no longer simply that of an exchange, but a cancel mark. From now on Chris exists *sous rature*.[50]

The tragedy tightens as one realises that it is only by destroying his identity as a painter that Chris could claim, in the privacy of a foggy night, an identity with a vengeful god, the fatal moment and the jolt of electricity. The demonic god arose from the corpse of the true enunciator, the artist. As this identification with death-dealing power surged at a precise moment, it also lasted only for an instant; the God of Electricity will have his own revenge. Even in the film as now constituted, the cut from the door closing on Johnny as he is led to the electric chair to the electric sign pulsing outside the window of the flop house hotel that Chris checks into after his moment of transfiguring sets up a deeply sinister rhythm. Here now is the God of Electricity, peering into Chris's window, alternating between bursts of illumination and total obscurity. Even with the scene on the power lines repressed, the flashing light picks up a mechanical and fatal rhythm, begun in Chris's train trip up to Sing Sing for the execution, in both a visual and aural overtone: the click-clack of the wheels and the eerie flashing of the landscape outside the train windows – the sinister, mechanical rhythm of the Destiny-machine.

The sequence that ensues becomes Lang's most savage visionary scene, a strict parallel to the sequence that ends *Dr. Mabuse, the Gambler* as Mabuse's hallucination of his victims surrounding him converts his counterfeiting den into one of the torturous circles of Hell. But here Lang uses sound rather than superimpositions or overlap-dissolves to convey Chris's mad visions, recalling Lang's comments to Lotte Eisner that if he were to re-shoot *The Testament of Dr. Mabuse*, he would use voice-over rather than superimpositions to convey Dr. Baum's vision of Mabuse.[51] We first see the pulsing light *before* Chris enters the room, as if it were awaiting his arrival. As he comes in the door, the underscoring very softly repeats a rhythmic almost mechanical vamp, synching with the pulsing of the light. The dominant sound, however is Chris's mournful whistling (the inversion of his bird calls when he felt like a kid with Kitty – and another link with Beckert) of 'Come to me, my Melancholy Baby'.

This reprise of Kitty's theme makes one uneasy, as Chris walks about the room, taking off coat, hat, scarf, jacket and tie. As he settles on the couch the reprise take on a new dimension. Having reached the phrase 'in love', Chris no longer whistles the tune, but instead reproduces Kitty's broken record: he repeats the two notes three times, then stops abruptly, realising what he is doing. The fourth repetition is taken over by the soundtrack. Once more Chris has become stuck, but not simply in a hopeless situation, like his marriage. A single moment of time has overtaken him, holds him in its endless, traumatic repetition, the sound of the record displacing his vision of Kitty's betrayal. Chris now has internalised the Destiny-machine, not as a series of mundane habits and anxieties, but as an endlessly repeating loop, that ultimate horror for Lang's protagonists of being imprinted with the one thing they wish they had never seen, like Joe and Katherine's view of the lynching. Chris realises now what he has been whistling and becomes suddenly silent as he takes off his shoes, as the underscoring becomes more insistent in its repetition.

Turning off the light switch, the erstwhile prophet of the God of Electricity, briefly plunges the room into darkness. In perhaps the strongest Expressionistic *noir* sequence in American film (with effects of hallucination conveyed, not by distortion in sets or stylised gesture, but entirely by the soundtrack and the rhythm of light, brilliantly realised by Krasner's cinematography), the following sequence dives down into the centre of Chris's madness, the tortured depressive side of his

mania on the power line. We witness a scene of torment and martyrdom as harrowing as any *Trauerspiel*. In an environment constantly switching between complete
darkness and the low-key lighting coming from the electric sign outside the
window, Lang catches Chris between two rhythms, a visual pulse of light and dark
and an audio *sprechstimme* of tormenting voices. When the light is switched off,
Kitty's voice calls seductively her first line from Chris's trauma-scene: 'Johnny, Oh
Johnny …', each word surrounded by an eerie repeating echo. Then comes Johnny's
response from the earlier love scene: 'Lazy Legs!' also reverberating. As Chris
searches the room, trying to find the source of the voices, they begin to whisper,
strongly but intimately, 'I'm here.' 'Jeepers, I love you, Johnny.' The voices echo and
repeat their love-calls to each other.

Chris settles on the bed, looking very much like Hans Beckert describing the
terror of hearing his voices. But there would seem to be an initial difference. Beckert's voices demanded things of him, addressed him directly. Chris initially hears
only the love-making of a couple he murdered. They speak to each other, not to
him. Once again he is crossed over, left outside the process of appellation. Chris lies
back in bed as the voices seem to stop for a moment. When they resume they don't
simply repeat the words they actually spoke in the trauma scene, but appear to
speak from beyond the grave, no longer simply echoing memories, but tormenting
fantasies. Kitty and Johnny say that by murdering them both Chris actually brought
them together, 'forever and forever and forever'. Unconsciously, Chris is authoring a
new fantasy, but unlike the visual images which allowed an outlet for his earlier
longing, this aural production (one might call it a private radio play rather than a
private movie) serves only to terrify and torture him.

Kitty's voice now addresses Chris directly, with lines repeated from her mockery
of him before her murder: 'You want to marry me?' Chris jumps from the bed and
paces the apartment, illuminated by the constant flickering, pulsating light. When
she calls out, 'You killed me!' he counters the accusation with his earlier rescue fantasy, 'No Kitty, it was him, you were innocent, you were pure, that's why he killed
you, that's why he had to die!' 'Then, addressing Johnny, You're the one I killed!' All
of this is met with mocking laughter and denials by the voices, ending with Kitty's
repetition, 'You kill Johnny? I'd like to see you try.' Chris screams her name louder
and louder as he grips the back of a chair, until the soundtrack falls silent. Having
stilled his voices for a moment, Chris (again recalling Beckert's gestures in the final
trial scene of *M*) wipes his face with his hand.

Chris is on trial here, tormented by the same accusing, mocking voices and sadistic laughter that echoed through the brewery cellar in *M*. But Lang stages more than
the torments of a guilty conscience. These aural hallucinations exceed the 'little
courtroom right inside, judge, jury and execution' that the moralistic reporter on the
train ride to Johnny's execution claimed prevents anyone from getting away with
murder. This hallucination completes the reversal of Chris's role as visionary artist.
Now he is trapped within his own fantasies, forced to listen to the endless copulation
of the ghosts of his victims. It is not simply the crime of murder that Chris suffers for,
but his own erotic anguish, the mockery by his lover, his exclusion from her love-
calls. This is the midnight hour which Benjamin sees as the archetypal moment for
the *Trauerspiel* as opposed to the bright daylight of classical tragedy. Chris does not
encounter justice in this hotel room, but the midnight moment, when, Benjamin
claims, time stands still, and 'the same ghostly image constantly re-appears'.[52]

After the moment of stillness, the voices begin again; Kitty calling for her lover,
Johnny. Chris, whose gaze has darted about the room looking for the source of the

voices, now looks sharply off screen. The electric sign in the window flashes with
particular intensity. The God of Electricity seems to be calling Chris through the
voice of his murdered mistress. Lang cuts to an angle we have not see previously,
showing both Chris and the window in long shot. As Chris whimpers and puts his
hands to his ears, the voice purrs, 'Jeepers, I love you, Johnny', the cycle starting up
again. The underscoring reaches a crescendo and we see a low angle shot of the
room's ceiling light. Lang cuts to a man in the corridor listening at Chris's door. He
and the hotel manager try to force the door when they hear a crash inside.

   In a reverse angle within the room we see only darkness, except a dim light from
the transom above the door. Then the sign outside the window flashes on, casting
the shadow of Chris's dangling legs onto the wall, suspended limply. This is the last
image that Chris will create: his visual defence against his aural torment; the final
private movie that he constructs with the aid of the God of Electricity; the coda to
his engineering of Johnny's execution – Chris's own death by hanging. The fatal
shadow pulses on and off for a few seconds until the men crash through the door.
The hotel manager flips the light switch as we see the other man lower the still-
breathing body of Chris to the floor. Holding him by the shoulders as he loosens the
noose, the man comforts him, saying, 'It's all right, old man.' Chris revives and
immediately hears Kitty's voice calling for Johnny, and exclaiming, 'Jeepers, I love
you Johnny!' Chris manages an ironic smile, before he collapses in sobs.

   Suicide plays an important role in Lang's dramaturgy. It can resolve a plot line
(Jellusic's suicide in *Spies*; Costa's suicide making his earlier, faked death real in
Ministry of Fear) or start one (Duncan's suicide which opens *The Big Heat*). But
most often suicides by major characters in Lang's films are interrupted one way (the
phone that interrupts Joan in *You Only Live Once*, the apothecary knocking the
poison from the maiden's hand in *Der müde Tod*) or another (Wanley's awakening
which undoes his apparently successful suicide). Liliom is the exception that proves
the rule; although he succeeds in killing himself, his consciousness continues, as we
follow him into the afterlife. But for Chris, unlike his *Doppelgänger* Wanley, this
interruption is no salvation, allows no return to a previous life. The seventeen-jewel
cashier has now literally become a broken record, trapped within an endless loop of
a replayed love scene in which he plays no part. The image of death he wished to
cast upon the wall, the antipode to Homer Higgins' portrait hanging on Adele's
wall, is effaced by snapping on the light switch. Death brings no closure to Chris;
instead he embodies the deadly repetition of the death drive, the horrific stuttering
of the Destiny-machine. In Freudian terms, the melancholy baby has become
trapped in true *melancholia*.

   Melancholia, according to Freud, is the failure of the mourning process which
gradually releases one's emotional investment in a lost or deceased loved one:

> The distinguishing mental features of melancholia are a profoundly painful
> dejection, cessation of interest in the outside world, loss of the capacity to love,
> inhibition of all activity, and a lowering of the self-regarding feelings to a degree that
> finds utterance in self-reproaches and self-reviling, and culminates in a delusional
> expectation of punishment.[53]

A fundamental unconscious ambivalence about the lost loved one sparks melancholia, a repression of some aspect of the original attachment. As Freud puts it, the
melancholiac 'knows *whom* he has lost but not *what* he has lost in him'.[54] Thus,
whereas in normal mourning the world is experienced as impoverished through the

loss of the beloved, in melancholia the ego itself becomes impoverished and divided against itself.[55] The melancholica has narcissistically identified with the loved one, and the ambivalent relation to the lost beloved surfaces as self-hatred and torment. The internalised, dead beloved acts like a sponge, or in Freud's image 'an open wound' absorbing all energy and 'emptying the ego until it is totally impoverished'.[56] The tormenting process involves a dire struggle:

> In melancholia, accordingly, countless separate struggles are carried on over the object, in which love and hate contend with each other; the one seeks to detach the libido from the object, the other to maintain the position of the libido against the assault.[57]

Chris's imagined colloquy with Kitty and Johnny literally stages the ambivalence of melancholia, rooted not only in his guilt over the murder of his beloved, but in a more fundamental ambivalence and narcissistic identification in his original love for Kitty. The role of exteriorisation and acting-out of this ambivalence in Lang's scene needs to be stressed. Chris's hallucination becomes an allegory of melancholia, not a clinical case. Freud again serves Lang as source for modern allegories of the complex interweavings of death and desire.

The scene of Chris sobbing, his face buried in the crook of his arm, dissolves into a winter landscape, a snow-filled park with two cops on patrol. One of only two images of nature in this claustrophobic film, this frigid locale cancels out the spring rain of the film's opening and the earlier crane shot of the trees arboring the Greenwich Village restaurant where Chris whistled like a bird for the predatory Kitty. The cops rouse Chris from sleeping on a snow-filled bench, rousting him into the streets of Christmas shoppers and his final encounter with the portrait of Kitty which closes the film. We can gather up now all the energies this final encounter releases: the vision of his own work, the god-like or demonic image-making power he once possessed and then denounced, now denied and destroyed; the vision of his dead beloved, painted at the moment he believed marked their union, an exchange of names which, in fact, turned out to be the effacing of his own; the appearance of the vengeful ghost of the one he murdered now confronting him, like his hallucinatory voices, with his crime; the image of his narcissistic identification with the lost loved one and the ambivalence of his love and hatred for her; and, last not least, the emblem of a commodity culture able still to make a profit from his work as he wanders abjectly past.

Kitty's eyes, open, staring, almost glassy, gaze out from the portrait invoking all these meanings. But now after her murder, as we see the portrait one more time, its staring eyes and slightly parted lips seem less the mark of a naive attempt at a portrait of one's beloved than the painting of a corpse. It was this portrait (more haunting than a Weegee crime scene photo) that accompanied the newspaper account of her death that Chris read in his cubicle, captioned, 'Self-Portrait of Katherine March, murder victim'. In many ways *Scarlet Street* reverses the relation between woman and portrait in *The Woman in the Window*. The only portrait that comes to life in *Scarlet Street* is that of Homer Higgins, minus one eye. The energy of *Scarlet Street* runs in a different direction.

Viewed from the ending, we could envision Chris's painting of Kitty's portrait as the first step in her murder. This visionary encounter on the streets of New York takes the form of all of Lang's key revelatory scenes: a revelation of death. But this is not simply the death of the beloved or even the death of the artist. If this *Self-Portrait* does fuse Chris with Kitty, how is he present in it? Since it lacks both his

likeness and his name, he can only be there as the artist's gaze and hand, that invisible point of origin on which all classical representation depends.[58] But we can only imagine this gaze through the image it has left, and that image looks back at us, and now in this final scene at its maker as well, complicating, perhaps even challenging, that dependence. Kitty's gaze from the canvas provides the most significant look at the camera/audience in this film; it presents perhaps Lang's most complex claim of enunciation, because it captures the gaze of an image as the look of death. The mystery possessed by this 'Mona Lisa without the smile' is, precisely, the gaze of death, the sightless eyes of the skull that hint at a vision that can see right through you, like the essential vision of Lang's film-making that Frieda Grafe described so well: 'the stripping bare of reality, reducing it to a skeleton, examining it like an X-Ray'.[59]

As Chris passes the Dellarowe Gallery, Lang ends the film with a demonstration of this vision. The camera cranes up to a high angle topographical image of the street, Chris's small figure almost lost in the crowd of shoppers. Then, shamelessly, an overlap-dissolve transforms the scene, not by a transition to another place or another image, but by slowly eliminating all the people but Chris, a man and woman near him seeming to fade out last, becoming shadows on a wall. The city street is empty except for Chris, no other people seem to exist in the world. As if a neutron bomb had exploded, all human life has disappeared, leaving only the architectural structures of the street viewed from Lang's high angle – and one lonely figure. An image again from Chris's painting, himself as an isolated wanderer in an empty city street, the shot closes out the film with an archetype of modernity, the night-time urban wanderer captured so well in Poe's 'The Man of the Crowd' or Maupassant's haunting 'La Nuit'.[60] Within this x-ray view what persist are not simply the eternal structures of fate, but the modern forms of human alienation, urban space, and a lonely haunted man caught within the melancholy gaze of the allegorist.

13

Secret Beyond the Door:
Broken Frames and Piercing Gazes

Pastiche and Palimpsest

That which lies here in ruins, the highly significant fragment,
the remnant, is, in fact, the finest material in baroque creation.
For it is common practice in the literature of the baroque to
pile up fragments ceaselessly, without any strict idea of a goal,
and, in the unremitting expectation of a miracle, to take the
repetition of stereotypes for a process of intensification.
    Walter Benjamin, *The Origin of German Tragic Drama*[1]

Scarlet Street made money and garnered critical praise for Lang as a director. In Diana Productions it seemed Lang had at last found the haven he sought in Hollywood, a place where his work was facilitated by talented collaborators, respected by the people who surrounded him and sheltered against the more brutal demands of the studio system. But, in fact, the mix was unstable; with its second production, *Secret Beyond the Door*, Diana Productions (and with it the hopes Lang had for semi-autonomy within the Hollywood system) crashed and burned. Although the causes for this disaster are manifold, the film which emerged from the wreckage bears some of the blame, a bizarre yet fascinating pastiche of Langian elements, a film whose near incoherence does not prevent it from being at points shockingly beautiful (or, at turns, risibly florid) and consistently fascinating, if never satisfying.

Secret Beyond the Door's disastrous reception both critically and at the box-office and the consequences of its failure also reflect the contradictory energies of a transitional moment in the history of Hollywood. Lang and Diana Productions sensed some aspects of this transition and felt they could ride its crest; instead they wiped out. As every history of Hollywood indicates, 1946 was the peak year of the industry, coming off an immediate postwar enthusiasm for the lifting of wartime restrictions and building on the all-time high attendance rates of the war era.[2] But from 1947 on, the decline of the industry set in, triggered by the large-scale demographic changes which preceded the new threat, and eventual triumph, of television.[3]

Cultural changes sent contradictory messages about the future of the movies. On the one hand there was a widespread claim that after the sobering experience of the war and particularly its aftermath (the atomic bomb and the revelation of the holocaust), the audience for movies craved more mature material, 'adult' movies.[4] The chaffing at censorship restrictions that *Scarlet Street* and other films during the war had initiated set the stage for continued confrontations not only with local censor boards, but, eventually, challenges to Hollywood's own self-censor, the Production Code Administration. Films imported from Europe, especially the Italian neo-realist films such as *Open City* (which Lang supposedly helped get shown in the US)[5] established new criteria for realism and made American restrictions appear puritanical. A new generation of scriptwriters and directors wanted to introduce more adult treatments of sexuality and morality, greater political controversy, and new models for character psychology and performances.[6] At the same time postwar reaction was also gathering strength, and suspicion of Hollywood's politics began to take on the virulence that outrage about its morals had sparked a generation before.

The time between the beginning of shooting *Secret Beyond the Door* (February 1947) to its release in Januar, 1948 almost precisely parallels the period in which the future fate of Hollywood was announced by three events. The 1947 decline in box-office receipts in retrospect might have been the most ominous sign, although at the time it caused little panic (Bernstein quotes the *Variety* headline 'Film Biz Dips to 'Only Terrific' From Used-To Be 'Sensational'').[7] More disturbing and certainly closer to home for Lang was the invasion of Hollywood by the House Committee on Un-American Affairs which held hearings into the Communist influence in the film industry in October 1947. This disturbing affair culminated in the prosecution of the 'Hollywood Ten'.[8] The committee called eleven 'unfriendly' witnesses whom they accused of being members of the Communist Party. The ten who refused under their constitutional rights to answer questions about party membership were cited for contempt of congress and were eventually sent to jail (including the scriptwriters of the spy film, *Cloak and Dagger* Lang had directed between *Scarlet Street* and *Secret Beyond the Door*, Ring Lardner Jr. – first choice to script *Secret*

Beyond the Door as well[9] – and Albert Maltz). The eleventh witness was another former Lang collaborator, Bertolt Brecht, who did testify, claimed he had never been a member of the Communist Party and then almost immediately left for East Germany. Earlier the Committee had also attacked Brecht's long-time collaborator (and the composer for *Hangmen Also Die*) Hanns Eisler, threatening deportation until he also left the country voluntarily. The 1947 hearings were only a prelude to the industry blacklists and mass hearings and their effects would loom over Hollywood for at least the next decade, with particularly sinister overtones for German émigrés like Lang who had left the Third Reich with the accusation of being *undeutsch* being levelled at them.[10]

The third event had been building for a long time and cast a long shadow: the Federal Paramount Decree in May 1948 which announced that under anti-trust laws the five major studios had to divest themselves of their theatre holdings and that distribution practices by all the defendants had to be re-organised.[11] This case had been before the courts for a decade and already by 1944 decisions concerning block-booking and other distribution practices (of more immediate impact on a minor studio like Universal which owned no theatres) had made Hollywood aware that their way of doing business over the last few decades was likely to end. The Paramount Decree spelled the end of the studio system and changed radically not just the way films were shown but how they were planned and produced. Further appeals and a generous schedule combined with delays on the part of the studios meant a complete divorce of studios from theatre ownership was not accomplished until well into the fifties, but Hollywood saw the writing on the wall. Although the divestment procedures and the HUAC hearings are unrelated (and even antithetical in their political orientations), it is generally agreed that uncertainty about Hollywood's future, reeling as well under a series of bitter studio strikes, prevented it from offering a united front against the HUAC and staving off the political attacks, as it had during the war.[12]

The breaking up of the studio system and distribution practices generally favoured independent producers, but the new industry environment ultimately endangered Diana's relation with Universal which had just undergone a major merger.[13] The studio's policy of forming relations with semi-independent companies, like Diana or Mark Hellinger's unit, followed a decision to move the studio (which had specialised in low-budget programmers) into high-budget A film releases.[14] *Scarlet Street* demonstrated the success the new policy might have. But in the post-1947 environment, the move did not play well. As Douglas Gomery puts it, 'The postwar years were not kind to Universal because management picked the wrong time to try to imitate the [Major Studios].'[15] If Diana had maintained the harmony between participants that it forged at its founding, and if their projects after *Scarlet Street* had enjoyed the same good fortune, Wanger, Lang and Bennett might have walked away from Universal with their production company intact. However, interior strife between Lang and Wanger, as well as problems with *Secret Beyond the Door*, condemned Diana never to make another film after its rupture with the studio. Lang's behaviour within Diana after *Scarlet Street* has been called 'neurotic' by Matthew Bernstein, and nothing prompts one to argue with that assessment (except, perhaps, to add paranoid, megalomaniacal, and ultimately self-destructive).[16] It is tempting to read *Scarlet Street* as Lang's paranoid vision of his partnership, with his star conspiring with her husband to rob him of his authorship.

Diana had become for Lang not only a means to produce his own films, but a sort of private fiefdom which he tried anxiously to protect from palace coups or surrender to the studio Huns outside the gate. McGilligan shows that Lang surrounded himself with a number of young co-workers, most of them women, nearly all of them political leftists.[17] Besides producing Fritz Lang films, this office was dedicated to manufacturing 'Fritz Lang' as a signature, not only putting him before the public eye, but defining for the public who he was as a film-maker.[18] Thus Lang and his office (along with Universal's publicity office) tried to come up with a catch-phrase that could identify Lang for audiences and critics – the equivalent of Hitchcock's 'master of suspense' or the 'Lubitsch touch'. But Lang seemed uncertain how to do this. While the most high-recognition Hollywood directors of the period – Hitchcock, Lubitsch, DeMille – carved out their identity by specialising in a specific type or genre of films (Hitchcock's thrillers, Lubitsch's romantic comedies, DeMille's historical spectacles) Lang seemed to want to root his reputation in more intangible qualities. 'Realism' (a term he was always attached to – without ever defining very clearly) was one aspect of his films he wanted stressed. Another was his targeting an adult audience, with culture and intellect.[19] His reputation for tyrannical control over details suggested one tack with the (incredibly unappealing) proposal, 'perfectionist deluxe'.[20]

The art house movie theatres which began to appear in the US after the war offered Lang one vision of who he might be in a new 'adult' Hollywood.[21] His German films, especially *M*, were shown in the new independent movie theatres popping up in urban areas and college towns which offered a mix of non-Hollywood films: older classic films; English films (such as the Alec Guinness comedies or Laurence Olivier's Shakespeare films, or psychological melodramas with new stars like James Mason); the neo-realist films from Italy (Rossellini's war trilogy, the first films of Fellini and De Sica). Some independent American companies mounted their own art films, such as Ben Hecht's *Specter of the Rose* (1947). A strong visual style; slightly more risqué plots or situations; a use of symbolism (often deriving from surrealism or Freudian analysis); the casting of an English actor new to Hollywood (Michael Redgrave, after James Mason turned the part down)[22] – these were elements of the art house films that Lang decided to include in *Secret Beyond the Door*. In spite of his claims of a realist style, Lang did not pick up influences coming from neo-realism, such as location shooting, casting non-stars, or introducing politically controversial subject matter, which were adopted by young directors like Joseph Losey, Nicholas Ray or Elia Kazan who were pioneering a new look for postwar American film (often with direct links to older Lang films – Losey did a remake of *M* which infuriated Lang, and Ray's premiere masterpiece, *They Live by Night* a tender and tragic account of an outlaw couple on the run, recalls *You Only Live Once*).

Lang's primary model for *Secret Beyond the Door* came from more mainstream films. In hiring Sylvia Richards as scriptwriter to this film Lang was doing more than putting his current mistress on the payroll.[23] Richards had a western and a melodrama to her screenwriting credit, and while her western expertise was expended on a script for the unrealised Diana production of *Winchester 73*, her script for the Joan Crawford melodrama, *Possessed* of 1947, helped tailor *Secret Beyond the Door* to the most recent fashion in women's melodramas, which forced gothic themes of madness through a Freudian filter. Using Freudian themes as new plot enigmas and an excuse for dream sequences with Expressionistic or surrealistic visual elements were aspects the popular woman's film and the new art house fare shared in such films as John Brahm's *The Locket* of 1946 (with its endlessly embedded flashbacks attempting to get at the childhood memory that made the heroine a kleptomaniac), the British *The Seventh Veil* of 1947 (in which sessions with a psychoanalyst uncover the root of pianist Ann Todd's ambivalent relation with her mysterious cousin played by James Mason); or most influential of all, Hitchcock's 1945 *Spellbound*.

Literally dozens of psychological melodramas with central women characters were released between 1945 and 1949, most of them involving a sort of Freudian detective plot in which buried memories are unearthed through psychotherapy or something similar in order to solve a mystery. Following Freud in an over-literal manner, dreams, parapraxis and memories are plumbed to get at the motive for a variety of crimes or strange behaviour. Freudian concepts simultaneously fulfil traditional plot functions and motivate new approaches to visual style and narration.[24] The narrative core of these films, uncovering a primal trauma, simplifies and even trivialises Freudian concepts, especially when the sexual etiology of the neuroses went unmentioned in all these films, producing a bizarre view of the human psyche as constantly prey to childhood experiences that have been repressed for no apparent reason. In fact, Sylvia Richards' script for *Possessed* shows that Freudian analysis was not the only device that could unearth memories and fantasies, since Joan Crawford delivers her voice-over flashback in that film, not via talking cures with an analyst, but in a hospital bed surrounded by doctors and prompted by an injection of some sort of truth serum, imaginatively called 'narco-synthesis'.

Nonetheless, these films' narrative structure, relying on memories, fantasies, dreams and their interpretation encouraged new visual styles with deep focus and low-key lighting, narrational styles heavy with flashback and voice-over, and a view of character motivation which, while hardly truly Freudian, was nonetheless more ambivalent and complex than the Hollywood character schemata had permitted until then. The series of psychoanalytical mysteries also shows the way a narrative pattern can cut across genre boundaries in Hollywood. Themes of repressed memories surfacing through dreams or hallucinations bleed across a number of genres, endowing them with a Freudian tone, such as Elina's memories and dreams in the horror film, *Cat People* the dreams of Ginger Rogers' blue dress in the musical, *Lady in the Dark* (based on the Broadway hit of Kurt Weill); or the flashing spurs that haunt Robert Mitchum in the western, *Pursued*.

A large number of the psychoanalytical mysteries tried to explain the behaviour of neurotic women but a key variant was introduced by Hitchcock in *Spellbound* which set the pattern followed by Lang in *Secret Beyond the Door*: a neurotic man whose illness is explained by a woman. An attractive but mysterious leading man (Gregory Peck in *Spellbound*, Michael Redgrave as Mark in *Secret*) seems to be alternatively normal and engaging and then, suddenly without apparent motive, cold, withdrawn, even sinister. His behaviour intrigues a young woman who falls in love with him. (In *Spellbound*, Ingrid Bergman, who plays a psychiatrist; Celia, the loving young woman in *Secret*, seems to have been in analysis herself and must have picked up its principles along the way – maybe by seeing *Spellbound*.) It becomes clear that there are certain cues that set off the man's bad behaviour which function like clues through which the young woman unravels his secret. Eventually he seems to be implicated in a murder. The clues are pursued through symbolic visualisations (the Dali-designed dream sequences of *Spellbound;* in *Secret* both Mark's hallucination and his 'collection of rooms' play this role, although a strict parallel does not exist). Through the young woman's clever decoding, it is discovered that, in fact, the young man suffers from a false sense of guilt due to a childhood trauma; he is not a murderer, and probably can be cured of his peculiar behaviour as well.

Lang's dependence on *Spellbound* might appear more shameless, if many of these motifs and structures were not present in the other psychoanalytical mysteries that proliferated around this time. Lang hired the composer for *Spellbound*, Miklos Rosza, who greatly added to the beauty of the film with one of his most powerful and experimental scores. Lang instructed him to compose a score very different from the previous film and forbid him to use the theremin, the electronic instrument so effective in giving the Hitchcock film an uncanny quality (even though Lang had pioneered the use of the theremin's electronic predecessor, the Ondes Martenot in *Liliom*).[25] Indeed, the influence of *Spellbound* on *Secret Beyond the Door* moves in both directions, direct borrowings and wilful deviations.

For instance, Lang seems determined to avoid the equivalent of the Dali-designed dream sequences of *Spellbound* and their role as major clues to be interpreted. *Secret Beyond the Door* does begin with an apparent dream sequence, but instead of it belonging to Mark, the troubled young man, it is associated with Celia. Lang, of course, could hardly be accused of imitating Hitchcock in his invocation of dreams. Instead of hiring Dali and building fun-house sets, he uses animation as he had done decades earlier for Kriemhild's dream in *Siegfried*. Walther Ruttmann was dead (and had been a Nazi collaborator), so Lang initially hired Ruttmann's great rival in abstract animation, Oskar Fischinger, who had provided the animation effects in *The Woman in the Moon*, and who was now a member of the Weimar émigré group in Hollywood, lured over by a contract with Paramount around the same time Lang had arrived. Fischinger was frequently hired by major Hollywood studios – Paramount, MGM, Disney (whose opening to *Fantasia* ripped him off) – and independent producers (Orson Welles' Mercury Productions for the never completed *It's All True*) without anything ever coming of it, and ultimately the same thing happened with *Secret Beyond the Door*, whose animated prologue was completed by the Disney studio.[26]

Curiously, when Lang spoke of *Secret Beyond the Door* in interviews, he did not refer to the debt it owes to *Spellbound*, but rather to his inspiration from *Rebecca*. This is more than camouflage. What Lang was attempting in *Secret Beyond the Door* was, I believe, a full scale appropriation of Hitchcock's Hollywood work and the genre which he had established, the suspense thriller from a woman's point of view. Because Hitchcock's work is now overshadowed by the films he did for Paramount in the 1950s it is easy to forget that in the 40s Hitchcock's films were produced in the wake of his greatest success, *Rebecca*. Hitchcock's ambivalence about this film and its producer, David O. Selznick, obscures its importance for his later career. Most of his films from the 40s reworked elements of *Rebecca*'s basic premise of a young and fairly innocent girl encountering a mysterious man whom she loves but is frightened by (*Suspicion, Shadow of a Doubt, Spellbound*) and being threatened by a large house controlled by an intimidating older woman (*Notorious, Under Capricorn*). These motifs show Hitchcock's debt to the tradition of women's gothic, a tradition centuries old, but revived by Daphne du Maurier's novel.

Hitchcock's debt to the women's film becomes even clearer when we consider another series of films, from the 40s, which Mary Ann Doane calls the 'paranoid woman's film' and Diane Waldman terms the 'gothic romance', linking it with this literary source.[27] Two plot elements define this series: a tormented wife whose ambiguous and mysterious husband she believes is (and often *actually* is) trying to kill and/or drive her mad, and a looming ancestral house frequently supplied with a forbidden room.[28] Even more than the psychoanalytical mystery, this series or sub-genre proliferates in Hollywood in the 40s, sparked undoubtedly by the success of *Rebecca* in 1940, including films by a large number of major directors between 1944 and 1948: George Cukor (*Gaslight*), Joseph Mankiewicz (*Dragonwyck*), Vincente Minnelli (*Undercurrent*), André De Toth (*Dark Waters*), Max Ophuls (*Caught*), Douglas Sirk (*Sleep My Love*), Jacques Tourneur (*Experiment Perilous*) – in addition to Lang and Hitchcock's contributions and many other less memorable offerings. But in the case of Hitchcock, the prominence of the *auteur* text in approaching his work has to some extent obscured the place of many of his films in this series.

Lang is working at the confluence of several styles in *Secret Beyond the Door*: the psychoanalytical mystery, interbred with the 'paranoid woman's' melodrama, especially under the sign of Alfred Hitchcock. The figure of Hitchcock clearly haunted Lang as he tried to position himself before the moviegoing public through Diana. The arc of their careers could be said to intersect at antithetical points. Hitchcock served as assistant director for *The Blackguard*, a British-German co-production shot in Ufa's Neubabelsberg studio as Lang was beginning *Metropolis* and McGilligan claims the young man watched the already celebrated master at the height of his power.[29] Hitchcock worked with Lorre soon after *M*, and was brought to the US by the same man who had brought Lang, David O. Selznick. But then the contrast sets in. Whereas Lang was allowed to languish after his arrival, searching for a project, Hitchcock soon after arrival was announced as directing the high-profile *Rebecca* based on du Maurier's bestseller (although, curiously, both directors initially spent some time working on unrealised projects about shipwrecks – Lang's *Hell Afloat* and Hitchcock's *Titanic*).[30] While *Fury* garnered Lang good reviews, *Rebecca* won the Academy Award and Hitchcock's star ascended with mainly high-budget, big star productions throughout the 40s. In 1947 we see Lang trying to attain the status Hollywood had already granted to the one-time anonymous assistant director who had once watched him command armies of extras.

That Lang influenced Hitchcock seems obvious, since the films that established Hitchcock's reputation, his English spy thrillers, seem to come very much out of Lang's *Spies*. But Hitchcock never cited a strong influence from Lang, and was more likely to remember *Der müde Tod* (possibly because Bernhard Goetzke, who played Death, also starred in *The Blackguard*, for which Hitchcock wrote the script and designed sets as well), than recall anything specific about *M* ('Wasn't there a whistling man in it?') or *The Testament of Dr. Mabuse* ('Mabuse – that's a long time back') despite prompting from François Truffaut.[31] But if the debt seems obvious, Hitchcock's originality cannot be questioned. The contrast between the styles of these two directors who helped define the thriller genre supplies endless material for critical comparison, as French critics have shown.[32] These two directors are probably the commercial film-makers who have been most profoundly influenced by Freud and especially the Freudian elaboration of the romantic intertwining of Eros and Thanatos. Stylistically, their most profound link probably comes, as Raymond Bellour has shown us, in their common engagement with the issue of enunciation in cinema, the contrasting way each makes their presence felt in their films as narrators.[33]

In *Secret Beyond the Door* the interrelation between the two directors takes on a tangible form. When Lang invoked *Rebecca* in referring to his film, he said, with disarming candour, 'talk about stealing', confessing his desire to appropriate something from Hitchcock's film.[34] In fact, one feels he wanted to incorporate something from nearly all of Hitchcock's major American films, and undoubtedly the director's success, as well. The borrowings from *Rebecca* are clear: the marriage to a mysterious man with a secret and his second wife's suspicion that he may have murdered his first wife, the husband's ancestral home catching fire in the climax in a fire set by a jealous female servant. The borrowings from *Spellbound* are equally evident, as I described. A key situation is lifted from *Notorious* as well, the wife's theft of a key from her husband in order to open a subterranean room he keeps locked. And Celia's belief she is about to be murdered by her neurotic husband, followed by her decision to stay with him anyway because she loves him, parallels the plot of *Suspicion*. *Secret Beyond the Door* appears as much a pastiche of Hitchcock motifs as of elements from Lang.

But this drama of appropriation and incorporation never simply smacks of plagiarism. Lang 'steals' from Hitchcock in order to transform him, to absorb his successful woman-centred suspense film formula into his own style; the alchemy doesn't entirely work, but we don't simply see gold turned into dross, either. Instead, underlying elements of Lang's style are highlighted which prevented the packaging of Lang as the new (old?) Hitchcock. The basic contrast lies in the way each director approaches the subjectivity of their characters and its narrative role. Hitchcock structures his films through central characters who serve as focalisations of the story: roughly, we see what they see and know what they know. Hitchcock occasionally shifts the focalisation from one character to another (for instance, back and forth between Devlin [Cary Grant] and Elsa [Ingrid Bergman] in *Notorious*) and certain brief scenes are even focalised through fairly minor characters (e.g. the saboteur, Fry in *Saboteur*). At significant, but relatively rare moments, the omniscience of the director intervenes dramatically and we are given viewpoints entirely outside the characters' experience. But with Lang, as we have seen, although he uses point of view shots dramatically, the melding of the focalisation with a character is much less dominant, and the authorial intervention more frequent. When Hitchcock misleads his audience (as in the lying flashback in *Stagefright*), he is more likely to do it through a character's subjective viewpoint (the flashback visualises the lie told by Jonathan Cooper), while Lang simply refuses the audience certain information (as in the robbery in *You Only Live Once*, or the ellipsis in *Secret Beyond the Door*).

Whereas Hitchcock will build most scenes out of a character's (or sometimes, characters') point of view, sculpting the space with the viewpoint of the character (think of Elsa's entrance to her husband's dinner party in *Notorious*), Lang insists, instead, on a primacy of space into which characters enter (the plot of this film – Mark's obsession with 'felicitous' rooms – stands as a sort of allegory for this primacy of space over character). A character's point of view, then, intervenes on the space, trying to make sense out of it, searching for the significant detail (as in Celia's point of view of the scarf on the floor in the room where Don Ignacio killed Isabella, the first overt shot from her point of view in that sequence), rather than constructing the space as a whole. Hitchcock reflects a stronger belief in the centrality of subjectivity, although his films are as fascinated as Lang's with its destruction through madness or terror. Lang, on the other hand, portrays systems as pre-existing and structuring subjectivity. The Destiny-machine which overwhelms Lang's characters never restricts itself to a psychological force. As we have seen, it forms the centre of his portrayal of human existence in modernity and of his probing of the nature of modern identity itself.

If both Lang and Hitchcock probe the terrors, passion, and violence implicit in patriarchal gender relations, Lang's portrayal of women is harder to place within the voyeuristic/sadistic mode that Mulvey sees Hitchcock as exemplifying.[35] Probing Lang's relation to *Rebecca* and Hitchcock's other gothic woman-centred suspense stories, we find Lang (and Richards his screenwriter) wilfully reworking the women

characters he takes from Hitchcock. The entrance of the young bride into the husband's house in Hitchcock leads inevitably to a confrontation with another (usually
older) woman figure whose authority she threatens: Mrs. Danvers in *Rebecca*, Mrs.
Sebastian in *Notorious*, and (after *Secret Beyond the Door*) Milly in *Under Capricorn*.
Lang raises the issue of authority between Celia and Mark's older sister Caroline in
Secret Beyond the Door, only to deflate it. Celia asks Caroline to keep her position of
authority managing the household, and although Caroline is ultimately blamed for
Mark's neurosis (as part of a childish prank) the film resolutely refuses to demonise
her. Anne Revere's unclichéd performance reveals the character's weakness, but also
her sincere appreciation for Celia's friendship and love for her brother.

     However, if Lang refuses to have the confrontation over household management
represented by both Mrs. Danvers and Milly, the ghost of Mrs. Danvers, particularly
her skulking and uncanny quality, pops up in the bizarre Miss Robey, with her scarf
masking her non-existent facial scar. This excessive character keeps flitting around
the margins of this story as she does around the corridors of the Lamphere house, a
possible menace, a possible ally, until in the end she becomes the *demon ex machina*
and decides to burn the house, as Danvers did at the end of *Rebecca*. If her unstable
character contributes to this film's incoherence, it is partly because Lang insists on
deflating her uncanny quality (until perhaps the ending) and defuses the drama
between Celia and her. Celia cannot be intimidated by her (one of Lang's transformations of the gothic pattern is to make Celia older and more experienced, and definitely more confident than most gothic heroines with a nutty husband).[36] When
she discovers Robey's secret (plastic surgery has removed the facial scar she got
when she rescued Mark's son from a fire, but she maintains the fiction of its presence in order to secure the family's sense of obligation to her), she pledges to keep it
a secret between the two women. Instead of Danvers' almost hypnotic evil as a
means of exerting power, Robey,when exposed, talks explicitly about her need for a
pay cheque.

     Broken into its elements *Secret Beyond the Door* displays an extraordinary range
of Langian themes and operates truly as an *auteur* film which cannot be understood
(or valued) without knowing the rest of Lang's work. The superior score by Rosza,
which Lang, in spite of his ignorance of music, discussed in detail with him (in contrast to Hitchcock's apparent lack of interest in the score for *Spellbound*),[37] added to
the extraordinary quality of Stanley Cortez's cinematography, draws us deep into
this flawed but rich work. Ironically Lang hated working with Cortez who was Bennett's choice for cinematographer over Lang's desire to stick with Milton Krasner.
Lang not only felt that Cortez was not his man, but railed against his slow pace of
work.[38] But Cortez's ability sharply to separate highly contrasting zones of shadow
and highlights and create sharp planes of focus makes *Secret Beyond the Door* one of
Lang's most beautiful and visually intriguing films, superior even to the fine work of
Krasner or Charles Lang, and the equal to the best cinematography in Lang's American work: Arthur Miller on *Man Hunt* and James Wong Howe on *Hangmen Also
Die*. But it must be confessed that the parts of *Secret Beyond the Door* do not equal
the whole, which is never able to interrelate these elements in the way Lang's best
film managed. Lang seems to have stuffed this film with vividly bizarre characters,
such as Miss Robey, or David, Mark's son who walks through the picture like a
miniature adult in suit and tie – the incredible shrinking man in his early stages –
without really devising plot lines that integrate them in a substantial way. However,
the very impossibility of holding this film together, and the tensions this generates,
constitute perhaps its most revealing and fascinating aspects.

Speaking and Seeing: A Woman's View and Voice

> The voice you hear is not my speaking voice, but my mind's voice.
>
> Opening lines of Jane Campion's *The Piano*

Both Hitchcock's style and the situation of the gothic 'paranoid woman's film' rely heavily on the point of view of female characters, seeming to call into question the Mulvey model of the dominance of the male gaze in the classical Hollywood system. Mary Ann Doane labours to prove that this attribution of a visual view-point in these films does not necessarily empower the woman character or provide a feminist alternative.[39] I would agree, primarily because the patriarchal assump-tions of Hollywood film operate most powerfully at the plot level, rather than being determined by an unconscious deep structure of the cinematic apparatus. A film like *Possessed* remains deeply disturbing for its portrayal of a woman's subjectivity, because techniques such as voice-over, visualisation of memories and fantasies and the use of point of view shots only serve to emphasise the reactionary assumptions of the plot. Female subjectivity is constructed in *Possessed* in order to be, as Doane shows, subjected to male analysis, judgement and recuperation according to patri-archal structures.[40]

Lang can hardly be seen as a feminist film-maker (although his office manager at Diana described him as 'an ardent feminist' and Lang considered using the fact that he mainly hired women as business associates and professed deep respect for them as a publicity angle to be offered to women's magazines – whatever all that is worth).[41] But *Secret Beyond the Door* stages a kind of incoherence of subjectivity that bleeds across gender roles (without explicitly analysing, let alone critiquing them) in ways that make the tidy patriarchal reading of the film by Jenkins and Doane rather problematic.[42] Celia's visual point of view dominates over any other character in *Secret Beyond the Door* but primarily as a thematised look, one express-ing a particular emotion or reaction, rather than as the main vehicle for narrative information as in a Hitchcock film. Celia's gaze is never simply perceptual, a phe-nomenological looking around. Rather, it is almost always a fascinated gaze, one transfixed in either horror or desire – or a combination of the two.

Lang inscribes Celia's subjectivity in *Secret Beyond the Door* in two registers: visu-ally through the use of point of view shots and other images of her ability to see the world around her (which I will analyse later); and, primarily, aurally through an extensive use of voice-over. Voice-over opened *Rebecca* (which probably influenced Lang's adoption of it – especially the invocation of dreams which the opening voice-over in both films includes), but only over Hitchcock's resistance.[43] During the 40s, voice-over emerged as a powerful narrative device, especially in the melo-dramatic genres of the women's film and *film noir*. In the women's film, voice-over adapted a first person confessional mode that appeared in fiction in women's mag-azines (like *Redbook*, the source of the original short story on which *Secret Beyond the Door* was based). In complete contrast to a non-diegetic, narrator voice-over (what Kaja Silverman calls a disembodied voice-over) this voice-over is deeply woven into the story. As Silverman puts it: 'the embodied voice-over designates not only psychological but diegetic interiority – that it emanates from the center of the story, rather than from some radically other time and place'.[44] This is especially true of the sort of voice-over that *Secret Beyond the Door* employs, which is only briefly tied to a flashback and for the most part speaks from an immediate relation to what is on screen rather than as a retrospective memory (in contrast to a *noir* confession such as Joe Gillis's post-mortem narration in *Sunset Boulevard*, or Lisa's voice-over in *Letter from an Unknown Woman*). Sarah Kozloff terms such non-retrospective voice-overs 'interior monologues', although she admits the distinction between immediacy and memory can be hazy.[45]

In *Secret Beyond the Door* there is no question that we are supposed to be within Celia's consciousness. The opening lines express this present tense immediacy rooted in the time and place of the narrative. After speaking of the meaning of dreams while Lang shows the animated 'dream pool', Celia's voice proclaims, 'But this is no time for me to think of danger, this is my wedding day!' The sound of this voice-over shows the qualities that Michel Chion finds typical of what he calls the 'I-voice': close miking which eliminates any sense of distance between us and the voice, so that it seems to speak to us directly, and a lack of reverberation which abstracts it from any specific space.[46] Thus the voice-over in *Secret Beyond the Door* embeds itself into the space and time of the story (although her voice-over does slip into the past tense, showing that instability Kozloff noted), but within a recessed private space of consciousness, truly, in Silverman's terms, at the deepest 'interior' of the film. After Mark leaves Celia at their honeymoon inn in Mexico, the cadence of her voice-over directly synchs with her actions as she paces the room (and even synchs with Rosza's score which takes up the rhythm of her litany of 'Why did he leave, why did he lie?', a musical motif which subsequently invokes, and occasionally substitutes for, her interior monologue), giving us access to her doubts as they occur.

For Chion these qualities allow such 'I-voices' to become a 'pivot of identifications'.[47] Most commentators agree that voice-over tends to increase viewer identification with a character through both increased access to their motivations and an increased sense of intimacy[48] (although I would add that if these monologues were written to seem nasty, irrational or offended shared cultural assumptions, such formal devices would hardly succeed in making us empathise with the speaker). Celia's voice-over or interior monologue primarily allows us access to her particularly private thoughts. As such, it primarily reflects her uncertainties, doubts and fears, and even repressed feelings. Thus the voice-over expresses her excitement over the knife fight, and her excited ambivalence about being stared at by Mark, while her spoken words express her desire to leave. At her wedding, the voice-over expresses her fear of marrying Mark, and desire to run away, countered by her fear of what people would say. Visually, we see her take Mark's hand and kneel before the altar, and only a flicker of doubt appears on her face.

The portrayal of Celia's subjectivity through voice-over or interior monologue presents her as a divided character. This division between her interior monologue and her actions would have been greatly increased if Lang's original recording of this voice-over had been used, in which the lines were actually spoken by a different actress than Joan Bennett. This would have staged Lang's conviction that the unconscious *is* another, 'someone in us we perhaps don't know'.[49] (Universal demanded the change, and Bennett agreed, which Lang saw as a great betrayal.)[50] Further, as we have seen, the voice-over most frequently reflects Celia's doubts, confusions and fear, thoughts which she is loath to either voice or act on. In this sense, Doane and Jenkins are right that the film undercuts an authoritative female discourse. But their objection to this would seem to argue for a sort of unified consciousness that their use of Lacanian psychoanalysis renders rather contradictory.

But there is no question that in *Secret Beyond the Door* Lang's portrayal of feminine subjectivity does not offer a reliable substitute for the masterful male gaze.

While her point of view plays a key role in the film, visual certainty and mastery elude Celia as much as subjective certainty in her interior monologue. Although the film begins with a number of signs of subjectivity other than a point of view shot (Celia's voice-over; the dream prologue, the flashback memory), her first point of view shot comes within the flashback during her trip to Mexico, and Lang introduces it as the centre of a dramatic scene and gives it the force of an unsettling revelation. An off screen scream attracts the attention of Celia and her friend who both turn and look off to the right. Lang cuts to a long shot as a young man pulls a knife and wraps his girlfriend's scarf around his arm. The camera, tracking back, reveals another man, bare-chested, with a knife poised. Lang then cuts to a wide shot that tracks in to a medium shot, isolating Celia and emphasising her off screen fixed stare. The following point of view shows a long shot of the fight as the men circle each other. Her voice-over tells of her excitement (Richards' writing – or perhaps Lang's given his strong involvement in the writing of this script[51] – struts its most florid, women's magazine prose): 'fighting for her with naked knives. Death was in that street.' As so often happens in Lang's 40s films, Celia's look is doubled, or mirrored, by looking at someone looking: a medium close-up of Celia looking off, cuts to the woman they are fighting for, watching the duel with some pleasure. Celia's voice-over makes it clear she identifies with the woman's voyeurism: 'I felt how proud she must be.'

Celia's gaze expresses erotic and even sadistic fascination: a voyeuristic absorption in the 'primitive passion' of these natives. But as her gaze found its double in the girl's regard of her rival paramours, she now becomes pulled into the action. The knife thrown by the younger man misses its target and embeds itself in the table of curios close to Celia's hand. The action is announced in typically Langian fashion, first the throw of the knife, then the scream of Edith, Celia's friend, and the off screen sound of knife entering wood and its almost musical quivering, like a plucked piano string – all before the camera tilts down, following the direction of Celia's gaze, finally to reveal the knife. The phallic violence of the scene has turned on its voyeur.

But this intersection of gazes has not yet found its apex. Celia reacts to the knife with a sort of shiver as her gaze searches for something off screen. Her voice-over explains, in *Redbook* style, 'Suddenly I felt that someone was watching me. There was a tingling at the nape of my neck as though the air had turned cool. I felt eyes touching me like fingers …' What Celia searches for as she continually scans off screen space from left to right and back again, is this invisible gaze, the further doubling of the scene of spectating. Celia had first found a feminine mirror-image and imagined herself watching in that woman's place. Now, after the knife throw, she feels her own specularity suddenly exposed. In Langian fashion the voice-over describes this male gaze as a hand as well as an eye. Lang cuts to Mark, straining to look to the right as everyone around him continues to watch the knife fight to the left. A close-up follows of Celia looking rather dismayed, but also rapt, almost mesmerised by Mark's gaze. The voice-over describes the gaze now in hypnotic terms, and also invokes its penetrating, x-ray aspect: 'There was a current flowing between us, warm and sweet, but frightening too, because he saw behind my makeup what no-one had ever seen, something I didn't know was there.' Celia turns to Edith and says she wants to leave.

Point of view for Lang usually troubles the scene, probing it for a dramatic possibility, if not a full-fledged visionary moment. Here Celia discovers a rather explosive eroticism through her pleasure in looking. But immediately she is captured in another's gaze, a gaze which poses not only an erotic invitation and even threat, but a recognition of her, a seeing into her erotic nature. Once again we see that the mastering male gaze plays a key role within the Langian system, but, even in scenarios of desire, it embeds itself in a more complex pattern than simple male vision and female objectification. Immediately after the fight in the market, Edith tells Celia, 'When you finally snapped out of your trance you looked as though you had seen Death himself.' Almost to herself, Celia mutters, 'That's not how he looked to me.' The gaze of death which underpins Lang's visual system is invoked here by the film's silliest character only to be disavowed by Celia. But the logic of the scene supports Edith's accidental insight. Celia has responded to a gaze at once deadly and desiring and it is the balancing act she will have to carry out with her own attraction to death that will drive the film. And after its dramatic introduction, Mark's point of view is fairly rare, and doesn't appear even at moments where one would expect it – such as his anguished look at the sprig of lilacs pinned to Celia's shoulder when she meets him at the station. This view triggers his emotional withdrawal, but his point of view is not given. If Celia's point of view cannot claim knowledge of the world, Mark's can even less, since Mark is obscure to himself as well.

Celia's gaze within the film is often deficient. She figures as one of Lang's semi-blind characters, not only through point of view shots which veil what she sees in Stanley Cortez's hard-edged shadows, but in the way she is surrounded by images of dark, ambiguous reflections, such as the animated 'dream pool' of the prologue which shimmers with reflected sparkles (stars? phosphorous? glints of sunlight?), while its ripples blur the strange forms lurking in the depths, moving from solid rocks to strange grasping roots and tendrils, like the ill-formed hands of baby monsters. The dream pool which introduces Celia's voice-over and represents, roughly, her unconscious, is echoed by: the wishing well surrounded by candles over which she makes her wish for Mark's love and receives her first kiss from him; the mirror in which her reflection first smirks then is alarmed when she playfully locks out Mark on their wedding night in Mexico; and the huge mirror occupying half the wall in her bedroom in Mark's house. All of these reflect her impulsiveness, her ignorance of the nature of her own attraction to Mark, and, ultimately, her loneliness, her reflection being the only face looking back at her in both bedrooms.

The flashback which interrupts the scene of Celia's wedding, in effect interrupts her first point of view shot. The film's opening images from the animated shot to the extraordinary vertiginous floating low angle tracking and craning shot of the interior of the Mexican cathedral (*Marienbad avant la lettre*), although visualising the thoughts spoken on the soundtrack, are definitively *not* rooted in the visual viewpoint of any character (as Gerard Legrand stresses in his essay on the film;[52] however Stephen Jenkins (mis)describes the shot as if the shot were Celia's point of view – presumably after gaining the power of weightlessness).[53] Then Celia emerges from the shadows and walks forward, ready to supply an anchor for the voice and the story, when Lang cuts to a flashback (introduced by the metaphor of drowning and seeing your whole life 'pass before you like a fast movie') to her life in New York and then her meeting with Mark in Mexico. Some ten minutes later, Lang deposits us back in the cathedral as Celia in her wedding dress continues to walk towards the camera, lifts her head and looks off. Lang cuts to her view, first of the priest, altar and altar boys, and then, pans to the right to pick up Mark, who walks towards her. Lang cuts to a close-up of Celia looking off screen towards him. In the succeeding point of view shot, he is swallowed by one of Cortez's inky shadows, only his outstretched hand illuminated. The sudden obscurity pleonistically visualises Celia's voice-over, 'Suddenly I'm afraid. I'm marrying a stranger, a man I don't know at all.'

As I have stated, Celia's point of view shots are generally of enigmas, mysteries she tries to unravel, and many remain uninterpreted for some time, such as her brief glance at Miss Robey peering at her through the curtain when she arrives at the Lamphere estate (and which Caroline mistakenly says was probably Mark's son David – the first Celia has heard of Mark having a son or even having been married before). Others seem to embody contradictions – such as her view from the window of Mark bandaging an injured dog, expressing an apparent kindness he has been withholding from her. Or the basically contentless point of view of the road from the car as she imagines in voice-over her dead brother asking her if she loves Mark and telling her that, if she does, she should stay with him. None of these shots have the penetrating insight of a Langian visionary scene. Rather Celia's visions confront her with a series of contradictory or incomplete signifiers, a jumble of signs, which she tries to arrange in some logical order.

But whereas in Hitchcock's *Suspicion*, the menacing and mysterious quality of Lina's world, her suspicion of her husband's murderous intents, are actually mis-recognitions on her part, projections and distortions of her fears, the obscurity of Celia's world precedes her point of view. Her house *is* dark and obscure and filled with old neuroses, and her husband *is* plotting to kill her. Thus the world around Celia wreathes itself in mystery and hides its secrets from her as she tries her best to penetrate its darkness. Jenkins isolates one motif of this obscurity, the shot of Mark with his back to the camera, by which, he says, Celia is 'denied the object of her look'.[54] I pointed out that in the scene he refers to, this shot cannot be considered Celia's point of view (she hasn't even arrived on the scene yet, which she does in the next shot). But beyond this instance, the image of Mark with his back to the camera forms a motif of the film, and most frequently these shots are *not* from Celia's point of view. Occasionally they are: as when she watches Mark make martinis after the incident when she locks the door in Mexico. But during the discussion after the party at Mark's rooms, Celia, who is looking in the other direction, does not see Mark's back which is turned to the camera, not to her. In other words, Mark turns his back on us, the spectators, or on the primary look of the camera; his obscurity is a condition of his portrayal in Lang's world, not of Celia's deficient vision. Lang makes it clear: the world of his films resists vision, hides from it, disguises itself, and *Secret Beyond the Door* narrates this struggle of vision and consciousness against obscurity.

The allegorical emblem of this epistemological obscurity is, of course, the locked door to Mark's secret Seventh Room, the room that Bluebeard forbids his wife to open. Mary Ann Doane quite rightly calls attention to what she terms the 'hypersig-nification' of this door (which we can translate as its allegorical function), and per-ceptively points out the moment when a shot of the door intervenes in the scene where Celia watches Mark from her window as he cares for the injured dog. As Doane says, the shot (from a low height and angle which makes it appear imposing and unstable) 'seems to appear from nowhere' and 'ruptures the spatial continuity of the scene'.[55] This single shot from a space outside the space of the scene visualises a phrase that occurs in Celia's interior monologue as she watches Mark ('What goes on in this mind that he can change so suddenly? He keeps it locked, like this door.'). Such a discontinuity returns to a technique Lang used in his first sound films, *M* and *The Testament of Dr. Mabuse*, a single shot of a different space being referred to in conversation (such as the cut to Mabuse's secret meeting room in *Testament* or to the nightwatchman drinking beer in *M*).

Lang's brief deviation from the Hollywood continuity system is allowed because of the symbolic nature of the locked door, a mode, which the other psychoanalytical films from the 40s also used, as Doane points out. But the example she compares it to, Hitchcock's use of an image of a series of doors opening in *Spellbound* as Constance (Ingrid Bergman) and John (Gregory Peck) kiss for the first time, actually contrasts with Lang's use, and not simply because of opposition between opening and locked doors. Hitchcock's doors provide a (pat, but powerful) metaphor for Constance's erotic surrender; they exist nowhere but in her consciousness.[56] Celia also speaks of doors opening when she first kisses Mark (another debt to *Spellbound*), but we don't see them. The locked door Lang does show us, although it lies outside the space of the immediate scene, *exists*, nonetheless within the space of the film. It is not simply an emblem of Celia's subjectivity, but of the enigmatic nature of her husband and of the world of the film.

Unlocking Bluebeard's Seventh Room

> … the key to my Self was tendered me, and for the first time I
> opened with astonishment and secret trembling the long-
> barred door – the inside looked like Bluebeard's chamber, and
> it would have strangled me had I been less fearless.
> *The Night Watches of Bonaventura*[57]

As unsatisfying as the plot structure of this film might be (with enigmas raised that are never fully developed or resolved, like David's conflict with his father, and allegorical motifs that are never clarified – like the succession of flowers that Celia invokes, daffodils, lilacs, carnations – with only lilacs ever having significance in the plot), its climactic scene in which Celia opens the locked door develops the theme of the obscurity of vision and knowledge as beautifully as *You Only Live Once* does, through an intricate interweave of sound, image and narrative structure. Lang wreathes in literal shadow dialectal images of vision and knowledge as Celia attempts to uncover Mark's secret by penetrating, like Bluebeard's wife, into the one room he keeps locked. Mark, when he first speaks to Celia and claims that she isn't what she seems to be, describes her as a 'Twentieth Century Sleeping Beauty' and clearly assigns himself the task of waking her up. But this scenario of female passivity awaiting the male kiss plays no role in the film as it develops. Instead, without naming it, Lang adapts a very different fairy tale, that of Bluebeard, in which female agency uncovers male guilt.[58] Lang dialectically develops the fairy tale, and Mark finally transforms from murderous Bluebeard into a male Sleeping Beauty, awaiting his wife's insight to wake him from his nightmare.

The sequence begins in Celia's room as she sits grasping the copy of Mark's key she has obtained. The clock perched on the mirrored mantelpiece chimes, marking the half hour. Lang cuts to the clock and the mirrored wall behind it, which doubles the room, but does not reflect Celia. Her interior monologue speaks of time seeming to stand still. Taking the key in one hand and a flashlight in the other, Celia embarks on her investigation, like a girl detective. Her voyage down the stairways and corridors into the wings of this labyrinthine and spatially discontinuous house (which seems to contain an endless series of connected rooms) moves through inky darkness. Her flashlight casts only a small circular nimbus of light, until it spotlights the number '7' on the locked door to the secret room. In close-up brightly shining light moves and glints off the lock and doorknob as Celia unlocks and opens the door. Lang provides a series of tropes of visual revelation that directly recall the revelation of the secret meeting room of the 'man behind the curtain' in *The Testament of Dr. Mabuse*. The door first opens onto darkness. Then the flashlight beam moves up and reveals – another visual barrier – a curtain. A reverse angle shows Celia entering, nearly invisible in the darkness, but her light brightly indicating her position. The reverse angle is shown again, as the beam moves across the curtain to reveal a light switch on the adjacent wall. Celia moves towards it, flips it on and light softly filters through the curtain, backlighting it. She parts the curtain and Lang again cuts to the reverse angle as she enters into the room on the other side and we see her astonished expression.

What she sees compounds and fractures the film's metaphors of vision as the scene nearly sinks under its contradictory roles. Frankly I can barely follow the significance this scene is supposed to have for the plot, but its development of the allegory of vision and knowledge shows more coherence. Celia's point of view reveals that the room is, in fact, a copy of her own bedroom. The effect of this doubling is dizzying for Celia and for us, as well. At the beginning of the sequence Celia sat in her bedroom ready to penetrate into the mysterious room her husband keeps locked. She made her way through darkened hallways, a locked door, drawn curtain, only to find – not a blood-soaked room strewn with the bodies of Bluebeard's previous wives – but, that she is back where she started, in her own bedroom! How are we to read this? As a psychoanalytical symbol of Celia's narcissism? I don't think so, she has not truly gone in circles, she has in fact penetrated into her husband's secret creation. What then does this mirror-play mean?

Celia continues to probe the room for clues to its secret. Her interior monologue does not at first identify it as *her* room, but as 'Elena's room', Mark's first wife, and therefore, since Mark collects rooms in which murders have taken place, as a confirmation of David's claim that his father murdered his first wife. But a panning point of view shot considers the room again, and Celia realises a difference between this and all the other rooms in Mark's collection. Mark stressed, as he displayed his collection to the party guests, that he did not recreate the rooms, but reassembled them; like a true connoisseur, his collection consists only of originals, not copies. Celia's interior monologue puzzles over the meaning of this discrepancy as she further explores the room. Behind the curtain she finds a bricked-up window (another echo of *The Testament of Dr. Mabuse*); as she opens the drawers in a dresser and table she finds them empty, whereas the other rooms were stuffed with the original props. She wonders if the room might not be finished, but recalls that Mark said it was. In interior monologue Celia then decides (following a line of reasoning impenetrable to me) that the fact that the room *is* a copy indicates that Mark only blames himself for Elena's death and did not actually murder her. Drawing a breath of relief, her interior voice declares her husband guiltless: 'You couldn't kill!'

But the sound of the traditional Langian emblem of the Destiny-machine, the chiming of a clock from off screen, freezes this exorcism of Mark's guilt, drawing Celia's attention. Just as in the beginning of the sequence, back in Celia's *real* bedroom, Lang cuts to the clock and the mirrored wall behind it, which doubles the room, but does not reflect Celia. The uncanny sense of *déjà vu* and running around in circles, aroused when we first recognised the room as a double of Celia's, returns, compounded. Celia's smile of relief dies on her face and gives way to alarm. She

notices something else on the mantlepiece that gives her the horrors. We hear the
last words that will be spoken in her interior monologue: 'The candle!' Then, for the
first time, Celia speaks her doubts out loud, as she says, 'It's my room! It's waiting
for me!' Lang cuts again to the mirror mantelpiece with its clock and two candles, as
for the first time in this sequence she appears in the mirror, darting past it as she
flees the room.

   Now it is certainly part of the weakness of this script that I can't figure why Celia
is initially convinced Mark did not kill Elena, and am not absolutely sure why she
then realises he means to kill her (the apparent motivation for her flight). But the
logic of the imagery and, to some extent, the narration, has allegorical power. The
room mirrors her room, but as she explores it, the details (or lack of details) make
it seem a simulacrum, a mere stage set, a harmless reproduction. But then Lang
focuses (rather indirectly for Hollywood films, which are generally so redundant)
on a detail that indicates something else: the candles. Spoiling the mirror-like symmetry of the room, one candle is shorter than the other. This horrifies Celia, not
because she shares Lang's mania for detail and love of symmetry, but because it is
a detail recently added to her own (real) room. She cut down one of the candles in
order to use the wax to make the impression of Mark's key to the Seventh Room.
Mark had noticed it a few days before, and remarked on how it spoiled the symmetry (he *does* shares Lang's mania). This detail signifies two things immediately,
from which Celia deduces more: Mark has not recreated a room out of his past
('Elena's room!') but a room from the immediate present ('My room!'), and that it
probably is not yet finished as he claimed, since he is still updating it. 'It's waiting
for me!' Celia exclaims out loud, meaning, presumably, that this room is not a
place where a murder *has* taken place, but a room where one *will* take place. Allegorically this room-doubling does not so much represent Mark's repetition compulsion as his need to create a setting in which he will act out the scene he refuses
to remember, forcing the present (and future) of his marriage back into the dead
past of his childhood.

   But most importantly, the scene in this room is the culmination of both Celia's
point of view and her interior monologue. Celia's voyage of discovery has not truly
been circular. She moves very literally (or rather very imagistically) through obscurity to an absolute clarity of both vision and understanding, the bright, doubled
specularity of the mirror. This is why her interior monologue, which had been the
voice of her repressed doubts, ceases now. She has found her voice and speaks out
loud her horrifying discovery. But it is a discovery she is not sure she can face, and
so she flees back into obscurity, running from the highly lit Seventh Room back into
the inky-dark corridor. Trembling in the darkness, she sees light coming from the
door to Room Number Three, where Don Ignacio strangled Constancia, Maria and
Isabella. With the most experimental moment in Rosza's score, Lang underscores
both Celia's uncanny terror in the dark and her desire to reverse her discovery, seeking out the obscurity of her earlier, limited vision in order to disavow what she has
learned, diving back into the darkness. Rosza explains that: 'when Michael Redgrave
opens the door behind which lie his secrets, Lang wanted an unusual sound and,
since I refused to use the theremin again, we experimented with having the orchestra play their music backwards, recording it back to front on tape, and then playing
it back as usual; the end result sounds the right way around, but has an unearthly
quality'.[59] Rosza's description would seem to indicate this was done when Mark first
shows his room, but it is clear that this eerie aural technique of reverse music happens here, as Celia slips back into the shadows, flattens herself against the wall to

avoid the light and the view of her husband, rushes through the corridors, door-ways and back up the stairs she had just descended.

As she climbs the stairs, Miss Robey enters the corridor and responds to Celia's plea for help, turning on the light, getting her jacket and the keys to the car (Robey's motives here are obscure to me: true friendship, or a desire to eliminate a rival? This again is less a developed ambiguity than a lack of both clarity and the information needed to make this bizarre figure an actual character). As she rushes downstairs, Celia nearly trips over the scarf from Room Three, presumably dropped by Mark. As she examines it, she again says to herself out loud the sort of conclusion she pre-viously restricted to her interior monologue: 'Constancia, Maria, Isabella!' This additional revelation is followed by another dash into the darkness as Celia rushes out the front door into an early dawn filled with Lang's emblem for partial vision, fog. In some of Cortez's most delicate yet powerful images, Celia rushes through a dream-like landscape of dark silhouetted trees and billowing mist. Disoriented and terrified in a space without markers, running this way and that, Celia finally stops in the foreground, turns and sees, as if materialising from the fog, a dark silhouette of a man. Rosza's pounding score ceases abruptly. The silence is followed by a slow fade to black. Over this total eclipse of the image we hear Celia scream, Lang once again drawing a voice out of the darkness of the screen. Then Rosza's score crashes in again, stressing the prolonged absence of image.

This fade to black literally leaves us in the dark, withholding a scene from the audience, one of Lang's most radical ellipses. Lang allows us to fill in the gap and encourages us to make a mistake. Our next image is of Mark emerging from his bathroom. Voice-over in the form of an interior monologue returns to the film, but now, for the first time it is Mark's consciousness we hear. As he walks into his bedroom, his voice-over says, 'It will be a curious trial. The People of the State of New York versus Mark Lamphere, charged with the murder of his wife, Celia.' In closeup, we see him pick up Don Ignacio's scarf as he intones, 'Exhibit A'. There follows a beautifully shot and boldly conceived sequence of Mark's imagined trial in which he continues to speak, but now in lip-synch. (This sequence was apparently cut by censors in Ohio,[60] and, in fact, is missing from many prints of the film, including the currently available video version.) The trial is clearly Mark's fantasy, shot in abstract sets with looming shadows, obscuring everyone's face (judge and jury), except Mark's, who appears simultaneously as defendant and prosecutor, accusing and excusing himself, claiming he had to assert himself against the women who controlled his life, and finally declaring, 'We are all children of Cain!' The judge's pounding gavel brings us out of this hallucination with a Langian sound rhyme as a servant knocks on Mark's door to tell him breakfast is served.

Everything we see and hear is calculated to make us believe Mark has murdered Celia; he even seems to confess to the crime. He then goes quietly downstairs for breakfast, says Celia is gone, fires Miss Robey (for disloyalty he says, and she assumes it is because Celia has told him about the removal of her disfiguring scar, which she had promised to keep secret), then stalks off, saying he wants to be alone. Upstairs he enters Celia's sitting room, picks up one of her gloves, then looks around startled. A cut reveals Celia, backlit and dark, standing in the narrow corridor that leads to her bedroom. Mark says he thought she had left (!), and she says she had, that she ran into Bob who had come to fetch David for a trip to New York and had got lost in the fog. She drove with him to the next town, but now she has come back because she loves Mark.

What the hell is going on here, that is not simply due to clumsy storytelling, or cuts Universal may have made in Lang's original version? Both of these factors may play a role in this obscurity, but a certain thematic and formal logic to this sequence does surface and a logical story can be pieced together. Things sort themselves out a bit when we realise that we have made false assumptions (cued, as David Bordwell says, by 'unreliable narration', but not by outright falsities).[61] The male silhouette that frightened Celia in the fog, was the anodyne Bob, not Mark, and Celia's scream came from being harmlessly startled, not from being murdered. Mark's interior monologue, which clearly shows him as mentally deranged at this point, does not confess to a murder he *has* committed but to one he is *still* planning (the same discovery Celia made in Room Seven, that a murder is imminent, rather than in the past). Once again, Lang redoubles his theme of mistaken perception not, as Hitchcock might, by having us share the characters' points of view (so that in the final scene in the car in *Suspicion* we, like Lina, interpret Johnny's out stretched hand as a threat rather than an offer of help), but by making us, as spectators, jump to the wrong conclusion, instead of questioning the ambiguous signs we are given. Lang may not handle this as elegantly here as he does in *You Only Live Once* or *Woman in the Window* (the revelation of Celia still alive seems too off-hand), but the narrative technique is the same as in the earlier films. It is also striking that during the breakfast scene Miss Robey makes a similar mistaken conclusion, that Celia betrayed her trust, whereas Mark's explanation to Caroline seems to indicate it was the aid Miss Robey gave to Celia's getaway that prompted the firing; he still knows nothing about the disappearing scar. Robey's mistaken conclusion will have dire consequences.

Now that we have the plot and the narrational structure sorted out, it is worth confronting the interpretation offered by Jenkins and endorsed by Doane of this ellipsis and Mark's following interior monologue. Jenkins argues that the film presents 'the gradual denial of Celia's discourse, and the assertion of Mark's discourse of which she becomes a function'.[62] In the scene in the fog he claims Celia 'is now "removed" from the text' (presumably the quotes around 'removed' are meant to indicate, 'not really', since she pops back in after a little more than five minutes). What *is* undeniably removed is Celia's interior monologue which does not recur in the last twenty minutes of the film. The replacement of Celia's interior monologue by David's indicates for Jenkins that '[Celia's] discourse is now definitively replaced by Mark's'.[63] Doane agrees with Jenkins about the role of the interior monologues, and adds even more fervently about the ellipsis: 'What the void on the image track gives witness to is the death of female subjectivity.'[64]

I think that it can be argued, as Doane does, that the paranoid women's film as a genre expresses patriarchal fear of woman and a pleasure in seeing them punished for their curiosity, and *Secret Beyond the Door* does not completely escape these assumptions. But on the level of textual analysis, I can't follow Jenkins and Doane's argument, unless one makes mechanical equations (e.g. eliminating Celia's voice-over = eliminating woman's subjectivity). In fact, earlier in the film, during Celia's first meeting with Mark, Lang actually drops out Mark's voice track – although his lips keep moving as he continues speaking – and replaces it with Celia's interior monologue. This indicates, as she says, that she is too excited to really listen to him, but a mechanical interpretation might isolate it as a feminist gesture. Contextualisation must precede interpretation if works are to uncover ideological assumptions and not simply be forced to illustrate them. There are disturbing aspects in the last section of *Secret Beyond the Door*, but I think they lie in Celia's willingness to be murdered by her husband, not in a loss of her subjectivity or discourse,[65] since her questions and explanations finally overcome her masochistic resignation and puncture Mark's patently psychotic discourse. In *Possessed*, in contrast, there is no question that Louise's discourse (voice-over and flashback, complete with visualised fantasy) is a function of male discourse, prompted by the doctor's injection, commented on and interpreted by the male doctors in a discourse that is presented as medical and authoritative. But to claim that Mark's voice-over, clearly presented as hallucinatory and psychotic, plays the same role strains credulity.

In a clear reversal of *Possessed*, Mark's psychotic discourse is submitted to probing, interpretation and revelation by Celia. Significantly, in contrast to most 'gothic romances', there is no alternative male figure of the sort that usually confirms the woman's suspicions and frequently rescues her, replacing the disturbed husband as lover. As Diane Waldman indicates: 'This character is a feature of all the Gothics which end with a confirmation of the woman's experience [she has apparently forgotten *Secret Beyond the Door*, but her error stresses the film's exceptional nature]; he is young, handsome, usually a detective ... or a doctor functioning as one.'[66] Celia's former fiancé Bob functions as a residual version of this role, but performs no major action, other than being mistaken for Mark in the fog. That Celia herself confirms her own suspicions through her final discussion with Mark in Room Seven, shows the increased role of female discourse in this film.

The final scene of the film in Room Seven, in which Celia confronts the now totally wacko and pop-eyed Mark, who stalks armed to kill her with Don Ignacio's scarf, hardly gives a convincing representation of psychoanalysis, but its narrative intentions are clear. Celia unlocks the door to Mark's memory (Doane's claim of a displacement here is untenable – Celia always considered the locked door as an emblem of Mark's inaccessible psyche);[67] Celia's discourse cures him. Mark's interior monologue conveys his insanity, not his authority (or, as in the scene at breakfast, reveals his claim to authority as unbalanced), just as Celia's interior monologue had been the voice of her repressed doubts and uncertainties. Thus Celia's interior monologue ends, not because her subjectivity is being expunged, but because she can now voice out loud what she previously had to keep tacit, that her husband intends to murder her. Far from losing her voice, Celia has learned to speak and located her problem no longer in her fear, or feelings of self-reproach for being an inadequate wife, but squarely in her husband. She uses her new-found voice to practise (an all too magically effective) version of the talking cure on her nutcase husband.

Secret Beyond the Door does not settle into an exemplar of patriarchal order and female victimisation. But the problem is – it doesn't truly settle into any coherent pattern, but swirls through several registers, generating allegorical figures more quickly than it takes responsibility for them (one of several aspects it shares with *Metropolis*). Its narrative of the mastery of a female voice and point of view develops more clearly, only to become muddled in the film's final moments. As Celia realises the significance of the locked door, she rises from the chair in which she previously passively awaited her murder, stands and points with her outstretched figure – the traditional, melodramatic gesture of female accusation of a male villain (see Lillian Gish in *Way Down East* – or Kriemhild confronting Hagen at the end of *Siegfried*). The almost invocatory power of this gesture, as much as her words, stops Mark in his tracks and causes his taut scarf to go limp. He then brings forth his traumatic memory of his mother locking him in his room. But recalling this only returns him to his murderous rage, until Celia corrects his mis-impression by informing him that Caroline locked him in the room, not his mother. (Hollywood's sidestepping of Freud's claim of a sexual etiology for neuroses once again trivialises the scene as a serious treatment of the unconscious and makes psychoanalysis, here as in *Spellbound*, simply a matter of clearing up false impressions. Presumably if it *had* been Mark's mother who locked the door, Mark would have gone ahead and strangled Celia!) Mark's rage was based on the same sort of misidentification Lang prompts in the audience through the ellipsis. After Celia sets him straight, Lang shows a close-up of Mark's scarf now going definitively limp. Like so many of Lang's heroes, Mark has suffered from a partial vision of reality.

Celia's melodramatic stance throws into relief the fact that her cure of Mark is theatrically conceived, a work of *mise-en-scène* as much as a talking cure. She waits for Mark in Room Seven, the theatrical scene he has already fitted so carefully with decor and props for her murder. She places lilacs in the vase to be sure of hitting as many cues as possible. In many ways this scene returns (as does the climax of *Spellbound*) to a pre-Freudian theory and treatment of traumatic mental illness, by re-enacting the original scene (this actually forms the plot of some of the earliest narrative films, such as D. W Griffith's 1909 film *The Restoration* or Leonce Perret's *Les Mystères des Roches de Kador* from 1912). Lang, in later interviews, saw his portrayal of a sudden cure as a great weakness of this film.[68] The purpose and meaning of the ending seem to blur as it revolves around re-enactment rather than realisation. At this point Celia's discourse *is* undercut, since aspects of the re-enactment are beyond her directorial control. Miss Robey actually supplies the key repetition – the locking of the door. Celia's insight into Mark is rendered useless by Robey and she must be carried out of the burning house by a masculine rescuer.

The melodramatic rescue (once again, as in *Metropolis* coming almost out of nowhere in order to reposition a flawed protagonist as an action hero)[69] re-masculinises Mark, and has him now *break* through the locked door (the lights in Room Seven have gone off, and Mark's forcing of the door now leads the couple into the light, out of the dark room). Meanwhile, Miss Robey seems to be arranging her own therapy, or acting out a repetition compulsion, as she sets fire to the Lamphere estate, nearly trapping Mark and Celia inside. Rescuing David from a similar fire was the heroic act which guaranteed her previous job security and disfigured her with the now-effaced scar. Presumably she is trying to kill Celia (she doesn't know Mark had slipped in to strangle his wife) in revenge for the firing she mistakenly blames on her. Or is she thinking of staging another rescue and getting her job back? Or has she simply seen *Rebecca* too many times and can't resist imitating Mrs. Danvers? Perhaps most curious, but ultimately just as confusing, Robey stands watching the flaming mayhem she has caused in front of wind-blown birch trees, recalling Dr. Baum hiding among the trees watching the flaming factories in the finale of *The Testament of Dr. Mabuse*. Lang did not have to call on *Rebecca* for a scene of conflagration, since his films are full of them. The climax of *Secret Beyond the Door* resembles a whirlwind in which Langian motifs spin and play without settling into a final pattern.

Architecture of Doom

> Our taverns and our metropolitan streets, our offices and
> furnished rooms, our railroad stations and our factories
> appeared to have us locked up hopelessly. Then came the film
> and burst this prison-world asunder by the dynamite of the
> tenth of a second, so that now in the midst of its far-flung
> ruins and debris, we calmly and adventurously go traveling.
>   Walter Benjamin, 'The Work of Art in the Age of Mechanical
> Reproduction'[70]

Let me return to Lang's acknowledgment of the debt *Secret Beyond the Door* owed
to *Rebecca*. He didn't discuss any of the similarities of plot or genre mentioned in
the previous sections. Rather, as he explained the idea of *Secret Beyond the Door* to
Peter Bogdanovich he invoked something else:

> You remember that wonderful scene in *Rebecca* where Judith Anderson [Mrs.
> Danvers] talks about Rebecca and shows Joan Fontaine the clothes and fur coats and
> everything? When I saw this picture (I am a very good audience), Rebecca was *there*,
> I *saw* her. It was a combination of brilliant direction, brilliant writing and wonderful
> acting. And – talk about stealing – I had the feeling that maybe I could do something
> similar in this picture when Redgrave talks about the different rooms.[71]

Although this confession may display both Freudian displacement and Brechtian
covering of one's tracks, it nonetheless highlights the centre of *Secret Beyond the
Door* for Lang and certainly one of its more successful ideas:[72] Mark Lamphere's
theory of 'felicitous rooms'.

Apparently little remains in the film from its source, the *Redbook* serial by Rufus
King except this conception of a collection of rooms.[73] Lang changed the collector
from a publisher to an architect (although Mark also publishes an architectural
journal, aptly named, as we will see, *Apt*). Mark Lamphere's profession prompts
many critics to seek autobiographical references here, given that Lang always
described the profession of his father, Anton Lang, as architect. Patrick McGilligan
claims Lang's father was more of a contractor and builder than an architect, but the
connection to architecture clearly existed.[74] Lang's accounts of his youth always
included the decision not to follow in his father's footsteps, but to pursue the fine
arts (one might evoke here the scene in *Secret Beyond the Door* where Celia asks
Mark's son David if he intends to be an architect, too, and he responds, forcefully,
'no!'). But critics have frequently pointed out that Lang's chosen field of cinema,
and especially Lang's own work, has a strong affinity to architecture, both in its
actual design and building of sets, and more generally in its construction and fragmentation of space.

Mark's theory aligns constructed spaces and the events that occur in them in a way
that on the one hand recalls cinema (or at least the way a director approaches sets),
and on the other hand proposes a peculiar form of determinism. 'My main thesis', he
explains to his bride on their honeymoon, 'is that the way a place is built determines
what happens in it.' He collects rooms that exemplify his theory, carefully reassem-
bling them somewhere in the bowels of the Lamphere estate (I would love to see the

floor plan of this country home!), and calls them 'felicitous rooms'. Lang elegantly introduces two of the film's main themes with this phrase: first and most obviously Mark's theory, but second and delayed in its effect, the ease of misinterpretation. Celia assumes this word means, as would most people through its cognates – felicitations, felicity – happy. After finding he has a collection of rooms in which murders have taken place – and all murders of women by men – she confronts him asking if he hadn't said he collected 'happy' rooms. He responds, 'Felicitous doesn't mean "happy", darling. Look it up in the dictionary. It means happy in effect, fitting, *apt*.'

Thus it is not the form or function that most draws the attention of architect, critic and collector Mark Lamphere, but a slightly crackpot theory (when Celia first hears it she says indulgently 'Mark, my sweet lamb, you're tetched in the head!') of occult influences, 'unholy emanations', from a certain structure which determines 'the actions of the people living in it'.[75] The connection to the scene from *Rebecca* is not as direct as Lang makes it (which is perhaps why it can be confessed), but it goes to the core of Lang's style: an ability to invoke something invisible, something absent, through the arrangement of objects and surroundings. For Lang, the empty rooms Mark collects exemplify the events which took place in them; we could say, reversing Mark's metaphor of emanation, that they are imprinted by the events, long after the people who enacted them have disappeared. We find again Lang's x-ray or neutron bomb vision, seeing through events to the essential structures. And the reversal of emanation/imprint returns us to Lang's central paradox of authorship. Are these rooms the cause of these events? Or simply their containers? In claiming that the murderers were driven to their crimes by the rooms they dwelled in, Mark provides a complex emblem for the Destiny-machine.

Lang presents the rooms to us with Mark as literal guide, as he takes us and his house-guests on a tour, narrating the history and pointing out the details of each

room (he apparently has seven of them, but we only see three on this tour, and a fourth, the seventh and last, when Celia takes us there). Jenkins describes Mark's tour narration as his 'voice-over' which is literally incorrect, since Mark speaks these lines within the diegesis. His speeches are not even examples of interior monologue, but rather firmly planted within the world of the film, occasionally, but by no means always, 'voice-off' – words spoken without Mark appearing on screen, but always located somewhere just beyond the frame. However, Jenkins' misdescription carries insight. Mark's tour-guide discourse functions, in fact, much more like Silverman's description of traditional masculine voice-over narration. Mark's voice exists within the world of *Secret Beyond the Door*, but he stands outside and narrates the story of each of his rooms. As Silverman says, voice-over, through its independence from the visual world, tends to assert itself as an enunciator.[76] This corresponds to Mark's role in not only telling the story of each room, but interpreting it as well, determining and articulating its meaning. In contrast, Mark's later psychotic interior monologue displays his lack of control over events and himself. In the scene at the train station, for instance, his interior monologue drones, 'I must get away from her, as far as possible', while his action contradicts the intention and he returns home rather than getting on the train – the same sort of split between thought and action that Celia's earlier interior monologues showed.

But in this collection of rooms Mark attempts to maintain control over both their stories (through his theories) and his growing psychosis (by creating a room for his own drama, allowing him both to plan and commit the murder he dreams of and therefore seem in control of this mad compulsive action). Silverman's insight holds here: both Celia's and Mark's interior monologues situate them inside the events, as their victims. Through his narration of his rooms Mark tries to assert a position outside his rooms, a position of knowledge, control and mastery, but it is important that he can never really achieve the position of enunciation to which he aspires, he still stands within the diegesis – hence the limitation of Jenkins' description. Jenkins also does not mention that Mark's narration is challenged, and his theory turned on its head by a woman's voice. 'The intellectual sub-deb' as she is referred to in the credits, who substitutes Mark's explanation of occult emanations from the room with a psychoanalytical reading. She first speaks up (appropriately given Freud's architectural metaphors for the unconscious) in the second room, the cellar where a man murdered his mother by tying her to a chair as flood waters filled the room. She explains that it is unusual for a son to murder his mother, but that 'in many cases the murder of a girl friend or a wife has its psychological roots in an unconscious hatred for the mother'. Mark, however, counters her reading, with a simpler motive, the son's greed for the old woman's life insurance payment.

In the third room, Don Ignacio's, the same young woman indicates that Ignacio's compulsion to murder his three wives could have been treated by psychoanalysis. Mark asks if that means the room played no role, and the woman responds negatively. The room is important, she maintains, but because of an unconscious association it carries from something that happened in it, a repressed childhood trauma and/or resolution to kill that took place there in a forgotten past. 'But he still killed!' Mark insists. The woman agrees, 'But he didn't know why, he just *had* to. But if he had been able to tell someone, like a psychoanalyst, what it was that happened here, no murder would have been necessary.' It is easy to dismiss this young woman,[77] but for two rather suspect reasons. One is the claim that an art work should not provide its own interpretation so baldly. However, allegories frequently give their argument in a clearly stated manner; it is the translation of this theme into imagery or language that constitutes the pleasure of the allegory. Further, as I hope I have shown, accepting the validity of this young woman's statement does not exempt the viewer from a complex process of reading the images of this film, in order not only to test it, but to work through its significance for the characters.

I believe the other reason many viewers and critics might doubt her authority is, quite simply, sexism. This doesn't necessarily tarnish the reader/viewer who comes to this conclusion since she may claim (with some validity) the sexism to be embedded in the film itself and its complicity with Hollywood attitudes which traditionally scorn a know-it-all woman. The credit name given to the character 'Intellectual sub-deb' and the whispered comment by another woman to Mark, 'She's a brain-psych major', would seem to support that the film is mocking this woman, judging that she is simply applying academic concepts straight out of her textbooks, rather than the sort of personal wisdom born of experience that Hollywood films tend to endorse ('There's no place like home'; 'No man is a failure as long as he has friends').

Although these signs do indicate a discomfort with this character, I think they are outweighed by other factors. It is her romantic friend, for instance, who wears the silly glasses (Hollywood code for a woman striking an intellectual pose not truly her own), while the sub-deb herself is attractive and serious, not at all caricatured.[78] Her discussion of psychoanalysis avoids jargon (think, in contrast, of Noele Noele's brief role in An American in Paris as a student abroad tossing off big words as she tries to evaluate Gene Kelly's painting). Most importantly, the film endorses her reading in the final scene: Mark does have an unconscious hatred of his mother which makes him feel compelled to kill his wife (wives?); he had even made a repressed vow some day to kill her. Talking about it with Celia does render the murder, 'unnecessary' (in fact when the woman says 'if he had been able to tell someone, like a psychoanalyst, what happened here', Lang cuts directly to a close-up of Celia, tipping us to the end of the movie, right then, if we read it carefully or retroactively).

Celia's apparently sudden application of the young woman's suggestion at the end of the film gains a degree of believability when we recognise Celia's inability to follow the advice at this moment. Rather than focusing on the woman's (or Lang's) suggestion of the role she might take, Celia stares at Don Ignacio's scarf. She gazes at it and at Mark as he delivers his narration with the same fascinated, trance-like, glassy stare that came over her in the marketplace in Mexico (in contrast to the sub-deb's, intent, focused observation of Mark and his story). She has not yet acknowledged her husband's illness (and presumably her own perverse fascination with it) which at this point she disavows in favour of lecturing herself about being a good wife. As Mark leads the group into the next room, she stays behind for a tête à tête with her former fiancé, Bob. Her refusal to voice her doubts, her claim to Bob, 'I know Mark, he wouldn't do anything unfair' is greeted by raucous off screen laughter, Lang's overt narrational mockery of the statement. Thus the climactic trip to Room Seven where Celia has her moment of visual insight and finds her voice, enables her to play the role that, at this earlier point, she can't even understand. As a basic principle of the talking cure, one cannot simply listen to an analysis of one's problem and be healed, but must work it through in one's own discourse. Both Mark and Celia have had to confront aspects of themselves for the final talk to have its effect.

What maintains Mark in his madness is partly his insistence on male authority, that 'thinking is the prerogative of men' as he tells Celia during their honeymoon.

Thus he remains stuck in his determinist reading of the room, deaf to the young woman's alternative interpretation, and condemned to be – a murderer. What does he gain from this position which is clearly psychotic? He does indeed gain something: the paranoid's conviction that he alone has cracked the system, that he has the only theory which explains events. Mark's delight in this power unfurls itself in his tour of his rooms. He is, we know, a failed architect. These rooms however are his creations, even though he has slavishly reassembled the originals. His art consists in explaining them, narrating them. Here we find the intricate variation on the *pas de deux* between would-be enunciator and the Destiny-machine, possibly the most successful and personal aspect of this film.

As Mark narrates the rooms we recognise in them the archetypal Langian images of death (hardly a semantic leap since they are all scenes of murders): empty rooms. Although the group crowds in, there is a barrier between them as spectators, witnesses, and each room as a scenographic space. No-one moves into that space. Yet 'empty' is, of course, an anthropocentric word. These rooms are filled with things. They present large-scale Langian arrangements of objects, but rather than showing a geometrical order, these objects are arranged to tell stories: they delineate the murders that took place here. While no-one moves into these rooms, they are not seen statically, because Lang's camera moves within them, tracing out relations between objects and thereby telling their story. Mark's claim to enunciation appears most strongly as his narrating voice synchs with the camera movement. In the first room, the camera moves from the wine glass perched on a table as Mark explains that the Count de Guise did not poison his wife Céleste, 'but, if you notice the handkerchief on the couch [the camera moves as if following Mark's pointing finger], there's a little blood. There was a rapier thrust [the camera tilts down to frame the rapier on the floor]'. I suspect again that Lang's confession to Bogdanovich obscures the real source of inspiration in *Rebecca*. The invisible presence invoked here is not a person (Mark's Room Seven specifically does *not* invoke his dead wife Elena, as Celia comments), but a past incident, a murder. Lang here follows Hitchcock's technique in the scene in which, as Max narrates the way Rebecca actually died in the boathouse, a roving camera cued to his voice traces out the patterns of that fateful night.

The same sort of camera movement occurs in the next two rooms. As Mark describes the flood waters rising, the camera obediently tilts up from the chair to which the mother was tied to the high-water mark on the wall. This dissolves directly to the next room, as the camera moves from a dinner table to an overturned chair and Don Ignacio's scarf. The camera tracks back for a broader view as Mark describes the sophistication of the room's furnishings. Just as Mabuse and Haghi seemed to control the actual enunciation of the film through the power of their gaze and control of technology, aligning their gaze with the lens of the camera and their will with the pattern of the film's editing, Mark dreams the same dream of enunciatory power, although Lang gives him different means: his apparent voice-over standing outside the scene but giving it meaning, and his apparent direction of the movement of the camera. Thus, of Lang's characters to this point, Mark perhaps most completely combines the role of artist with the role of enunciator, framing his perverse desires three-dimensionally in his rooms. There is no contradiction between his art and his murderous intent, as there was for Christopher Cross, because his *is* an art of death, just as he claimed Don Ignacio pursued the fine art of murder.

Mark combines the film-maker's and the architect's art in his Seventh Room. Like all of Lang's psychopaths (and some of his slightly less mad characters as well) his ultimate work of art is private, less a private movie in this case, than a private theatre in a private room. But, of course, the antinomies of Mark's role as an artist overwhelm him at the end. As the artist of the Destiny-machine, he becomes its victim rather than its master; as the artist of death, he must obey a scenario because, as the sub-deb put it, 'he doesn't know why, he just has to'. His position of supposed knowledge, control and exteriority to the drama has disappeared. He is, simply, just another victim. As architect of death, the logical acme of Mark's work, as Frieda Grafe says, citing Hegel, is the construction of his tomb.[79] But due to Celia's intervention, Mark does something else; he remembers, and then he re-experiences and reverses his childhood trauma. Room Seven at the climax again recalls Baum's room with the curtain with lovers trapped in a sealed room, menaced now by fire rather than water. Mark breaks out of his private theatre to find his world in flames.

As I have already said, this flaming corridor reprises Lang's traditional conflagration ending. But whereas in the German films this conflagration seemed to represent an apocalypse, whether religious (*Der müde Tod*) or social (*The Testament of Dr. Mabuse*), here it destroys Mark's past, both in the form of his ancestral home and his collection of rooms. As Grafe concludes, for Lang, the ultimate form of architecture is not truly the tomb, but the ruin. He builds in order to destroy. One might describe *Secret Beyond the Door* as the ruin of a great film, or the ruin of a great film-maker. Through its collapse, structures are revealed that are more astonishing than the more structurally sound edifices of lesser film-makers.

14

Coda: *House by the River*

Effacing the Traces and Writing the Abject

> I have to initiate you into our mysteries, my dear friend [...]
> To exclude the element of chance, one must eliminate the
> traces, for every deed leaves a trace which chance can attach
> itself to. But every attempt to wipe out the trace creates new
> ones. You may take that to be a law.
>
> Ernst Junger, *A Dangerous Encounter*[1]

The credits for *Secret Beyond the Door* stressed the ascendance of Lang's name. *Scarlet Street* opened with the 'Walter Wanger Presents' title card, then 'A Fritz Lang Production'. *Secret Beyond the Door* substituted a simple possessive for the second title card: 'Fritz Lang's' appeared on the screen followed by *Secret Beyond the Door*. Lang claimed ownership of the film. This high point of Lang's name on the screen in America was ironic, given that Lang had only prevented Universal completely re-cutting the film by by threatening to take his name off it. Putting his name back on the screen did not save the film from the studio interference, especially the re-recording

and to some extent rewriting of Celia's narration. Lang's name represented an invest-ment to Universal, carefully positioned by the publicity Diana had churned out, and worth preserving, they felt. Claiming the film with his name on the screen still didn't mean he controlled it completely – only so far as negotiations and threats had allowed.

In *House by the River,* Lang's name only receives the directorial credit it had found in most of his previous Hollywood films; there was no chance to claim this film as 'Fritz Lang's'. Lang's name appears (as was traditional for most directors) as the final name in the opening credits, superimposed like the rest of the credits over shots of the river. As Lang's name comes on the screen, shots of the river bank dis-solve to an image of dark water and George Antheil's score becomes overwhelmed by the sound of these nocturnal currents. Lang's name fades away and we are left briefly with the image and sound of the flowing river. Although Lang may have had nothing to do with the opening credits, it is hard not to see his name as sinking or drowning in these obscure waters. Given the themes of this film, it might be most appropriate to see his name as being flushed away.

Patrick McGilligan has called *House by the River*, 'Fritz Lang's real descent into the "B" world'.[2] Released through Republic Pictures which had been known for its low-budget programmer westerns and serials, the description is only partly apt, since *House by the River* represented a speciality prestige film for Republic, which, like Universal, emerged from World War II in considerable profit and with a desire to produce a few higher-budget A films. The year before, 1948, two famous direc-tors produced modestly budgeted (although many times the budget of the average Republic film), but strongly artistic films at Republic, Frank Borzage's masterpiece *Moonrise* and Orson Welles' experimental *Macbeth,* while the year before that Republic had released Ben Hecht's *Specter of the Rose,* the archetypal low-budget American art film.[3] But for Lang, coming on the heels of the collapse of Diana, the production deal worked out with Fidelity Pictures and Republic must have felt like a precipitous come-down. Lang later tended to ignore the film in interviews or mention it only in passing, and even when responding to praise of the film, charac-terised it simply as a job he had to take. In an interview in *Positif* in 1968 Lang attributed the circumstances of the film's production to the anti-Communist witch hunt:

> I didn't know why, but I had no contract. My agent was simply told there was no
> work for me. My lawyer was told that no-one had accused me of being a
> Communist, but that I might have been one. I made the film because I had not had
> work for a year and a half.[4]

As Janet Bergstrom has shown in her research on *The Blue Gardenia*, in later inter-views Lang tended to invoke the blacklist to explain his participation in lower-budget films, often without much basis.[5] Lang's explanation may reflect his tendency to blame his problems on outside circumstances, or even a certain para-noia, but right after the Producers' Association issued the Waldorf statement pledg-ing no member of the Communist party would be knowingly hired in Hollywood, paranoia seemed a rational approach to the world.

Ironically, Lang's seemingly abject position – the loss of his fiefdom and dreams of independence, a considerably shorter shooting schedule than he had allowed himself when he was producer, and a cast whose star power barely lit up the mar-quee – yielded one of his most unified, disciplined, and imagistically powerful films. *House by the River* does not have the explosive power of *Secret Beyond the Door*, nor the achievement of *Scarlet Street* or the social trilogy. We are dealing here with a modest work, almost a *Kammerspiel*, with definite stretches of rather pedestrian film-making (the too-long court inquest – particularly after Lang's compressed montage 'trials' in *Scarlet Street* and *Secret Beyond the Door* – and the rather tentative love scenes between John and Marjorie). But *House by the River* engages strongly with Lang's major themes, supplying a quite satisfying diminuendo to the films of framed desire.

Although *House by the River* uses a limited number of sets, its central sets making up the house of Stephen and Marjorie Byrne with its lawn dipping down to the river hardly qualifies as a B-film set. The interior of this house with it huge staircase has been uniquely designed and lit to invoke a turn-of-the-century upper middle-class home. Never, not even in Stanley Cortez's lighting of the (more magnificent) mansion in Welles' *The Magnificent Ambersons*, has the semi-obscurity of gas lighting been as well conveyed as here in Edward Cronjager's darkest of low-key lighting setups. One feels the cloistering darkness of a Victorian house, filled with the idle passion of the well-to-do on a summer's evening eventually turning into the gloom of death. As in no other film, this house evokes Walter Benjamin's comment:

> The bourgeois interior of the 1860's to the 1890's – with gigantic sideboards distended with carvings, the sunless corners where potted palms sit, the balcony embattled behind its balustrade, and the long corridors with their singing gas flames – fittingly houses only the corpse.[6]

The film's scrupulous attention to period detail – the line engravings in the newspaper rather than photographs, the *carte de visite* size photos in the family album – show a care in the production of this film that indicates possible art house ambitions for its release.

Responding to the enthusiasm the *Positif* interviewers showed for this film, while dismissing it as a job ('a director needs money to live'), Lang confessed to liking the film's 'nocturnal atmosphere'.[7] To more intimate friends, it seems, he expressed more involvement. McGilligan quotes Lang's close friend from later years, filmmaker Pierre Rissient claiming Lang recalled *House by the River* with 'enormous emotion': 'He would describe shot by shot the first ten, twelve minutes of the film.'[8] I would claim that the beginning of the film, along with a few later sequences, can stand alongside the best of Lang's film-making in terms of the narrative precision of image, sound and the emotional associations evoked. The first images establish the river bank locale, Stephen Byrne writing in a gazebo in his yard overlooking the river, while his neighbour Mrs. Ambroise hoes her garden. Although the images are peaceful enough, Lang again benefits from a strong musical score, this time by another figure of twenties avant-garde culture, Georges Antheil, former self-proclaimed 'bad boy of music', friend of Ezra Pound, student of Stravinsky and composer of the provocative score for Leger's *Ballet Mécanique*,[9] now happily, or at least successfully, working in Hollywood. The odd rhythms of his score give these opening shots an undefinably sinister atmosphere.

A shot, cued by Mrs. Ambroise's off screen look, solidifies this atmosphere: a carcass of a bloated, dead cow floats down the river, an almost shocking bit of reality pasted between shots of carefully designed studio sets, with a repulsive quality one can almost smell. Over an image of Stephen writing we hear Mrs. Ambroise proclaim off screen the first line of the film: 'I hate this river!' Lang's American films create associations out of juxtapositions that can pass unnoticed, and this film masterfully constructs undertones and subtexts from rebus-like joinings of images which otherwise fulfil conventional narrative continuity. Thus the cut from this floating offal to Stephen's writing might pass unnoticed, were it not that throughout this opening Lang embeds numerous juxtapositions associating Stephen's writing with the filth of the river, even before he finally makes the comparison explicit in dialogue.[10] Mrs. Ambroise complains to him about the river and its tide carrying the same refuse back and forth; 'in with one tide, out with the other'. As Stephen and Mrs. Ambroise talk in the foreground, Lang frames Emily, the Byrnes' maid between them as she approaches from the background. The irony of her appearance at this point is proleptic. After Stephen murders her, it is her body which the river tides will wash back and forth, in a scene that deliberately recalls this one.

As Emily enters the foreground, Stephen says, 'It's the people that should be blamed for the filth, not the river.' Lang cuts to Emily holding out a package, a manuscript of Stephen's returned by a publisher. Once again, his writing is associated with filth through juxtaposition. Stephen's remarks to Mrs. Ambroise make the association explicit: 'My manuscripts are like the tide out there, they always come back.' He tosses away his cigarette as he says this, maintaining the thread of detritus, things cast off. The association of images and sounds make it clear that the manuscripts are not simply a representative of the eternal return, but of the return of filth, as the rejected prose comes home. This penumbra of associations continues when Mrs. Ambroise nudges her literary neighbour and advises him to make his writing more popular by spicing it up, 'make them racy'. As we hear the middle-aged Ambroise's words off screen Lang focuses on Emily in the gazebo glancing at Stephen's pages as she puts down the returned manuscript; visually, she embodies the attraction Ambroise advises him to add to his work: young, buxom, sexy. In a rather disturbing manner Lang links 'filth' and sexuality. But it is not just the sense of something dirty that operates in this opening, but what Julia Kristeva calls, the 'abject', that which is cast off, rejected, thrown away with disgust, offal. The abject represents that which the subject rejects, but which is too undefined, too disturbing to take on the definition of an object.[11]

Emily emerges from the gazebo to express her concern that the plumber has not arrived to fix the downstairs (that is, of course, the servant's) tub. Stephen gives her permission to use the upstairs bathroom. Frieda Grafe has pointed out that architecture in Lang expresses power relations, particularly the hierarchy of classes, vividly embodied in *Metropolis* with its class-determined layers.[12] Connections between layers which undermine these divisions or bring them into contact – stairways, elevators and corridors – take on a dynamic role. Like the breaks in routine in *The Woman in the Window* and *Scarlet Street*, this slight displacement of the bourgeois order of the household, Emily's upstairs bath, will have fatal consequences. Emily curtsies nicely and walks back to the house. Stephen's lingering gaze at her as she walks away heightens the earlier association of her with racy, spicy thoughts. She has clearly captured Stephen's imagination, enough that Mrs. Ambroise has to snap him out of his reverie by asking him how does *Mrs.* Byrne like the new maid?

Mrs. Ambroise heads back to her house, Emily up to the bathroom; Stephen is left alone, as Antheil's score re-enters. For the next five minutes of the film, not a single word of dialogue will be spoken; Lang will let images and sounds speak with both narrative clarity and an expanding range of overtones. Stephen saunters into the gazebo, opens up the package, reads the rejection letter, then crumples it violently and throws it away, bringing a degree of anger and violence into the theme of the cast-off, the abject. A curiously excessive moment follows as Lang cuts to a close-up of an insect walking across a page of the manuscript Stephen has been working on. This Buñuelian image (and this is certainly the film in which Lang comes closest to Buñuel) continues the theme of the abject (*Leviticus* XI, 41: 'And every creeping thing that creepeth upon the earth *shall be* an abomination'). Georges Sturm associates it with the scarab or dung beetle, but it doesn't look like one to me.[13] As it wanders across Stephen's novel, it recalls more strongly the insect that medieval painters would place (often in *trompe l'oeil*) on their canvas to indicate the inevitability of death and decay. Surprisingly, Stephen reacts to this insect gently, turning from his anger at rejection to care for this small living thing which he delicately shakes off the paper. While demonstrating that Stephen 'wouldn't hurt a fly'[14] the action also shows his mercurial quality, switching from anger to kindness almost without transition, an indication of Stephen's strange drifting quality, the unmoored nature of his emotions.

His emotions flow in another direction with the next shot. Stephen looks up from the page to see (in long shot) the light going on in the upper bathroom window. Lang cuts back to Stephen who smiles, turns and sits at his writing table (which faces the river, away from the house). Lang now makes explicit the basic technique of this film – what Stephen will later call 'reading between the lines' – the grasping of unspoken association between images (and sounds). Intercutting images of Emily's bath with Stephen staring off vacantly at his desk, Lang ties her bath directly to Stephen's fantasy. A close-up shows the lines Stephen has just written: 'Therefore sleep would not come to Roland Forbes, as it will not come to any man with a troubled mind.' He puts the page down and scores through the lines and then shakes his pen in such a way as to cause a blot on the manuscript. He himself rejects his own work, effaces his writing at this point, expressing the sort of dissatisfaction that he describes his fictional character as experiencing.

Stephen rocks back and forth in his chair, and Lang cuts to the long shot of the bathroom window, a view behind his back. As Stephen continues rocking, the intercut images reflect his imagination without becoming literal fantasy images; in their relatively anodyne quality, they displace the undoubtedly more explicit images that race through Stephen's mind.[15] A closer view of the bathroom window appears as Lang draws us into this scene. Provocatively, this exterior view dissolves into a high angle medium close-up of Emily's bath, as her hand reaches in and pulls the plug. A loud sucking noise is heard. The eroticism of her body is displaced onto the waste water going down the drain, picking up overtones of the river and its freight of filth. The warm humidity of the bath becomes visible in the next shot: a mirror clouded with condensation. Emily appears in the mirror as an obscure phantom, until her hand enters and wipes the surface clear. For Stephen, mirrors and water will constantly be associated in this film.[16] This image anticipates the dumping of Emily's body into the river, but also shows the coming into focus of a fantasy image, born from the murky depths of water and reflection, like the 'dream pool' in *Secret Beyond the Door*. Emily takes delight in her image, but also looks at it critically, prepares it to be an attractive sight, as if anticipating a gaze focused on her (like the male gaze embodied in the camera that films this 'private ' moment), pinching her cheeks. Lang cuts directly to Stephen still rocking and staring off, creating an almost Kuleshov-effect of an impossible eyeline match coming from this juxtaposition. Emily is not only filmed from a male voyeuristic point of view, she appears here as a reflected image, framed within the mirror. She is another woman framed as the image of male desire in this series of Lang films. As in *Scarlet Street* the process of framing a woman as an image initiates a movement towards her murder.

Stephen rises, buttons his jacket and, picking up a flower from his writing table, walks back into the house in a casual manner. As he nears the door, Lang gives the final and culminating image of the alternation between Stephen and Emily's bath: another medium close-up of the bathtub, only now the water level is low, and forms a spiralling whirlpool as it drains, a sucking, gurgling noise rising from it. This gurgling noise continues over a shot of Stephen heading into the house. He pauses as he hears it and turns his head, Antheil's score stopping suddenly to allow this sound to dominate. Lang shows us the drainage pipe coming down the side of the house in this early stage of indoor plumbing (another rich period detail), as the gurgling continues – Emily's bath-water flowing down towards the sewer and the river. A low angle, highlighted, medium close-up of Stephen follows as he recognizes the source of the noise and looks up from the drainage pipe toward the bathroom window. Following his gaze, the camera tilts up to the window. Stephen smiles broadly as the sucking-gurgling-flushing sound continues.

This is truly an obscene moment, again worthy of Bunuel. The eroticism of the previous scene drains into this passionate plumbing. The noises are bathroom noises; not just the tub drain is evoked, but the sound of a flush toilet, even sounds of digestion and excretion. The drainage pipe pulls together the associations of the opening sequence into the most explicit instance of what I have previously termed Lang's cloacal vision. Both associations of this term function here: first, the subterranean sewer, one of the pathways from the upper-class second floor bathroom into the depths of filth, directly connected with the river itself. Second, the cloaca as a passageway for filth, a toilet, a sewer carrying dead things, the corridor of the abject. This is the source of Stephen's perverse passion, as he contemplates with a smirk a servant girl's dirt carried through the plumbing of his house. The following shot

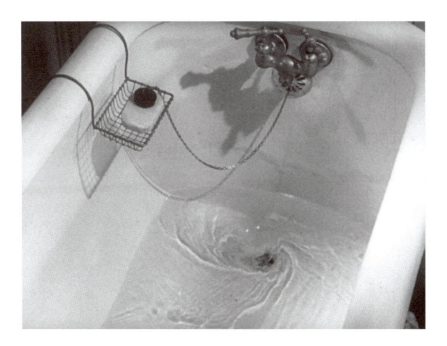

shows Emily's innocent infraction of class rules as she appropriates some of her mistress's perfume, dabbing it behind her ear and above her breasts. Her body remains off screen; we only see her framed mirror reflection, illuminated by the gas jet which flames to one side.

Stephen enters the house, a dark looming interior swimming with small pools of light, glinting off banisters and wainscoting, the camera dollying in as he stands before a mirror situated at the staircase and lights a candle. He primps in front of the mirror, as Emily did in the preceding shot, arranging his tie, then looking away from himself and taking a drink. His investment in the mirror is different from Emily's; it has none of her youthful exuberance. One suspects he takes a drink because he is not entirely pleased with what he sees when he regards himself, although his narcissism is indubitable. A heavy silence broods over the scene, ever since the score was hushed to call attention to the noise of the plumbing. Lang cuts to a new angle of Stephen as he takes another drink, then reacts to the off screen click of a door latch and moan of a hinge opening. Like a naughty boy, Stephen blows out the candle and looks up at the landing.

Emily's transformation into a framed image continues as Lang portrays her exit from the bathroom by a shadow cast on the wall, a dark silhouette within the bright rectangle of light thrown through the open door. Lang shoots this shadow play from a low angle, as if from Stephen's point of view. As Emily shuts the door, the shadow disappears. We see Stephen, shot from above, lurking in the shadows by the stairway, the unusual angle and the low-key lighting coming from one side, make him look reptilian. A low angle shot (again invoking Stephen's point of view) of Emily coming down the stairs shows just her bare legs coming from her bathrobe, framed between the struts of the banister. The portioning of her body out into separate parts – hands, face, and legs – framed for the predatory male gaze has been systematically accomplished. Looking up, Stephen smiles in voyeuristic pleasure and takes another drink. The leg-show continues, the camera craning down to follow her downstairs, focused still on the lower part of her body. Lang cuts back to Stephen drinking and gloating at his voyeur thrill. The intercutting between Emily and Stephen which began with them in separate spaces, has now moved into proximity and rooted itself in Stephen's lustful look.

We then see Emily framed in long shot as she continues her descent, when, out of the silence, the off screen clink of Stephen's glass is heard. Emily gasps in fright. She backs up against the wall. Stephen smiles sardonically in his hidden darkness. We hear Emily's panicked breathing unnaturally amplified on the soundtrack, then see her in medium close-up, terrified, searching the darkness for the source of the sound. Stephen smiles and speaks her name tauntingly, 'Emily'. Emily is initially relieved to realise it is her boss, and tells him she left everything in the bathroom neat and tidy for his wife. But Stephen blocks her way coming down the stairs, lets her go, then grabs her arm, remarking on her perfume. He moves forward to kiss her as if the borrowed perfume gave him access. She struggles and demands to be let go. He threatens to tell his wife about the perfume. Emily says she doesn't care and demands to be released, raising her voice.

With Emily's scream, Stephen's point of view darts out the window to Mrs. Ambroise in her yard in the distance. He tells Emily to be quiet, forcing his hand over her mouth, but she wriggles out of his hold and screams more loudly. Lang cuts outside to a long shot of Mrs. Ambroise who stops still and looks around. We think for a moment she has heard Emily's cry for help. But no sound penetrates out here. Lang cuts back inside where Emily continues screaming and Stephen begins to strangle her. Back outside we see why Mrs. Ambroise looked around: searching, she finds her bundle of plant ties and goes back into her house. Inside Stephen's house, Emily's scream has ceased and we see Stephen framed from the waist up, watching out the window. 'That's better', he says, and the camera tracks back, revealing Emily below the frame, as she falls from his hands, dead.

In this sequence Emily has moved from a living person to an abstracted, erotic image framed and split into separate parts within Stephen's lustful gaze and imagination. But when she refuses his advances Stephen treats her as an annoying object resisting his will, trying to keep her quiet with physical force – until she dies. As he realises she is dead he drops her, like the other useless things, the cigarette butt, the rejection letter. Stephen's problem in *House by the River* becomes getting rid of this embarrassing object, Emily's body, now that it longer has the possibility of giving him pleasure. Stephen feels no guilt from his murder, merely panic that it might cause him problems, and, later, delight in the increased contact with reality he feels it gives him. Almost immediately as he crouches over the fallen, lifeless, limp body and whispers 'merciful God', the fear that he might be caught descends on Stephen, as a knock sounds at his door.

Lang's direction of the performance of Louis Hayward shows a bold originality, conveying Stephen's almost infantile panic by refusing to let him stand up. His first reflex motion recoils from the body he crouches over. As he pulls back, his wrist becomes tangled in the sash of Emily's robe. He shakes his hand free with an impatient gesture of disgust, and then *crawls* across the floor towards the door. He edges along the staircase, looking back at one point towards the thing that was Emily and sharply pulling his legs away from contact. He slivers through the darkness of the room, among its potted plants and carved wooden nooks and crannies, barely visible

in its deep pools of shadow, as the knocking continues, trying to keep out of sight. The immediate de-familiarisation of the space of the house which his crawling produces is uncanny. The house looms gigantically as Stephen seems reduced to an infant, and its darkness appears less to threaten, than to shelter, the murderer.

Stephen peeks around a corner and we see from his point of view the shadow of a man at the glass door, still knocking. Lang then cuts to a large close-up of an eye peering through something. It is unclear at first whose eye this is, and its enlargement, by far the closest shot so far in the film, startles us. But in the next shot Stephen huddles back into his corner, and we realise the eye must be looking into the room, a magnified fragment of the man at the door whom we still have not seen except as a silhouette. In the next shot the eye returns, an almost disembodied image of the gaze itself, the threatening view of surveillance that Stephen fears abjectly. Once again Lang embeds the voyeuristic male gaze within another threatening view which observes it. In long shot Stephen, hiding in the foreground, watches as the shadow-man finally leaves the doorway. He creeps forward, and slowly, for the first time since he murdered Emily, stands up. He turns and walks back towards the camera, but stops still. In reverse angle we see what he sees: the room, Emily's body on the floor and the shadow-man passing the back windows. The camera tracks with Stephen as he comes to the back door and, relieved, lets in John, his patient, good brother in this Cain and Abel story, whom he will prevail upon to help him get rid of Emily's body.

From this point on, Emily remains out of sight. Her body and the attempts to conceal it will occupy the first half of the film (a grim version of *The Trouble with Harry*), but it will now no longer be shown; it has dropped below the frame of the image. When John examines Emily (who Stephen claims accidentally fell down the stairs), he bends down below the frame, and his announcement that she has been strangled comes from off screen. Lang collaborates with Stephen's desire to remove her from sight, thrust her aside. Lang dissolves from Stephen discovering a large wood sack in his basement to the sack stuffed with its burden being laced up. 'She'll soon be in the river', Stephen explains, 'and it will all be forgotten.' From here on Emily exists as an object, heavy, awkward, which the two brothers carry between them, terrified of discovery, out of the house and down to the boat at the river dock. They seek the cover of darkness, even hiding on their bellies behind a low wall when Mrs. Ambroise emerges.

'That filthy moon!' Stephen cries as their boat moves over dark water, shimmering with moonlight, execrating the pale eye which hangs over them, illuminating their attempt at oblivion. The anchor tied to the body is tossed overboard, and then the brothers struggle to tip Emily into the river over the edge of the boat. Lang cuts suddenly to a gleaming fish that leaps out of the water, perfectly white and glowing like a phantom, a nicely done process shot as the fish makes an arc up from the inky water into light and air, then back again into obscurity, leaving behind a placid surface. Startled, Stephen nearly falls from the boat into the river. 'Did you see that?' he cries, 'something bright, something flashed out there in the water!' Like the looming eye peering into his house, like the moon he besmirches, the leaping fish has terrified Stephen with the idea of visibility, light flaring into his darkness. I have said that Stephen feels no guilt over this murder, and I think his behaviour (such as his delight and exaltation at the party held on the same evening as the murder) in the rest of the film demonstrates this. But he does fear, to the point of madness, exposure, being caught in the eye, not so much of the law, as of an avenging spirit. This is not a mere emblem for subjective guilt, but a primal terror.

For in Lang's films, the dead almost always return. The image of the river with its tides exemplifies this rhythm of ebb and return. Lang frequently expresses this eternal recurrence by repeating earlier scenes with variations, but in *House by the River* he pushes such repetition to a truly uncanny horror. In his famous essay 'The "Uncanny"', Freud discussed how 'an unintended recurrence of the same situation' can cause a feeling of 'helplessness and of uncanniness'.[17] After Stephen returns home from disposing of Emily, Lang precisely re-stages the situation preceding her murder. The exact same camera movement follows Stephen from the door to the mirror, where he again pauses and strikes a match. Mirrors will trouble Stephen from now on, more than his uncertain narcissism can explain. He brings the flaming match close to his face and scrutinises it. Suddenly the same off screen sound that introduced Emily is heard: the click of a door latch followed by the creak of an unoiled hinge. This startles him and he looks up, no longer in lustful anticipation, but in fear, the forgotten match burning his finger, so that he extinguishes it with a sharp wrist motion. Earlier he had blown the candle out to conceal himself as he watched Emily emerge from her bath. But he is no longer in a position of mastery, and the sudden darkness is involuntary. When Lang repeats the shadow of a woman cast on the wall by the bathroom light, a shudder of the uncanny drives out any anticipation of erotic voyeurism. Stephen is subjected to this image now; it no longer gives him the thrill of a private show.

A high angle shot of Stephen shows him transfixed, staring upwards, and the following shot repeats the cheese-cake image of female legs protruding from a bathrobe, framed by the struts of the banister. Horrified, Stephen repeats the name he earlier called tauntingly in order to frighten the young girl he subsequently killed, now a low, choking whisper – 'Emily?' Lang shows the woman's form, backlit, dark against the wallpaper, a revenant. Is Stephen caught, like Chris Cross in an echoing traumatic moment, where erotic promise turns to nightmare and the dead victim revisits the murderer? Instead the dark figure speaks his name in a different voice. It is his wife, Marjorie, coming from her bath, and Stephen whispers her name now, with relief. The dead have not yet returned for Stephen Byrne, but their *mise-en-scène* has been repeated. Stephen regains his composure and is able not only to lie about Emily's absence, but to take her place as lady's maid, helping his wife dress for a party.

The dressing takes place in a *mise-en-scène* of mirrors, redoubling his wife's semi-dressed figure. The scene gains an erotic intensity, as Marjorie moves from a large wall mirror to sit before a smaller mirror over her vanity table, Lang filming the couple in the mirror. But as Marjorie puts her arms up to pull her husband down for a kiss, a strange glint leaps from the back of her silver hand mirror lying in front of the vanity mirror which frames the couple as they are about to embrace. Lang returns here to the most basic film techniques, scratching directly on the film stock to create this uncanny flash of light by scoring off the film's emulsion, as he had in Freder's trauma in *Metropolis*, and with Liliom's sparkling star. The glint of light draws Stephen's attention away from his wife's lips, as we see the dark river superimposed over the mirror, and the gleaming fish leaps from the back of the shimmering hand mirror. Lang cuts to Stephen staring into the mirror, his wife confused by his distraction. A close-up of the hand mirror follows, superimposed with darkly scintillating water and the sound of flushing. Marjorie asks him what the matter is as he grabs his head, and he explains he has a headache.

On the most obvious level, Lang conveys that Stephen is haunted by the scene he just endured, so that elements of it seem to recur to him, cued by visual similarities: his wife coming down the stairs, the light reflecting off the silver hand mirror. But Lang's very precise *mise-en-scène* expresses more. Stephen has moved from masterful

male director of imagined scenes to their terrified spectator. The dark waters which offered him a place where things sink and are forgotten have become a reflective surface from which things leap out and terrify him. It is worth noting that the mirror flashes *before* Stephen looks at it, drawing his attention to it, rather than simply being a surface on which he projects his guilt. The mirror initiates a play of images, the ultimate battle for enunciation between Stephen Byrne, author, and the Destiny-machine, speaking in the name of the dead servant girl. The battle is far from over, the opponents have simply entered the lists. Stephen gazes again at the hand mirror, and in the succeeding close-up the water has vanished, as if he has gained control over his visual field. The shot dissolves into Stephen's exuberant face as he dances at the party, where he shows high spirits and a new confidence as a lady-killer. Stephen is determined to master this deed, to gain from it a new identity as a writer and ladies' man.

The Flow of the Writer's Hand

> For a while yet I can write all this down and express it. But
> there will come a day when my hand will be far from me, and
> when I bid it write, it will write words I do not mean. The time
> of that other interpretation will dawn, when not one word will
> remain upon another, and all meaning will dissolve like clouds
> and fall down like rain.
> Rainer Maria Rilke, *The Notebooks of Malte Laurids Brigge*[18]

As Georges Sturm has shown, *House by the River*, especially the opening sequences, resembles in many ways the first film in the enframed desire series, *The Woman in the Window*.[19] After the accidental murders (although the murders carry very different degrees of guilt in each, neither was premeditated), both murderers undertake to hide the traces of the crime, most particularly the dead body of the victim. In both films this attempt to cover one's tracks proves less than successful with the body recovered, and the fear that the investigation might target the protagonist. But from this point on the films take very different tacks. Wanley continues to undertake the Sisyphean labour of trying to remove any signs that point towards his guilt, and ultimately succumbs to their accumulated weight. Stephen Byrne, in contrast, restructures the direction of the investigation by allowing it to target his brother. He takes a hand in the events himself, and simultaneously begins building a career for himself as an author based on both the publicity from Emily's disappearance and a new understanding of his mission as a writer drawn from his actual experience as a murderer. Although he begins in a position similar to Wanley's, he then takes on the active role of an artist found in the other films of this series, in which the act of murder and artistic creation tend to merge, only to encounter at the end a mutual exclusion.

Marjorie confides in John that Stephen seems to delight in Emily's disappearance, and John is particularly upset by the way Stephen besmirches Emily's reputation. Stephen re-fashions Emily into his own nasty fantasy, referring to her as 'a promiscuous servant girl' who he claims must have wandered off naked (since none of her clothes are missing). Marjorie suspects Stephen 'fancies the whole thing as a great big melodrama with himself in the leading role'. Unwittingly, Marjorie describes Lang's movie itself. Stephen wants, in contrast, not simply a leading role in a drama of the signs of good and evil, but the position of enunciator. His picture appears engraved in the newspaper, and Emily opens the family album only to find that the photograph of Stephen on which it is based, is missing. The image of this blank page within the album, only the frame for Stephen's picture remaining, his image gone, indicates not only that he took the photograph and gave it to the newspaper in order to generate publicity, but that he is now declaring control over his image, revoking it from the domains of domesticity.

Lang dissolves from Marjorie holding the album and laughing as she exclaims that Stephen is like a child, wanting to see his picture in the paper, to a close-up of that missing photograph, now framed. The camera pulls back to reveal a Langian shop window display: Stephen's photo next to a bust of Shakespeare (seeming to look askance at this interloper) a pile of copies of Stephen's previously unsuccessful novel, *Night Laughter*, and finally an announcement that the 'eminent author, Stephen Byrne' will autograph copies of his book there. Stephen takes no boyish delight in having his picture appear in the paper. Rather, he is launching a publicity campaign, deftly positioning himself as both author and commodity. Stephen makes it clear to Marjorie that Emily's disappearance gave his writing career the jump-start it needed, but he also indicates his future novels will be even better because 'they'll be about things I know'. The notebook containing the sheets of his new novel bears the title *Death on the River*. His murder of Emily provokes his rebirth as a writer, bringing him a knowledge and experience he never had before.

Stephen wishes to transform the vision shown in the dark mirror into an expression of exultation; he wishes to take the image missing from the family album and turn it out into the world, advertising a commodity bearing his name and signature. The murder of Emily began as a prank he arranged, a little drama of seduction that toppled into attempted rape and murder, apparently out of his control. But what he wishes to do now is to claim it as his own creation, to embrace the abject he tossed away from him and make of it his private 'melodrama' – his new novel, held within the closed notebook which he allows no-one to open and read, because it is not 'ready' yet. His murder was the accidental result of his drunkenness and lust, but now he wants to claim it, or at least absorb it into his creative work, taking nourishment from the abject – that is his fantasy.

But the circular rhythm of the film, the ebb and flood of the tide reveal the hand of the Destiny-machine, endlessly recycling the same situations as it asserts independence from this self-proclaimed enunciator. Earlier Lang repeated the scenography of the prelude to the murder on the staircase. Now he begins the film all over again, and the abject declares itself independent of Stephen's control. Stephen sits in the gazebo writing. From off screen we hear Mrs. Ambroise repeat her opening line: 'I hate this river!' Asked what the problem is now, she explains, 'That horrible thing floated by again, that dead animal.' Stephen, annoyed at the intrusion into his writing, crosses out several lines in his manuscript and tells her the cow must have sunk a long time ago. Looking off, Mrs. Ambroise corrects herself, 'Why it's a sack of some kind, probably filled with rubbish.' Stephen looks up and we get the withheld shot of the floating sack, filmed exactly as the carcass had been. Stephen stares in horror, rising from his writing table and gathering together the pages of his novel. The association of Emily with a 'dead animal' and 'rubbish' reveals the primal nature of Stephen's sudden panic; it is not simply guilt or fear of discovery that galvanises him into action, but the reflux of the abject, and the possible return of the dead which threatens his new-found position as enunciator.

Stephen looks out to the river again and no sack is visible. The river is playing with him, inviting him into a macabre game of hide-and-seek. He rushes down to the dock and gets in the rowing boat, taking with him (as Lang shows in close-up) the manuscript of his novel. A dissolve links the image of Stephen rowing off from the dock with a close-up of the family album and the empty frame where his picture once was. In order truly to penetrate into this game with death, Stephen would have utterly to efface himself, but is his egotistic drive to be an enunciator capable of this sort of sacrifice? The trip down the river, as night comes on, in pursuit of Emily's floating body elicits one of Lang's most haunting and atmospheric sequences. The river becomes animated, filled with flowing strands of seaweed and looming branches, that seem alternately to beckon towards and to grasp at Stephen as he rows by, the dark water itself, billowing and shimmering, soliciting his searching gaze into formless nothingness.

Submerged trees and water reeds glisten in the darkness, creating an ambiguous visual field, until Stephen catches a glimpse of the half-submerged bag near the shore. He grounds the boat and takes a boat hook to try to snare the bag, wading waist deep into the water. Lang shows the pole futilely beating the water as the bag remains just out of reach. But then the hook snags it and he draws it towards him, the bag ripping as it comes. A cascade of long blonde hair flows from the tear, causing a moment of revulsion in Stephen. This hair recalls the long strands of river moss more than Emily's shoulder length hair. What transformations has the river wrought in this abject water-logged body, turning it into something rich and strange? The bag then turns and moves away, Stephen's hook flailing at the river as it tries to reach it again, while it floats off teasingly.

Stephen scrambles into the boat again, ready for pursuit, but as he searches the river around him, all he sees (we see) is the empty melancholy landscape, the bare trees, the murky waters. No bag, no body – Emily is hiding once again. As Stephen seems to beseech the river to give up its secrets, Lang makes his most mocking comment on his quest. We see again the mystery of the leaping fish, darting out of the water, flashing in the moonlight and diving back again. Stephen turns at the sound, but this time he does not see the fish (only we witness this bit of dark laughter at Stephen's plight, his attempt to see into the obscurity of death and the Destiny-machine). Stephen is granted no vision, he only sees the dark water where the fish once was and now is no more. He stares off. Lang shows the empty horizon of the river bank, then tilts the camera down into the darkness of the river and fades out. Stephen's search of the river is pointless. He can only rush to his brother's house and cry out, 'It's come up, John, it's come up! Emily's come back.' He nearly sobs as he repeats Mrs. Ambroise's opening complaint, 'It will be passing up and down the river until they find it, *up and down* the river, it will go on for weeks!'

However, when Stephen learns that John's name is indelibly inscribed on the bag containing Emily's body, he turns towards the camera with a sickening look of satisfaction. This abject thing still falls within the realm of words, as a writer, his area of expertise. He sees he can still manipulate the plot, setting his brother up as the fall guy. Thus when the detective arrives with the bag that once contained Emily's body, Stephen is again seated in the gazebo, writing with confidence and satisfaction, making the detective wait while he finishes writing a line ('wanted to get my thoughts down before they go away'). He identifies the sack as his brother's with unruffled ease. Likewise at the inquest Stephen shows complete aplomb as he lies under oath, in complete contrast to John's obvious discomfort (and guilt at concealing his brother's murder).

Stephen's devotion to his new novel, his new confidence and sense of authorship extend to extra-literary events. Not only does he encourage suspicion of his brother, he constructs motives for his supposed affair with Emily ('John's a cripple, he knows he hasn't a chance with a girl of our class. It's not hard to believe that he carried on with a servant girl!'). In addition, with some insight for repressed emotion, he begins to construct an affair between his wife Marjorie and John, sitting confidently in front of Marjorie's vanity mirror, buffing his nails, as he spins these tales (or paranoid theories? Could Stephen actually believe them?). Significantly, however, he avoids looking into this mirror (there are still things he cannot control). Marjorie responds that he has a 'filthy mind', the one comment that seems to get a rise out of him.

However, Stephen can still regard himself in the downstairs mirror, the one by the staircase. Lang creates an expectation of repetition by showing Stephen examining himself in this mirror for the third time. This time Stephen shows the greatest satisfaction, sticking his finger in his mouth in order to moisten it and slip off his wedding ring (clearly, he is going out philandering). Rather than reprising his former awkwardness, or terror, before the mirror, the sequence that follows shows Stephen in complete command of his environment and planning his first deliberate murder, that of his brother John. Marjorie tells him she is worried John might commit suicide from the pressure of the accumulating suspicion (and we could add, guilt; John is the only one who feels guilty in this film). Stephen realises this gives him a perfect situation for getting rid of his brother, and establishing his guilt in the eyes of all. Stephen sneaks around the house after Marjorie thinks he has left, gathering from the secret recesses of a Victorian desk the earrings that he took from his wife in order to make Emily seem like a thief. His movement through these corridors, doorways and stairways is flawlessly timed to avoid Marjorie's gaze as he slips out of the house unseen (although a billowing curtain in one window sets up the scenario for his later demise). He invades John's house through the window and places the apparently incriminating evidence, the earrings, in the loudly ticking clock. But will such cavalier treatment of the image of the Destiny-machine be tolerated?

Stephen finds his brother down by the dock. Against the background of the nocturnal river, he tries to explain to him the power he has drawn from Emily's murder. 'I've gained something', he reveals, explaining that he has overcome some fundamental fear he had possessed which had always held him back, and had made his writing inferior. Now he has conquered that fear and he has written 'something good'. John is horrified: 'It took a murder to do that'. Stephen indicates that that doesn't seem too high a price to pay. John perhaps says it most eloquently, without fully realising what he is saying, 'You stepped right out of Emily's murder as though you were shedding your skin'. Like that abomination in *Leviticus*, the snake that 'goeth on its belly', Stephen has renewed himself by contact with death; through an act of murder, he has re-fashioned his identity. A dark theory of artistic creation sketches itself here.

Stephen illustrates his new Satanic egotism by knocking his brother in the head with a boat chain, then tossing his unconscious body into the river. The various motives possible for this fratricide – fear that John will tell the police; jealousy over his attention to Marjorie; anger over John having just socked him in the mouth – all could explain the action. But the supplement of Stephen's desire to commit another murder, intentionally this time, seems just as compelling. He drags John's body out of frame and we hear an off screen splash as Lang fixes our attention on empty space, the bare boards of the dock. This image of emptiness dissolves to a shot of the notebook holding the manuscript for Stephen's novel, the title clearly readable: *Death on the River* by Stephen Byrne. The equation of the two works, Stephen's two masterpieces, is evident, based on death and nothingness.

The camera pulls back and we see a pile of manuscript pages as Marjorie reads them. The act of writing completes its circuit, finding its reader. Stephen had (accidentally?) left the manuscript out on his desk when he hurriedly took out the earrings. Stephen emerges from the darkness of the hallway, framed in the doorway, to see Marjorie with his *magnum opus*. But in contrast to his earlier anger when she picked up a page the wind had blown off his writing table, his reproach, 'How many times have I told you to keep away from my desk?' lacks outrage. He is actually pleased she is reading it, anxious to hear her opinion. Marjorie is astounded at his question, and his reaction seems almost a parody of the totally absorbed artist: 'Well, don't you think it's good? Can't you appreciate its quality, quite apart from its content?' He seems only slightly annoyed when she says the novel shows her husband is a murderer. He congratulates her for reading between the lines, although he had thought he had disguised it better. It is not her reading *per se* that worries him, but the fact that she is unlikely to keep silent about what she has read.

That could be solved by the final acts of Stephen's melodrama enacted according to his direction and script. John's death will be seen as suicide, a veritable confession of his guilt. But the guilt will be compounded; John will be discovered to have killed again before he did himself in, and Marjorie will be his second victim. As Stephen closes in on his wife, he makes the same blocking movement he did on the stairs with Emily, then grabs her by the hand, as well. As he holds Marjorie he confesses to and reinvokes Emily's murder, explaining that she wore Marjorie's perfume, and that he hadn't meant to kill her: 'But I didn't realise how easy it would be.' This is one of the sources of his satanic confidence, the realisation of how easy it is to kill a human being. He squeezes Marjorie's throat, and like Emily, she drops below the frame, into that unimaged space of the abject, of death itself.

But apparently it is easier to kill someone when you aren't trying to, than when you are. An off screen tapping competes on the soundtrack with Marjorie's strangled attempts to breathe. Stephen's attention again is drawn off screen, although the shot that follows shows only the empty, dark doorway to the room. But the next time we see this doorway a dim figure stumbles into the light – John, still dripping and wet from being thrown in the river for dead. Once again the river gives up its dead, what Stephen thought he had got rid of, returns. He should know by now that the river is his worst accomplice, but he repeats the hubris of all of Lang's murderous enunciators, not realising his mode of murder will turn on him, and that the dead always return.

Stephen backs away in preternatural horror and lets the still breathing Marjorie fall to the floor. He runs down the corridor, but suddenly stops and stares. The window blows open a door with the hinges creaking loudly and a white curtain blowing through it. Lang is ready now to give Stephen a visionary moment, a glimpse of his private movie, projected on the wind-blown screen. Reprising the motif of the wraiths of victims haunting their murderer, the image of Emily appears superimposed on this white curtain. In a sense it repeats the shadow play we have seen twice, the door opening and the figure of a woman cast on a wall. But this is different – not a shadow, but a bright apparition, not an inert wall, but a billowing surface which endows the image with movement and intention. Emily's arms reach out towards Stephen as if enacting the erotic welcome he fantasised she might give him as she stepped from her bath. Stephen stares wide-eyed in horror and – for the third and last time – intones her name: 'Emily'.

As he dashes through the doorway fleeing this vision, the curtain becomes entangled around his neck (recall Emily's sash that clung to him right after her death). Struggling with it, Stephen pulls it tighter around his neck, strangling himself as he begs 'Emily' to let him go. The curtain obeys Stephen's request better than he did

Emily's dying plea; Lang shows the curtain rings popping from the rod as Stephen struggles, the curtain tightening. Released, Stephen plunges over the stairwell with a howling scream, crashing on the floor below, where Emily had lain when Stephen had created his first fiction and claimed to John that she had fallen down the stairwell. Lang wastes no time getting out of here. He cuts briefly to John and Marjorie as the lovers embrace for the first time, but the camera moves on, over to the flood of papers that have fallen on the floor, the detritus of Stephen's great novel, whose title and signature ends the film.

In his brief but penetrating comments on *House by the River*, Enno Patalas clearly discerns the battle between Stephen's creation of himself as a novelist and the forces which destroy him. For Patalas, however, this drama takes place within Stephen, with his conscience and his unconscious in combat with him. 'All his acts aim at hiding his crime, but in such a way that it will be uncovered. He desires punishment as much as he fears it.'[20] Patalas's point applies particularly to Stephen's novel – isn't it a confession, however cleverly he may have disguised it, simply waiting for someone to read between the lines? And leaving it out on his desk, after he even carried it with him in the boat when he went in pursuit of Emily's body – isn't this clearly a parapraxis, showing he unconsciously wants Marjorie to read it, desires to be found out?

I certainly would not dismiss this reading, but I believe that Lang's dramaturgy here and in most of his films is less psychological, more external, more allegorical. Stephen shows delight in the murder, not remorse, and this is what makes him both repellent and fascinating. That which destroys him seems rather to come from elsewhere, from outside him. Certainly one can read Emily's phantom on the curtain as the projection of Stephen's madness, but seeing it as the actual return of the vengeful dead remains an option. As Frieda Grafe observes (in the same book) in Lang's films 'Objects become the vectors of action. They usurp the position of the subject

[…] The impression of fatality that comes from Lang's films is produced by these objects.' Whether one reads them as allegories of mental processes (the tendency in a psychological era) or not, objects and the relations between them in Lang take on a will of their own, thus becoming the dominant force in the films, what I have called the Destiny-machine. It is this pattern of repetition, recurrence and final vengeance that kills Stephen Byrne.

The fictional world of Lang's film, that world he created through his frames and his juxtaposition of images and sounds constitutes more than a space of action, more than a stage for characters. At key moments it generates its own images, as if possessed of a primal artistic will. In visionary moments, characters behold these images and attempt to discern their meaning, which generally panics them and not infrequently causes their death. But it would seem the world throws up these allegories whether they are observed or not. Stephen doesn't see the second leaping fish; but it presents to the viewer an emblem of his fate. A small example of this sort of allegory comes soon after Emily's 'disappearance', as John discusses Stephen's behaviour with Marjorie. John is feeding Marjorie yarn which she gathers into a ball. As John learns that certain things of Marjorie's are missing and realises that Stephen is manufacturing evidence to make Emily appear to be a thief, he pulls the yarn suddenly taut. This is a psychologically revealing gesture, and not a particularly rich one, expressing John's anger at his brother's behaviour, destroying the reputation of the innocent young woman he murdered. But when the conversation turns to Stephen's pleasure in the incident of Emily's disappearance, the yarn John holds begins to twist itself into miniature hangman's nooses. John does not cause this, it is not his gesture, but an action of the object itself. John, in fact, doesn't seem to notice it. The yarn generates spontaneously the signs of death and punishment. Of course, this is Lang's fictional world, not a statement about reality. But perhaps paranoia within Lang's world could be best understood as a viewpoint which sees the world as organising itself as though it were simultaneously artist and artwork. Whether we see them or not, the world in Lang's films constantly makes significant gestures.

This brings us to the heart of the enframed desires series for which *House by the River* provides such a succinct summary. Like his earlier master criminals, Lang's artists (Chris Cross, Mark Lamphere, Stephen Byrne) compete with the world in creating significant images. This act of hubris takes on the appearance of a crime, as Lang shows most clearly in this last film that his artists draw their greatest inspiration from the abject, from the breaking of primal taboos, particularly the act of murder. Chris Cross's naiveté, as he sits in innocent delight on the toilet painting a displaced image of his sexual desire, allows him to become a 'great artist' only because a primal repression shields him from the true sources of his inspiration. Once his innocence is punctured his art literally becomes an act of murder/suicide. Mark Lamphere creates his works of art in order to merge with the artistry of objects, to distil for himself their fatal power. Wishing to identify with this force, he creates his simulacrum of a room as the site for the murder he feels he must commit. Because of the intervention of interpretation by the woman he loves, he is the only one of this group of artists who survives. Stephen Byrne suffers the opposite fate. He rewrites his act of accidental murder in order to claim it with his signature, not expecting an act of reading by his wife who finds out his meaning all too well. Desiring to stop her from telling what she reads, he tries to kill her, asserting an author's tyranny not only over events but over readers as well. He discovers, like Mabuse, that he is only an incident in a plot and that his own writing hand has

15

The Blue Gardenia

Contradictions of a Decade

Mass culture is not to be reproached for contradiction ...
but rather on account of the reconciliation which bars it
from unfolding the contradiction into its truth.
                Theodor Adorno, 'The Schema of Mass Culture'[1]

The 1950s in America was an era of contradiction. Dominated by a powerful reaction which tried to turn back the reforms of the New Deal era under the guise of anti-Communism, it was also the era in which resistance to American Civil Rights policy reached a crisis that could no longer be ignored, creating a movement that incubated the transformations that surfaced in the 60s. For Lang, it was a period that was marked by insecurity – the threat of the blacklist at the beginning of the decade and a final breach with Hollywood at the end. In Robert Parrish's account of the famous meeting of the Directors' Guild in 1950 where Cecil B. DeMille demanded that Joseph Mankiewicz, the president of the Guild, support a policy requiring every member to sign a loyalty oath, Lang was one of the directors who

attacked DeMille's super-American stance. Lang rose and told the room that for the first time in the United States the fact that he spoke with a foreign accent made him feel afraid.[2] Nonetheless the 50s was also the decade of Lang's greatest productivity, with nine feature films produced in Hollywood and two in West Germany. While the films Lang directed in the 50s all (other than the dismissable *An American Guerrilla in the Philippines*) showed a sustained mastery of directorial skill, they seemed less centred on the key issues this study has traced, and the films appeared less closely linked in theme and stylistics.

The HUAC returned to Hollywood in 1951. The original Hollywood Ten reported to serve their prison terms in 1950. Whereas the 1947 hearing had been an invasion of Hollywood welcomed by a fairly small group of reactionaries, the return engagement was to a large extent prompted by (former) liberals who wanted to have themselves cleared of suspicion of Communism, such as *Scarlet Street* star Edward G. Robinson, who requested a hearing before the committee to establish his loyalty. Other former leftists or Communists sought a means of public repentance and a return to Hollywood payrolls.[3] The new round of hearings no longer targeted a small group like the original nineteen 'unfriendly witnesses' subpoenaed in the first hearings, but set out broadly to expose Communist party members working in Hollywood. Known as the 'mass hearings', these continued from 1951 to 1954.[4] The price for clearance became set: a public confession or explanation was not enough; one had to name names of other Communist party members. Clearance by informing became the only route back into employment and many high profile figures took it, such as director Elia Kazan, playwright and scriptwriter Clifford Odets and novelist and scriptwriter Budd Schulberg. The list of accused Communists swelled through this process and the blacklist burgeoned to 212 officially 'named' former or current party members, including screenwriters, composers, directors and actors.

But besides the highly public processes of testifying before the committee and either confessing, naming names and being cleared, or resisting, taking the Fifth Amendment and being cited for contempt (or being forced into hiding to avoid subpoenas), there was also a less public process of making deals. This was particularly important for figures who had not been named as Communist party members but were perceived as 'fellow-travellers' sympathetic to Communist causes and members of so-called 'front groups' believed to be set up by the Communist Party to attract liberal supporters. Such people might find they were 'grey-listed', not officially named by the HUAC committee, but not being employed either.[5] Lang felt he had been grey-listed.[6] Although Lang was never called to testify before the HUAC, and had by all evidence never been a CP member, the process of clearing his name in the early 50s was both harrowing for Lang and elicited less than heroic behaviour on his part.

Lang's lawyer was Martin Gang, a former supporter of liberal causes, who became in the early 50s the primary means of attaining clearance for film-makers who felt they had been grey-listed.[7] Lang indicates he used Gang to clear his name working through the American Legion, which Ceplair and Englund have called 'the supermarket of the clearance industry through the threat of boycotting films to which suspected "subversives" had contributed …'.[8] The American Legion had its own more extensive list of 'subversives' quite independent of the HUAC which targeted not simply Communists, but their 'dupes', liberals or leftists who now found themselves labelled subversives. Those named were given a chance to clear themselves by writing a letter explaining why they had joined a particular 'front' organisation and were asked asked to name others who had joined. In interviews he gave even in the late 60s, Lang still repeated the grovelling and apologetic tone that must have characterised his original letter as he explained why he was associated with liberal or anti-fascist groups.[9] No-one today should claim the luxury of judging such compliance, but that Lang was repeating the same excuses long after the threat was removed indicates the degree of fear the grey-list must have inspired in him. Did he name names? The American Legion was not legally constituted to demand such a service, although it requested it. More likely they accepted Lang's excuses of extreme naiveté in associating with Communists, and his nearly abject acknowledgment of their power.

Few people emerge from this period as heroic, and the moral contradictions are not to be simplified. Many Popular Front liberals felt as betrayed by Stalinist policies as by home-grown reactionaries. An atmosphere of pervasive corruption, cowardice and paranoia-inspiring threats pervades not only Hollywood policies but 50s cinema. It has often been pointed out that Kazan and Schulberg's highly influential *On the Waterfront* can be read as an apologia for being a stool-pigeon. More broadly, a strong theme emerges in 50s American cinema of the exposé, the revelation of widespread corruption hiding under placid surfaces. The anti-Communist hearings were only one aspect of a national drama of purging corruption through public testimony and revelation. The Kefauver hearings into organised crime staged a similar drama, albeit this time with more conventional criminals and tangible threats. The 50s became an era in which the creation of an ever more comfortable bourgeois *intérieur* (supplied now with a powerful anchor in television and insulated from urban distraction by relocation to the suburbs) also encountered an increasingly glaring spectator-oriented public sphere of mass media (including, again, the television).

The contradictory energies of the 50s are displayed with particular clarity in its popular culture. On the one hand, an embrace of reaction, a desire for conformity and normality and a certain sexual puritanism, embodied particularly in the image of suburban, white, middle-class, heterosexual family as the foundation of society, reflected in Hollywood comedies and especially in the new medium of television. On the other hand, the expanding consumer culture encouraged an ever more intense hedonism, a fascination with sexuality in its most palpable forms (the era of *Playboy* and, in film, Jane Russell and Marilyn Monroe, a featured actress in Lang's *Clash by Night*). Likewise, popular culture reflected an obsession with social deviance, from the juvenile delinquent to the beatnik, which, while often displayed within a disciplinary discourse of disapproval, also provided new models of behaviour and emotional expression. The emergence of rock and roll as a commercial form, the popularity of James Dean, and – across the increasingly questionable divide to high culture – the emergence of method acting, abstract Expressionism, and beat poetry, all outlined a breach in forms of expression that would become generational, with the younger generation valuing an immediacy of emotional expression, associated with sincerity, 'realism', and, not infrequently, violence. Perhaps more than anything else it was this new sensibility which would contrast sharply with the distanced and pessimistic style of Lang and make his films look old-fashioned. Whereas in the thirties and forties Lang found genres or series which corresponded to his style – such as the socially conscious 'message' film of the thirties, or the *film noir* of the 40s – in the 50s one feels him groping for an equivalent niche.

Thus the strong films that Lang makes after *American Guerrilla*, the western *Rancho Notorious* and the realist melodrama *Clash by Night*, on the surface seem to be made by different directors (as might two other back-to-back films, the realist

Human Desire, 1954, outstanding for its location shooting, and the almost entirely studio-shot and beautifully stylised *Moonfleet*, 1955). *Rancho Notorious* can be linked to a number of other films Lang directed in the 1950s – *Moonfleet* and the two Indian films, *The Indian Tomb* and *The Tiger from Eschnapur* which deal with exotic locales in either time or space: the old west, eighteenth-century England, a mythical India. All of these films unwind within an extremely artificial and constructed fantasy world and make often brilliant use of the motifs of adventure literature that Lang had introduced in *Spiders*, as well as the plots and situations of Zane Grey, Robert Louis Stevenson and Karl May. These films would repay a more detailed study than I can give them in this work, since they deviate explicitly from my central theme of modernity. In some ways these productions fit into a broad segment of 50s cinema, the Technicolor, wide-screen (*Moonfleet* was Lang's only film in CinemaScope) escapist fantasies which were extremely popular in the 1950s and included westerns, swashbucklers and spectacular films dealing with ancient civilisations. But the techniques of illusionism so important to the 50s, not only colour and wide-screen, but also location shooting and big-budget reconstructions, only emphasise how unreal Lang's films in this vein look. Lang insisted on the constructedness and artificiality of his archetypal fantasy worlds, and did not try to endow them either with emotional immediacy or even believability. As critic Jonathan Rosenbaum has said, these are creations of pure surface.[10]

Thus *Rancho Notorious* doesn't strive for historical accuracy in details (in contrast to *House by the River*): a wanted poster bears a photograph, not an engraving. While big-budget westerns in the 50s revelled in location shooting in National Parks adding a touristic fascination to the genre, *Rancho Notorious* remains restricted to back-lot shooting, a familiar western town set and the strangest reconstruction of south-west rock formations ever crafted from plywood and paint. One can find these factors in other lower-budget westerns, but Lang's film stressed the west as a lost period, retrieved only in fading memory and folk legend, with the image of an aging star at the centre. Lang uses the song 'The Ballad of Chuck-a-Luck' as an off screen narrator who treats the story as a 'legend', 'a souvenir of a bygone year', and an 'old, old story' – to quote lines that are sung under the opening credits. Vern's quest for the man who killed and raped his fiancée turns into a search for the former dance hall beauty, Altar Keane, played by Marlene Dietrich, whose legend is conveyed through flashbacks as the fond memories of aging raconteurs. This contrasts with the emotional immediacy, intensity of violence and sense of landscape that directors like Anthony Mann, Nicholas Ray, or even Samuel Fuller were squeezing from the genre. Even Ray's *Johnny Guitar* which has some surface similarities to *Rancho Notorious* (set primarily within the realm of outlaws and featuring a legendary star, Joan Crawford as a dance hall proprietor with a similarly ambiguous relationship with the law) has an emotional immediacy in Sterling Hayden's performance and a contemporary political reference as an allegory of McCarthy era witch-hunts that the elegiac tone of *Rancho Notorious* avoids.

The film's emphasis on vengeance and obsession brings it close to other 50s westerns which increasingly dealt with unstable characters, but Vern's obsession seems to fade as he reaches Chuck-a-Luck, the ranch where outlaws on the run can hide out, and finds Altar Keane, the legendary beauty. Keane's line to him as she finds herself drawn to the younger man, 'why don't you ride away and come back ten years ago?' captures the film's overwhelming sense of belatedness. Lang's starting point for his original story was the idea of archetypal western characters, the gunfighter and the dance hall singer, who are showing their age.[11] Thus the western could become part of Lang's fatal landscape and the frontier itself was dominated by the image of the spinning wheel of fate, an explicit emblem of the Destiny-machine. Just as in *Siegfried*, Lang portrayed a realm of legends declining into the realm of history, so in *Rancho Notorious* he shows a legendary world that seems to be running down and dying out.

In *Clash by Night*, on the other hand, Lang comes closest to the new realism of post World War II American cinema, with a strong emphasis on location shooting, a script which challenged the stability of the American family with a drama of infidelity, and dialogue from a playwright whose work provided one of the first arenas for experiments in method acting (Clifford Odets had dedicated the original play to Lee Strasberg – who also directed it on Broadway – the most influential innovator of 'the Method' in American acting). Although screenwriter Alfred Hayes strongly reworked Odets' original play, changing the locales, redefining characters and transforming the ending and most of the last act, McGilligan's claim that 'only a few lines of Odets' epigrammatic dialogue were salvaged' simply isn't true.[12] Hayes' script makes good use of Odets' dialogue which persists throughout the film, and many of Hayes' new lines sound like Odets.

It is not surprising that, as Bernard Eisenschitz discovered, producers Jerry Wald and Norman Krasna originally considered Nicholas Ray, possibly the film-maker who best understood the new movements in acting and dramaturgy that a play like Odets' represented for the American cinema to direct this production.[13] The casting of the film reflects a compromise between old and new Hollywood that is frequent (and often wonderfully effective) in 50s films. Robert Ryan (who had played the lesser role of Joe Doyle in the original Broadway production) crafted a powerful emotional performance equal to his groundbreaking acting in films by Ray and Mann. A future Strasberg pupil, the young Marilyn Monroe, made one of her earliest dramatic appearances, and although her lack of discipline drove everyone on the set crazy, her immediate sensuality typified the new erotic tone of the 50s and greatly enlivens the film. On the other hand, Barbara Stanwyck gives a very traditional and strong performance as Mae Doyle.

Apparently both Joan Crawford and Bette Davis were also considered for this role, indicating that the producer recognised that for all its innovative energy, the play could be positioned as a woman's melodrama.[14] Hayes' restructuring of the plot to eliminate the play's climactic murder made infidelity rather than homicide the central issue of the film, and built up Mae into the dominant role, tailor-made for Stanwyck. Such changes made the transition into a more traditional genre work smoothly. But the uniquely realist quality of the film does not disappear. This is certainly the most 'adult' drama that Lang ever filmed, with a strong sense of psychological conflict defining the characters, a basic verisimilitude of motivation (even the film's happy ending reconciliation is carefully crafted by Hayes to seem the result of mature people realising their responsibilities and deciding to tolerate each other's failings). Likewise the 'documentary' footage that Lang and cinematographer Nicholas Musuraca (the master of light and shadow for Tourneur's *I Walked with a Zombie* and *Out of the Past*, now showing his skill at location shooting) shot on location in Monterey not only forms a visually strong prologue to the film, but roots the drama in an environment of fishing boats and their catch, the sea and its inhabitants (seagulls, seals and fish) and the cannery with its fast-moving conveyor belts and disciplined workers. As in other realist films of the 50s this location work gives the emotional fireworks some ballast in the real world.

Frieda Grafe quotes Lang as saying in 1930 that he would never include the ocean in his films, that its elemental power terrified him and he would never risk trying to render it in a film.[15] She also notes that by 1952 in *Clash by Night* Lang seems to have overcome this fear. Besides the documentary footage of the sea and its relation to animal and man, shots of ocean breakers appear under the film's credits, as the river had in *House by the River*. These same shots appear later as Mae Doyle, after her marriage to Jerry, the big-hearted, but childlike, fisherman, stands at her window at night smoking and – well, if Stanwyck's impatient manner of inhaling doesn't convey her unsatisfied sexual longing, the pounding surf outside the window must. There is a way that for all its competence *Clash by Night* doesn't seem a uniquely Langian film. The ocean has come into his closed world, as either a tamed pictorialism or a clichéd metaphor. Lang allows a strong script to be carried by powerful and individual performances, deftly articulating drama and conflict with camera and editing, but one feels Lang flaunting his craft, rather than mining his deepest material and personal obsessions.

Even the sequences that seem most like Langian inventions rarely rise to the imagistic lucidity one expects. The projection booth (which in the final scene of the original play is the locale of Earl's murder by Jerry, as the insipid dialogue of a romantic movie plays on), supplies a nice background for a fight between Earl and Jerry, but never takes on the titanic quality of the Destiny-machines found in other Lang films. More complex, the use of an alarm clock in the sequence in which Jerry realises his wife and Earl are having an affair, although directly inspired by Odets' play, does supply some of the complex layers one expects from Lang. In Odets' play the alarm clock enters into the action when Earl and Mae come home after Jerry's uncle has told him the rumours about their affair and, growing suspicious, Jerry has found perfume and a box of nightgowns hidden in Mae's drawer. He picks the clock up as he talks to them and the alarm suddenly goes off as his discovery of the nightgowns is mentioned. In Lang's version (and again Hayes may be responsible for the change) Jerry begins looking at the clock before they arrive, concerned about their extended trip to the amusement park. It then ticks audibly through the sequence of their arrival and the subsequent conversation. He picks it up and it goes off as the nightgowns are brought in and his discovery of them is apparent. But in contrast to the Odets script, Jerry clings to the clock throughout the scene, during Mae's confession, as if trying to both hold on to something stable and to keep his hand occupied so he doesn't turn violent. At the end of the scene, as he raises his hand as if to strike Earl, the alarm goes off again, distracting him from his violent gesture and he throws the clock across the room rather than throwing a punch at Earl.

The small changes are significant and demonstrate the nuanced border between Lang's style and the psychological realism of Odets' play. For Lang, as always, the clock mainly represents something beyond a character's psychology, whereas in the play it expresses Jerry's inability to hold back his anger at his discovery of his wife's infidelity. The clock for Lang first indicates the time passing before Mae and Earl get home, the time in which Jerry's suspicion grows. It then twice becomes a sign of Jerry's anger for Lang, but its very repetition stresses its mechanical nature. Rather than the clock becoming the equivalent of a psychologically revealing gesture, it images Jerry as a machine going out of control, a cog in a wheel of larger circumstances, rather than an emotional centre.

In the 40s, psychoanalysis provided Lang with images that could translate individual psychology into exteriorised allegories. The tortured souls of the framed desire series transform their perverse desires into dreams, paintings, architecture and mystery novels. But in the 50s a new style of acting and storytelling created emotional catharsis through strong identification with characters at their most revealing and vulnerable moments rather than through symbolic exteriorisation (think of Odets' line, retained in the film, when Mae says to Earl, 'you're cruel and sarcastic because you think I've seen you naked for a second' and the way Dean, Brando, Clift or Lee Remick based characterisation on such moments of revelation). Such psychological interiority and emotional display contrasted strongly with Lang's more ironic, distant approach. Although Lang could direct a film like *Clash by Night* with great skill and insight, it never equals the best work of directors like Ray, Kazan, or Aldrich dealing with similar material. And while at points *Clash by Night* seems to veer towards the older Langian melodramas (the high angle shot of Jerry as Mae agrees to marry him standing on her porch above him directly recalls the similar shot of Chris Cross when he gets permission to write to Kitty early in *Scarlet Street*), Lang seemed to realise that the era of *Scarlet Street* and *Secret Beyond the Door* had passed.

Instead, the contradictions and outright dishonesty of the public exposé, as he had seen it enacted around him at close hand, might have offered Lang a way to work out his own discomfort with the idea of emotional exposure and expression though a process of collision with publicity. With *The Blue Gardenia,* Lang returns both to his more traditional mystery-thriller genre and literally revisits many aspects of *The Woman in the Window.* But the theme of the exposé also emerges in a manner which makes what first seems like a forties *film noir* (with cinematographer Nicholas Musuraca returning to his skilled manipulation of light and shadow) into a film which navigates the contradictions of the 50s. In many ways Lang seems to return to his emphasis on the social landscape, the terrain of modernity of the films from the twenties. The psychological drama of *The Blue Gardenia* takes on a public dimension that the dramas of framing desire managed to avoid for the most part, with the figure of the newspaper reporter coming to the centre for the first time in a Lang film.[16] In many of Lang's films a newspaper headline or a journalist plays the role of a sort of chorus. But in a number of Lang's major 50s films the theme of bringing a story before the people becomes central. Yet Lang's view of such exposés remains ambivalent. The journalists' motives are always at least ambiguous, and sometimes venal. The 50s for Lang led not to emotional authenticity, but to a deeper exploration of reification.

Off the Hook

> Beechwood 4-5789
> You can call me for a date any old time.
>
> The Marvelettes[17]

Lang's first films from the 50s do not seem immediately like Lang films (although a careful examination of *Rancho Notorious* does reveal Langian treatments of death and fatality). But with his fourth film of the decade, *The Blue Gardenia*, it is clear that no-one else could have made this film. Once again Lang undertook a film made by an independent producer, this time Alex Gottlieb releasing through Warner Brothers. Lang supposedly got the job through the intervention of the studio head of Columbia, Harry Cohn, definitively getting Lang off the grey-list.[18] Although basically dismissed by Lang as a quickly made and impersonal assignment, this lower-budget B-film has in the last few decades gained attention and been the subject of careful analysis, partly from a feminist perspective, with fine essays by E. Ann Kaplan, Janet Bergstrom and Douglas Pye.[19] As with *House by the River*, Lang linked this film and his dissatisfaction with it to the McCarthy era. As Janet Bergstrom points out, Lang's claim that he only took the film after a period of enforced idleness (repeated by Lotte Eisner who gives the period as eighteen months)[20] can't be supported by the actual facts. Only seven or eight months separate the final shooting of *Clash by Night* and Lang's beginning of pre-production work on *The Blue Gardenia*, not at all an unusual period between films in Hollywood.[21] Lang may have confused the period with the time that elapsed between *Secret Beyond the Door* and *House by the River*. However, seeking clearance through Martin Gang and the American Legion would have probably taken place around the period of *The Blue Gardenia*, so in essence Lang's story makes sense, even if he exaggerated the period of unemployment.

The number of clearly deliberate echoes of previous Lang films (from plot echoes of *The Woman in the Window* to identification by blind mendicants as in *M*), and use of Langian devices (such as visually rhyming overlap-dissolves between scenes), seems to indicate Lang's personal involvement in this film, in spite of later dismissals. *The Blue Gardenia* doesn't show the same degree of control and imagination that *House by the River* exhibits. But not least of the interests in this admittedly modestly budgeted and swiftly shot film is its foregrounding of the telephone, an instrument almost as central to Lang's films as the omnipresent clocks. The telephone as a means of communication plays a more ambivalent role in Lang's dramaturgy than clocks which almost always announce that time is up for Lang's characters. The telephone can deliver a life-saving message (as in *You Only Live Once*) – or not (*The Woman in the Window*). Most fundamentally the telephone functions in Lang as a system that connects but subtly subordinates people, one of the structures of modernity that exists outside of individuals' control and subtly determines aspects of their lives.

The 50s saw a period of increased systematisation, as utopian ideals of the Depression and wartime era became realised as instruments of social order and control (such as the grid-like developments of the suburbs, seen as a cure for urban overcrowding, or the increased gathering of information on citizens that originated in social aid programs of the New Deal era). From *The Blue Gardenia* on, Lang's films seem to reflect this increased systematisation and reification (or perhaps return to this earlier theme, never completely abandoned). The telephone serves as the central system in this film, but it is only one aspect of the way the environment has been organised. Although Lang again may not have had much control over the opening credit images, they start the film with a banally brutal image of systematic order: an overpass in the Los Angeles freeway. The first image of the film's narrative then picks up reporter Casey Mayo and his photographer moving along an LA boulevard in a convertible placing the characters within this system. The archetypal image of the 50s promise of new technology and order – the enormous postwar spending on a federal highway system, and the creation of freeways around and through metropolises – already grounds the film in an abstracted order of stop and go.

The Blue Gardenia deals with telephone switchboard operators, the anonymous women (such as the one glimpsed briefly towards the end of *Dr. Mabuse, the Gambler*) who were central to the introduction of this new communication technology and who gave the telephone a specific gender within popular representations.[22] In the ambiguous history of the gendering of modern technology as feminine (which

Andreas Huyssens has discussed in relation to Lang and Harbou's *Metropolis*),[23] the telephone plays a special role. The telephone's association with the domestic, with the voice, and with the love of talk, all led to an atypical association of the technology with traditional feminine spaces and stereotypes. As one early telephone historian put it, 'The girls had softer voices, more patience, and nimble fingers.'[24] The large-scale hiring of women as switchboard operators, following the earlier influx of female operators of sewing machines and typewriters, belied cultural clichés of male control of the machines emerging from the new technology. Telephone companies re-inforced this association with the feminine in their advertising images of exclusively female operators, bringing a simultaneously sexy and maternal humanisation to what by the 50s (in the US at least) was becoming an increasingly mechanised process.

The Blue Gardenia gives Lang's portrayal of modern identity – defined by an assigned place within an established system – a gendered twist. After a series of films centred on female protagonists (*Secret Beyond the Door*, *Rancho Notorious* and *Clash by Night*) Lang may have become identified as a woman's director. But, in contrast to the previous films, *The Blue Gardenia* projects a view of women focused through the new sexuality of the 50s. This new reified idea of sexuality becomes most clearly exemplified in the film by an icon of American patriarchal sexuality in 50s popular culture: the bachelor's 'little black book' which files potential sexual partners and their telephone numbers. The film opens with reporter Casey Mayo and sketch artist Harry Prebble interviewing and sketching Crystal, a switchboard operator, for a newspaper feature on the long distance operators of Los Angeles. Flirting with Mayo, Crystal gives her vital statistics: age, nationality and, with a seductive air, phone number: 'Granite 1466'. Although Mayo doesn't pick up on this implied come-on, Prebble does, writing the number across his sketch of Crystal's face. Mayo continues throughout the film to refer to Crystal as 'Granite 1466'. He and Prebbles make it clear via their comparison of their 'little black books' that the collection of phone numbers equals the collection of women as objects of sexual conquest. Mayo's black book includes not only numbers but another 'code', a series of exclamation points which apparently rate the women as sexual performers. Lang's theme of modern identity being reduced to numbers and figures has never been stronger, but it gains here an almost brutal sexual twist: men are the coders, women the coded. Nowhere in Lang's film has the sense of male dominance been so blatant.

If Lang records this process of sexual subjection and reification without flinching, the equating of women with phone numbers nonetheless leads to the systematic twists that thwart all his characters when they assume their mastery of a system guarantees their potency. 'Granite 1466' is the number shared by three women room-mates, all of whom work as switchboard operators: Crystal, Sally (a dumb blonde serving as strained comic relief), and Norah, the film's pretty and victimised heroine. When Harry Prebble calls Granite 1466 he actually gets Norah who is distraught over a letter from her boyfriend stationed in Korea, breaking off their engagement. Harry characteristically doesn't listen to her long enough to understand she is not the girl he is calling for (does it really matter?) and Norah in her emotional state accepts a blind date over the phone. Phone calls play a central role in structuring the film, with Lang focusing on the way the phone system (imaged by the switchboard at which Norah works) involves uncertain identification as well as a reduction of identity to a single string of numbers.

On their blind date Prebble gets Norah drunk, and takes her back to his studio where he tries to force her to have sex. In a near stupor, Norah hits him with a fire poker, and passes out. She regains consciousness some time later, and rushes back home. The next day Prebble is found dead and the evidence indicates his murderer was a woman. The film's mystery plot involves the identification of Prebble's murderer and reporter Mayo's attempts to communicate with her directly through a newspaper column he entitles 'Letter to an Unknown Murderess'. Naming the murderess 'The Blue Gardenia', he asks her to call him, ending his column with the plea, 'go to the nearest phone booth and invest a dime on the rest of your life. Dial Madison 6025 and ask for yours, very earnestly, Casey Mayo.' Irked by his attempt to circumvent the police investigation, his detective friend has a woman call claiming to be the Blue Gardenia and then cuts in, admonishing Mayo to give any suspect who calls 'our number, Michigan 5211'. Norah, already the victim of a phone call not intended for her, becomes surrounded by the numbers of the system that wants to entrap her, both press and police, dual investigations proceeding, as in *M*. But Lang makes it clear that on the phone we can never be sure who is on the other end of the line. Mayo's plea is answered by dozens of calls from women who claim to be the murderess. Norah, meanwhile, is tormented by a call which asks her in a sinister voice, 'Is this the Blue Gardenia?' She hangs up in a panic, explaining to Crystal it was a wrong number, only to learn it's Crystal's boyfriend pulling a gag. Norah finally does call Mayo and confesses, but her call is interrupted when she sees a policeman passing and flees, leaving the receiver dangling off the hook in the public telephone booth. When she finally meets with Casey, he doesn't recognise her voice from the phone call (recalling Kent in *The Testament of Dr. Mabuse* who only recognises Baum's voice when he heard it recorded or over a loudspeaker), and is never sure whether she is the girl who called him the first time, or as she claims, merely a friend of the girl he is looking for. In spite of her elusive identity, he falls in love with her.

The *deus ex machina* ending which reveals Norah is not the murderer, may seem to stretch credulity, but it relates to the telephone theme with admirable coherence. The murderer, in fact, is Prebble's former girlfriend who arrived at his studio after Norah had fled his advances. Her existence was indicated early in the film when Prebbles is told he has a phone call from a girl during his sketching at the long distance switchboard. He takes it, boasting, 'I have more phone numbers than the phone company.' The caller is a woman who tells him desperately she 'needs to see him and talk to him' (as Janet Bergstrom's research on the film's original script reveals, the woman is pregnant, a fact only vaguely hinted at in the existing film).[25] Prebble brushes her off, telling her to call him at home. 'How can I?' she responds. 'You've changed your number and I can't get it from the operator.' Prebble therefore represents the evil genius of this system in which men have all the numbers and access to the lines of communication, and woman have none, even though they are the operators who make the actual connections. Although Prebble dies for his treachery, Norah remains in the final scene just a phone number to Casey Mayo, even if she is *the single* number he needs (Crystal cautions her not to respond too quickly when he calls her). Mayo expresses his future monogamy by tossing his little black book to his paper's photographer. The film ends with the image of this goon drooling over the book, having apparently cracked its code.

E. Ann Kaplan has claimed in her important essay on *The Blue Gardenia* that Lang undermines the dominant male discourse of *film noir* in this film by providing an alternative female discourse in the person of Norah, rather than privileging the male investigator (here the newspaper man Casey Mayo).[26] Elizabeth Cowie in her essay 'Film Noir and Women' has questioned such a definition of *noir* as a male form. She has argued that a female discourse is central to *noir* films like Anthony

Mann's *Raw Deal* of 1948, extending the definition of *noir* to include such women's melodramas as *Secret Beyond the Door*.[27] But *The Blue Gardenia*'s accent on Norah's point of view contrasts with the more famous *film noir* based on a work by the same (woman) author, Vera Caspary, *Laura*, which has a similar plot of a detective investigating a murder and falling in love with a woman he encounters during the investigation. *Laura* is initially focalised in the memory of Waldo Lydecker, and then in the interrogations of the detective. Halfway through the film Laura, who was believed murdered, reappears. The film never shifts to her viewpoint. In contrast, while *The Blue Gardenia* doesn't achieve the strong foundation in female point of view seen in *Secret Beyond the Door* (from which Celia is only briefly absent), its key dramatic scenes are from Norah's point of view. However, scenes from Norah's viewpoint alternate with scenes focalised on Casey Mayo's and his investigation. *The Blue Gardenia* stages a central conflict between male and female points of view and intensifies the film's sense of sexual duality through (as Kaplan points out) a sharp differentiation and conflict between spaces coded as male and female.[28]

But there is no question that the world *The Blue Gardenia* portrays (as opposed to the narrative Lang presents) is dominated by a male discourse. The women may operate the switchboard but, as Prebble shows, men control who sends and who receives messages. Thus Norah creates an elaborate *mise-en-scène* for the reading of a letter from her boyfriend in Korea, including champagne and dinner, turning off the lights, lighting candles and carefully positioning his photograph, which she toasts with her champagne and speaks to, before she tears open the envelope.[29] But in this letter, conveyed by the man's voice-over, her lover explains that he is breaking off his long-term relation with Norah and tells her he is going to marry a nurse he met in Tokyo. His letter ends 'with affection and best wishes for your future', a phrase Norah repeats bitterly out loud, adding 'yours very truly'. Prebble's phone call interrupts this scene of a man's message torpedoing a woman's fantasy.

Norah moves from one male discourse of betrayal to another throughout the film. Prebble transmits a predatory male message through several media. As a sketch artist he captures women on paper and canvas in cheesecake caricatures and clearly feels the control he exerts over his models' images extends to their bodies. Lang seems to grant him the villain's traditional illusion of control over cinematic enunciation when he dissolves from Prebble's sketch of a woman in a dress to Norah in the exact same pose in the dress she has picked out to celebrate her birthday and read her lover's letter in. This control over images is matched by his *savoir faire* over the telephone, whether brushing off his spurned lover, or asking Norah over the phone if she will join him for dinner. When he convinces the very drunk Norah to return with him to his studio he will also try to arrange all aspects of the *mise-en-scène*, turning off lights, edging her to the couch and putting on mood music, a record of the film's theme song 'Blue Gardenia', on his record player.

As Norah's room-mate, Sally, reads the break-up letter Norah received from her boyfriend, she exclaims with disgust, 'Men!' and Lang dissolves directly to Prebble holding a menu at the 'Blue Gardenia' restaurant and ordering the dinner and drinks before Norah has even arrived, stressing to the waiter that the 'Polynesian Pearl Divers' must have plenty of rum. He approaches the date like a battlefield and assures himself strategic advantage. The Blue Gardenia restaurant itself presents a fascinating environment of 50s bad taste 'exoticism': outfitted with oversized wicker chairs, tropical plants, Filipino waiters in Hawaiian shirts and Nat 'King' Cole, perhaps the only African-American seen in a Lang film in the 50s, displayed as an exotic creature bedecked with orchids and reflected by an oddly placed mirror. The Blue Gardenia radiates a male fantasy environment, a trap for women designed as an over-ripe garden of the fulfilled wishes of the hedonist, where Casey Mayo and Harry Prebble run in to each other and wish each other 'Happy Hunting'.

Lang constructs Norah's return to Prebble's studio apartment as an uncanny echo of Wanley's trip home with Alice Reed with genders reversed. Besides the essential similarities in plot structure of a tipsy, relatively innocent character brought home by a more sexually experienced one, Lang seeds the scene with *déjà vu* details. Like Reed's apartment, Prebble's studio has a huge mirror over the fireplace mantle. Like Wanley, Prebble cuts his finger on the wire of a champagne bottle. In terms of plot, the essential repetition comes as this tipsy tryst suddenly veers into violence. However, no hot-tempered lover intervenes here (at least not yet). As Prebble forces himself on the semi-conscious Norah, she resists violently, finally picking up and swinging the fire poker when Prebble refuses to leave her alone.

But in addition to the obvious similarity to *The Woman in the Window*, the scene in significant ways also recalls *House by the River*. Here the gender exchange is more chiasmic. Norah is the one who has drunk too much and who apparently kills, more or less accidentally. But the aggression of Prebble strongly recalls Stephen Byrne's near rape of Emily. In some ways Norah is Emily returned and vengeful, quick and smart enough to defend herself from a male attack. The moment of Norah's self-defence recalls the imagery of *House by the River* more than the murder and its aftermath in Alice Reed's apartment. This artist's studio swims in Musuraca's shadows and highlights as Prebble sets the scene for seduction, turning off the lights (and unconsciously recreating the *mise-en-scène* Norah earlier created for the reading of her letter). It is in stark contrast to the gleaming brightness of the apartment in *The Woman in the Window*. Prebble's looming bulk seems part of the darkness trying to overwhelm Norah as she struggles against him. Cornered, she stands against the mirrored fireplace trying to get away from him, but he literally won't let her go.

The act of violence is rendered in a brief staccato montage of the sort Lang had used since the 20s. Gathering strength in medium close-up, Norah pushes Prebble away from her, off screen to the left, the mirror behind her reflecting her as she reaches down out of frame. A very brief shot follows (less than two seconds) of a mirror (reflecting only a palm frond) being shattered. Then an even shorter shot (less than a second!) flashes: a slightly low angle image of Norah in medium close-up swinging her arm violently. Prebble's screaming face is reflected in a shard of the mirror, then the glass falls and his face disappears, leaving us with dark broken glass. Although this shot lasts nearly three seconds, Prebble's image is nearly sub-liminal, reflected in the glass for about half a second.

This jagged montage (in which the brevity of the shots reflects the violent shat-tering of the mirror) primarily expresses Norah's clouded vision in her drunken and distraught state – she collapses in a dead faint in the following shot. This indi-rect and fragmented presentation of her violence against Harry Prebble will later reflect her lack of memory of the event and create the essential lacuna for this mys-tery plot: what happened when she struck Prebble? But in contrast to the psycho-logical exploration of character that was becoming fundamental to the 50s style, Lang provides a symbolic series of metaphors, very much in the twenties avant-garde tradition. Lang shows his fascination with consciousness as it is over-whelmed, vision when it becomes opaque, through imagery that recalls not only the superimposed visions of *House by the River*, and the animated dream of *Secret Beyond the Door*, but reaches back to Freder's collapse in *Metropolis*.

Over Norah's unconscious figure Lang superimposes dark water (as if it escaped from the broken mirror, as in *House by the River*) which forms a swirling whirlpool (a

traditional Hollywood image for loss of consciousness). Then over the whirlpool, a series of animated forms appears, directly based on the 20s work of Ruttmann and Fischinger, concentric arcs with solar flares, which move briefly across the screen, overwhelming our vision of Norah. The whirlpool continues and slowly fades away, as we see Norah raise herself and return to consciousness. Lang conveys her point of view of the studio with wavering images shot through a distorted lens, and then a shot of the shattered mirror, similarly distorted. Norah staggers to her feet and, still reeling from her ordeal, exits the studio, leaving behind her shoes, a dropped handkerchief, and the Blue Gardenia corsage Prebble bought for her at the restaurant.

If Norah's distorted vision and loss of consciousness align with well-established Langian themes, the plot structure at this point makes an important modification of his usual narrative practice. The essential mystery-creating ellipsis appears here, and the film turns on the fact that we don't really know what happened when Norah swung the poker. Typically for Lang's misleading narration (or as Douglas Pye nicely calls it 'suppressive narration'),[30] we are cued to believe she killed Prebble with her blow, but, equally typically, we are wrong. But, untypically, this gap in the narration is motivated and naturalised by Norah's amnesia and limited point of view. She wakes up the next morning with her memory of the evening after her visit to the Blue Gardenia 'a complete blank'. This is, in fact, a more conventional way of creating a gap in the plot and alignment with the main character's subjectivity is a more familiar Hollywood approach. This is one of the reasons why, in spite of its many fascinating aspects, *The Blue Gardenia* never equals *The Woman in the Window* or *House by the River* in originality of narration.

Lang also develops the theme of an incomplete vision familiar from his other American films, but this time within a gendered division of discourse, in which woman's vision, rooted in her own subjectivity, is somehow deficient, and will collide with a male investigation based on logical inference and access to the mass media. Norah's amnesia and limited knowledge, represented by the shattered mirror, can never be fully restored by her own recall, a point made clear when another switchboard operator drops her hand mirror and the fragments seen from Norah's point of view dissolve into a brief flashback of Prebble's mirror shattering. Norah's memory of events after the meeting at the restaurant begins to return, but only in an image of shattered, incomplete vision. Ultimately the clue that leads to her exculpation comes from something she recalls hearing rather than seeing, the record of 'Blue Gardenia'.

Booking Cinderella

a Dialectical Fairy Scene

Walter Benjamin[31]

The Blue Gardenia punctures fairy tales and fantasy worlds in a bitter parodic manner, and with violent overtones. Mayo refers to Prebble during his visit to the long distance switchboard as the wolf let loose among a plethora of Red Riding Hoods, accenting the predatory image of sexual relations that threads through the film. Norah's room-mate Sally devotes her time to reading violent 'Mickey Mallet' murder mysteries (a slight inversion of the name of the misogynist, hard-boiled, and virulently anti-Communist private eye of the 50s, Mike Hammer, who exemplifies the new energies of the decade through his sharp contrast with the earlier

Sam Spade created by Dashiell Hammett, who was then serving time for refusing to name names to the HUAC). Sally is described by Crystal, the third room-mate, as 'a lucky girl living a life of passion and violence'. Lang dissolves from Sally playfully thrusting a large carving knife as she does the dishes to the cover of the latest Mallet novel *My Knife is Bloody* garnished with a huge knife about to slit a woman's throat, lying next to the now sleeping Sally, apparently happily dreaming a scenario of murder and violence. Lang then cuts to Crystal, who smiles and turns sensuously in bed, speaking her lover's name. The correlation is clear; the fantasy life of these frustrated and lonely young women consists of sex and violence and perhaps involves an equation between the two.

The fairy tale given the most bitter twist in this film is *Cinderella*. Norah left her shoes as well as her corsage behind when she fled Prebble's studio, giving the detective the principal clue to her identity. When Mayo publishes his 'Letter to an Unknown Murderess' in his paper, asking the 'Blue Gardenia' killer to call him and confess, he uses the shoe size of Norah's abandoned pumps to screen out the dozens of women, again bored and frustrated and hoping to spice up their lives through a connection to a passionate murder, who call and confess. Cynically, Lang transforms the Prince's search for the girl who left her glass slipper behind into a detective-like investigation. Norah's sudden flight from Prebble's studio also becomes a bitter re-reading of the fairy tale, Cinderella running away, not when her dress turns to rags, but when Prince Charming attempts date rape.

After Prebble's murder, *The Blue Gardenia* follows the genre pattern of investigation, accenting Lang's particular theme of the attempt to pin down identity through objects that stand in for the unidentified person. Lang's imagery does its most interesting work in this vein. Right after the broken mirror at work summons up Norah's first fragmentary memory, Lang dissolves from a view of the back of her head to a close-up of a Blue Gardenia corsage. As the corsage is handed to Casey Mayo, the camera pulls back to a long shot (a technique Lang uses increasingly in the 50s to open scenes) and shows Mayo questioning the blind woman who sold the corsage to Prebble and Norah at the restaurant. Besides the echo of *M* (the blind identifying a murder suspect), the cut from the back of the head of the woman who can't really remember, to a woman who is blind but has a tenacious memory continues Lang's play with incomplete vision and knowledge. The blind woman provides Mayo with additional clues towards Norah's identity, picked up aurally: from the unique rustle of her dress, she is sure that the woman was wearing taffeta; and the quality of her voice, 'friendly and quiet'. Lang dissolves from this comment back to Norah at the switchboard, feeding that friendly voice into her mouthpiece, as she answers a call and makes a connection.

Following the pattern set in *The Woman in the Window*, when Norah discovers Prebble has been murdered, her world transforms into a paranoid's playground of uncertain and threatening perceptions. Cops appear almost everywhere she turns, she accuses her room-mates of spying on her; and joking phone calls seem to carry accusations. Although somewhat awkwardly done, compared to the earlier film, Lang makes it clear that Norah, like all the characters in the film, lives in an environment of constant surveillance, but only notices it when feelings of guilt or fear of discovery render the guardians of order suddenly apparent. Like Wanley, she tries to destroy evidence that would link her to the murder, and thereby erases some part of her identity. She burns the black taffeta dress, a remnant of her romantic fantasy, donned when she thought she would read a love letter from her fiancé and worn for her date with Prebble. As in the tale of Cinderella, the magical ball dress becomes reduced to nothing. This burning in an outdoor incinerator draws a cop in a patrol car, who admonishes her for breaking restrictions on incinerator use at night, much like the traffic cop stopping Wanley for a minor infraction in *The Woman in the Window*.

Norah's ability to identify her lost shoes in detail serves as the equivalent to Cinderella's perfect fit and brings her into contact with Casey Mayo who hardly appears to be Prince Charming. As Norah flirts with confessing to Mayo, her drama of female guilt and paranoia, typified by shrouded vision and limited recall, intersects with Mayo's male discourse, the journalist's desire to ascertain the facts and grab a headline. Norah calls from a gas station near the Santa Monica pier, gloomy and adrift with fog, only to vanish into off screen space after a cop walks her way. She reappears walking through the fog to Mayo's newspaper building, and enters the spacious press room after hours, whose empty obscurity is punctuated by an electrical sign flashing outside. Casey greets her from the shadows, then leads her to his highlighted desk, then out to the brightly lit coffee shop, only to have her vanish again into the fog at the end of the scene.

Within the duality of genders that structures this film, the Langian theme of messages that have gone astray takes a peculiar twist involving male messages addressed to women of uncertain identity. Prebble's call to Crystal, which is taken by Norah, sets the plot in motion. But Prebble's reaction when Norah arrives reveals that his message had not really been targeted specifically, just aimed at any woman who might succumb to his charm. Mayo's column also throws out a line with romantic trimmings, hoping the Blue Gardenia murderer will bite. His newspaper message to the Blue Gardenia is vaguely addressed: 'Letter to an Unknown Murderess'. The title carries an ironic (intentional?) echo of Max Ophuls' masterful film of woman's narration and desire from 1948, *Letter from an Unknown Woman*, but inverts its gender of enunciation and address. Lang's male messages solicit women their writers don't really know, possessing only vague indications to identify them (Crystal's telephone number, Norah's shoe size). Norah twice decides that she is addressed by these messages, first, as an answer to her loneliness and betrayal, and then as a way out of fear and guilt, only to discover herself trapped both times within a male scenario where there is little concern for who she is, or how she feels, other than in terms of a fulfilment of a male projection of seduction, or headline grabbing.

Mayo writes his column as a letter, addressed to a specific but unnamed reader. While Norah eventually will feel herself interpellated by it (responding to the name Mayo has given her, 'the Blue Gardenia') and read it as an offer of help, the film subtly but repeatedly compares Mayo's letter to the traumatic letter she received breaking off her engagement. The idea for the letter comes to Mayo when his boss assigns him his next story, to cover the next H-bomb test. When Casey asks what he should do about 'my girlfriend, the Blue Gardenia', the editor replies, 'You've left dames before: write her a letter!' Mayo's column therefore is initially presented as a male strategy for avoiding female entanglement and emotional scenes, a brush-off letter, precisely like the one Norah received from Korea. As Norah reads the column, its filmic rendition recalls the reading of her birthday letter: we hear it in Mayo's voice-over, until Norah reaches the end, Mayo's signing off signature, 'yours, very earnestly, Casey Mayo'. This explicitly parallels Norah's bitter words as she crumpled the earlier letter, 'Yours, very sincerely, yours, very truly'. Casey has simply given her a third variation. As Janet Bergstrom observes, 'This closing, which earlier seemed like the ultimate proof of her fiancé's insensitivity, is here taken by Norah as a sign of just the opposite: Casey May's sincerity.'[32] As in the earlier scene, Norah speaks these words out loud; however, (for the first time in the film) she looks directly into the camera, indicating her acceptance of this message as addressed to her.

The parallels to the earlier letter undermine the 'earnest' sincerity of Mayo's offer for the viewer (there is no indication that Norah recognises the similarity; for her Mayo's letter initially seems to offer a way out of the alienation and anomie produced by the first one). That these parallels are intentional is indicated in the script, as Janet Bergstrom points out.[33] Before writing the letter Mayo supplied another parallel, the most disturbing one. Casey indicates to his photographer friend that if the Blue Gardenia comes to him he will turn her over to the cops 'with best wishes for her future'. Besides confessing the duplicity of his offer to help, this phrase is precisely the one used to close Norah's birthday letter, as the former fiancé bids Norah farewell, a phrase again, bitterly repeated by Norah. Mayo makes his motives explicit, 'I'm a newspaper man, I live on headlines. I want to be the guy to nail her.' Mayo's predatory intentions (including all the associations possible with 'nail her': martyrdom, capture and sexual conquest) align him not only with the former fiancé, but with Prebble and with the generally aggressive male discourse of the film. Thus Mayo's zest for the hunt is de-individualised; not only as a male trait but as the force behind his newspaper. Within the letter Mayo makes the institutional identity of his discourses explicit: 'I want to help you. When I say "I", I mean my newspaper and me.' The fairly conventional montage that bridges Mayo's typewriter tapping out the first line of his 'Letter to an Unknown Murderess' column to Norah reading it, shows the presses rolling and a variety of readers also absorbing the new edition. While Hollywood boiler plate, the sequence conveys a discourse mediated through public institutions and mass readership, the broadcast male discourse of the society, being received by a lonely frightened woman as a personal message of concern – a 50s Destiny-machine working smoothly.

Uncertainty about the senders and receivers of phone calls, letters and even kisses permeates this film. During Prebble's attempted seduction a half-passed out Norah responds to Prebble's 'Happy Birthday, Norah', with a passionate kiss and the question, 'Why did you have to write that letter?' The kiss and the question are obviously addressed to the now ex-boyfriend in Korea, but Prebble is happy to receive them, and uses her response as the opening wedge in his attempt to force her to have sex with him. Are people who they say they are? When Norah finally meets Mayo face-to-face, she claims not to be the Blue Gardenia or the girl who spoke to him on the phone, but merely a friend of the suspected murderer, and Mayo seems uncertain whether to believe her or not. The charade continues when Crystal shows up at the meeting arranged at the coffee shop the next day ('Three-forty, just in time for the Sunset Edition'), but then reveals to Casey that Norah, sitting in the next booth, is indeed the Blue Gardenia. Casey, now enamoured with Norah, is more surprised at this revelation than we might expect, and confesses to Norah he intended to turn her over to the police. With a Langian *déjà vu* of a repeated traumatic moment, a furious Norah gathers her room-mate, saying 'Come on, Crystal, I made another mistake!' However, the cops get her at the door. We see Norah being booked at the station, with a close-up of her fingers being inked and fingerprints taken. As in much of Lang, the final official establishment of identity comes as the sign of guilt and capture by the systems of the state. But the government record is not the final moment of identification. Norah is immediately greeted by newspaper photographers who call out to the cops, 'Come on, Mac, we've got deadlines to make!' and are then told, 'O.K. She's all yours.' Flashbulbs pop in Norah's face as she tries to shield her eyes from the glare with her ink-stained hands. Like Eddie Taylor, Norah Larkin has been captured and processed for public consumption. But, in contrast to Eddie's more impersonal plight, Norah's potential lover has played a role in her public exposure.

Casey Mayo will, however, undertake the further investigation that frees Norah from both legal charges and guilt feelings. But, in striking contrast to the psychoanalytical discourse of *Secret Beyond the Door*, although a scene Norah cannot remember stands at the centre of the mystery, there is no real attempt to re-awaken her memory. Her amnesia is accepted as a blank that cannot be filled; only another story can substitute for Norah's guilt and her lack of vision/memory. The investigation of Norah's lack of memory is blocked in several ways. When Casey is questioning her at the coffee shop as they share hamburgers, he seems to attempt something like Celia's jarring of Mark's memory through recreating a *mise-en-scène*. When Norah says the last thing the Blue Gardenia recalls is the Nat 'King' Cole record playing, Casey plugs some nickels in the jukebox and brings on the song. Norah looks at the coffee cup in front of her and remembers that Prebble gave the Blue Gardenia coffee 'but it only made her groggier' (because, as Lang shows in an almost subliminal shot, Prebble spiked it with liquor). But the memory goes no further, partly because Norah is maintaining the fiction that she is not the Blue Gardenia and therefore she cannot resurrect any new memories. Instead, the playing of the song refers back to Prebble's control of *mise-en-scène*. Lang shows the song's effect in the present with a cut to the waiter, as the song coming on causes him to eavesdrop about the meeting Mayo is arranging the next day with the Blue Gardenia. We learn later that he is planning to tip off the cops. Therefore, rather than opening up Norah's memories, the song evokes male plots which entrap her, one past and one future.

But Norah's memory remains a blank, primarily because there is nothing to be recovered. Her act of violence was as ineffectual as its portrayal was vague. She cannot produce the missing part of the puzzle because she doesn't have it, it takes place outside her consciousness (it isn't even clear if her awakening in Prebble's studio comes before or after the murder – nor does it make much difference). Female subjectivity in *The Blue Gardenia* does not make the journey undertaken in *Secret Beyond the Door* from obscurity and mystery to speaking out and analysing the situation, but remains a blank, an empty place, a syncope. What does this woman want, anyway?

But the merry-go-round of mis-attributed acts, the sorting out of the source of deeds, has not gone full circle yet. It is revealed, only after Norah has been arrested, that the eavesdropping coffee shop waiter, not Mayo, called the cops and turned Norah in. And, of course, the mystery can only be solved, and a happy ending produced, by the discovery that, in fact, Prebble's murder is not Norah's doing. The thin clue on which this plot reversal pivots involves a detail of Prebble's *mise-en-scène* for seduction, his careful selection of the proper mood music for each situation. Mayo and his photographer buddy are sitting in an airport when the *Liebestod* theme of Wagner's *Tristan and Isolde* comes on the soundtrack. Casey reacts strangely at first, looking around, and asks the (late Godardian) question: where is the music coming from? The photographer explains, 'it's canned – they can everything these days', as Lang cuts to a loudspeaker piping the music into the airport waiting room. Mayo recognises the theme as the record the cops said was playing when Prebble was killed. But Norah's last memory was of the 'Blue Gardenia' playing. The gap in the plot has finally opened, with a switch in soundtrack.

Pursuing the source of Prebble's Wagner record, Mayo convinces the police to visit the record store Prebbles frequented. The manager tells the sales girl in the back of the store, whom Lang shoots from the back as she holds an album with the title 'After

Dark', that the police want to talk to her. We are returned to the realm of things we can't see clearly and don't entirely know, as the woman slowly turns her face and we can recognise Prebble's desperate caller from earlier in the film, as the *Liebestod*, pre-sumably non-diegetically this time, comes on the soundtrack. She marches into the ladies' room, breaks a glass, and a second later a scream announces the discovery of her attempted suicide. From her hospital bed she narrates a flashback that fills in the lacuna: how she stopped in at Prebble's studio to demand he tell her if he were going to marry her; he tried to calm her down by playing Wagner, but when she saw the handkerchief Norah had dropped on the floor, she hit him with the poker, as the *Liebestod* swelled to a climax. We realise that Norah's whole misadventure was just a sideshow to someone's else's grand passion, complete with operatic accompaniment. Running away from her own drama of abandonment, she wandered blindly into some other tragedy, whose complete story we will never know.

In the hall of justice the three room-mates emerge to a barrage of photographers, as flashbulbs pop once more, but the women pose and are apparently delighted at this publicity. Norah rehearses a big sigh of relief for the camera. Crystal gives Casey their phone number again, he divests himself of his 'little black book', and the film ends with a return to the image of the freeway overpass. The traffic speeds on. The blaze of flashbulb photography, the fact that the happy ending will be chronicled in the next edition, doesn't erase the breach the film chronicles between the private dark and shadowy landscapes of personal passions, and public records and exposés apparently dedicated to tracking down and exposing elusive identities, but only in an abstract reified form. Whether a phone call will allow Casey and Norah Larkin to bridge a gap that has also become increasingly gendered remains an open question.

16

The Big Heat

Circuits of Corruption

> Being on the telephone will come to mean, therefore, that
> contact is never constant, nor the break clean.
> Avital Ronell, *The Telephone Book*[1]

The Blue Gardenia wades waist deep in the pre-fabricated wish-fulfilment environments of the 50s, almost as if it were a 90s retro parody: the Polynesian restaurant
which gives the film its title; Nat 'King' Cole crooning the similarly named theme
song in tones as smooth as velvet, decked out like a cabana boy; the 'little black
book' of alphabetised, untrammelled sexual favours accessible if you simply let
your fingers do the walking; the bachelor's pad with stereo and mirrored fireplace;
the frictionless, free-flowing freeway system. But like the best 50s American film-
makers, Lang does not celebrate this lush, comfort-designed, smooth ride, but
rather casts grit in its path, exposing the rough edges of the relations between the
sexes, the violence implicit in the new male culture, and the obvious lack of comfort

in the places where most people live and work, the crowded flat where the girls have a strict schedule for the use of the bathroom, or the high-pressured impersonality of both switchboard and newspaper office.

The Big Heat also moves through this contradictory environment whose smooth surfaces mask the fissure between the good life for the few and the cramped and hectic worlds of the mass of people: the gangster bar, The Retreat, brightly lit and hard-edged with the 'James Meehan Trio' playing, hardly the seedy locale of a 30s or 40s gangster film; Vince Stone's apartment with built-in bar, and modern furnishings; Lagana's mansion with an imposing portrait of his mother on the wall; but, also, the empty shell of a middle-class home; hotel rooms so anonymous it is hard to tell them apart; the chain-link fence and twisted metal of the automobile junkyard.

The Big Heat stands as Lang's finest American film of the 50s and one of the crowning films of his career. It completes a development towards a seemingly classical style, in the sense that the film appears to be constructed with a pure economy of storytelling in mind, with few of the experiments Lang tried in the 30s and 40s, with almost no image that stands out for its compositional beauty, no editing that seems to play tricks with traditional continuity, no overt directorial flourishes of any kind. But in many ways Lang's nearly telegraphic clarity of narrative technique leaves him time to develop the subterranean relations between images and sounds which have always been a part of his style, but which, especially since *House by the River*, have functioned on a powerful but almost subliminal level. Lang's style in the 50s began to resemble camouflage: the films strive to resemble the very environment they critique. Lang's classicism cloaks a distance and irony which penetrated to the cold rage for order that underlies the emotional expressivity of 50s culture.

Thus a tension between placid surface and hidden corruption structures *The Big Heat,* and the drama deals with a struggle between those forces which try to keep the lid on, and those which want to force the hidden violence out into the open. In most 50s films this melodramatic pattern of righteous violence overcoming evil repression is paralleled by an emotional drama of self-realisation and self-expression, usually represented by a love affair. Think of *On the Waterfront* (Kazan), *On Dangerous Ground* (Ray), *The Big Knife* (Aldrich), or even *Underworld USA* (Fuller). Although many things in the script of *The Big Heat* and its source novel by William P. McGivern point in this direction and remain operative in Lang's film, his directorial approach does not accent Detective Dave Bannion's emotional breakthrough. Instead, this drama of surface and depth focuses mainly on social structures and roles, the system of corrupt order and the violence it takes to expose it. *The Big Heat* stands as Lang's most powerful and complex exposé story, partly because of the ambiguity of the exposé's relation to Bannion's emotional life, and its unflinching unfolding of the breach between genders already sketched in *The Blue Gardenia*.

The opening few minutes of *The Big Heat* present a Liebnitzean monad of the whole film. As Colin McArthur points out, the film's major characters are all introduced (although the protagonist, Dave Bannion, only enters in the first shot of the second sequence),[2] the plot's central enigma is set in motion (will Tom Duncan's suicide note ever be delivered?), the tone of genre violence and the theme of cover-up indelibly sketched, and a geography of the interlocking spaces of power in the modern city laid out with the telephone system tracing the hierarchies of power. The breakdown into shots always follows the centre of narrative interest, and even more than in *The Blue Gardenia*, Lang uses the precise camera movements in and out which the small mobile camera mount known as the crab dolly (introduced in *The Blue Gardenia*) allows. Janet Bergstrom quotes a German newspaper article covering the shooting of *The Blue Gardenia* in which Lang describes his camera movement as 'the constant companion of the actor; it becomes a sharp observer of the events, capturing a drama more intensely as it draws quickly nearer when something decisive is done or said. ... The camera in motion, therefore, becomes an important and "living" participant in the film.'[3] These camera movements do not distract from the action, but they most certainly dissect and analyse it, an essential part of Lang's new classical style.

The film opens with a high-angle medium close-up of a desk top on which a gun rests; a hand enters the frame and picks up the revolver, then the camera pulls back and reveals a badge and an envelope addressed to the district attorney. We hear the revolver fire and the man's head falls onto the desk. Lang opens the film without an establishing shot, accenting the emblematic play of objects. The narrative economy of the sequence derives partly from its near abstraction, its almost inhuman presentation of an act of violence and self-destruction. Gun, badge and letter dominate this scene, the human figure is nearly eclipsed. Lang could not set up the inciting incident of the film, or its dominant stylistic concerns with greater clarity than in this single shot. Who is this man, what do these objects mean, where are we? All these questions are quickly cued by the dramatic opening to the film.

The second shot cuts back from the medium close-up of the collapsed suicide to reveal a location, a well-appointed domestic interior, dominated by a staircase, the desk in the foreground. The man's wife, still in her nightgown, comes downstairs, drawn by the noise. Lang cuts in to medium shot as she pauses on the landing, posed next to a large grandfather clock showing the time to be three o'clock. The camera tracks towards her husband's slumped-over body, as if presenting her point of view from the stairs, but then she enters the shot as if following the camera's lead, appearing as a dark silent silhouette against the brightly it desk. A somewhat low-angle medium close-up gives her delayed reaction shot, and we realise her silence was not

the product of shock; she observes the off screen scene coldly, her head turning as she surveys the desk. The following close-up, a carefully arranged composition of the significant objects – gun grasped by the dead man's hand, badge and addressed envelope – reveals it is the envelope that attracted her interest. Apparently unfazed by her husband's suicide, she reaches for the envelope as the camera pulls back to medium shot, opens it and reads the letter, expressing irritation. She crosses to the telephone. The sound of a passing car draws her attention to the window, and she closes the blinds before she lifts up the receiver and dials, asking to speak to Mike Lagana. After a pause, she says harshly, 'I know it's late, wake him up! Tell him it's Tom Duncan's widow.'

We cut to a muscular young man in a bathrobe standing before a middle-aged gangster lying in bed whom the next shot reveals swathed in satin sheets and silk pyjamas, his claw-like hand outstretched, telling him there's a call 'on the private line'. After repeating 'Widow?' Lagana takes the phone, tells her he appreciates her call, that they will certainly get together, and that now she should call the police. Handing the receiver back to the young man, who gives him a cigarette and lights it, Lagana tells him to call Vince Stone. The young man makes the call, then tells Lagana, 'His girl says he's playing cards.' Lagana takes the receiver and, as the camera moves in on him, explains, 'This is not a social call, Debbie. Tell Vince I want him right away.' We cut to hit man Vince Stone's apartment where no-one is asleep, as his girlfriend, Debbie, sprawled seductively on a divan, replies that she loves to call Vince to the phone for Lagana, she 'likes to see him jump'. She calls out to Vince, whom Lang shows playing cards in the other room with the commissioner of police, in a sing-song voice: 'Oh Vince, it's HIM', pantomiming an elaborate salaam. Vince leaps from his chair, runs into the living room of a fancy, modern, well-lit apartment, takes the phone and tells Debbie to see if anyone in the other room wants a drink and to shut the door. Debbie steps over the couch, complaining that she doesn't know about the politicians in the next room, but she's so bored she

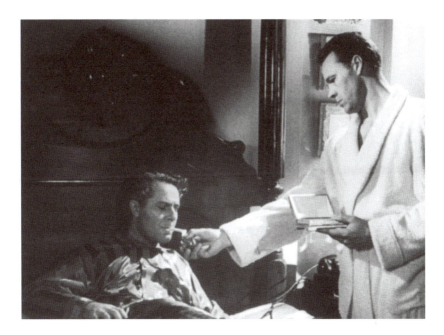

needs a drink, pausing in the doorway to admire herself in a mirror. Vince explains finally to Lagana, 'I didn't know it was the private line ringing or I would have answered myself.' He assures his boss he 'will see to it'.

In the first four minutes of the film, phone calls link three different levels of a corrupt society, emphasising the relay of information by having intermediaries first answer the phone and then call their superiors. The chain of voices relaying commands evokes a realm where 'private' lines mean dirty business, and the sexuality of underlings expresses their superior's power and their own subservience. Lang's view of the systematic nature of the modern arrangement of power recalls his earlier German films. A violent action, the suicide, unlooses a flurry of communication that traces the lines of command as the gangster and his minions scurry to control the damage. In effect this sequence combines elements of the opening of *Mabuse* and the police procedures of *M*, a communication between the levels of power which reveals systematic procedures as in *M*, absorbing an act of violence into a carefully managed design, as in *Mabuse*. Here, however, the police play poker with the gangsters and establish a path of corruption that snakes through the city on private lines, rather than discussing public policy over the phone.

This opening picks up the theme of the astray message present in Lang's film from the beginning of his career, the jamming of communication systems so that a message cannot be delivered to its addressee. The purpose of these opening phone calls is certainly to convey information (Bertha Duncan tells Lagana about her husband's suicide and his attempt to inform the district attorney of the bribery system he was involved in; Lagana contacts his hit man to arrange the pay-off which will keep Bertha Duncan from turning her husband's letter over to the district attorney). But the real purpose behind the calls is to block the suicide note's attempt at communication and confession. The letter of public confession becomes repressed as a new message system sets up a detour through the private lines.

It is precisely this blocking of communication that supplies the motive for the film's plot, which can only be resolved when, after Bertha Duncan's death, the letter finally surfaces. If the opening telephone calls successfully block the final message of a dead man, at least for most of the film, the tension caused by Detective Bannion's investigation can also be charted through a series of phone calls, all of which interrupt the seeming tranquillity of his family life. The first call comes during dinner from Tom Duncan's former girlfriend Lucy Chapman who claims there must be more to his death. After speaking to Bannion, Chapman is killed. When Bannion follows up the possible connection he is reprimanded by the chief of police who says he has been 'getting calls from above' complaining about Bannion's investigation. Bannion's visit to an underworld hang-out leads to the bartender immediately calling Lagana to inform him of Bannion's continued investigation. Bannion's wife receives a threatening and obscene phone call at home, and shortly afterward she is killed by a car bomb intended for him. Bannion tries to track down her killers through tracing phone calls to the mechanic who placed the bomb, and by placing calls to them at the underworld bar. In the last seconds of the film, after the gangsters have been defeated and Bannion has been returned to his job as detective, he immediately receives a phone call sending him out on another case.

The image of Vince Stone reassuring his boss over the phone that the suicide letter can be suppressed ends the first sequence of the film. Lang uses an overlap-dissolve to bring us into the second sequence and a visual shock to bridge the transition, transferring from the apparatus of hearing to devices of vision. Vince's image dissolves into a medium shot of a police photographer, his camera aimed below the frame. Vince's image has just faded out, when the huge flash of the camera pops and an optical effect bleeds the image to total whiteness for several frames. Lang's camera pulls back revealing Tom Duncan slumped over his desk and a long shot of the now bright living room, filled with cops. The camera then tracks to the right to reveal Dave Bannion, the hero of the film, looking sleepy and rumpled as a cop apologises to him for having to rouse him out of bed. A forensic cop enters the frame and explains it's 'a suicide, no question'. The camera pivots to the left as Bannion crosses to his partner, Burke, and affirms that no note was found. He moves towards the staircase in the background to go upstairs and speak to the widow.

As Gerard Leblanc and Brigitte Devismes argue in their thorough and insightful analysis of the film and its documents (original scenario, shooting script, Lang's sketches, studio memos, etc.), this scene shows Bannion's naive faith in the evidence immediately presented to his sight; the limits of Bannion's vision are reflected in this opening flash that briefly erases the image from the screen.[4] Like the flashes from the newspaper photographers in *The Blue Gardenia*, the camera represents the glare of a public seeing. Lang subtly indicates that this seeing is profoundly compromised because it photographs a false scene as a fact (the suppressing of the letter falsifying the *mise-en-scène* of Duncan's suicide), and literally with the flash which momentarily blinds the viewer. Further, as Leblanc and Devismes also point out, the overlap-dissolve briefly superimposes Vince Stone over the police photographer, so that it seems Stone snaps the picture. In *The Big Heat* Lang continues to use overlap-dissolves as a subliminal way to express central metaphors.

The following shot takes us to the bedroom of Bertha Duncan, seconds before Bannion knocks on her door. Lang immediately confronts us with another device of vision, a three-faced mirror before which Bertha sits at her vanity table. The doubling of her images does not hint at dreams, as in previous Lang films, but at duplicity and deception. Bertha is, as Lang noted in the margin of his script, 'arranging her face'.[5] She dabs her eyes with a cloth, apparently to supply the tears lacking as she confronted her husband's death. She hears Bannion's knock, and, as the camera pulls back, crosses to a chair, arranging her pose and her robe, and in a tremulous voice asks him to come in. As Lang's marginal note in the script emphasises, we see Bannion's entrance reflected in the mirror.[6] As the mirror was the place where Bertha prepared her illusion, Bannion enters the room under her power; he will only see what she wants him to see, his vision has been curtailed. Bertha sobs, struts across the room, explains her husband was in poor health, and Bannion, shot in close-up, seems moved and convinced by her performance. He leaves satisfied.

The first two sequences culminate in the newspaper insert that follows: a small article that explains Duncan's suicide was due to his health problems. The official story plasters over the corruption, the details of which we still don't know. The next shot shows Bannion reading the paper as the camera pulls back and reveals his modest living/dining room and his wife Katie (Jocelyn Brando, Marlon's sister who unfortunately always looks to me like her brother in drag) setting dinner on the table. The series of well-appointed interiors that opened the film – Duncan's, Lagana's, Stone's – contrast with this image of lower-middle-class felicity, a modest, calm stability founded on the fact that Detective Bannion has not looked too deeply or seen too far. Bannion maintains the sort of domestic tranquillity that the 50s saw as ideal, a home in an archetypal suburban development, by not only limiting his vision but drawing clearly defined lines between his family and scum or trash.

This dividing line moves in two directions. The first comes in complete contrast to both his home life and the performance of the grieving widow he so admired in

Bertha Duncan's bedroom, as he responds to his first phone call and meets bar girl Lucy Chapman at the underworld hang-out, a brightly lit, modernly designed nightclub called The Retreat.[7] Chapman begins by denying the truth of the newspaper account. She continues to deconstruct other elements of the story as Bannion has understood it, especially the ideal nature of the Duncans' marriage which Bertha had described, indicating she and Duncan were lovers and he was about to divorce his wife and marry her. Bannion refuses to believe her. He leaves Lucy contemptuously as she questions the sanctity of marriage and class differences ('the only difference between me and Bertha Duncan is that I work at being a B-girl, and she has a wedding ring and a marriage certificate!'), accusing her of planning blackmail, and telling her she could talk herself into a lot of trouble. Which she does.

The drawing of this line, below him, with contempt for the lifestyle of a B-girl who compares herself to a cop's widow, causes Bannion no immediate problems. But his anger soon afterward becomes directed at the crime boss Lagana, following the second phone call to his house (this time an anonymous caller who uses obscene language when his wife answers the phone). This call leads directly to the murder of Bannion's wife, his resignation from the police force and his decision to shake up the system he was originally willing to dwell within.

If the opening glimpse of Lagana's bedroom radiates illicit luxury, the grandeur of an upper-class lifestyle greets Bannion as he pulls up to Lagana's mansion. Bannion is stopped on his way into the house by a beat cop, one of ten cops a day assigned to protect Lagana and his family. Bannion refuses to be stopped by the butler as he passes through the pillared portico into the Lagana mansion. As he waits in the hallway, a dance party for Lagana's teenage daughter is in full swing behind him, with a live band and servants patrolling with drinks on silver trays. Lagana ushers him into his library where a framed portrait of the other end of the Lagana lineage, his recently deceased mother, beams down on their discussion.

When Bannion begins to question Lagana about Lucy Chapman's murder the gangster objects strenuously, 'I have an office for that sort of thing. This is my home and I don't like dirt tracked into it.' Bannion responds with what can only be called an argument about class, contrasting his home with Lagana's, 'We don't talk about those things in this house, do we? No, it's too elegant, too respectable. Nice kids – party – picture of Mama up there on the wall. No, it's no place for a stinking cop! … I'm going to tell you something. You know you couldn't plant enough flowers around here to kill the smell. Cops have homes too, only sometimes there isn't enough money to pay the rent, because a cop gets hounded off the force by your thievin' cockroaches for trying to do an honest job. What's the matter, you think I live, under a rock or something? Your creeps have no compunction about phoning my house!'

The genre logic of this scene, carefully crafted in Sydney Boehm's screenplay, sets up the dynamics of the plot and of Bannion's character. Bannion now emerges as an archetypal 50s action hero who reaches the point where he can no longer repress his anger. In this scene Bannion, so far presented as an honest, but none-too-perceptive, cop and loving family man, breaks protocol and confronts the gangster boss, venting anger rather than searching for information, following a 50s (and to some extent late 40s) belief that anger equals authenticity. Crucially, his anger takes physical form when he punches out Lagana's bodyguard. The hero delivers both emotional rhetoric and a devastating right to the chin.

The tension Bannion's transformation sets up – not only with his job and his superiors, but with his domestic tranquillity – drives the film from this point on. Lucy Chapman and the bar represented the antithesis of his suburban home and family: as she says, no wedding ring, no marriage certificate, and, as the bartender says after she is murdered, 'not much more than a suitcase full of nothing between [her] and the gutter'. Lagana, on the other hand, represents family and home, only grown to gargantuan proportions, a man whose success can give his family everything they want and who, like Bannion, wants to protect the sanctity of his home from the dirt that gets tracked in. Like so many 50s heroes, Bannion becomes allied with the outcasts of society, the marginal and abject, in his fight against Lagana. He will have to invade the imposing domestic spaces shown in the film's first sequence, Bertha Duncan's house, Lagana's mansion, Vince Stone's apartment, in order to bring down the 'big heat' – the pressure which will reveal the stink behind the flowers. In doing so he also destroys his own domestic space, and releases a critique of the dominant culture whose destructive force is difficult to get back into the bottle.

The Construction of Authority

> … the social gest[us] is the gest[us] relevant to society, the gest[us] that allows conclusions to be drawn about the social circumstances.
>
> Bertolt Brecht, 'On Gestic Music'[8]

The French publisher Armand Colin has done film studies a great service by publishing a thorough study of *The Big Heat*, *Le Double scénario chez Fritz Lang* including shooting script, the original scenario, and Lang's floor plan diagrams of the sets outlining camera position, and actors' movement, along with a careful comparison to the film as it exists, done by Gerard Leblanc and Brigitte Devismes. Documents like these reveal the production process of *The Big Heat*, supplying an account of the various forces which entered into its creation. A line-by-line comparison between the original scenario by Sydney Boehm, finished before Lang was hired to direct, and the final shooting script (including many notes in Lang's handwriting) provides a way of determining Lang's contribution to this process through the changes he made. Careful examination of the diagrams Lang devised for camera set-ups and the blocking of action, as well as the final film, allows a thorough description and analysis of Lang's *mise-en-scène*, the way in which he visualised and interpreted the script.[9]

Colin McArthur argues in his BFI monograph on *The Big Heat* that this sort of investigation of the production process of films, 'solid, empirical historical work', is precisely what *auteur* studies need to overcome their limitations.[10] The materials exist to do this thoroughly for nearly all of Lang's films (especially the American ones) and I hope that my critical monograph will encourage this undertaking. Increasingly sophisticated views of artistic texts have realised that no text exists in isolation. A discussion of process of production and reception history opens the textual system to the dynamics of social history. I have included in my analysis some discussion of the production context and critical reception. However, this monograph primarily deals with the images and sounds coming from the screen. I avoid hermetically sealing these texts from the context in which they are produced and understood. But I do not claim to offer a full history of either their production or reception, which would take a number of tomes larger than this one. Neither production nor reception can be banished from the way a film affects us, nor can they be excluded from each other (producers envision the process of reception and hope to control it; critics understand films on the basis of cues given by producers as to genre and style). But I would like to emphasise that empirically founded studies of production and reception still require organising and theoretical assumptions, still demand an act of reading and interpretation.

A careful consideration of the production history of a film, especially a Hollywood film, seems to work against a critical approach that sees the director as the enunciator of the film, what McArthur calls the 'Romantic notion of the director as "onlie begetter"'.[11] As I have tried to indicate both in my introduction and through my readings, the concept of Lang as enunciator of his films is a conflictual and not a biological one, in which Lang interacts with both collaborators and larger cultural forms such as genre, period style and ideology. In other words, I would maintain that the director as enunciator need not be thought of as a Judaeo-Christian creator *ex nihilo*, but as an Aristotelian demi-urge who works with pre-existent material, and the nature of that material will always function as one of the causes of the creation. But while this helps explain some of the empirical aspects of Lang as director, working with material he is given and transforming it (or not), I would like to emphasise again the lesson Lang teaches us about enunciation. Not only is it an agonistic process involving a struggle, but also a hubristic one, in which any claim to total authorship invites its own destruction. The Fritz Lang that these films deliver to us, when viewed as an aggregate and carefully read, is a creature formed by the texts and their reading, as much as a creator; a signature forged through a conversation which seeks to bridge a historical gap between director and critic.

The original scenario for *The Big Heat*, written before Lang was hired, already contained the series of phone calls that opens the film. The author of the device is therefore Sydney Boehm, rather than Lang. But once Lang filmed the sequence, it became part of the Lang corpus and its significance in that context is different than it would be in the corpus of another director. Similarly, Leblanc and Devismes point out that the filming of Tom Duncan's opening suicide was discussed by producer Robert Arthur in a memo to Lang after Jeff Shurlock advised him that a suicide in full view of the camera, such as Boehm's original scenario described, would be considered too violent for the Production Code Administration. Filming it as an off screen action would be a preferable approach. Leblanc and Devismes call this section of their analysis, 'When the producer directs'.[12] The document clearly shows the sort of palimpsest a Hollywood film becomes, with suggestions, contributions and pressures exerted from a number of sources, and one could title it just as well, 'when the censor directs', or, given McArthur's further contextualisation of this concern in terms of contemporary complaints from foreign governments about the increased violence in American films,[13] 'when international politics direct' or even 'when economics direct'. Reminding viewers that no-one writes in a vacuum and that cinema, as a major economic investment, is always subject to a host of pressures is important. But the term 'director' becomes silly as we move in this direction.

Every film is a palimpsest and the film historian must unravel its contributing threads. But the best such production history that I have encountered, Peter Baxter's study of *Blonde Venus*, *Just Watch: Sternberg, Paramount and America* reveals that, after the history of the diverse competing forces that contribute to the palimpsest have been sorted out, there remains the work itself, which takes on a significance of it own. As Baxter says of his study:

> It conceives of a text as on the one hand a discrete, symbolic object, exhibiting its own coherence – material, formal and semantic – along with its own internal contradictions, and on the other as an event in the discursive process of mass entertainment, itself a primary constituent of American social being in the twentieth century.[14]

Thus *Blonde Venus* as it exists is, in my opinion, a much more interesting text than any of its possible versions represented by earlier scripts. Paradoxically (but only if taken literally; logically, if we bear in mind the complex dialectical and historical process of constructing an author), *Blonde Venus*, with all the different forces contributing to it, stands as a more revealing and complex Sternberg film, than his original treatment would seem to promise. This is not necessarily true, of course (I think Lang's treatment of *You and Me* may have been a better film if realised as he originally envisioned it). And it is partly true only because we are considering an actual film, fully realised in sound and images rather than a sparse treatment. But only a naive understanding of authorship would claim that only complete control within a sort of social vacuum yields an authorial text, or, conversely, that a complex network of collaborators and social pressures automatically rules out authorship.

With Lang, of course, the issue of control is to some extent empirically ascertainable, and his struggle to maintain it plays a key role in the dialectic of his authorship. Material is transformed critically by bringing it into the orbit of Lang's corpus, as the telephone calls in the opening of *The Big Heat* demonstrate. This does not deny other's (such as Boehm's) contributions, but it does define their significance within a critical reading of Lang's corpus. The filming of the opening suicide, however, raises a different sort of question when put in the context of Lang's career. In *Metropolis*, within the sequence where the false Maria drives the upper-class young men of Metropolis crazy (cut from the American release print, but replaced in the Munich restoration and the Moroder release version), Lang films a suicide in almost the exact same way, in terms of off screen space. Coincidence? Possibly. But in fact, Arthur's memo to Lang after summarising his conversation with Shurlock, actually states, 'therefore in my opinion we should film the suicide as *we have discussed*' (my emphasis).[15] In other words, there is no reason not to assume that Lang himself suggested the framing as a way to deal with the problem of graphic violence, as he had solved it before.

The examination of Lang's diagrams for the actual shooting and staging of scenes offers an analytical view of his process, indicating what he held to be at stake in his control of the small details of action and angle of view, precisely those areas of film-making over which he exerted what seemed to many of his collaborators (some cinematographers and many actors) an obsessional and tyrannical control. This can be shown in the sequence that follows Bannion's second visit to Bertha Duncan, after his conversation with Lucy Chapman. In spite of his contemptuous treatment of Chapman, one fact – the Duncans' vacation home at Lakeside, another sign of upper-class luxury – has raised Bannion's suspicions. After his return trip to the Duncan house, Bannion is called into the office of his immediate superior, Lieutenant Wilks. Lang's diagram of the scene plots four different camera angles, scene and the camera movements which are used in this eight shot scene. In addition, it marks out the pathway that Wilks will take walking around his desk as he speaks to Bannion who remains seated throughout the scene. A smaller sketch of this movement is also drawn in the margin of the shooting script, although Leblanc and Devismes point out both diagrams somewhat simplify Wilks' actual path.[16]

Devismes and Leblanc begin their analysis of this scene with the observation that Lang avoids the more conventional shot/reverse shot approach that might be chosen for this encounter between Bannion and his superior, in which Wilks will dress down Bannion for continuing to investigate Duncan's suicide.[17] Lang uses four camera positions: a wide two shot of the office showing both Bannion and Wilks (a shot which moves around a bit, drawing closer at first, and circling the action in the latter part of the scene); a medium close-up of Bannion; a three-quarter shot of Wilks; and then a final two shot filmed from behind Wilks. However, the claim that Lang avoids a shot/reverse shot pattern does not really hold up under close examination (the authors seem to be labouring under the misconception that shot/reverse shot always involves point of view shots, which is only one – less frequent – possibility). The four camera positions represent two pairs of reverse angles, as the cut from Bannion sitting to Wilks standing makes clear, a cut which is, contrary to Leblanc and Devismes' claim that the characters do not look at each other, based on an exchange of glances. The final shot, taken from the fourth position, reverses the angle of the preceding two shot, which has moved from an initial view perpendicular to the back wall, to an angled view of the wall with a window behind Wilks' desk. Presumably what Leblanc and Devismes mean is that we do not have a succession of similarly framed alternations between medium close-ups of Wilks seated at his desk and Bannion across from him, edited with the give and take of the dialogue, which would be an extremely static way of shooting the scene, probably more like television coverage than most film-making in the 50s.

Lang's approach is not that unusual, but nonetheless expressive. The decision to make Wilks and Bannion appear in different-sized framings reflects the common Hollywood practice of stressing one character within a scene (often, as here, the protagonist and most sympathetic character, but sometimes simply the most forceful) by giving him or her a closer framing (what cinematographer Gordon Willis calls 'relative screen size'). Thus Bannion gets two medium close-ups in this scene, while the closest we get to the more ambiguous Wilks is one three-quarter shot. Lang's more original and complex contribution to the scene comes with the actual blocking, Wilks' nearly constant movement, circling around his desk. Leblanc and Devismes point out that this movement encircles Bannion, as if Wilks were laying a trap for him, and that he moves from an apparently friendly confidence at the beginning of the scene to clear opposition.[18]

Wilks is certainly dancing around Bannion and the crux of this meeting – that he is ordering Bannion to stop his investigation; and Lang's choreography expresses this. But there is more here. First off, as McArthur points out, Wilks is an oddly composite character in the film, a literal condensation of two polar characters in McGivern's original novel, Inspector Cranston, 'the single unblemished figure in the upper echelons of the police department' and the Wilks of the novel, who is 'totally corrupt'. The film's Wilks is 'a highly ambiguous figure, semi-corrupt although ultimately straight'.[19] Lang brilliantly (and in a manner I am tempted to call Brechtian) constructs the ambiguity of this character before us, not through an exploration of an ambivalent interior or tension-ridden psychology, but in terms of exterior social behaviour.

In the opening of the scene Wilks, jacket off, shirt sleeves rolled up, is washing his hands. Although a Pontius Pilate reference may be operating here,[20] Lang primarily presents this as an everyday action, as he had similarly shown Lohmann washing up in his office in *M* (the design of the lavatories in the two films even seems similar). As Devismes and Leblanc point out, in the course of the scene the conversation between Wilks and Bannion moves from a friendly intimacy to a hierarchical confrontation. But rather than deception, it seems to me the change is based on two factors: first, Bannion's refusal to take the 'friendly' warning to lay off (i.e. his transformation from blinkered cop to action hero), and, second, Wilks' transition within the scene from a personal self to an official self. It is precisely this switch which Lang stages before our eyes and accents through his choreographing of Wilks. Like Bertha Duncan preparing her face in the mirror, only less metaphorically, Wilks prepares himself officially to order Bannion to stop. In his rolled-up shirtsleeves Wilks tells Bannion he has been getting calls from 'upstairs' about Bannion's second visit to Bertha Duncan. Bannion asks if she complained and Wilks responds, 'someone did'. At the beginning of the conversation Wilks attributes the pressure and the question to someone else. But as he turns towards Bannion in the three-quarter shot, buttoning his sleeves, he begins to place himself within the system he just differentiated himself from: 'I'm the one who has to explain, you don't keep an office like this very long, stepping on corns.' Lang's marginal notes at this point indicate he considered having Wilks at the mirror examining himself, making the comparison to Bertha Duncan explicit, but apparently decided not to. The action of buttoning the sleeves is subtler, and more expressive of Wilks donning his public persona, which is not a simple deception. Wilks now crosses behind his desk and takes his jacket off a hanger. He tells Bannion he is simply asking him, 'not even ordering', to stop bothering Mrs. Duncan. As Wilks puts on his jacket, Bannion indicates that Lucy Chapman's murder may be connected to Duncan's suicide. Wilks rounds the table, leans against it as he listens to Bannion, then circles him to the other end of the desk, tapping him on the shoulder, and advising him that Chapman's murder is outside their jurisdiction. He now rounds the desk and, for the first time, sits behind it – now fully and properly dressed – across from Bannion as he tells Bannion again to stop pestering Mrs. Duncan. Lang cuts to the angle from behind Wilks as Bannion rises and asks 'You still asking me?' The reverse angle shows Wilks

fully ensconced in the position of authority behind his desk as he says, 'No more. I'm telling.' As Bannion leaves the office in angry silence, Lang returns to the shot from behind Wilks' back. Progressively, his donning the suit and assuming his position behind the desk has allowed him to identify with, rather than differentiate himself from, 'the calls from upstairs'. Now his face is removed from us altogether. Lang portrays the conflict in this character in an exterior manner through social *gestus*. Nothing in the scene draws attention to this process, except, perhaps, the things Lang avoids, such as Hitchcockian close-ups making Wilks' drama into a psychological one, or any moralistic denunciation of his hypocrisy. More important than condemning it, Lang shows us how an official takes on the persona of his job. There may be no better example of Lang's termite approach, observing the crucial 50s social tension between self and public presentation.

While the theme of *The Big Heat*, the exposure of hidden corruption, corresponds to the basic logic of melodrama as Peter Brooks finds it in the works of Balzac – the exposure of signs of evil and the restoration of the signs of virtue through the exertion of pressure or violence,[21] Lang's dramaturgy avoids the methods of melodramatic portrayal. This is why I find Leblanc and Devismes' more melodramatic reading of Wilks' circling movement as the laying of a trap, inadequate. Evil has no single representative in this film, and overt actions like Bannion barging into Lagana's mansion yield nothing but trouble. The image of the phone system persists throughout the film to express the almost incorporeal spread of corruption through the city. The dissolve from Bertha Duncan watching Bannion leave from her window after he has questioned her about Lucy Chapman to a police office teletype printing out the discovery of Lucy's body on a county highway, not only expresses a cause and effect relation (Bertha obviously phones Lagana to let them know Lucy is making trouble), but also a mechanical impersonality and displacement of violent action into the circuits of communication, a Langian reduction of a character to information. The systematic nature of the mob's control of the city makes it a perfect example of the modern Destiny-machine. The interlocking nature of this pervasive corruption is also imaged in Bannion's second meeting with Wilks following his invasion of Lagana's home. As Leblanc and Devismes point out, this scene begins with another significant overlap-dissolve – from the close-up of Lagana which ends the previous scene to Wilks already in the process of chewing out Bannion for his visit to Lagana. Wilks speaks, but Lagana has been imprinted over the scene; Wilks only mouths Lagana's words, responding again to what he calls 'the squeeze from upstairs'.

When a mob car bomb intended for Bannion blows up his wife Katie instead, Bannion's meeting with Police Commissioner Higgins (with Wilks in attendance) shows him moving up the echelons of corruption. Once again the conversation centres on phone calls, as Bannion cuts through Higgins' hypocritical condolences for his wife's death and plans for a phony investigation of her murder, by telling Wilks to 'trot on down to your office and wait for him [Higgins] to call your orders. Oh, he'll phone you, just as soon as he gets his orders from Mike Lagana.' This infuriates Higgins and makes him demand Bannion's suspension, to which Bannion responds by throwing his police badge onto Higgins' desk 'permanently'. But when Higgins asks for his gun as well, Bannion responds that the gun is his, bought and paid for. With this recurring 50s expression of disgust for corrupt systems (think of Cooper throwing his sheriff's badge in the dirt at the end of *High Noon*), Bannion asserts the sort of independence and individuality which Lang's films never cease questioning. In a corrupt city dominated by a system that operates as a Destiny-machine, what effect can Bannion's personal revenge actually have?

Rogue Cop

> 'This light guided me. More surely than the light of noon-
> day. To the place where he (well, I knew who!) was awaiting
> me – a place where none appeared' […] 'To a place where
> none appeared', Bannion repeated. 'Maybe there wasn't
> anyone there, Father. Maybe there was never anyone waiting
> for us after the darkness of the night. That's a rather comical
> idea, don't you think?'
>
> William P. McGivern, *The Big Heat*[22]

Bannion's resignation from the police force is followed by the emptying out of his former home. Lang shows this house in the process of being stripped bare, shot from a slightly high angle which captures its stark, almost geometrical, emptiness. If

the scenes of Bannion's earlier domestic bliss strike some critics as unconvincing, [23] these images reveal the emptiness that (at least potentially) underlay that tranquillity, exemplifying Lang's x-ray vision, seeing through to the emptiness at the heart of things, death in life. The images, especially Bannion's point of view shot glancing towards the kitchen before he goes out the door, recall Joe's horror when he returns to his empty apartment towards the end of *Fury* and whimpers, 'Katherine, don't leave me.' Katie Bannion has left for ever, as Lang put it, 'blown to smithereens.'[24] Lang uncovers the hollow core of the dream of the suburban home, the centre of 50s ideology.

Lang films in the 50s put homes in an uncertain light. Mae Doyle returns home at the opening of *Clash by Night*, and when she is welcomed back, she responds (in one of Hayes' lines worthy of Odets), 'Home is where you go when you run out of places.' When Casey Mayo asks Norah Larkin if she is an LA girl, she responds automatically, 'No, I live in Los Angeles, but it's not my home', a comment her domestic life would certainly seem to affirm. In *Moonfleet,* young John Mohune returns to his family estate to find it overgrown and partly in ruins, and in *Human Desire* Jeff admits lots of soldiers in Korea were happy to get away from home. Frieda Grafe exaggerates when she claims that Lang does not portray houses in which people dwell, but rather the imposing facades of public buildings,[25] since the American films particularly are filled with homes; but, in fact, these homes (from the social trilogy on) are always precarious, threatened with emptiness, houses from which one is turned out, more often than sheltered within.

But if Bannion's home life is now effaced, the memory of it plays a structuring role for his character throughout the rest of the film. He undertakes a work of mourning, as well as revenge, for his dead wife and the 50s ideal she represented. Bannion's ties to the realm of the dead differentiate him from Lang's hubristic enunciator characters. While Bannion does take the law into his own hands, he displays little of the egotism of Lang's master criminals, or even his criminal artists. Bannion reacts mechanically, a function of the Destiny-machine rather than its master. His attempt to identify one of his wife's killers by having his brother-in-law phone The Retreat at 9:30 exactly and ask for the name he has been given (a detail Lang added to the script),[26] shows his desire to synchronise the phone with the clock and use the rationality of the system as part of his methodical investigation. But there is no scene that shows an emotional passion beneath this methodical behaviour. Bannion's ego and his desire (other than for revenge) seem to have perished with his home life. Even his obsession is remarkably unemotional and inexpressive. He in many ways resembles a dead man walking, and perhaps recalls Kriemhild more than any other Lang character.

The same question persists in this film that occurs in all of Lang's films involving mourning: is the one left alive capable of working through the mourning process and realising ultimately that they are, in fact, still alive? Or will they become encumbered with death and slip into melancholia, identifying more with the dead than with the living? This question, so vital to Lang in his works in Weimar Germany, surfaces with a new intensity in 50s America. Bannion's abandonment of his previous life creates a deep fissure in his character as he moves into an anonymous world of hotel rooms and nightclubs, the world of Lucy Chapman, rather than Katie Bannion. (Debbie Marsh will comment sarcastically when she enters Bannion's hotel room, 'Hey, I like this – early nothing!') But unlike a 40s private eye, Bannion does not really belong to this world, and this creates the essential tension between normality and deviance that structures so many 50s films.

In the 40s, the *film noir* most often centred on the private eye, rather than the G-man who had dominated the final films of the 30s gangster cycle. In the core films of the *noir* series, the private eye often gave in to the seductions of a femme fatale, as in *Out of the Past*, creating a scenario of mutual betrayal, fallen hero and no-good woman. The 50s *film noir* detective more frequently is a member of the police force, a public employee maintaining law and order, rather than a self-employed go-between sorting out sordid affairs behind the cops' backs. But in the strongest 50s *film noirs* the cop hero generates tension within the police force. He chaffs against police procedure and carries out his own personal quest for justice or revenge, often becoming a 'rogue cop' (the title of another McGivern novel, also made into a film soon after *The Big Heat* and showing many similarities in theme and character – and demonstrating the difference a director makes), like Bannion, operating outside the police.

This divided hero, representing law and order but literally an outlaw, appears in some of the strongest films of the 50s, including *The Big Heat*'s *doppelgänger* Joseph H. Lewis' *The Big Combo*, scripted by Philip Yordan and photographed in the darkest shades of *noir* by John Alton (and the figure also appears in the 'last' *film noir*, Welles' *Touch of Evil*).[27] By operating outside the law, the rogue cop affirms an ideal justice untrammelled by official corruption or incompetence, but he also risks becoming indistinguishable from the gangsters he fights (a line whose equivalent could be found in most films in the series is Debbie's caution to Bannion that if he murdered Bertha Duncan there wouldn't be much difference between him and Vince Stone). Thus the plot must resolve the cop's quest not only by defeating the gangster, but with a renunciation of violence by the cop (the climactic scenes of both *The Big Heat* and *The Big Combo* end with the gangster begging the cop to kill them, and the cop refusing). Further, while the femmes fatales in 40s *film noir* usually end up dead with nothing mitigating their own self-description, 'I'm no good' (other than the beauty of the passion they display), the rogue cop films are obsessed with redeeming a woman's virtue, often in the form of rescuing her from a romantic entanglement with the gangster (a plot device in both *Rogue Cop* and *The Big Combo*, as well as *The Big Heat*).

The image of Bannion closing the door on his shattered dream of an all-American home, dissolves to the antithesis of that dream, Debbie Marsh, singing to herself and dancing a solitary rumba as she shakes a martini in the bar of Vince Stone's apartment. While the moral contrast is evident – the hedonistic mistress of a gangster in a home bar replacing the wistful look at the now empty domestic kitchen – Lang does not stress the judgemental overtones. Instead, after these images of emptiness and death, Debbie's energy brings the film back to life. Her vitality stimulates the rest of the film, as her death will bring it to an end. Debbie, like a small number of Lang heroines (Sonja in *Spies*, Jenny in *Man Hunt*), represents Lang's most sympathetic view of women, women allowed to be both sexual and tender, partly because they exist outside the realm of matrimony.

Debbie dwells in an environment of hedonistic narcissism. She repeatedly stops and examines herself in the many mirrors around Vince's apartment. Even in Bannion's 'early nothing' hotel room she immediately gravitates to the mirror. Vince describes her 'career' as, 'six days a week she shops, on the seventh she rests'. Or, as she herself describes her 'expensive fun' to Bannion: 'clothes, travel, expensive excitement', summing it all up with the statement, 'I've been rich and I've been poor – *believe me* rich is better.' But beneath the obvious trappings of luxury, what is most striking about Debbie is not only her playful liveliness, but her perceptive sarcasm. It is unclear if Vince even realises she is needling him when she says she has a new perfume which repels men and attracts mosquitoes, or burlesques his subservience to Lagana. She is even willing to needle Lagana himself, although he misses it entirely.

Debbie's life also bores her. Her spontaneity and interest in defying authority combines with her boredom to make her respond in a surprising manner when Bannion kicks Stone out of The Retreat after he burns a bar-girl's hand with his cigarette for picking up a pair of dice too quickly. After Stone's goon frightens off a college boy who objects to Vince's action, Bannion intervenes and calls the goon 'a thief'. Lang cuts immediately to Debbie who reacts with curiosity, and continues to watch this confrontation closely, especially when Bannion stares down Stone and tells him to leave 'while he can still walk'. Debbie offers to buy Bannion a drink, an action which can only be seen as an appreciation of his defying her lover. Bannion refuses the drink, saying he would choke on 'Vince Stone's money'. Debbie's dominant reaction to Bannion seems to be curiosity, a curiosity that soon takes a sexual form when she catches up with him outside, takes his sleeve and suggests going back to his hotel room, shrugging off his insults. In the room Debbie deposits herself on the bed almost immediately and tells Bannion she is there to do 'research'. Her cleverness and sarcasm allow her to brush off Bannion's continued insults.

Colin McArthur has claimed that the story arc of *The Big Heat* follows Bannion's alienation from humanity and his gradual reintegration into the community.[28] Much of 50s American action cinema (and one might claim much of American cinema throughout its history) tells some variation of this story. McGivern's novel, particularly through its strong Catholic subtext and references to St. John of the Cross fashions this action as a sort of redemption, and presents Bannion as going through a successful mourning, as the penultimate lines of the novel indicate, 'Something had ended this morning he knew. Now he was starting over, not with hatred, but only sadness.'[29] McArthur claims that, 'in both film and novel Bannion's rehumanisation is tracked through his relationship with Debby Ward (Debbie Marsh in the film)'.[30] This story can be found (and tracked) in the film, and would seem to be present in the original scenario. But I feel that Lang does not truly invest in this tale of redemption and reintegration into the community, and in fact, if anything, undermines and questions it. One can certainly claim a sort of moral awakening for Debbie, but at the price of disfiguration and ultimately death. Lang's film savours the bitterness of this exchange and instead of sketching a redeeming, even if unconsummated, love affair at the centre of his film, tells the much less conventional story of a love affair that does not (cannot) happen, because the hero remains in love with a dead woman, and, through her, with death itself.

Lang dissolves from a shot of Lagana on Stone's terrace overlooking the city at night, an archetypal genre image of the gangster standing before the city he dominates ('the city is yours' sign which beams down on the gangsters in *Underworld* and *Scarface*) to Bannion beginning his investigation in an automobile junkyard. The classical gangster film of the 30s was arranged on a vertical axis, charting the rise and fall of the little Caesar or public enemy. But Bannion, like many of Lang's heroes, plumbs the depths, moving down not only the social scale but into realms that embody death and decay, such as this automobile graveyard with its grotesque denizens, the huge Aitkins guzzling Coca-Cola and his crippled book-keeper, Selma Parker. But as in classical myth, it is from these depths that Bannion is granted aid, as if the dead were more audible in these desolate surroundings. Bannion must shake up the corrupt city from its abject foundations.

The 'big heat' refers to the pressure that will finally descend on the corrupt city and purify it. Bannion evokes it only once, as he makes his final visit to Bertha Duncan's house, the site of his original duping and blindness, now able to see the woman and her house for what it is. This is a scene that Lang added to Boehm's original scenario, drawing on a scene in McGivern's novel, but changing it significantly, as well.[31] He first notes that nothing in the house has changed yet, meaning that Bertha has not yet begun to live the high life her blackmail of Lagana will bankroll, but also that it is his vision of the house that has transformed; he now sees the exploitation on which the Duncan household is founded (and, in fact, Mrs. Duncan has added a pearl necklace to her ensemble). Bannion looks at Duncan with the contempt he previously held for Lucy Chapman, whose murder Bertha exults over, and adds that it was her husband's love affair with Lucy that made him feel uncomfortable about being paid off by Lagana. The complete moral blindness of Bannion earlier in the film is now exposed. When Bannion accuses Bertha of protecting Lagana 'for the sake of a soft plush life', she folds her arms in satisfaction and says, 'The coming years are going to be just fine, Mr. Bannion.' In frustration, Bannion not only threatens Duncan, but puts his hands around her throat with intentions of murder, intoning: 'With you gone the big heat falls, the big heat for Lagana, for Stone and for all the rest of the lice.' Bannion no longer seeks simple revenge, but a transformation of the city. His scope and imagery is apocalyptic. Resembling Kriemhild, he dreams of a world scorched and levelled by the fire of justice.

As I mentioned, although deriving from McGivern's novel, Bannion's visit to Duncan has been changed significantly.[32] As part of McGivern's narrative of Bannion's gradual conversion away from hate and violence, it is Bannion's conscience that stops him from killing Duncan: 'Bannion's arm came down slowly until the muzzle of the gun pointed at the floor. "I don't have the right to kill you", he said in a low, raging voice.'[33] In Lang's film it is only the arrival of a pair of cops (summoned by another phone call relay – first Bertha Duncan to Lagana, then Lagana to the cops) that makes Bannion take his hands off Bertha's throat. Therefore, if Lang were developing Bannion's gradual rehumanisation, he deliberately avoids a major signpost of his moral ascent.

McArthur's main argument for the centrality of the reintegration and rehumanisation of Bannion comes from his relation to other characters, the number of people who come forth to aid him in his quest for justice: the crippled Selma Parker in the automobile junkyard; the brother-in-law's army buddies; his partner Burke, and, towards the end, Lieutenant Wilks; and, most crucially, Debbie Marsh. Again there is no question that both the novel and the original scenario are organised around this archetypal American plot of the reintegration of a loner hero (who traditionally at some point declares he doesn't need anybody) into a broader community through mutual aid and a love affair (think of *Rio Bravo* or *Underworld USA*). In the film, as Bannion is leaving his empty house, his partner Burke articulates the democratic ideology behind this story line explicitly, telling Bannion: 'You're on a hate binge. You've decided people are all scared rabbits and you spit on them … . No man's an island, Dave. You can't set yourself against the world and get away with it.' In the original scenario similar advice is given Bannion by the priest, Father Masterson, who has been cut from the film, with Bannion responding, 'I don't need anyone, not you, not the department, no-one!'[34]

But if the explicit verbal message of the script cannot be denied (and certainly it forms one layer of the palimpsest of the film), Lang's *mise-en-scène* points in another direction. In the film Bannion does not utter the archetypal phrase about not needing anyone. He simply ignores Burke's homily. Lang, however, supplies a more eloquent response through the powerful images of the empty interior, the hollow space that once held Bannion's life. It is this image that ends the scene, overwhelming any spoken platitudes. Further, if friendship based on aid and especially a love affair chart the conversion of the hero in most American narratives of re-integration (think of Tolly Devlin's changing relation to Cuddles in *Underworld USA*), Bannion's interaction with those that aid him seems extraordinarily inexpressive. In every scene with someone who aids him, Bannion is polite and appreciative, but markedly unemotional and always focused on his goal. Lang's conception of Bannion's character allows no deviation from his purpose; hardly a single line of dialogue is given him as he interacts with those that help him, that does not immediately serve his investigation, as in his conversation with Selma Parker, where even his gratitude is phrased in formal, official tones.

In other words, without making this a pejorative term, Bannion *uses* the people who aid him, and has absolutely no other relation to them. Selma Parker identifies Larry Jordan as the man who arranged the car bomb that killed his wife, but, after the identification is made, she hobbles off as Bannion waves her away, and is never seen again. The sequence which for McArthur most clearly marks Bannion's reintegration, the gathering of his brother-in-law's army buddies to guard the apartment where his daughter is staying when Lagana orders the police guard called off, also maintains Bannion's emotional isolation. He first questions their competence, then, when reassured, politely thanks them. But there is no forging of comradeship. He doesn't join their poker game, or *Rio Bravo* style, start up a community-sing. Likewise, when Bannion emerges from the apartment block and finds that Burke and Wilks have taken over the suspended police detail, he is again appreciative, perhaps even a bit moved by Wilks' conversion and willingness to endanger his pension by coming to his aid. But his reaction is notable for its reserve and for his continued refusal of fellowship. When Wilks asks if he wants company, Bannion firmly and laconically refuses. What we see in these scenes is not the forging of a new community, but an image familiar from Lang's Weimar thrillers – the armed mobilisation of the city, the conversion of an apartment living room into a bivouac for an army squad. Domesticity has been definitively effaced from this film and the paramilitary logic of 50s society has emerged into the open. Now the good people have guns as well as the gangsters. Ernst Junger's image of total mobilisation simply had a domestic veneer in 50s America and in Lang's film has been blown away.

Bannion's emotional reserve needs careful description. He is not an alienated psychopath seething with hatred for the human race (indeed a portrayal in that vein, such as Robert Ryan's performance in Nick Ray's *On Dangerous Ground*, could lead to the highly psychologised interior performance I am claiming Lang avoids). Bannion responds to the aid given him – Glenn Ford's kind eyes and occasional half smile showing his humanity – but minimally, and never deviates into fellowship. Rather than a neurotic, Bannion is driven by instrumental reason: every word he speaks, every action he takes is calculated to further his ends. To defeat the Destiny-machine of the city's pervasive corruption Bannion must adopt its machine-like operation. In this respect, Bannion is like Lang in the 50s, adapting his style to the system.

His relationship with Debbie Marsh, which, if conventional Hollywood patterns were followed, should provide the centre of his conversion, carefully, if subtly, avoids emotional interaction. Thus in her first trip to his hotel room in which her motivations are obviously erotic curiosity and an immediate attraction to Bannion (as well as, as Bannion, with his ability to see the purposes underlying actions, tells her, the desire to get back at Vince Stone for leaving her at the bar), Debbie encounters a complete check. Every one of Bannion's questions, although disguised as small talk, aims at eliciting information from her, which Debbie (pretty perceptive about motives, herself) tells him she is not going to offer ('I didn't come up here to talk out of school'). Debbie's attempt to edge him toward the erotic causes an almost toxic reaction on Bannion's part (in a muted way his most expressive acting). It also turns him nasty as he insults Debbie with an even worse version of the contempt he showed Lucy Chapman: 'I wouldn't touch anything of Vince Stone's with a ten foot pole.' Lang underscores the viciousness of this remark by having it lead directly into the film's most famous scene: Vince Stone destroying Debbie's face with scalding coffee. Both men have treated her with derision.

But an initial encounter like this could simply set up the transformation into a love affair the conversion and rehumanisation plot calls for, especially after Debbie's definitive break with Stone and her redemptive suffering. But if anything, during Debbie's second trip to Bannion's hotel room after she has been burned, Bannion displays his single-minded focus even more mechanically. As Debbie comes in sobbing in pain and fear, he systematically asks her who was at the apartment, maintains his distance and offers not a single word of comfort or sympathy, his willingness to hide her at his hotel being simply pragmatic. Debbie finally explodes at this treatment and confronts him with his coldness and his responsibility in her injury ('You don't care. You don't care what happened to me. You don't care about anything or anybody. I was followed when I came here with you, – that's why I got this!'). This could constitute the emotional centre of the scene in a conventional approach, and indeed it does mark the moral centre. But Lang withholds Bannion's reaction to Debbie's comment – if he has any – filming him from the back. His politeness does kick in as he offers Debbie a drink, but Lang refuses to develop a sense of intimacy or compassion on his part.

If Bannion's third scene with Debbie shows him at his most polite, the refusal of intimacy or emotion is most clearly thematised and directly tied to his mourning and alignment with the world of death. When Debbie asks him about his wife he responds with what Debbie calls 'a police description', the Langian motif of a person reduced to information, here especially bitter since it is Bannion describing his beloved: 'Twenty-seven years old, light hair, grey eyes'. When Debbie asks for more personal details, Bannion stands up and removes himself from Debbie's proximity, standing with his back to her (and to us) at the window. Debbie apologises for bringing her up (the second time she has evoked the erotic and gotten a toxic reaction on Bannion's part). She redirects the conversation into a more comfortable groove: the progress of Bannion's investigation. For the two shot of their discussion, Lang creates one of the more unusual (although typically Langian) compositions in the film, a high-angle shot from a height a little above Bannion, with his back on the left of the frame and Debbie seated in the chair in the corner on the right. As Leblanc and Devismes indicate, this underscores the lack of eye contact between them.[35] However, since the cuts between their close-ups are based on eyelines, the angle serves mainly to stress the disparity between them, allowing a two shot even though one is standing and the other sitting.

After detouring away from Katie Bannion, the centre of this conversation becomes Bertha Duncan as Bannion explains to Debbie, that Bertha is holding her husband's suicide confession as blackmail over Lagana, and that she therefore constitutes a stone wall for Bannion who wants the contents of the letter to surface. 'If she dies the letter goes to the newspaper. I almost killed her an hour ago. I should have.' Debbie responds to this with the archetypal line, indicating that Bannion couldn't kill Bertha, that if he did, he would be like Vince Stone. However, Bannion shows no repentance for his earlier attempted murder, only a regret it was interrupted. It is Debbie who is preserving a high standard of morality, rather than Bannion. Once again Lang denies us an insight into Bannion's reaction to Debbie, this time by interrupting the scene with another phone call, informing him of the danger to his little girl, since the police guard has been removed. He rushes out, throwing a revolver on the bed, and saying perhaps his nastiest (unintentionally?) line to Debbie, 'Keep that for company.' Freudian overtones are unnecessary to make clear that the only companionship Bannion can offer her is a deadly mechanism.

Systematically, then, Lang has raised the possibility of an erotic relationship building between Debbie and Bannion, based on sexual attraction, sacrifice, need, emotional expression and a higher morality. Just as systematically he has dodged it, using this emotional possibility as a foil for Bannion's single-minded focus on his revenge. Contrary to more traditional psychological drama, this contrast does not generate emotional tension between Debbie's offer of emotional sustenance and Bannion's death-ridden obsession. There will be no culmination in which Bannion breaks down and acknowledges he needs Debbie, no scene (like the one between Sandy and Tolly in *Underworld USA*) where a wiser character dresses Bannion down and shows him the value of what Debbie is offering. Lang's view remains exterior, morally observing, rather than creating empathy or psychological drama. Bannion remains a representative of what Siegfried Kracauer, in his study of the detective novel, called the '*ratio*'. In his methodical investigation and elimination of his foes, Bannion employs violence not as emotional expression but as a tool of instrumental reason.[36]

The Big Heat Falls Alike on the Just and the Unjust

The Big Heat differs from the classical detective novels Kracauer studied in its fascination with violence. For Tzvetan Todorov, the increase in violent action, as the detective actually struggles with the criminals he pursues, separates the 'thriller' as developed by Hammett and Chandler, with its visceral dragging of violence into the centre of the plot, from the classical detective story in which the violence occurs before the narrative and the detective primarily uses his (or her) intellect to explain it.[37] As I have indicated, in *The Big Heat*, violence primarily takes on the melodramatic role of exerting pressure on the surface of reality into order to make it yield up the truth. This is the apocalyptic energy of the 'big heat' which, to paraphrase William Blake, will melt apparent surfaces away and display the truth which was hidden. For Bannion this revelatory violence takes the form of strangling, most clearly in the scene where he finally encounters Larry Jordan, throttles him and says, 'When I let go, start talking'. Bannion squeezes off the breath of life in order to start the flow of words, extorting information from the recalcitrant gangster. He tries the same thing with Bertha Duncan, but gets interrupted.

But there is another current of violence in this film which involves not gasping for air, but burning with fire. Exerted primarily by the gangsters and primarily against women, it moves from Lucy Chapman's off screen cigarette burns ('I saw them', says Bannion to the coroner as he snuffs out his own cigarette, 'every single one of them'), to the flaming car Bannion pulls his wife from, to Stone putting his cigarette out on the B-girl's hand (a detail Lang added to the original scenario),[38] to the boiling pot of coffee Debbie receives in the face, matched, then, by the scalding she gives Vince in the climactic scene. The effect of such heat on a woman's skin remains perhaps the most indelible image from this film, particularly in its final unveiling by Debbie, who seems to delight in the horror her face inspires in Stone as she rips off her bandages. It is this image of female flesh burned and scarred that underlies the *ratio* of Bannion's investigation.

Bannion's investigation takes the initial mis-step of not taking Lucy Chapman seriously because of his preconception about the moral status of a B-girl. Bannion's earlier domestic life sharply contrasts with the bachelor culture portrayed by *The Blue Gardenia*, but he looks on unattached women with the same reification as Harry Prebble, only instead of prowling the hunting ground, he remains ensconced at home, avoiding women of dubious reputation. However, the film makes it clear that the moral standing of Lucy and Bertha Duncan is actually the inverse of their marital status: Lucy's love led to Tom Duncan's 'soul-searching'. *The Big Heat* adopts the basic dualism of the rogue cop series most clearly in its treatment of women, but the ideology which divides women along a grid of sexual morality consistently reveals itself to be dangerously fallacious. The burden of a dichotomy of wife and whore which blinds Bannion's initial reception of Lucy's information becomes visualised, almost allegorised, in Debbie's burned face, glamorous on one side, hideous on the other. But rather than recalling traditional Christian allegories of the diseased woman's body as an emblem of the dangers of lust, or, as McArthur reads it, as a sign of her dubious morals,[39] Debbie's face carries the imprint of male violence, a violence that she tries to get Bannion to accept his responsibility in causing, but which we never see him do. By the end of the film Bannion achieves his exposé, and seems to renounce violence as he refuses to shoot Vince Stone, but his quest is littered with the bodies of dead women. As Bannion gets up from Debbie after she dies, Lang slowly overlap-dissolves to a newspaper rising, as if from her dead body, proclaiming: 'LAGANA, HIGGINS, INDICTED! Duncan Confession Exposes Crime Syndicate'. With a nearly allegorical superimposition Lang reveals the deadly foundation of Bannion's success.

We could diagram the women involved in Bannion's exposé this way:

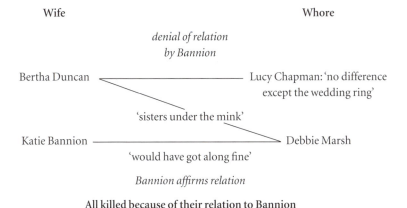

But what is striking about Bannion's investigation is not the women it accumulates as passive victims, but the fact that Lucy Chapman and Debbie Marsh, respec-
tively, initiate and resolve the process for him. In spite of his instrumental logic,
Bannion on his own achieves very little. It is Debbie Marsh who truly carries out his
revenge (along with a bit of her own) and breaks through the stone wall of Bertha
Duncan. The most thorough and perceptive critics of this film, Leblanc, Devismes
and McArthur have all described the ambiguity of Bannion's relation to Debbie's
shooting of Mrs. Duncan. Is this Bannion's ultimate instrumental use of the women
around him, getting Debbie to commit this murder for him? Actually, McGivern's
novel is most explicit about this; Debbie explains as she calls Bannion after shooting
Bertha, 'She had the note, and you couldn't kill her. Well I could. It was easy.'[40] But
to what extent is Bannion actually manipulating Debbie? As McArthur says of Bannion's last conversation with her in which he describes Bertha as the obstacle to
defeating the gangsters, 'Bannion's remarks here are tantamount to asking Debbie
to kill Bertha Duncan.'[41] Leblanc and Devismes concentrate on the visual action at
the end of the scene, where Bannion throws a revolver on the bed for Debbie (the
one, in fact, that she will use to kill Bertha), and rushes out, leaving the hotel room
door open, as if, after explaining how necessary Mrs. Duncan's death is, he gives her
the means and clears the way for her to do it.[42] Similarly, the hook between scenes in
which Burke and Wilks ask Bannion if he is going to Bertha Duncan's house and
Debbie's arrival there merges the action of the two characters. Bannion answers,
none too convincingly, 'no', followed by a dissolve to the Duncans' door bell ringing
as she comes downstairs. Debbie stands at the door, but the connection between
scenes makes it seem that she simply completes Bannion's (denied) intention.

But one should not minimise Debbie's own achievement in her murder of Bertha
and scalding of Vince (as she says to Vince, 'The lid's off the garbage can, and *I* did
it!'). The motif of Debbie looking at herself in mirrors in the first half of the film

conveyed her narcissism, her concern with her beauty. One could also point out that this concern has economic as much as psychological motives; Debbie is aware that her ticket to the wealth she has enjoyed has been her beauty and ability to attract a rich protector like Vince Stone (she says to Bannion in their first hotel meeting, 'Did you think I was an heiress or something before I met Vince?'). Checking her face is like reading the stock market quotes, making sure her future is secure. Thus, just before he douses it with boiling coffee, Vince watches Debbie examining herself in the mirror and says, 'That's a real pretty kisser', and she replies 'Isn't it though?' Vince's violence displays not simply psychopathic rage, but a calculated sadism, destroying Debbie's collateral in a sexist society. As she says as she is dying, 'Vince shouldn't have ruined my looks, it was a rotten thing to do.'

Debbie's duality, reflected both in her emblem, the mirror and the bifurcation of her face, takes on another twist when she visits Bertha Duncan. Lang reveals Bertha's financial windfall from her husband's death in stages (in contrast to the original scenario which speaks of her diamond ring in the first scene with Bannion),[43] so that Bertha's mink coat visible as she lets Debbie in the front door, has a sort of climactic effect; she is now fully dressed in her role as bloodsucker. Debbie enters wearing her mink coat (and Gloria Grahame's ability to make it swish is one of the few arguments against animal rights activists). Since her scalding, Debbie has avoided mirrors and here the blocking – the two women moving towards the camera abreast, then turning and facing each other directly – invokes mirroring. Debbie articulates the *Doppelgänger* effect when she explains to Bertha, in one of the film's best lines, 'We're sisters under the mink.' But if Bertha is Debbie's double, she looks through a glass darkly. Bertha is the image of herself that Debbie definitely rejects, the calculating bloodsucker who doesn't care where the money comes from. Thus as Bertha goes to make another death-dealing phone call (telling Vince Stone to come pick Debbie up), Debbie uses Bannion's revolver to drill her at the same desk where her husband died. Bertha flops under the desk onto the floor, as Debbie tosses the gun down, too. She will use a different weapon on Vince.

The direct visual connections tying Debbie's murder of Bertha to Bannion continue with an overlap-dissolve from the shot of the abandoned revolver, thrown on the floor by Debbie as it was earlier tossed on the bed by Bannion, to a shot of Bannion, his back to the camera, looking into a window display. This is one of the last display windows Lang will film in his career. Bannion's identity as a man without any desire, except to carry out his revenge, is starkly imaged by the complete contrast between this shot of window-shopping and every other one in Lang's *œuvre*. Although we see a mannequin wearing women's clothes, this plate glass window appears primarily as a reflecting mirror. Bannion does not look into it: there is nothing there he wants. Instead he uses it to keep an eye on the building across the street, Stone's residence, and turns his head towards us only as he (and we) see, in the window's reflection, a car drive up and a man enter the building. Exactly what Bannion intends by watching Stone's apartment is unclear. If his intentions are homicidal, Debbie is there before him, and Bannion only enters after Stone shoots her, supplying a crime he can charge Stone with red-handed.

The final conversation between Bannion and Debbie as she dies not only completes the conversation Bannion earlier refused, but allows Bannion to realise and affirm that Katie and Debbie 'would have gotten along fine', a statement that erases, or at least denies, the sexist (and class) dichotomy which structured so much of the film. But he is only able to speak this way to her when (because?) she is dying. What are we to make of his death-bedside manner? Several forces are operating here and while any one of them makes sense, they are, as often happens in American cinema's dream logic, rather mutually exclusive. First, Bannion's work is accomplished; he can again return to the living and express the tenderness (for his wife, as well as for Debbie) that he has repressed throughout the second half of the film. This would indicate that the process of revenge, including its violence, has been cathartic for him, his mourning has been completed. In a second reading, the sexist dichotomy has not been purged from the film, merely upheld by a fatal sacrifice. Debbie could kill Bertha Duncan because she is already tainted, and the stain on her virtue could only be eliminated with her death, and it is only the purified, dying Debbie who could be equated with Katie (McArthur seems to read Debbie this way).[44] A third reading, (for me the most Langian, but perhaps only the most Gunningian) would see Bannion as still immersed in the realm of death and able to commune tenderly with Debbie precisely because she, too, now approaches that world. The tone of his voice here not only expresses a tenderness totally lacking since his wife's death, but an immersion in a memory of past time as he invokes not only his dead wife, but his life with her which has been destroyed. His speech mourns the domestic tranquillity he once possessed, that middle class *intérieur* we saw emptied out.

In constructing Bannion, then, Lang invoked the typical action hero of the 50s, the man who takes the law into his own hands, restores justice and in the process gains (or regains) a new sense of community and an ability to love, the drama, as McArthur says, of rehumanisation and reintegration. However, a close examination, especially of the author-text rather than the genre-text (these are, as McArthur does not seem to acknowledge, different approaches and highlight different aspects of the text they are applied to) shows Lang resisting the emotional catharsis and psychological approach of most such films. Boehm's original scenario actually included a happy ending where Debbie (who in this version did not kill Bertha, – who was shot by Lagana instead – and therefore has no legal charges hanging over her) survives. A surgeon even indicates her scars can be healed, and a marriage with Bannion seems to be in the future. Bannion and Burke leave the hospital as dawn breaks to go to have breakfast with Bannion's daughter. Here the drama of reintegration is fully imaged, with a return to both the force and the family, a replacement wife for Bannion and middle-class redemption for Debbie. Lang eliminated all this and returned to a more pessimistic ending drawn partly from McGivern's novel. Rather than portraying a romance of transformation and redemption, Lang maintains a distanced observation, highlighting moral ambiguities and social *gestus*.

The last images of the film portray a return to normality as Bannion is back at his desk and the routine of the office begins again. The version of the scenario (dated 4 March) that introduced this new ending describes it as 'nearly a repetition of the first scene' (referring obviously to a different beginning than Duncan's suicide). Even without this literal circularity, one feels that the film is beginning again and that the 'The End' imprinted on the scene intervenes arbitrarily. The absorption back into the everyday routine could be seen as the final step of Bannion's re-integration, but even McArthur comments, 'The bleak cycle has begun once more', picking up on the film's final sense of limbo. Bannion's mechanical routine does not visibly differ from his earlier behaviour. The success of Bannion's revenge is portrayed in a cold headline, a new newspaper story cancelling out the previous newspaper story of Duncan's suicide which filled the screen earlier. There is no community shown welcoming the news, no reunited family to find happiness in its promise of a new life. For an apocalypse, very little has changed; perhaps Bannion only brought the 'little heat'. Has Bannion returned from the realm of the dead, or is he still wandering among them? Lang again refuses to tell us. Perhaps the ultimate critique of 50s culture is that normal life does not look so very different, whether the mob has been defeated or not, whether Bannion has completed the work of mourning or not. Bannion's last line as he exits to go out on another case is, 'Keep the coffee hot, Hugo.' Something is kept warm – but coffee? Can *you* drink it after you watch this film?

17

While the City Sleeps/
Beyond a Reasonable Doubt

The News is Made at Night

Night has come: alas, that I must be light! And thirst for the
nocturnal! And loneliness!
Friedrich Nietzsche, *Thus Spoke Zarathustra*[1]

Both the novel of *The Big Heat* and Boehm's original screenplay placed Dave Bannion's investigation against the background of an electoral campaign for mayor,
and included the character of a journalist, Furnham, sympathetic to Bannion and
trying to uncover municipal corruption. Other than a brief reference to the elec-
tions by Lagana, this context has nearly disappeared from Lang's film and Furnham has vanished entirely, the place of a reporter character taken simply by shots
of newspaper stories or headlines. Given the importance of journalists in Lang's
other contemporary films from the 50s, this excision is rather surprising, but I
believe that Lang decided to concentrate entirely on Bannion's exposé of the mob,
an action which is obsessional and never displays the split between personal
motives of career advancement and uncovering the 'truth' that we find in Casey
Mayo, Ed Mobley or Tom Garrett, Lang's trio of 50s journalists.

Lang's last two American films were a package deal with producer Bert Friedlob,
both lower-budget films released through RKO, a studio tottering towards collapse.
As Gerard Legrand points out, the two films not only share many elements, but
actually function as a matched pair.[2] Both films star Dana Andrews, an actor whose
work in Otto Preminger's films of the 40s and early 50s (especially *Daisy Kenyon*,
Fallen Angel and *Where the Sidewalk Ends*) had embodied perfectly Preminger's
moral ambiguity, portraying characters that were unsavoury and unresponsive on
the surface, but capable of a certain existential morality when it was demanded of
them. Andrews is a minimalist actor, and in Preminger's films manages to convey a
sense of hidden (or repressed) depth of feeling. In the 50s, however, his minimal-
ism had become, using Patrick McGilligan's phrase, 'monochromatic'.[3] Andrews'
performances, and even his characters, in these two films share a similar feeling of
betrayed promise, an intellectual acuity that slides in and out of focus, a predatory
attitude towards women, and a general sleepiness which is explained diegetically in
the first movie by his late nights spent in police headquarters, but seems mainly to
reflect the actor's growing alcoholism in the second.[4] Rarely has Lang maintained
such a degree of distance from his protagonist, (especially in *Beyond a Reasonable
Doubt* where we learn very little about Garrett's motivations), and one is slightly
unclear whether to feel Andrews' performance perfectly fits this distance, or, rather,

that Andrews' lack of engagement with the audience exaggerates Lang's intentions. However, I tend towards the former reading.

In both films Lang gives the plot a double goal, in which the main action the characters undertake is given a double motivation by an authority figure (publisher in the first film, editor in the second). In *While the City Sleeps* the various members of a news organisation – the editor of its flagship paper, the head of its news wire service, and the manager of its picture service – all try to break the story of the capture and identity of a serial killer. But their real motivation is a competition set up by their new publisher in order to select the executive manager of the organisation. The murderer, his crimes and apprehension, are framed by the corporate struggle for the new position. In *Beyond a Reasonable Doubt* (setting aside for the moment its twist ending) Tom Garrett is accused of murder and stands trial, but, in fact, his situation was stage managed by his former editor and future father-in-law who wants to prove it is dangerous to sentence someone to capital punishment through the use of circumstantial evidence by making an innocent man seem guilty through manufactured evidence. In both cases suspenseful stories of crime and punishment are framed within journalistic investigations.

Both films have a similar look, as well, partly a spareness of set design that undoubtedly is due to budget restrictions, but also a lighting style, especially in *While the City Sleeps* that almost totally lacks the chiaroscuro that Lang's films usually flaunted . Other than the subway scenes in the climax of *While the City Sleeps*, and the scenes around the strip club and its alleyway in *Beyond a Reasonable Doubt*, these films take place in high-key lighting and the shadows have been burned away. Burnett Guffey masterfully produced the last of Lang's carefully highlit and shadowed sequences in *Human Desire* (1954). Although shadows are more frequent in *Beyond a Reasonable Doubt*, they rarely mark out pools of darkness sparkling with highlights as in the earlier films. Whether a contemporary concern about shadowy scenes reproducing well on television had an influence here (the fact that both these films were shot in wide-screen format might argue against a concern for television sales, although, unlike CinemaScope, RKO's Superscope allowed the films to be projected in a variety of aspect ratios)[5] or other technical factors intervened, Lang's last American films have a stark untextured feeling that makes them seem flat and claustrophobic.

One wonders if Lang's increasing loss of vision might also have played a role. In 1942 Brecht had recorded in his diary a chilling story of Lang visiting an eye specialist who asked him to read the letters on a chart. Lang responded that first the light should be turned on, then learned that the light was already on.[6] In the next decade his eyesight continued to deteriorate. But if Lang's declining eyesight has a stylistic consequence in his late Hollywood films, it takes the form, not of a gathering darkness, but a blinding brightness, like the photographer's flashbulb blasting into the camera in *The Big Heat*. Is the bright, shadowless light of these last Hollywood films a reflection of his need to pour on as much illumination as possible to be able to see? Or is it simply another sign of a general change in 50s film-making style, especially in lower-budgeted films? Whatever explanation might be given for this stylistic change, the more highly illuminated, almost over-exposed look of these films carries a thematic freight as well.

For a number of Lang critics these last two American films represent a final winnowing of Lang's vision, a minimalist style cut to its essentials. Jean Domarchi laid down the terms for such an appreciation of these late Lang films in his *Cahiers du Cinéma* review of *While the City Sleeps* in 1956, stressing not only Lang's distance, but his abstraction and linear narrative construction.[7] Jacques Rivette, in his famous review of *Beyond a Reasonable Doubt*, 'The Hand', most incisively described Lang's last Hollywood style: 'as though what we were watching were less the *mise en scène* of a script than simply the reading of this script, presented to us just as it is, without embellishment'.[8] For Rivette this minimalist (or to use his Hegelian vocabulary, negative) approach renders the film diagrammatic, with characters reduced to concepts, moving in a world of quasi-abstract necessity in which no concession is made to the details of the everyday or the pictorial. As the furthest development of the closed universe of Lang's vision, *Beyond a Reasonable Doubt* would seem to constitute the apogee of his career, or its *reductio ad absurdum*.

The *Cahiers* critics had taken Bazin's ideal of a film without an overt style in a direction he had never expected, towards a praise of the classicism of the Hollywood studio film, and their enthusiasm for the last of Lang's American films is due partly to this ideal, a style eschewing tricks of montage or Expressionism of composition, a style seemingly without a style. Yet these last Hollywood films also create an atmosphere in which it is as difficult to breathe as it is to enjoy Andrews' performances. The demonstration of Lang's plotting certainly stands out in these films, but his earlier longing for utopian politics, or the ambivalent portrayal of the dialectics of desire seem drained away. Possibly Jonathan Rosenbaum is right in saying that only in Lang's outright escapist films (*Moonfleet*, the Indian films) with their evocation of childhood fantasy, does a sense of Lang's delight in cinema remain.[9]

The working title of *While the City Sleeps*, *The News is Made at Night*, as well as its two opening images (in the pre-credit prologue) – a night view of the port of New York with the caption 'New York City Tonight' and a high-angle, typical *noir* shot of a city street glistening with rain – promises a nocturnal vision. But after this opening, there is nothing *noir* in the look of this film which takes place within a realm of glaring visibility. The final release title seems more appropriate to the film's vision; while the city sleeps, the film's protagonists, especially Dana Andrews' character Ed Mobley, wander sleepless and bleary-eyed in brightly lit apartments, police stations and bars. This panoptical world, bereft of shadows or privacy, is captured in the art direction of the central newsroom of the Kyne empire whose glass-enclosed compartments expose all the offices of the various departments to mutual observation. Gerard Legrand refers to it as a 'glass beehive'.[10] The scene in the news office opens as Ed Mobley observes the head of the wire service, Mark Loving, leaning over his secretary, Nancy Liggett, who is Ed's girlfriend. He immediately places a call asking her to tell her boss to keep his distance. This is a realm in which everyone watches everyone, like the department store in *You and Me*, and there is no such thing as a private moment.

After Walter Kyne Jr., the moronic and slightly sinister son who takes over the news empire after his father's death (whom Vincent Price's performance endows with an unexpected weight and added repulsion), sets up the competition for the position of executive director, the various heads of departments eye each other through their glass partitions with paranoia, each trying to anticipate the others next move. It is as though Lang multiplied Chris Cross's cashier's office and juxtaposed a succession of identical cubicles, all occupied by equally deceitful clerks. When crusty editor John D. Griffith (Mobley's ally and the most likeable of these sharks) finally gets the scoop on the murderer's identity, he must communicate to his staff in whispers and pantomime unconcern, aware that Mark Loving might see him and get suspicious if anything unusual seems to be happening. The third competitor, Harry Kritzer, the head of the picture services, spends less time in this glass beehive, since his plan to gain the top position involves romancing Kyne's wife and getting her to convince her husband to promote him. But he doesn't escape from the panoptical environment, complaining when he visits Kyne's home that he suspects there are sliding panels in the wall and microphones hidden behind the pictures. A direct development of Lang's themes of the carceral society in the thirties, the blight of visibility is now related to people's work, not their putative crimes, as everyone watches everyone else and tries to anticipate and counter their actions.

Further, *While the City Sleeps* sharpens Lang's sense of visual aggression. The film's pre-credit prologue introduces Robert Manners, the serial killer, as he first spies out, then kills, a young woman. Dressed like Brando in *The Wild One*, Manners' murders directly follow a sudden erotic vision which seizes the image of a woman and pushes the young man's psychopathic reactions into overdrive. Manners' deadly vision functions like a compressed version of Lang's artists of desire: in almost every instance the women he attacks are first seen as an image, a framed reflection or a shadow cast on the wall. As Emily's shadow captivates Stephen Byrne in *House by the River*, as Cross's portrait of Kitty presages her murder, for Manners a woman imaged is a woman marked for death. Thus, as he delivers a bottle of medicine from the drug store to the film's first victim, he glimpses her through the front door frame and then through the frame of her bathroom door, another of Lang's double frames. On the bathroom wall he sees a shadow of the young woman, presumably nude as she puts on a bathrobe. Later he prepares to attack Dorothy Kyne after seeing her reflected in a mirror as she hikes her skirt to adjust her stocking.

The killer's connection with the visual is not only passive. The first murder is presented in such a way as to merge Manners' aggression with the camera itself. Manners has pushed the button on the lock of the young woman's apartment, so he gains access without announcement. As she kneels by her tub preparing her bath, she hears the off screen noise of the door opening. She turns toward the camera. The camera tracks in on her, as if it had taken over the killer's point of view, and the young woman looks at it in wide-eyed, unmoving terror. Then, as the camera closes in on her, she throws up her hand and screams, her eyes never moving from the lens (the final invasion of her space accomplished with a zoom). Her screams erupts as the shot quickly fades to black. Out of this darkness the title of the film comes, followed by the cred-

its. The camera movement not only mimes the killer's violence (and not simply his physical approach), it literalises the link in the killer's pathology between sight and violence, image and death. The camera as the medium of his sight and violent desire rushes towards the woman and then the screen fades to total darkness, this threatening vision effaced in an obscurity that figures death.

The first shot after the credits picks up the aftermath of the crime, whose actual violence has been elided, with a shot of the bathrobe abandoned on the floor, as the camera tilts up and to the left to reveal a photographer in the next room snapping a picture. Once again Lang burns out an over-exposed frame to portray the camera's flash, picking up the theme of aggressive visuality, an over-transparent world whose obviousness is the opposite of the visionary moment Lang portrayed in earlier films, yielding not insight, but dazzlement, blinding flashes. While the rest of the characters may not be as fatally prey to images of desire as Manners is, they live in the same hyper-visual, exposed world. As the cameraman walks out of frame, Lang's camera moves past him, over to the wall, where the killer has inscribed his message, 'Ask Mother', which then fills the frame. The film's undeveloped and pat explanation of Manners' mania through a mother fixation is less interesting than the killer's attempt to communicate at each of his crime scenes, leaving clues that the police and Mobley interpret as mockery and braggadocio. In many ways they are the horribly reduced equivalent of the works left by Lang's artist-criminals, attempts at authorship, signatures attached to crimes.

In discussing *While the City Sleeps* Lang frequently referred back to *M*, his other treatment of a serial killer.[11] The comparison certainly doesn't put the later film in its best light, especially if one compares Peter Lorre's performance to John Drew Barrymore's, or Ernest Laslo's photography to Fritz Arno Wagner's. But, if the later film hardly achieves the crystallisation of Lang's style and themes that *M* represents, the comparison nonetheless highlights the view Lang took of 50s America and the late development of his style. Hans Beckert terrifies the whole city, with all its inhabitants isolated in their common anxiety. In *While the City Sleeps* Manners' crimes are seized upon as a gimmick to sell papers, while normal life seems to continue regardless (contrast the Berliners who surround the bus suspecting the child murderer may have been caught to the subway riders who barely give Manners a second glance as he jostles past them in full flight). Before he dies, Kyne Sr. reads the news of the opening murder on the teletype machine he has installed next to his hospital bed (which is installed in his newspaper office). Furious at the limited play his paper has given the murder, he instantly sees an opportunity, as he puts it, to 'scare silly' every woman in the country. If Beckert's crimes seemed to move through Berlin like a disease, the terroristic impulse of Manners immediately possesses Kyne as he reads the story. Rather than simply conveying information as in *M*, the media in *While the City Sleeps* mime the murderer's actions, determined to terrify the public in order to sell more papers.

The contagion of Manners' murderous perversion and lethal vision pervades the city through the influence of the media which attempts to terrorise and titillate the public with the drama of his succession of murders and the process of his identification. The photographs supplied by Kritzer's picture service develop visual themes from Lang's earlier portrayals of visual journalism in *Fury* and *You Only Live Once*, attempting to circumscribe identity and fix guilt. The front page of the *Sentinel* after the second murder shows on the left a photograph of 'The Scene of the Latest Slaying' with the position of the murdered woman's body draped over her bed outlined by a thick white line, a large white X marking the door through which the murderer entered, and a broken line with an arrow laying out his pathway as he forced his way in. Another white arrow above the outline of the absent body points to an insert of the victim's face, smiling in a photograph taken earlier. The murder scene and victim have been processed and abstracted as information, reduced to graphics that resemble Lang's own shooting diagrams. The victim becomes an empty space supplemented by a smiling photograph, and the caption emphasises her position as one of a series ('latest slaying'). The violence of modernity's modes of representation and information matches the aggression of the crime itself.

Next to the crime scene photo/diagram is a drawing labelled 'This is the Killer'. Above the caption is an outline of a young man's face with dark hair, the face left completely blank. The caption above the drawing reads: 'Fill in this Face'. The blank-faced drawing's dark hair is based on the one physical clue the police have obtained from the crime scene, strands of hair found in the victim's fingernails. The blank face visualises the idea of mystery, an identity waiting to be filled in. Like the caption to the photograph of Eddie Taylor's hat which indicated that identifying the owner of the hat would yield the killer, it is an invitation to the general public to join in the investigation, to try to find the killer. However, Lang here is less involved in the potential mistakes to which this could lead, than the blank face as the ultimate template for the guilty party in his films: the faceless self awaiting an imprint of a specific identity which can condemn it. This 'fill in the blank' face provides his ultimate image of modern identity, or non-identity, the abstraction of all facial features until all that remains is simply the presumption of guilt.

Rather than portraying again the populace aiding the pursuit of criminals and Lang's dual vision of the modern city as the site of carceral surveillance and total mobilisation (as in films from *M* to *You Only Lie Once* to *The Big Heat*), Lang shows the killer himself picking up the invitation to 'Fill in this Face', sketching in a (slightly idealised, like a comic book hero) self-portrait onto a copy of the newspaper as he lolls on his bed. Again Lang draws a parallel between Manners and the artist-criminals of the enframed desire series of films in the 40s, especially Stephen Byrne, who also 'wanted to see his picture in the papers'. The relation to Hans Beckert is illuminating. Beckert wrote to the press and had his handwritten note reproduced in the papers. Like Manners, his impulse to kill seems to come partly from a

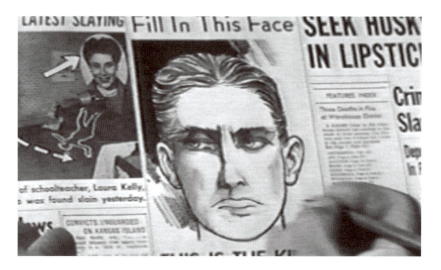

moment of piercing erotic vision, as when he sees the little girl framed in the mirror of the cutlery display. But Beckert's primary drama, his private theatre, seemed to dwell in the fantasy world he could inhabit with child-bride victims, while Manners seems more involved with his interaction with the media and police than the grim satisfaction his victims provide him. His act of filling in the picture accepts the frame the media gives him for his identity, and the act of inscribing his own face reacts to the general, abstracted and faceless identity offered to a modern city dweller. Manners defies this form of effacement, but only through modernity's own debased form of celebrity, the gimmick of publicity.

If the faceless outline published on the *Sentinel*'s front page could be anybody, like the numerous vague 'descriptions' offered in Lang films (which, as Joe Wilson said in *Fury*, could fit a million guys), we are faced again with the situation introduced in *M* in which the murderer no longer represents the extraordinary and bizarre, but rather the unremarkable average citizen. The killer's potential similarity to anyone, is what the investigation, and Mobley's reports in particular, try to undo, creating instead a specific face and personality to match the crime and fix the culprit. However, in doing this Mobley continuously reveals his own similarities to the man he is hunting, so that (in a motif common in *noir* films of the 50s) he becomes, as E. Ann Kaplan put it, a *Doppelgänger* of the serial killer.[12] This is clearest in Mobley's predatory attitude towards women, a sleazy, self-amused leering that permeates this film as it does *The Blue Gardenia*, often recalling Manners' hysterical reaction to titillating images of women (as when the camera itself lingers on the shadow of Dorothy Kyne doing her exercises, apparently nude, then rounds the partition in order to ogle her in her bathing suit). The one active woman character in the film, the columnist Mildred Donner (played by the original tough girl, Ida Lupino) plays on the axiomatic nature of this male gaze, when she attracts the interest of Mobley and a bartender by gazing into a slide viewer. As Lang said, Lupino, 'played it so wonderfully that you immediately knew what the picture was: she was naked'.[13] In actuality, in typical Lang mockery of male voyeurism, the slide is revealed to be of a nude baby on a rug.

But Mobley particularly reveals the duplicity and potential violence in his attraction to his girlfriend Nancy. (In fact, when Nancy hears the serial killer described as 'a real nut on dames' she responds 'and this description begins to fit Mobley!'). Earlier in the film, while kissing Sally goodnight at her apartment doorway, Mobley slides his hand down the edge of her door, finds the button which releases the lock and pushes it. Besides the obvious sexual displacement of this action undertaken in close-up, its major significance lies in the fact that this is Manners' main *modus operandi*, as we saw in the pre-credit murder scene. After being attracted to a potential victim, Manners similarly fixes the lock so he can enter freely. Mobley leaves, but lingers on the stairway observing Nancy's legs framed by the banister. He discovers the means by which Manners entered his victim's apartment because he shares (along with most of the men in this film) his combination of duplicity and desire. Thus his plan to catch the murderer by using Sally as bait not only shows his willingness to use the woman he loves as a means to an end in a particularly dangerous fashion, but locates her as the centre of a peculiar exchange between himself and Manners, one underscored by the scene in which Manners finds the flowers Mobley left outside the apartment door, with a note inscribed, 'To Dearest Nancy who deserves a better fate then Ed Mobley'. Undoubtedly. But what fate is Mobley setting her up for? Whose desire is Manners following up and whose murder is he committing?

Television, Person to Person

> I never appear on television, except *on television*.
> Prof. Barry O'Blivion in David Cronenberg's *Videodrome*

Before Mobley finally grapples with Manners in the subway tunnel, they have another 'face to face' encounter, albeit of a mediated sort. Mobley's second television broadcast in the film is delivered, as he says, in the 'hope that the killer might be listening to me'. Indeed he is, and Lang constructs Mobley's broadcast as a direct address to Manners by cutting between them, but via the technological – and visual – hook-up of television. Like the telephone in *Dr. Mabuse, the Gambler*, the new technology interrelates a series of disparate places, but through the device of the glance, and with the possibilities of shared communication both multiplied and curtailed. The sequence begins in Mark Loving's offices as Nancy turns on the television, bringing on the Kyne emblem placed over a map of the United States, which introduces Mobley's broadcast. As she and her boss listen, Mobley's face appears on the monitor. As he delivers the news of the latest murder, Lang cuts to the television studio (contained within the same Kyne Enterprises building) with Mobley in the background of the shot, a television camera and soundman framing him in the foreground. Lang then cuts into a closer shot of Mobley as he speaks, framed more or less as he would be on the television screen, although not yet shown on the monitor. However, he speaks and looks directly at the camera in the mode of a television commentator.

As Mobley indicates his hope that the killer is listening to the broadcast, Lang cuts to Manners in his bedroom, still in his pyjamas, his bed unmade, sitting astride a chair as he watches the TV. The television monitor is visible at the edge of the left foreground, but the cutting basically operates as shot/reverse shot stressing Mobley's direct address to the killer. Lang next presents a reverse angle which does not bridge two distant spaces (the television studio and Manners' bedroom) but shoots Manners from behind, over the shoulder and reveals in the background of

the shot the television with Mobley continuing his broadcast, placing the two elements within Manners' bedroom. But Lang continues the idea of television as a network connecting a number of people and places; as Mobley mentions in his commentary his criminologist friend who helped him profile the killer, Lang cuts to Lieutenant Kaufman, also watching the broadcast, then returns for a last time to the wide shot of the television studio, Mobley flanked by the technology of broadcast. The place of a television broadcast is, in effect, every place and no place, public space and private space meshed, yet not truly interacting,

But as Mobley declares, 'I am going to say a few things to the killer, face to face.' Lang intercuts between Manners and his TV exclusively; this conversation will take place between man and monitor. Lang opens this section of the sequence with a two shot showing the TV on the left and Manners seated on the right, as Mobley both evokes and threatens Manners' anonymity: 'Mr. Unknown, you will not for very long remain unknown.' He cuts to a shot of Manners alone in the frame looking almost directly into the camera lens as he smiles in amusement. In the succeeding close shot of the TV, Mobley seems to meet this gaze, looking directly out from the television, as he lists the murderer's first identifying trait, his strength. In the matching reverse angle Manners smiles broadly in response (both Mobley and the killer make strangling motions with their hands as Mobley describes the latest killing). In the succeeding reverse angle the television camera tracks in on Mobley, enlarging his size within the monitor as he links the unknown killer to the previous murder. The cut to Manners shows his eyes widening in alarm and fixed on the camera as his mouth opens and he drops the comic book he has been clutching, apparently stunned by his identification as 'the lipstick killer', and Mobley's next revelation that, 'you read the so-called comic books'.

Lang breaks this shot/reverse shot pattern with a shot of Manners' comic book ('The Strangler', its cover emblazoned with an image of the dead body of a woman) falling to the floor. The shot is somewhat startling, excessively emphasised by its deviance from the shot/reverse shot pattern. Stephen Jenkins insightfully pointed out that this shot can be related to other shots in Lang films of objects falling between the parted legs of male characters, the drops of blood when Eddie Taylor cuts his wrists in prison, the knife Chris Cross drops when he hears of his painting

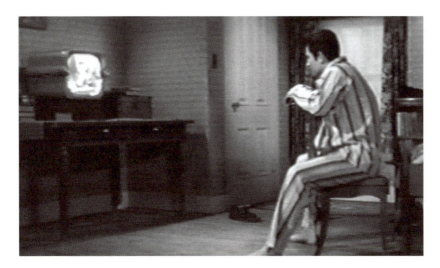

being on display under Katherine Marsh's name.[14] In all these cases the shot marks a crisis, a moment of near collapse and imminent danger for the character. Lang may also have wanted to emphasise the comic book as part of his (never very successful) explanatory mechanism for the killer. Gruesome comic books, such as the legendary EC crime comics, *Vault of Horror, Tales from the Crypt, Shock Suspense,* and *Crime Suspense,* had recently been blamed as a cause of juvenile delinquency, and with the testimony of the notorious Dr. Wertham, had been the target of both journalistic exposés and congressional hearings.[15]

Primarily, the shot of the fallen comic book expresses a transition in Manners' attitude from smirking enjoyment to the growing panic, a fear of discovery, a feeling of having been rendered visible, that marks the greatest fear of Lang's characters, like Beckert after the chalk M has been placed on his back. The sequence reaches a point of reversal here; previously Manners has watched the television in self-satisfied invulnerability, aware that he could watch Mobley, but Mobley could not watch him. However, as Mobley piles on item after item staking out Manners' identity in the process of moving towards his capture, Manners feels this invisibility and invulnerability slipping away and reacts in panic. It is as though the look at the camera that Mobley projects from the television could actually be trained on Manners as he watches. This is, of course, literally impossible, but it constitutes Lang's metaphoric image of the new medium: television not simply as a new form of visual entertainment, but as a means of surveillance. You don't just watch television Lang claims: it watches you.

The cutting pattern in the next few shots underscores this perception. An over-the-shoulder shot follows, like the one which began the alternation between Manners and Mobley, as Mobley describes the murderer as having dark brown hair. The medium shot centred on Manners recurs next, his eyes shifting in alarm, as Mobley explains that the killer is about twenty years of age. Lang then returns to the close shot of the television as Mobley smiles nastily and looks straight into the lens and delivers his lowest blow to the killer's self-esteem: 'You're a mama's boy!' Manners now appears in facial close-up for the first time, his eyes focused slightly to the left as his mouth turns into a snarl of hatred. As Mobley continues his analysis ('the normal feeling of love that you should have for your mother has been twisted into hatred for her and all of her sex'), Manners' mother, as if on cue, knocks on the door. He quickly switches off the television and hides his comic book.

In many ways Mobley's broadcast to the killer plays the same role as Casey Mayo's column 'Letter to an Unknown Murderess' in *The Blue Gardenia*; he even addresses the killer as 'Mr. Unknown'. The tone of the two contrasts completely, of course, from Mayo's cajoling seduction and offer of help, to Mobley's confrontational challenging, provoking and insulting, but the ploy to make the criminal feel directly and personally addressed by the journalist and hence expose him/herself is the same. The difference in tone relates most obviously to a difference in gender (seductive sympathy considered effective with women, derision and anger the proper way to provoke a young man), but perhaps also suited to the two different media, the more distanced column/letter compared to the 'in-your-face' style of television. The enunciatory mode of television, a look directed to the viewer/camera, seems, of course, to mimic the Langian technique of direct address to the cinema camera. However, important differences appear: the look at the camera in Lang threatens to break through the fictional world of the film and establish a direct contact with the viewer. A television announcer's look at the camera indicates a mode of non-fictional, informational, direct address, delivering the news, or persuading someone to buy something. The illusion that one is addressed by the television, that, in fact, the announcer does look at us, is essential to its non-fictional modes, and therefore does not have the startling effect that the look at the camera in the midst of a fictional film evokes. In this sequence Lang beautifully plays with the paradoxes of this new medium, its seeming ability to see into the world in which it is received. The television becomes a new image of the panoptical environment.

But if Mobley's broadcast appears as the parallel to Mayo's column and bears the same duplicity (neither journalist really wants to communicate with the murderers they address; they simply want to expose them for their other viewers/readers), it contrasts most starkly with a parallel scene from *M*: Beckert's interaction with his mirror in the film's second sequence. Recall: Beckert sits alone in his room and performs in front of his mirror, making a series of faces which become increasingly grotesque. The mirror embodies his private theatre where he can both admire himself narcissistically and (ultimately) terrify himself by enacting his transformation into a monster. Here, alone with no witnesses, he doubles his own gaze, becoming both performer and spectator, actor and audience. Doing this, Beckert not only mimes the split in his consciousness between everyday, ordinary self and monstrous murderer, he reveals his own torment, haunted by the monster he becomes, torn between the protest he intones later at his trial: 'Can Not!', and the dire command 'Must!'

But Manners seated before his television performs no similar drama. This may be taken as a sign of the lesser power and insight of this film and certainly the acting ability and performances of Lorre and John Drew Barrymore contrast sharply. But it is not simply an aesthetic impoverishment that occurs here, so much as an extreme change in visual registers, a technological, social and experiential transformation within modernity which Lang observes with great insight. Compared to Beckert, Manners is an impoverished character possessed of a modern sense of selfhood which has been further restricted. Manners' passivity contrasts to Beckert's perverse, but active, imagination. Manners is positioned as a spectator, not a performer, as he sits in his room. He smirks with pleasure at the television broadcast because he narcissistically enjoys the report of his fame (whereas Beckert tells us in his final speech that when he reads the next day of his murders he is repulsed), driven less by a complex image of desire than (as Mobley puts it) 'his sick and warped ego [which] demands to be fed with the milk of self importance'.

Manners' mirror is the public eye of television. His murders, although clearly the product of a traumatised libido, primarily reflect, not a scenario of desire, but an attempt to construct an ego, not simply from the act of murder, but from the resulting publicity (again reminiscent of Stephen Byrne). He interacts well with the media and information-driven society he dwells in. He sketches in his own face in the place provided in the newspaper, he watches the television report of his murders, he falls into Mobley's trap of pursuing Nancy (lurking briefly among the shop windows, but – unlike Beckert – finding no vision of a child's paradise within them, no reflection of his desires, just a momentary hiding place). Like Beckert, he hopes to discover an idealised romantic image of himself in the blank spaces of the newspaper, or reflected by the television screen. But instead he encounters, not Beckert's phantasmal monster, but the smugly accusing and mocking face of Mobley denouncing him as a mama's boy and flaunting his own ability to see into Manners' private world, and deflate his fantasies. Unlike the infinite and terrifying depth of the mirror, the television screen exhibits the realm of exposure, of a glaring visuality.

Besides its rather science fictional anticipation in the surveillance devices Lio Sha uses in *Spiders*, and those that Joh Frederson uses to communicate with his foreman Grot in *Metropolis*, television makes a rather inconspicuous debut in Lang's films the year before *While the City Sleeps*, in the living room of Carl and Vicki Buckley in *Human Desire* as part of that film's detailed and observant set design. But the privileged place it occupies in *While the City Sleeps* not only reveals it as the exemplar of the new visual realm of exposure that Lang explores in the 50s, but as the harbinger of a new era in media journalism. Mobley writes as well as appearing on television, but it is his public and visual performances that Lang stresses (when we first see him he is having make-up applied for his imminent telecast, his face prepared to meet the television camera and millions of viewers). But the key action of the film's opening scenes comes with the death of Amos Kyne, the patriarch of the news empire that his nebbish son Walter will inherit. The script makes clear that this passing from one generation to another marks a stage of decadence in the vision and professionalism of journalism, but Lang's *mise-en-scène* at least metaphorically assigns Kyne's passing to the triumph of television.

From his office hospital bed, Amos Kyne has called in the key players in his media empire in order to tell them how to handle the new sensation he dubs 'the lipstick killer'. As the others leave, Kyne retains Ed Mobley and confides in him his concerns about who will head his empirc after he dies and regrets that Mobley himself never seemed to want the job. When Mobley replies that he has never desired power, Kyne responds that the issue is not power but, 'the responsibility of the free press to the people. In this country it's the people that make the decisions. If they are to make their decisions right, they have to have all the facts.' As Kyne articulates the principles of a classical liberal public sphere, Mobley, concerned about his broadcast due in a few minutes, moves over to the television and switches it on. As Kyne's off screen lecture pauses in mid-sentence, Lang shows the television screen in close-up, the image appearing with the logo of the Kyne empire, the K within a circle which appears like a talisman throughout the film, as persistently as the Y-shaped emblem of the Mohunes appears in *Moonfleet*. When Lang cuts back to long shot, if we are perspicacious, we notice Kyne collapsed in his bed in the background. A second later Mobley attracts our attention to him as he says, 'I didn't mean to cut you off, but ...' then rushes over to the unconscious Kyne, as the television announces the Kyne's media presentation of Mobley's broadcast, Lang cutting to the television as the Kyne emblem appears as a network covering the United States. As Lang cuts Kyne's death scene, clearly the television killed him; he checks out as the tube is switched on.

The death of Amos Kyne forms a tissue of references all of which mark a sense of an era passing, whether intentionally conceived or not. As print journalism seems contrasted to the new medium of television, so also a classical era of cinema seems to be marked. Robert Warwick, the actor playing Kyne, had starred in some of the first American feature films around the time that Lang entered cinema, with wonderful performances in such early features as Tourneur's *Alias Jimmy Valentine*, and therefore embodied four decades of film history. Likewise, as Gerard Legrand points out, *While the City Sleeps* seems seeded with references to RKO's greatest film, *Citizen Kane*,[16] from the resemblance of Kyne's emblem to the monogram on the gate to Xanadu to the death of the newspaper magnate early in the film (albeit shot in a highly different manner from Welles' gothic opening – although both deaths are immediately followed by reports in new, non-print, media, the newsreel in *Citizen Kane*, the television broadcast in *While the City Sleeps*). With both filmic references Lang marks past eras in film history, eras now giving way to the new regime of television.

It would be a mistake to read the figure Lang constructs – with the lethal effects of television juxtaposed with Kyne's discussion of a free press – too literally. Lang most certainly marks an era with this direct substitution of one media with another, as Mobley's immediately following broadcast becomes Kyne's obituary. By 1956 television's transformation of the media landscape was evident (RKO, the studio which released *While the City Sleeps*, as it dissolved under Howard Hughes' management in the 50s, would become the television production studio for the queen of television, Lucille Ball, as its facilities became Desilu Productions, with Karl Freund, the cinematographer for *Metropolis*, shooting episodes of *I Love Lucy*). In fact, most of the 'all-star' cast of *While the City Sleeps* were featured in their own television series around this time. But Kyne's terroristic approach to the 'lipstick killer' story makes it clear that, despite his articulation of the values of the public sphere, he practised sensational reporting with gusto. Television simply extends a project of abstraction and dehumanisation inherent in Lang's portrayal of modernity since the twenties, and fully operative in print journalism as well as the new medium.

Mobley's broadcast to the unknown murderer reveals not only television's heightened role in realising the late stages of the project of modernity, but also its role as the fulfilment of Lang's own modern vision (or nightmare). From its first anticipations in his silent films to the featuring of the medium in his last film, *The Thousand Eyes of Dr. Mabuse*, Lang primarily conceived of television as a means of surveillance, rather than a means of representation like cinema (although, as *Fury* made clear, film could play this role as well). While Mobley's look at the camera during the television broadcast certainly carries some of the overtones of the enunciatory claims of earlier Lang characters (Mobley is not only analysing and defining the identity of the murderer, he is also setting up his own plot to capture him, using his on-air announcement of his engagement to Nancy as a lure), as I mentioned earlier, Lang is also simply recording the mode of address of television journalism. Mobley's interplay with Manners shows both the intrusive character of this new medium, seeming to spy out Manners in his bedroom, following the fiction of television's apparent intimacy and direct address exploited in many early television programmes which interviewed celebrities in their own homes. Mobley cannot, in fact, see Manners, and the journalist never has to undergo the discomfort that Casey Mayo experiences when he encounters and becomes personally involved with the flesh and blood embodiment of his unknown murderess. Instead, Mobley remains blind to Manners within his apparently all-seeing medium. The film ends with Manners reduced to a photograph, headline and printed confession in the *Sentinel* and its affiliated newspapers, and the last shot shows Mobley smothering a persistently ringing telephone with his hat, as he moves at last towards sleep (and other things) in the film's final dirty joke.

Inside Out

> It was clear to me that the letter had been turned, as a glove,
> inside out, re-directed, and re-sealed.
> > Edgar A. Poe, 'The Purloined Letter'[17]

Walter Benjamin referred to Edgar Poe's short story 'The Man of the Crowd', (a story which follows the mysterious, possibly criminal, eponymous character and his surveillance by the story's narrator, but without any discernible crime ever taking place) as 'something like the X-Ray picture of a detective story'.[18] Rather than presenting a crime and its detection, Poe's story seems to explore the parameters and conditions, the *données*, of the detective story, like a logical demonstration rather than a narrative. *Beyond a Reasonable Doubt* would seem to play a similar role in Lang's *œuvre*, a film, as Jacques Rivette claimed, which almost diagramatically demonstrates the mechanisms of Lang's narrative processes, and turns his most frequent patterns

inside out. While Lang's most famous American films frequently portrayed the plight of innocent characters mistakenly identified as murderers (as in *Fury*, *You Only Live Once*, and *The Blue Gardenia*), *Beyond a Reasonable Doubt* chronicles the process of freeing a condemned prisoner, believed to be innocent, who in the end turns out to be truly guilty. Whereas a series of Lang films show guilty (or guilty-appearing) characters systematically getting rid of the evidence that might condemn them (*The Woman in the Window*, *House by the River*, *Human Desire* – even Norah burning her taffeta dress in *The Blue Gardenia*) in *Beyond a Reasonable Doubt* protagonist Tom Garrett has himself photographed with compromising evidence and intentionally plants it in places (the murder site, his car seat and glove compartment) where he is sure it will be found. The role of misleading signs of innocence and guilt becomes reversed. Following the logic of Poe's 'The Purloined Letter' – but also of the blinding light of exposé in Lang's late Hollywood films which conceals through a glaring visuality – the evident and discoverable serve as a cloak for the truly hidden and secret.[19]

Likewise, *Beyond a Reasonable Doubt* can be read as one of Lang's ultimate and most devious parables of authorship. Tom Garrett, a former journalist, now turned successful novelist, appears to have two projects for his future: marrying Susan Spencer, the daughter of his former editor, Austin Spencer, and writing a second book to follow up and solidify his first success. His former editor and future father-in-law has his own project, a critique of capital punishment, particularly when based on circumstantial evidence, which often takes the form of a pointed attack on Thompson, the district attorney, whom Spencer feels is 'trying to reach the Governor's chair over the bodies of executed men'. Austin Spencer's project seems to dovetail with Garrett's plans for a new book, although their collaboration conflicts with Tom's plans to marry Susan, first delaying it and ultimately leading to a break in their engagement. Austin Spencer persuades Garrett to collaborate on an exposé of capital punishment which would prove an innocent man could be condemned to death based solely on circumstantial evidence. This work will not be another novel, since as Spencer puts it, 'a fictitious story wouldn't prove anything; it could only be proven by a fact, that no-one could deny'.

Thus this new work, whose form is never exactly specified (obviously a work of non-fiction, presumably a book, although Spencer may make use of it in his newspaper) will be based on actual events enacted and staged by Spencer and Garrett which appear to incriminate Garrett for a crime which he did not commit. Spencer selects a crime from the newspaper (illustrated by the diagrammatic crime photos Lang featured in *While the City Sleeps*, with arrows marking the murder site) for which the police have no strong suspect, the murder of Patty Gray, a burlesque dancer whose strangled body was found abandoned on a hillside. Garrett and Spencer then go about manufacturing evidence which could be construed as pointing to Garrett's guilt. The only description the police have of a suspect is a vague one based on another dancer's brief glimpse of the man Patty left with the night she was killed: a man of medium build with a grey coat and a brown hat who smoked a pipe and drove a dark late model car. Precisely the sort of vague description which would fit a million guys and so often entraps Lang's innocent protagonists, the description here functions like the blank-faced newspaper illustration in *While the City Sleeps*, an outline of an identity which Spencer and Garrett seek to fill in with Garrett's features.

Like so many of Lang's films, *Beyond a Reasonable Doubts* traces the construction of an identity against the dual background of modern attempts at surveillance and recording identity amid the general anonymity of modern existence. Garrett can step into the role of murderer because the murderer could be anyone. Not only does Garrett reverse the scenarios of entrapment of the innocent, he also displays an affinity for the construction of a false identity exerted by Lang's earlier master criminals through their skill at disguise. Like Mabuse, Garrett can fashion himself into someone else, only instead of the disguise showing a blatant theatricality and mastery of caricature (along with the delight in becoming someone else), this assumed identity possesses no strong characteristics. Garrett simply becomes himself with a few slight variations. His assumed identity is truly *nemo*, the modern man as no-one.

Lang portrays this construction of identity as evidence with a mirror shot which both recalls and contrasts with the shot of Haghi in front of his dressing-room mirror in *Spies* preparing his clown persona as Nemo. As Spencer buys Garrett a grey coat to resemble the one mentioned in the police description, Garrett stands modelling it in front of a three-faced full-length mirror (anticipating the greatest 50s fable of identity, Hitchcock's *Vertigo*). After the salesman leaves, Spencer prepares to photograph the buying of the coat. Garrett suggests, however, that Spencer position himself in such a way that he, too, will appear in the picture, reflected in the mirror. Spencer's appearance will reflect the constructed nature of the photograph and therefore the process itself. Instead of a man simply putting on a false face, as in *Spies*, Lang here shows the construction of identity as a collaboration and a fragment of a constructed narrative, with author and subject both caught in the mirror. Thus Lang composes an image (from a different point of view than Spencer's photograph) in which we see Garrett posed in the fitting room wearing the coat, Spencer with his camera on the right and, on the left in the mirror behind Garrett, Spencer repeated again in reflection as he snaps the picture. Lang includes the motif so frequent in his 50s films of the camera's flash starkly over-exposing a frame.

Photographing the process of fashioning Garrett's new identity and including Spencer in the photo represents an essential stage in their collaborative project. Spencer and Garrett will not only construct evidence and plant it, they will also record their process, thus lifting it from the realm of mere fiction of Garrett's previous novel and guaranteeing its non-fictional aspect (recall Godard's claim that every film could be dissolved into the non-fictional documentary of its process of production). In other words, Spencer and Garrett construct a double scenario. The evidence is planted in order to be discovered and (mis)read by the police and district attorney as signs of Garrett's guilt. But simultaneously, other evidence is created and another story is recorded: the photographs of the construction of Garrett's guilt, which will deconstruct the first scenario, prove it to be a fictitious construct and, in the process, establish Garrett's innocence. In order for Spencer's exposé to work, the second scenario must be withheld, must hide behind the first. Spencer and Garrett construct the first in order that the police and Thompson the DA might discover it, and must believe they are uncovering something the culprit wishes to conceal (his guilt). But after the first reading has proceeded to its culmination – Garrett's conviction for a murder he did not convict – then the *coup de théâtre* will take place and the second scenario will be revealed, the one which was truly and cleverly hidden (even concealed from Susan, daughter and fiancée, which creates the tension that breaks up the engagement). This revelation will reveal the misreading by the minions of the law, and demonstrate the dangers of sentencing someone to capital punishment based on circumstantial evidence, accomplishing Spencer's purpose and, presumably giving Garrett material and publicity for his next best-seller.

Who then is the author of this work-in-progress? While Garrett is assumed to be the writer ('That's the way I make my living', he explains in his last line of the film), we never see him writing (other than doodling during his trial and then tearing up the paper, an image broadcast in the television coverage of his trial). Susan at one point inspects his typewriter and says, 'You were on page four three weeks ago and you're on page four now! You're not a slow writer, you just don't write!' While this may be a subterfuge to conceal his true project from Susan, there is no question that Austin Spencer takes on the visible role of authority in the constructing of the crime. He proposes the theme to Garrett, points out the case they will duplicate in the newspaper and tells Garrett where and how to stand as he takes the photographs which will establish his innocence (although, as in the fitting room, Garrett occasionally makes his own suggestions). Spencer aims the camera and holds the evidence for safe keeping in his wall safe. Although he maintains a circumspect silence during Garrett's arrest and trial, it is clear that Spencer constructs this arrest and conviction as his own plot, even designating a privileged reader for it: District Attorney Thompson, whom Spencer manipulates into misreading the evidence. Both Garrett and Spencer seem to enjoy the way they mislead Thompson, and Lang cuts from Thompson making a rather theatrical gesture of satisfaction after Dolly Moore's testimony to a medium shot of Garrett concealing his own smirk of amusement.

As an unreliable narrator, one who devises scenes and situations so that they will be misread, withholding information (the photographs and other documents Spencer keeps locked in his safe), Spencer not only acts as an author, but resembles Lang's own techniques of devious narration. As both the constructor of artifice and the holder of the truth, Spencer is a particularly powerful author figure, awaiting his moment for the revelation which will climax his staged drama and demonstrate his thesis about capital punishment. Immediately after Garrett's amusement at

Thompson's confidence Lang dissolves to a close-up of a radio announcing the second day of jury deliberations and the possibility of an imminent verdict in Garrett's trial. The progress of the trial is chronicled in headlines, and radio and television broadcasts, Lang making clear that it is a media event, fully covered by the various forms of journalism. Spencer's exposé unfolds in the glare of publicity. However, Lang pans to show Spencer removing the secret evidence from his safe and placing it in envelopes. The media have no idea that they, too, are being manipulated as part of Spencer's plot and that he holds in his hands evidence that will determine and probably reverse the outcome of these deliberations.

As Spencer takes the evidence out to his car, presumably to transport it to the courtroom and deliver it to the district attorney at the moment of Garrett's verdict, the car radio continues to comment on the trial, making the point that Garrett was working on his 'second novel'. The key turning point of the film occurs precisely as Spencer seeks to reveal his authorship, display the documents of his hidden narrative and reverse the course of events. As he backs out of his garage, an oncoming truck slams into his car, turning it over and causing it to burst into flames as Spencer screams within. Lang stages the death of the author pyrotechnically in the last of his Hollywood conflagrations, including another image-effacing flash frame of blinding light as the flames engulf the screen. The fire will destroy not only the author of the plot, but also the evidence he carries that shows there was a plot, a second 'non-fictional' narrative lurking under and reversing the surface story of guilt the DA has presented. In the last shot of the sequence Lang shows flames surrounding the now tilted and driverless steering wheel as the radio continues to broadcast, announcing, 'And so the fate of Tom Garrett today rests solely in the hearts and minds of twelve jurors.' The hubris of authorship, of the assumption of the control of the media and even of the course of the unfolding of the film has met its characteristic Langian outcome. Control eludes the would-be enunciator/author with fatal consequences and another essential undelivered message, the evidence of Spencer's plot, goes astray. The radio broadcast which shortly before seemed dependent on Spencer's control of information, now has the last word, and locates Garrett's fate outside Spencer's control.

The first double story has been demolished in a burst of flame; Lang superimposes the car's flames over Garrett's cell as he dissolves to the next scene, with Garrett lying calmly reading, awaiting the jury's delayed verdict when his lawyer enters. He advises the lawyer to relax too, since there is nothing they can do about the verdict. But when he learns about Austin Spencer's death, and realises that now there truly is *nothing* he can do about the verdict, he gives way to panic, grabbing and shaking his lawyer and frantically divulging Spencer's plot. However, without the author's authority and supporting evidence to back the story up, it has no status as 'non-fiction' and is ridiculed as improbable in court. 'It is highly significant', District Attorney Thompson declares, 'that the defendant comes up with this incredible, fantastic story about an alleged plan now after Mr. Spencer's death.' However, the judge grants the defence an opportunity to present tangible evidence in support of its claim. The search for the photographs at first yields nothing until it occurs to Susan Spencer the photos might have been with her father in the car.

Lang cuts to this new evidence, bits of black chemical waste encased in sheets of glass, as the assistant district attorney describes them as the remnants of photographs charred beyond recognition with no possibility of recovering the images they once held. Not even that residual trace of writing so useful to Lang's secret agents has been retained. Susan holds the sections of glass up to the light coming through the office window, as if hoping some transparency might reveal a trace of image, but they remain dark and impenetrable, like the black, deeply shadowed windows of the office buildings seen outside. Here the ambition of the exposé to reveal all in a blinding flash of truth has reached the limits of opacity, the ultimate blindness that haunts all of Lang's cinema, but especially his late films. The products of Spencer's auto-developing camera, these photographs did not even leave behind a negative which could reproduce their image, only a unique original, now reduced to ash. No Lang situation shows more vividly the limits of visual representation.

The undoing of an author-like character, an enunciator who hubristically seems to control the unfolding of the film's story, whether Lang's master criminals or his artists who try to capture the object of their desire in an image, forms the core of Lang's *œuvre*. However, the demonstration of their final impotence, the snatching away of their enunciatory power, usually marks the end of a Lang film. Therefore, while the death of Austin Spencer seems to fulfil a Langian design, it does so in an apparently deviant manner; destroying the author's control midway through the film. The film seems now to slide back into a more familiar Langian scenario, the entrapping of an innocent man, despite his pleas of innocence and even the efforts of his former fiancée, Susan Spencer, who uses the power of her dead father's paper to get Garrett's case reconsidered. Finally, a familiar Langian device intervenes, the discovery among Austin's paper of a letter addressed to District Attorney Thompson describing his own scheme, including 'the dates, the places, the explanation'. The delayed communication surfaces with its almost magical liberating effects, as Thompson himself asks the governor to pardon Garrett.

In the midst of this apparently happy ending, as Garrett meets with Susan Spencer in the warden's office, the script gives the film its final twist, which not only provides an unsuspected denouement, but demands that the viewer reconsider its parable of authorship one more time. As Serge Daney has observed, *Beyond a Reasonable Doubt* demands to be watched twice, first for its suspenseful unfolding and second to enjoy its wit in reverse.[20] Like so many characters in Lang's films, from Professor Wanley to Emil Czaka, the almost-freed Tom Garrett makes one of those off-guard slips that seems like an unconscious confession of an *Id* desiring punishment. Garrett refers to the woman murdered under the name Patty Gray, as 'Emma', revealing he knows her real name, Emma Blooker, and therefore actually knew the woman he claimed never to have met. As Susan confronts him with his slip, he confesses the truth: that he *did* murder Patty Gray or Emma Blooker, that she was a former wife from his youth who had disappeared then reappeared just as he was about to marry Susan and had threatened to blackmail him. He claims Austin Spencer's scheme showed him a way to commit the murder and get away with it. Susan leaves stunned and apparently repulsed and Lang lingers on Garrett standing alone in the warden's office. As Lang dissolves to the next scene, a newspaper front page and headline are superimposed over Garrett, reading: 'Garrett is Innocent'.

With this confession and ironic image Lang not only offers his final dark image of the value of the journalistic exposé, but opens a reconsideration of the whole previous film text. We now no longer see Garrett as Spencer's collaborator, willing to take on the role that he suggested while Spencer held the camera and seemed to direct the show. Instead Spencer was Garrett's dupe, a man whom he manipulated so perfectly that he left him with the illusion intact that he was the author and director of the scheme. He creates, as Georges Sturm puts it, a *mise-en-scène* within a *mise-en scène*,[21] in fact a *mise-en-abîme* on the issue of authorship and direction. In many ways, as Raymond Bellour pointed out, Garrett therefore resembles Joe

Wilson in *Fury*, using the processes of a trial for his own aims, only here to create an extraordinary alibi, rather than punish a murderous mob.[22] And in contrast to showing us Joe's plot as it unfolds as he did in *Fury*, Lang here behaves like Austin Spencer, creating a misleading narration, withholding essential information until the final few minutes of the film. Behind Garrett's manipulation of events and their perception by other characters, we see Lang's own manipulation of our point of view.

Thus the second viewing of the film recommended by Daney allows us to watch for the clues to Garrett's authorship, re-reading them – such as the real significance of Garrett's half-concealed smirk during the trial. Garrett's manipulation of Spencer is flawless, letting him suggest both the murder case to use and proposing Garrett as the apparent murderer, decisions Garrett had to foresee ahead of time, but which gave Spencer the illusion of having freely chosen them (almost like a theological paradox of free-will and providence). While his desire to have Spencer appear in the photograph seems entirely logical, the framing of the cameraman within Garrett's composition visually indicates Spencer's unwitting absorption into Garrett's plot (much like Bannion appearing in Mrs. Duncan's mirror early in *The Big Heat*). As he cleans his car before placing the incriminating evidence of body make-up and stocking, Garrett also shows that he knows the fact that blackmailer Heidt told Alice Reed in *The Woman in the Window*, that the complete removal of fingerprints can seem as suspicious as incriminating marks themselves, that in effect, careful erasure can be a powerful mode of authorship.

The basic figure of *Beyond a Reasonable Doubt* consists of the palimpsest formed by the superimposition of Spencer's plot over Garrett's in such a manner that the staging of evidence by Garrett and Spencer covers and obscures Garrett's original action. But Lang has also left room within his design for the construction of still other stories. Instead of simply being Spencer's dupe, District Attorney Thompson actually arrives at the true story (masquerading as the false construction) of Tom Garrett's guilt, partly by following up bits of evidence *not* planted by Garrett and Spencer, such as the withdrawal of three thousand dollars from Garrett's bank account and the re-deposit of most of the money soon after. The motive that Thompson assigns for Garrett's murder of Patty Gray/Emma Blooker – the need to rid himself of her so that he could 'fulfil his commitment to Miss Spencer', perfectly matches the explanation Garrett finally gives Susan for the murder. Likewise, his explanation of the withdrawal and re-deposit of the money – that Garrett paid Patty/Emma the money then ransacked her apartment and retrieved most of it after he murdered her – also fits the facts and seems very likely. Rather than a mechanical reader responding to misleading cues, Thompson appears as a clever investigator.

However, one main clue that he produces leads in another direction and reveals the maze of potential stories that Lang made sure persisted around the edges of the basic figure. The initial police reports indicate that Patty Gray's murderer smoked a pipe. This is the one aspect of the description that Garrett and Spencer do not pick up on or attempt to recreate. However, Thompson finds in a search of Garrett's house and garage a number of matchbook covers which bear the imprint of a pipe rim, as if a pipe smoker had used them to tamp down his tobacco. Here Garrett's explanation seems adequate: that he has visitors who smoke pipes and undoubtedly leave their matchbook covers behind. Thompson doubts the explanation, but Lang has shown Austin Spencer using a matchbook in precisely this manner and tossing it aside in Garrett's garage. Why do Spencer and Garrett avoid this one detail of the police description and why does Lang emphasise it? Philippe Arnaud makes it clear in his reading of Lang's notes on the film's script that this detail functions as a red herring, designed, in fact, to mislead the viewer into another possible story construction.[23] Lang and the scriptwriter (but with Lang apparently stressing this alternative explanation in his notes to the script), at several points hint that Spencer might actually be the murderer (the pipe being the main clue – as well as the fact that Lang cuts to Spencer each time it is mentioned in court – but also Spencer's apparent previous knowledge of the strip club and the dancers). Unquestionably this remains merely a red herring, but if the viewer is prompted to suspect Spencer, it would reveal Garrett's *modus operandi* of using the apparent exposé of capital punishment as an alibi for murder. Thus one false turn in the maze of stories could lead towards the correct solution.

The knitting together and subsequent unravelling of plots and motivations, intentions and apparent authorship, hidden guilts and over-obvious alibis, do make *Beyond a Reasonable Doubt* seem more like a demonstration of Langian narrative principles than a film in itself. Lang worried before and after the film's production about the audience's attitude to the main character Garrett, who in the last few minutes is revealed to be a murderer after being the protagonist, presumed innocent, throughout the previous part of the film.[24] But possibly more radical (or more dangerous) from the point of view of audience involvement than this apparent moral switch is the discovery that so much of the film has been withheld from us, not simply Garrett's guilt, but a whole backstory of a youthful marriage, a sudden reappearance of a deceitful and errant wife, a decision to commit murder and the carrying-out of the act, and then the decision to cover it up. All of these events could be more psychologically interesting and potentially more dramatic and involving than the rather methodically dull character we are allowed to observe, idly doodling on a piece of paper or reading as his fate is being decided – particularly with Dana Andrews' low-key performance.

Once again it is hard to decide if this is the extreme point of Lang's abstraction, his demonstration that this rather humdrum character we have watched is actually capable of murder, or simply a sign of a flawed and inexpert script, as André Bazin, and to some degree Lang himself, seemed to have felt.[25] However, Arnaud's research makes it clear that Lang did in fact work hard on analysing and revising the original script, and so many elements correspond to devices within his previous *œuvre* that it is hard to dismiss the film as bungled or impersonal. Among Lang's papers related to this film, the Eisenschitz and Bertetto volume reproduces two pages of notes, representing two different stages of the film's scenario. In spite of minor differences between them, they both cover the opening events of the film. Lang has arranged the events in two columns which reveal the basic narrative approach of the film. On the left, the column is labelled, 'What the audience sees and knows', while the right column is headed, 'What happens – but we don't show', or, in the later version, 'What happens but the audience *doesn't know!*' Lang carefully charts out all the unseen events (e.g. Emma's phone calls, her meeting with Garrett, his withdrawing money and paying her, the murder, his ransacking of the apartment and recovering money, etc.) and their temporal relation to the events that are shown (in Russian formalist terms, outlining the *fabula*'s relation to the *syuzhet*). If one can dismiss problems of performance and casting, low-budget set design, and a cinematographer hardly up to the standards of Lang's earlier films as being outside his control, the structure of the film remains very much under his scrutiny, yielding simultaneously a brilliant demonstration of unique narrative construction and a supremely inhuman film.

The final reframing of the film which establishes Garrett as the 'author' of the plot, reveals a new method for the Mabuse figure, the grand enunciator: a criminal who, instead of making his presence known by his daring acts and the chaos he sows, remains entirely concealed beneath the apparently normal processes of law and exposé. As an author who 'doesn't write' Garrett appear as a *deus absconditus*, able to sit back and pare his nails as his plot is worked out by others more passionately involved than he is. Patty/Emma's apparently catastrophic entrance into his life appears within the body of the film only through the phone call that interrupts his lovemaking with Susan Spencer early on. Garrett's first impulse is to follow the example of Mobley at the end of *While the City Sleeps* and let the phone ring. However, Susan tells him to take the call. He claims later that the call was from his publisher demanding that Garrett get to work on his next book, thus placing Emma's reappearance in his life under the guise of a demand for authorship. However, what he had first said to Susan as he takes the call seems even more apropos: 'I'll get rid of this.' Getting rid of Patty/Emma is precisely the phrase both Thompson and the assistant district attorney use to provide the motive for Garrett murdering her, and the phrase with its overtones of discarding some annoying thing evokes Stephen Byrne's attempt to conceal the body of Emily in *House by the River* (as Garrett's apparent plan to turn his experience into a book recalls Byrne's novel written after the murder). In his nonchalant attitude to the murder, even his passionless confession, Garrett appears the most inhuman of Lang's murderers, a man entirely absorbed with his own projects and the way to get rid of obstacles with the least risk but never displaying either the master criminals' will-to-power or the artists' obsessions with desire.

Realising that Emma's phone call to Garrett is one of the things that happens that we don't know (or don't know fully), doubles Lang's use of the device of the delayed message in the film: not only Austin Spencer's explanation, but the significance of

this phone call is withheld from us for most of the film. Thus the phone call interrupting the love scene between Garrett and Susan near the opening of the film (the
second scene after the credits) is matched by the phone call which interrupts the
signing of Garrett's pardon in the film's final scene. This last call actually comes in
the middle of a question from a reporter about Garrett's relationship with Susan.
Once again Lang withholds the actual content of the call, but the context and the
reaction of the governor – remanding Garrett back to his cell, and declaring 'There
will be no pardon' – make it clear the call has conveyed Susan's information that
Garrett confessed to committing the murder. There is no mystery here. One thinks
of the phone call in *You Only Live Once* which superseded the law, interrupted
Joan's suicide, announced Eddie's escape from electrocution and accomplished the
bringing together of separated lovers. Systematically this phone call has the opposite effect in this film. A pardon rather than a suicide is stopped in midcourse, an
execution reinstated, and one lover informs on another. The law, not desire triumphs. The last shot of the film shows Garrett's still characteristically inexpressive
face as he looks at the unsigned pardon off screen, resting on the governor's desk.
The newspaper photographers take more pictures, their flashbulbs again clearing
the screen of any image with their burst of light, before Garrett is led off and the
film ends. The door closing behind him is the last image appearing in Lang's last
American film.

18

The Circle Closes on the Last Mabuse

Return to the Scene of the Crime

Home is where you go when you run out of places.
Mae Doyle in the Fritz Lang/Alfred Hayes' version of
Clash by Night

One cannot approach Lang's return to Germany without a sense of the uncanny – in German terms *das unheimlich* – that profoundly unsettling feeling that in the midst of the supposedly familiar (or 'homelike' to give a literal translation of *das heimliche*) something profoundly unfamiliar has arisen, not from the foreign and alien, but from the deepest reaches of both memory and forgetfulness. Freud points out that repetition in itself evokes a sense of *das unheimlich*,[1] and Lang's return to his former homeland recycles material from his earlier film-making career during the Weimar period for two new films. Yet this return to Germany from exile also yields a profound sense of the untimeliness of history, the knowledge that nothing can ever truly be repeated, and that in repetition lies not so much the promise of rebirth as the harbinger of death. Repetition involves a profound mourning for the passage of time.

Lang himself spoke of his return as 'like a circle that was beginning to close – a kind of fate'.[2] It is only when envisioning the ending of a life or a career that such a pattern could be recognised or such a fate accepted. Lang was referring specifically to the offer from West German producer Artur Brauner to make a new film based on *Das indische Grabmal* scripted by Thea von Harbou and directed by Joe May in 1921. Lang claimed that the earlier script was a collaboration between Harbou and himself (one of their first) and that Lang had been slated to direct it, but, at the last moment, May announced that he himself would take over the film. Whether or not Lang's account is completely accurate (even in his remake, only Harbou is credited with the original story), the experience of regaining a project taken away from him, reversing an episode of youthful impotence that occurred before he had attained fame and power, undoubtedly gave Lang a circular sense of completion, the granting of a long delayed promise. In 1965 Lang explained his decision to Peter Bogdanovich by saying, 'You should make a picture you started.'[3] Was Lang aware he was echoing one of his last lines as 'Fritz Lang' in Godard's *Contempt*, the line before he explains that he is about to shoot the scene of Ulysses' first glimpse of his homeland on his return?[4] For Lang, the return from exile began under the spell of the recovery of something lost, finishing a film begun decades earlier. In the years between, of course, Lang had experienced world-wide fame, undergone the break-up of his marriage with Harbou, witnessed the rise of the Nazis and survived exile, a world war and a Hollywood career. Was he now beginning over again, wiping away those years of both triumph and trauma?

This two-part film, *The Tiger of Eschnapur* and *The Indian Tomb*, was shot partly on location in India. Once again Lang appears to shadow the career of Jean Renoir who also shot his first film after his Hollywood career, *The River*, in India – although one could hardly imagine films more different, or visions of India more contrasting, than Lang's and Renoir's. As in the Asian film of another 50s refugee from the Hollywood studio system, Josef von Sternberg's *Anatahan*, produced and shot in Japan, Lang created an India of his imagination, drawn from the Orientalism of such German painters as Ludwig Deutsch and Rudolph Ernst, as well as the Arabian novels of Karl May. Lang's films also revive a tradition of German Orientalist silent films, including: Joe May's original *Das indische Grabmal* and sequences of his *Die Herrin der Welt*; Lang's own *Hara Kiri* and *Die Spinnen*; as well as the German–Indian films of Franz Osten (*Shiraz* and *A Throw of Dice*) from the late 20s. But while in debt to a long tradition of European Orientalist fantasies (with all the richness of imagery and dubious ideology that that entails) Lang's Indian films relate even more strongly to the contemporary late films of Sternberg and Renoir. Like *Anatahan* and *The River*, *The Tiger of Eschnapur* and *The Indian Tomb* attempt to establish an alternative film-making style to the classical Hollywood narrative forms, while making full use of the devices of visual spectacle each director had perfected in different ways. All these films express a debt to the silent cinema in which the directors began their careers, especially to the visual language forged in that era and a form of imagistic rather than psychological narrative. But in the case of Lang and Renoir the more recent innovation of colour photography formed a cornerstone of this desire to recapture the visuality of the earlier cinema in a modern form.

The bitter attacks on Lang's Indian films by West German reviewers (in spite of their popularity and commercial success) decried them as anachronisms, returning to an outmoded dramaturgy, an attempt to revive a style of epic film-making that had perished with Kriemhild and the Nibelungs. Such criticism shows tremendous myopia, since Lang's control of colour photography (particularly the ways the colours and hues of costumes relate to the colour values in the various decors) represents a truly modern aspect of film-making. The non-realistic, semi-abstract plot and characters would inspire the most advanced film-makers of the 60s, such as Jean-Luc Godard and Jean Marie Straub.[5] But on a more profound level, Lang does create an untimely style of film-making and even attempts a work of resurrection – one that goes further back than his own silent films to realms of myth and magic. German critics compared the films to *Die Nibelungen*, a work that Lang refused to remake when Brauner suggested it after the Indian films, partly, he claimed, because of the difficulty of treating a mythical subject in sound cinema.[6] However, as I tried to show, *Die Nibelungen* chronicles the decay and betrayal of a mythical world, as the supernatural heroes Siegfried and Brunhild descend into the world of treacherous human civilisation. In the Indian films, representatives of the enlightened arts of the West, architects and engineers, penetrate into ever more ancient layers of the city and palace of Eschnapur, discovering a realm of magic and divine power, which can either betray or redeem.

The *Tiger of Eschnapur* ends with its hero Berger, the German architect, and his lover Seetha nearly perishing in the desert from thirst and heat as they try to escape from Eschnapur. Before he collapses, Berger fires his automatic into an overpowering sun which burns out the screen. As if Lang were directly attacking the over-exposed, blinding light which dominated his last Hollywood films, in these films his protagonists seek refuge within cavernous realms of magic and concealment. But this is a realm of other gods and powers than those found in the Odenwald or the volcanic mountains of Iceland; Lang lets the nationalist super-heroes he had created in the 20s rest in their tombs. The mythical figures that emerge here are frankly sensuous mother goddesses, whose images, sculpted or painted, are enclosed in caves. The most magical moment in these films occurs when a spider, responding to Seetha's prayers to the image of Shiva, weaves a web over the entrance to the cave in which Seetha and her German lover hide from the Maharajah's troops, the glistening web convincing the searching soldiers that no-one has passed into the cave recently. This salvation accomplished by the smallest of the goddess's creatures endows the film with a gentle fairy-tale quality, quite in contrast to the epic mythical imagery of Siegfried's battle with Fafner the dragon.

But if a certain innocence radiates from the film's folk-tale plot, nonetheless the gods, or rather goddesses, remain jealous and vengeful when betrayed, with the lovers' refuge immediately invaded when Berger eats the fruit consecrated to the goddess, and Seetha loses the goddess's favour when Berger accidentally witnesses her secret ritual dance before the huge image of the goddess in the lower levels of the city. As in *Dr. Mabuse, the Gambler*, a magical performance, in this case a fakir performing the traditional rope trick, serves as camouflage for a murder. The cavernous depths of Eschnapur contain images of living death in the leper colony imprisoned there, and characters face mortal danger when they lose their way in this labyrinth, as Maria did in the catacombs under the city of Metropolis. Magic and the divine return to the screen in Lang's Indian films, but they remain ambiguous forces. The goddess may offer benevolence and protection, but Lang persists in seeing mythical forces as ultimately dangerous and inimical to humans, sinister and misleading.

All of Lang's exotic films of the 50s, both in Hollywood and West Germany, *Rancho Notorious*, *Moonfleet*, and *The Tiger of Eschnapur* and *The Indian Tomb*, present colourful worlds of the past whose exotic locations, drenched in history and legend, provide a seeming respite from the harsh black and white worlds of his contemporary exposés. But Lang's characters never recover a lost paradise for long. Ultimately in all these films the past emerges in terms of loss: the scars on Jeremy Fox's shoulder from the teeth of watchdogs set on him in his youth, in which the terrified John Mohune recognises the embodiment of his mother's nightmarish tales of her childhood; or the tales of lost fame and elegance that Vern evokes from Altar Keane as he probes her memories at Chuck a Luck ranch. These apparently escapist films seek out hidden or subterranean worlds which promise protection and riches, but are finally revealed to be tombs, whether the literal crypt of the Mohunes in *Moonfleet* in which young John Mohune encounters the rotting skeleton of his ancestor; the leper cave in the Indian films; or the Chuck a Luck ranch in *Rancho Notorious*, which Vern denounces to Altar as a morgue and a graveyard – metaphors that a few minutes later, after the final shoot-out, are rendered literal. Lang's attempt at reviving a visual style which kept faith with the silent Weimar cinema recaptured a magical world, but one whose treachery and corrupt foundations cannot be glossed over. As in all of Lang's resurrections, the return of the past reveals the uncanny presence of death in life. As beautiful as the Indian films are – with their colour, elegance of costume and decor, graceful and sensual actors' movement and lush lighting – they remain a portrayal of an enclosed world, a tomb from whose funereal richness and imprisoning luxury the characters spend most of the film attempting to escape.

Having completed the film the earlier realisation of which was interrupted, and having turned down the offer to remake another one of his mythical or legendary Weimar films (Brauner suggested both *Die Nibelungen* and *Der müde Tod*), Lang next decided to undertake a different sort of resurrection. In turning down the remakes Lang declared that he did not wish to repeat himself;[7] his West German films refer back to his Weimar films, not through repetition, but completion: bringing an interrupted process to an end, finishing off a series. Lang agreed to complete his Mabuse series with a third film. He claimed in interviews that his first reaction to doing another Mabuse film was, 'Look, for me the son-of-a-bitch is dead. Buried.'[8] Or 'I already killed that son-of-a-bitch!'[9] But the previous Mabuse film had demonstrated that being dead and being unable to influence events are two different things. In this film the return of the dead became the premise of the plot, allowing Lang to acknowledge explicitly the difference between the eras of the films, and make the time that had elapsed between them part of the new plot. *The Testament of Dr. Mabuse* had marked the transition from the Germany of the inflation era to a Germany on the verge of Nazi takeover, as well as the transformation Lang and cinema had made from silence to sound. Why not make a film which marked Germany's survival of both the Third Reich and defeat in World War II, and its movement into the postwar economic miracle? The spectre of Mabuse, the persistence of his criminal legacy would brood over a trilogy that embraced the history of Germany in the twentieth century.

Compared to the glorious colours, opulent settings and luxurious costumes of the Indian films, *The Thousand Eyes of Dr. Mabuse*, with its stark black and white, minimal sets, and lousy process shots, takes on the appearance of an act of mourning, sackcloth and ashes. Lang returns to the harsh look of his late-Hollywood, low-budget films, although the shadows and highlights achieved here are richer. The theme of the exposé immediately opens the film, as the investigative reporter of Lang's late-Hollywood films collides with his long-lasting theme of the interrupted message. The film's first scene shows the murder, en route to a television studio for his news broadcast, of reporter Peter Barter, who has just told his station managers that he has the 'hottest news story of the year'. Instead of Barter delivering his exposé (presumably concerning the return of the Mabuse gang), a young woman reporter takes his place before the camera and announces his death (like Ed Mobley delivering Amos Kyne's obituary on the air immediately following his death).

Jonathan Crary's insightful treatment of Lang's Mabuse series locates the thematic core of the films in the way 'these films compellingly chart the mobile characteristics of various perceptual technologies and apparatuses of power'.[10] *Dr. Mabuse, the Gambler*, as Crary points out, employs 'an array of spectacular techniques of dazzlement, immobilization and suggestion'. Mabuse's hypnotic power was embodied in his gaze and his control over the visual experience of others, whether through his attempts to mesmerise von Wenk with glimmering glasses and crystals, or to fascinate a theatre audience with optical illusions. With the coming of sound cinema, Mabuse (or his heir Dr. Baum) exerts power, less through a control of vision, than the amplification, recording and broadcast of his voice, establishing, as Crary puts it, 'tactics of simulation, recording and telecommunication in which auditory experience is primary'.[11] The culmination of these systems of perceptual control and illusion comes in *The Thousand Eyes of Dr. Mabuse* in which, to quote Crary, 'the cathode ray tube becomes a dominant component of the Mabuse system'.[12] In contrast to Lang's late-Hollywood films, television, the new form of publicity and exposé, does not primarily serve as the tool of an investigative reporter. Lang kills this figure off in the film's first minutes, thus keeping him off the air. The exploration of Barter's ransacked apartment by Police Commissioner Kras only reveals his notebook labeled 'Television Journal' with all its papers ripped out, a tape recorder with all of its recordings missing, and a television set with its picture tube smashed. Lang has snatched the technology of observation and exposure from the hands of the reporter and returned it to the pervasive, paranoia-generating system of the unseen master criminal and grand enunciator.

The first moments of *The Thousand Eyes of Dr. Mabuse* unwind as if Lang had never left Germany, so smoothly does he resume the style of editing and sound links that characterised his last German films, *The Testament of Dr. Mabuse* in particular. The first twelve or so minutes of *The Thousand Eyes* consist of a dozen short scenes, nearly all of them less than two minutes in duration and most of them less than a minute, which switch rapidly from location to location, each of them ending with a sound link which propels us into the next scene, in spite of temporal ellipsis or spatial distance. This breathless opening not only conveys a sense of fast-breaking action as we see television reporter Peter Barter shot in his car in the first minute and a half, but also embeds this opening murder into a network of prophecy, investigation and suspicion. As in the earlier Mabuse films, Lang demonstrates the cinema's ability to portray the complexities of crime and detection within a modern metropolis and an interlocking landscape of information (and dis-information).

Lang returns to the terrain of modernity, resurrecting a montage style which he had been forced to tame in his Hollywood films. But the nature of this network of interlocking crimes and the fear they inspire has changed since the silent films which first established Lang's imagery of the modern environment as the topography of terror. In the openings of *Dr. Mabuse, the Gambler* and *Spies*, Lang moved breathlessly through the synchronised unfolding of a murder and heist, or elliptically through a series of interlocking thefts and assassinations. Each sequence found its centre either in Mabuse at his telephone, timing all the actions, or Haghi, announcing to the camera his authorship of these crimes. In *The Thousand Eyes of Dr. Mabuse*, the grand enunciator remains hidden or at least camouflaged. The essential question of Lang's master criminal films: 'Who is behind all this?' is no longer explicitly articulated, let alone answered. In a further development of the dispersion that Nicole Brenez noted in *The Testament of Dr. Mabuse*,[13] the opening crimes cannot be attributed to an identifiable enunciator-figure. They seem to wander astray in a flurry of associations, cued by Lang's free-roaming, associative editing.

The *mise-en-scène* of the film's opening shot formally anticipates Barter's murder, foreshadowing his elimination before it occurs. The camera pulls back from a medium shot of Barter in his white sedan to reveal a black sedan creeping in from off screen right. This sinister vehicle moves into the foreground and eclipses the white car, the camera now framing the man within the black car who will kill Barter. From a close-up of this expectant assassin drumming his fingers on the case that holds his weapon, Lang cuts to the roster of the homicide bureau including the name of Commissioner Kras, the protagonist of this film, heir to Lohmann.[14] The cut is proleptic, like the anticipatory composition of the previous scene; no murder has taken place, yet Lang has already brought us to the homicide bureau. The theme of anticipation and prolepsis turns into literal prophecy in the next few shots, as Commissioner Kras receives a phone call from the psychic Cornelius who claims to have a vision of an impending murder, which he describes as if it were unfolding before him: 'There are two cars I see in particular stopping for a light … I see two men, calamity for one – an evil plan – murder!'

Providing the film's first strong sound link, Cornelius's declaration, 'murder!' triggers the cut to the assassin in the black car, as he removes his futuristic rifle from its case, shoulders it, and shoots Barter. In the following close-up, Barter slumps onto his steering wheel. Reproducing the staging of the murder at the traffic light of Dr. Kramm from *The Testament of Dr. Mabuse*, Lang then cuts to a traffic cop waving cars on.[15] A topographical high angle shot shows the traffic begin to move – except for Barter's immobilised car. Lang then cuts to a close-up of a clock reading one minute to four. The traditional image of mortality in Lang here also signals the deadline of modern information broadcasting, four o'clock marking the time for Barter's broadcast, as this close-up introduces the television studio. The woman reporter substitutes for him, and following another shot of the clock (now reading four), the report of Barter's death is broadcast, with the cause of death described as a heart attack. The next cut – back to the hitman in the car reporting the success of the assassination over a phone to someone he addresses as 'Doctor' – immediately undercuts this broadcast (mis)information.

The following cut takes us to the man who is receiving the assassin's report, but unlike the portrait shots of Mabuse or Haghi pictured at their control desks as they receive the reports of their henchmen, we see only a closely framed shot of a microphone and broadcasting apparatus with hands resting upon it. No face is revealed, only an off screen voice is heard. As if to compensate for this exclusion of facial identity, the camera tilts down to reveal a clubfoot, as the 'doctor' issues further orders to the murderer. As we then cut back to the car carrying the assassin, our own curiosity and frustration are voiced by the chauffeur of the black car who tells the murderer (again echoing lines from *Testament*), that he would like to see the doctor in person. Cautioned about the dire fate of others who have shared his curiosity, the driver shudders, but responds, 'I still want to know what the fellow really looks like, this doctor.' Lang cuts directly to Cornelius in the midst of conversation, saying he 'can't explain things like this'. As the camera pulls back we realise he is speaking to Kras about his visions, but the immediate link makes it seem that Cornelius is reacting to the driver's curiosity.

In the conversation between Kras and Cornelius about his visions, Lang recycles his antinomy of vision and blindness. Kras scoffs as Cornelius in a strained accumulation of metaphors describes the darkness that enwraps him ('It is impossible to suppress the viscous black magic that permeates, foggy as a graveyard in the night under a dark cloud'). His visions, Cornelius claims, emerge as sudden piercings of this obscurity. He responds to Kras's scepticism by removing his dark glasses and revealing his white, pupil-less eyes, the startling visual equivalent of his hyperbolic language. Without his eyes, Cornelius declares, he sees far better than many. A phone call immediately confirms Cornelius's prescience as a police official calls to inform Kras that an autopsy has revealed Barter's death was not due to a heart attack, but to a steel needle embedded in his skull – a murder, as Cornelius had predicted.

Lang's sound links now embed the opening murder into the process of investigation, as Lang cuts from Kras's phrase ('a long steel needle rammed in his head') to a close-up of this needle seen through a magnifying glass, being examined by a police technician. Lang returns to the scientific processes of police investigation so lovingly detailed in his last films before the war. The cut from the lab technician takes us to a roving shot of Barter's ransacked apartment, the camera moving among the scattered objects until Kras's hand enters the frame and defines this somewhat sinister prowling image as a police investigation. The scene links the earlier detailing of police procedure in the late-German films with the recurring scenes of crime locations in the late-Hollywood films. But Kras claims that nothing will be found here. Not only are the records of Barter's investigation missing, but even the blotter from his desk (the repository of vestigial messages still possible to decode in *Spies*) has been taken, and no fragmentary inscription remains on the window panes (as in *Testament*) – only a smashed television set, which, Kras assures the assistant dusting it, will yield no fingerprints. The bulb of a police camera flashes, but compared to the over-exposed frames of the Hollywood films, its effect is weak. Kras remarks that all they have is a long steel needle (clearly lost within a haystack of non-evidence).

In the following shot, Lang introduces a meeting at police headquarters (directly recalling the crisis meetings in *M*) with a report on this needle and the futuristic gun which fired it into Barter's skull. Throughout the film, Lang seeds references to cutting-edge technology – this experimental rifle, Mabuse's various devices of surveillance, or millionaire Travers' private rocket-launching company – using this new technology to stress the contemporary setting of the film. But, as the meeting reveals, all this updating only increases the film's senses of untimeliness. 'I feel like I've already gone through this case', an official declares, accenting the *déjà vu* quality of this recycled and resurrected plot. He gives his unease a name: 'Mabuse', a name completely unfamiliar to the other members of the department. The official explains who Mabuse was (giving a compressed synopsis of the first two films in the series), and mentions Mabuse's legacy, his testament. Lang cuts from the meeting to the single direct image of Mabuse this film provides, a shot of an overgrown graveyard, through which the camera moves, finally locating and zooming in on a small marker stuck in the ground, reading 'Dr. Mabuse no. 37'. As Lang shows this unimpressive marker on the screen, we hear the official in voice-over say that old-time criminals still claim Dr Mabuse 'can never die'. The official describes Barter's

murder as an exact duplicate of the killing of Dr. Kramm by Mabuse's gang. But he is the only one who remembers Mabuse or these events, and he speculates that Mabuse's record has been disposed of by his accomplices. The name Mabuse, which Lohmann could still recall and locate in the police archives, now dwells in oblivion. However, the chief speculates that a record of Mabuse's case must exist somewhere.

Continuing the sound links, Lang cuts immediately to a close-up of old worn binders bearing Mabuse's name and case number as the chief's speculation continues on the soundtrack. The camera follows a hand which opens up and arranges the microphone and apparatus for broadcast, the camera then tilting down to reveal again the clubfoot we associate with 'the doctor' from the earlier scene. The radio signal is received by men travelling in a van, who monitor the message closely as it announces, 'This is Dr. Mabuse speaking' and informs them of the arrival of the American 'Henry B. Taylor'. Lang cuts to Taylor (or as he is later called, Travers) at his hotel room in the midst of a business deal.[16] When asked whether his rocket programme is a private firm or a branch of the American government Taylor/Travers announces it doesn't matter, the two interests are so intertwined. Lang cuts back to the men in the van receiving Mabuse's orders to watch Taylor's every move, and informs them of his location in a suite at the Hotel Luxor. In the following shot the police note that before his death Barter was last seen at the Hotel Luxor. The next scene, another police meeting, pulls together the threads of the opening scenes around this location, as a detective details a series of unsolved murders and thefts, all revolving around the Hotel Luxor. From this point on it is clear that the Luxor forms the centre of this web of references, crimes, memories and conspiracies. A locale takes on the pivotal role that the figure of Mabuse or Haghi played in the earlier films, character giving way to architecture.

Recycled Vision, Feigned Blindness, Total Exposure

> Drüben auf dem Grabe steht noch der Geisterseher und
> umarmt Nichts!
> Und der Widerhall in Gebeinhause ruft zum lezten Male –
> *Nichts –*
> On the grave beyond, the visionary is still standing and
> embracing Nothing!
> And the echo in the charnel-house cries for the last time
> *Nothing!*
>
> *The Night Watches of Bonaventura*[17]

Throughout this extended opening sequence Lang used his earlier technique of links between scenes via sounds and images which appear to complete or comment on each other. This omniscient joining of scenes separated in space and time – flaunts Lang's control of narration, displaying an ability to reveal a greater depth of knowledge than the characters' (cutting from the woman journalist who reports Barter's 'heart attack' to Barter's actual assassin; or from the police official wondering where Mabuse's files are, to the binders in the possession of the clubfooted man who calls himself Mabuse). But Lang also withholds knowledge from the audience or actually misleads them (the man with the clubfoot will be revealed *not* to be Mabuse – that is the head of the gang – but simply a dispensable operative). Most characteristically, Lang will make connections that are only apparent on a second viewing of the film. For instance, the cut from the chauffeur saying he would like to see what the doctor looks like to the psychic Cornelius, seems mainly to continue the motif of not being able to see, with Cornelius's invocation of his blindness and the darkness which surrounds him. However, by the end of the film we realise that Cornelius actually heads the gang as the avatar of Mabuse; in a sense the chauffeur's wish has been granted by this cut to Cornelius, only we do not realise it. But if the wish is partly fulfilled, it is also partly denied: in Cornelius we only see Mabuse's disguise, his true face will only be revealed at the film's climax.

Cornelius claims the gift of prophecy and clairvoyance, second sight. However, his prediction of the murder can be so accurate only because, in fact, he is its instigator. The 'evil plan' he claims to have foreseen is his own. While Cornelius's astrological trappings and seances recall the occult powers of the earlier Mabuse, especially Sandor Weltmann's fakir-like illusions, his tricks do not even employ the powers of hypnosis (although at the end it is claimed he had Marion Ménil under an hypnotic spell). They are all stage-managed illusions, pure and simple, situations he has set up in order to gain power over characters by seeming to predict their fates, becoming one of Lang's most devious enunciator figures – an author posing as a reader. Rather than resurrecting the visionary tradition of the Weimar films, Cornelius recycles the motif as a farce. Both his visions and his blindness are fake. The initial image of Cornelius doffing his dark glasses and exposing his white, sightless eyes causes a shudder. But in a later scene, as he speaks to the millionaire Travers, Cornelius's eyes, shown in close-up, clearly show the edges of white contact lenses. Initially it is unclear what we are to make of this. Is it simply a failure of illusionism, 'a naked artifice of props' as Jonathan Rosenbaum describes the wires visibly manipulating the snake in *The Indian Tomb* (or, even more risible, the stuffed

tiger Berger bravely battles in *The Tiger of Eschnapur*)?[18] But Lang reveals that Cornelius's fakery is diegetic when the seemingly comic character of Mistelzweig (the Interpol operative masquerading as an insurance salesman) confronts him and tells him, 'those white contact lenses, I laughed when I saw them, probably you saw them in a film'. If this latest avatar of Mabuse recycles the earlier master criminal's protean identity and aspires to his position of grand enunciator, his disguise leaves something to be desired, his models being B-movies.

All of Lang's master criminal films involve a play with disguise and illusion which generates metaphors of stage-managing and, ultimately, film directing. When Cornelius's exclamation of 'murder!' over the phone to Kras seems to literally trigger the assassin's action through a direct cut, Lang is visualising Cornelius/Mabuse's command over the plot as an apparent control of the editing of the film itself, the exclamation becoming a command, the cut expressing cause and effect. But, as Lang has demonstrated over and over again, the ultimate control of the film rests with the narrator and author, with Lang himself as the agent of narration. Throughout *The Thousand Eyes of Dr. Mabuse* characters are framed within plots devised by others without the characters being aware of their own manipulation by these unseen forces. But Lang parallels the fates of these blindly manipulated characters with his own manipulation of the film viewer, blindly following misleading cues, unaware of the total design until the end of the film.

Thus we are repeatedly cued to see the clubfoot as the one identifying sign we have of Dr. Mabuse. After Marion Ménil tells Travers that the sadistic and pathologically jealous husband she has been fleeing has traced her to the Hotel Luxor, the first shot of her husband entering her room frames his now familiar clubfoot. We assume that this terrified woman is married to Dr. Mabuse and her mysterious behaviour (lies, her attempt at suicide) is explained by this dire situation. Lang even shows this huge, deformed foot trampling on the roses Travers had sent to

Marion. After this seeming madman threatens Marion with a knife, then knocks the gun, with which she tries to defend herself, out of her hand, Travers bursts into the room. Picking up the pistol from the floor, he responds to the man's looming threat and Marion's command, 'Shoot him!' The clubfooted Dr. Mabuse falls dead. Travers and Ménil now face the problem, reprised from *The Woman in the Window*, of how to dispose of the dead body without causing a scandal. Marion's physician, Dr. Jordan, agrees to help, bringing the ambulance from his clinic to the hotel. The dead man will be taken out with the doctor claiming he is the still-living victim of a heart attack. Left alone in the hotel, Marion comforts Travers who is stunned by having killed a man. She assures him he saved her life. Besides, she adds, Travers had asked if she would marry him if she were free. Now, she says, as she kisses him passionately, I am.

Lang cuts from this close-up kiss to the body of the clubfooted man in the ambulance, covered with a sheet. Suddenly he stirs, pulling the sheet off himself, as if revivified by the kiss in the previous shot. 'Well, it worked,' he says, 'just like the Doctor said it would.' But then his off screen look becomes startled. We cut to the other side of the ambulance interior and see Barter's assassin, futuristic rifle at his shoulder, as he fires and we hear the off screen scream of the clubfooted man. This is one of several nodal points in this devious film where Lang suddenly overloads the scene with contradictory cues, destroying our earlier assumptions but not supplying new ones. The clubfooted man, we realise, is not dead, but alive. Further, we assumed (because he said so) that *he* was the doctor, Dr. Mabuse, the one who gave the orders. Now we hear there is another 'doctor' (the real Dr. Mabuse? Dr. Jordan?) who has planned this scene of a fake murder. As we are processing this new information, our informant is suddenly killed. The man we thought was dead, and whom Jordan and the others were pretending was still alive, really is alive, that is, *was* still alive, and now is really dead. This is the shortest of all of Lang's resurrections, but certainly an emblematic one in its *mise-en-abîme* of reversals and contradictions. Jordan told Travers he would later announce that the man eventually died of a heart attack, recalling again the alibi for the assassination of Barter which opened the film. Lang seems to return to the opening of a film when the same assassin fired the same rifle, but makes us feel more lost than ever. We realise we have been witnessing a charade, a scene staged, but by whom and for whom? The one visual sign we had of Mabuse's identity, the clubfoot, has now been removed from the film. Who has given the assassin orders to kill this man?

The staging of this false murder, followed by a real one, not only involves role-playing, fake props (Marion's gun which fired only blanks) and pre-scripted dialogue, but a complex arranging of spectatorship. I referred earlier to Travers bursting into the room to protect Marion from her knife-wielding 'husband'. The metaphor here is literal, since he enters the room by smashing through a large mirror, an action which hardly seems to phase Marion. This outright surreal image is realistically-motivated by a plot device involving surveillance and voyeurism. A few scenes earlier, the slimy manager of the Hotel Luxor, Berg, had approached Travers, knowing his growing affection for Marion whom he rescued from a suicide attempt, and also of his putting her under surveillance, presumably for her own protection. Berg tells Travers he can help him increase his knowledge of this mysterious woman.

Berg takes Travers into the room which adjoins Marion's and reveals behind a closet door what he calls a 'technical device', a two-way mirror, transparent from this room; allowing a clear view into Marion's private life, while appearing to be an ordinary mirror in Marion's room. The device even has a speaker, which allows one to hear whatever happens in the next room. At first we see the maid cleaning the room, running the vacuum cleaner and then, nicely, polishing the surface, as Lang cuts from the window side to the mirror side within Marion's room. Lang immediately introduces the voyeuristic aspects of this set-up, both erotic and investigative, as Marion enters the room and has the maid help her hook her bra and then pulls on her slip. Lang cuts to Travers in close-up staring, as Marion puts on her lipstick inches away from him. A messenger arrives with the roses Travers sent her. Again Lang intercuts his gaze as he watches this presumably private moment of Marion smiling as she reads his note, embracing the roses lovingly and then collapsing in tears. It is only after this scene that Travers turns to the manager and denounces 'this appalling spectacle'. Explaining he is hardly the sort of man who finds spying charming, Travers indicates, somewhat contradictorily, both that he wants the place boarded up and that he will rent the room as an additional apartment.

It is from this room and through this window/mirror that Travers later watches the drama of Marion Ménil's encounter with her clubfooted husband and then enters abruptly into the scene. Our understanding of this drama therefore remains incomplete without considering the other side of the scene – its reverse angle – Travers' position as spectator, the character for whom the scene has been arranged. After Dr. Jordan called, warning Marion that her husband was coming to the Hotel Luxor, she ran from Travers' hotel suite back to her own room. Lang shows her rifling through her purse and then opening a closet door. He cuts on this action to Travers likewise opening the door to the closet in the adjoining room containing the two-way mirror. He slides back the covering for the mirror, revealing the scene in the next room, like a theatre curtain drawing back. The camera repositions itself, framing the room as the husband knocks at her door. Through the early part of the scene Lang alternates between shots filmed from within Marion's room and shots from the other side of the mirror, either framing the action through the mirror, or showing Travers watching. As the action turns violent, however, Lang's camera remains in Marion's room, cutting between her and her husband, until Travers bursts through the mirror, showering the scene with shards of glass.

Framing the scene in this manner emphasises its theatrical quality, Lang anticipating through composition a fact not yet revealed (that we are watching a scene staged in order to further involve and compromise Travers and make him susceptible to Mabuse's manipulation). But besides hinting at the fictive and illusory quality of this staged scene, incorporating Travers watching unobserved through the glass heightens the theme of voyeurism and surveillance so central to this film. The erotic dimension of the obsessed and potentially jealous lover (the manager had told Travers the mirror was first installed for a jealous husband who wanted to 'catch his wife in the act') plays an important role here with many echoes in Lang's earlier films. As a primal scene of jealousy, the scene recalls Chris Cross's witnessing of the love scene between Kitty and Johnny in *Scarlet Street* which was similarly framed through a transparent partition. In *The Thousand Eyes* however, the lover hears his beloved proclaim her love for him (as Marion confesses to the clubfooted man that as much as she hates him she loves Travers) and then heroically rescues her from a murderous attack. In other words, Travers acts out in this scene the fantasy scenario Chris will try to maintain against the reality he pathologically denies. But, of course, Travers' heroism is simply a role devised for him within Mabuse's plot. In a sense, even his act is fictitious, although he is unaware of it, as he fires blanks into the man who is a phony husband, has been a phony doctor, and will be a phony corpse.

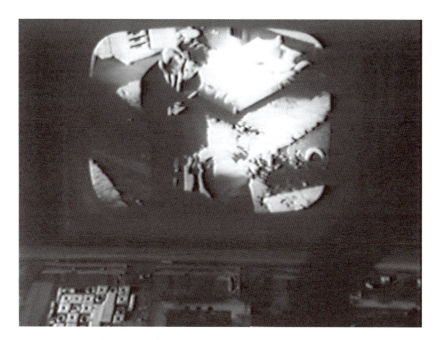

But is Travers' spectatorship of the little play arranged for him the true 'other side' of this scene, its ultimate reverse angle? In this game of Chinese boxes, Lang's framing of vision gets even more complicated. Before the scene grows violent, right after the husband wags his finger at Marion and declares, 'You'll never be free of me, never', Lang interrupts his pattern of alternation between shots in Marion's room and shots from Travers' room and introduces – literally from nowhere – a shot of Marion and her husband *framed within a television monitor*. The shot continues the argument between husband and wife without a glitch, as the husband tells Marion that after 'her theatrical suicide attempt the papers were full of her and her new lover'. We see the monitor sitting above a control panel of dials, although the close framing does not reveal if anyone is watching. Even more astounding, after Travers breaks through the mirror and enters the scene and shoots the husband, Lang cuts on the action of the husband falling to another high angle view of his 'death', framed again on the same monitor; then an unidentified hand enters the frame and turns the monitor off. As it fades to black, the figure of a man passes in front of it.

Talk about *mise-en-abîme*! Travers watches this scene believing it is real and that no-one knows he is watching. Before we learn that this was a scene staged for his benefit, Lang reveals that someone else is also watching it, from Lang's traditional topographic high angle viewpoint, and through another 'technical device' – not a two-way mirror this time, but a television monitor. Therefore yet another reverse angle to this scene exists, one we cannot locate in any familiar space or location – except recognising that it appears on television, the no place and every place of late modernity. The visionary moment, which penetrated through the surface to an emblematic revelation of a deeper reality, so crucial to Lang's Weimar films – and which became increasingly problematic in the Hollywood films, becoming either assimilated with technology (the newsreel in *Fury*) or madness (the hallucinations of Chris Cross in *Scarlet Street* or Stephen Byrne in *House by the River*) – can only appear in this film in the parody of Dr. Cornelius's phony visions and seances. In its place, developing the sense of over-exposure from his last Hollywood films, Lang presents a world saturated with observation, a world without secrets, subject to technological scrutiny by faceless functionaries. Every scene possesses another side, but instead of penetrating to a depth of truth and revelation, this other side reveals only another observer, threatening exposure and blackmail.

The startling impact of this sudden eruption of the television image on the film viewer comes largely from its unexplained nature, Lang's duplicitous narration again in full operation. Only much later does Lang reveal the nature and source of these video images that suddenly pop up in the middle of scenes, creating a new level of narration that, since it remains unexplained, threatens to rupture the whole diegesis. Could these images, we wonder, simply be the viewpoint of another audience, watching Lang's film on television, somewhere, entirely outside the diegesis? Lang only threatens such modernist, narrative self-reflexivity. The Hotel Luxor, we learn, is honeycombed with surveillance video cameras which convey television images to a secret control room. As Marion later explains to Travers, 'they see and hear everything'. But Lang withholds this explanation until long after we have been seeing – and puzzling over – these intrusive video images.

The first of these images intervenes in a sequence already filled with traditional means of surveillance: Mistelzweig dances close to Travers and Ménil with a busty blonde, who is herself revealed to be a spy for Commissioner Kras (as Mistelzweig is later revealed to be an Interpol agent). Two spies dancing with each other: he spies on Travers, while she spies on him! Lang cuts from the blonde delivering her report on Mistelzweig to Kras in the hotel bar back to the ballroom with a shot of Travers and Marion in the foreground as they discuss the possibility of her getting a divorce from her tyrannical husband. The low visual resolution of the shot registers immediately, as if we were suddenly watching a poorly duped print. The camera pulls back, but instead of moving away from the couple and revealing more of the ballroom, the frame of a television monitor comes into view and a control panel below it. We were actually watching our protagonists on television. The revelation of this added frame is bizarre, nearly comic, certainly mysterious. Although their dialogue continues, the image on the monitor dissolves for a moment into horizontal bands, due to some electronic interference. As Travers receives an important message from his business assistant, the camera dollies in on the monitor, swallowing the frame, without offering any clue to its function or location. The next cut brings us back into the primary diegesis without missing a beat, as Marion reacts to Travers' sudden absorption in business matters with a line which (at least in its English version) seems to pun on the bizarre visual transformation we just witnessed: 'You see, you can't just switch off either.'

As Crary claims, this seamless, yet baffling, transition from one medium to another could reflect the grand transformation in media and technology then occurring, the transition from the film medium to the regime of electronic imagery.[19] But it is not primarily in terms of television's supplanting of cinema that Lang introduces the new technology here. Rather, the television cameras installed in every room of the Hotel Luxor (as well as the corridors, ballroom, and bars) are a further elaboration of the culture of surveillance that has characterised the terrain of modernity since Lang's earliest films. The mesh of visual observation has simply become finer, with hardly a moment escaping. Marion explains in the film's final scenes, as the lovers are trapped in Mabuse's central control room: 'from here he watches every room in the hotel; then he plays his role as clairvoyant. He has seen everything, heard everything.' Thus Cornelius's pretended visions not only predict events he himself has planned, but reveal details of one's life no-one else could have witnessed, whether incriminating or minor, such as the cut Travers received on his finger from a broken glass, an incident Cornelius revealed to him on their first meeting. 'But I was alone', Travers marvelled, 'That's something no-one could know.'

While Lang's last film does offer a grim account of the triumph of television, a theme he had broached already in his last Hollywood films, this new medium fulfils a long-standing technological fantasy in Lang's cinema, rather than marking the eclipse of an older mode of representation by a newer one. Television in *The Thousand Eyes of Dr. Mabuse* simply realises the role Lang had envisioned for it in his science-fiction scenarios already visualised in *Metropolis* and even *Spiders* – an almost magical means of surveillance. In his first films Lang had already glimpsed the total exposure of the terrain of modernity. Part of the untimely feeling of *The Thousand Eyes of Dr. Mabuse* comes from this sense of a science-fiction story already come true, strangely anachronistic in its futuristic wonder at technology already in place. The secret of the Hotel Luxor lies not only in the thousand video eyes seeded through its ceilings and walls, but in its origin and history – its heritage, or as Mistelzweig puts it, its horoscope. Mistelzweig explains at one point that buildings have horoscopes and fates just as people do, the moment of the laying of their cornerstone marking the moment of their birth and the setting of their fate. From this perspective as well, the centre of both Lang's and Mabuse's plot lies in the Hotel Luxor itself, as a piece of panoptic architecture and as a place in time, a building with a history.

The Site of Remembering and Forgetting in Late Modernity

> In its buildings, pictures and stories, mankind is preparing to
> outlive culture, if need be.
> Walter Benjamin, 'Experience and Poverty'[20]

Mistelzweig locates the fate of the Luxor in its original construction (its cornerstone laid in May 1944) under the Third Reich. But the hotel did not simply come into being under the Nazis; it was conceived as part of the Nazi system. The hotel, Mistelzweig explains, was constructed as a place to gather all the foreign diplomats under one roof, and make them easier to spy on. 'There was a curse on this place from the start', he claims. Dr. Jordan/Cornelius/Mabuse received from the hotel managers the original Gestapo plans for this hotel panopticon. Therefore his video surveillance simply upgrades or fulfils the original Nazi intentions (remember that television was more completely developed and put into operation in Berlin under the Third Reich than in any other country before the end of World War II). When Cornelius reveals himself to Travers in the hotel's control room in the film's penultimate scene, he speaks of himself as Mabuse's heir, but the terms he uses to refer to Mabuse – 'a madman or a genius' … 'he had great power, with a plan for all mankind' – could apply as well to Hitler.

If Lang's claim, that *The Testament of Dr. Mabuse* was a prescient protest against the Third Reich and that Mabuse was intended as a Hitler figure, must partly be seen as a retrospective exaggeration, the references in *The Thousand Eyes of Dr.*

Mabuse to the survival of Nazi ambitions in postwar Germany cannot be denied. But with this last film the trajectory of the whole series becomes clear. Mabuse's will-to-power becomes at every stage less overtly theatrical and melodramatic (albeit always involved in the staging of scenes and the creation of spectators), less personal, and more abstract and technological – more invisible. Mabuse's scenes can now be staged in intimate hotel rooms, and the spectators no longer need hypnosis to become fascinated and manipulable. The erotics of voyeurism and the lust for knowledge gained through visual surveillance are more effective than literal hypnosis in creating enthralled spectators. It does not matter any more if Mabuse is alive or dead, not simply because his legacy can create any number of avatars, but because his methods have become absorbed into the structure of the all-pervasive technological system of modernity.

A few years after World War II, at the nadir of Lang's Hollywood career, between *House by the River* and *An American Guerrilla in the Philippines*, Lang filed a story outline with the Screen Writers' Guild, entitled 'The Story of L B 2' or, alternatively, 'Here Speaks L B 2'. Lang envisioned this sketch as a comedy adventure film, very much in the mode of Hitchcock's later *North by Northwest*, involving an American businessman in Europe mistaken for the liaison of a neo-Nazi group because he is unwittingly wearing a necktie selected as a signal by the group. The group is raising funds for the return of Hitler and it announces the signs by which its agents can be recognised through broadcasts over short-wave radio delivered in a voice which purports to be the voice of Hitler himself, having survived the war and preparing a comeback. Experts listen to the broadcasts and clearly identify the voice of the Führer. At first they believe the broadcasts are simply a montage patched together from recordings of Hitler's earlier speeches, but references to current events render that thesis untenable. The American businessman is persuaded to help agents of the United Nations track down the source of these broadcasts. Ultimately it is revealed that rather than a neo-Fascist resurgence, the broadcasts are simply a con game carried out by a Hungarian vaudevillian and his German accomplice who made livings before the war imitating Hitler. Surprised at the willingness of Germans to donate to this hopeless cause, they decided to exploit this desperate desire for the return of Hitler.

For Lang, the comic tone he wished to bring to this search through the often nightmarish and constantly surreal landscape of postwar Europe, would be guaranteed by the punch-line discovery that the voice of Hitler, seemingly from beyond the grave, is nothing more than a simple swindle. Lang ends his treatment for the film with the statement: 'The world learns the identity of the self-proclaimed Führer. The legend of Hitler is destroyed. The entire world gives a sigh of relief. ... The entire world explodes with Homeric laughter.' [21] In this sketch Lang tries for once to tell the story of an unsuccessful resurrection as an outright comedy. The terror re-emerges only as a farce and the world rejoices as a nightmare that threatened to become recurring is dispelled. In a sigh of relief, in a burst of laughter, Lang believes the world can forget its recent trauma. But Lang's – let alone the entire world's – joy and relief were premature. The decade of the 50s, with its experience of the Hollywood blacklist and the congealing of the Cold War must have struck Lang, like many German émigrés, as the possible return of an all-too-familiar cycle.

In some ways *The Thousand Eyes of Dr. Mabuse* retells 'The Story of L B 2', but the possibility of resuscitating Mabuse or Hitler through the technology of imitation and broadcast no longer ends in laughter. [22] Although Lang's film has rarely been treated in terms of the postwar processing of the Nazi trauma in Germany, Lang proposes a vision of German history which sees continuity rather than rupture and which refuses to either memorialise or forget the past. The complete amnesia displayed about Mabuse by police and others obviously stands in on one level for a German desire to forget the Third Reich. The Nazi past pervades *The Thousand Eyes of Dr. Mabuse* without needing to be rendered visible. Like Mabuse's technology, it is embedded in the structure of things, powerful because it lacks a spectacular presence. One might object that Lang's cops and robbers story remains an inadequate medium for describing the Nazi legacy. For all its ability to crystallise and sum up many of Lang's themes, no-one can deny that, next to a film like *M*, *The Thousand Eyes of Dr. Mabuse* shows many inadequacies: poor performances, stretches of uninspired story-telling, and a central love affair, the soporific qualities of which contrast sharply with its prototype in the truly sensual love affair between Tremaine and Sonja in *Spies*. But these admitted inadequacies cannot diminish the more dominant control and precision of imagery, editing and genre logic that also characterise Lang's final film. The total shape of Lang's career is once again clarified by his last German film. Lang began within the genre of 'sensation films', and even his forays into art cinema, the main commodity the Weimar cinema offered for export, never disavowed this background, but rather sought ways to exploit the immediacy of the mass medium of film at the same time as refining its visual language; to combine popular genres with artistic ambitions. Thus Lang at both ends of his career (and indeed throughout his Hollywood period) was accused of creating kitsch rather than art, condemned for being the popular entertainer he always wanted to be.

But inadequacy of representation in this case refers to more than simply the gulf between high art and low art that film criticism, particularly any criticism which takes the idea of an author seriously, so often finds itself contemplating. As Adorno stated, the Nazi experience defines the limits of representation. I find Lang's allusive and indirect invocation of the Nazis in *The Thousand Eyes of Dr. Mabuse* more powerful than most of his overtly anti-Nazi films of the Hollywood era for this very reason. In addition, unlike styles of realism or naturalism, allegory always acknowledges an inadequacy of representation, a gap – if not an abyss – between signifier and signified. Within the conventional adventure *topoi* of popular genres like the detective story, the experience of modernity is less represented than allegorised, caught in images and locales, modes of behaviour and types of objects, as much as in the predictable plots. Thus Lang returns for this last film to the locale that defined the detective story for Kracauer as an allegory of modern experience, the modern hotel.[23]

The Hotel Luxor exemplifies and gathers together Lang's grasp of the terrain of modernity and his specifically architectural approach to allegory, unfolding emblems in their manifold spatial structures. As Frieda Grafe claims, architecture for Lang primarily expresses structures of domination.[24] Rather than inert structures, Lang's buildings act as devices – machines – regulating the behaviour of those within, designed to channel their movement, and facilitate their observation as much as to provide shelter. As grand machines – Lang's ultimate Destiny-machines – these buildings always contain secrets. On the one hand, there are the secrets built into the structures which provide the source of their power: Mabuse's secret counterfeiting plant; the machine rooms of which Freder knows nothing and which his father strives to keep concealed from him in *Metropolis*; the spy centre concealed within Haghi's bank; the secret temple of the goddess beneath Eschnapur into which Berger wanders with disastrous results; the Luxor's hidden control room. But

if these secret centres of power allow the buildings to accomplish their work of subjection, there remains an aspect of most of these buildings, which, like all of Lang's
Destiny-machines, works against total control. Often this is figured not only in spatial terms but in temporal ones: the space which cannot be controlled contains in
some sense the building's own history or even pre-history. Thus, the revolt within
Metropolis arises from its deepest and most ancient level, forgotten by the master of
Metropolis, the catacombs; Mark Lamphere's forgotten childhood secrets are
enshrined in his seventh room and their discovery leads directly to the destruction
of his ancestral home; the conspirators of Eschnapur will be destroyed by their own
undermining of the city's foundations; and the curse that broods over the Luxor
dwells in its cornerstone with its fatal date, May 1944, when Nazis ruled and when
the tide had turned in the war, slating Berlin to become a city of ruins.

The public and heterogeneous space of the classical hotel lobby typified for Kracauer the modern terrain of the detective story, the realm of alienated experience.
In *The Thousand Eyes of Dr. Mabuse*, the space of meetings and encounters shifts
slightly to the hotel bar just off the lobby (with Lang constructing a set which often
looks onto the lobby just beyond), but the function remains the same, a place of
meetings, erotic encounters, role-playing and mutual observation. Lang is fascinated by passageways, the intermediary spaces which join up other spaces, transi-
tory spaces, not only the lobby, but the corridors and elevators. The true detective of
this film, Mistelzweig, penetrates into the secret of the Luxor by observing the
hotel's elevators, and noting the contradiction in the numbers illuminated on its
control board in the lobby. The elevators with their dials and succession of illuminated numbers (which Mistelzweig counts off as he watches) exemplify the abstraction that characterised Lang's Destiny-machines. But Mistelzweig finds their flaw:
an elevator car which leaves one floor, seems to proceed directly to the lobby, but its
door opens on emptiness. Mistelzweig realises the elevator made a stop on a floor
not indicated on the dials, the secret floor of Mabuse's command centre where Travers and Marion are held hostage.

Mistelzweig positions himself to observe both elevator and lobby, noting the
entrance of Dr. Jordan into the hotel and then into the elevator. Standing at the control panels and switching on and off his various cameras whose images appear on a
bank of monitors in the background, Jordan/Mabuse demonstrates his visual control – although the images we see reveal police arriving and searching the hotel – as
he describes his already foiled plan of world domination to Travers ('with your
rockets I could have controlled the universe and sent it into chaos: I could have
pushed the proverbial button – and I would have!'). But when he emerges from the
control room and gets on the elevator he depends on the last resort of Haghi in
Spies, the anonymity of his undisguised face. He removes his makeup, false beard
and wig, in the elevator mirror. However, Mistelzweig, who has been watching the
elevator carefully, identifies him, calling out his various names – Dr. Jordan, Cornelius – before he declares that the escaping man is Dr. Mabuse. The ensuing car
chase proceeds across the terrain of modernity, Mabuse monitoring the police communications over the short-wave radio, the police plotting the getaway car's course
on the autobahn, until Mabuse makes a sharp turn off a barricaded bridge and his
car plunges into the river below. The dark water of the river swallows Mabuse's car
– Lang's recurrent image of temporary oblivion. Like Emily in *House by the River*,
Mabuse has sunk beneath the surface – never to return? Brauner wanted more
Mabuse films, but Lang refused to participate; he had once more killed the son of a
bitch. As Lang put it, 'I said, "No, I am not doing another." He [Brauner] has already

made two more, and I cannot stop it.'[25] A total of three more Mabuse films were made in West Germany without Lang. In spite of a number of projects Lang proposed after *The Thousand Eyes*, this was his last film. He died in 1976 in Hollywood, sixteen years after his final film.

The Death of Cinema; Cinema and Death

> Some may consider that, intending to talk about Baudelaire, I
> have succeeded only in talking about myself. It would certainly
> mean more to say it is Baudelaire who was talking about me.
> He is talking about you.
>> Michel Butor, *Histoire Extraordinaire*[26]

> I await the death of cinema with optimism.
>> Jean-Luc Godard

Fritz Lang's career, from his first scripts for Joe May in 1917 to *The Thousand Eyes of Dr. Mabuse* released in Germany in 1960, parallels precisely the period marked out by Bordwell, Thompson and Staiger as the era of the 'Classical Hollywood Cinema'.[27] Although the focus of that epoch-marking book in film studies is specifically American, the period it covers, beginning with the stabilisation of feature-film-making with a style based on the dramatic analysis of space through editing, and ending with the emergence of television as the new dominant medium, has international relevance and truly demarcates an epoch. Lang's total career encompasses this central period of film history, from its establishment as a stable narrative form to its growing acknowledgement, in both mode of production and film style, of the emerging electronic media. One can't avoid seeing Lang's development as expressing something of the essence of this history, not only because he made influential films within this period, but also because his films focused on themes of vision and representation, on issues of technology and modernity, and on the agonistic nature of enunciation in a new medium.

Throughout Lang's career, film was frequently referred to as the 'art form of the twentieth century'. As we enter into the twenty-first century (having already clocked cinema's first century), this phrase may have lost its original promise of a radically new art form. As the new art of a new century, film made use of new technology (following in the wake of photography, the first machine art), and would claim as its audience the new populace of the century – the masses, the vast numbers of workers finally granted some time for entertainment and immediately targeted by commercial entrepreneurs. This promise may now sound hollow, ironically because it was, at least partly, fulfilled; but the term now also takes on a retrospective and historical dimension. Film *was* the art form of the twentieth century, particularly of what Eric Hobsbawm has termed the 'short twentieth century' lasting from 1914 to 1991, a period almost synchronous with Lang's career.[28] Cinema recorded not only the stories and events of the twentieth century, its tastes and fashions, but also its forms of aesthetics and experience, especially those new configurations of space and time that I have termed the terrain of modernity – experiences which often called on terms from cinema to create images adequate to them: montage, flash-back, close-up view, superimposition, fast-motion, dissolve.

Fritz Lang's cinema is impregnated with the history of the century in which it occurred. But the central argument of this reading of his films has been that Lang's films do not simply reflect that history, but speculate upon it, revealing its possibilities as well as its actualities, uncovering its assumptions as well as its fantasies, its conditions as well as its desires. Lang understood, more fully, I would claim, than any other director, that cinema would provide the image by which the twentieth century, the era of late modernity, would grasp itself. He understood how to use montage structures not only to portray the interlocking conditions of space and time, but to narrate breathtaking tales of suspense and danger, to make an audience both grasp and reflect upon this experience through a new form of story-telling. He likewise understood that the cinema would have to provide the twentieth century with visions of both its future (as the allegorical mirror of contemporary social problems) and its past (as the equally allegorical image of the way myth descends into the human realm of history).

Lang likewise meditated on the unique visual power of this new medium, the key, he claimed, to its transformation of culture and creation of a new mass audience. Pursuing his belief in the promise of the new medium as a universal language – a utopian dream he shared with many of the first generation of narrative filmmakers, from Griffith and Chaplin to Eisenstein and Vertov – Lang rediscovered the methods of allegory and forged an analogy between cinema and traditional metaphors of vision and revelation. As a visual medium, cinema did not simply record the visual world. It did more; it could render visible meanings that lay beneath the surface of everyday experience. But it is perhaps in the failure of modernity to establish a realm of transcendence that the central paradox of Lang's cinema lies. No vision of heaven or bliss was adequate to the modern terrain he portrayed so well; in fact, that terrain was founded on the collapse of such transcendence, the disenchantment that Max Weber had described to Lang's generation, and that Liliom discovered in the celestial waiting rooms.

Although no film-maker was more drawn to magic than Lang, he was too honest to create a counter realm of transcendent meaning to balance out the bitter lessons of modernity. If one finds fascist tendencies in Lang's Weimar work, they lay partly in his temptation to create a cinema that could supply this realm of transcendence, renew the ancient myths, and celebrate the mysteries of a new syncretic religion that could reconcile man and technology, labouring and managerial classes. But Lang's films never truly succeed in doing this. *Die Nibelungen* films mark the death song of myth rather than its rebirth, while *Metropolis* always remains a complex and flawed allegory rather than an inauguration of a new mythology or cult. Lang's allegories remain what Benjamin declared the genre to be: a form that shows a yearning after transcendence while remaining fixed within an immanent world of mourning. This is not to say that vision did not play a role in Lang's cinema, especially during the Weimar period. But instead of opening upon the vistas of eternity, Lang's visionary moments represented sudden piercing insights into the emptiness of things, whether Freder's vision of the voracious destruction of the workers on which the city of Metropolis was founded, or the maiden's vision of the presence of Death at her wedding table in *Der müde Tod*.

I have used the term Destiny-machine to indicate that Lang's essential vision of modernity, his insight into the century in which he worked, is primarily worked out in terms of being systematic and inhuman, apparently closed and inescapably framed. Vision in Lang is like an x-ray that penetrates through apparent surfaces to the structures that underlie them. But these underlying structures are not metaphysical forces, or Platonic ideas. I use the image of the machine not only to convey their systematic nature, but also their constructedness – machines are made by humans. But I adopt the idea of destiny to indicate that the machines become so powerful humans forget they made them, and perceive them as powers within themselves, outside history. This forgetting is itself a destiny, a fate, an enchantment difficult to awake from. Lang himself seems at points to have been subject to this forgetting, but the traces of another possibility shine through in his ability to capture the eruption of a desire for something else. But above all, Lang as film-maker of the twentieth century documents the systematic entrapment of mankind in its own creations – mankind's thrall to a technological realm as threatening as the frozen and inert Odenwald.

Thus while vision has a piercing and revelatory side, Lang was perhaps even more aware, especially as his career moved through the rise of Fascism, exile, World War II and its Cold War aftermath, of the other side of sight, the attempt to control all things within an objectified field of vision. I know of no other director who has as thoroughly pictured the modern world in terms of prison, or prison in terms of pitiless observation. What is often termed Lang's paranoia could more accurately be viewed as his understanding of the systematic nature of modernity and his realisation of the central role of surveillance in the modern assertion of power. Working within the popular genres of the detective story and the spy thriller, Lang made this drama of observation the central modern drama. In a systematic society everyone is marked with an identity which can be categorised and archived. Lang portrayed both the efficacy and failures of this system, the play between impersonation and disguise, on the one hand, and identification and apprehension, on the other.

When I claim that Lang worked out the agonistic relation of the author in the new mechanical and systematically industrial medium of motion pictures, I am not proposing a contest between a traditional romantic artist and a soulless new medium. On the contrary, while Lang's view of modernity may be bleak at points, one never doubts his delighted embrace of the possibilities of the new technology of cinema, his fascination with the realms of experience it opens up, his initial utopian hopes for the fulfilment of its promise. Lang's bitterness expresses disappointment with the present rather than nostalgia for the past. Therefore the new terms of authorship dictated by the cinema opened doors for Lang as a film-maker rather than simply providing obstacles. As I have indicated, Lang's repeated tale of the defeat of a grand enunciator as he sees the system he thought he controlled elude his grasp, supplies an allegory for authorship in film. Lang's authors, whether master criminals or obsessed painters, architects and novelists, all are undone by their own creations.

But I firmly believe that Lang himself understood the importance of letting his own creation go, of discovering the limits of his own control and authorship. If I were writing a biography I don't think I could make this claim. But as an author embodied in his films, Lang always conveyed the limited view of his hubristic characters, allowing us to understand that their dream of total control was necessarily beyond the grasp of the artist's hand, and ended only in madness. Lang's own attempt to control his films as a director so totally was agonistic, a struggle which he knew was condemned to failure; this new medium would always outrun his intentions. Lang's assertion of authorship in cinema enacted the drama of its own impossibility. In this way Lang's authorship is not reducible to a romantic, idealistic notion of genius. It is rather a modern process in which the author bears the imprint of society, technology and history in the attempt to provide an image of these forces. As much as Lang's hand shaped his films, they were also imprinted on him. He carries a mark, like the prisoners in Kafka's penal colony.

Lang chronicled the deaths of his grand enunciators. But he also showed their creations themselves becoming images of death, not only in the case of master criminals who surrounded themselves with the corpses of those they betrayed, but also with his artists who fused acts of creation with acts of murder. From his first masterpiece, *Der müde Tod*, Lang's films narrated attempts to undo the work of death, failed resurrections which, instead of attaining the transcendence of the Last Judgement, merely demonstrated the presence of death-in-life. But Lang's failure to attain transcendence testifies to his refusal to disavow the reality of death. One could claim that nearly all Lang's films attempt to come to terms with death, first struggling against it and finally, in some way acknowledging it. After acknowledge-ment must come mourning, as Freud indicated – indeed acknowledgement is to a large degree the main accomplishment of the work of mourning. Few artists have shown how difficult this work of mourning can be, or how seductive the surrender to melancholia can appear. One might claim Lang's vision of the twentieth century was one steeped in the work of mourning, dedicated to acknowledging the degree of deadliness the systematic processes of modernity have introduced.

I spent an evening with Fritz Lang in 1970 in a hotel suite at the Sherry Nether-lands in New York when I was twenty years old. Lang received my girlfriend, the painter Claribel Cone, and me warmly, partly because he saw us as members of a new young generation that he felt might transform society. He scorned his older friends that were also visiting him, partly because he felt they had made rude com-ments about my shoulder-length hair and Claribel's clothing. Taking us into a corner he told us he no longer wanted to spend time with anybody but young people. 'These other people in this room', he whispered dramatically, 'although they do not know it, they are already dead, *already dead!*' He described a scene from a film he wanted to make about my generation, a scene which is obviously the same one described by Lotte Eisner, although I remember it a bit differently.[29] A young girl has taken LSD during an orgy in a hippy loft. Shy and a bit fearful, she leaves the loft and goes out to the stairwell. Here two coloured balls come bouncing down the stairs to meet her and then, as if possessed of a will of their own, bounce in front of her. They lead her up the stairway to the roof of the building. When the girl pushes open the door to the roof it appears magically like a Garden of Earthly Delights. She begins to dance with the bouncing balls, taking off her clothes. As she dances eroti-cally with them, she unknowingly reaches the edge of the roof and falls. Lang would have cut then to her impaled on an iron fence below, her fate commented on caus-tically the next morning by passersby. Succinctly in this last private movie Lang brought together the visionary scene and the presence of death, as well as the devi-ous promise of desire in what he saw as the 60s generation's attempt to transform the world through sensual ecstasy. Like all of Lang's films this proposed scene com-bines clichés and originality, the worlds of Kafka, Bosch and Timothy Leary, in one more parable about the fragility of desire and the triumph of death.

Ultimately, perhaps, Lang's films do not so much portray the twentieth century as mourn for it, mourning its unfulfilled promises while acknowledging its cruel-ties and delights. At the moment of its invention, the cinema was received, as Noel Burch pointed out, as a triumph over death, a way to preserve personal immortal-ity with the record for all eternity of not only one's appearance but one's gestures, and, with the phonograph, one's words.[30] This image of a technological eternity, a life embalmed and forced to reiterate a never varying succession of gestures and words is worthy of Lang's most terrifying nightmares, the Destiny-machine as eternal repetition. Rather than denying death through a simulacrum of life, cinema as a historical machine at its best allows us to mourn life and time's passing, experiencing again that evanescent beauty which Baudelaire saw as the particular domain of the modern arts. Lang understood that every image of life includes the spectre of death.

My brief meeting with Lang was in some ways no more intense than an uncanny encounter I had years after his death with words in his handwriting. I had prepared a slide of a document reproduced in the wonderful volume on Lang edited by Bernard Eisenschitz and Paolo Bertetto, *Fritz Lang: La Mise en scène*, Lang's notes for *Beyond a Reasonable Doubt*, in which he divided the film's opening scenes into the two columns, 'What the audience sees and knows' on the left and 'What happened – but we don't show' on the right. My attention was drawn to an obscure line at the bottom of the right column, enlarged as I projected it on the screen for my class. The line is in Lang's handwriting, but seems to have been partially erased, or whited out. Closer examination showed it read: 'The dead never leave you.' The exact meaning of this phrase in this context will always be a subject for speculation. It doesn't seem to fall into the category of unshown events in the film, although it is not irrelevant to protagonist Tom Garrett's situation – suddenly finding his life invaded by a wife he hadn't seen for years and thought had divorced him, then deciding to murder her in order to maintain his new lifestyle – but it also doesn't describe anything specific in the film. Is it a more general comment? It certainly could apply to many, if not most, of Lang's films. Mourning is not only a way of remembering the dead, but also a process of letting them recede, of overcoming the haunting of the living by the dead, and Lang's films again and again present characters who are haunted by the death of either loved ones (*Der müde Tod*), or victims (*House by the River*) or both (*Scarlet Street*). Or is it possible that this note does not refer to a film, but is a personal note of Lang's and, if so, how would one define the difference between its role in his life and in his films? And why, finally, was it erased, particularly in the manner it was – obscured, but still readable?

Clearly there are no answers to these questions, and I am treating this bit of Lang's writing not really as evidence, a clue which might solve the mystery of Lang (it may well have no inherent significance at all), but as an emblem, not only for Lang's own treatment of death, but for his role as author. If I sense the gesture of Lang's hand in this writing, I also know it is not truly a gesture I can follow back to its source and thereby trace and recover in terms of its true meaning. Instead, it remains an invitation to speculation, an enigma, the pursuit of which could be endless.

The author's hand here erases as well as writes. The resonance of this partly-obscured trace with its message expressing terror and perhaps resignation brings me back to another author who created my most indelible image of Lang the author, Jean-Luc Godard (and in spite of many anecdotes I have read indicating a different personality, the man I met in 1970 was the man I saw on the screen in *Contempt*). If Lang mourned for the twentieth century through his images, Jean-Luc Godard has mourned for the death of cinema, chronicling its century of imagery in his *Histoire du Cinéma*. In Godard's history the world revealed by the cinema has been swallowed by video and Godard demonstrates the great and ambiguous promise of this new(er) technology, rendering everything available, everything repeatable. In the first episode in which the images and sounds of war and fascism invade the screen intermingling the actual and the fictional to yield an authentic image of history, Godard suddenly introduces a shot from *M*: the close-up of the

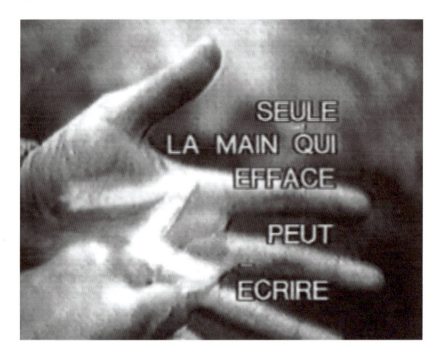

hand being marked with the fatal letter, ready to imprint it on Beckert's back. Over the image Godard prints the words: SEUL LE MAIN QU'EFFACE PEUT ECRIRE.

Only the hand which erases can write. In Godard's video, this means many things, beginning perhaps with the Nazi attempt to not only eliminate the Jews and other victims, but to eradicate even their memory. I believe it also includes a reference to Socrates' claim in Plato's *Phraedrus* that writing, the act of inscription, will destroy living memory. Most certainly it refers to the way cinema has provided the imagery of our memories of the war and the holocaust, simultaneously preserving the trace of these events for our conscience, yet also, perhaps, anaesthetising our responses to them through their familiarity. But the phrase also holds for me the key to all modern authorship, specifically authorship in the cinema, and especially the authorship of Fritz Lang. For the modern author, the emblematic gesture lies not only in the writing of words but in their partial erasure. Every author must imagine his own death, must sign his own death sentence. The dead never leave you, even if you erase them. But if we think of the way that Death in the last moments of *Der müde Tod* finally vanishes and thereby opens up a space for the lovers' reunion, we can see that part of the author's task in erasing is clearing a space for a new inscription. Lang appears in this writing, but he also disappears, vanishes, but not without a trace. The trace which remains invites me not to become lost in infinite speculation, but to return again to Lang's films, to watch again these assemblies of words and images and sounds which are among the most precious records of the twentieth century.

Notes

Preface

1 David Bordwell's *Making Meaning: Inference and Rhetoric in the Interpretation of Cinema* (Cambridge, MA: Harvard University Press, 1989) would of course be an exception, although which reaches the opposite conclusion to mine.

2 Thomas Elsaesser, 'Traps for the Mind and Eye', *Sight and Sound*, vol. 7 no.8 (NS), August 1997.

Introduction: Standing Outside the Films – Emblems

1 *Die Nachtwachen des Bonaventura/The Night Watches of Bonaventura*, ed. and trans. Gerard Gillespie (Austin, TX: University of Texas Press, 1971), pp. 208–9.

2 Jorge Luis Borges, 'Borges and Myself', in *The Aleph and Other Stories 1933–1969,* trans. Norman Thomas Di Giovanni (New York: E. P. Dutton, 1978), p. 152.

3 See, Gerard Genette, *Paratexts: Thresholds of Interpretation,* trans. Jane E. Lewin (Cambridge: Cambridge University Press, 1997). Since there are a variety of prints of *M* in circulation, there are also a variety of credit sequences and credit images. The one I am describing appears in the recent reconstruction of *M* by the Munich Film Museum and Taurus Film, as well as in older prints. The same or similar image appear in posters for the film.

4 It was, of course, Jacques Rivette who first drew attention to the theme of the hand in Lang in his review of *Beyond a Reasonable Doubt*, 'The Hand', at least by implication. See Jacques Rivette, 'The Hand' in *Cahiers du Cinema: 1950's Neo-Realism, Hollywood, New Wave,* ed. Jim Hiller (Cambridge, MA: Harvard University Press, 1985), pp. 141–4 (originally published in *Cahiers du Cinema* 7, 6 November 1957).

5 Patrick McGilligan, *Fritz Lang: The Nature of the Beast. A Biography* (New York: St. Martin's Press, 1997).

6 Michel Foucault, 'What is an Author?', in *Language, Counter-Memory, Practice: Selected Essays and Interviews* ed. Donald F. Bouchard. trans. Donald Bouchard and Sherry Simon (Ithaca, NY: Cornell University Press, 1977), pp.113–38. See also Wayne Booth, *The Rhetoric of Fiction* (Chicago, IL: University of Chicago Press, 1961).

7 Foucault, p. 129.

8 Ibid., p. 117.

9 Roland Barthes, 'The Death of the Author', in *The Rustle of Language,* trans. Richard Howard (Berkeley: University of California Press, 1989), pp. 49–55.

10 Barthes, p. 53; Foucault, p. 116.

11 An important exception is Colin MacCabe's 'The Revenge of the Author' in *The Eloquence of the Vulgar: Language, Cinema and the Politics of Culture* (London: BFI, 1999), pp. 33–42.

12 Peter Wollen, *Signs and Meaning in the Cinema,* expanded edition (London: BFI, 1998), p. 115. See also Stephen Jenkins, 'Introduction', in Jenkins (ed.), *Fritz Lang: The Image and the Look* (London BFI, 1981), p.7.

13 One account of this is given in Peter Bogdanovich, *Fritz Lang in America* (London: Studio Vista, 1967), p. 34.

14 The analysis of Hölderlin's poem given in the film derives primarily from Maurice Blanchot's essay 'Hölderlin's Itinerary' included in *The Space of Literature,* trans. Ann Smock (Lincoln, NE: University of Nebraska Press, 1982), pp. 269–76. However, the analysis is not identical and there may be another source as well. This constitutes another quote as well.

15 McGilligan, pp. 178–9.
16 Mark Shivas, 'Fritz Lang Talks about Dr. Mabuse', reprinted in Andrew Sarris (ed.), *Interviews with Film Directors* (Indianapolis, IN: Bobbs Merrill, 1967), p. 260.
17 Quoted in McGilligan, p. 174.
18 Shivas, p. 260
19 Ibid.
20 Ibid.
21 McGilligan, pp. 178–9
22 Ibid., p. 176.
23 Shivas, p. 260
24 I am not sure where this interview was originally recorded, I have seen it as part of an introduction to a screening of *The Testament of Dr. Mabuse* on French television. I thank Trond Londemo of the University of Stockholm for drawing my attention to it.
25 Bogdanovich, p. 127.

Chapter 1: The *Märchen*: *Der müde Tod* – Death and the Maiden

1   Walter Benjamin, *The Origin of German Tragic Drama*, trans. John Osborne (London: NLB, 1977), p.166.
2   See Kristin Thompson, '*Im Anfang war* … some links between German fantasy films of the teens and the twenties', in Paolo Cherchi Usai and Lorenzo Codelli (eds), *Before Caligari: German Cinema 1895–1920* (Pordenone: Edizioni Biblioteca dell'Immagine, 1990), pp.138–61 for a discussion of Wegener's views of cinema; Georg Lukacs, 'Thoughts on an Aesthetic for the Cinema' (1913), trans. Barrie Ellies-Jones, in *Framework*, no. 14, Spring 1981, pp. 2–6.
3   Vincente J. Benet Ferrando, 'Symbole, metaphore et stabilité narrative dans *Der müde Tod*' in Bernard Eisenschitz and Paolo Beretto (eds), *Fritz Lang: La mise en scène* (Paris: Cinématheque Française, n.d [1993]), pp. 99–109.
4   Benjamin, pp. 159–236. The most thorough and insightful discussion of Benjamin's understanding of allegory I have read occurs in Rainer Nagele, *Theater, Theory, Speculation: Walter Benjamin and the Scenes of Modernity* (Baltimore, MD: Johns Hopkins University Press, 1991).
5   Benjamin, pp. 168–70.
6   Miriam Hansen, *Babel and Babylon: Spectatorship in American Silent Film* (Cambridge, MA: Harvard University Press, 1991), pp. 194–5.
7   Horapollo, *The Hieroglyphics of Horapollo,* trans. George Boas (Princeton, NJ: Princeton University Press, 1978), Bollingen Series, vol. XXIII.
8   Vachel Lindsay, *The Art of the Moving Picture* (1915; New York: Liveright, 1970).
9   Benjamin, p. 187.
10 Hansen, p. 171.
11 Benjamin, p. 166.
12 Ibid., p. 185.
13 Benet Ferrando, p. 99.
14 Sigmund Freud, 'Mourning and Melancholia', *Standard Edition of the Complete Psychological Works of Sigmund Freud*, trans. James Strachey, 24 vols (London: The Hogarth Press, 1953–74), vol. XIV, pp. 237–58.
15 Anton Kaes's recent work on Weimar cinema and its relation to the trauma of W.W. I, which I heard him present as 'The Return of the Undead' at the conference 'Film and Animism'. Zentrum für Literaturforschung, Berlin, Feb. 1999, goes further in tracing this theme. His work *Shell Shock: Film and Trauma in Weimar Germany* (Princeton, NJ: Princeton University Press, forthcoming) will develop it at length. I am indebted to discussions of it with him.
16 Freud, 'Thoughts for the Times on War and Death' and 'On Transience', *Standard Edition*, vol. XIV, pp. 273–3308.
17 Freud, *Beyond the Pleasure Principle*, *Standard Edition*, vol. XVII, pp. 1–64.
18 Freud, 'On Transience', p. 307.
19 Benet Ferrando, p. 100.

20   Marc Vernet, 'The Look at the Camera', *Cinema Journal*, vol. 28 no. 2, Winter 1989, p. 48.
21   Ibid.
22   Ibid., p. 60.

Chapter 2: The Decay of Myth: Siegfried's Death, Kriemhild's Revenge

1   Sigmund Freud, *The Interpretation of Dreams, Standard Edition*, vol. V, p. 515.
2   Fritz Lang, 'Worauf es beim Nibelungen-Film ankam Fritz Lang' from *Die Nibelungen ein deutsches Heldenlied*, reprinted in Fred Gehler and Ulrich Kasten (eds), *Fritz Lang Die Stimme von Metropolis* (Berlin: Henschel Verlag, 1990), p. 171. My thanks to Emily Godeby for help with translation.
3   Lang, 'Stilwille im Film von Fritz Lang' in *Jugend,* no. 3, 1 February 1924, reprinted in Gehler and Kasten, p.163.
4   Lang, 'Worauf es beim Nibelungen-Film', p. 171.
5   Sabine Hake, 'Architectual Hi/stories: Fritz Lang and *The Nibelungs*', *Wide Angle*, vol. 12, no. 3, July 1990, p. 41.
6   Goebbels quoted in Georges Sturm, *Fritz Lang: Films/Textes/References* (Nancy: Presses Universitaires de Nancy, 1990), p. 61.
7   George Lukacs, *The Theory of the Novel*, trans. Anna Bostock (Cambridge, MA: MIT Press, 1971), pp. 29–39.
8   Thea von Harbou, 'Le film des Nibelungen et sa genèse' (1924) in Alfred Eibel (ed.), *Fritz Lang Trois Lumières* (Paris: Flammarion, 1988), p. 51.
9   Lukacs, p. 34.
10   Lang, 'Worauf es beim Nibelungen-Film', p. 171.
11   Ibid.
12   Wilhelm Worringer, *Form in Gothic* (New York: Schocken Books, 1964), p. 41.
13   Siegfried Kracauer, *From Caligari to Hitler: A Psychological History of the German Film* (Princeton, NJ: Princeton University Press, 1947), pp. 93–5.
14   Ibid., p. 94.
15   Ibid., pp. 92 and 93.
16   David J. Levin, *Richard Wagner, Fritz Lang and the Nibelungen: The Dramaturgy of Disavowal* (Princeton, NJ: Princeton University Press, 1998), p. 104.
17   Kracauer, p. 94.
18   Levin, pp. 113-15.
19   Walter Benjamin, *The Origin of German Tragic Drama*, pp. 165–6 and passim.
20   Peter Bogdanovich, *Fritz Lang in America*, p. 28.

Chapter 3: *Metropolis*: The Dance of Death

1   Susan Buck-Morss, *The Dialectics of Seeing: Walter Benjamin and the Arcades Project* (Cambridge, MA: MIT Press, 1989), p. 173.
2   I will not attempt to list the negative comments by critics here, but Lang gives his own demurral in Peter Bogdanovich, *Fritz Lang in America*, p. 124.
3   Fritz Lang, 'The Future of the Feature Film in Germany', 1926, reprinted in Anton Kaes, Martin Jay, Edward Dimendberg (eds), *The Weimar Republic Sourcebook* (Berkeley: University of California Press, 1994), p. 622.
4   Jeffrey Herf, *Reactionary Modernism: Technology, Culture and Politics in Weimar and the Third Reich* (Cambridge: Cambridge University Press, 1984).
5   The financial fate of *Metropolis* and its effect on Ufa is detailed in Klaus Kreimeier, *The Ufa Story: A History of Germany's Greatest Film Company 1918–1945*, trans. Robert and Rita Kimber (New York: Hill and Wang, 1996), pp. 156–7.
6   Ibid., p. 156.
7   Richard A. Lanham, *A Handlist of Rhetorical Terms* (Berkeley: University of California Press, 1969), p. 3.
8   Ibid.

 9 Angus Fletcher, *Allegory: The Theory of a Symbolic Mode* (Ithaca, NY: Cornell University Press, 1964), p. 84.

10 See Tzvetan Todorov, *Theories of the Symbol*, trans. Catherine Porter (Ithaca, NY: Cornell University Press, 1982), pp. 198–207; Hans-Georg Gadamer, *Truth and Method* (New York: Seabury Press, 1975), pp. 63–73.

11 See Fletcher, pp. 15–16.

12 Ibid., p. 55.

13 Lang, 'The Future of the Feature Film in Germany', p. 622.

14 Vachel Lindsay, *The Art of Moving Pictures*, p. 199.

15 Ibid., pp. 200–5.

16 Miriam Hansen, *Babel and Babylon*, pp. 189–94.

17 Ibid., p. 184.

18 Thea von Harbou, *Metropolis* (New York: Ace Books, 1963), p. 66.

19 Oswald Spengler, *The Decline of the West*, trans. Charles Francis Atkinson (New York: Alfred A. Knopf, 1928), vol. II, *Perspectives on World History*, pp. 504–5.

20 For science fiction see Peter S. Fisher, *Fantasy and Politics: Visions of the Future in the Weimar Republic* (Madison, WI: University of Wisconsin Press, 1991), especially p. 115; for a profound consideration of technology and politics in Weimar and after, see Herf, especially pp. 152–88.

21 Kracauer, p.162.

22 Freund quoted in Frederick W. Ott, *The Films of Fritz Lang* (Seacaus, NJ: Citadel Press, 1979), p. 125.

23 Fletcher, pp. 40–56.

24 Ibid., pp. 158–80.

25 Quoted in Peter Sloterdijk, *Critique of Cynical Reason*, trans. Michael Eldred (Minneapolis: University of Minnesota Press, 1987), p. 436.

26 Fletcher, pp. 70–146.

27 Roger Dadoun, '*Metropolis: Mother-City – "Mittler – Hitler"*', trans. Arthur Goldhammer, *Camera Obscura*, no. 15, Fall 1986, p. 155.

28 Spengler, p. 504.

29 Bogdanovich, p. 124. The critic who has most carefully considered the relation between the medieval and the modern in *Metropolis* is R. L. Rutsky, 'The Mediation of Technology and Gender: *Metropolis*, Nazism, Modernism', *New German Critique*, no. 59, Spring/Summer 1993, pp. 18–32.

30 Sigmund Freud, *Civilization and its Discontents, Standard Edition*, vol. XXI, pp. 69–71.

31 Rutsky, p. 16.

32 Harbou, p. 47.

33 Wilhelm Worringer, *Form in Gothic*, p. 83.

34 Harbou, p. 59.

35 Lang, 'The Future', p. 623.

36 Raymond Bellour, 'Ideal Hadaly (on Villiers' *The Future Eve*)', *Camera Obscura*, no. 15, Fall 1986, p. 131.

37 Line from a poster based on a poem by Walter Mehring Lang remembered seeing in 20s Berlin. Lang quoted in McGilligan, *The Nature of the Beast*, pp. 122–3. The poster is reproduced in Georges Sadoul, *L'art Muet (L'Après Guerre en Europe 1919–1929)* (Paris: Denoël, 1975), pp. 446–7, the line reading: Berlin, stop for a moment! Remember, your dancing partner is Death. (Berlin halt ein! Besinne dich. Dein Tänzer ist der Tod)

38 Dadoun, p. 145.

39 Rutsky, again, has probed these patterns with insight, see especially pp. 5–7.

40 Dadoun, p. 145.

41 Harbou, p. 9.

42 Ibid., p. 21.

43 Ibid., p. 18.

44 J. Laplanche and J.-B. Pontalis, *The Language of Psychoanalysis*, trans. Donald Nicholson-Smith (New York: W. W. Norton, 1973), p. 335.

45 Bertolt Brecht, *Poems 1913–1956*, pp. 124–5.

46 All quoted in McGilligan, p.100; 166; 127.

47 Lang, 'The Future', pp. 622–3.

48 Kracauer, p. 164.

49 Sadoul, p. 342.

50 Georg Kaiser, *Gas II. A Play in Three Acts,* trans. Winifred Katzin (New York: Frederick Ungar, 1963), pp. 15–16.

51 Andreas Huyssen, 'The Vamp and the Machine: Fritz Lang's *Metropolis*' in *After the Great Divide: Modernism, Mass Culture, Post-Modernism* (Bloomington: Indiana University Press, 1986), p. 78.

52 Rutsky, pp. 12–16, especially.

53 Ibid., pp. 24–7.

54 Ibid., pp. 25–32.

55 Benjamin, p. 233.

56 Henry Adams, *The Education of Henry Adams* (Boston, MA: Houghton Mifflin, 1918), pp. 380–90.

57 Rutsky, pp. 19–21.

58 Klaus Theweleit, *Male Fantasies,* vol. I, *Women Floods Bodies History*, trans. Stephen Conway (Minneapolis: University of Minnesota Press, 1987), pp. 418–19.

59 Huyssen, pp. 74–5.

Chapter 4: Mabuse, Grand Enunciator: Control and Co-ordination

1 Siegfried Kracauer, 'The Hotel Lobby', in *The Mass Ornament: Weimar Essays*, trans. and ed. Thomas Y. Levin (Cambridge, MA: Harvard University Press, 1995), p. 175 (section of his study, *The Detective Novel).*

2 Nicole Brenez, 'Symptome, exhibition angoisse: réprésentation de la terreur dans l'oeuvre allemande de Fritz Lang', *Cinématheque*, no. 3, Spring/Summer 1993, discusses this theme with insight.

3 Kracauer, p. 175.

4 Discussions in English of the Film Reform movement in Germany appear in Sabine Hake, *The Cinema's Third Machine: Writing on Film in Germany 1907–1933* (Lincoln: University of Nebraska Press, 1993), pp. 27–41 and with great insight in Scott Curtis, 'The Taste of a Nation: Training the Senses and Sensibility of Cinema Audiences in Imperial Germany' *Film History*, vol. 6, no. 4, Winter 1994, pp. 445–69. The essential source in German is, of course, Anton Kaes (ed.), *Kino-Debatte: Texte zum Verhaltnis von Literatur und Film 1909–1929* (Tubingen: Max Niemeyer, 1978).

5 Fritz Lang, 'Kitsch, Sensation–Kultur und Film' in E. Beyfuss and A. Kossowsky (eds), *Das Kulturfilmbuch* (Berlin: Carl P. Chryselius Ed., 1924), reprinted and translated into French in *Positif*, no. 358, December 1990, pp. 151–3.

6 Ibid., p. 152.

7 Ibid., p. 151.

8 Ibid., p. 152.

9 The still is reproduced in Helmut Farber, 'Trois Photos de Tournage de *M*', in Bernard Eisenschitz and Paolo Bertetto (eds), *Fritz Lang*, pp. 140–1.

10 Kracauer, p. 183.

11 Carlo Ginsburg, 'Clues: Roots of an Evidential Paradigm', in *Clues, Myths and the Historical Method*, trans. John and Anne Tredeschi (Baltimore, MD: Johns Hopkins University Press, 1989) p. 123.

12 Rosalind Williams, *Notes on the Underground: An Essay on Technology, Society and the Imagination* (Cambridge, MA: MIT Press, 1990).

13 Lewis Mumford, *Technics and Civilization* (New York: Harcourt Brace Jovanovich, 1934), pp. 75–7.

14 Williams, p. 52.

15 Judith R. Walkowitz, *City of Dreadful Delight: Narratives of Sexual Danger in Late-Victorian London* (Chicago, IL: University of Chicago Press, 1992), p. 17.

16   G. K. Chesterton, 'A Defense of Detective Stories', in *The Defendant* (London: R. B. Johnson, 1901), p. 158.

17   Anthony Giddens, *The Consequences of Modernity* (Stanford, CA: Stanford University Press, 1990), pp. 18–19.

18   Uco/Decla-Bioskop Program for *Dr. Mabuse Part I*, foreword reprinted in Gunter Scholdt (ed), *Norbert Jacques Fritz Lang Dr. Mabuse: Roman/Film/Dokumente* (Ingebert: W.J. Rohrig Verlag, 1987), p. 173. I thank Emily Godeby for help with the translation.

19   Sir Arthur Conan Doyle, 'The Final Problem', in *The Complete Sherlock Holmes* (New York: Doubleday, 1930), p. 471.

20   Marcel Allain and Pierre Souvestre, *Fantomas* (New York: William Morrow, 1986), p. 11.

21   Quoted in Georges Sadoul, *L'art Muet*, p. 532.

22   Uco/Decla-Bioskop Program for *Dr. Mabuse Part I*, p. 173. I thank Emily Godeby again for help with the translation.

23   English, of course offers a pun here between the visual regime of watching, and the timepiece known as a watch. German *Uhr* does not offer the same pun. However, the role of the watch as a form of surveillance, especially as a supervisor or timekeeper overseeing work processes, had of course been long established in the factory system and was institutionalised and taken to extremes in Taylor's process of 'scientific management'. There is a way that Mabuse resembles a Taylorite efficiency expert with his stopwatch in hand. Later in *Mabuse* one of his henchmen complains that he can't take the pace of the gang's operation and is thinking of quitting.

24   Ravi S. Vasudevan, 'Film Studies, New Cultural History and the Experience of Modernity', *Economic and Political Weekly*, 44, 4 November 1995, p. 2811.

25   Giddens, pp. 19–20.

26   Georg Simmel, *The Philosophy of Money*, trans. David Frisby (London: Routledge, 1990), pp. 445–6.

27   Noel Burch, 'Notes on Fritz Lang's First *Mabuse*', in *In and Out of Synch: The Awakening of a Cine-Dreamer*, trans. Ben Brewster (Aldershot: Scolar Press, 1991), pp. 207–8. Also Burch, 'Fritz Lang: German Period', in same volume, pp. 6–7.

28   A thorough, insightful and fascinating treatment of the emblematic shot and its evolution is given by Livio Belloi in his thesis 'Le Regard et ses voltes: Aspects du cinéma des premiers temps', Université de Liège, 1997, pp. 200–88, which goes much more deeply into the issues raised here.

29   Walter Benjamin, *Charles Baudelaire: A Lyric Poet in the Era of High Capitalism*, trans. Harry Zorn (London: Verso, 1983), p. 43.

30   See my article, 'Tracing the Individual Body: AKA Photography, Detectives, Early Cinema and the Body of Modernity' in Vanessa R. Schwartz and Leo Charney (eds), *Cinema and the Invention of Modern Life* (Berkeley: University of California Press, 1995).

31   Gerald D. Feldman, *The Great Disorder: Politics, Economics and Society in the German Inflation 1914–1924* (Oxford: Oxford University Press, 1997), p. 390.

32   Is Mabuse also coded as Jewish, particularly in this scene where he acts as stock speculator, a profession that Weimar associated with Jews (as it did, as Anton Kaes pointed out to me, psychoanalysts!)? Certain reviewers saw it this way, as in the review from the *Münchener Gazette*, from 1925 quoted by Gunter Scholdt, which described Mabuse as a 'typical picture of the criminalistic Jew'. Scholdt (ed), p. 149. However, this review also attacks the film as a Jewish product from author Norbert Jacques and publisher Ullstein and Thea von Harbou as 'a teachable student of the Jewish master'. I thank Emily Godeby for help with the translation.

33   Giddens, p. 25.

34   Simmel, p. 431.

35   Feldman, p. 513. I want to thank Anton Kaes for encouraging me to think about Mabuse in terms of the inflation.

36   Detlev J. K. Peukert, *The Weimar Republic: The Crisis of Classical Modernity*, trans. Richard Deveson (New York: Hill and Wang, 1989), p. 64.

37   Ibid., chart of dollar exchange rate of the paper mark 1914–1923, p. 5.

38   Ibid., pp. 5–7.

39   Peukert, pp. 62–5.

40 Feldman, p. 535.
41 Feldman, p. 575.
42 Fyodor Dostoevsky, *The Gambler*, in *The Short Novels of Dostoevsky* (New York: Dial Press, 1945), pp. 22–3.
43 Ibid., p. 21.
44 Ibid., pp. 98–9.
45 Benjamin, pp. 134–5.
46 Ibid., p. 136.
47 Ibid., p. 135.
48 Charles Baudelaire, 'Le Jeu', in *Les Fleurs du Mal*, trans. Richard Howard (Boston, MA: David R. Godine, 1982), p. 101.
49 Quoted in Maria M. Tatar, *Spellbound: Studies on Mesmerism and Literature* (Princeton, NJ: Princeton University Press, 1978). p. 133.
50 Quoted in Patrick McGilligan, *The Nature of the Beast*, p. 85.
51 Henry Tyrrell, 'Some Music Hall Moralities', reprinted in George C. Pratt, *Spellbound in Darkness: A History of the Silent Film* (Greenwich, CT: New York Graphic Society, 1973), p. 17.
52 One discussion of this theme by Bellour can be found in Janet Bergstrom, ' Alternation, Segmentation, Hypnosis: Interview with Raymond Bellour', in *Camera Obscura*, nos 3–4, Summer 1979, pp. 100–2.
53 Quoted in Alan Gauld, *A History of Hypnosis* (Cambridge: Cambridge University Press, 1992), p. 430.
54 Bergstrom, pp. 100–2.
55 Baudelaire, p. 82.
56 See Anton Kaes, 'The Cold Gaze: Notes on Mobilization and Modernity', *New German Critique*, no. 59, Spring/Summer 1993, pp. 105–17
57 Williams, p. 51.

Chapter 5: Haghi

1 *The Night Watches of Bonaventura*, p. 143.
2 Lotte Eisner, *Fritz Lang*, trans. Gertrud Mander (New York: Oxford University Press, 1977), p. 59.
3 Georges Sturm, *Fritz Lang: Films/Textes/References* (Nancy: Presses Universitaires de Nancy, 1990), p. 56.
4 Detlev J. K. Peukert, *The Weimar Republic*, p. 16.
5 Nicole Brenez, 'Symptome, exhibition, angoisse', p. 10. This is a particularly insightful essay. The translation of the German version of *Spione* would be: 'God Almighty, what powers has their hand in this game?' One might add that the murder of the man in the open car may be patterned on the assassination of Rathenau. See Robert G. L. Waite, *Vanguard of Nazism: The Free Corps Movement in Postwar Germany 1918–1923* (Cambridge, MA: Harvard University Press, 1952), p. 219.
6 Prints of *Spies* vary greatly. There is a print widely distributed in the US which derives from a British/American release and is more than a third shorter than German prints, cutting out most of the subplot dealing with Jellusic. The cutting of this version is extremely carefully reworked and one wonders if Lang might have had a hand in the shortening. The German prints I have seen also vary a bit. In the prints prepared for export to the US and Great Britain, we still cut directly to Haghi after the intertitle question, but with his back to the camera as he speaks to his underlings. Although the issue is posed more elegantly and directly in the German prints with the close-up, both versions raise and answer the question of agency right at the beginning of the film.
7 Andreas Huyssen, 'The Vamp and the Machine', pp. 67–8.
8 Lang, quoted in Eisner, p. 96.
9 Ibid.; Brenez, p. 6.

10 Max Horkheimer and Theodor W. Adorno, *Dialectic of Enlightenment*, trans. John Cumming (New York: The Seabury Press, 1972), p. 60.

11 David Bordwell, *Narration in the Fiction Film* (Madison: University of Wisconsin Press, 1985), pp. 59–60.

12 Reproduced in Bernard Eisenschitz and Paolo Bertetto (eds), *Fritz Lang*, p. 122.

13 Raymond Bellour, 'Le Regard de Haghi', *iris*, no. 7, second semester, 1986, p. 5.

14 Ibid., p. 7.

15 Ibid., p. 5.

16 Réné Descartes, *Meditations on First Philosophy* in *The Philosophical Writings of Descartes*, vol. II (Cambridge: Cambridge University Press, 1985), p. 15. French and Latin versions in *Meditationes de Prima Philosophia/Méditations metaphysiques* (Paris: Librairie Philosophique J. Vrin, 1960), pp. 23, 24.

17 *The Night Watches of Bonaventura*, p. 213.

18 Eisner, p. 394.

19 This encounter appears in the English language print, but is actually truncated in the generally more complete German prints.

20 This connection is less clear in the German version, which locates the microphone in the office of the Japanese spies, Haghi's means of spying on them as they spy on Sonja. The effect is the same, but in the shorter version it is actually more direct.

21 Walter Benjamin, *Charles Baudelaire*, p. 48.

22 Noel Burch, 'Fritz Lang: German Period', pp. 11–17.

23 Quoted in Frederick W. Ott, *The Films of Fritz Lang*, p. 148.

24 Actually the English language version is more elliptical, while the German version devotes more than twenty shots to the period between Tremaine's awakening and the wreck.

25 Søren Kierkegaard, *Either/Or*, vol. I, trans. David and Lilina Swenson (Princeton, NJ: Princeton University Press, 1971), p. 30.

26 According to the English language print. The German simply has him ask for 'a little music, please'.

Chapter 6: *The Testament of Dr. Mabuse*

1 Franz Kafka, 'The Great Wall of China', trans. Willa and Edwin Muir, in *The Complete Stories* (New York: Schocken Books, 1971), p. 244.

2 This is true of the English language print, the German message does not appear to be in code.

3 Sigmund Freud, 'A Note upon the "Mystic Writing-Pad" ', *Standard Edition*, vol. XIX, pp. 225–32. This metaphor of Freud's has been the subject, of course, of Jacques Derrida's influential commentary, 'Freud and the Scene of Writing', in *Writing and Difference*, trans. Alan Bass (Chicago, IL: University of Chicago Press, 1978), pp.196–231.

4 Nicole Brenez, 'Symptome, exhibition, angoisse', p. 14.

5 David Bordwell, *Narration in the Fiction Film*, p. 160.

6 Noel Burch, 'Fritz Lang: German Period', pp. 17–20.

7 Michel Marie, *M, le Maudit, Fritz Lang Etude critique* (Paris: Nathan, 1993) p. 34.

8 Brenez, p, 11.

9 Herman Melville, *Moby Dick or The Whale* in *Romances of Herman Melville* (New York: Tudor Publishing, n.d.), p. 857.

10 Siegfried Kracauer reported Lang's claim in *From Caligari to Hitler*, p. 66. Lang repeats the story in 'La nuit viennoise, un confession de Fritz Lang', *Cahiers du Cinéma*, no. 169, August 1965, p. 52, and in Peter Bogdanovich, *Fritz Lang in America*, pp. 63–4.

11 Kracauer, pp. 66–7.

12 For the imagistic aspect of intertitles and words in German Expressionist films, see Philippe Dubois, 'L'écriture figurale dans le cinéma muet des années 20', in Francesco Pitassio and Leonardo Quaresima (eds), *Scrittura e Immagine: La didascalia nel cinema muto* (Udine: Forum, 1998), especially pp. 75–85.

13 Michel Chion, *The Voice in Cinema*, trans. Claudia Gorbman (New York: Columbia University Press, 1999), pp. 31–47.

14 Ibid., p. 37.
15 Ibid., pp. 37-42.
16 Jonathan Crary, 'Dr. Mabuse and Mr. Edison' in Russell Ferguson (ed.), *Art and Film Since 1945: Hall of Mirrors* (Los Angeles, CA: Museum of Contemporary Art, 1996), p. 271.
17 Chion, p. 42.
18 Jorge Luis Borges, 'Death and the Compass' in *Labyrinths*, pp. 86–7.
19 Ibid., pp. 17–29.
20 Chion offers an insightful analysis of this and the opening phone call as well, pp. 66–73.

Chapter 7: *M*: The City Haunted by Demonic Desire

1 Walter Benjamin, *The Origin of German Tragic Drama*, p. 44.
2 Georg Trakl, *Autumn Sonata*, trans. Daniel Simko (Mount Kisco, NY: Moyer Bell, 1989), p. 19.
3 Noel Burch, 'Fritz Lang: German Period', pp. 20–30 (original version, with diagrams not included in English translation in *Revue d'Esthétique* special number 'Cinéma, théorie, lecture', 1973, pp. 227–48); Roger Dadoun, 'Le pouvoir et "sa" folie', *Positif*, no. 188, December 1976, pp. 13–20; Anton Kaes, ' The Cold Gaze', pp. 105–17. Kaes' forthcoming book for the BFI on *M* promises to develop the rich insights of this essay.
4 Noel Burch, 'Fritz Lang: German Period', pp. 21–2.
5 Ibid., pp. 20–30.
6 Michel Chion, *The Voice in Cinema*, pp. 17–18; 30–47.
7 Burch, *passim*.
8 Thierry Kuntzel, 'The Film Work', *Enclitic*, vol. 2 no. 1, 1978, pp. 40–61; Michel Marie, *M le Maudit*, pp. 101–16; Marie-Claire Ropars-Wuilleumier, *Le Texte divise* (Paris: Pup, 1981), pp. 93–104.
9 Marie, p.101.
10 This version, a project of 100 Jahre Kino Europarates and Taurus Films, with image reconstruction by the Munich Film Museum and sound restoration by Donat Keusch and Christian Zajac will be my principle version, although others have been consulted.
11 Kuntzel, p. 41.
12 Robert Bresson, *Notes on Cinematography*, trans. Jonathan Griffin (New York: Urizen Books, 1977), p. 21.
13 Burch, p. 21, and passim.
14 Georg Simmel, 'The Metropolis and Mental Life', in *Of Individuality and Social Forms* (Chicago, IL: University of Chicago Press, 1971), pp. 328–9.
15 Thus the restored print. Other prints continue the cries over all the shots, less effectively, in my opinion.
16 Kuntzel, p. 59.
17 Bertolt Brecht, 'Utterances of a Martyr', trans. John Willet, in *Poems 1913–1956* (New York: Methuen, 1976), p. 15.
18 Kuntzel, p. 59.
19 Peter Bogdanovich, *Fritz Lang in America*, p. 86.
20 Ibid., pp. 28–9.
21 Marie, p. 116.
22 Martin Buber, *I and Thou*, trans. Ronald Gregor Smith (New York: Charles Scribner's Sons, 1958), p. 18.
23 Kuntzel, p. 60.
24 Lotte Eisner, *Fritz Lang*, p. 109.
25 As much for his personal expression of enthusiasm for the film, which I could not take lightly, as for his article, 'La Machine-Cinéma', in *Cinéma et littérature 8: Les Temps des Machines*, Valenca, 1990, pp. 49–55.
26 R. L. Rutsky, 'The Mediation of Technology and Gender', p. 29.
27 Jacques Rivette, 'The Hand', p. 141.
28 Quoted in Frederick W. Ott, *The Films of Fritz Lang*, p. 148.
29 Siefried Kracauer, *From Caligari to Hitler*, p. 122: photo with caption facing p. 129.

30 Kaes, p. 108.
31 Ibid., pp. 114–15.
32 Burch, p. 23.
33 For instance, Burch, p. 23, and *M, a Film by Fritz Lang*, trans. Nicholas Garnham (New York: Simon and Schuster, 1968), which is based on the transcription from *L'Avant-scène Cinéma*, no. 39, July-August 1964, p. 20.
34 And identified by Marie, p. 34, as a characteristic of *M*.
35 Burch, p. 24.
36 Maria M. Tatar, *Lustmord: Sexual Murder in Weimar Germany* (Princeton, NJ: Princeton University Press, 1995), p. 158. My good friend and collaborator Travis Preston first alerted me to the significance of the Peer Gynt play to *M*. I am also indebted to his observations about the relation between Beckert and the children.
37 Henrik Ibsen, *Peer Gynt: A Dramatic Poem*, trans. Peter Watts (London: Penguin Books, 1966), p. 69.
38 Henri Lefebvre, *The Production of Space*, trans. Donald Nicholson-Smith (London: Blackwell, 1991).
39 Kaes, pp. 114–15.
40 Burch, p. 25; 'De "Mabuse" a "M": Le Travail de Fritz Lang', *Revue d'Esthétique*, special number: 'Cinéma, théorie, lecture', 1973, p. 237.
41 Dadoun, p. 16 (my translation).
42 Quoted in Ott, p. 156.
43 In 'La nuit viennoise, un confession de Fritz Lang', *Cahiers du Cinéma*, no. 169, August 1965, p. 52 (my translation).
44 Rainer Maria Rilke, *The Notebooks of Malte Laurids Brigge* (New York: W.W. Norton, 1964), pp. 94–5.
45 The Mabuse poster appears in Gunter Scholdt (ed.), *Norbert Jacques…*, p. 153. The *Fantomas* film poster appears in *1895*: L'année 1913 en France numéro hors serie Oct. 1993, p. 244.
46 Burch, p. 21.
47 Dadoun, p.19.
48 Ibid.
49 Marie, p. 52.
50 Quoted in William Leach, *Land of Desire: Merchants, Power, and the Rise of a New American Culture* (New York: Pantheon Books, 1991), p. 60. Besides being an expert on shop windows, Baum was, of course, the author of *The Wonderful Wizard of Oz*.
51 Kracauer, p. 221.
52 See Baum, quoted in Leach, p. 60.
53 Eisner makes the point that Lang wanted 'to say that the ultimate reason for the murders is the unequal distribution of wealth. Frau Beckmann is forever at the tub; hence she has no time to look after Elsie properly or fetch her from school', *Fritz Lang*, p. 128.
54 Marie, p. 53.
55 Kuntzel, pp. 43–4.
56 Quoted in Patrick McGilligan, *The Nature of the Beast*, p. 157.
57 Burch, p. 21, p. 29.
58 See Ott, p. 155.
59 Dadoun, p. 20.
60 Ibid.
61 Higham and Sheenby, *The Celluloid Muse*, p. 123.
62 Quoted by Bernard Eisenschitz in his valuable essay 'Le Production, le tournage' in *M le Maudit un film de Fritz Lang* (Paris: Le Cinématheque Français/Editions Plume, 1990), p. 35.
63 Dadoun, p. 20.
64 The most complete version of this anecdote is told by Lang in Bogdanovich, pp. 126–7.
65 Kracauer, p. 219.
66 Bogdanovich, p. 20.

Chapter 8: You Ought to Be in Pictures: *Liliom* and *Fury*

1   Bertholt Brecht, 'On Thinking about Hell', trans. Nicholas Jacobs, in *Poems 1913–1956*, p. 367.

2   Ibid., trans. Frank Jellinek, p. 131.

3   The weighing of evidence is done well in Patrick McGilligan, *The Nature of the Beast*, pp. 174–81.

4   Curt Riess, quoted in ibid., p. 191.

5   Lang's divorce is detailed in ibid., pp. 181–3.

6   Ibid., pp. 157–8 and 169–73.

7   Noel Burch, 'Fritz Lang: German Period', p. 30. Burch's later reflections are on p. 31.

8   Ibid., p. 3.

9   Kristin Thompson, 'Early Alternatives to the Hollywood Mode of Production: Implications for Europe's Avant Gardes', *Film History*, vol. 5 no. 4, December 1993, pp. 386–404.

10 Ibid., p. 388.

11 Ibid., p. 395.

12 Lang tells stories of his adjustments to Hollywood procedures in many places. See, for example, Charles Higham and Joel Greenberg, *The Celluloid Muse: Hollywood Directors Speak* (Chicago, IL: Henry Regnery, 1969), p. 106; Peter Bogdanovich, *Fritz Lang in America*, p. 32.

13 Theo Lindgren speaks of these detailed 'scenarios' being used during the Berto of *M* and *The Testament of Dr. Mabuse*. Quoted in Alfred Eibel (ed), *Fritz Lang Trois Lumières*, pp. 72–3. Lotte Eisner quotes Lindgren on the same topic, p. 144. A wonderful selection of these diagrams that Lang prepared for *The Big Heat* has been published in Gerard Leblanc and Brigitte Devismes, *Le Double Scénario chez Fritz Lang* (Paris: Armand Colin, 1991). Several related plans are reproduced in Bernard Eisenschitz and Paolo Bertetto (eds), *Fritz Lang: La mise en scène*, for *The Woman in the Window*, p. 281; *Cloak and Dagger*, p. 306; *Rancho Notorious*, p. 357; *The Blue Gardenia*, p. 371; and *Moonfleet*, p. 396.

14 Such sketches, some in Lang's hand, some in those of his art directors, are reproduced in ibid.: *Die Nibelungen*, pp. 78, 82, 84; *The Testament of Dr. Mabuse*, pp. 90, 152–8; *M*, 149–51; *Man Hunt*, pp. 232, 237; *Ministry of Fear*, p. 267; *The Woman in the Window*, p. 281; *Cloak and Dagger*, p. 307; *Rancho Notorious*, pp. 347, 349, 351; *Moonfleet*, pp. 394–5. The art directors' sketches for *Man Hunt* have been published in Bernard Eisenschitz, *Manhunt de Fritz Lang* (Paris: Editions Yellow Now, 1992), pp. 147–253.

15 Such accounts are numerous. For a sampling, see McGilligan, pp. 243–4, 265 (Henry Fonda); p. 254 (Sylvia Sidney); p. 311 (Edward G. Robinson); p. 338 (Lilli Palmer); p. 359 (Michael Redgrave). Perhaps most vivid is Marlene Dietrich's description in the interview film, *Marlene* (1983) by Maximilian Schell of Lang chalking her marks in *Rancho Notorious*, but doing it based on his six foot stride rather than her considerably smaller one.

16 Manny Farber, 'White Elephant Art vs Termite Art', in *Negative Space: Manny Farber on the Movies* (New York: Praeger Publishers, 1971), pp. 134–44; Lang is quoted in Bogdanovich, p. 20.

17 Walter Benjamin, 'Commentaries on Poems by Brecht', in *Understanding Brecht*, trans. Anna Bostock (London: NLB, 1977) p. 60.

18 Brecht, 'Jan 19, 1942', *Journals 1934–55,* trans. Hugh Rorrison, ed. John Willett (New York: Routledge, 1996). p. 193.

19 Lang, quoted in Bogdanovich, p. 38.

20 Brecht, *Poems 1913–1956*, p. 131.

21 See details of the pre-production for *Liliom* in McGilligan, pp. 193–6.

22 Ibid., p. 197.

23 Ibid., p. 199.

24 Ibid., p. 201.

25 Bernard Eisenschitz, 'Le Production, le tournage', p. 23. McGilligan, p. 190, seems to cast doubts on whether this script actually dated from this earlier period, which the reference Eisenschitz turned up in *Kinematograph* from1929 should settle (McGilligan, following Eisner had looked for evidence a bit later in 1933). The script for *Scandal in Vienna*, a project of

Lang's from the early 1950s, has been published in French translation in Fritz Lang, *Le montagne des superstitions et autres histoires*, trans. Christine and Jacques Rousselet, ed. Cornelius Snauber (Paris: Pierre Belfond, 1991) and in German translation in *Der Berg des Aberglaubens und andere Geschichten* (Vienna: Europa Verlag, 1988).

26 René Daumal, 'Avant la présentation de "Liliom"', reprinted in *Positif*, no. 188, December 1976, p. 7 (originally published in *Aujourd'hui*, 13 March 1934).

27 See Garrett Stewart *Between Film and Screen: Modernism's Photo-Synthesis* (Chicago, IL: University of Chicago Press, forthcoming).

28 Daumal, p. 7.

29 Eisner, p. 153.

30 Brecht, 'Deliver the Goods', trans. Humphrey Milnes in *Poems 1913–1956*, p. 379.

31 McGilligan describes Lang's trans-Atlantic trip and arrival, pp. 201–3.

32 On Sagan, see McGilligan, p. 202. On Eisenstein in Hollywood, see, among others, Ivor Montague, *With Eisenstein in Hollywood* (New York: International Publishers, 1969).

33 French and German translations of this screenplay treatment have been published in Fritz Lang, *Mort d'une carrièriste et autres histoires*, trans. Christine and Jacques Rousselet, ed. Cornelius Schnauber (Paris: Pierre Belfond, 1987) and *Der Tod eines Karriere–Girls und andere Geschichten* (Vienna: Europa Verlag, 1988).

34 Bogdanovich, p. 126.

35 For instance, Nick Smedley's carefully researched article 'Fritz Lang's Trilogy: The Rise and Fall of a European Social Commentator', *Film History*, vol. 5, pp. 1–21.

36 The best treatment of the way self-censorship functioned in Hollywood in the 1930s is Lea Jacobs, *The Wages of Sin: Censorship and the Fallen Woman Film 1928–1942* (Madison: University of Wisconsin Press, 1991).

37 The discussion I will carry out throughout this work of the motif of the shop window in Lang could be seen as an extension of this brilliant insight by Frieda Grafe: 'If one wants to locate in Lang a critique of the system, a critque of capitalism, it is in this direction that one should search: the exposition of merchandise, the exposition of desire. *The Woman in the Window*: the image of a woman as a trap for the gaze. Lorre in *M*, seeing himself among the objects, seeing the reflection of his own gaze.' In [Enno Patalas, Frieda Grafe, Hans Prinzler], *Fritz Lang*, trans. Claude Porcell (Paris: Rivages, 1985), p. 25. This French edition of the book originally published in German (Munich: Carl Hanser Verlag, 1976) was published without authors' names due to a disagreement about the use of illustrations, but the written text is the same.

38 Brecht, 'Oct. 22, 1942', *Journals*, p. 261.

39 In [Patalas, Grafe, Prinzler], p. 103.

40 Bogdanovich, pp. 20–2.

41 Ibid., p. 22.

42 Vincente Sanchez-Biosca, 'Fury ou comment est ne John Doe' in Eisenschitz and Bertetto (eds), pp. 191–202.

43 Ibid., p. 193.

44 Quoted in Mark Shivas, 'Fritz Lang Talks about Dr. Mabuse', p. 260.

45 André Bazin, 'The Evolution of the Language of Cinema', in *What is Cinema? Vol. I* (Berkeley: University of California Press, 1967), p. 32 ; Lang gives his opinion in Bogdanovich, p. 28.

46 Bogdanovich, p. 31

47 Jean Douchet, 'Dix-sept plans' in Raymond Bellour (ed.), *Le cinéma Americain: Analyses de films*, vol. I (Paris: Flammarion, 1980), p. 221.

48 Stewart supplies a strong reading of the photographs scattered throughout *Fury*.

49 Paramount advertisement quoted in Katherine Helgensen Fuller, 'You Can Have the Strand in Your Own Town', *Film History*, vol. 6 no. 2, Summer 1994, p. 173.

50 Eisner, p. 161.

51 Ben N. Hall, *The Best Remaining Seats: The Story of the Golden Age of the Movie Palace* (New York: Bramhall House, 1961), pp. 36–41; Fuller, pp. 173–4.

52 Still reproduced in Bogdanovich, p. 31.

53 Scene described in McGilligan, pp. 226–7.

54 [Patalas, Grafe, Prinzler], p. 100.

55 Particularly reviewers Kenneth Fearing in *The New Masses* and Robert Stebbins in *New Theater*, both leftist publications. See the summary of their reviews in E. Ann Kaplan, *Fritz Lang: A Guide to References and Resources* (Boston, MA: G.K. Hall, 1981), pp. 168–9.

56 Sanchez-Biosca, p. 193.

57 Ibid., p. 194.

58 Reynold Humphries also discusses Joe's look at the camera and his position as enunciator, although in an incredibly obscure manner, in *Fritz Lang: Genre and Representation in his American Films* (Baltimore, MD: Johns Hopkins University Press, 1989), p. 37.

59 Ibid.

60 Ibid., p. 195.

61 Douchet, pp. 216–17.

62 Ibid., pp. 228–9.

63 Sanchez-Biosca, pp. 197–8.

64 Ibid., p. 197.

65 Joseph Mankiewicz quoted in McGilligan, p. 232.

66 Sanchez-Biosca, p. 199.

Chapter 9: *You Only Live Once*

1 Heinrich von Kleist on the painting *Monk by the Sea* by Caspar David Friedrich, *Berliner Abendblatter 12*, Blatt, 13 October 1810, pp. 47–8. My thanks to Inge Baxman and John Butler-Ludwig for helping me locate this quote.

2 Frieda Grafe in [Grafe, Enno Patalas and Hans Prinzler], *Fritz Lang*, pp. 24–5

3 For the concept of haptic space pioneered in art history by Alois Riegel, see his pithy summary in the essay 'Late Roman or Oriental?', trans. Peter Wortsman in Gert Schiff (ed.), *German Essays on Art History* (New York: Continuum, 1988), pp. 173–90. For a careful discussion of the concept and its application to film history, see Antonia Lant, 'Haptical Cinema', *October*, pp. 45–73. A similar sense of Lang's visual style may be behind Jean Roy's claim of a deep affinity between the eye and the hand in Lang. See Jean Roy, 'L'oeil, le regard, l'écran: essai sur Fritz Lang', *Cinema 80*, no. 255, March 1980, p. 108.

4 Fritz Lang, 'The Future of the Feature Film', in Anton Kaes, Martin Jay and Edward Dimendberg (eds), *The Weimar Republic Sourcebook*, p. 623.

5 Laura Mulvey's classic essay, 'Visual Pleasure and Narrative Cinema' can be found in Laura Mulvey, *Visual and Other Pleasures* (Bloomington: Indiana University Press, 1989), pp. 14–28; Stephen Jenkins, ' Lang: Fear and Desire', in Stephen Jenkins (ed.), *Fritz Lang: The Image and the Look* (London: BFI, 1981), pp. 38–124.

6 Roy, p. 105.

7 Martin Heidegger, 'The Age of the World Picture' in *The Question Concerning Technology and Other Essays*, trans. William Lovitt (New York: Harper and Row, 1977), pp. 115–54.

8 Ibid., p. 150.

9 As Grafe puts it, 'the world of appearance becomes transparent in order to reveal the law whereby it functions' (p. 31).

10 Both Roy and Grafe point out the importance of blindness in dealing with vision in Lang. Roy, 'L'oeil', p. 105; Grafe, pp. 62–4.

11 The treatment for *Men without a Country* is given in French translation in Lang, *Mort d'une carrièriste*, pp. 67–94.

12 George M. Wilson, *Narration In Light: Studies in Cinematic Point of View* (Baltimore, MD: Johns Hopkins University Press, 1986), p. 17.

13 Jean Luc Godard, *Godard on Godard*, ed. and trans. Tom Milne (New York: Viking Press, 1972), p. 216.

14 Wilson, p. 17.

15 Ibid., pp. 33–6.

16 David Bordwell's careful and insightful discussion of the narration in detective films in

Narration in the Fiction Film, pp. 64–70, is very helpful in describing the weave of controlling knowledge in this genre, which Lang both conforms to and somewhat alters in this sequence.

17 Ibid., p. 67.
18 Wilson, pp. 19–22.
19 For a definition of the dialogue hook, see Bordwell, p. 158.
20 Wilson, p. 21.
21 Ibid., pp. 29–34.
22 Quoted in the *Third World Newsreel Teach Our Children* as an intertitle. Reproduced in David E. James, *Allegories of Cinema: American Film in the Sixties* (Princeton, NJ: Princeton University Press, 1989), p. 218.
23 This sequence is essential to Wilson's reading of the film, pp. 18–22.
24 Wilson provides a different consideration of this shot in ibid., pp. 18–19; Reynold Humphries provides a rather confused account in *Fritz Lang: Genre and Representation*, pp. 30–6.
25 Novalis, *Hymns to the Night and Other Selected Writings*, trans. Charles E. Passage (New York: Bobbs Merrill, 1960), p. 5.
26 Friedrich Hölderlin, *Hyperion or The Hermit in Greece*, trans. Willard Trask (New York: Frederick Ungar Publishing, 1965), p. 115.
27 A discussion of Towne and Baker, generally ignored in discussions of American screenwriters, can be found in Matthew Bernstein, *Walter Wanger: Hollywood Independent* (Berkeley: University of California Press, 1994), pp. 117–26.
28 Bernstein, p. 120
29 Ibid.
30 McGilligan, p. 126. E. Ann Kaplan summarises an interview with Lang by Eileen Creelman in the New York *Sun* for 28 January 1937, in which Lang indicates he had wanted the woman's part to be even more central to the film. Kaplan, *Fritz Lang: A Guide*, p. 170.
31 Bernstein, p. 121.
32 Rosza's account of working with Lang is reprinted in Alfred Eibel (ed.), *Fritz Lang Trois Lumières*, pp. 111–14.
33 Wilson, p. 36.
34 Bogdanovich, p. 35.
35 Wilson, p. 36.
36 Erwin Panofsky, '*Et in Arcadia Ego*: Poussin and the Elegiac Tradition', in *Meaning in the Visual Arts* (Chicago, IL: University of Chicago Press, 1982), pp. 295–320.
37 Wilson, p. 37.

Chapter 10: *You and Me*

1 Peter Bogdanovich, *Fritz Lang in America*, p. 39. In fact, as Rob White pointed out to me the stage direction (actually 'exit, pursued by a bear') occurs in *The Winters Tale*, Act III Sc III.
2 Poster for *You and Me*, reproduced in Frederick W. Ott, *The Films of Fritz Lang*, p. 182.
3 See, especially, Theodor Adorno's somewhat neglected essay 'The Schema of Mass Culture', in *The Culture Industry: Selected Essays on Mass Culture*, ed. J.M Bernstein (London: Routledge, 1991), pp. 53–84.
4 Charles Higham and Joel Greenberg (eds), *The Celluloid Muse*, p. 108.
5 *The New Yorker*, 1938, in Clipping File for *You and Me*, New York Public Library, Billy Rose Theater Collection.
6 Review, *New York Times*, 6 June, 1938 in Clipping File for *You and Me*, New York Public Library, Billy Rose Theater Collection.
7 On Lang's Paramount contract, see Patrick McGilligan, *The Nature of the Beast*, pp. 250–1.
8 *New York Times*, 6 June 1938. Nugent, besides being a reviewer, was a scriptwriter, eventually writing several scripts for John Ford, *The Searchers* among them.
9 The termination of the deal with Paramount is described in McGilligan, p. 256.
10 Bogdanovich, p. 38.
11 Lang said the same thing to Higham and/or Greenberg, p. 108.

12   Roland Barthes, 'Mother Courage Blind', in *Critical Essays*, trans. Richard Howard (Evanston,
     IL: Northwestern University Press, 1972), pp. 33–6.
13   Bertolt Brecht, *Journals 1934–1955*, pp. 243, 259.
14   This was for a score for the film directed by William Dieterle, who had also worked in Weimar
     theatre and cinema, eventually titled *Blockade*, released in 1938. Wanger decided not to use
     Weill's score, after initial enthusiasm. See Weill's letters to Lotte Lenya from Hollywood,
     January–March 1937, in *Speak Low (When You Speak of Love): The Letters of Kurt Weill and
     Lotte Lenya*, trans. Lys Symonette and Kim Kowalke (Berkeley: University of California Press,
     1996), pp.196–221.
15   Ibid., pp. 235–46, 250, 253, 261, 269.
16   Bertolt Brecht, 'A Short Organum for the Theatre', *Brecht on Theatre*, trans. and ed. John
     Willett (New York: Hill and Wang, 1964), p. 201.
17   Brecht, 'The Modern Theatre is the Epic Theatre', in ibid., p. 35.
18   Bogdanovich, p. 39.
19   Ibid.
20   Rick Altman, *The American Film Musical* (Bloomington: Indiana University Press, 1989.), esp.
     pp. 16–58.
21   Ibid., pp. 62, 69, 77.
22   Ibid., pp. 62–79.
23   Lang's treatment in French translation is included as Fritz Lang, '*You and Me* Story Outline' in
     Bernard Eisenschitz and Paolo Bertetto (eds), *Fritz Lang*, pp. 207–13.
24   Altman, p. 47.
25   Lang, '*You and Me*', in Eisenschitz and Bertetto, p. 209.
26   *Variety*, 8 June 1938, p. 38.
27   Altman, pp. 45–53.
28   Salka Viertel, *The Kindness of Strangers* (New York: Holt, Rinehart and Winston, 1969),
     pp. 206–8.
29   Review of *You and Me* from *New York Herald Tribune* in Clipping File for *You and Me*, New
     York Public Library, Billy Rose Theater Collection.
30   Lang, '*You and Me*' in Eisenschitz and Bertetto.
31   Ibid., p. 210.
32   Altman, pp. 74–9.
33   *New York Sun*, 2 June 1938; *New York World Telegram*, 2 June 1938; in Clipping File for *You and
     Me*, NYPL, Billy Rose Theater Collection.
34   *New York Journal American*, 2 June 1938 in Clipping File for *You and Me*, NYPL, Billy Rose
     Theater Collection.
35   Bertolt Brecht, 'Hollywood', *Poems 1913–1955*, p. 382.
36   The department store as emblem of modern consumer culture is discussed in Rosalind H.
     Williams, *Dream Worlds: Mass Consumption in Late Nineteenth-Century France* (Berkeley, CA:
     University of California Press, 1982); William Leach, *Land of Desire*; Elaine S. Abelson, *When
     Ladies Go A-Thieving: Middle-Class Shoplifters in the Victorian Department Store* (Oxford:
     Oxford University Press, 1989), which deals particularly with surveillance and shop-lifting in
     department stores.
37   See Leach, pp. 73–4.
38   Altman, pp. 50–8.

Chapter 11: *The Woman in the Window*: Cycles of Desire

1   Johann Wolfgang von Goethe, *Faust Part One and Two*, trans. Charles E. Passage
    (Indianapolis, IN: Bobbs Merrill, 1965), pp. 85–6.
2   Edgar Allan Poe, 'The Oval Portrait' in *Poetry and Tales*, (ed.), Patrick F. Quinn (New York:
    The Library of America, 1984), p. 482.
3   This is, of course, Helen's line describing the effect of perfume on a girl: 'it does something for
    a girl's soul, kind of'.

4   Stephen Jenkins, 'Lang: Fear and Desire' in Jenkins (ed.), *Fritz Lang: The Image and the Look*, especially pp. 40–4; 63–123.

5   Laura Mulvey, 'Visual Pleasure and Narrative Cinema', pp. 14–28.

6   See Friedrich Nietzsche, *Thus Spoke Zarathustra*, trans. Walter Kaufmann in *The Portable Nietzsche*, ed. Walter Kaufmann (New York: Viking Press, 1967), pp. 129–30.

7   J. H. Wallis, *Once Off-Guard* (New York: E.P Dutton, 1942).

8   Accounts of this journal are numerous, with perhaps the most revealing being the description by Pierre Rissient in Alfred Eibel (ed.), *Fritz Lang Trois Lumières*, pp. 312–13.

9   Ibid., p. 313.

10 Siegfried Kracauer, *From Caligari to Hitler*, pp. 119–20.

11 Wallis, p. 53.

12 Lang claims responsibility for this change of ending in numerous later interviews and in his article 'Happily Ever After' (1948), in Harry M. Geduld, *Film Makers on Film Making* (Bloomington: University of Indiana Press, 1969), pp. 224–31. However, in an interview with Eileen Creelman in the *New York Sun*, 17 April 1945, summarised in E. Ann Kaplan, *Fritz Lang: A Guide*, p. 417, he claimed the ending was the producer's idea, not his.

13 In Charles Higham and Joel Greenberg (eds), *The Celluloid Muse*, p. 113.

14 Peter Bogdanovich, *Fritz Lang in America*, pp. 63–4.

15 Ibid., p. 63.

16 Georges Sturm, *Fritz Lang*, p. 119.

17 Ralph Waldo Emerson, 'Compensation', *Essays* (New York: Thomas Y. Crowell, 1961), p. 84.

18 A carefully-researched account of Lang's work at Fox on these films, can be found in Nick Smedley, 'Fritz Lang Out-foxed: The German Genius as Contract Employee' *Film History*, vol. 4 no. 1, 1990, pp. 289–304.

19 Noel Burch, 'Fritz Lang: German Period', p. 3.

20 Patrick McGilligan, *The Nature of the Beast*, p. 209; Anthony Heilbut, *Exiled in Paradise: German Refugee Artists and Intellectuals in America from the 1930s to the Present* (Berkeley, CA: University of California Press, 1997), p. 65

21 An insightful account of *Man Hunt* and its exemplary place within the thriller genre can be found in Martin Rubin, *Thrillers* (Cambridge: Cambridge University Press, 1999), pp. 226–41. Bernard Eisenschitz, *Man Hunt par Fritz Lang*, provides a thorough analysis as well as an account of the production of the film. As always, Jacques Aumont provides key insights in 'L'oeil était dans le tombeau ou We did not see what Thorndike saw' in Eisenschitz and Bertetto, pp. 249–62.

22 Kracauer, pp. 73–4.

23 There have been many discussions of the relation between Brecht and Lang in making this film. Lang's various interviews give his account, generally from years after the event. Brecht's work diary chronicles his work on the script and the variation of his estimates of Lang and his other collaborators, as well as his final disappointment with the outcome. Bertolt Brecht, *Journals 1934–55*. Probably the most insightful discussion remains Ben Brewster's 'Brecht and the Film Industry', *Screen*, Winter 1975/76, pp. 16–45, which also includes a discussion by Brewster, Colin MacCabe and others.

24 Jean-Louis Comolli and François Géré, 'Two Fictions Concerning Hate' in Jenkins (ed.), p. 145. This long analysis, originally published in *Cahiers du Cinéma*, no. 286, March 1978, remains the most detailed discussion of the film.

25 Brecht, *Journals 1939–1955*, pp. 243, 261.

26 Brecht seems to have intended something like this; see his entry for 18 Octpber 1942 in his work diary: 'Thus the German terror has the same impersonal character as the Czech assassination', p. 260.

27 Richard Hofstadter, *The Paranoid Style in American Politics and Other Essays* (New York: Random House, 1967), p. 36.

28 Andrew Sarris, 'Fritz Lang', *Interviews with Film Directors*, p. 257.

29 James Naremore, *More than Night: Film Noir in its Contexts* (Berkeley: University of California Press, 1998), especially pp. 1–39.

30 Benjamin develops the analogy of ideas and the constellation in *The Origin of German Tragic Drama*, p. 34. My definition is my own, although inspired by this discussion of Benjamin's.
31 Naremore, pp. 5, 9–11.
32 See Naremore's discussion of this scene, p. 89.
33 Heinrich von Kleist, *Amphitryon*, trans. Marion Sonnenfeld (New York: Frederick Ungar, 1962), p. 80.
34 Reynold Humphries quite perceptively picks out the series of straw hats through this film from Mazard to Lalor to Heidt to this cloakroom. However, he multiplies the single straw hat behind the attendant into ' a whole line of such hats', *Fritz Lang*, pp. 105–6.

Chapter 12: *Scarlet Street*: Life Is a Nightmare

1 Walter Benjamin, '*Trauerspiel* and Tragedy' in *Selected Writings: Vol. I 1913–1926*, eds Marcus Bullock and Michael W. Jennings (Cambridge, MA: Harvard University Press, 1996), p. 57.
2 Karl Marx, *The Eighteenth Brumaire of Louis Bonaparte* (New York: International Publishers, 1963), p. 15.
3 Lang interview in Charles Higham and Joel Greenberg (eds), *The Celluloid Muse*, p. 115; Peter Bogdanovich, *Fritz Lang in America*, p. 66.
4 Patrick McGilligan, *The Nature of the Beast*, p. 321.
5 Higham and Greenberg (eds), p. 115.
6 Jean Renoir, *Letters*, eds Lorraine LoBianco and David Thompson (London: Faber and Faber, 1994), pp. 122–3.
7 Edward Benson, 'Decor and Decorum, from *La Chienne* to *Scarlet Street*: Franco-U.S. Trade in Film during the Thirties', *Film and History*, vol. 12 no. 3, September 1982, pp. 57–65; E. Ann Kaplan, 'Ideology and Cinematic Practice in Lang's *Scarlet Street* and Renoir's *La Chienne*', *Wide Angle*, vol. 5 no. 3, 1983, pp. 32–43; Thomas Brandlmeier, 'Lang-Renoir, Renoir-Lang', *epd film*, October 1984, pp. 19–22.
8 Jacques Rivette, 'The Hand', pp. 140–4.
9 Stephen Jenkins, 'Lang: Fear and Desire' in Jenkins (ed.), *Fritz Lang*, p. 103.
10 McGilligan, p. 318.
11 Quoted in ibid., p. 310.
12 In fact, a fascinating version, undeservedly neglected in discussions of these films, of *La Chienne* was released in 1936 between the Renoir and Lang version. *Las Mujeres Mandan*, directed by the powerful Mexican director, Fernando de Fuentes, actually introduces the Legrand/Cross character with a sequence of domestic comedy adapted from W. C. Fields' *It's a Gift*, portraying this character as the archetypal comic hen-pecked husband.
13 See Conley's reading of the film in *Film Hieroglyphics: Ruptures in Classical Cinema* (Minneapolis: University of Minnesota Press, 1991), pp. 20–45. Gematria is the kabbalistic method of biblical interpretation in which the rearrangement and substitution of letters yields hidden meanings. Conley's essay is fascinating, witty and often insightful, but I can't help feeling, as Johnny Prince says about one of Chris's paintings, 'The guy must be a hop head, seeing things like that!' Lang's forthright confession of the scatological theme in relation to Chris can be found in McGilligan, p. 318.
14 Georg Kaiser, *From Morning to Midnight* in *Five Plays*, trans. J.M Ritchie (London: Calder and Boyars, 1971), p. 33. Although the plot of *Scarlet Street* closely follows *La Chienne*, its imagery more closely recalls Kaiser's play.
15 A connection made by Conley, p. 26, although his further reading of 'Jew' in the sign seems uncalled for.
16 [Enno Patalas, Frieda Grafe, Hans Prinzler], *Fritz Lang*, p. 124.
17 Jenkins, pp. 99–100.
18 'L'autre homme en nous' in Fritz Lang, *Mort d'une carrièriste*, pp. 43–4.
19 Conley, p. 24. A brief definition (with references to Freud's writings) of the 'primal scene' is given in J. Laplanche and J.-B. Pontalis, *The Language of Psychoanalysis*, pp. 335–6. An essential discussion by Freud comes in 'From the History of an Infantile Neurosis' [The 'Wolf Man' case], *Standard Edition*, vol. XVII, pp. 41–7 and passim.

20   Jenkins, p. 99.
21   Ibid., p. 55.
22   A still reproduced in Bogdanovich, p. 68, seems to show Chris with the pick *after* the murder, so it is quite possible the scene was originally longer than the current four stabs. The fascinating story of the banning of *Scarlet Street* is detailed by Matthew Bernstein in 'A Tale of Three Cities: The Banning of *Scarlet Street*', *Cinema Journal*, vol. 35 no. 1, Fall 1995, pp. 27–52.
23   Quoted in ibid., p. 33.
24   Jacob Boehme, *The Signature of All Things* (Cambridge: James Clarke, 1969), p. 10.
25   Matthew Bernstein, *Walter Wanger*, p. 198. Bernstein provides the most thorough account of Diana productions, pp. 197–216.
26   McGilligan, p. 316.
27   Bernstein, *Walter Wanger*, p. 199.
28   Ibid., pp. 202–3.
29   Ibid., p. 206.
30   Ibid., p. 201.
31   Noel Burch, 'Fritz Lang: German Period', p. 3.
32   Walter Benjamin, *The Origin of German Tragic Drama*, pp. 125–7.
33   I read this anecdote, oddly enough, in Daniel Yankelovich and William Barrett, *Ego and Instinct: The Psychoanalytic View of Human Nature – Revised* (New York: Random House, 1970), p. 127.
34   Quoted in Michael Hamburger, *Reason and Energy: Studies in German Literature* (London: Weidenfeld and Nicolson, 1970), p. 12. This is a notoriously difficult passage to translate. Thomas Pfau gives this more literal, but less comprehensible rendering: 'The presentation of the tragic rests primarily on the tremendous – how the god and man mate and how natural force and man's innermost boundlessly unite in wrath – conceiving of itself [rests] on the boundless union purifying itself through boundless separation'. Friedrich Hölderlin, 'Remarks on *Oedipus*', in *Essays and Letters on Theory*, ed. and trans. Thomas Pfau (Albany, NY: SUNY Press, 1988), p. 107
35   McGilligan, p. 318.
36   This encounter, of course, forms the starting point of Stephen Heath's classic essay 'Narrative Space' in *Screen*, no. 17, Autumn 1976, p. 68.
37   Diane Waldman, 'The Childish, the Insane and the Ugly: The Representation of Modern Art in Popular Films and Fiction of the Forties', *Wide Angle*, vol. 5 no. 2, 1982, pp. 52–65.
38   Fritz Lang, 'Hommes sans patrie', in *Mort d'une carrièriste*, p. 79.
39   Bogdanovich, p. 67.
40   Lang discusses Decker in his interview in Higham and Greenberg (eds), p. 116. Edward G. Robinson's collection of modern art may also play a role in the film's sympathetic view of modernism.
41   Walter Benjamin, *The Origin of German Tragic Drama*, p. 151.
42   Bogdanovich, p. 66.
43   See Gilles Deleuze and Felix Guattari, *Anti-Oedipus: Capitalism and Schizophrenia*, trans. Robert Hurley *et al.* (Minneapolis: University of Minnesota Press, 1983).
44   From Bertolt Brecht, 'Ten Poems from a Reader for Those who Live in Cities', *Poems 1913–1956*, p. 131.
45   Ibid., p. 69.
46   Bernstein, *Walter Wanger*, pp. 204–5.
47   Bogdanovich, p. 69.
48   Ibid.
49   Jean Douchet, 'La tragédie du héros Langien', in Bernard Eisenschitz and Paolo Bertetto (eds), *Fritz Lang*, p. 293.
50   *Sous rature* is translated by Gayatri Chakravorty Spivak as 'under erasure'. It refers to a practice originated by Heidegger and developed further by Jacques Derrida of using a word while also cancelling it out: 'Since the word is inadequate it is crossed out. Since it is necessary it remains legible.' Gayatri Chakravorty Spivak, 'Translator's Preface', in Jacques Derrida,

Of Grammatology (Baltimore, MD: Johns Hopkins University Press, 1976), p. xiv. With Chris Cross this state of being becomes literal as well as figurative.

51   Lotte Eisner, *Fritz Lang*, p. 134.

52   Benjamin, *The Origin of German Tragic Drama*, p. 135.

53   Sigmund Freud, 'Mourning and Melancholia', p. 244.

54   Ibid., p. 245.

55   Ibid., p. 246.

56   Ibid., p. 253.

57   Ibid., p. 256.

58   See, of course, the discussion of Velasques' *Las Meninas* in Michel Foucault, *The Order of Things: An Archeology of the Human Sciences* (New York: Random House, 1970), pp. 3–16.

59   Grafe, p. 16.

60   Edgar A. Poe, 'The Man of the Crowd' in *Poetry and Tales,* pp. 388–96; Guy de Maupassant, 'La Nuit', translated as 'Night: A Nightmare', in *The Complete Short Stories of Guy de Maupassant* (Garden City, NY: Hanover House, 1955), pp. 795– 8. See also my discussion of the x-ray of urban space, in 'From Kaleidoscope to the X-Ray: Urban Spectatorship, Poe, Benjamin and *Traffic in Souls* (1913)', *Wide Angle*, vol. 19, no. 4, pp. 25–63.

Chapter 13: *Secret Beyond the Door*: Broken Frames and Piercing Gazes

1   Walter Benjamin, *The Origin of German Tragic Drama*, p. 178.

2   See, for instance, still the best one volume history of American cinema, Robert Sklar, *Movie-Made America: A Cultural History of American Movies* (New York: Random House, 1976), p. 269.

3   See John Belton, *Wide Screen Movies* (Cambridge, MA: Harvard University Press, 1992) for a good description of changing movie demographics after World War II, as well as Sklar, pp. 279–83.

4   See, for instance, Sklar, p. 280.

5   Patrick McGilligan, *The Nature of the Beast*, p. 348.

6   See, for instance, the account of Abraham Polonski's arrival in Hollywood during the wartime 'Popular Front' period in Larry Ceplair and Steve Englund, *The Inquisition in Hollywood: Politics and the Film Community 1930–60* (Berkeley, CA: University of California Press, 1983), pp. 191–7.

7   Matthew Bernstein, *Walter Wanger*, p. 212.

8   The best account of the Hollywood Ten and related anti-Communist activity in Hollywood remains Ceplair and Englund, *Inquisition in Hollywood*, because of its placement of the events within a broad context. For the Hollywood Ten specifically, see pp. 325–60.

9   Bernstein, *Walter Wanger*, p. 209.

10   For an account of Weimar émigrés and the anti-Communist campaign in postwar USA, see Anthony Heilbut, *Exiled in Paradise*, pp. 364–94.

11   For the most useful summaries of the decree and its effects, see Ernest Borneman, 'United States versus Hollywood: Case Study of an Anti-Trust Suit', and Tino Balio's abridgement of Michel Conant's *Anti-Trust in the Motion Pictures*, 'The Impact of the Paramount Decree', both in Tino Balio (ed.), *The American Film Industry* (Madison: University of Wisconsin Press, 1985).

12   Ceplair and Englund, pp. 244–53; Sklar, pp. 257–62.

13   Bernstein, p. 210.

14   Ibid.

15   Douglas Gomery, *The Hollywood Studio System* (London: BFI, 1986), p. 160.

16   Bernstein, p. 215.

17   McGilligan, pp. 348–50.

18   Ibid., p. 345.

19   See Bernstein's discussion of Diana publicity meetings, p. 201.

20   McGilligan, pp. 346–7.

21 See Douglas Gomery, *Shared Pleasures: A History of Movie Presentation in the United States* (Madison, WI: University of Wisconsin Press, 1992), pp. 180–8; and the dissertation by Barbara Wilinsky, 'Selling Exclusivity:The Emergence of Art Film Theaters in Post World War II American Culture', Northwestern, 1997.

22 Bernstein, p. 209.

23 On Lang and Richards' personal relationship, see McGilligan, pp. 352–4.

24 David Bordwell offers some insightful comments on the way psychoanalysis was integrated into Hollywood practice in David Bordwell, Janet Staiger, and Kristin Thompson, *The Classical Hollywood Cinema: Film Style and Mode of Production to 1960* (New York: Columbia University Press, 1985), pp. 20–1.

25 Miklos Rosza, *Double Life* (New York: Wynwood Press, 1989), pp. 151–2.

26 William Mortiz, 'The Films of Oskar Fischinger', *Film Culture*, nos 58–59–60, 1974, pp. 37–188, unfortunately does not reveal much about Fischinger's dealings with Lang on this film. Bernstein simply indicates Fischinger's tests were 'unsatisfactory' and that Disney shot the sequence, p. 213.

27 Mary Ann Doane, *The Desire to Desire: The Woman's Film of the 1940s* (Bloomington, IN: Indiana University Press, 1987), p. 123; Diane Waldman, '"At last I can tell it to someone!": Female Point of View and Subjectivity in the Gothic Romance Film of the 1940s', *Cinema Journal*, vol. 23, no. 2, Winter 1983, pp. 29–40.

28 Waldman, pp. 123–4, 134. Waldman's definition of gothic romance: 'a young inexperienced woman meets a handsome older man to whom she is alternately attracted and repelled. After a whirlwind courtship … she marries him. After returning to the ancestral mansion of one of the pair, the heroine experiences a series of bizarre and uncanny incidents, open to ambiguous interpretation, revolving around the question of whether or not the gothic male really loves her. She begins to suspect that he may be a murderer', pp. 29–30.

29 McGilligan, p. 122.

30 Hitchcock's relation to Selznick is detailed in Leonard J. Leff, *Hitchcock and Selznick* (New York: Weidenfeld & Nicolson, 1987).

31 François Truffaut, *Hitchcock* (New York: Simon and Schuster, 1967), pp. 61–2.

32 See Fereydoun Hoveyda, 'Les Indes Fabulées', *Cahiers du Cinéma*, no. 99, September 1959, pp. 56–8 for an early example.

33 Bellour, 'Hitchcock the Enunciator', *Camera Obscura*, no. 2, Fall 1977, pp. 72–8; also 'Le Regard de Haghi'.

34 Bogdanovich, p. 73.

35 Laura Mulvey, 'Visual Pleasure and Narrative Cinema', pp. 23–4.

36 This point is also made by Elizabeth Cowie in 'Film Noir and Women', in Joan Copjec (ed.), *Shades of Noir* (London: Verso, 1993), p. 149.

37 Rosza, pp. 150–1.

38 Bernstein, pp. 207, 211.

39 Doane, p. xx.

40 Ibid., pp. 57–8, 60.

41 McGilligan, pp. 349–50.

42 Stephen Jenkins, 'Lang; Fear and Desire', pp. 104–9: Doan, pp. 150–1 basically endorses Jenkins.

43 Leff, p. 42.

44 Kaja Silverman, *The Acoustic Mirror: The Female Voice in Psychoanalysis and Cinema* (Bloomington: Indiana University Press, 1988), p. 53.

45 Sarah Kozloff, *Invisible Storytellers: Voice-over Narration in American Fiction Films* (Berkeley: University of California Press, 1988), pp. 5–6.

46 Michel Chion, *The Voice in Cinema*, p. 51.

47 Ibid.

48 See Kozloff, p. 63.

49 Bogdanovich, p. 73. Lang seems to indicate this was only an unrealised idea, but Bernstein, p. 212, and McGilligan, p. 363, both indicate this voice-over was originally recorded by another actress whom Bernstein names as Colleen Collins, p. 215.

50 Bernstein, pp. 212, 214.

51 Bernstein, pp. 207, 215.
52 Gerard Legrand 'Le génie des lieux', *Positif*, no. 94, April 1968, p. 63.
53 Jenkins, p. 104.
54 Ibid.
55 Doane, p. 138.
56 Legrand also compares these two scenes, p. 62. Cowie notes the similarity as well, but suggests
     a connection to Bartók's opera, *Bluebeard's Castle*, may be more apropos (p. 154).
57 *The Night Watches of Bonaventura*, p. 237.
58 Cowie also argues for the importance of the Bluebeard story for interpreting *Secret Beyond the
     Door*, pp. 150, 156–7.
59 Rosza, p. 151.
60 Bernstein, p. 214.
61 David Bordwell, *Narration in the Fiction Film*, p. 83.
62 Jenkins, p.106.
63 Ibid., p. 107.
64 Doane, p. 151.
65 Cowie, however, offers a defence from a feminist/psychoanalytical point of view of Celia's
     decision to return and the transformation it indicates which I find quite tenable, pp. 157–8.
66 Waldman, p. 36.
67 Ibid.
68 Bogdanovich, p. 74.
69 We might recall that mama's boy Freder was also locked in a room in Rotwang's house, which
     reportedly Lang had Gustav Fröhlich beat until his hands were bloody (McGilligan, p. 116) as
     he grasps Maria's scarf – but here I believe we are entering into Lang's symptomology, rather
     than figures in the text.
70 Walter Benjamin, 'The Work of Art in the Age of Mechanical Reproduction', in *Illuminations*,
     p. 236.
71 Bogdanovich, p. 73.
72 It is the one element of the film which he claims was good in the interview in Charles Higham
     and Joel Greenberg (eds), *The Celluloid Muse*, p. 118.
73 McGilligan summarises the serial, p. 356.
74 McGilligan, p. 7.
75 These are phrases Mark uses in the film during the tour of his rooms.
76 Silverman, p. 51.
77 As Legrand does in his generally insightful review of the film, p. 62.
78 Interestingly, Legrand mistakenly attributes the glasses to the 'sub-deb', ibid.
79 Frieda Grafe in [Grafe, Enno Patalas, Hans Prinzler], *Fritz Lang*, p. 46.

Chapter 14: Coda: *House by the River*

1   Ernst Junger, *A Dangerous Encounter,* trans. Hilary Barr (New York: Marsilio Publishers,
     1992), p. 102.
2   Patrick McGilligan, *The Nature of the Beast*, p. 369.
3   Douglas Gomery, *The Hollywood Studio System*, pp. 184–7.
4   'Fritz Lang a Venise (Entretien)', *Positif*, no. 94, April 1968, p. 12.
5   Janet Bergstrom, 'The Mystery of *The Blue Gardenia*', in Joan Copjec (ed.) *Shades of Noir*,
     pp. 97–101.
6   Walter Benjamin, *One-Way Street*, in *Selected Writings*, p. 447.
7   'Fritz Lang a Venise (Entretien)', p. 12.
8   McGilligan, pp. 369–70.
9   See his autobiography *Bad Boy of Music* (Garden City, NY: Doubleday, 1945), written a few
     years before *House by the River*.
10 Georges Sturm's essay on this film perceptively picks out most of these associations woven
     through the opening scene. See 'La nymph du scarabée', in Bernard Eisenschitz and Paolo
     Bertetto (eds), *Fritz Lang*, pp. 323–3.

11 Julia Kristeva, *Powers of Horror: An Essay on Abjection*, trans. Leon S. Roudiez (New York: Columbia University Press, 1982), pp. 1–17.
12 Frieda Grafe, in [Grafe, Enno Patalas, Hans Prinzler], *Fritz Lang*, p. 48.
13 Sturm, p. 326.
14 Ibid. Lotte Eisner stresses the contrast, 'the man who cannot hurt an insect will five minutes later kill a human being', *Fritz Lang*, p. 287.
15 Sturm reads this the same way, albeit a bit more literally, p. 330.
16 Sturm makes this point, p. 329.
17 Sigmund Freud, 'The "Uncanny"', *Standard Edition*, vol. XVII, p. 237.
18 Rainer Maria Rilke, *The Notebooks of Malte Laurids Brigge*, p. 52.
19 Sturm, p. 332.
20 Patalas, in [Grafe, Patalas and Prinzler], pp.132–3.

Chapter 15: *The Blue Gardenia*

1 Theodor Adorno, 'The Schema of Mass Culture', p. 70.
2 Robert Parrish, *Growing up in Hollywood* (New York: Harcourt Brace and Jovanovich, 1976), p. 208. Patrick McGilligan's quote of Parrish's account made me aware of it, *The Nature of the Beast*, p. 376 Curiously, Larry Ceplair and Steven Englund, *Inquisition in Hollywood*, p. 369, attribute this statement to Rouben Mamoulian, although their source seems to be Parrish, so this is most likely a simple error.
3 Ceplair and Englund, pp. 364–5.
4 See John Cogley, 'The Mass Hearings', an excerpt from his *Report of Blacklisting, I The Movies* in Tino Balio (ed.), *The American Film Industry*, pp. 410–31.
5 Ceplair and Englund, pp. 386–8.
6 Peter Bogdanovich, *Fritz Lang in America*, pp. 83–4.
7 McGilligan, pp. 375, 379; Ceplair and Englund, pp. 389–93.
8 Ceplair and Englund, p. 392.
9 Bogdanovich, pp. 83–4; Charles Higham and Joel Greenberg (eds), *The Celluloid Muse*, pp. 120–1.
10 Jonathan Rosenbaum in conversation.
11 Ibid., p. 77.
12 McGilligan, p. 389.
13 Bernard Eisenschitz, *Nicholas Ray: An American Journey* (London: Faber and Faber, 1993), p. 174.
14 McGilligan, p. 389.
15 Frieda Grafe, in [Frieda Grafe, Enno Patalas, Hans Prinzler], *Fritz Lang*, p. 58.
16 Eleanor Stone, the woman reporter in *Western Union* is an exception, but I don't think an important one.
17 *The Marvelettes' Greatest Hits,* William Stevenson, Marvin Gaye, G. Gordey, 'Beechwood 4-5789' (Detroit, IL: Motown Records, 1966), side 2, track 6.
18 Higham and Greenberg (eds), p. 121.
19 Lang's dismissal of the film can be found in Bogdanovich, p. 84. The reinterpretation can be found in E. Ann Kaplan, 'The Place of Women in *The Blue Gardenia*', in E. Ann Kaplan (ed.), *Women in Film Noir* (London: BFI, 1972); Janet Bergstrom, 'The Mystery of *The Blue Gardenia*'; and Douglas Pye, 'Seeing by Glimpses: Fritz Lang's *The Blue Gardenia*', *CineAction!*, Summer 1988, as well as Stephen Jenkins' essay on 'Lang: Fear and Desire'.
20 Lotte Eisner, *Fritz Lang*, p. 321. Eisner's account of the Blacklist is wildly inaccurate, making *Senator* Joseph McCarthy a member of the *House* Committee on Un-American Affairs(!), and getting her dates all wrong.
21 Bergstrom, p. 100.
22 Carolyn Marvin, *When Old Technologies Were New: Thinking About Electric Communication in the Late Nineteenth Century* (Oxford: Oxford University Press, 1988) discusses the gender dynamics of the early telephone operators, pp. 84–5.
23 Andreas Huyssens, 'The Vamp and the Machine'.

24 A. W. Merrill, et al., *Book Two: History and Identification of Old Telephones,* quoted in Avital Ronell, *The Telephone Book: Technology, Schizophrenia, Electric Speech* (Lincoln: University of Nebraska, 1989), p. 301.

25 Bergstrom, pp. 105–6.

26 Kaplan, pp. 83–9.

27 Elizabeth Cowie, 'Film Noir and Women', pp. 121–65.

28 Kaplan, p. 85.

29 Pye, 'Trusting the Tale: Lang and Suppressive Narrative', in Micheal Koller and Clare Stewart (eds), *Fritz Lang: Traps for the Mind and Eye* (Melbourne: Melbourne Cinematheque, 1998), p. 28, also makes the point of Crystal's *mise-en-scène.*

30 Ibid.

31 This was the original subtitle for Benjamin's Arcades Project. See Susan Buck-Morss, *The Dialectics of Seeing,* pp. 33–4.

32 Bergstrom, p. 108.

33 Ibid.

Chapter 16: *The Big Heat*

1 Avital Ronell, *The Telephone Book,* p. 20.

2 Colin McArthur, *The Big Heat* (London: BFI Film Classics, 1992), pp. 50–3.

3 Janet Bergstrom, 'The Mystery of *The Blue Gardenia*', p. 118 n. 26. The original article was written by Friedrich Porges 'Eine Kamera, die alles sieht: Fritz Lang erfand das "Opernglas" System' from the *Berliner Morgenpost,* 27 February 1953.

4 Gerard Leblanc and Brigitte Devismes, *Le Double scénario chez Fritz Lang,* pp. 204–5.

5 Ibid., p. 23.

6 Ibid.

7 Colin McArthur also points out the way the Bannion household operates in opposition to both the previously seen homes and The Retreat, p. 58.

8 Bertolt Brecht, 'On Gestic Music', in *Brecht on Theatre* (ed.) John Willett, pp. 104–5.

9 Leblanc and Devismes, p. 205.

10 McArthur, p. 43.

11 Ibid., p. 46.

12 Leblanc and Devismes, p. 19.

13 McArthur, pp. 24–5.

14 Peter Baxter, *Just Watch: Sternberg, Paramount and America* (London: BFI, 1993), p. 7.

15 'Inter-Office Communication April 10, 1953, to Mr. Fritz Lang on the part of Robert Arthur.' This memo is quoted in Leblanc and Devismes, p. 19, in French and I have translated it back into English, so the phrasing may not be exact.

16 Leblanc and Devismes, pp. 77–89.

17 Ibid., p. 87.

18 Ibid., p. 88.

19 McArthur, pp. 16–17.

20 Leblanc and Devismes, '… Wilks is compromised and has "dirty hands" ', p. 86.

21 Peter Brooks, *The Melodramatic Imagination* (New Haven, CT: Yale University Press, 1976), pp. 125, 154.

22 William McGivern, *The Big Heat* (London: Simon and Schuster, 1988), p. 73. Bannion is quoting St. John of the Cross.

23 Peter Bogdanovich, *Fritz Lang in America,* p. 10.

24 Ibid., p. 85.

25 Frieda Grafe, in [Grafe, Enno Patalas, Hans Prinzler], *Fritz Lang,* p. 50.

26 Leblanc and Devismes, p. 38.

27 Tom Flinn in his article 'The Big Heat and The Big Combo: Rogue Cops and Mink-Coated Girls' compares these two films and discusses the figure of the 'rogue cop', *Velvet Light Trap,* no. 11, 1974, pp. 23–38.

28 McArthur, pp. 18–22, 66–76.

29 McGivern, p. 183.
30 McArthur, p. 20.
31 Leblanc and Devismes, p. 146–7.
32 McArthur also makes this point, although he does not draw my conclusion, p. 20
33 McGivern, p. 160.
34 Leblanc and Devismes, pp. 35.
35 Ibid., p. 150.
36 Siegfried Kracauer, *Le Roman Policier* (Paris: Payot, 1972).
37 Tzvetan Todorov, 'Detective Fiction', in *The Poetics of Prose*, trans. Richard Howard (Ithaca, NY: Cornell University Press, 1977), pp. 47–8.
38 Leblanc and Devismes, p. 39.
39 McArthur, p. 74.
40 McGivern, p. 167.
41 McArthur, pp. 72–3.
42 Leblanc and Devismes, p. 151.
43 Ibid., p. 23.
44 McArthur, p. 74.

Chapter 17: *While the City Sleeps/Beyond a Reasonable Doubt*

 1 Friedrich Nietzsche, *Thus Spoke Zarathustra*, p. 219.
 2 Gerard Legrand, 'L'effacement des traces', *Positif*, no. 248, November 1981, p. 65.
 3 Patrick McGilligan, *The Nature of the Beast*, p. 418.
 4 Ibid.
 5 James L. Limbacher, *Four Aspects of Film* (New York: Brussel and Brussel, 1968), p. 112.
 6 Bertolt Brecht, *Journals 1934–1955*, p. 225.
 7 Jean Domarchi, 'Lang le constructor', *Cahiers du Cinéma*, no. 63, October 1956, pp. 40–1.
 8 Jacques Rivette, 'The Hand', p. 140. McGilligan attributes this quote to Stephen Jenkins.
 9 Jonathan Rosenbaum, in personal conversation, September 1999.
10 Legrand, p. 65.
11 Peter Bogdanovich, *Fritz Lang in America*, p. 102.
12 E. Ann Kaplan, 'Patterns of Violence toward Woman in Fritz Lang's *While the City Sleeps*', *Wide Angle*, vol. 3 no. 4, 1980, p. 57.
13 Bogdanovich, *Fritz Lang in America*, p. 106.
14 Stephen Jenkins, 'Lang: Fear and Desire', p. 55, for illustrations, pp. 58–9.
15 For one contemporary account of the concerns over comic books see Robert Warshow 'Paul, the Horror Comics and Dr. Wertham' (1954), in *The Immediate Experience* (New York: Atheneum, 1976), pp. 83–104.
16 Legrand, p. 65.
17 Edgar A. Poe, 'The Purloined Letter', in *Poe: Poetry and Tales* (New York: Library of America, 1984), p. 696.
18 Walter Benjamin, *Charles Baudelaire*, p. 48.
19 Philippe Arnaud in his essay 'Beyond a Reasonable Story' in Bernard Eisenschitz and Paolo Bertetto (eds), *Fritz Lang*, also compares the film to Poe's story, see p. 423.
20 Serge Daney, quoted in Georges Sturm, *Fritz Lang, Films/Textes/References*, p. 157, from *Cine-journal 1981–86* (Paris: Cahiers du Cinéma, 1986), pp. 15–18.
21 Sturm, p. 157.
22 Raymond Bellour, 'Double Vu', in Eisenschitz and Bertetto (eds), p. 440.
23 See especially the note he quotes without analysing in detail 'suspicion on Spencer' about a scene not shot, but clearly revealing Lang's intention – Arnaud, p. 426.
24 Lang discusses this concern in Bogdanovich, p. 109, and in letters to Lotte Eisner reprinted in Eisner, *Fritz Lang*, p. 359.
25 Bazin's review of *Beyond a Reasonable Doubt*, 'Un incroyable film' originally appearing in *Radio-Cinéma-Télévison*, no. 405, 20 October 1957, p. 46, is summarised in E. Ann Kaplan, *Fritz Lang: A Guide*, pp. 208–9. Lang's comments on the script are in Charles Higham and Joe Greenberg (eds), *The Celluloid Muse*, p. 123.

Chapter 18: The Circle Closes on the Last Mabuse

1 Sigmund Freud, 'The "Uncanny" ', pp. 236–8.

2 Peter Bogdanovich, *Fritz Lang in America*, p. 111.

3 Ibid.

4 'Je termine mon film, il faut toujours terminer qu'est qu'on a commencé', *L'Avant Scène*, nos 412–13, May– June 1992, p. 86.

5 As Jonathan Rosenbaum has pointed out to me in conversation, it was probably the Indian films with their mythological material, that made Godard envision Lang as the director of *The Odyssey* in *Contempt*.

6 Lotte Eisner, *Fritz Lang*, p. 390.

7 Bogdanovich, pp. 115–16.

8 Mark Shivas, 'Interview with Fritz Lang', in Andrew Sarris (ed.), *Interviews with Film Directors*, p. 261.

9 Bogdanovich, p. 116.

10 Jonathan Crary, 'Dr. Mabuse and Mr. Edison', p. 271.

11 Ibid., p. 273.

12 Ibid.

13 Nicole Brenez, 'Symptom, exhibition, angoisse', p. 11.

14 The name of this character is given in filmographies, variously as Kraus (Bogdanovich, Eisner, Kaplan) Krass (Sturm, Ott), and Kras (Jenkins, McGilligan). The writing on this roster actually looks to me more like 'Kros', but since no-one offers that alternative I will stick with Kras, in spite of my general faith in Sturm's credits.

15 Eisner (pp. 390–1) offers a comparison between the two scenes.

16 In the English-dubbed version of this film, the only one I had access to, this character, played by Peter Van Eyck, is first referred to as 'Taylor', but then within a few scenes his name is given as Travers. All filmographies refer to him as Travers, except Sturm who calls him by both names, indicating Travers is an alias, something not made clear in the English-dubbed version. The reporters identify him as Travers, the millionaire, but if it is an alias, why do his business associates also call him Taylor, then stop doing so later on? Presumably sloppiness in dubbing may explain this.

17 *The Night Watches of Bonaventura*, pp. 246–7.

18 Jonathan Rosenbaum, *Moving Places: A Life at the Movies* (Berkeley: University of California Press, 1995), p. 261.

19 Crary, pp. 273–4.

20 Walter Benjamin, 'Experience and Poverty', in *Selected Writings: Volume 2 1927–1934*, p. 735.

21 Lang's treatment is included in Fritz Lang, *Le montagne des superstitions et autres histoires*, pp. 13–23, with additional information on pp. 211–13.

22 The licence plate of Mabuse's car during the final chase scene, L B S 21, may well be a reference to this connection as one of Lang's private hieroglyphs or gags.

23 Siegfried Kracauer, 'The Hotel Lobby', pp. 173–85.

24 Frieda Grafe in [Grafe, Enno Patalas, Hans Prinzler] *Fritz Lang*, p. 48.

25 Shivas, p. 261.

26 Michel Butor, *Histoire Extraordinaire*, trans. Richard Howard (London: Jonathan Cape, 1969), p. 170.

27 David Bordwell, Janet Staiger and Kristin Thompson, *The Classical Hollywood Cinema*, p. xx.

28 Eric Hobsbawm, *The Age of Extremes : A History of the World, 1914–1991* (New York: Pantheon, 1995).

29 Eisner, p. 416.

30 Noel Burch, *Life to Those Shadows*, pp. 26–7.

BIBLIOGRAPHY

Abelson, Elaine S., *When Ladies Go A-Thieving: Middle-Class Shoplifters in the Victorian Department Store* (Oxford: Oxford University Press, 1989).

Adams, Henry, *The Education of Henry Adams* (Boston: Houghton Mifflin, 1918).

Adorno, Theodor, *The Culture Industry: Selected Essays on Mass Culture*, ed J. M. Bernstein (London: Routledge, 1991). 'The Schema of Mass Culture', trans. Nicholas Walker.

Alain, Marcel, and Pierre Souvestre, *Fantomas* (1911), n.tr. (New York: William Morrow, 1986).

Altman, Rick, *The American Film Musical* (Bloomington: Indiana University Press, 1989).

Anon., *Die Nachtwachen des Bonaventura/The Night Watches of Bonaventura* (1804/5), ed. and trans. Gerard Gillespie (Austin: University of Texas Press, 1971).

Antheil, George, *Bad Boy of Music* (Garden City, NY: Doubleday, 1945).

Balio, Tino (ed.), *The American Film Industry* (Madison: University of Wisconsin Press, 1985). Tino Balio, 'The Impact of the Paramount Decree'; Ernest Borneman, 'United States versus Hollywood: Case Study of an Anti-Trust Suit'. John Cogley, 'The Mass Hearings'.

Baudelaire, Charles, *Les Fleurs du Mal* (1857), trans. Richard Howard (Boston, MA: David R. Godine, 1982).

Barthes, Roland, *Critical Essays*, trans. Richard Howard (Evanston, IL: Northwestern University Press, 1972). 'Mother Courage Blind' (1960).

———, *The Rustle of Language*, trans. Richard Howard (Berkeley: University of California Press, 1989). 'The Death of the Author' (1968).

Baxter, Peter, *Just Watch: Sternberg, Paramount and America* (London: BFI, 1993).

Bazin, André, 'Un incroyable film', *Radio-cinéma-télévision*, no. 405, October 1957.

———, *What is Cinema? Vol. I*, trans. Hugh Grey (Berkeley: University of California Press, 1967). 'The Evolution of the Language of Cinema'.

Belloi, Louis, 'Le regard et ses voltes: Aspects du cinéma des premiers temps', Université de Liége, 1997.

Bellour, Raymond, 'Hitchcock the Enunciator', *Camera Obscura*, no. 2, Fall 1977.

———, 'Le Regard de Haghi', *iris*, no. 7, second semester 1986.

———, 'Ideal Hadaly (on Villiers' *The Future Eve*)', trans. Stanley E. Grey, *Camera Obscura*, no. 15, Fall 1986.

———, 'La Machine-Cinéma', *Cinema et litérature 8: Les Temps des Machines*, Valenca, 1990.

Belton, John, *Widescreen Movies* (Cambridge, MA: Harvard University Press, 1992).

Benjamin, Walter, *Illuminations*, ed. Hannah Arendt, trans. Harry Zohn (New York: Harcourt, Brace and World, 1968). 'The Work of Art in the Age of Mechanical Reproduction'.

———, *The Origin of German Tragic Drama* (1963 [1925]), trans. John Osborne (London: NLB, 1977).

———, *Understanding Brecht* (1966), trans. Anna Bostock (London: NLB, 1977).

————, *Charles Baudelaire: A Lyric Poet in the Era of High Capitalism* (1969), trans. Harry Zohn (London: Verso, 1983).

————, *Selected Writings: Vol. I 1913–1926*, eds Marcus Bullock and Michael W. Jennings (Cambridge, MA: Harvard University Press, 1996). *One-Way Street* (1928), trans. Edward Jephcott and Kingsley Shorter; '*Trauerspiel* and Tragedy' (1916) trans. John Osborne.

————, *Selected Writings: Vol. II 1927–1934*, eds Michael W. Jennings, Howard Eilanf and Gary Smith, trans. Rodney Livingstone et al. (Cambridge, MA: Harvard University Press, 1999). 'Experience and Poverty' (1933).

Benson, Edward, 'Decor and Decorum, from *La Chienne* to *Scarlet Street*: Franco-U.S. Trade in Film During the Thirties', *Film and History*, vol. 12 no. 3, September 1982.

Bergstrom, Janet, 'Alternation, Segmentation, Hypnosis: Interview with Raymond Bellour', *Camera Obscura*, nos 3–4, Summer 1979.

Bernstein, Matthew, *Walter Wanger: Hollywood Independent* (Berkeley: University of California Press, 1994).

————, 'A Tale of Three Cities: The Banning of *Scarlet Street*', *Cinema Journal*, vol. 35 no. 1, Fall 1995.

Beyfuss, E., and A. Kossowsky (eds), *Das Kulturfilmbuch* (Berlin: Carl P. Chryselius Ed., 1924). Includes Lang's 'Kitsch, Sensation – Kultur und Film'.

Blanchot, Maurice, *The Space of Literature* (1955), trans. Ann Smock (Lincoln: University of Nebraska Press, 1981). 'Hölderlin's Itinerary'.

Boehme, Jacob, *The Signature of All Things* (Cambridge: James Clarke, 1969).

Booth, Wayne, *The Rhetoric of Fiction* (Chicago, IL: University of Chicago Press, 1961).

Bogdanovich, Peter, *Fritz Lang in America* (London: Studio Vista, 1967).

Bordwell, David, *Narration in the Fiction Film* (Madison: University of Wisconsin Press, 1985).

————, *Making Meaning: Inference and Rhetoric in the Interpretation of Cinema* (Cambridge, MA: Harvard University Press, 1989).

————, Janet Staiger, and Kristin Thompson, *The Classical Hollywood Cinema: Film Style and Mode of Production to 1960* (New York: Columbia University Press, 1985).

Borges, Jorge Luis, *The Aleph and Other Stories 1933—1969*, trans. Norman Thomas Di Giovanni (New York: E.P. Dutton, 1978). 'Borges and Myself'.

————, *Labyrinths: Selected Stories and Other Writings*, ed. and trans. Donald A. Yates and James E. Irby (New York: New Directions, 1964). 'Death and the Compass'.

Brandlmeier, Thomas, 'Lang-Renoir, Renoir-Lang', *epd film*, October 1984.

Brecht, Bertolt, *Poems 1913–1956* (New York: Methuen, 1976). 'Deliver the Goods', trans. Humphrey Milnes; 'Hollywood' (1942), trans. Michael Hamburger; 'On Thinking about Hell' (1941), trans. Nicholas Jacobs; 'Ten Poems from a Reader for Those who Live in Cities' (1926–7), trans. Frank Jellinek; 'Utterances of a Martyr' (1918), trans. John Willet.

————, *Journals 1934–55*, ed. John Willet, trans. Hugh Rorrison (New York: Routledge, 1996).

————, *Brecht on Theatre*, ed. John Willet, trans. Hugh Rorrison (New York: Hill and Wang, 1964). 'The Modern Theatre is Epic Theatre' (1930); 'On Gestic Music' (1957); 'A Short Organum for the Theatre' (1949).

Brenez, Nicole, 'Symptome, exhibition, angoisse: représentation de la terreur dans l'oeuvre allemande de Fritz Lang', *Cinématheque*, no. 3, Spring/Summer 1993.

Bresson, Robert, *Notes on Cinematography* (1975), trans. Jonathan Griffin (New York: Urizen, 1977).

Brewster, Ben, 'Brecht and the Film Industry', *Screen*, vol. 16 no. 4, Winter 1975/76.

Brooks, Peter, *The Melodramatic Imagination* (New Haven, CT: Yale University Press, 1976).

Buber, Martin, *I and Thou* (1933), trans. Ronald Gregor Smith (New York: Charles Scribner's Sons, 1958).

Buck-Morss, Susan, *The Dialectics of Seeing: Walter Benjamin and the Arcades Project* (Cambridge, MA: MIT Press, 1989).

Burch, Noel, *In and Out of Synch: The Awakening of a Cine-Dreamer*, trans. Ben Brewster (Aldershot: Scolar Press, 1991). Includes 'Notes on Fritz Lang's first *Mabuse*'; 'Fritz Lang: German Period': the original French version of this text, published in a special number of *Revue d'Esthétique* ('Cinéma, théorie, lecture', 1973), contains diagrams not included in the translated version.

————, *Life to Those Shadows*, ed. and trans. Ben Brewster (Berkeley: University of California Press, 1990).

Butor, Michel, *Histoire Extraordinaire* (1961), trans. Richard Howard (London: Jonathan Cape, 1969).

Cahiers du Cinéma: 1950s Neo-Realism, Hollywood, New Wave, ed. Jim Hillier (Cambridge, MA: Harvard University Press, 1985). Jacques Rivette, 'The Hand' (1957), trans. Tom Milne.

Ceplair, Larry, and Steve Englund, *The Inquisition in Hollywood: Politics and the Film Community 1930–60* (Berkeley: University of California Press).

Chesterton, G. K., *The Defendant* (London: R.B. Johnson, 1901). 'A Defense of Detective Stories'.

Chion, Michel, *The Voice in Cinema* (1982), trans. Claudia Gorbman (New York: Columbia University Press, 1999).

Conley, Tom, *Film Hieroglyphics: Ruptures in Classical Cinema* (Minneapolis: University of Minnesota Press, 1991).

Copjec, Joan, (ed.), *Shades of Noir* (London: Verso, 1993). Janet Bergstrom, 'The Mystery of *Blue Gardenia*'; Elizabeth Cowie, 'Film Noir and Women'.

Crary, Jonathan, 'Dr. Mabuse and Mr. Edison', in Russell Ferguson (ed.), *Art and Film Since 1945: Hall of Mirrors* (Los Angeles, CA: Museum of Contemporary Art, 1996).

Curtis, Scott, 'The Taste of a Nation: Training the Senses and Sensibility of Cinema Audiences in Imperial Germany', *Film History*, vol. 6 no. 4, Winter 1994.

Dadoun, Roger, 'Le pouvoir et "sa" folie', *Positif*, no. 188, December 1976, pp. 13–20

————, '*Metropolis: Mother-City – Mittler – Hitler*', trans. Arthur Goldhammer, *Camera Obscura*, no. 15, Fall 1986.

Daumal, René, 'Avant la présentation de "Liliom"' (1934)', *Positif*, no. 188, December 1976.

Deleuze, Gilles and Félix Guattari, *Anti-Oedipus: Capitalism and Schizophrenia* (1972), trans. Robert Hurley et al. (Minneapolis: University of Minnesota Press, 1983).

Derrida, Jacques, *Writing and Difference* (1967), trans. Alan Bass (Chicago, IL: University of Chicago Press, 1978). 'Freud and the Scene of Writing'.

Descartes, Réné, *Meditationes de Prima Philosophia/Méditations metaphysiques* (1641; Paris: Librairie Philosophique J. Vrin, 1960), *Meditations on First Philosophy*, in *The Philosophical Writings of Descartes*, vol. I, trans. John Cottingham, Robert Stoothoff and Dugald Murdoch (Cambridge: Cambridge University Press, 1985).

Doane, Mary Ann, *The Desire to Desire: The Woman's Film of the 1940s*
        (Bloomington: Indiana University Press, 1987).

Domarchi, 'Lang le constructor', *Cahiers du Cinéma*, no. 63, October 1956.

Dostoevsky, Fyodor, *The Short Novels of Dostoevsky*(New York: Dial Press, 1945).
        The Gambler (1866).

Douchet, Jean, 'Dix-sept plans', in Raymond Bellour (ed.), *Le cinéma americain:
        Analyses de films*, vol. I (Paris: Flammarion, 1980).

Doyle, Sir Arthur Conan, *The Complete Sherlock Holmes* (New York: Doubleday,
        1930). 'The Final Problem'.

Dubois, Philippe, 'L'écriture figurale dans le cinéma muet des années 20', in
        Francesco Pitassio and Leonardo Quaresima (eds), *Scrittura e ImmagineL La
        didascalia del cinema muto* (Udine: Forum, 1998).

Eibel, Alfred (ed.), *Fritz Lang Trois Lumières* (Paris: Flammarion, 1988). Reprints
        Thea von Harbou's 'Le film des Die Nibelungen et sa genèse' (1924).

Eisenschitz, Bernard et al., *M le maudit un film de Fritz Lang* (Paris: Le
        Cinématheque Française/Editions Plume, 1990). Eisenschitz, 'Le Production,
        le tournage'; Vincente Sanchez-Biosca, 'Fury ou comment est ne John Doe'.

Eisenschitz, Bernard, *Manhunt de Fritz Lang* (Paris: Editions Yellow Now, 1992).

———, *Nicholas Ray: An American Journey* (London: Faber and Faber, 1993).

———, and Paolo Bertetto (eds), *Fritz Lang: La mise en scène* (Paris:
        Cinémathèque Française, n.d. [1993]). Philippe Arnaud, 'Beyond a
        Reasonable Story'; Raymond Bellour, 'Double vu'; Vincente J. Benet
        Ferrando, 'Symbole, metaphore et stabilité dans *Der müde Tod*'; Jean
        Douchet, 'La tragédie du héros Langien'. Helmut Farber, 'Trois Photos de
        Tournage de *M*'; Lang, '*You and Me* Story Outline'; Georges Sturm, 'La
        nymph du scarabée'.

Eisner, Lotte, *Fritz Lang*, trans. Gertrud Mander (New York: Oxford University
        Press, 1977).

Elsaesser, Thomas, 'Traps for the Mind and Eye', *Sight and Sound*, vol. 7 no. 8 (NS),
        August 1997.

Emerson, Ralph Waldo, *Essays* (New York: Thomas Y. Cromwell, 1961).
        'Compensation' (1841).

Farber, Manny, *Negative Space: Manny Farber on the Movies* (New York: Praeger
        Publishers, 1971). 'White Elephant Art vs Termite Art' (1962).

Feldman, Gerald D., *The Great Disorder: Politics, Economics and Society in the
        German Inflation 1914–1924* (Oxford: Oxford University Press, 1997).

Fisher, Peter S., *Fantasy and Politics: Visions of the Future in the Weimar Republic*
        (Madison: University of Wisconsin Press, 1991).

Fletcher, Angus, *Allegory: The Theory of a Symbolic Mode* (Ithaca, NY: Cornell
        University Press, 1964).

Flinn, Tom, '*The Big Heat* and *The Big Combo*: Rogue Cops and Mink-Coated Girls',
        Velvet Light Trap, no. 11, 1974.

Foucault, Michel, *The Order of Things: An Archaeology of the Human Sciences*
        (1966), n.tr. (New York: Random House, 1970).

———, *Language, Counter-Memory, Practice: Selected Essays and Interviews*, ed.
        Donald F. Bouchard, trans. Donald Bouchard and Sherry Simon (Ithaca, NY:
        Cornell University Press, 1977). 'What is an Author'.

Freud, Sigmund, *The Complete Psychological Works of Sigmund Freud*, ed. and trans.
        James Strachey, 24 vols (London: The Hogarth Press, 1953–74). Vol. V: *The
        Interpretation of Dreams* (1900). Vol. XIV: 'Mourning and Melancholia'

(1917), 'On Transience' (1916), 'Thoughts for the Times on War and Death'
    (1915). Vol. XVII: *Beyond the Pleasure Principle* (1920), 'From the History of
    an Infantile Neurosis' (1918), 'The "Uncanny"' (1919). Vol. XIX: 'A Note
    upon the "Mystic Writing-Pad"' (1925). Vol. XXI: *Civilization and its
    Discontents* (1930).

Fuller, Katherine Helgenson, 'You Can Have the Strand in Your Own Town', *Film
    History*, vol. 6 no. 2, Summer 1994.

Gadamer, Hans-Georg, *Truth and Method* (1960), n.tr. (New York: Seabury Press,
    1975).

Gauld, Alan, *A History of Hypnosis* (Cambridge: Cambridge University Press,
    1992).

Gehler, Fred, and Ulrich Kasten (eds), *Fritz Lang Die Stimme von Metropolis*
    (Berlin: Henschel Verlag, 1990). Reprints Lang's articles 'Worauf es heim Die
    Nibelungen-Film ankam Fritz Lang' (1924), and 'Stiwille im Film von Fritz
    Lang' (1924).

Genette, Gerard, *Paratexts: Thresholds of Interpretation*, trans. Jane E. Lewin
    (Cambridge: Cambridge University Press, 1997).

Giddens, Anthony, *The Consequences of Modernity* (Stanford, CA: Stanford
    University Press, 1990).

Ginsburg, Carlo, *Clues, Myths and the Historical Method* (1986), trans John and
    Anne Tredeschi (Baltimore, MD: Johns Hopkins University Press, 1989).
    'Clues: Roots of an Evidential Paradigm'.

Godard, Jean-Luc, *Godard on Godard* (1968), ed. and trans. Tom Milne (New York:
    Viking Press, 1972).

Goethe, Johann Wolfgang von, *Faust Part One and Two* (1808/32), trans. Charles E.
    Passage (Indianapolis, IN: Bobbs Merrill, 1965).

Gomery, Douglas, *The Hollywood Studio System* (London: BFI, 1986).

——, *Shared Pleasures: A History of Movie Presentation in the United States*
    (Madison: University of Wisconsin Press, 1992).

Gunning, Tom, 'Tracing the Individual Body: AKA Photography, Detectives, Early
    Cinema and the Body of Modernity', in Vanessa R. Schwartz and Leo
    Charney (eds), *Cinema and the Invention of Modern Life* (Berkeley:
    University of California Press, 1995).

——, 'From Kaleidoscope to the X-Ray: Urban Spectatorship, Poe, Benjamin
    and *Traffic in Souls* (1913)', *Wide Angle*, vol. 19 no. 4, October 1997.

Hake, Sabine, 'Architectural Hi/stories: Fritz Lang and *The Nibelungs*', *Wide Angle*,
    vol. 12 no. 3, July 1990.

——, *The Cinema's Third Machine: Writing on Film In Germany 1907–1933*
    (Lincoln: University of Nebraska Press, 1992).

Hall, Ben N., *The Best Remaining Seats: The Story of the Golden Age of the Movie
    Palace* (New York: Bramhall House, 1961).

Hamburger, Michael, *Reason and Energy: Studies in German Literature* (London:
    Weidenfeld and Nicholson, 1970).

Hansen, Miriam, *Babel and Babylon: Spectatorship in American Silent Film*
    (Cambridge, MA: Harvard University Press, 1991).

Harbou, Thea von, *Metropolis* (1927), n.tr. (New York: Ace Books, 1963).

Heath, Stephen, 'Narrative Space', *Screen*, vol. 17 no. 3, Autumn 1976.

Heidegger, Martin, *The Question Concerning Technology and Other Essays*, trans.
    William Lovitt (New York: Harper and Row, 1977). 'The Age of the World
    Picture' (1952).

Heilbut, Anthony, *Exiled in Paradise: German Refugee Artists and Intellectuals in America from the 1930's to the Present* (Berkeley: University of California Press, 1997).

Herf, Jeffrey, *Reactionary Modernism: Technology, Culture and Politics in Weimar and the Third Reich* (Cambridge: Cambridge University Press, 1984).

Higham, Charles, and Joel Greenberg, *The Celluloid Muse: Hollywood Directors Speak* (Chicago, IL: Henry Regnery, 1969).

Hobsbawm, Eric, *The Age of Extremes: A History of the World, 1914–1991* (New York: Pantheon, 1995).

Hofstadter, Richard, *The Paranoid Style in American Politics and Other Essays* (New York: Random House, 1967).

Hölderlin, Friedrich, *Hyperion or the Hermit in Greece* (1797–9), trans. Willard Trask (New York: Frederick Ungar Publishing, 1965).

————, *Essays and Letters on Theory*, ed. and trans. Thomas Pfau (Albany, NY: SUNY Press, 1988). 'Remarks on *Oedipus*'.

Horapollo, *The Hieroglyphics of Horapollo*, trans. George Boas (Princeton, NJ: Princeton University Press, 1978), Bollingen Series, vol. XXIII.

Horkheimer, Max, and Theodor W. Adorno, *Dialectic of Enlightenment* (1944), trans. John Cumming (New York: The Seabury Press, 1972).

Hoveyda, Fereydoun, 'Les Indes Fabulées', *Cahiers du Cinéma*, no. 99, September 1959.

Humphries, Reynold, *Fritz Lang: Genre and Representation in his American Films* (Baltimore, MD: Johns Hopkins University Press, 1989).

Huyssen, Andreas, *After the Great Divide: Modernism, Mass Culture, Post-Modernism* (Bloomington: Indiana University Press, 1986). 'The Vamp and the Machine: Fritz Lang's *Metropolis*'.

Ibsen, Henrik, *Peer Gynt: A Dramatic Poem* (1867), trans. Peter Watts (London: Penguin Books, 1966).

Jacobs, Lea, *The Wages of Sin: Censorship and the Fallen Woman Film 1928–1942* (Madison: University of Wisconsin Press, 1991).

James, David E., *Allegories of Cinema: American Film in the Sixties* (Princeton, NJ: Princeton University Press, 1989).

Jenkins, Stephen (ed.), *Fritz Lang: The Image and the Look* (London: BFI, 1981). Jenkins, 'Lang: Fear and Desire'; Jean-Louis Comolli and François Géré, 'Two Fictions Concerning Hate' (1978), trans. Tom Milne.

Junger, Ernst, *A Dangerous Encounter*, trans. Hilary Barr (New York: Marsilio Publishers, 1992).

Kaes, Anton (ed.), *Kino-Debatte: Texte zum Verhaltnis von Literatur und Film 1909–1929* (Tubingen: Max Niemeyer, 1978).

————, 'The Cold Gaze: Notes on Mobilization and Modernity', *New German Critique*, no. 59, Spring/Summer 1993.

————, *M* (London: BFI Film Classics, 2000).

————, *Shell Shock: Film and Trauma in Weimar Germany* (Princeton, NJ: Princeton University Press, forthcoming).

————, Martin Jay and Edward Dimendberg (eds), *The Weimar Republic Sourcebook* (Berkeley: University of California Press, 1994). Reprints Lang's 'The Future of the Feature Film in Germany' (1926).

Kafka, Franz, 'The Great Wall of China' (1933), trans. Willa and Edwin Muir, in *The Complete Stories* (New York: Schocken Books, 1971).

Kaiser, Georg, *Gas II. A Play in Three Acts* (1920), trans. Winifred Katzin (new York: Frederick Ungar, 1963).

———, *Five Plays*, trans. J. M. Ritchie (London: Calder and Boyars, 1971). *From Morning to Midnight* (1917).

Kaplan, E. Ann (ed.), *Women in Film Noir* (London: BFI, 1978). Kaplan, 'The Place of Women in *The Blue Gardenia*'.

———, 'Patterns of Violence toward Women in Fritz Lang's *While the City Sleeps*', *Wide Angle*, vol. 3 no. 4, 1980.

———, *Fritz Lang: A Guide to References and Resources* (Boston: G.K Hall, 1981).

———, 'Ideology and Cinematic Practice in Lang's *Scarlet Street* and Renoir's *La Chienne*', *Wide Angle*, vol. 5 no. 3, 1983.

Kierkegaard, Soren, *Either/Or* (1843), vol. I, trans. David and Lilina Swenson (Princeton, NJ: Princeton University Press, 1971).

Kleist, Heinrich von, *Amphitryon* (1807), trans. Marion Sonnenfeld (New York: Frederick Ungar, 1962).

Koller, Michael, and Clare Stewart (eds), *Fritz Lang: Traps for the Mind and Eye* (Melbourne: Melbourne Cinematheque, 1998). Douglas Pye, 'Trusting the Tale: Lang and Suppressive Narrative'.

Kozloff, Sarah, *Invisible Storytellers: Voice-over Narration in American Fiction Films* (Berkeley: University of California Press, 1988).

Kracauer, Siegfried, *From Caligari to Hitler: A Psychological History of the German Film* (Princeton, NJ: Princeton University Press, 1947).

———, *Le Roman policier* (Paris: Payot, 1972).

———, *The Mass Ornament: Weimar Essays* (1963), ed. and trans. Thomas Y. Levin (Cambridge, MA: Harvard University Press, 1995). 'The Hotel Lobby'.

Kreimeier, Klaus, *The Ufa Story: A History of Germany's Greatest Film Company 1918–1945*, trans. Robert and Rita Kimber (New York: Hill and Wang, 1996).

Kristeva, Julia, *Powers of Horror: An Essay on Abjection*, trans. Leon S. Boudiez (New York: Columbia University Press, 1982).

Kuntzel, Thierry, 'The Film Work', *Enclitic*, vol. 2 no. 1, 1978.

Lang, Fritz, 'La nuit viennoise, un confession de Fritz Lang', *Cahiers du Cinéma*, no. 169, August 1965.

———, 'Happily Ever After' (1948), in Harry M. Geduld (ed.), *Film Makers on Film Making* (Bloomington: University of Indiana Press, 1969).

———, *Mort d'une carrièriste et autres histoires*, trans. Christine and Jacques Rousselet, ed. Cornelius Schnauber (Paris: Pierre Belfond, 1987), *Der Tod eines Karriere-Girls und andere Geschichten* (Vienna: Europa Verlag, 1987).

———, *Le montagne des superstitions et autres histoires*, trans. Christine and Jacques Rousselet, ed. Cornelius Schnauber (Paris: Pierre Belfond, 1991), *Der Berg des Aberglaubens und andere Geschichten*, trans. Hermi Amberger (Vienna: Europa Verlag, 1988). Unrealised scripts from Lang's Hollywood period.

Lanham, Richard A., *A Handlist of Rhetorical Terms* (Berkeley: University of California Press, 1969).

Lant, Antonia, 'Haptical Cinema', *October*, no. 74, Fall 1995.

Laplanche, J., and J.-B. Pontalis, *The Language of Psychoanalysis* (1967), trans. Donald Nicholson-Smith (New York: W.W. Norton, 1973).

Leach, William, *Land of Desire: Merchants, Power, and the Rise of a New American Culture* (New York: Pantheon Books, 1991).

Leblanc, Gerard, and Brigitte Devismes, *Le Double scénario chez Fritz Lang* (Paris: Armand Colin, 1991).

Lefebvre, Henri, *The Production of Space* (1974), trans. Donald Nicholson-Smith (London: Blackwell, 1991).

Legrand, Gerard, 'Le génie des lieux', *Positif*, no. 94, April 1968.
————, 'L'effacement des traces', *Positif*, no. 248, November 1981.
Leff, Leonard J., *Hitchcock and Selznick* (New York: Weidenfeld and Nicholson, 1987).
Levin, David J., *Richard Wagner, Fritz Lang and Die Nibelungen: The Dramaturgy of Disavowal* (Princeton, NJ: Princeton University Press, 1998).
Limbacher, James L., *Four Aspects of Film* (New York: Brussel and Brussel, 1968).
Lindsay, Vachel, *The Art of the Moving Picture* (1915; New York: Liveright, 1970).
Lukacs, Georg, 'Thoughts on an Aesthetic for the Cinema' (1913), trans. Barrie Ellies-Jones, *Framework*, no. 14, Spring 1981.
————, *The Theory of the Novel* (1914), trans. Anna Bostock (Cambridge, MA: MIT Press, 1971).
MacCabe, Colin, *The Eloquence of the Vulgar: Language, Cinema and the Politics of Culture* (London: BFI, 1999). 'The Revenge of the Author' (1989).
Marie, Michel, *M, le Maudit, Fritz Lang Etude Critique* (Paris: Nathan, 1993).
Marvin, Carolyn, *When Old Technologies Were New: Thinking About Electronic Communication in the Late Nineteenth Century* (Oxford: Oxford University Press, 1988).
Marx, Karl, *The Eighteenth Brumaire of Louis Bonaparte* (1869), n.tr. (New York: International Publishers, 1963).
Maupassant, Guy de, *The Complete Short Stories of Guy de Maupassant*, n.tr. (Garden City, NY: Hanover House, 1955). 'Night: A Nightmare' ('La Nuit', 1883).
McArthur, Colin, *The Big Heat* (London: BFI Film Classics, 1992).
McGilligan, Patrick, *Fritz Lang: The Nature of the Beast, A Biography* (New York: St Martin's Press, 1997).
McGivern, William, *The Big Heat* (1952; London: Simon and Schuster, 1988).
Melville, Herman, *Moby Dick or The Whale* (1851), in *Romances of Herman Melville* (New York: Tudor Publishing, n.d.).
Montague, Ivor, *With Eisenstein in Hollywood* (New York: International Publishers, 1969).
Mortiz, William, 'The Films of Oskar Fischinger', *Film Culture*, nos 58/59/60, 1974.
Mulvey, Laura, *Visual and Other Pleasures* (Bloomington: Indiana University Press, 1989). 'Visual Pleasure and Narrative Cinema' (1975).
Mumford, Lewis, *Technics and Civilization* (New York: Harcourt Brace Jovanovich, 1934).
Nagele, Rainer, *Theater, Theory, Speculation: Walter Benjamin and the Scenes of Modernity* (Baltimore, MD: Johns Hopkins University Press, 1991).
Naremore, James, *More than Night: Film Noir in its Contexts* (Berkeley: University of California Press, 1998).
Nietzsche, Friedrich, *The Portable Nietzsche*, ed. and trans. Walter Kaufmann (New York: Viking Press, 1967). *Thus Spoke Zarathustra* (1883–5).
Novalis, *Hymns to the Night* [1802] *and Other Selected Writings*, trans. Charles E. Passage (New York: Bobbs Merrill, 1960).
Ott, Frederick W., *The Films of Fritz Lang* (Seacaus, NJ: Citadel Press, 1979).
Panofsky, Erwin, *Meaning in the Visual Arts* (Chicago, IL: University of Chicago Press, 1982). '*Et in Arcadia Ego*: Poussin and the Elegiac Tradition' (1936).
Parrish, Robert, *Growing up in Hollywood* (New York: Harcourt Brace and Jovanovich, 1976).

Patalas, Enno, Frieda Grafe, and Hans Prinzler, *Fritz Lang* (Munich: Carl Hanser
    Verlag, 1976), *Fritz Lang*, trans. Claude Porcell (Paris: Rivages, 1985). The
    authors withdrew their names from the French edition.
Peukert, Detlev J. K., *The Weimar Republic: The Crisis of Classical Modernity*, trans.
    Richard Deveson (New York: Hill and Wang, 1989).
Poe, Edgar Allan, *Poetry and Tales*, ed. Patrick F. Quinn (New York: The Library of
    America, 1984). 'The Man in the Crowd' (1840); 'The Oval Portrait' (1842);
    'The Purloined Letter' (1844).
Pratt, George C. (ed.), *Spellbound in Darkness: A History of the Silent Film*
    (Greenwich, CN: New York Graphic Society, 1973). Reprints Henry Tyrrell,
    'Some Music Hall Moralities' (1896).
Pye, Douglas, 'Seeing by Glimpses: Fritz Lang's *The Blue Gardenia*', *Cineaction!*,
    Summer 1998.
Renoir, Jean, *Letters* (1913–78), eds Lorraine LoBianco and David Thompson,
    trans. Craig Carlson, Natasha Arnoldi and Michael Wells (London: Faber
    and Faber, 1994).
Riegel, Alois, 'Late Roman or Oriental?', trans. Peter Wortsman, in Gert Schiff (ed.),
    German Essays on Art History (New York: Continuum, 1988).
Rilke, Rainer Maria, *The Notebooks of Malte Laurids Brigge* (1910), trans. M.D.
    Herter Norton (New York: W.W. Norton, 1964).
Ronell, Avital, *The Telephone Book: Technology, Schizophrenia, Electric Speech*
    (Lincoln: University of Nebraska, 1989).
Ropars-Wuilleumier, Marie-Claire, *Le Texte divise* (Paris: PUP, 1981).
Rosenbaum, Jonathan, *Moving Places: A Life at the Movies* (Berkeley: University of
    California Press, 1995).
Rosza, Miklos, *Double Life* (New York: Wynwood Press, 1989).
Roy, Jean, 'L'oeil, le regard, l'écran: essai sur Fritz Lang', *Cinema 80*, no. 255, March 1980.
Rubin, Martin, *Thrillers* (Cambridge: Cambridge University Press, 1999).
Rutsky, R. L., 'The Mediation of Technology and Gender: *Metropolis*, Nazism,
    Modernism', *New German Critique*, no. 59, Spring/Summer 1993.
Sadoul, Georges, *L'art Muet (L'Après Guerre en Europe 1919–1929)* (Paris: Denoël,
    1975).
Sarris, Andrew (ed.), *Interviews with Film Directors* (Indianapolis, IN: Babbs
    Merrill, 1967). Sarris, 'Fritz Lang' (1967); Mark Shivas, 'Fritz Lang Talks
    about Dr. Mabuse' (1962).
Scholdt, Gunter (ed.), *Norbert Jacques Fritz Lang Dr. Mabuse:
    Roman/Film/Dokumente* (Ingebert: W.J. Rohrig Verlag, 1987). Reprints
    Uco/Decla-Bioskop documentation and contemporary reviews.
Silverman, Kaja, *The Acoustic Mirror: The Female Voice in Psychoanalysis and
    Cinema* (Bloomington: Indiana University Press, 1988).
Simmel, Georg, *The Philosophy of Money* (1907), trans. David Frisby (London:
    Routledge, 1990).
———, *Of Individuality and Social Forms*, ed. Donald N. Levine (New York: Urizen
    Books, 1971. 'The Metropolis and Mental Life' (1903).
Sklar, Robert, *Movie-Made America: A Cultural History of American Movies* (New
    York: Random House, 1976).
Sloterdijk, Peter, *Critique of Cynical Reason* (1983), trans. Michael Eldred
    (Minneapolis: University of Minnesota Press, 1987).
Smedley, Nick, 'Fritz Lang Out-foxed: The German Genius as Contract Employee',
    Film History, vol. 1 no. 4, 1990.

————, 'Fritz Lang's Trilogy: The Rise and Fall of a European Social
      Commentator', *Film History*, vol. 5 no. 1, March 1993.
Spengler, Oswald, *The Decline of the West* (1918/22), trans. Charles Francis
      Atkinson, 2 vols (New York: Alfred A. Knopf, 1928), vol. II, *Perspectives on
      World History*.
Spivak, Gayatri Chakravorty, 'Translator's Preface', in Jacques Derrida, *Of
      Grammatology* (1967; Baltimore, MD: Johns Hopkins University Press,
      1976).
Stewart, Garett, *Between Film and Screen: Modernism's Photo-Synthesis* (Chicago,
      IL: Chicago University Press, forthcoming).
Sturm, Georges, *Fritz Lang: Films/Textes/References* (Nancy: Presses Universitaires
      de Nancy, 1990).
Tatar, Maria M., *Spellbound: Studies on Mesmerism and Literature* (Princeton, NJ:
      Princeton University Press, 1978).
————, *Lustmord: Sexual Murder in Weimar Germany* (Princeton, NJ: Princeton
      University Press, 1995).
Theweleit, Klaus, *Male Fantasies* (1977), trans. Stephen Conway, 2 vols
      (Minneapolis: University of Minnesota Press, 1987), vol. I, *Women Floods
      Bodies History*.
Thompson, Kristin, '*Im Anfang war* … some links between German fantasy films of
      the Teens and Twenties', in Paolo Cherchi Usai and Lorenzo Codelli (eds),
      Before Caligari: German Cinema 1895–1920 (Pordenone: Edizioni Biblioteca
      dell'Immagine, 1990).
————, 'Early Alternatives to the Hollywood Mode of Production: Implications for
      Europe's Avant Gardes', *Film History*, vol. 5 no. 4, December 1993.
Todorov, Tzvetan, *The Poetics of Prose* (1971), trans. Richard Howard (Ithaca, NY:
      Cornell University Press, 1977).
————, *Theories of the Symbol* (1977), trans. Catherine Porter (Ithaca, NY: Cornell
      University Press, 1982).
Trakl, Georg, *Autumn Sonata*, trans. Daniel Simko (Mount Kisco, NY: Moyer Bell,
      1989).
Truffaut, François, *Hitchcock* (New York: Simon and Schuster, 1967).
Vasuvedan, Ravi S., 'Film Studies, New Cultural History and the Experience of
      Modernity', *Economic and Political Weekly*, 44, 4 November 1995.
Vernet, Marc, 'The Look at the Camera', *Cinema Journal*, vol. 28 no. 2, Winter 1989.
Waite, Robert G. L., *Vanguard of Nazism: The Free Corps Movement in Postwar
      Germany 1918–1923* (Cambridge, MA: Harvard University Press, 1952).
Waldman, Diane, 'The Childish, the Insane and the Ugly: The Representation of
      Modern Art in Popular Films and Fiction of the Forties', *Wide Angle*, vol. 5
      no. 2, 1982.
————, ' "At last I can tell it to someone!": Female Point of View and Subjectivity in
      the Gothic Romance of the 1940s', *Cinema Journal*, vol. 23 no. 2, Winter 1983.
Walkowitz, Judith R., *City of Dreadful Delight: Narratives of Sexual Danger in Late-
      Victorian London* (Chicago, IL: University of Chicago Press, 1992).
Wallis, J. H., *Once Off-Guard* (New York: E.P. Dutton, 1942).
Warshow, Robert, *The Immediate Experience* (New York: Atheneum, 1976). 'Paul,
      the Horror Comics and Dr. Wertham'.
Weill, Kurt, and Lotte Lenya, *Speak Low (When You Speak of Love): The Letters of
      Kurt Weill and Lotte Lenya*, trans. Lys Symonette and Kim Kowalke (Berkeley:
      University of California Press, 1996).

Williams, Rosalind H., *Dream Worlds: Mass Consumption in Late Nineteenth-Century France* (Berkeley: University of California Press, 1982).

———, *Notes on the Underground: An Essay on Technology, Society and the Imagination* (Cambridge, MA: MIT Press, 1990).

Wilinsky, Barbara, 'Selling Exclusivity: The Emergence of Art Film Theaters in Post World War II American Culture', Northwestern, 1997.

Wilson, George M., *Narration in Light: Studies in Cinematic Point of View* (Baltimore, MD: Johns Hopkins University Press, 1986).

Wollen, Peter, *Signs and Meaning in the Cinema*, expanded edn (London: BFI, 1998).

Worringer, Wilhelm, *Form in Gothic* (New York: Schocken Books, 1964).

Yankelovich, Daniel, and William Barrett, *Ego and Instinct: The Psychoanalytic View of Human Nature*, rev. edn (New York: Random House, 1970).

INDEX